5468796 Architecture

I0804228

platform.MIDDLE

platform.MIDDLE

Thank you to Michelangelo Sabatino, Reed Kroloff and the Illinois Institute of Technology's College of Architecture for hosting the **platform.MIDDLE** Symposium and for their support of this publication.

FOREWORD

Reed Kroloff

There are plenty of books on housing: a quick search on Amazon yields more than 50,000 titles (and that's after cross-listing "architecture" with "housing" to tighten the list). So why this one? Why now?

5468796 Architecture, the Winnipeg-based phenom firm founded in 2007 by Johanna Hurme and Sasa Radulovic (joined soon after by Colin Neufeld), has made housing something of an obsession. The firm's work has included a number of striking multi-family projects – some 15 in all, one for every year they've been in practice, including thousands of units (and that doesn't include the single-family homes, which of course also count as housing).

This attention to one of the most pressing problems of our age was an important part of what inspired then-Acting Dean Michelangelo Sabatino of Illinois Institute of Technology's College of Architecture (IIT) to name Hurme and Radulovic the 2019 Morgenstern Fellows – a program funded by a visionary donor intent on bringing in leading architectural thinkers to investigate challenging architectural problems through research-based teaching. While at IIT, Hurme and Radulovic convened a symposium intended to tease out ideas for creating models of housing that made sense in our contemporary world, even – or especially – if they broke convention. And by convention, that meant not only in architecture, but the entire system of development, design and construction.

Supported by IIT's Phyllis Lambert Fund, the IIT conference was the genesis of this book (also supported by the Lambert Fund). When the conference ended, Hurme and Radulovic realized that the material gathered there suggested a possible armature upon which a different kind of publication on contemporary housing could be built, one that functioned less as a catalog of what had been and more as a manual for what could be.

"platform.MIDDLE," which you are reading now, summarizes the conference. It's concluding chapter, "Reflection," is a short instruction set for how to attack the challenge of housing in a modern world – as recommended by the conference and curated by Hurme. "platform.MACRO" researches beyond the scope of the architect. "platform. MICRO" describes a set of general conditions by which to test these conclusions.

That is followed by "projects.MODELLING," essentially an expansion of "MIDDLE's" instructions using 5468796's practice as a sample set for testing the hypotheses.

Call it the scientific method in architecture. Call it an academic approach to a market problem. Call it research-based practice. Call it what you like. The point here is that it works. Support from Morgenstern and Lambert provided Hurme and Radulovic a context, some funding, and a platform for testing their research; exactly what academia does at its best. Their practice, and even more importantly, their gimlet-eyed view of this part of the architectural world provides the proof. It's all here. Don't let the amount of material intimidate you. Open a chapter, grab a hammer (or a calculator or a proforma sheet) and get to work.

NO MIDDLING MATTER

Trevor Boddy

I imagine it should come as no surprise that one of the most focused and useful housing conferences I have ever attended should be mid-continental. Organized by Winnipeggers Johanna Hurme and Sasa Radulovic and hosted by Crown Hall at the Illinois Institute of Technology, the event was broad-shouldered and to-the-point, as poignant as a Studs Terkel commentary and bracing as a November breeze off Lake Michigan or Manitoba. Coastal cities have made a hash out of contemporary architectural culture – import-export ports too ready to host shiploads of formalist gymnastic equipment, quaysides filled with palettes of beguiling but inoperable theoretical gadgets.

Things are done different, mid-continent. There is something about the flatlands surrounding Chicago and Winnipeg, their being defined by infinite webs of trains, trucks and throughways, that sobers with reality-checking, humbles with verdant reminders of horizons lined by wheat and corn. This framing and sense of being in-between seems to have helped the reconsideration of housing, architecture's most essential but lowest-status endeavor.

That current lowly status generates wave after wave of loudly trumpeted but inevitably partial solutions. These include the chimera of mass production, from Fuller's Dymaxion House to Soviet pre-cast concrete panel systems and everything else modular, and on to the digital printing of houses, the craze of the moment. Then there are the serial romances of typology and planform, from brownstones and perimeter blocks, to Wiessenhof Siedlung's paradise on a Stuttgart hill, to tower-and-podium, then duplex, triplex, fourplex, have you any wool? Mid-continentalism means trading fuzzy thinking for focus, practicality, a needed editing-back, but most of all, it means sharing a sense of housing's destiny being the improvement of lives in small, often invisible ways. The architects and developers lined up for Platform were selected for their convergence with this goal. Most of those invited have small firms, and their built accomplishments are painfully under-publicized. In bringing this group together to show work, talk solutions, and ultimately to produce this book, Platform organizers at IIT and Hurme and Radulovic's firm of 5468796 are dedicated to a flow of information and inspiration for those on the front lines of the contemporary housing crisis. True to their selected name for the project, they have indeed created a platform.

The work of John Ronan Associates was a revelation to me when a midwestern snowstorm gave fellow Vancouverite Marianne Amodio and I an extra, unexpected day to tour Chicago and see the buildings John had presented at Platform. The notion of hybridity is central to JRA's work, but just as much to the mission of large cities in the 21st century. This means hybrid building programs, hybrid and layered social ambitions, hybrid construction vocabularies, even a hybrid colour sense, with more shades of embellishment included than excluded. JRA's Independence Library and Apartments, commissioned under former Mayor Rahm Emanuel, is a proud and singular accomplishment. It is a shining and playful monument for residents at the scale of their own neighbourhood – a maker of community. It makes perfect sense that a local library be topped by affordable housing for seniors, and that the whole complex be bright and welcoming. The common sense of housing moves like these has largely escaped designers ringing the Atlantic and Pacific.

SOM's futureHOME 2050 joins a long parade of the "houses of tomorrow" that stretch back for a century or more, most often presented at World's Fairs. Despite its curved glass and gleaming metal, there is something nostalgic about this, the only single-family house shown at Platform. Stacking such houses vertically on a services spine-tower only further emphasizes its unreality – the world has moved on from this kind of futurism, even with this half-believed dash for density. Chicago has also moved on from its large and troubled public housing estates, with Cabrini Green almost entirely demolished and rebuilt at much lower densities. SOM's AMLI 90 for a former housing projects site is a revival of the slab apartment block, showing the typology has a future, especially with residential units as carefully conceived as here.

MA + HG have earned deep respect in Vancouver for their acute and detailed analysis of the whole housing production system, their findings illustrated in an engaging range of diagrams, supported by deep mines of data. Their Tomo Co-Housing block on South Main Street has a clever range of unit types, with a sheltered sunny courtyard defined by the L-massing and a large resident's amenity space on the arterial street side. MA + HG's Union Street housing is a double house set in the backyard of a century old two storey wooden residence the new units introduced there arranged on non-orthogonal geometries that improve their privacy, plus avoiding the banality of "the shack out back."

Two projects from Montreal's KANVA transform small industrial buildings into amenable housing, and are ingenious in detail. One development called Irene adapts a brick workshop into lodging so seamlessly that the resulting architecture seems as if it has been ever thus. Another named Fabricca adds a second skin of openable metal panels and shutters to accommodate building systems while also allowing cross-ventilation and existing walls to breath. For his part, Rafael Lengoria offers "Ibero-American Housing Lessons," with those from the likes of Chile's Pritzker-winning Alejandro Aravena offering a fresh take on public housing, but the works of Spaniard Ricardo Bofill seeming pompous and overblown when set on pages beside them.

Saskatoon's Curtis Olson describes work with SHIFT to craft modest multi-family complexes in the Riversdale neighbourhood, an inner suburb having the highest ratio of aboriginal residents of any North American city, and with almost no tradition of townhouses. Rich Sciortino describes work with another inner-city developer, Brinshore, who are redeveloping some of the 140 acres of the Robert Taylor Homes, an infamous Chicago towers project. He made clear that creating new and humane communities in these settings requires a complex negotiation with funding and approving authorities, because truly affordable housing only exists in the suburbs, given the much lower land costs there.

One of the most useful sections of this volume is the portfolio of Case Studies which concludes it. These are more in-depth studies of key buildings that had been shown briefly in the talks, with richer illustrations and more depth of plans and details. Particularly useful are its comparative data sets and analyatic diagrams indicating density and plan configurations – this is the base-datum of comparables so needed in housing studies, but which is (usually) so difficult to find. The other breath of fresh air at this uniquely positive and productive housing conference was the fact that there was a review panel featuring designers and commentators from other cities – cross-dialogue and international inquiry are fundamental to this this symposium. How often have we all attended housing conferences where the slides whip by, and design firm after firm are toddled off the podium, leaving only muddles of barely remembered images, unsupported by discussion and synthesis.

Every year the chorus of crisis grows louder, a widespread and now shouted sentiment that housing is becoming one of the most intractable problems facing even the most advanced and wealthy of nations. The range of designs and ideas on show at Platform exemplifies the gathered and interpreted information needed to improve all housing, not just the missing middle. I have proposed that the flatlands teams who dominated the Platform presentations have found advantages – not just an avoidance of glamor and wealthy patrons – in being devised at the middle of the continent.

That phrase "missing middle" might equally apply to architectural thinking itself, routinely seduced by the notion of building-as-artwork, like the art galleries which are a too-frequent subject of final year theses, followed by career-long ambitions from too many architects to build one, usually disastrously. At the other end of the spectrum is the pure spatial commodity flow of the high-rise office or condo tower plus the suburban tract house, where thinking is turned off and replication machines crank out square feet by the millions. Yes, this "missing middle" of architectural thinking itself is something of a muddle, complex due to its very importance and contingency, shaped by a matrix of finance, regulation and an ever-human desire for pleasant accommodation. Having said this, wisdom can accrete from being in the middle.

The phrase "fair to middling" is too often thought to be a put-down: a forty-watt success; a partial accomplishment. But a "fair to middling" take on contemporary housing is a heroic breakthrough in an architectural-intellectual landscape dominated by architecture-as-sculpture and architecture-as-consumable. In resisting easy answers, in asking everyone to explain and debate, in compiling comparable drawings and data, Platform stakes out a needed and inevitable position in this landscape. This is no middling matter.

Calgary
Vancouver
Saskatoon
Winnipeg
Montreal
Chicago
Houston

INTRODUCTION

5468796 Architecture

Housing affordability in North America has reached a crisis point. Against the backdrop of rapid urbanization and an accelerating environmental emergency, we need solutions for city building that are more socially and economically sustainable, as well as multi-family housing that is more equitable and livable.

The origins of our current condition are various and touch every aspect of modern life, from the inherited urban fabric to the commodification of housing, political realities and outdated policy frameworks. In the West, we live in a prevailing culture that values the individual over the communal, where success is measured more by square feet than by social connection or sense of community.

It is important to note that many of these problems fall outside of the traditional sphere of architecture. As such, the profession is not able to respond to the root cause of every issue. We also recognize that it is not an architect's role to engineer social change through design – admittedly, the profession has tried and failed in this arena many times over. However, to us this does not mean that architects or planners should be devoid of responsibility. On the contrary, challenging the profit-driven private development formula should be the prerogative of every architect engaged in housing architecture.

Initiated by Dean Michelangelo Sabatino and Morgenstern Chairs Johanna Hurme and Sasa Radulovic of 5468796 Architecture, "platform.MIDDLE: Architecture for Housing the 99%" took place at the College of Architecture at the Illinois Institute of Technology on April 12 and 13, 2019. The symposium explored the current state of multi-family housing in North America and the architect's role in shaping its future, bringing together practitioners, critics and developers from across Canada and the United States, with an emphasis on market-driven economies.

The participants highlighted the major challenges that can impact an architect's ability to deliver better outcomes, as well as opportunities to broaden the reach of architecture through housing. The goal of "platform.MIDDLE" was to provide a venue for engagement and a call to action. The workshop unfolded through a number of short presentations and moderated discussions.

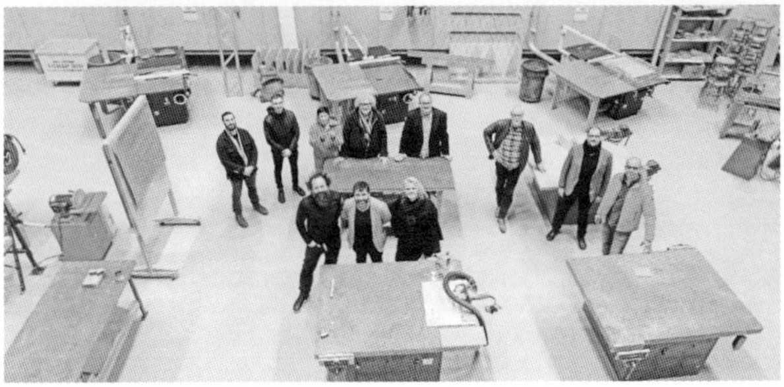

This volume distills the "platform.MIDDLE" symposium into written essays, forum transcripts and detailed case studies to highlight the relevant work, theoretical underpinnings and personal ethos that drives each individual and practice. When studied as a whole, this book demonstrates the variety of processes and approaches – formal and informal, top-down and bottom-up – that can be implemented to enact meaningful change through the profession of architecture and its related disciplines.

Participant matrix

Participant	**Role**	Architect	Developer	Educator	**Scale**	Small	Medium	Large	**Tools**	Advocacy	Engagement	Technology	Colour	Fabrication	Finance	Installation	Research
5468796		●		●		●	●	●		●	●	●	●	●	●	●	●
Curtis Olson			●			●	●			●	●				●		
David Brininstool			●				●	●			●				●		
John Ronan		●		●		●	●	●			●	●	●			●	●
KANVA		●	●	●		●	●			●	●	●	●	●	●	●	●
Lluís Ortega		●	●	●		●	●	●					●			●	●
MA+HG		●		●		●	●			●	●		●	●	●	●	●
Martin Felsen		●		●		●	●	●			●		●				●
Peter Landon		●		●		●	●	●			●		●				●
Rafael Longoria		●		●		●	●									●	●
Rich Sciortino			●				●	●			●				●		
RNDSQR			●	●		●	●			●	●				●	●	
SOM		●		●			●	●			●	●		●			●
Trevor Boddy				●			●	●				●				●	●

Itinerary . April 12 . 2019

Kick off [12:00-12:10]

Michelangelo Sabatino
Interim Dean, College of Architecture IIT

Michelangelo Sabatino trained as an architect, historian and preservationist. His research broadly addresses intersections between culture, technology and design in the built environment. From his research on preindustrial vernacular traditions and their influence on modern architectures of the Mediterranean region, to his current project, which looks at the transnational forces that have shaped the architecture, infrastructure and landscape of the Americas over the course of the 19th and 20th centuries, he has trained new light on larger patterns of architectural discourse and production. He earned a Laurea in Architecture at the Università di IUAV (Venice) and a doctorate in the Department of Fine Art, University of Toronto, and pursued a post-doctoral fellowship in the Department of History of Art + Architecture, Harvard University.

MS Let's have a very energetic and very personal discussion, and let's walk away from this workshop having learned as much as we can from each other.

Framing [12:10-12:30]

Johanna Hurme + Sasa Radulovic
5468796 Architecture Morgenstern Chair IIT

Johanna Hurme + Sasa Radulovic are co-founders of 5468796 Architecture in Winnipeg, Canada. Since 2007, the firm has received national and international recognition, including the Rice Design Alliance Spotlight Award, the RAIC Emerging Architectural Practice Award, WAN 21 for 21, the Architectural League of NY Emerging Voices, and the Design Vanguard issue of Architectural Record. In 2012, 5468796 represented Canada at the Venice Biennale, and in 2013 they received the Prix de Rome Award in Architecture from the Canada Council for the Arts (CCA). In addition to practice, Johanna and Sasa are activists, advocates, educators and lecturers. They have initiated a number of design related events and programs that serve to improve public appreciation of architecture, including Table for 12 + 1200, Chair Your Idea and Design Quarter Winnipeg. Johanna is also the past Chair of the Winnipeg Chamber of Commerce Board of Directors and Chair of the WCC's Our Winnipeg Task Force. Sasa is an active member of the Board of Directors of the UofM Partners Program, an organization that promotes communication between professionals, industry, educators and students.

JH Our interest has been in the housing realm for a long time, not necessarily because we chose to work in it but because these were the kinds of projects we were lucky enough to receive early on in our careers.

What has been a glaring difference between where we both originally came from in a European context to a North American one is the lack of the missing middle.

We are going to have an honest and uncomplicated conversation about the tricks of the trade and what we can all do together to further the topic of livability.

SR There are no universal truths and that is why we are looking at a variety of contexts, from the west coast to the east coast and north to south.

The entire field of multi-family housing requires an architect, therefore we have an obligation to address it. There really is no excuse.

Itinerary . April 12 . 2019

Keynote.1 [12:30-13:15]
Good design is for everyone

Peter Landon
LBBA Architects

Keynote.2 [13:15-14:00]
Hybrid typologies

John Ronan
John Ronan Architects

FORUM.1 [14:00-14:30]

Keynote.3 [15:00-15:45]
Housing revisited

Arathi Gowda + Andrew Obendorf
Skidmore, Owings & Merrill LLP

FORUM.2 [15:45-16:15]

Keynote.4 [16:15-16:45]
Taking charge

Marianne Amodio
MA+HG Architects

FORUM.3 [16:45-17:30]

Keynote.5 [17:30-18:00]
Total architecture

Tudor Radulescu + Rami Bebawi
KANVA

FORUM.4 [18:00-18:30]

Itinerary . April 13. 2019

Keynote.6 [8:30-9:00]

Housing cultures

Trevor Boddy
Writer + Curator

Keynote.7 [9:00-10:00]

Ibero-american housing lessons

Rafael Longoria
University of Houston

Perspectives [10:00-11:00]

Curtis Olson
Shift Development

Living in cities

Rich Sciortino
Brinshore Development LLC

Form follows finance

Alkarim Devani
RNDSQR

LIFE

FORUM.5 [11:00-11:30]

case.STUDIES [11:30-12:30]

Lluís Ortega
Sio2 Arch, JL-Office

102 Dwellings

Marianne Amodio
MA+HG Architects

Union

John Ronan
John Ronan Architects

Independence Library + Apartments

Radulescu + Bebawi
KANVA

Edison

David Brininstool
Brininstool + Lynch Ltd

630 N. Franklin

Marianne Amodio
MA+HG Architects

Marianne holds a Masters Degree of Architecture (honours) from the University of Manitoba, and is a registered Architect with the Architectural Institute of British Columbia. She began her eponymous firm, Marianne Amodio Architecture Studio in 2009. The practice was awarded the Arthur Erickson Award for Emerging Architect, followed by the AIBC Award for Emerging Firm. In 2016, the firm welcomed Harley Grusko AIBC and was renamed MA+HG Architects. Marianne is currently a member of the City of Vancouver Regulation Redesign Advisory Committee and a former Board Member of the Chinatown Heritage Area Planning Committee and the Council of the Architectural Institute of British Columbia. Marianne's past service also includes Chair of the City of Vancouver's Creative Advisory Panel for Housing Innovation and member of the City of Vancouver Mayor's Advisory Committee for Housing. She gleefully co-hosts Pecha Kucha Vancouver and mentors a growing brood of Intern Architects.

Rafael Longoria
University of Houston

Rafael Longoria is an ACSA Distinguished Professor of Architecture at the University of Houston and principal of LONGORIA+, a Houston-based architecture and urban design collaborative. He is a numerary member of Mexico's Academia Nacional de Arquitectura and a senior fellow of the American Leadership Forum. He serves as Advanced Studies Coordinator and Director of the Atrium Press at the Gerald D. Hines College of Architecture & Design. Longoria is a founding editor of AULA: Architecture and Urbanism in Las Américas, and has served on the editorial boards of The Journal of Architectural Education, Cite, (In)forma, and the Rice University Press. From 2004 to 2005, he was President of the Association of Collegiate Schools of Architecture.

Rafael holds degrees from the Rice University School of Architecture and the Graduate School of Business of The University of Texas at Austin. Publications include *The Green Braid: Towards an Architecture of Ecology, Economy, and Equity, a collection of sustainability essays and projects* co-edited with Kim Tanzer.

Andrew Obendorf
Skidmore, Owings & Merrill LLP

Andrew Obendorf was a studio design leader at Skidmore, Owings & Merrill LLP, and since 2022 is an architect at Gensler. At SOM, he led design efforts-use, cultural, residential, retail, healthcare and government buildings throughout the world. Notable projects include the recently completed NATO Headquarters in Brussels, Belgium; 100 Mount Street in North Sydney, Australia; the Christ Hospital Joint and Spine Center in Cincinnati, Ohio; and the Bank of China Headquarters in Ningbo, China. Research initiatives have included futureHOME2050 at the Museum of Science and Industry, AMLI 900 for Hanley Wood, and AMIE1.0 (Additive Manufacturing Integrated Energy), a 3D-printed building in collaboration with the University of Tennessee and Oak Ridge National Labs. Andrew received a Master of Architecture from the University of Illinois. He is a Professor of Practice at the University of Tennessee, a licensed architect in Illinois and Ohio and a member of the American Institute of Architects (AIA).

Arathi Gowda
Skidmore, Owings + Merrill LLP

Arathi Gowda was an associate director and sustainable team leader at Skidmore, Owings & Merrill LLP, and since 2022 is Principal at ZGF. At SOM, she was responsible for championing the environment during the design and construction phases of Architecture, Planning and Interior projects. Arathi brings her knowledge of analysis and passive design techniques to projects, focusing on helping teams realize integrated design solutions that consider the impacts of the built environment on multiple scales. Gowda was awarded the 2016 Chapter Mission Award by the United States Green Building Council – Illinois Chapter. She serves philanthropically with several organizations including the advisory boards for Carbon Drawdown at Illinois Green Alliance and the Marshall Bennett Institute of Real Estate. Gowda holds a Bachelor of Architecture degree from Carnegie Mellon University. She is a registered architect in Illinois, a certified planner with the American Institute of Certified Planners, and a LEED Accredited Professional.

Tudor Radulescu
KANVA

Tudor Radulescu is the cofounding partner of KANVA, established in collaboration with Rami Bebawi in Montreal, Quebec. The firm has won many prestigious awards and competitions including the 2018 World Architecture Festival Future Experimental project of the year, the 2017 Prix de Rome from the Canadian Council for the arts, the 2015 Royal Architecture Institute of Canada (RAIC) Emerging Architectural Practice Award, several RAIC Awards of Excellence, Canadian Architect Awards of Excellence, Ordre des Architectes du Quebec Awards of Excellence and Grands Prix du Design Awards.

Since 2003, Tudor has carried out the design for a wide range of projects. He is committed to experimentation towards the advancement of building practices and material innovation, and the impact on the condition and development of contemporary culture through architectural design. Tudor holds a Master of Architecture and a Bachelor of Science in Architecture from McGill University.

Rami Bebawi
KANVA

Rami Bebawi is the cofounding partner of KANVA, established in collaboration with Tudor Radulescu in Montreal, Quebec. KANVA's work elicits an experience, a memory, a reaction. The firm is made up of passionate architects, artists, and scenographers whose work is at the forefront of thinking, imagining, drawing and constructing. KANVA demonstrates architecture's transformative power through a range of disciplines and scales, from the ephemeral to the institutional, including student housing, large-scale public art installations, mixed-use buildings, commercial projects, public spaces, and cultural institutions.

Leading KANVA into its 18th year, Rami has established himself as a dynamic leader who is continually pushing the creative potential of every project. He believes in the promotion of cross-cultural and cross-discipline sharing of experiences and knowledge, to create rich narratives and sensitive approaches for every project. Rami holds a Master of Architecture and a Bachelor of Science in Architecture from McGill University.

David Brinistool
Brinistool + Lynch Ltd

David Brininstool is a founding partner of Brininstool + Lynch, established in Chicago in 1989. The firm has brought rigor, vision, and elegance to diverse projects since its founding. Their work is firmly rooted in the proud architectural legacy of Chicago; it unabashedly celebrates its kinship with the rigorous modernism of Mies van der Rohe, as well as its sympathy for Frank Lloyd Wright's marriage of building and landscape. And, in the pragmatic Chicago tradition, Brininstool + Lynch is a firm whose work is as much driven by process as it is by product. The result is architecture that is as enduring and timeless as it is graceful and powerful. An adjunct professor at the Illinois Institute of Technology, David holds an MA and a BS from the University of Michigan. He is the past Vice President and Director of the American Institute of Architects and a member of the Council on Tall Buildings and Urban Habitat and the Society of College and University Planning.

Alkarim Devani
RNDSQR

Alkarim is the co-founder and principal of RNDSQR, a visionary inner-city builder and developer with multiple holdings in many of Calgary's inner-city communities. His broad experience covers the fields of real estate, business, marketing, construction, land development and community outreach.

Alkarim is a born and raised Calgarian, with a deep commitment to the world class trajectory of the inner-city. His passion for design and innovation drives his city- building vision. Grateful for the opportunities he's been afforded, he works to actively improve the lives of the city's residents by creating spaces that are vibrant, beautiful, and sustainable – connecting individuals with their city and one another. Alkarim is a dedicated and active member of the community and development industry. He regularly contributes his time to numerous volunteer organizations, as well as a number of industry-led boards and committees.

Lluís Ortega
Sio2 Arch, JL-Office

Lluís Ortega holds a PHD from the ETSAB, Universitat Politècnica de Catalunya (UPC), an MA in Philosophy from the Universitat de Barcelona and obtained his Master of Science (AAD) degree from Columbia University. He is an Associate Professor at IIT in Chicago and Visiting Professor at the Universidad Torcuato di Tella in Buenos Aires. Lluís is a founder of F451Arquitectura, which now operates under the name Sio2 Arch, and is the founder and co-principal at JL-Office with Julia Capomaggi.

Lluís has overseen several specialized publications as the director of the architectural magazine *Quaderns d'Arquitectura i Urbanisme* (Barcelona, 2003-2005), Platform GSD 2008 (Actar/Harvard University, Barcelona/ Cambridge, 2010), the reader *La digitalización toma el mando* (Editorial Gustavo Gili, Barcelona, 2009) and as editor in chief of IIT Press (2015-2018). He is the author of *Atlas of Suprarural Architecture*, with Ciro Najle published in 2016 and of *Total Designer*, published in 2017.

Rich Sciortino
Brinshore Development LLC

Rich Sciortino is a founder and co-owner of Brinshore Development, one of the Midwest's leading affordable housing developers. Since its inception in 1994 Brinshore has developed over 100 real estate projects that include over 6,000 residential apartments. Brinshore's projects span 12 states and range from urban infill to master-planned communities that all incorporate exceptional architectural and landscape design along with innovative programming.

Rich serves on several non-profit boards including the LISC/Chicago (Board Chair) which facilitates neighbourhood development through support of local organizations; All Chicago which combines financial assistance and advocacy to end homelessness in Chicago; and Space Fund which creates art-based and cultural hubs to serve as catalysts for neighbourhood development. Sciortino holds a bachelor's degree in Finance from the University of Connecticut, a law degree from Tulane University and an MBA from Northwestern University.

Martin Felsen
UrbanLab

Martin Felsen directs UrbanLab, an architecture and urban design firm based in Chicago. UrbanLab is involved in projects at all scales, from large, urban plans to residential, commercial and recreational projects. UrbanLab blends design and research to produce progressive, site-specific projects, resulting in a new aesthetic for resilient architecture, landscapes and public space. UrbanLab's recent book *Bowling* speculates on how city-scaled forms can become an architecture-based urbanism — a conjecture of what a comprehensible city could be to combat contemporary crises. The firm was awarded the AIA College of Fellows Latrobe Prize, the History Channel's "City of the Future" competition, and many design awards from the AIA. UrbanLab's work has been published and exhibited widely, including in the 2010 and 2012 Venice Architecture Biennale and the 2015 and 2017 Chicago Architecture Biennial. Martin is a Fellow of the American Institute of Architects, and Director of the Master of Architecture program at the Illinois Institute of Technology.

Peter Landon
LBBA Architects

Founder and Principal of LBBA, Peter Landon is known for his community-based city planning, development and design work. He is a champion of "social conscious" and diversity in design and supports neighbourhood revitalization efforts across Chicago. A personal commitment through his career has allowed LBBA to successfully balance context, technology, design, environment, and economy in a variety of modest, space efficient, socially and economically mixed urban mixed-use housing developments.

Peter's work has won numerous awards, including multiple AIA Chicago Distinguished Building Awards, Divine Detail Awards and Richard H. Driehaus Awards for Architectural Excellence in Community Design. Peter continually participates in conferences, panel discussions, lectures and advisory groups. He is actively involved with citywide inclusionary zoning initiatives and the Children's Memorial Redevelopment commission.

Trevor Boddy
Writer + curator

Trevor Boddy is a critic and curator of contemporary architecture/urbanism, a travel writer, educator, lecturer and a Vancouver-based consulting urban designer. His most recent books are: *CITY-BUILDER: The Architecture of James K M Cheng* (Images, Melbourne); *Glacier Skywalk*; and *Stantec: Airports* (both Figure 1 Press, Vancouver). His book *The Architecture of Douglas Cardinal* was awarded the Alberta Book of the Year Award, and his writing on buildings and cities has garnered Canadian and international awards, including the Royal Architecture Institute of Canada Advocacy Award, the Jack Webster Journalism Award, and UIA/CICA's Pierre Vago Prize. As a curator, Boddy created the 2014 "Rethink: Behind San Diego's Skyline" (for Bosa), and the "Vancouverism: Architecture Builds the City" exhibition for the 2008 London Festival of Architecture.

Trevor has held academic positions at UBC, Oregon, Manitoba, Carleton and Toronto. He holds a BA from the University of Alberta and a Master in Architecture from the University of Calgary.

John Ronan
John Ronan Architects

John Ronan is the founding principal of Chicago-based John Ronan Architects. He serves as Lead Designer on all projects and is known for his abstract yet sensuous work which explores materiality and atmosphere. John has been named a member of Architectural Record's inaugural Design Vanguard issue, was selected to The Architectural League of New York's Emerging Voices program in 2005 and is the recipient of the 2017 American Academy of Arts and Letters Architecture Award. His design output has been covered extensively by the international design press and his work has been exhibited internationally. John Ronan Architects is the recipient of numerous design awards including two AIA Institute National Honor Awards.

John holds an MA with distinction from the Harvard University Graduate School of Design and a Bachelor of Science degree from the University of Michigan. He is currently the John and Jeanne Rowe Endowed Chair Professor of Architecture at the Illinois Institute of Technology College of Architecture.

Curtis Olson
Shift Development

Curtis Olson is a trained engineer, musician and the CEO of Shift Development, a property development company at the heart of a collaborative, creative community in Saskatoon. He has earned a reputation for introducing solutions for urban infill projects such as in the Fairbanks project, Saskatoon's first warehouse-condo conversion; The Hayloft, which transformed an abandoned, dilapidated 1930s grocery store into a vibrant live/work space and house concert venue; and The Two Twenty, which introduced the first co-working space to Saskatoon. Curtis proved the market for urban townhouses in the Riversdale neighbourhood with Element Urban Village. Curtis believes every Shift Development project is an opportunity to create rich urban lifestyles, with high walkability (average walkscore reaching 89.4) and that are connected to the pulse of the city. In a city dominated by suburban, car-centric development, the path has innumerable challenges and is ripe with opportunity for innovation.

GOOD DESIGN IS FOR EVERYONE

LBBA Architects

Like many other cities across North America, Chicago has a housing affordability crisis. Despite the considerable data that is available and the critical importance of the subject matter, we have not been able to find the political strength to turn development toward inclusionary zoning or design.

In Chicago, a family of four earning 60% of the area median income (AMI) should be able to rent housing at 30% of their income to meet the definition of affordability, but roughly 50% of all renters spend more than this target percentage.[1] Yet as a city, Chicago continues to direct the majority of its money toward high-end projects while areas with greater need fail to draw political or architectural attention. Despite their clear upward potential, many south and west side neighbourhoods have been hollowed out due to a lack of viable housing and employment opportunities, a shortage that is felt with particular acuteness by Chicago's Black community.

Although Chicago has an ambitious five-year housing development plan to expand resources, energize neighbourhoods, and support owners and renters with policies such as transit-oriented development, it takes an average of three to five years to complete a single affordable housing development with 80-100 units. In spite of these challenges, the city maintains a vibrant network of grassroots neighbourhood development groups that create partnerships between for-profit developers and non-profit organizations to address issues related to homelessness, family housing, aging in place and sustainability, among other concerns. LBBA Architects is embedded in this development community. Our approach to affordable housing is not simply to find a suitable site and erect a building. Rather, we immerse ourselves in the community to better understand the breadth of virtues and challenges, in order to create comprehensive, sustainable and progressive urban development.

Woodlawn Park Redevelopment

Over more than three decades in practice, LBBA has completed over 5,100 residential units, the majority of which are multi-family housing projects in Chicago. Many of these projects actively re-imagine and transform existing communities, neighbourhoods and buildings. Among these is the recently completed Woodlawn Park Redevelopment, done with POAH (Preservation of Affordable Housing, City of Chicago) which re-imagines the failed 1960s Grove Parc Plaza project to create over 400 new affordable and mixed income residential units in total. The development plan emphasizes community renewal and a linkage between the University of Chicago and the CTA green line. LBBA completed 165 units in three phases: the new buildings are oriented to better face the street and are complemented by landscape features to produce a sustainable, pedestrian friendly streetscape that is intended to act as a catalyst for neighbourhood revitalization.

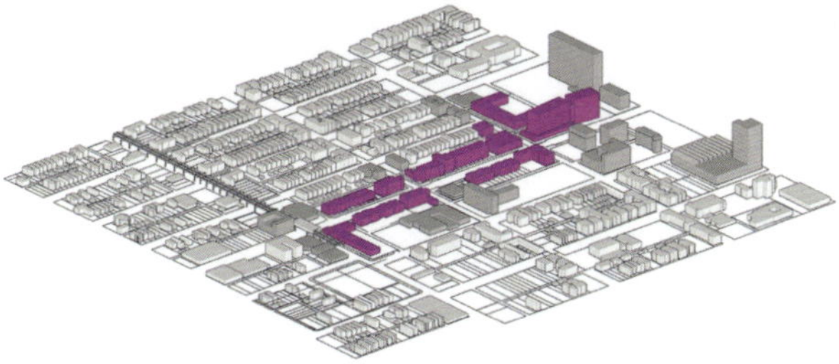

Woodlawn Park features community garden areas and green buffers that offer privacy and safety to ground-floor residents.

Terrace 459 at Parkside of Old Town

On the site of the troubled Cabrini Green public housing development, LBBA was involved in a redevelopment plan that provides more than 700 mixed income homes intended to nurture a sense of safety and community. In the multi-phased approach, LBBA worked on Terrace 459 in 2016 and Elm 551 in 2021. Terrace 459 at Parkside of Old Town contains a mixture of 106 affordable and market rate housing units distributed between one mid-rise building and walkups that together frame a generous green space. The buildings are constructed out of a checkered pattern of low-cost, repetitive, pre-cast concrete elements finished with bright colours, bringing vibrancy and personality to the units and the surrounding environment.

We believe that in order to repair a hole in the urban fabric, one must reach beyond the boundaries of a single building in order to strengthen the surrounding areas.

Terrace 459 at Parkside at Old Town.

Legends South Redevelopment

Legends South is one of Chicago's most ambitious efforts to revitalize public housing that, once completed, will include 2,400 mixed income rental and affordable home-ownership units. Under the Chicago Housing Authority's "Plan for Transformation," these phases reconnect the formerly isolated super block high-rise site to the street grid by adding new streets, scaling the blocks for more comfortable walking distances, and establishing a variety of public, semi-public, and private courtyard spaces.

On the former site of the infamous Robert Taylor Homes public housing development, LBBA worked with other architects to create a mixture of low and mid-rise affordable and market rate housing. The multi-phase project aims to reconnect the former high-rise site to the surrounding neighbourhoods through the construction of new streets and re-scaling of new blocks toward a pedestrian friendly environment. This long-term project has left a number of blocks and lots temporarily vacant; however, these spaces have been adapted to accommodate urban farms which provide food and employment for neighbourhood residents. Buildings are sensitively designed throughout the project site to match the architectural style of the surrounding neighbourhoods while emphasizing walkability through a variety of public, semi-public and private spaces.

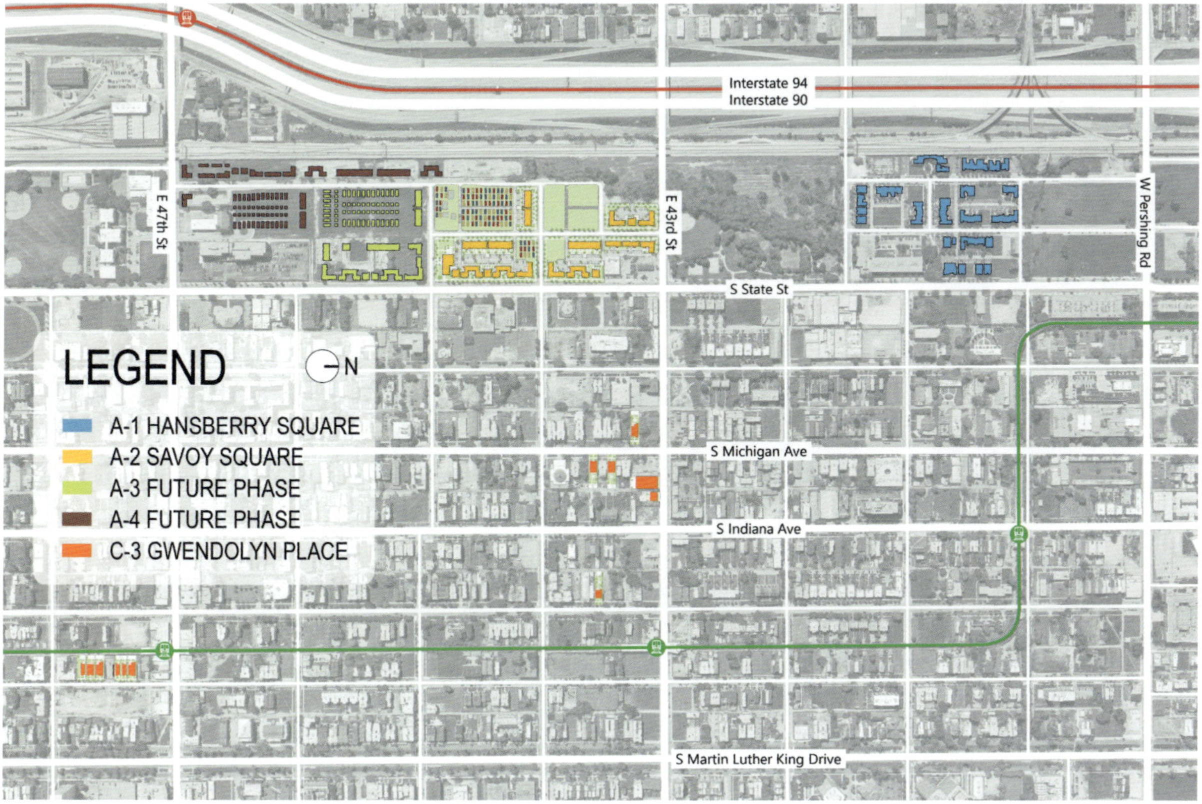

The Legends South Development re-imagines a formely troubled high-rise housing site. The project offers housing at a more sensitive scale while making room for urban agriculture and green space.

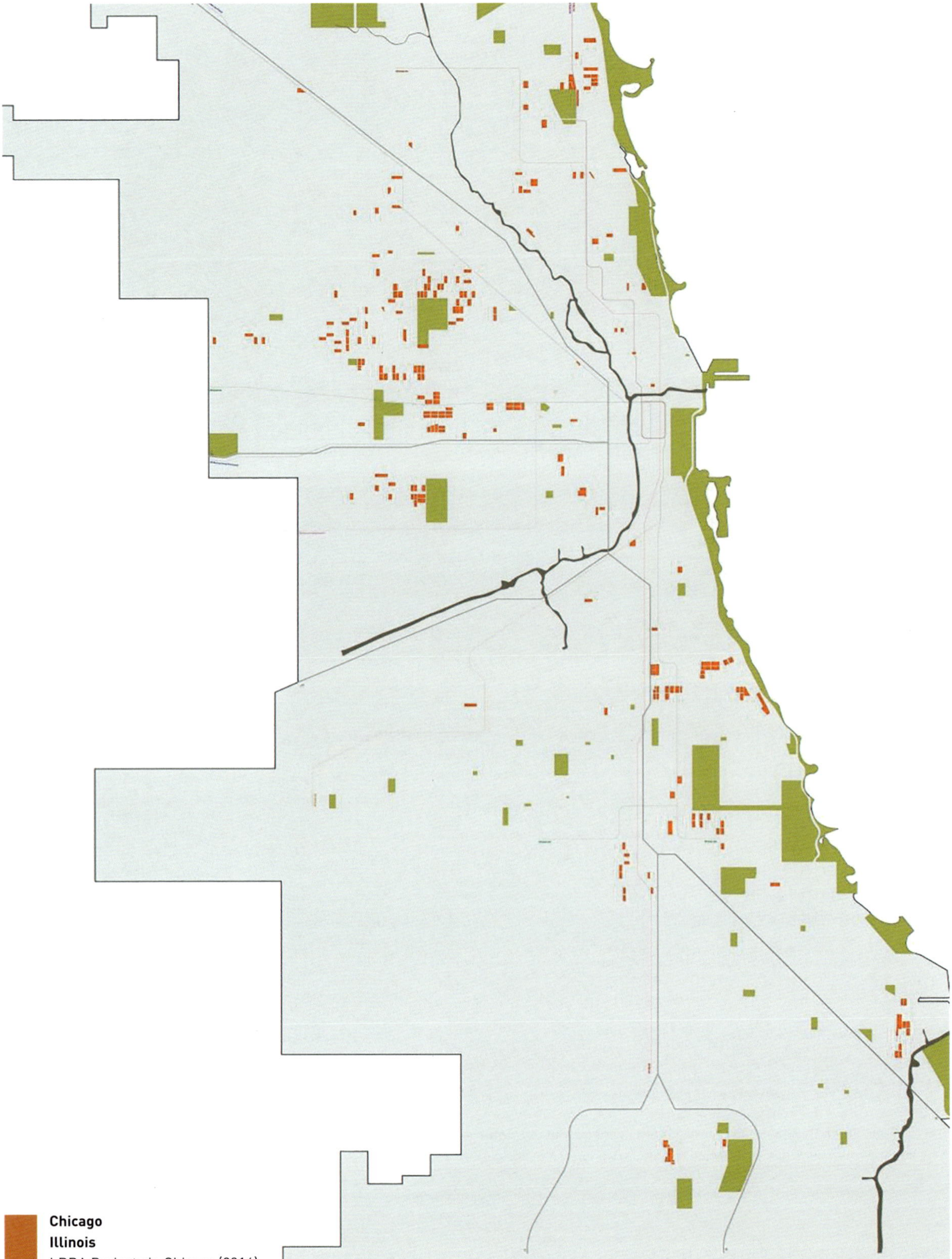

Chicago
Illinois
LBBA Projects in Chicago (2016)

Completed as part of the Tierra Linda scattered-site project, this six unit multi-family project is built to Passive House standards.

Tierra Linda

Many of LBBA's community-based projects focus not only on the architecture, but also on the rehabilitation of the surrounding neighbourhood. For over 25 years, LBBA has worked with the Latin United Community Housing Association (LUCHA) on different projects, including a scattered-site housing project called Tierra Linda, which transforms existing buildings and empty lots in the Humboldt Park neighbourhood into safe, accessible, sustainable and affordable units. One of the six-flat Tierra Linda buildings is the first affordable, multi-family Passive House in the City of Chicago. The Tierra Linda project operates on the belief that safe, dignified and environmentally-conscious housing can and will bolster a neighbourhood in decline.

Across a range of projects, LBBA creates socially driven designs for the city of Chicago by keeping buildings where possible, patching the spaces where we cannot, and letting the beauty of the cracks shine through. In the face of rapid gentrification and an affordability crisis, LBBA leverages community partnerships, creative funding models and professional expertise to create meaningful, affordable and healthy communities across the city.

platformMIDDLE
Architecture for Housing the 99%
FRIDAY 12:00 noon-7:00 p.m.
S. R. Crown Hall, Center Core
SATURDAY 8:30 a.m.-12:30 p.m.

HYBRID TYPOLOGIES

John Ronan Architects

Chicago has an infamous reputation when it comes to affordable housing. Following WWII, the city used eminent domain to clear large swaths of its troubled urban fabric and rebuilt with high-rise public housing projects under the guise of urban renewal. Although these buildings – constructed to replace blighted neighbourhoods and urban slums – were perceived as desirable at first, their shortcomings would soon become apparent.

A combination of failures in urban planning, architectural theory and public policy, guided at the time by the Chicago Housing Authority, permeated this grand social experiment. An expedient design and construction process resulted in highly repetitive units with little natural daylight or ventilation, as well as buildings that offered little communal space. The resulting slab-block towers were easily controlled by gangs, permeated by crime and fell quickly into disrepair. One of the policy failures was to charge residents a percentage of their income rather than a flat rate or percentage of market value, creating a vicious cycle in which lower earning residents were de-incentivized to improve their financial circumstances in the short term. The buildings quickly became unhealthy and unsafe places for residents.

By the 1990s, this failed experiment had reached its end stage. Federal and local governmental support had disintegrated alongside public perception of such buildings. The federal government mandated their demolition by way of withholding public housing funding. In their place, local agencies turned toward a new solution. "Scattered-site" housing projects were distributed throughout the city to avoid concentration in any one geographic area. These projects were typically constructed as low to mid-rise buildings in neighbourhoods all over Chicago. Despite their relative success, such projects commonly fail to combine public housing with public amenity. In recent years, there has been growing support for projects which leverage hybrid typologies to better serve both residents of individual buildings and their surrounding communities. John Ronan Architects (JRA) have produced a number of such hybrid projects since their inception in 1999.

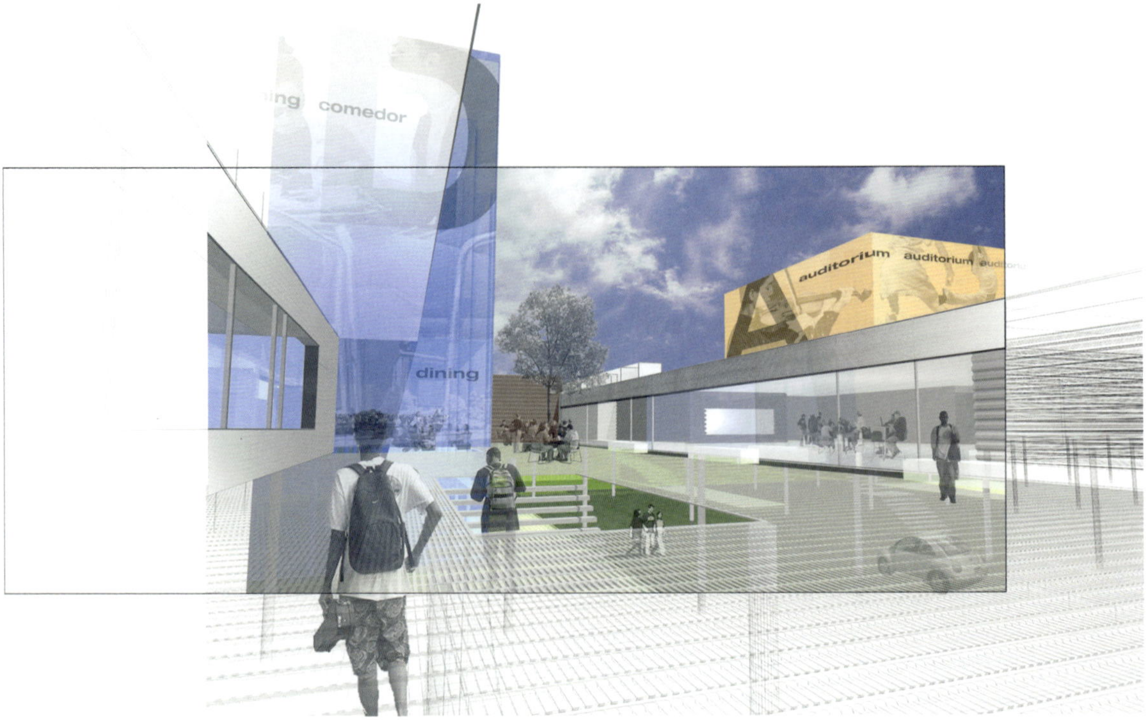

Perth Amboy
High School

In 2003, JRA won a competition for a large high school in New Jersey with 3000 students wherein ideas regarding urban and social hybridity originated. Perth Amboy High School was to be located in a relatively impoverished, largely immigrant community which lacked significant cultural and communal assets.

The winning JRA scheme offered the community a building that would serve not only as a new school, but also as a civic cultural centre. Communal elements, including the library, gym and auditorium were to be shared with the wider community while school was not in session.

The project was designed around three superimposed elements: towers holding the communal spaces, classrooms and an articulated site surface "mat." Parking was located in the middle of the site beneath a striated superstructure which offered covered outdoor spaces, communal spaces and courtyards below and between. The colour-coded and graphic-emblazoned towers, serving the library, gym and auditorium, were embedded and served as anchor points to the classroom blocks which were divided in to six academies.

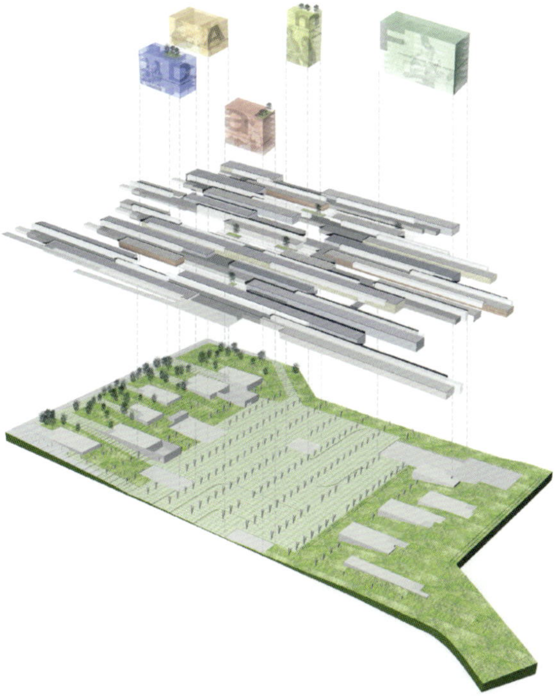

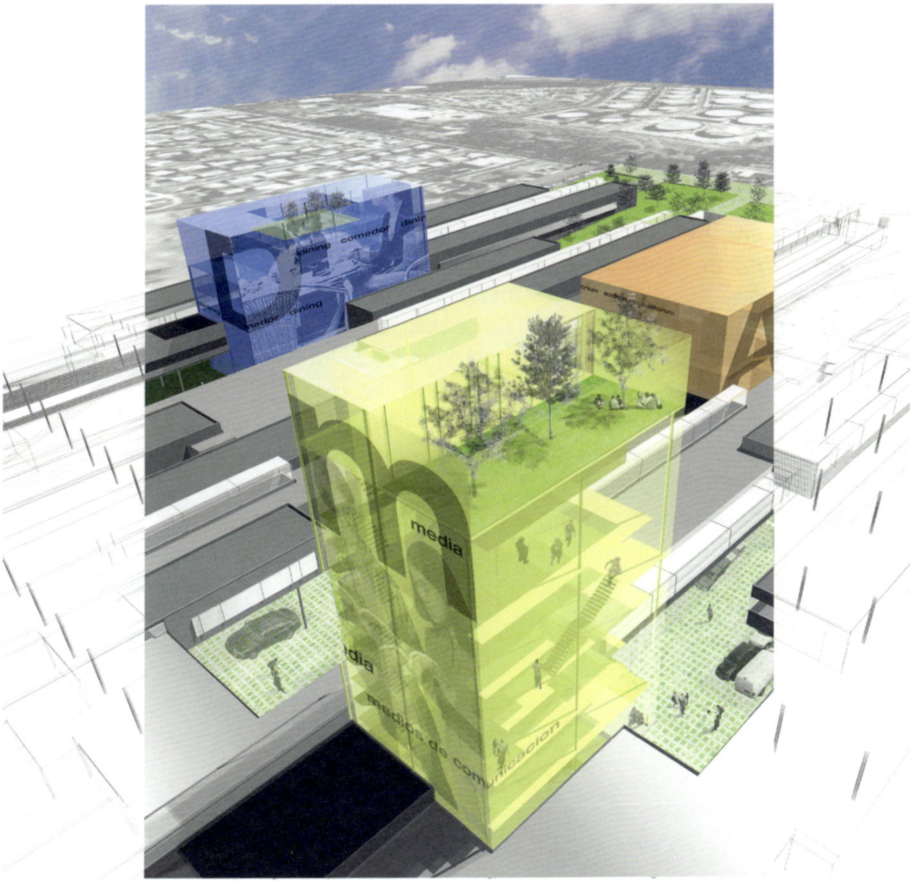
dining
comedor
media
media
medios de comunicación

South Shore High School

While the Perth Amboy project awaited funding, JRA received a commission from the City of Chicago for a compact high-school prototype that would fit on a single city block. JRA utilized the research and insights from Perth Amboy in the new South Shore High School building, which was organized as three bars: body, mind and spirit, that housed recreation, academies and arts. The 220,000 square foot facility would be located on a site measuring 266'x600' to serve 600 students in two academies. Since public school projects have a large number of strict formal requirements – such as 30'x30' classrooms, masonry construction, etc. – the design becomes more about the siting and configuration of the building circulation spaces. The three bars (body, mind and spirit) are shifted to create outdoor spaces for entry, athletics and a reading garden. The strategic breakdown of these three zones allow for hybrid configurations and use by the public outside of school hours.

JRA's South Shore project re-imagines a high school building as a community hub that is activated throughout the day, week and year.

Independence Library + Apartments

By the time Mayor Rahm Emanuel came into office in 2011, the City of Chicago had already enjoyed the success of such hybrid projects. Building on this achievement, they set out to combine public buildings with public housing projects. Using U.S. Department of Housing and Urban Development funding, the idea was to combine rental housing with a library. In 2016, JRA won a competition to design the Independence Library and Apartments, which would serve as a prototype for this new hybrid typology.

To execute the project, JRA had to not only engage with the owner and typical suite of consultants, but also with sixteen different community groups that were involved in the building process. The project also required an accelerated design and construction schedule, with only nine months between initial concept design and groundbreaking, and an additional year and a half to build.

In order to complete meaningful, socially-oriented projects, the architect must not act as an isolated creative genius, but rather as a connector and director who organizes and coordinates the activities of all those involved.

In a conscious attempt to transcend the brutal pragmatism that characterized Chicago's post-war affordable housing projects, such projects aim to recognize, integrate, and improve the physical and social contexts in which they exist through conscious design decisions. Through creative typological thinking accompanied by a sensitive understanding of community needs, projects might be generated that offer safe and dignified housing for all. In the end, it is not about using planning and design to isolate people by wealth or income, but rather about integrating every member of our society into the life and well-being of the city.

JRA's Independence Library combines affordable senior housing and a public library.

FORUM.1

Sasa Radulovic
5468796 Architecture
Professor - Morgenstern Chair IIT

David Brininstool
Brininstool + Lynch Ltd

Peter Landon
LBBA Architects

John Ronan
John Ronan Architects

SR What have you learned from project to project?

PL There is a lot of continuity. In the beginning of our practice we were doing a job, and it evolved into a different job and I said we would need more money. The client said we don't have any money, can you just pick it up on the next job because it's all one big job. And that worked. We see it that way – as one big job. What we learn on one, we bring to another.

PL I think things move slowly in these communities because people don't change quickly - it takes generations to change. If you look at Robert Taylor Homes or Cabrini Green, because they were built so suddenly and all at once, there was no opportunity to learn from the failures. Maybe it's good that it's slow, maybe it's good because it because it gives you a chance to learn, to see what other people are doing, and you don't have one big mistake that's compounded.

DB Our practice is not involved with affordable housing, we're market rate. As land prices rise, where is the give? There is a lot of pressure to keep the construction cost at a point that makes sense to the market. Very early on we learned to engage contractors in the design process.

JR One thing that Peter is facing that David is not is the regulatory framework. When you're designing affordable housing, there are these filters that your design has to pass through: federal, state, local. They make the project more expensive. It's actually more expensive to build affordable housing than it is to build market. That's the irony. That's why you don't see more of it.

SR How important is construction cost versus life cycle cost?

DB Our market used to be 90% for sale and 10% apartment. Along came a financial implosion and now it's the opposite. When it was primarily for sale units, the construction cost pressure was even higher to be competitive. Now that we're doing more rental, we are probably doing higher quality buildings from a construction and durability standpoint. Developers are either hanging on to them or flipping them to institutional clients. That's one of the things driving sustainability in the private sector – these buyers require that these projects meet certain ADA and green building standards.

DB We're starting to see that the land cost per unit is what is escalating the fastest, it's doubled. The rental rates haven't doubled, the sales rates haven't doubled. What's left in that formula to make up the difference? Construction costs. And design fees, of course. It's a lot of pressure in that market.

SR Peter, we had a chance to visit a few of your projects. One aspect that we noticed is the focus on public space like community gardens. Obviously more care was paid there. We like to think that these outdoor spaces create better communities.

PL When the scattered site projects first started, they wanted a separate door to every unit, so we had all these doors on the outside with a small private space for each unit. When they started to tear down all the high rises and implement these plans for transformation, they said there was no "hanging out." You couldn't hang out on the front stoop. So everyone hung out in the parking lot behind the building. So we started incorporating areas in the back with shared spaces for the moms and kids instead of private spaces.

SR How long do your tenants stay in these affordable housing projects? Do they stay for a while or is it a stepping stone?

PL They stay. And they stay. And their kids stay. It's really hard in this country to change class. You're lower income, its hard to break out. Job prospects don't get better, they get worse over time. Aging in place is an important issue - making sure that if the units are not accessible, they are at least universal design.

JR My library project is senior housing so it's the last stop, really. An important difference in the project I show is that it was a competition, which we won. The developer more or less had to build what we designed, they couldn't take liberties. For example the balconies were staggered, but there was a cost premium because it's cheaper to line them up. Somehow it survived value engineering.

SR John, your project has an elevated garden. I assume that adds to the value of the housing.

JR As far as the garden goes, you need it. Look how much it improves the library and the apartments.

You have to make an argument for your project, they're not going to do it just because you're the architect. You need a reason and you have to be persuasive.

JR As an architect you have to know more than design. You have to know the process by which the project will come about. You have to understand the regulatory framework, the politics, construction costs, and many other things that have nothing to do with design in the strict sense. You have to be able to get in there and get a seat at the table.

SR David, have your strategies changed as you moved from condominiums to apartment design?

DB I was going to make a comment about common areas. When we started doing condominiums 20 years ago, people were trying to replicate the private space that they had in their suburban homes. We're seeing that the amount of common area in developments has exploded.

Part of it is the market, developers are trying to attract the same people. There's also an attitude among young professionals that is oriented toward having a shared experience. I hope it's an indication that we're becoming a more urbanized culture.

JR There's also a political component to that though. New tenants move in and ask the city: where's my park? The city puts it back on the developer – you're going to put the park in your building.

If developers want to up zone, the city will ask for things in exchange. That's why on my project, the city embraced the garden. As the neighbourhood gets denser, there's a commensurate increase in public space that's needed.

PL You could easily meet the requirement for outdoor amenity space with balconies, but there is a movement to be more collective. Instead of something small, create something substantial. It's become a much more integrated and socialized environment.

DB Since the land is really at a premium, any shaping of the building you do can also capture a bit of public space. It's not a park, but these little spots are valuable too.

JH Could you highlight anything that you think could go into the architect's expanded realm? Is there anything you see as an opportunity for us as a profession to further the livability agenda?

PL The one thing we haven't talked about is the social construct that we're operating in. As architects we promote what we feel is great architecture, and that's not always what the general public wants. We've had a real breakdown in the conversation between our profession and our consumers.

We're operating in a vacuum. To move forward, there must be a greater conversation between our profession and the public at large. I don't see it happening at the rate we need it to.

PL We look at the projects in Europe and we say, how are they doing it? How do they convince people to put in the resources? I think it's a whole different social construction. It's more a top-down process. In our country, the market place rules. The market only knows what it already knows, it doesn't know the next thing. Developers chase the market, they don't usually create it. When we look around and we see such a mediocre built environment, it's a bigger question than what we're teaching in school or how much architects are paid. It's a much bigger issue.

JR I think there are a lot of areas where architects could be more involved. The low hanging fruit is the zoning codes that the city abides by. Chicago's by-law was written for another era when people worked downtown and went back to their single family home in the suburbs.

The codes and regulations aren't keeping up with the innovation that's happening in the city and the way people are actually living.

www.jrarch.com

HOUSING REVISITED

Skidmore, Owings & Merrill

Although Jonas Salk's research on world population and human values might suggest that we are at a point of potential collapse, it may be argued that we are advancing on a positive journey toward making the world a more sustainable and balanced place for all living things.[1] As a species, we are in a period of rapid urbanization. It is estimated that by 2050, 6.5 billion people will be living in cities. Currently, our cities produce 75% of the world's carbon emissions. Over the 20th century, architects have moved from a built-to-last model to a more linear process of constant production and demolition. It is evident that we have reached the limits of this capacity.

A seminal 1972 work titled "The Limits of Growth" simulated exponential economic and population growth with a finite supply of resources and found a point of collapse that we are approaching with great speed.[2] However, there are alternate scenarios where we might stabilize and find a new equilibrium. An economic theory called the Kondratiev Cycle discusses global innovation and its effects on the worldwide economy. According to this model, we are now entering an era of environmental protection, bio/medical technology and holistic health. These future-focused studies inspire and provide an operational framework for three speculative, research-based community housing projects at three different scales conducted by Skidmore, Owings & Merrill (SOM) over the past decade.

SOM's futureHOME 2050 project is a prototypical sutainable, modular home that is imagined to be both aggregated among existing Chicago neighbourhoods and as a module within a high-rise tower.

futureHOME 2050

In partnership with Chicago's Museum of Science and Industry and the Chicago Botanical Garden, SOM designed an exhibit which imagined the future home of 2050. The project was intended to make a statement about living 30 years in the future through a prototypical building that functioned both as a home and as a component of the museum, demonstrating both the potential for shared living and the evolution of private space. The project team was composed of researchers, futurists, architects and engineers from around the world who brought a diversity of outlooks on the future of housing. The project built upon existing research from SOM, leveraging new technologies for construction, healthy living, on-site energy generation and sustainability.

The net-positive house features a 3D-printed base, joints and central service core, a milled cross-laminated timber structure, a dynamic curtain wall façade and a photovoltaic roof array. The building systems are designed to lower energy consumption by 50% when compared to contemporary building standards and reduce reliance on municipal water infrastructure by utilizing environmental features such as geo-exchange wells, bi-directional vehicle charging, underfloor heat, natural ventilation, smart grid connection, compost, rainwater collection and grey water treatment.

At the same time, the project anticipates and accommodates the dynamic role of the future family, presenting a narrative in which multi-generational households are better equipped to respond to economic and environmental challenges.

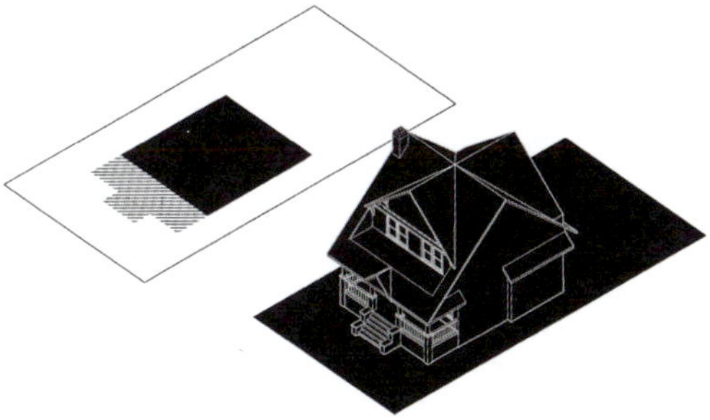

Chicago lot

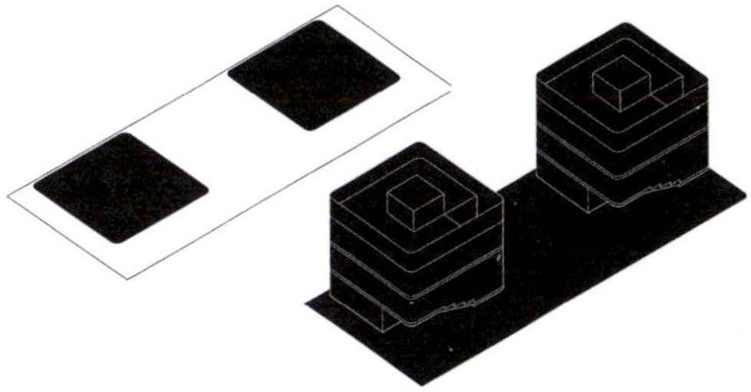

futureHOME 2050 x 2

2050
futureHOME Drive

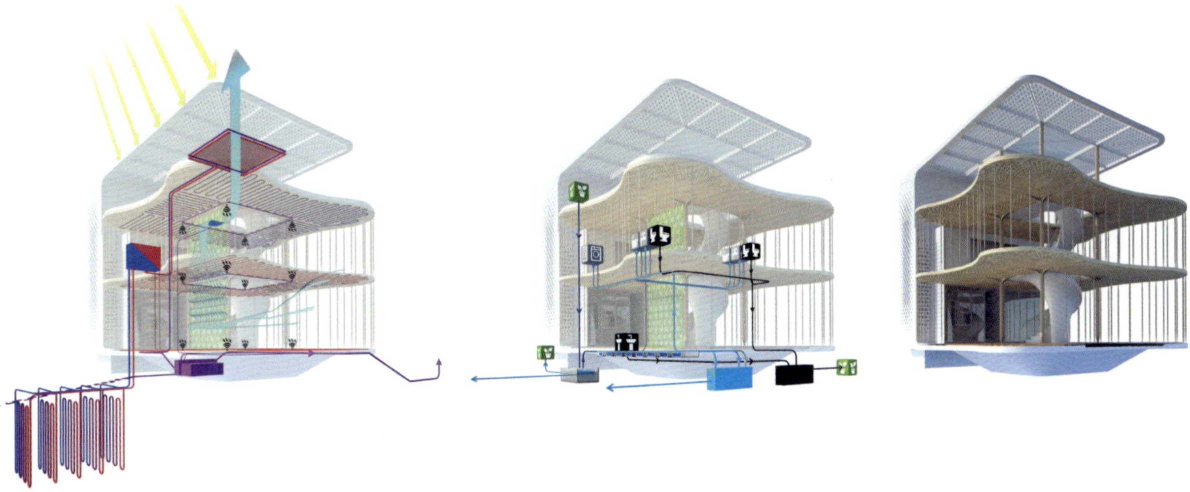

The house is entered through a glass-louvered performative solarium which serves to provide food, clean the air through phytoremediation, and bio-filtre grey and black water. The main floor living spaces anticipate new technologies and modes of entertainment, work and food preparation, while upstairs a multi-generational family is afforded both privacy and places to entertain. Consideration was also given to how the house might provide density and integrate into the existing urban fabric in Chicago. Two of these house modules are designed to fit on a typical double lot with a shared community garden space between.

SOM's futureHOME 2050 concept is imagined as a modular element within a high-rise composition that refigures a typical Chicago neighbourhood block into a tower. The diagrams depict structural, energy and water positive designs in one module.

Around the world, cities are growing with great speed while consistently outperforming national averages for carbon emissions. Cities comprise a small percentage of land area, but provide the extreme majority of our gross domestic product and employment. In Chicago, as in many cities across North America, increased urban density through multi-family housing (as opposed to detached single-family housing) is well suited to accommodate projected urban growth, reduce per-capita building operational energy, optimize infrastructural construction and renovation costs, and reduce transit related energy consumption. With this understanding, lessons learned in the futureHOME 2050 were applied to a higher density model.

By taking the original house design and replicating it vertically along a shared backbone as opposed to horizontally along a street, the typical Chicago block, complete with a diverse mixture of housing, gardens, amenities and public space, is transformed into a community high-rise tower that provides increased density, a sense of community and sustainability.

AMLI 900+

The next project, completed in 2018 with real estate media firm Hanley Wood and developer AMLI Residential, re-imagines the AMLI 900 building, a 440-unit, 24-storey apartment tower built in Chicago in 2007 by Solomon Cordwell Buenz. The goal of the project was not to erect a new building, but rather to evaluate the existing building, prescribe a new set of social and performative goals, re-imagine how the project might change ten years later, and investigate the future design challenges of multi-family housing.

SOM's AMLI project re-imagines an existing high-rise, high-density typology. By reworking the dimensions of the typical unit, establishing new community areas, and including new sustainability features, the AMLI project demonstrates a compelling alternative to the highly criticized mid-century public high-rise buildings.

The team used survey data, sustainability goals, solar analysis and computational fluid dynamic models to redesign the building a decade after its completion according to principles of wellness and healthy living (anticipated by the Kondratiev Cycle) at the scale of the unit, group, community and city. The size and proportion of the room modules were changed to increase flexibility with regard to multi-generational living, family type and use as well as to increase the quality of air and daylight in each unit. A performative outdoor terrace acts as an amenity, operable wall and thermal buffer between the unit and the outside air. Since the developer is interested not only in rent, but also in how they might attract and retain long-term tenants, they benefit greatly from flexible and adaptable units that respond to people's changing needs over time.

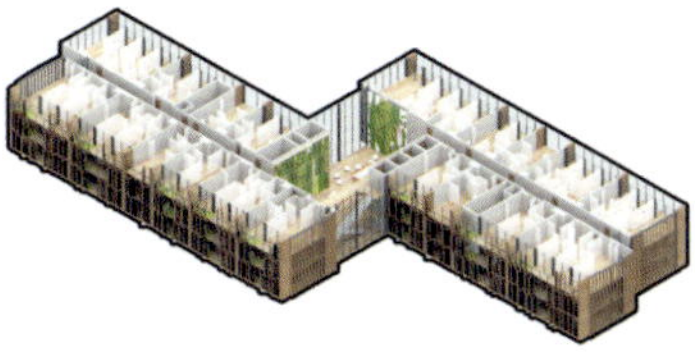

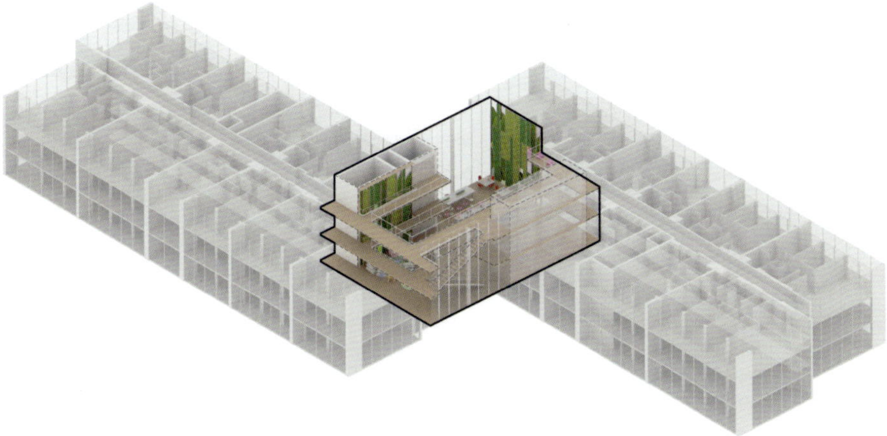

AMLI 900

AMLI 900+

At the scale of the floor, tenants expressed a preference for feelings of security, personalization, intimacy and connection to others. In the new design, the individual unit size is slightly decreased in order to allow natural light into the corridors and provide an additional 2,200 square feet to be redistributed as communal resident or "neighbourhood" amenity spaces. This found area creates a series of three-storey performative atrium spaces that group three floors (57 units) of the building together into a central neighbourhood hub with a single elevator access point. The atrium is used to collect and distribute fresh light and air via natural ventilation to the corridor spaces beyond. The atrium also includes a phytoremediation wall and a community-focused open space that might be used for communal dining, a flexible workspace, a winter garden, a fitness centre or an entertainment venue, encouraging a heightened sense of community and personal identity.

The building is thereby composed as a community of eight vertically stacked neighbourhood bundles with 57 units per neighbourhood. At the ground level, the existing building features a parking garage, vehicle drop-off area and lobby space. In anticipation of a personal vehicle reduction and public transit usage increase, the new design envisions a gradual re-purposing of the garage to host an urban farm, local grocery store and street activating retail space along with additional amenity spaces that better connect the residents to the city beyond. The rooftop of the building is transformed to take advantage of the great views and includes fitness spaces, photovoltaic panels and community areas.

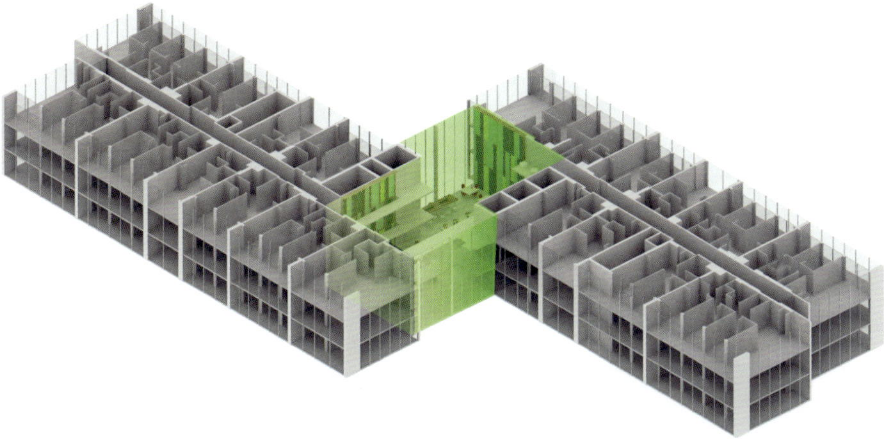

While the existing building is oriented north to south, the new design calls for the building to be turned 90 degrees in order to reduce overall energy consumption and take advantage of daylighting and views. A mass timber construction system coupled with the building reorientation, high-performance envelope, an advanced building management system, shared energy between units, and on-site renewable energy generation pushes the building toward a low embodied carbon, all-electric, net-zero target. Though the initial construction costs would be higher than the existing building, it is calculated that through the improved amenity spaces and sustainable energy initiatives, the market rate per unit would be significantly increased alongside an intended increase in resident retention, health, well-being and sense of community.

At a time when cities are experiencing rapid growth and change, a serious yet optimistic, speculative yet attainable vision for housing provides a unique opportunity to challenge and rethink traditional construction methods, building practices and modes of living. Through this innovative set of experimental projects, SOM leverages emerging technologies, building science and social theory to imagine a future that is socially and environmentally sustainable. Despite the contemporary challenges of population density, energy resource depletion and material consumption, through architectural innovation we can make positive progress toward a world that is a better-balanced place for all living things.

FORUM.2

Martin Felsen
UrbanLab

Arathi Gowda
Skidmore, Owings & Merrill LLP

Andrew Obendorf
Skidmore, Owings & Merrill LLP

MF There seems to be a kind of large scale investigation happening in the three projects you presented. You look at the whole world, then there's a local investigation where you see architecture trying to accomplish some of the metrics you're looking at. I noticed a bit of tension as you try to funnel a lot of these larger statistics, problems and ideas into your projects. How do you resolve that as practicing designers?

AG We've done a lot of data aggregation with AIA National. When you look at energy use, multi-family housing produces a lot of emissions when compared to other sectors. We try and look at these meta narratives because it helps inform us.

AO I think you have to scare the daylights out of people every once in a while and understand how poorly we're performing in a lot of these markets and also around the world.

Chicago is not a high-performing city in terms of the buildings we are constructing. Having that fear in your mind when you are going into a project is a great asset, because you understand how important it is and how wasteful a lot of things are.

AG We talk about visible and invisible strategies. As designers we care about the way things look and we know visually what will draw people, but it is the invisible things that are going to get us. We are constantly thinking of ways to seduce. So you have a garden space, but it's actually a performative garden space with daylighting and energy use. That's how we need to be thinking as designers.

MF The projects you showed, they're for a certain class of people. There's a kind of social sustainability that you're after. How do you talk about it in the office, the idea of affordability that came up in the last panel. How accessible are these ideas? How can we make them more widespread given their expense?

AO You need to leverage those white-collar projects to understand how they work, to understand the process that goes into designing it and making them feasible. If you can apply these technologies, understand how they work and execute them, you can help further the research.

With all inventions, what does the first one cost versus the hundredth? That's how we think about it. By understanding them you drive up the availability.

AG I think it's important to note, the AMLI project was designed to Passive House standards. We shared a few theoretical projects today. How do you make every project perform this way? It is important for us to advocate for collective thinking.

I know we don't think about certifications or policy in school, but these kinds of programs drive the market. In California and London when we aggregate data across our firm, the code is harder and it accelerates the trends and brings cost down. We've more than quintupled the rate of code adoption for energy efficiency in this country. That's huge. We can be better designers if we buy things at cost together.

MF The reason that SOM's reputation is so high and has been there for decades, is that you share information, you disseminate, you publish. There's been an open knowledge database that your firm has tried to establish where you try to open up the secrets and not have proprietary information. There is a social function that grounds the firm. How do you plan to get the next generation of information out to students, faculty, researchers and the general public?

AO We engage with a lot schools. For example, I teach at the University of Tennessee College of Architecture and Design. They have a great program that brings together a practicing office with students, faculty and scientists. So we are all thinking about things in different ways but running down parallel paths, tackling the same problems. The results start to leapfrog very quickly. It's about engagement. It's about publishing. When you start any of these projects, the first Google search sends you down a path of finding out what's been done before, so making information available is very important.

TAKING CHARGE

MA+HG Architects

Established in 2009, MA+HG Architects is an architectural practice based in Vancouver that strives to address environmental, economic and social sustainability in the city through the primary lens of missing middle housing projects.

Behind San Francisco, Vancouver is the second most unaffordable housing market in North America.[1] Landlocked between mountains and the Pacific Ocean, there is a limited landmass on which to build. At the same time, the population of Vancouver is expected to grow by 45,000 residents per year toward an estimated population of 1.2 million by 2041. It is estimated that these new residents will require approximately 500,000 additional housing units, with current growth only projected to accommodate half of the expected need. The housing industry in Vancouver cannot build fast enough and does not have enough land on which to build.

Despite the clear need for increased density, 68% of this limited land mass is zoned for single-family housing. Only at the end of 2018 was a by-law passed to allow duplexes in single family zones – a small step that took eight years to implement. Increasing density anywhere other than along transit corridors and existing high-density neighbourhoods has been an intense battle despite the relatively low number of truly single-family dwellings, since many existing homes have secondary suites. Retaining the character of these single-family neighbourhoods (a thinly veiled colloquialism for low density and decidedly un-modern housing) is a priority for many Vancouver residents.

The resistance to alternative housing models and the lack of affordable housing is amplified by the commodification and widespread financial corruption of the Vancouver real estate market, which has resulted in year-over-year spikes in land prices and real estate values. There is a clear lack of affordable housing for the average resident and a deficiency of housing security, especially among renters who in 2018 made up 46% of Vancouver's population.

This set of unique spatial, social, economic and zoning pressures has defined much of the residential architecture in Vancouver. Formulaic and quantifiable developer pro formas and data driven zoning restrictions have reduced the architect's job to designing the skin around a predetermined program and massing. As a result, Vancouver's housing stock is made up primarily of podium towers, six-storey double loaded corridor apartments buildings and "character" single-family houses, with little in between.

Over the last number of years, these issues have changed how we perceive our relationships to our homes, communities and environments, resulting in a grand re-envisioning of Vancouver's future. A political shift in both provincial and civic government has led to rapid policy changes – including an empty homes tax and a speculation tax – in order to push back against years of formulaic for-profit development and cool the real estate market. Such policies support the desire for walkable, neighbourly urban environments, a community of sharing spaces that promotes increased social interaction toward an overarching sense of joy and belonging. This model relies less on quantity and actively questions how much space one truly needs as a function of economic, environmental and social factors. We believe one of the best ways to save money and have a smaller carbon footprint is to simply build less.

To describe the relationship between these new forces and our work in this arena, we have appropriated the psychological term "social density" to mean both the density in an area in terms of the number of people and the number of interpersonal reactions that are likely to happen in a given setting.

For our purposes, we achieve social density through three key strategies: densification, sociability and sharing, and the preservation of heritage buildings. A timeline of projects proposed and completed by MA+HG Architects over the past decade demonstrates these principles, as well as an inverse relationship between the area in square feet per occupant and community – as one's personal footprint gets smaller, the principles of liveability, sociability and community become increasingly more important.

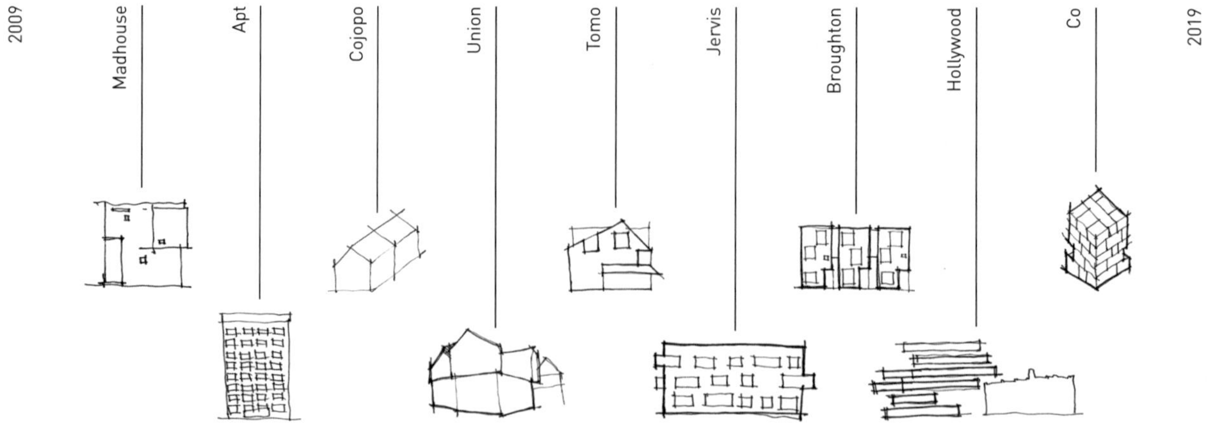

Vancouver
British Columbia

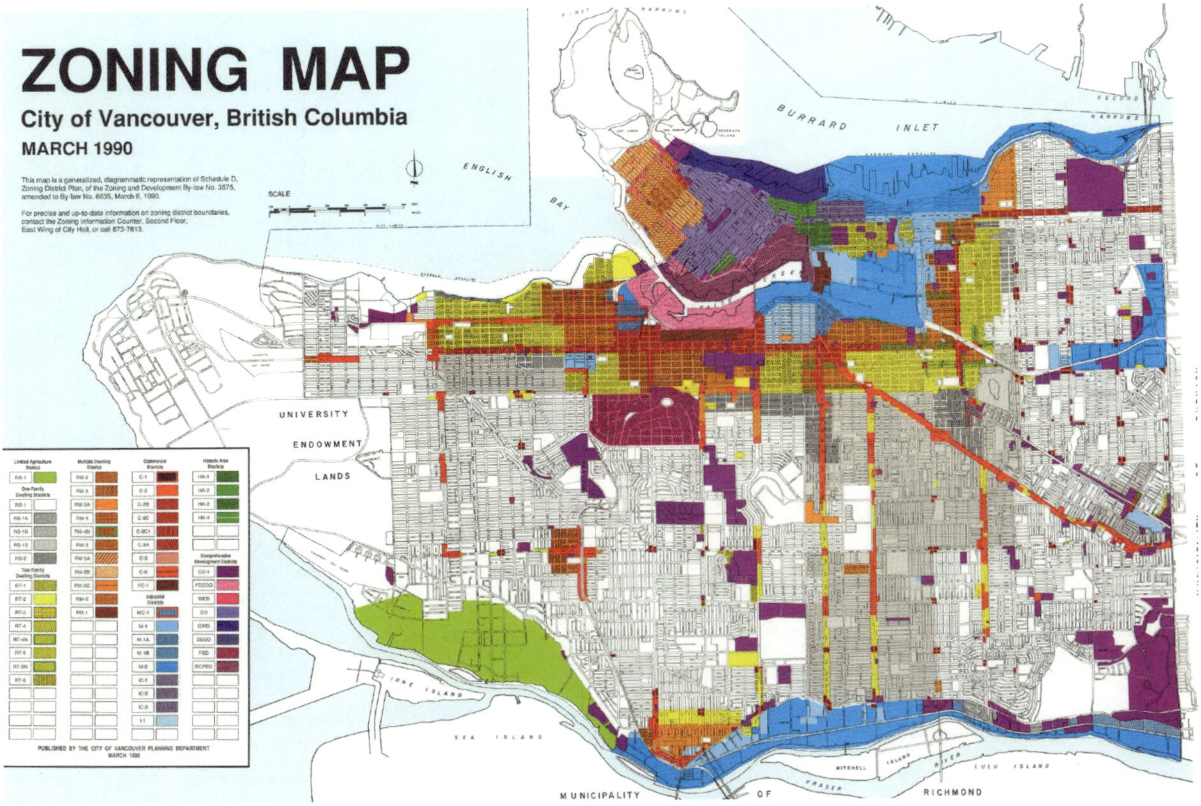

SOCIAL DENSITY

Densification

01 More than three units per standard sized lot (33x122).
02 Elimination / reduction of setbacks = more efficient use of land.
03 Elimination / reduction of parking = more space for people.
04 Employing smaller units with liveability features: higher ceiling heights, dual aspect units.
05 Make it beautiful.

Sociability & sharing

01 Creating connections between units.
02 Thoughtful design at moments of intersection.
03 Rethinking "family".
04 Creating maximum interaction: sharing amenities, functions, outdoor space, tools...
05 Integrate with nature.

Save heritage buildings

01 Recognizing places of shared memory + history.
02 Saving heritage buildings makes density acceptable.
03 Make it beautiful.

"Single Family," up to 3 units only.

"Everything Else," where different uses, typologies and scales are permitted, including multi-family residential.

Tomo

621 sq m
6684 sq ft
Min. Site Area

20 m
65 ft
Frontage

13.87 m
45'-6
Height

1.47
FSR

53%
Site Coverage

Tomo (which stands for "together more") is one example of an affordable middle-housing solution that addresses these elements of social density. Situated between a bustling transit thoroughfare and a quiet single-family community, Tomo is a pure example of a missing middle project in Vancouver. The project is a co-housing dwelling situated on a double-wide lot that was originally zoned for single-family use with up to 5,000 square feet of buildable area, based on a floor space ratio (FSR) of 0.75. MA+HG Architects completed a rezoning process in the fall of 2018 under the Affordable Housing Choices Policy for Co-Housing that allowed for increased density on certain sites in Vancouver with a demonstrated need for enhanced affordability. In this case, affordability is ensured by a covenant that limits the resale value of the units to 25% below market rates at the time of each sale in perpetuity. The project also establishes

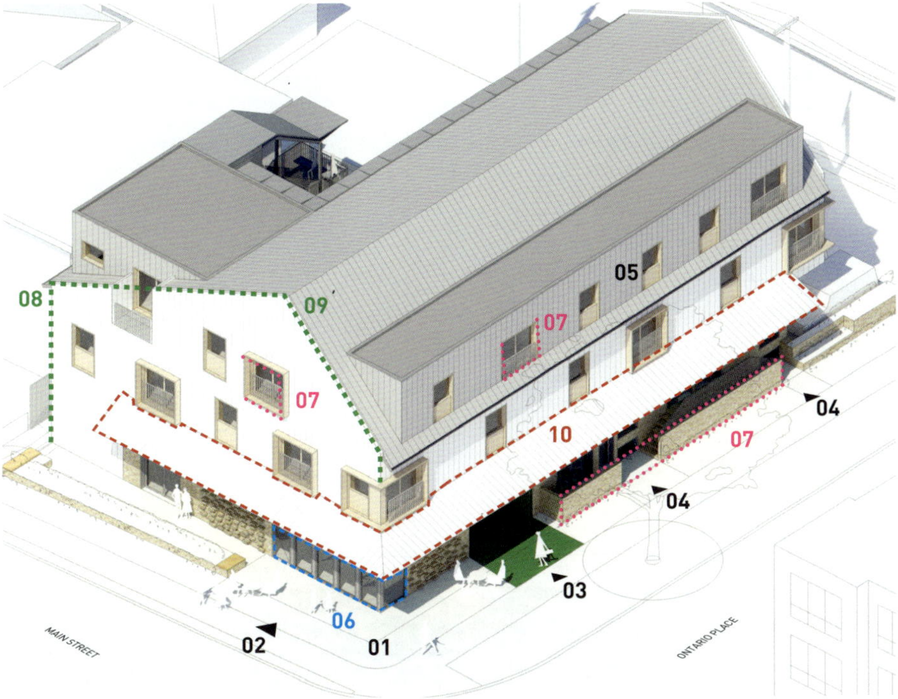

01 Community interface: The front yard creates a soft zone between public and private realms, where Tomo residents, neighbours and passers-by intermingle.
02 The entry at Common House activates the northeast corner of Main St. and Ontario Pl.
03 The residential entrance marks the arrival from Main St. into a residential scale environment.
04 Entrances to the townhouses along Ontario Place activate the street and give a residential scale while still allowing for privacy.
05 A residential scaled façade along Ontario Pl. and Main St. provides a soft, approachable edge.
06 Generous glazing creates social transparency in and out of the Common House.
07 Public / private interface at neighbour stoops and Juliette balconies: These semi-private spaces encourage residents to linger where they can cast eyes on the street, but still feel at home.
08 The southeast roof line is scaled to two storeys to respect the context and mediate the streetscape.
09 The building profile is shaped by the familiar "gable" form that maintains a residential character and scale.
10 The street canopy creates greater comfort for residents as well as other pedestrians.

a link between sociability and affordability; residents save money through the sharing of spaces, resources, and time. The rezoning of the project allowed for approximately 15,000 square feet of buildable area, populated by 12 co-housing units which range from 500-square-foot studios to 1,000 square foot, three-bedroom units.

The architectural parti and form respond to a desire for new architectural typologies between a single-family home and a typical six-storey apartment building. The "sharing parti" prioritizes the traditional backyard by wrapping the building around a central south-facing courtyard. This courtyard format allows generous access to shared outdoor space, while the inclusion of a "common house" along the front side allows this shared space to extend out into the public streetscape. A single large gabled roof form echoes the traditional architecture of the surrounding neighbourhood and gathers all public and private spaces together. This gesture becomes an outward expression of the co-housing community of twelve families, who have figuratively and literally gathered together under one roof. The public and private realms are well articulated through materiality and disposition, with the resident stoops and the common house at the corner of the project acting as a transitional zone between the two.

Tomo is intended to be the first of many housing developments that prioritizes principles of social density. The project strives to serve the missing middle through typological innovation, buildability, affordability, sociability and sustainability.

Co-

Sometimes policies don't go far enough. Despite recent improvements, Vancouver remains a surprisingly conservative city that continues to impose strict parameters on height and density in response to community sentiment. To challenge these restrictions and the strong preference for single-family traditional housing, MA+HG Architects undertook a research project named Co-, commissioned by Rize Alliance, which proposes an innovative yet pragmatic new high-density housing model for Vancouver. Based on principles of social density and shared community, the study challenges local by-law and zoning rules, but abides by all Part 3 National Building Code of Canada requirements.

Co- proposes a membership-based multi-family housing model that is grounded on ideas of community, building porosity, access to outdoor space and the sharing of amenities. By shifting square footage away from individual unit sizes toward amenity spaces, more units are allowed, amenity spaces are bolstered, and traditional notions of public-private space are challenged. The project started with an analysis of the typical area of an individual unit in Vancouver, then reallocates approximately 40% of this area toward additional units and communal amenity space. By eliminating redundant private areas within an individual suite, communal spaces such as shared kitchens, courtyards, lounges, laundry areas and exercise facilities are created.

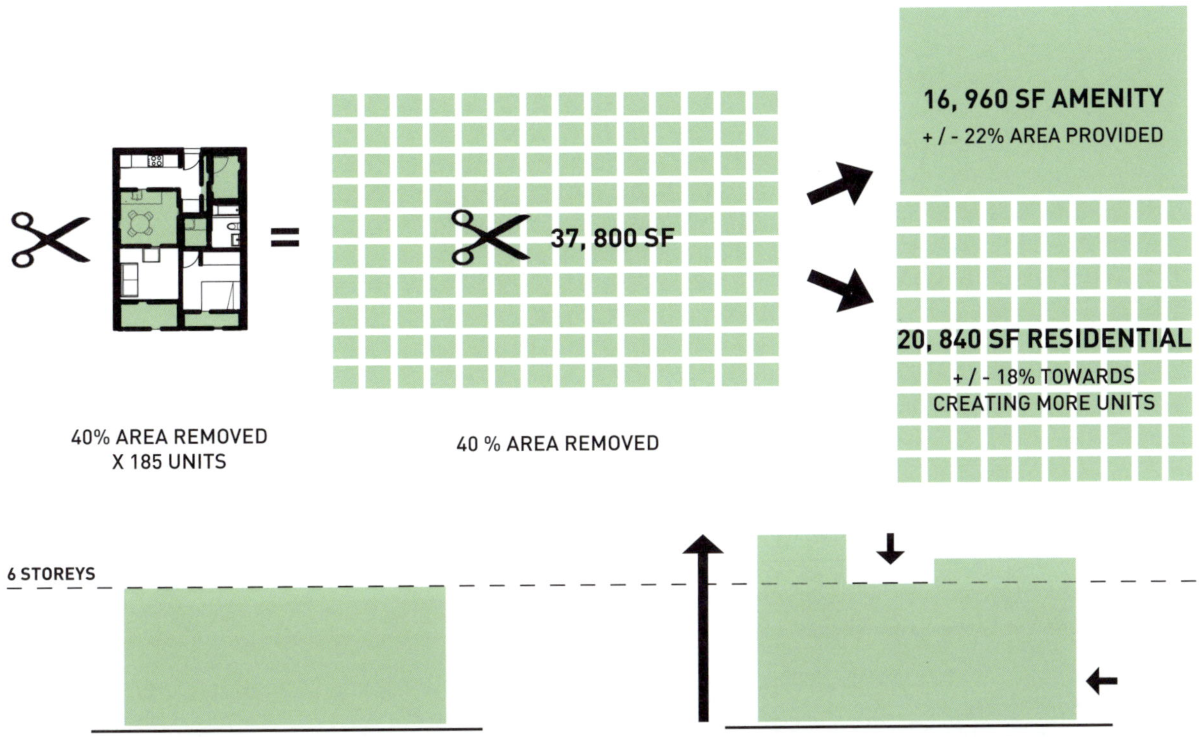

MA+HG Architects' Co- housing reconsiders North American planning principles by shifting space away from the individual unit and toward new collective amenity spaces.

The amenity spaces allow sociability to play a more significant role in everyday life: activities that would traditionally be conducted in solitude are instead conducted communally.

Co- includes 185 affordable units that may be rented at below-market rates. At the same time, the increased unit count offsets additional construction costs brought on by the building typology. A highly porous and expressive architecture that contains both ample green space and access to sunlight, challenges the current building by-laws and offers an alternative to homogeneous six-storey construction.

Modular units compose a variety of dwelling configurations ranging from studio to three-bedroom units, which allows the development to house a highly diverse, multi-generational community. Activities and amenity spaces are specifically designed to catalyze community relationships and spirit at a variety of scales, from the neighbour to the block, from the neighbourhood to the village, all the way up to the city at large. Stoops, recreational spaces, breaks in the building, patios, kitchens, lounges and commercial retail units are shared in a variety of ways, from tenant to tenant, family to family, floor to floor, building block to building block and resident to pedestrian.

Minimal & liveable private space

Shared essential amenities that are part of your daily routine

Access to co-amenities across the city

One might reasonably ask if such a model is financially feasible. After a $150 decrease in monthly rent which accounts for increased build costs and profit, an increase in revenue of 22% for the developer was calculated. The intention of this work is to reveal creative opportunities for development that support affordability, community interaction and sociability in tandem with our drive toward the formation of a sharing economy and of homes that inspire happiness.

Each of these projects is based on the fundamental tenets of sharing and community. They propose new typologies that challenge us to rethink traditional single-family neighbourhoods and strive for new modes of living. In a city with exorbitantly high land prices, where it is common practice to tear down and build anew, our work aims to be beautiful and livable while maintaining a strong connection to its context. The ideas presented are not necessarily new; in many ways they represent a return to the way things used to be and the ways in which we used to live. Ultimately, they reveal how architecture is fundamentally about problem solving. We hold great faith in the power of architecture to creatively respond to issues of middle housing, and how, particularly in the case of social density, creativity is a quantifiable good.

FORUM.3

Rafael Longoria
University of Houston

Marianne Amodio
MA+HG Architects

Trevor Boddy
Writer + Curator

RL One of the questions that keeps coming up throughout this symposium is whether architects are the best people to do housing. From everything we have seen today, I'd say the answer is yes. What do you think you were prepared and not prepared to do from your architectural education?

MA I don't think I was prepared to walk into a city that had this sudden affordability crisis. I moved to Vancouver in 2005, it was bustling because of the Olympics. Coming from Winnipeg, it was already unaffordable. Because of that our perspective was different and our expectations were different. We never expected to be able to buy a house. We wanted to be close to nature in a livable, walkable community. Vancouver is still all of those things. The expectations of people who grew up there is that they should be able to afford a house. It's a shock to them that what their parents have isn't available to them. Coming to terms with that has been challenging. When it comes to added density and smaller spaces, we deal with a lot of anger. People are upset that this is where we have to go.

TB You're incredibly active on civic and planning committees. Can you talk about reconciling that with your design practice? It seems to me you're working as a planner, advocate and architect.

MA I've been lucky enough to sit on a number of mayoral advisories for housing, due to our earlier work. For me, it's impatience.

I don't want to sit around and wait for them to decide that in 20 years, 20% of the population gets to live on 80% of the land mass.

It's absurd. And it takes so long for these changes to come around. I really want to be involved in pushing the city and advocating for this change that is really needed.

RL I'm surprised to hear there is this anger in Vancouver. How can a place that appears to be an architect's dream come true have this dark side?

MA There are a lot of problems in Vancouver right now. I have a five-year-old practice with my husband and we have an opportunity to shape a city. I feel grateful for that. It's a beautiful city and the people are excellent. We love it and we'll always continue to live there. For a lot of people, the changes came so quickly that it was hard to manage emotionally. Our city has altered so much.

A lot of it is perception. We must have neighbourhoods that look like single-family neighbourhoods, but really that's a lie when there are six people living in a single-family house. Why do we degrade the renter or the people who can't afford to live in the front of the property? We relegate renters to laneway houses, transit corridors and towers while 20% of the population lives in these single-family dwellings that data shows are emptying out because no one can afford to live there. If we recognize the truth, we can make changes that will benefit everyone.

When I ask people if they would prefer to live in a 30-storey tower next to a subway or a four-storey building in a single-family neighbourhood, the answer is obvious. Everyone would choose to live in a walk-up, but we're not zoned for that. It makes me mad and it's so undemocratic. I don't think it's the right answer.

TB I'd like to ask a different kind of question and get into the designs you've done. People who teach architectural history and theory like Raphael, Michelangelo and myself know that the success of shared facilities in housing complexes in multiple cultures and at multiple times in history is not always good. There can be enormous resistance. What can be different in yours?

MA I think it's different because it's a choice.

We're moving to a sharing economy. We see a lot of co-working spaces, car sharing – what it does is catalyze community. In a tower you barely know your next door neighbour. But you create these areas for community living, sharing and collaboration.

TB There's getting to know, and getting to know far too well. How do you decide which amenities are shared?

MA We have this project called Apt, it's a 12-storey apartment building where all of the units are 150 square feet. It has 15,000 square feet of amenity space and it used to be a senior's home. Half of the project was changing the covenant to be suited for millennial work force housing. We renovated the amenity space into shared kitchens, lobbies and work spaces. Bathrooms were not on the list. When you're living small, you have to think about where's the line? We can pretend, but it's closer to more conservative than maybe we'd all like.

RL These are market-rate developer projects. How did the developer react? What came first, did the developer ask you to think of different ways to do it? Or did you change the brief?

MA We have a history of doing this kind of work and dealing with small scale, so the developer approached us to create a design. They were curious. If we try to do something different, what would it look like? What does it mean for our pro forma and construction cost? We were grateful to be paid to put it all together into a cohesive project.

TB Real estate is a commodity and it tends to be sold by the square foot. How did you hold the hand of the developer and put a price on the collective space? Did you come up with a pro forma or financial model?

MA The Co- project is rental. The city has a program to incentivize developers to add more density in exchange for controlled rental rates. The way we spoke to the developer about it was tying the unit size to a portion of the amenity space. So when they rent the space, their square footage includes a portion of the amenity area that the tenant uses.

We did another project like this where we looked at micro units with amenity space. Almost every week the amenity kept get smaller and smaller. They were trying to fit the zoning constraints, but it was becoming containers for people. We had to walk away.

RL Would you say there are a lot of progressive developers in Vancouver?

MA We are lucky enough to work with a couple of the best developers in Vancouver. They are often long-time property owners, so land values don't come into play as much. It's harder to create a project like Co- or Tomo if you bought the property yesterday.

RL How can you make housing more affordable in Vancouver?

MA I used to think I could answer that question, but I sat around a table with some very intelligent economists and policy makers. The problems aren't just related to land mass. There is widespread financial corruption from foreign bodies. There are a lot empty apartments – we call them piggy banks. There's nothing we as architects can do about that.

At the same time, like SOM, we believe in remaining positive and finding the silver lining. Half of our clients are families who are coming together to buy properties so they can all live in it. To me that's a beautiful thing, rather than everyone living in their 2,500 square foot houses and never talking to each other. To me, architecture is a political act. We talk about what's important to us and what we value through what we choose to build.

TB Vancouver creates an atmosphere of innovation. We've always been a dense, constrained city. We were innovative in housing 100 years ago, 50 years ago and now. These are the causes we need to think through, like MA+HG have done. We're kind of a laboratory. We're the hottest hot money city in the world. We're a safety deposit box. But that's happening everywhere to a certain degree. These are the trends that will shape cities.

The nice thing about the case studies and examples that we are hearing about at this symposium, is that we can start to cross-reference them to create connections and solutions.

MIDDLE
platform
platform MIDDLE
Architecture for Housing the 99%

KAWS
PEANUTS
AQUAFINA

TOTAL ARCHITECTURE

KANVA

KANVA is a multidisciplinary studio located in Montreal whose work strives to expand the scope of architecture through multi-family housing projects, large-scale installations and public spaces. Founded by Tudor Radulescu and Rami Bebawi, KANVA has undergone a series of self-reinventions in response to challenging economic circumstances. Through this process, they have developed considerable expertise in development, construction, finance and design. As a result, they are able to counter the typical hyper-specialization of practice by taking projects into their own hands not just as architects, but as consultants, advocates, developers and general contractors. This approach has enabled the firm to not only finance and build their own projects, but also afforded them a credibility that allows for increased creative flexibility in their built work.

In the 1970s, Dutch soccer coach Rinus Michels developed a style of play called Total Football in which, through all-around skill and creativity, eleven players would act interchangeably as a single unit as opposed to an aggregated sum of discrete positions and functions.[1] KANVA believes strongly in such cross-competence; studio members bring a wide variety of skills to the team that act in tandem with traditional architectural knowledge, coming together to make up a total architecture.

This comprehensive approach to building encompasses design, management, construction, finance and operation. By combining these elements into a total architecture, the firm has developed expertise in their craft regardless of whether or not they serve in every capacity for each project. It also affords them a high degree of validity when acting in a non-comprehensive capacity.

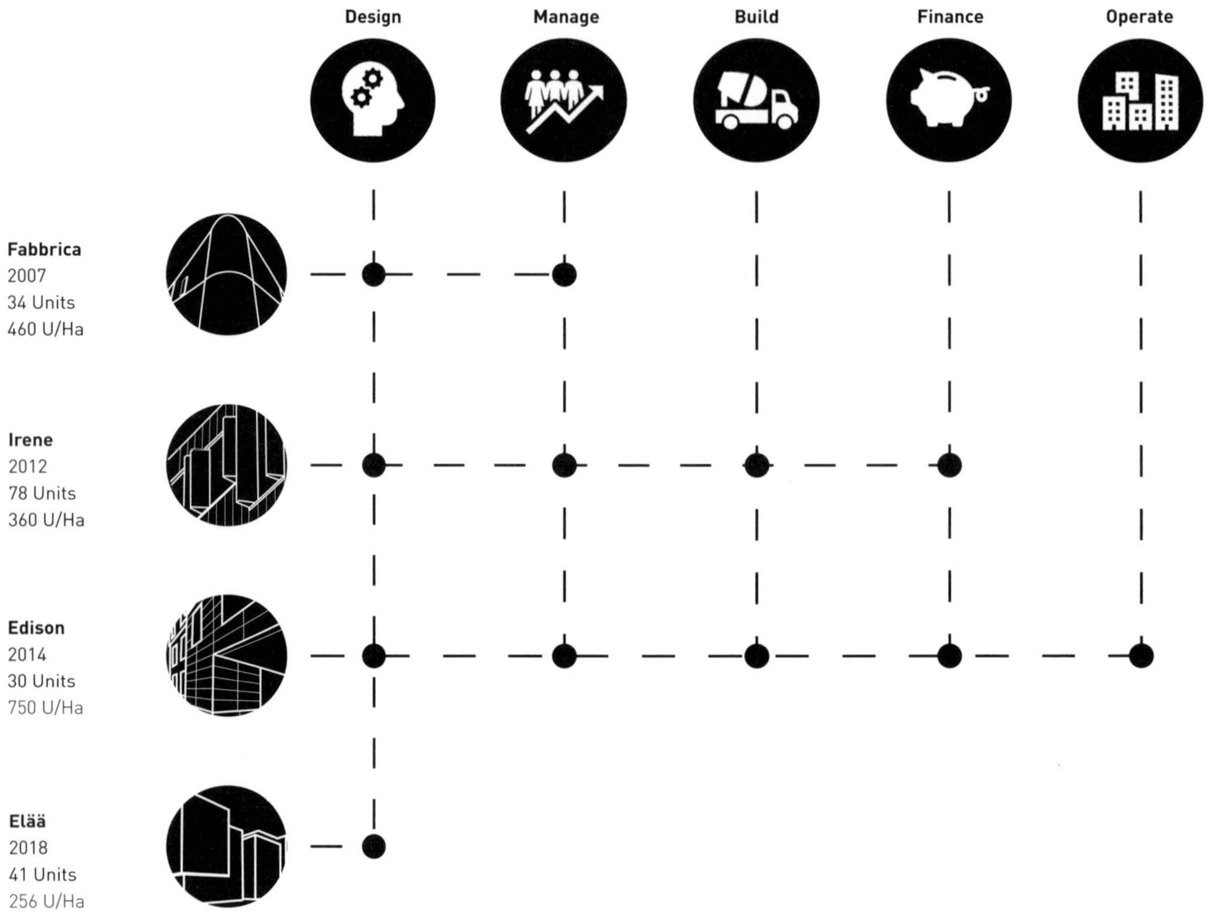

Four projects highlight the firm's range of experience over the last fifteen years. Starting in 2007 with the Fabbrica project, where KANVA handled design and management, the firm developed its abilities in the Irene, Edison and Elää projects towards a total architecture. All of the lessons learned from taking on additional responsibilities allow KANVA to become better architects and to deliver better projects.

Total architecture

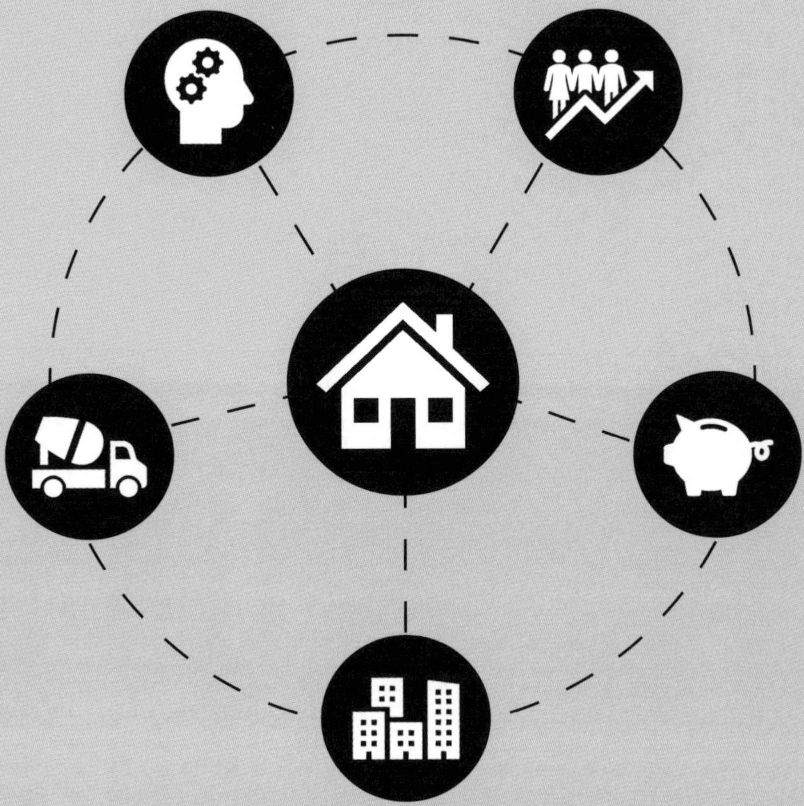

Design
Architecture, Art, Graphic Design, Urban Design, Landscape Architecture, Interior Design

Management
Marketing, Public Engagement, Sales, Development, Communications, Legal

Build
General Contracting, Supplier, Installer/Builder

Finance
Mortgage, Capital Investment, Evaluation, Risk & Value Analysis, Construction Finance

Operations
Leasing, Accounting, Maintenance, Tenant Management

Fabbrica

Fabbrica reimagines an existing industrial building in a revolving neighbourhood as a sensitively designed multi-family housing project. Through a close understanding of market trends and building requirements, KANVA identified an opportunity for meaningful development and infill density. Although its outward design presence is subtle, the project demonstrates how an intimate knowledge of Montreal, a willingness for calculated risk-taking, and a creative vision for the reuse of a heritage building can bolster an under-valued neighbourhood.

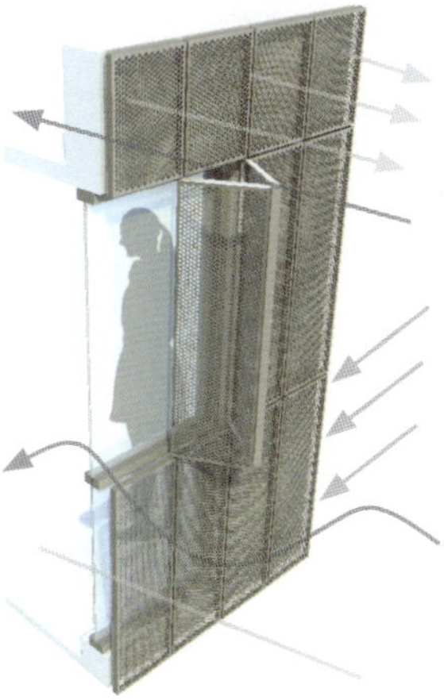

Irene

Irene is an urban mixed-use development that was designed, financed and constructed by KANVA in 2012. An adaptive re-use project, Irene integrates a perforated aluminum clad volume on top of an existing early 20th century industrial building. The new double-skinned façade acts not only in contrast to and in dialogue with the old building below, but also as a performative veil that allows for privacy and natural ventilation while integrating and concealing mechanical systems.

Edison

Edison is a student housing project that demonstrates a genuine work of total architecture. Using an innovative photoengraved concrete method, Edison responds to the site's history by weaving together a visual narrative with shared amenities. Due to its unique design and programming, evaluators had difficulty assessing the building's value. In order to prove the project's financial viability, KANVA took on the responsibility of attracting tenants and operating the building for a number of years before its eventual sale.

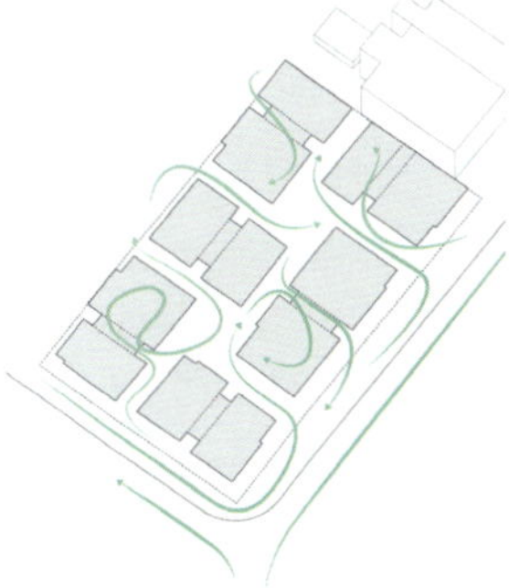

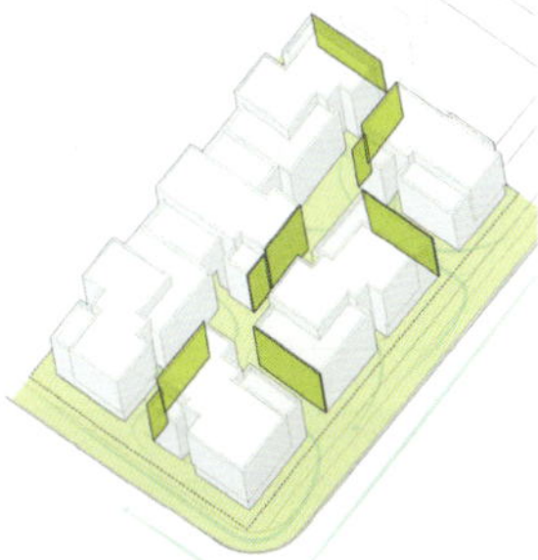

Elää

Situated along the St. Lawrence River in Montreal, the borough of Verdun is made up of a series of well-populated urban parks and alleys. Elää is a multi-family housing project that creates a microcosm of its surroundings through its composition of alleys and public spaces. As a result of the firm's past experience managing, building and financing projects as well as the use of an inexpensive charred wood façade, KANVA was able to make informed arguments and find room in the budget for outdoor communal amenity spaces.

Across these four projects, KANVA demonstrates their approach to total architecture. For Edison, insightful interior design and management strategies leverage a close understanding and empathy for student needs and behaviours. At Elää, an unexpected urban design scheme includes passages and courtyards, which echo its surrounding context. In a number of these projects, a graphic design strategy developed in-house puts forward the architecture and its narratives as visual identities and primary sales elements.

For Edison and Irene, *guerrilla* public art installations and public events root the buildings in their social context by inviting community participation while serving as secondary marketing strategies. Prior to the construction of Edison, 30 used bed frames were purchased online and placed on site to promote the future building, elicit feedback and generate discussions around the project. At the Irene project, community youth were invited to participate in the creation of large-scale graffiti and murals on the interior walls of the existing industrial building.

ArchigraphiK was KANVA's urban art graffiti workshop that provided secondary students from different Montreal schools with an outlet for expression as well as a chance to interact with their city's built heritage. The workshop entailed staging and documenting an intervention in a local space slated for demolition.

Through events, public engagement, art, massing and building technology, these projects reveal the story of their own place in time and in the life of the city.

Development and management mean not only being able to fight to obtain permits for projects that fall outside normal architectural categories, but also to identify opportunities for meaningful work despite significant financial risk. In some instances, this may mean placing bids on projects without the necessary funds. In others, this may mean acting in a capacity outside the typical architectural scope by bringing together a diverse combination of institutional, public and private stakeholders in order to invent a project where one might not otherwise exist. An offer was placed on Fabbrica without sufficient financing to finalize the purchase, however the agreement gave the firm a window of time to generate a pro forma, ratify its potential and obtain the necessary support to make the project happen.

When such projects arise out of unique circumstances, it is often necessary to become involved in marketing and sales. Here again, the architecture itself can play a central role. Through effective communication of the quality and energy of a given building, users are better able to connect with it. Through graphic design, art and events, the architectural and narrative qualities of the building are represented in new ways to attract tenants.

Prior to the construction of Edison, KANVA staged a pop-up installation, *30 lits*, that included 30 bedframes on the site of the new building, allowing the public to visualize and engage with the project prior to its realization.

The total architecture project extends to project management and construction. In order to optimize a project and organize a construction site, the architect must move away from an ideological dreamland and "get their hands dirty."

An intimate and direct knowledge of construction allows the architect to anticipate the needs of the builder toward an optimized construction sequence. In recent projects, KANVA has included phased construction schedules in their tendered construction sets so that the contractor has a template with which they might improve their budget and timeline.

By supervising and participating in construction, KANVA develops a close understanding of the building processes that inform their design decisions.

Total architecture also includes the ability to negotiate contracts and manage legal affairs and procedures where possible. Legal disputes are commonplace in the business of architecture. However, despite having suits filed against them during their years of practice, KANVA's depth of experience and direct approach has allowed them to almost entirely settle all claims without extensive legal procedures. In the only instance, KANVA used their knowledge of the construction and legal process to lead the depositions of the parties involved and the matter was resolved.

Innovation is important in a building; however, innovation does not stop with design. An innovative spirit rooted in cross-competence and interdisciplinary knowledge can not only give rise to high quality architectural projects, but also allows for significant longterm financial benefit.

Edison involved the exploration of an innovative concrete construction technique: photoengraved concrete panels that enabled the building to tell a story.

When considering innovative solutions for housing the 99%, architects must be just as confident as other professionals at the table. Although the process is challenging and often slow, KANVA believes in making a difference in their environment one project at a time. With any luck, incremental innovation engendered by total architecture will, over time, erode invisible barriers and encourage other architects, builders and developers to create meaningful and responsive middle housing projects.

FORUM.4

Michelangelo Sabatino
Dean, College Of Architecture IIT

Rami Bebawi
KANVA

Trevor Boddy
Writer + Curator

Rafael Longoria
University of Houston

Tudor Radulescu
KANVA

RL How did you start implementing the vertical integration with your projects?

RB There are many reasons. One of them is because after school we both went in different directions. I went into construction for a few years and Tudor was doing medical architecture. We had $50 left in our bank account and we bought a bottle of champagne and decided we would figure out something else. At the same time, the stock market crashed and people decided to place money into buildings. So we had access to money and people who were ready to invest in any building in Montreal. The city was suddenly re-booming. We had past clients who didn't know how to develop and wanted us to do everything.

There was a multitude of things, and also because Tudor has gained such an exceptional knowledge of our city, he can almost predict where things are going to move forward or stop. I've never seen someone so aware of the real estate market, urban development, population demographics, so much to the extent that we were saying together: would it be possible for us to do residential in any other city but our own?

Without that knowledge of a city, can you participate without being generic?

RB We had a young developer client on another project who had no clue what he was doing. As we were helping him figure it out, we were learning for ourselves. Midway through his project we said, if he can do it, we can do it.

RL How did you get the financing?

TR When we started our firm I was 26, Rami was 27. We were not members of our professional association yet. We are not very risk averse. We did not have families or mortgages. We said, if we mess up, we mess up. Our first project, Fabbrica – we just dove in.

RB In a pragmatic way, we had to make a purchase offer and put together a pro-forma, and yes we were lucky enough to find people with private equity who did not want to invest in the stock market. We asked, would you be willing to invest 25%? Once they said yes, we secured the purchase of the building.

I remember it very clearly – a cab ride to the bank.

We said, here is the building we have secured, we have 25% of the equity, we have nothing else. Will you finance us? The bank said yes. That has to do with how we spoke to the bank manager one on one. After 25 minutes they said, let's try.

That banker retired a month ago. We called him to say thank you, you're the one that said yes and took a risk. Because of your yes, we got yeses for the other projects.

TB Thank you for your presentation – it's nice to see your holistic analysis of small projects. I like your five point path, I think it's a really good model. The other thing you get points for is that I don't know if I've ever heard another architect talk about bankruptcy. It's one of the ghosts of our profession.

TR It's true, we're not ashamed to talk about bankruptcy. At the same time we're not ashamed to talk about profit. It's a problem Canadians have and artists in general, that you're a sell-out if you make money, which we think is so wrong. The fact that we own the student residence and make sure we live well, it helps our practice be sustainable. In the years when we have less projects or they are taking longer than expected, the development side can help out.

TB You create handsome and well thought out buildings. You can see the discipline of cost, you are careful what you spend money on. From my perspective on the west coast, you have a kind of cohort with other firms in town. You're not designing the same things, but there's an approach to heritage, skin, metal and screens that I think is a sort of housing culture in Montreal.

RB There is a movement in Montreal toward creativity and innovation. There is a lot of competition and an enormous amount of architectural firms. I don't think it's just a great initiative from architects. The public is asking for innovation.

The public's desire for quality has surpassed the city, which is technically supposed to lead.

There is something else I wanted to share. Before Tudor and I were able to go on this curve of success, at the start two of the people we met were Johanna and Sasa. We met them the first time we had ever won a medal. Out of the blue, they shared everything they knew. That stuck with us and we decided to implement that philosophy in our own way. It helps in Montreal. If you find an innovative material, you put out the plans so everyone can use it.

Let's all make it better together.

TB That's a really good point – it exists in the architectural and development community. Montreal is a boiling pot right now. Going back to something Marianne said, in Vancouver we have an advanced group of developers, they are with the market and with the people who want alternatives to live in, they are the ones leading things. City Hall is being pulled along kicking and screaming, slowing things down and putting things in the way.

These housing cultures to me are extremely interesting. A combination of ideas, personalities and economic opportunities. How can we bring these things together with the public? How can we tell our narrative and talk about the nature of innovation, revealing all sides of what we do.

Generally the more open we are, the better we are. Nothing is ever lost through sharing information.

RL I think your answer about getting into development should be really educational, particularly for students here. If he can do it, we can do it. Really what it takes to be a developer has very little to do with mathematics and everything to do with a lack of risk aversion. That is what stops many architects from becoming developers. There are some who do it – what is rare is those who become architect developers and are also doing high-quality architecture. It's very easy, when you have the pressure of paying the bills, to cut corners with the design.

TR When we design buildings – whether its through volumetric studies or zoning by-laws or materiality – we believe the innovative parts add value. When we say innovation, it's not always about creating new technology, it can be something as simple as using old technology in innovative ways. We used to do a lecture called Good Design is Good Business. We believe this is true when we design for ourselves and it's easy to get people on board when we can convince ourselves. It also gives us the right tools to convince our clients when we are doing it for them.

RB For the majority of our projects, we are architects only. To add to that, in order to push forward this quality and innovation, there must be a strong link to suppliers. They are taking risks with us, it implies that they are with us in the office, we go into their shops, we build the samples with them. Then they get into research and development with us to push it to another level. When we have meetings for finance, insurance, construction, or even with lawyers, we ask that everyone gives us five minutes and we tell them the narrative.

That sharing of the story actually brings the risk down. Everyone is willing to commit on a whole new level.

We bring in construction people doing mock-ups, but first we tell them why we are doing it. They are listening, and then they will get up and lead the project more than us. We can control the quality when everyone comes on board.

HOUSING CULTURES

Trevor Boddy

More than any other form of architecture, housing is too often considered simply as either an economic commodity—units to be rolled out to meet various market needs—or else as private realms of inhabitation—live-in sculptures that map our inner lives. It is not that housing-as-real-estate-product, or housing-as-formal-expression are wrong-headed, but that these readings are incomplete. Yes, housing arises out of economic conditions, and yes again, housing demonstrates an unusually intimate interplay of physical forms with mental ambitions, but these two axes of interpretation are not enough, because its social and historical dimension is crucial. Housing can be an art-form, there is certainly a housing industry, but there are also cultures of housing.

I am particularly interested in distinctive regional housing cultures—how unique local combinations of ideas, typologies, plan-forms and building technologies evolve over time. One of the great, if under-discussed, pleasures of world travel is to ground oneself in the urban patterns and potentials of varying local housing cultures, be they the perimeter blocks of Mittel-Europa, the hutongs of China, the organic clusters of West Africa, or countless others. Vancouver has one of the most powerful housing cultures in North America, but it is unusual in having evolved more recently than the brownstones of Brooklyn or even the hill-clinging Los Angeles villas of Frank Lloyd Wright and the Case Study Houses.

What stands out is that so much of Vancouver's innovation has been pursued through a building configuration that many regard as sub-architectural—the high-rise apartment tower. This is an introduction to the residential folkways, the anthropological evolution of high-density housing in Vancouver.

Geography is destiny in shaping Vancouver's housing culture. Squeezed between the Coast Range mountains to the north, the Pacific Ocean to the west, the American border to the south, and Canada's most fertile farmlands to the east, innovation in housing form and has always been a necessity here, not an option, because land prices have always been high, and pressure constant for increased residential densities. Prior to European contact, Indigenous inhabitation was mainly seasonal in what is now downtown Vancouver, with permanent villages instead tied to salmon-harvesting on the Fraser River ten kilometers to the south. Sparked by real estate deals in the 1880's anticipating the arrival of the Canadian Pacific Railway, Vancouver is one of the youngest and least organic major cities in the world, passing in two decades from forest primeval to bustling metropolis with almost no intervening stops of farmlands or villages.

The 600 block of West Hastings Street at the turn of the 20th century depicts an urban centre in the midst of rapid change and growth. Photograph by Richard Henry Trueman.

Through the first half of the 20th century Vancouver evolved the same streetcar suburbs seen around the continent, lined with wood-frame, wood-clad housing (brick was infrequent and expensive, reserved for apartment and commercial buildings). Leading post-war architects such as Ron Thom, Fred Hollingsworth, Barry Downs and Arthur Erickson made their reputations with modest wood frame modernist houses nestled into evergreen forests. The West End of the downtown Vancouver peninsula developed a tradition of small floor plate mid-rise towers by the mid-1950s, soon making it the densest neighbourhood in the west coast of the Americas.

Arthur Erickson was not satisfied with this configuration as architecture or urbanism, so produced a visionary sketch for a future West End intended for a planning study called "Plan 56." The Plan 56 drawing shows 50-storey plus residential towers elegantly sweeping up from a continuous podium. Most apartments have large decks facing the harbour, and there are multiple blocks where green roofs cap a continuous podium. This drawing anticipates most of the architectural and urban practices that came to be called "Vancouverism" 30 years later. Moreover, having these extremely early green features in combination with its mountain-echoing organic massing and harbour vistas, the drawing is a perfect illustration of Vancouver's housing culture, demonstrating a continuity between post-and-beam houses in the forest with the high density mega-development to come.

Project 56 conceptual sketch elevation, 1955.

In the mid-1980s, the large swath of a former railyard on the north shore of False Creek was to host Expo 86 before being sold in one large piece several years later. In anticipation of Hong Kong's 1997 transfer back to China, Vancouver's always-strong Asian ties of immigration and investment were only increasing through this period. The purchaser was Li Ka-Shing's Concord Pacific, and housing configurations and densities more alike Hong Kong, China, than Canada were proposed there from the beginning.

James Cheng's Marinaside Crescent project, located on the site of Vancouver's Expo 86, features a tower and podium model that includes a variety of living configurations.

A key designer advancing Vancouver's housing culture was James K. M. Cheng, initially with his 888 Beach completed in 1993, where small plate high rise towers were set on a full block podium of townhouses for the first time (for more on his designs, urbanism and biography, please see my 2017 monograph CITY-BUILDER: The Architecture of James K. M. Cheng, published by Images Press of Melbourne.) Growing up in Hong Kong, Cheng had studied at the University of Washington (where Steven Holl was a classmate), before completing graduate school at the Harvard Graduate School of Design (Richard Meier was a key influence there.) Cheng's firm went on to design the Marinaside neighbourhood for Concord Pacific, then a string of other developments marked by fine proportions and detailing, plus a dedication to public space and amenity.

When his Residences on Georgia for Westbank was approved in 1994, city planners anticipated its townhouses would accommodate families, while the small apartments in the towers would be filled with singles, seniors and students. But housing cultures change faster than planners can track, and the choices of a wave of refugees fleeing war in the former Yugoslavia proved that small apartments were fine for families in amenity-rich neighbourhoods such as the West End, many of these paid for by developers tied to projects such as Residences on Georgia.

A crucial concept for Vancouver and its housing culture is hybridity, so much so that I gave a title of "HybridCity" to my "retroactive manifesto" commissioned for a Vancouver Art Gallery exhibition. The Vancouverist tower-on-podium typology is a hybrid of the small plate residential towers of Hong Kong with the brownstones and Back Bay Boston townhouses Cheng knew as a student there. There is both geographic and architectural sense to the local quip that to make a Vancouverite you just cross a Hong-Konger with a New Yorker! Another manifestation of hybridity is Cheng's Spectrum, where four residential towers are set on the roof of the world's first downtown Costco store.

A manifestation of a quick-blooming housing culture, downtown Vancouver is now a forest of thin towers with streets edged with townhouses, an unusually successful reconciliation of density with amenity. Small-plate towers offer unique advantages for creating livable streets and condos. By pushing the buildings higher and squeezing them thinner, the same amount of building volume is offered than lower and bulkier buildings, with more (if occasional!) penetration of light, air and fragment views.

40

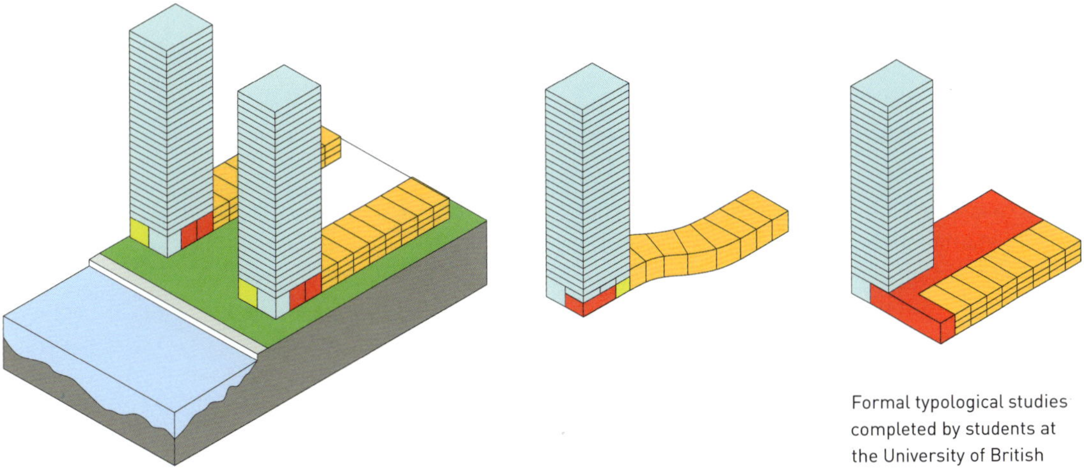

Formal typological studies completed by students at the University of British Columbia investigate possible configurations of a tower and podium model popularized by James Cheng.

James Cheng's River Green project elaborates on the hybrid tower-podium model. The building complex establishes a new terraced ground plane garden above at-grade parking that steps down toward a riverside park, features which were paid for by the developer.

Why did Vancouverites embrace residential towers so enthusiastically when they remained a hard sell through much of the rest of the Anglosphere? The answer to this is cultural, as in mid-20th century Britain and United States, high rises became associated with public housing and visible minorities. This was less an issue in countries like Canada and Brazil, where residential towers have always flourished as a middle-class housing option. For Toronto and Vancouver, high-rise housing projects became crucial to transit-oriented development. From the top of Toronto's CN Tower, one can map major transit lines and stations by seeing the towers surrounding them. A key difference for Toronto's housing culture is that it commonly employs the use of high-rise slab-block construction, as opposed to Vancouver's point-tower-and-podium. And when Concord Pacific built their CityPlace project in Toronto in the 1990s, planners insisted it be point-towers without podia, showing how difficult transmission of housing cultures can be.

The core problem Vancouver's late 20th century housing culture could not solve is affordability. With ever-increasing international investment, it now has the most expensive housing in the world, topped solely by sister city Hong Kong.

Victims of our own success in fostering livability with density, real estate prices in Vancouver are almost completely detached from local incomes and economy, with housing units now averaging more than 1,200% the value of annual household incomes. Housing in Vancouver has been priced as a global commodity as opposed to a local necessity – and our towers now need to be rethought of as safety deposit boxes for nervous global money.

This precipitated a political reaction in a change of both provincial and municipal governments in 2017-18, both dedicated to solving the affordability crisis. It will take decades. In the meantime, the "middle" is missing in Vancouver in all senses: middle income, mid-rise, middle not luxury amenity.

Returning to issues of design, the latest wave of luxury towers demonstrate more design innovation than those of twenty years ago. Despite the early prevalence of the tower and podium model, innovative slab-block projects are now found in greater Vancouver. One of the first to shift was James Cheng, with his River Green, flanking the Fraser River in Richmond, humanizing slab-block construction with creative massing and landscape design. Surmounting above-grade parking (necessitated by high water tables) covered with ponds and planting, River Green's high-rise slabs are articulated and edged by terraced gardens stepping down to a continuous riverside park. As is typical in Vancouver, these extensive public amenities are paid for not by the city, but by the developer, who pass on these costs to the purchaser.

Bonus density is encouraged by planners in exchange for developer-funded public amenities – but this is a financial model only possible in fast-growth cities such as Vancouver. Sorry, Winnipeg!

Arthur Erickson's Waterfall Building is a hybrid housing project arranged around a central courtyard that is constructed above a server farm, whose excess heat creates a conditioned micro-climate in the semi-public space.

Other hybrid building types have contributed to its housing culture. One of the last projects Arthur Erickson's designed was 2004's Waterfall Building, a mid-rise courtyard condominium planned to be set on top of a commercial web-server facility, a street-flanking waterfall for exhausting surplus heat. This water-screen creates a sense of enclosure while permitting the passage of light and street views. Erickson was delighted this live-work complex achieved housing densities comparable to some Yaletown blocks of tower-podia.

Michael Green Architects' Ronald McDonald House combines treatment and housing facilities for families caring for sick children and is constructed using tilt-up CLT panels and a brick façade.

A more recent project by Michael Green Architects showcases hybridity in building technology and program distribution. Constructed using tilt-up CLT panels and a brick façade, the 2014 Ronald McDonald House of British Columbia sensitively combines ground-floor shared amenities with private spaces above for several dozen families temporarily caring for sick children.

With Vancouver's diverse and innovative housing culture well established in the late 20th and early 21st centuries, what lies on the horizon? International influences for one, with new projects by global starchitects including BIG and Shigeru Ban set to punctuate Vancouver's urban and architectural landscape.

BIG's Vancouver house is a hybrid housing tower and podium whose sculptural form navigates complex setback requirements from the adjacent buildings and elevated roadway.

Kengo Kuma's Alberni tower balances extensive ground-floor public amenity space with housing above. The façade strategy of this project responds to new building code requirements that have rendered the all-glass Vancouverist façade unfeasible.

Shigeru Ban's Terrace House project was designed as a contemporary response to Arthur Erickson's terraced concrete Evergreen Building, complete with a mass timber "birdhouse" overlooking the surrounding city and harbour. Due to high land and construction costs, the project's future is uncertain.

BIG's recently completed Vancouver House twists upward from a triangular base, navigating complex three-dimensional setbacks and daylighting requirements. Unlike the designs of Arthur Erickson and James Cheng, whose work moves from inside out, the Vancouver House unit layouts (outsourced to another design firm) are subservient to the highly sculptural exterior.

Vancouver's new preference for iconic and marketable exterior form is also seen in the Alberni project by Tokyo's Kengo Kuma. For Vancouver high-rise condos, lower floors consistently fetch lower prices than higher ones. BIG's response was to craft a building with a small triangular base that transforms into a rectangular floor plate twice its size as it rises. Kuma's solution was to make a sweeping cut to the lower section his Alberni tower, hollowing out the bottom floors of the building, then giving the space back to the city in the form of a public park and plaza. Kuma also responds to new building code restrictions on fully glazed towers – window-walls being a staple of early 2000's Vancouverism – with variegated fenestration patterns and metal panels, creating visual textures more interesting than former models.

However, the global starchitect era of luxury housing for downtown Vancouver may be coming to an end, with the announcement in early 2020 of the bankruptcy of PortLiving's Terrace House project after only two storeys were built. Designed by Tokyo's Shigeru Ban in homage to Arthur Erickson's 1974 Evergreen Building next door, a similarly-detailed brutalist concrete base matching prior construction acts as a base for a "birdhouse" of an additional eight storeys of penthouses constructed in mass timber, a spectacular perch over-looking the harbour. On a site only 66 feet wide in a mid-block between Pender and Hastings Streets, land and construction costs were high and selling prices less than needed for this hybrid construction. For Vancouver, there is an affordability crisis, even for luxury housing!

These days, Vancouver is increasingly turning to mid-rise housing, demonstrated with the billions spent in the past five years for new buildings flanking both sides of Cambie Street, from King Edward Street five kilometers down to Marine Drive. An enormous missed opportunity for urban design and architectural innovation, the buildings here are competent but dull, that deadly combination so typical of things Canadian.

The next evolutionary stage of Vancouver's housing culture is more likely to be designed by small local firms than international names, and will be smaller in scale, more humble in its ambitions. Housing cultures are cyclic and incremental, and there will surely be a new wave of innovation to talk about in a decade or two, building on what has been imagined and built here to date.

IBERO-AMERICAN HOUSING LESSONS

Rafael Longoria

A decade ago, the University of Houston created a traveling studio with a research agenda focused on tracing the urban development of Ibero-American cities—with an emphasis on documenting recurrent housing typologies and the flows of architecture between Europe and the Americas. Since then, a series of five Pan-American Studio publications have documented recent projects in Argentina, Spain, Chile and Mexico.

"Mexico City Dialogues: New Architectural Practices," a 2005 exhibition at the Center for Architecture in New York City, catalogued the work of a talented generation of emerging architects. The exhibition, curated by Jose Castillo, identified common themes across a range of emerging practices dealing with the complicated restrictions and opportunities present in Mexico City. Primary among these commonalities were the forays of these young architects into real estate development as a complement to their design practice.

Derek Dellekamp, one of the architects featured in that exhibition, has developed a set of innovative housing projects as a response to changing demographics and economic pressures in the fashionable Condesa neighbourhood of Mexico City. His four-story CB 29 Building occupies a lot where a free-standing house previously stood. Three intertwined apartments are organized between a front and back garden, and around a central courtyard. The resulting building is an elegant and creative re-imagining of communal and private spaces that manages to maintain the scale of the original house.

Dellekamp's project for a new neighbourhood outside the city of Oaxaca extends the typological and spatial innovations he began with market housing to an even more challenging project: subsidized housing. His ingenious solution was a sophisticated mix-and-match modular system that allows one, two and three-story courtyard houses to be arranged in seemingly infinite combinations on a gridded block site plan.

No architect in Latin America has received as much acclaim for designing subsidized housing as Alejandro Aravena. We visited Aravena in his Santiago office to learn about his incremental growth approach, just before he won the Pritzker Prize in 2016. Unlike many Latin American architects who focus on high-end residential projects for wealthy patrons, Aravena's long-standing collaboration with Chile's Catholic Church allowed him to focus on social housing projects in addition to designing a remarkable series of academic buildings for the Pontificia Universidad Católica de Chile.

Dellekamp Arquitectos CB 29 building is a recent example of middle-housing innovation in Mexico City.

His flexible multi-family designs, in which "half-a-house" is constructed to be filled over time by its working-class occupants, is perfectly suited for a culture where adding to one's house is preferable to moving. And unlike many architects, Aravena welcomes ceding control to the residents of the final appearance of their own houses.

The house that Aravena designed for New Orleans Lower Ninth Ward, as part of the Make It Right foundation Hurricane Katrina rebuilding efforts, successfully applied his "half-a-house" principles to a single-family model. Instead of the row-house model with gaps-for-growth between units that he has implemented all over Latin America, at the Lower Ninth Ward, Aravena modified a shot-gun type house with a long porch parallel to the ridge occupying half the roofed space. Occupants then have the option of infilling as much of that long porch as needed over time.

ELEMENTAL's Quinta Monroy project contructs a simple yet flexible one half of a home at low cost, affording residents the ability to build into the frame and complete to their own liking over time.

Foreign Office Architects' Carabanchel Housing features an operable bamboo façade.

Spain contains some of the best and worst examples of multi-family housing ever built. Before the global financial collapse of 2008 brought their economy to a halt, the Spanish government went on a remarkable construction spree. Along with celebrated cultural landmarks (like the Guggenheim in Bilbao), entire new neighbourhoods of affordable housing were created around the country—including housing projects by some of the biggest international star architects.

The Madrid suburb of Carabanchel has many striking buildings that have been widely published around the world, such as Foreign Office Architects' elegant apartment block with an ever-changing folding bamboo-mat façade. While in Sanchinarro, another Madrid suburb, MVRDV's iconic Mirador building with an elevated public courtyard, designed as a hole in the massive housing slab, dominates the view of the surrounding landscape.

Both Carabanchel and Sanchinarro are useful to make the case that providing quality architecture, by itself, does not necessarily result in successful communities. Unfortunately, the streets and urban spaces of these neighbourhoods did not receive the same degree of attention and resources as some of the individual buildings.

In contrast, the new suburban housing development in Terrassa, a town near Barcelona, created public spaces as compelling as its new individual mixed-used buildings. The neighbourhood masterplan by Manuel de Solá-Morales is designed as a series of splayed housing fingers that span from a leafy street lined with ground-level commercial spaces, to a small forest on the rear side. Particularly interesting is Flores & Prats' Edificio 111 which packs 111 dwellings, 111 parking spaces, and 4 retail spaces on relatively small site, while managing to create an amazing variety of apartment plans and public spaces. The central patio is intended to promote communication and communal familiarity both as a gathering space, and as the visual focus of the many balconies around it.

Flores & Prats' Edificio 111 in Barcelona is arranged around a central courtyard with overlapping and undulating public spaces.

Ricardo Bofill's expressive Walden 7 development is based on a relatively strict module that is combined to create a variety of living and working spaces.

Building good housing in the neglected periphery of big cities is an enormous challenge. Ricardo Bofill's Walden 7, one of the landmark Spanish buildings of the 1970's, was a valiant attempt to create a vibrant community in what was then a desolate industrial landscape at the edge of Barcelona. The interwoven 14-storey towers offer many small moments and spaces for meeting and resting throughout – topped by a communal roof garden and pool. Each apartment is based on a 300-square-foot module, with modifiable partition walls that allow for a range of dwelling sizes and configurations. Run by a residents' council, the complex allows for businesses and services to be located both in the ground floor and in some strategic units.Through this careful integration of live-work spaces, meeting places, and a wide range of unit types, Walden 7 (whose name is inspired by the utopian science-fiction novel Walden Two by B.F. Skinner) has become a successful self-supporting community.

As good as some of the recent work is, the housing experiments of the 19th century also remain very relevant. Prior to winning the competition to plan Barcelona's expansion beyond its medieval walls in 1859, Ildefons Cerdà i Sunyer published a ground-breaking study documenting the dismal living conditions of the city's poor in the Barrio Gótico. Sixty years before the New York 1916 Zoning Resolution, Cerdà identified and implemented some of the key goals of that pioneering zoning ordinance: access to sunlight and ventilation. In his widely celebrated plan, the original layout of the perimeter buildings allowed a large public open space in the middle of each chamfered block – a few of which still survive intact.

Though there exist extraordinary individual architectural projects within this new city fabric, it is the urban plan itself that is most remarkable for its sensibility towards promoting healthy housing conditions throughout. The classic Barcelona Eixample apartment allows for a variety of configurations and occupant types that has proven well-suited to changing needs over the years. These buildings are typically six floors high, with retail at the ground level, a single central entrance and circulation core, and two apartments per floor, stretching from the street side to the courtyard side. One of the remarkable characteristics of this archetype is the versatility offered by the positioning of the core, just inside of the two front rooms. This makes the front rooms available to be rented as commercial spaces, small separate residential units, or to be integrated into a larger household configuration.

Residential courtyards developed on multiple levels on the interior of a Barcelona city block are highly desirable despite the seeming lack of privacy.

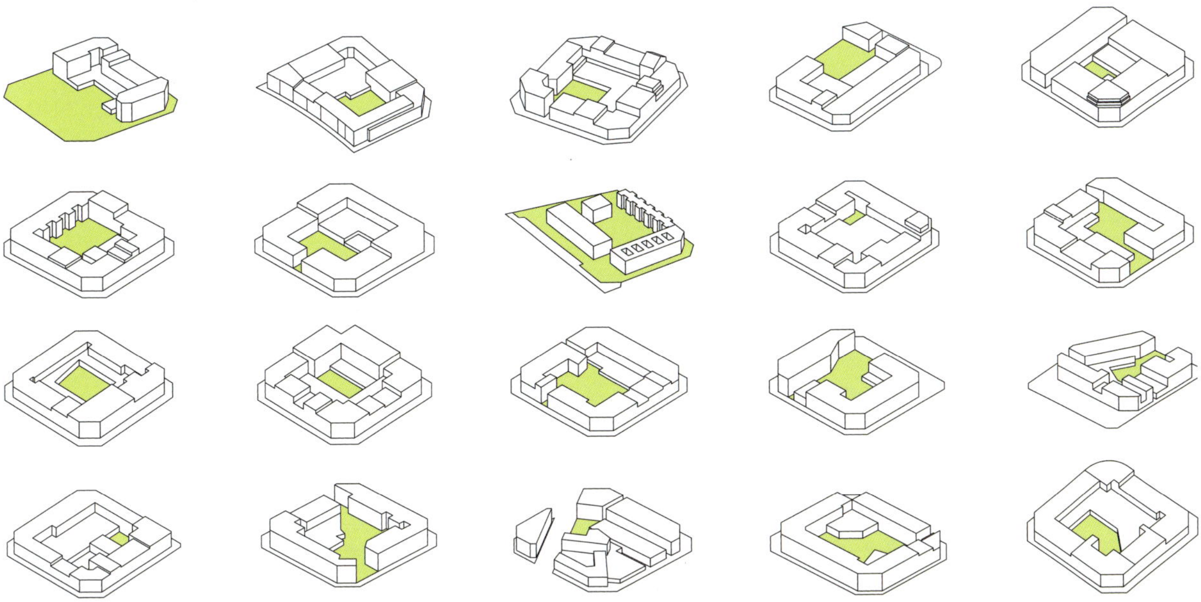

The Pan-American Studio investigated Eixample blocks, creating a catalogue of formal configurations for a variety of sites, living conditions, and public-private thresholds.

Regardless of whether we are looking at historical models or recent work, studying recurrent typologies or singular masterpieces, common elements that make up high-quality multi-family housing span time and place. These essential characteristics include:

- Careful consideration at a variety of scales — including the dwelling, the building and the neighbourhood;
- A rich variety of communal spaces and amenities;
- Connectivity and proximity to food, businesses and gathering spaces;
- Including mixed uses with programmatic flexibility in the ground floor and beyond;
- Financial, legal and programmatic inventiveness;
- Designing with the climate;
- Contextual sensitivity, and wherever possible, considering adaptive re-use;
- Never forgetting the continued relevance of a commitment to firmness, commodity and delight.

EXIT
S. R. CROWN HALL

LIVING IN CITIES

Curtis Olson

Great neighbourhoods don't happen by accident: they're built by community. Founded in 2009, SHIFT Development has produced a series of urban infill projects and ventures in Riversdale, a neighbourhood in transition in the core of Saskatoon. We see neighbourhoods as ecosystems made up of people, businesses and the built environment. Healthy neighbourhoods are made from healthy communities, where each component comes together to provide a better quality of life for each and every resident and visitor. Great neighbourhoods don't just look right, they feel right – something that we believe you have to experience on foot to truly understand.

Proximity breeds community. We have chosen to be hyper-focused in terms of where we operate – Riversdale is where we live and it is where we do business. It is no accident that each of our projects – now numbering over a dozen – is within a five-minute walking radius from our office. We consider ourselves more than developers. We are community members with a vested interest in the success and long-term health of our neighbourhood. Whatever we put our hand to, we start with community need, doing what we can to contribute to the livelihood and daily experience of every member.

Prior to starting SHIFT, we (partners Curtis Olson and Carrie Catherine) were living and working in Victoria. As musicians, we have a deep affinity for urban environments – the place where culture happens – and share a wealth of experience in cultural industries. Urbanist Jan Gehl believes "a good city is like a good party: people stay longer than really necessary, because they are enjoying themselves." To us, this quote captures the energy and spirit we've brought to every project we undertake.

Our approach to development does not place architecture on a pedestal. Rather, we have a shared belief that buildings are nothing more than boxes to be filled. If you build the right box, you can foster connection, community, cultural development and all of the great things that make living in cities worthwhile.

We returned to our hometown of Saskatoon from the west coast in order to step outside of our comfort zone, raise our family and help build the neighbourhood that we wanted to live in. In 2011 we created Saskatoon's first and largest co-working space, The Two Twenty. Inspired by a desire to share resources, the development grew organically when we stumbled onto a building with more space than we needed to house our own offices. In response, we found like-minded partners and expanded our circle of connections in order to make the project possible. Spanning two storeys and 35,000 square feet, The Two Twenty has become a second home for over 200 community members and an incubator for entrepreneurs and innovators, with shared meeting rooms, a kitchen and a cafe as social connectors. Some of our tenants have gone on to open their own small businesses in the neighbourhood.

SHIFT's The Two Twenty is Saskatoon's first co-working space that serves a burgeoning creative community.

Saskatoon
Saskatchewan

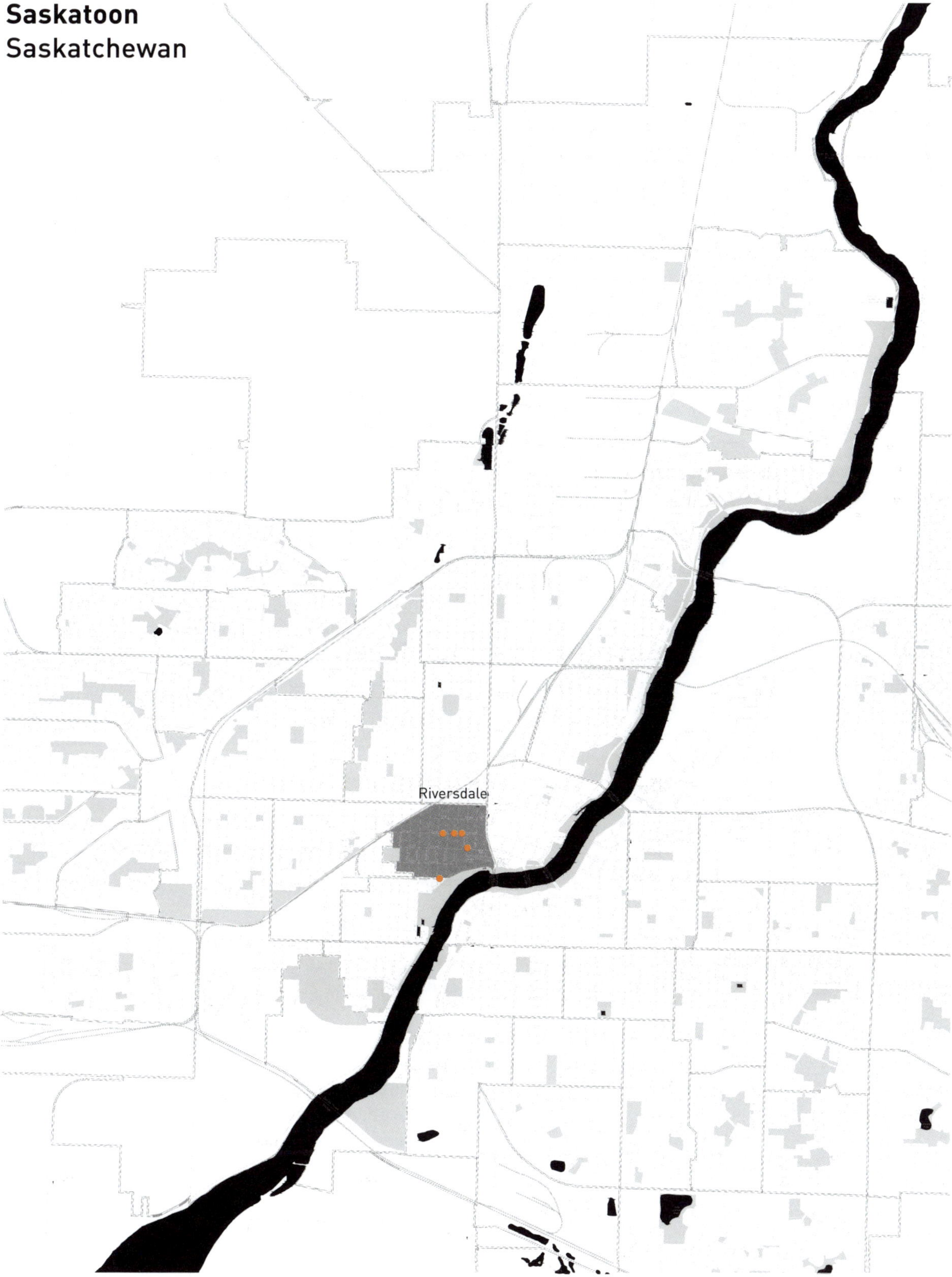

Our belief in the power of a sharing economy extends to our multi-family initiatives. In addition to commercial development, SHIFT has focused its energy on missing-middle housing, with completed projects including two courtyard-centred townhouse developments – Mosaic in 2014 and Element Urban Village in 2019.

Following the success of The Two Twenty, Mosaic arose from a desire to create more options for people wanting to experience urban living in Riversdale. The project consists of 12 two storey townhouse units ranging from studios to larger street-front live/work units, organized around a central courtyard and an active community of residents with shared values. Many of the original buyers still live in Mosaic today. Element consists of 17 townhouses, arranged in three bars. Six units face south toward Victoria Park, capturing lush green views with sight lines of the river beyond. The remaining units share an intimate, semi-private courtyard complete with individual decks and a communal barbecue space.

When SHIFT was established, active investment in the core was in short supply and 90% of development was driven by the suburban expansion of new neighbourhoods on the periphery. In downtown Saskatoon, 28% of developable land is a surface parking lot.

When you consider the timeline of issued building permits by neighbourhood from 2006 to 2015, the Central Business District only received 6% of the total value and included a new art gallery and a police station. In ten years, only three new buildings were completed in the city centre that were not publicly funded, large-scale institutional projects. All of SHIFT's projects are located just outside of this downtown boundary, in a neighbourhood rife with its own social challenges and lack of meaningful investment.

We believe numbers tell a story and we use them as a critical tool in assessing the success or failure of a specific initiative, both in our work and in understanding the context in which we operate. The statistics described in the preceding paragraph can be read as a failing grade on the output of the city's current policy framework on downtown renewal.

As a residential developer working at a unique scale in the urban fabric, we have run into countless roadblocks that were not foreseen at the outset. Zoning by-laws are the invisible hand that define what is and is not possible on a given site. It has been a significant challenge to evolve some of the existing city guidelines, many of which can have unintended consequences when applied to inner city lots.

Offsite levy charges are one example of a policy that works against "missing middle" infill in the city centre. Devised as an infrastructure cost for new neighbourhood development, offset levies are also charged to infill sites even though these projects rely entirely on existing infrastructure. As a result, there is more economic benefit to building high rise infill rather than mid-rise, since these costs are typically divided by the number of units when determining a project's pro forma.

Communal in-between spaces at Element Urban Village foster a sense of belonging and connection.

10

In addition, when we submitted our applications for Mosaic and Element, we were treated like a land developer in a new subdivision and required to pave back alleys in a neighbourhood where everything else is gravel. In an industry with thin margins and high construction costs, any unplanned expenditures can have a huge impact on a project's bottom line and become a determining factor in whether or not it proceeds from the design stage to construction.

Through trial and error, we always look for ways to experiment and uncover good urban solutions. With experience, we have learned that innovation is best supported through longterm ownership in order for us to see the full return on our investments. This is especially true in the case of energy-saving initiatives, which typically require more cost at the outset in order to make the project more sustainable over the course of its lifecycle.

In Saskatoon, the traditional trajectory funnels people toward what is familiar: single-family homes on large suburban lots. In order to propose an alternative to the status quo and attract people to something different, you will not win with dollars and cents. Rather, you have to draw people in with beauty, imagination and the potential for a lifestyle that you cannot get anywhere else.

Marketing is an essential tool to help shift perspectives. For Element, when prospective buyers ask how big the yards are, our response is that your front yard is six acres and the city cuts the grass. At the same time, we are careful not to over promise on some of the challenges of the neighbourhood we live in and set proper expectations for buyers. We are also conscious of our role in shaping one of the oldest and poorest neighbourhoods in Saskatoon. Riversdale has a large Indigenous population and we are constantly striving to develop with a spirit of inclusion, in order to foster a culture of compassion and a celebration of diversity. Through our work, we are able to deliver benefits back to the community through programming, giving initiatives and artist residencies.

Element Urban Village is situated along Victoria Park, taking advantage of existing public amenities.

We believe it is on the fringes and in the margins where invention occurs and new ideas are allowed to bloom. Our mission is to build spaces that create the conditions for great urban lifestyles. To us, that means building in areas that include a cluster of residential and commercial spaces that serve a wide range of people and needs. We are in a love affair with Riversdale, and as the neighbourhood continues to evolve, we will do the same.

FORM FOLLOWS FINANCE

Rich Sciortino

Founded in 1994, Brinshore Development is a residential development firm based in Chicago. In recent years, the firm has led the redevelopment of Robert Taylor Homes, a 100-acre site in Chicago originally populated by large brutalist buildings that contained over 4,000 apartments. Since the failure and subsequent demolition of the massive public project due to overcrowding, neglect and violence, Brinshore has worked alongside the Chicago Housing Authority to repopulate the site with medium and low-rise buildings in a mixed-income setting. The renovation and re-imagination of post-war social housing projects with mid-rise middle housing has helped the firm grow across the United States over the last few decades.

In order to properly address social housing – or affordable housing – in the United States, it is crucial to understand the framework in which it operates. For Mies van der Rohe, form followed function, however for affordable housing development, form follows finance. Unquestionably the most critical criteria for financing affordable housing is the availability and procurement of public subsidization. Recently, in Chicago and in other cities where more affordable housing is much needed, density bonuses have been offered for adding 10-20% of affordable units into projects. In Chicago, 10% of these affordable units must be built on-site while 10% may be built off-site. Because the on-site square footage of the original project is so valuable, developers scramble to find ways to construct the 10% of required units off-site.

Legends South re-imagines the site of the troubled Robert Taylor public housing project in Chicago.

These supplemental affordable housing requirements in market-rate development stand apart from a dedicated affordable housing market in the United States.This market is anchored on a single federal tax credit program, distributed through state-level governments and agencies, called the Low Income Housing Tax Credit (LIHTC). The LIHTC was created as part of the 1986 Tax Reform Act to subsidize affordable rental housing development throughout the United States. It is the largest federal program that incentivizes affordable housing, estimated to cost $9.5 billion per year. The program supports approximately 110,000 affordable units each year. Support is made available for both new construction and rehabilitation projects.

The LIHTC operates by issuing tax credits to state and municipal governments and agencies, which create specific rules and frameworks for eligibility. The developers keep or often sell these tax credits to outside investors. Properties are required to meet annual tests to confirm that units are rented to households with low-income. It has been argued that per unit subsidy costs are higher than necessary due to intermediate parties involved in organizing, financing and managing the fund, as well as various government mandates. At the same time, it is concerning that the LIHTC expires after ten years, leaving privately owned developments at risk of re-allocation to the private market.[1]

The LIHTC drives the affordable housing business, which in turn impacts the architecture. The state agencies responsible for disbursing the LIHTCs influence what you can and cannot build. In limiting the amount of subsidy given to a project, these agencies limit the project size.

Typically, affordable housing units that fall under this category range from 25 to 150 units. These sizes are challenging to maintain and find efficiencies within. In some instances, plans are required to be no less than 85% efficient, limiting the amount of common and amenity spaces in affordable housing projects. These rules, alongside others, place tight constraints on what and how one is able to build. To execute an affordable housing project, a clear vision is required that encompasses both these imposed restrictions and a self-imposed set of design standards and public responsibilities.

The Hyacinth Place development in Chicago offers a mix of for-sale and rental units.

The Dorchester was completed in partnership with the Chicago Housing Authority and combines an art centre with mixed-income housing.

In many cases in the United States, affordable housing design must act inclusively across demographics. In that spirit, there is as much effort and consideration given to programming and resident relationships as there is to architectural expression. Creativity and thoughtfulness are required to ensure that the architecture and the programming work together to create and maintain healthy, vibrant and long-lasting communities.

Even when designing a small project, we attempt to integrate complementary programming that serves to support both the tenants and the larger community – be it an art centre, daycare or healthcare facility. These complementary facilities help to build a narrative for each development focused on a specific theme that encourages architectural consideration at a variety of scales and moments throughout the project. It is important to our work that honest, simple touches – windows, landscape, lighting and artwork – even in the most mundane of places allow the tenant to feel special, safe and comfortable. Though it is not as easily done as it is said, we expect and hope to see small and sincere moments of beauty throughout a project from our architects and designers.

Although it is largely impossible to interpret and accommodate the various needs of individuals over an extended time, the desire for a beautiful space that one can take pride in calling a home is everlasting. Where possible, we advocate for keeping and renovating existing public housing projects as opposed to demolishing them due to their negative stigma. With the right approach, moments of beauty may be found, brought out or invented in what people often otherwise perceive as off-putting structures. We believe that, beyond financial structuring and complexity, affordable housing in the United States is about promoting inclusion and allowing dignity through beautiful, considerate architecture.

DEARBORN
STREET

LIFE

RNDSQR

RNDSQR is a placemaker in Calgary's inner city. As a small team focused on making a big impact, we use design to promote collision points and collaboration. Our work to date includes commercial, residential and mixed-use projects across a range of scales, with an intentional emphasis on established communities.

RNDSQR Life is a multi-faceted programmatic tool and partnership program that sees every building the company completes in the context of its larger neighbourhood. By creating and supporting a network of like-minded entrepreneurs who share our ethos and design aesthetic, we can encourage residents to shop local and help foster a small business ecosystem.

RNDSQR Life is a key strategy for our "missing middle" housing projects where mixed-use development may not be appropriate based on neighbourhood scale and fit, or where the project's proforma, density and affordability goals do not support the inclusion of internal amenity area. In response, we seek out amenity space for the building in the larger community, in order to support a symbiotic relationship between residents and small businesses, reinforcing connections and promoting walkability. The more people are living in dense urban neighbourhoods, the more impetus the city has to improve networks for pedestrians and cyclists. The more people are out moving in their communities, the more foot traffic for small businesses will continue to grow.

A longterm goal for RNDSQR Life envisions an integrated package of small business amenities built into the monthly rental cost. As a trial at Peaks and Plains, six months worth of coffee cards for the cafe across the street (and a member of our partnership program) were included in the rent. The pilot project had 100% uptake and helped support a sense of belonging amongst residents and familiarity with staff.

For General Block in Bridgeland, two single-family lots were amalgamated into a two-storey commercial hub. Tapping into our existing network, three members of our partnership program leased the main floor. With a public realm designed around places to sit, linger and enjoy the theatre of the street, these businesses see thousands of visitors each week, helping create a community gathering place and activating the nearby park. In response to Covid-19 lockdowns, RNDSQR launched a limited run of Small Business Care Boxes to support the local business community. In the span of three days we created a new program, curated products from all of our favourite entrepreneurs and raised over $70,000 to support them.

As developers, we have a social responsibility to build homes for people, not units on a spreadsheet. We also have a civic responsibility to knit our projects into the urban fabric, activate the public realm and help cultivate the daily encounters that lead to meaningful relationships. RNDSQR Life provides us with a critical path to reach this goal, with multiple benefits for the end user and community at large.

FORUM.5

Johanna Hurme
5468796
Architecture
Professor -
Morgenstern Chair IIT

Trevor Boddy
Writer + Curator

Curtis Olson
Shift Development

Rafael Longoria
University of
Houston

Rich Sciortino
Brinshore
Development LLC

JH From those of you in the development world, what is the biggest factor that holds you back from improving the quality of housing in your context? Is there something we as architects can do to improve the quality? Is there some way the formula can be tracked to achieve better outcomes in terms of city building?

RS This won't come as a surprise to anyone but it's really about cost containment. That's where this is all headed – trying to find ways to deliver something that is appealing, while at the same time holding down costs. Our cost structure for affordable housing isn't that different from luxury housing. Building inner city affordable housing is impossible without new policy. The cost of building in Houston is half of what it is in the city of Chicago. Where is affordable housing in Chicago? It's in the suburbs.

Without new policies, nothing is ever going to change in large municipal cities in the United States.

CO We always try to find the cracks that people have overlooked because there is too much friction or an unknown. We try to go after opportunities where we can improve density and find ways to bring the land cost down.

Architects need an eye for the proforma.

In our projects, we've rezoned everything that we've touched. Buying something at market rate and building what is allowed prescriptively does not pencil out. We're always looking for that lift through zoning. Most developers in Saskatoon wouldn't touch these sites, but we're fine getting our hands dirty and being patient.

RL We keep going back to this fascination with the no zoning regulations in Houston. It does make costs lower, but the fact that there's so much available land, some of it very cheap, is what makes a house affordable. The single-family market is still very accessible, particularly at the edges.

TB This is a little bit depressing. I'm going to make you more depressed by evoking a word called sprawl.

What's invisible in this country are the implicit subsidies to sprawl.

We in Canada do not have a deductibility of mortgage payment interest the way you do in the US. That's the single largest intervention in the housing market in the Americas. The amount of money that's diverted that effectively supports sprawl is unbelievable. It's as artificial as any other program, but it's so hard to get rid of.

In Canada, we do not nationally finance roads. In the US, the interstate highway system is a huge subsidy to sprawl, making it possible to live an hour and half away from the urban centre. It's getting harder and harder to support these suburbs. Some of them are collapsing in on themselves. There are all of these indicators that we've expanded out as far as we can and we need to fold back in. But it's hard. When you have a low-density city and you need to increase the density and bring more people within its boundaries, you have to fight the good fight over and over again.

We have to take a stand as architects against sprawl.

We've got very advanced regional planners in Vancouver. Andy Yan puts the extra price of the commute onto the house price. If you take the house price an hour away plus the cost of driving back and forth, all of a sudden the saving is gone. The advantages of cities are pretty evident.

RL The brief of the symposium in particular calls for multi-family housing as a more sustainable way of living.

JH We've been trying to fight that battle with politicians and decision makers, to prove the economic model for tighter communities as an overall city budget. The story gets fairly long, it's tough to prove that over an election cycle or in a campaign speech. As the University of Ottawa has studied, the biggest reason for sprawl is home price. You can buy a suburban home in Winnipeg and many parts of Canada at a lower cost. We have no policy that makes infill development affordable or comparable. That tends to be our battle. Do you have any suggestions? What does it take to get the general public to see infill as an acceptable model for living, or is that a losing battle?

CO I had a moment of awakening at our Element townhouse project, where I live with my family. We helped get a new mayor elected in Saskatoon a few years ago. I know him very well and we invited his family over for Sunday brunch. When he came for the first time, he was absolutely floored. He knew that we had done this project and seen the marketing, but still had no idea what we had actually built. He had to be standing in the unit, looking at the view of the river and park in order to make those connections.

As we try and attract new clientele into this Riversdale neighbourhood, you can argue and explain for days, but when they step in the door and have an experience being in a vibrant co-working space or a great townhouse, you don't have to argue or explain anything.

The challenge is to get them in and understand that it is actually possible.

We lack the culture in Saskatoon. Everyone expects single-family houses, that's what realtors tell them they need and that's what they buy.

Where we've realized our strategy has fallen short is with an ownership model for the condominiums we are building. The first question owners have is "what's resale?" We're shifting to a rental model – they have a different set of criteria and are more adaptable to coming into the neighbourhood.

TB There's something buried in there that's very important. It's so critical to show people your work and walk them through your project. Be generous to visitors. Err on the side of opening things up and having constant accessibility.

case.STUDIES

102 Dwellings

Sio2 Arch

Social Housing
Barcelona, Spain
2011

GFA
115,000 ft² [10,677 m²]

Site area
21,170 ft² [1,967 m²]

Floor area ratio
5.43

Covered area
73%

Efficiency [Gross/net]
84%

Unit types

Bedrooms	0	61	40	0
Storeys [within units]	102	0	0	0

Parking stalls 129

Units

42% Average unit
759 ft² [70.5 m²]

34% Smallest unit
618 ft² [57.4 m²]

63% Largest unit
1,126 ft² [104.6 m²]

Typology

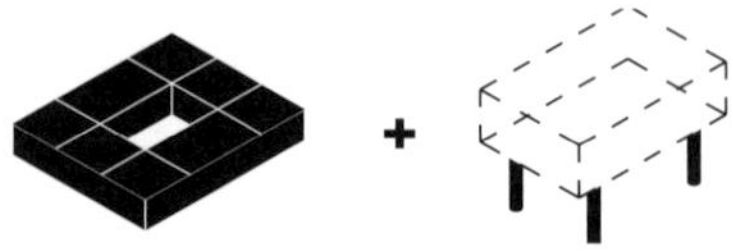

Occupancy

Residential
90%

Commercial
10%

Construction

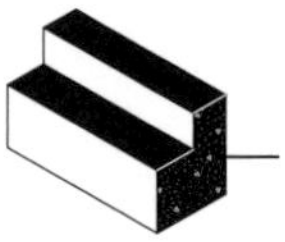

Concrete structure

107
LOCALS EN VENDA de 69 m2 +
Informació i vendes 629 12 36 64

In Spain, social housing is handled by a mixture of public authorities and private agencies and various partnerships between the two. To support this model, every design for a social housing project is chosen through competition. Typically, the unit types and sizes are predetermined, so architectural innovation is directed toward adding value to the development via expanding urbanity. Despite the tight restrictions on program, budget and unit layout, Sio2 Arch conjures additional architectural value through volumetric and urban manipulation. This strategy is clearly displayed in their 102 Social Housing project in Barcelona, where a careful shaping of the building volume in response to site and a diverse yet precise approach to building porosity and fenestration provides high quality units at a below-market price.

The building is composed of 102 housing units, ground floor commercial space, a central courtyard and 150 parking spaces. Operations of subtraction – including the removal of a central core, clipping the building corner, and shortening the building height along one side of the complex – allow the units to receive generous access to daylight and enable cross ventilation.

The building is organized around five central cores as well as communal elevated terraces and pathways gathered around an interior courtyard. These collective areas are marked by a distinctive blue colour that contributes to a sense of community and interiority. The diverse yet cohesive building envelope features staggered shading devices and balconies which gather together a range of unit types. At the same time, the courtyard acts as a new public street within the block, serving both the ground floor commercial spaces and the units above.

The 102 Social Housing project demonstrates the potential for quality living spaces and high-quality architecture, which is sensitively oriented to its context, to create a heightened sense of community with limited means. Through simple but well articulated massing operations, fenestration strategies and a limited material palette, the project provides much-needed housing with ample access to natural light and ventilation while maintaining existing and establishing connections with its urban context.

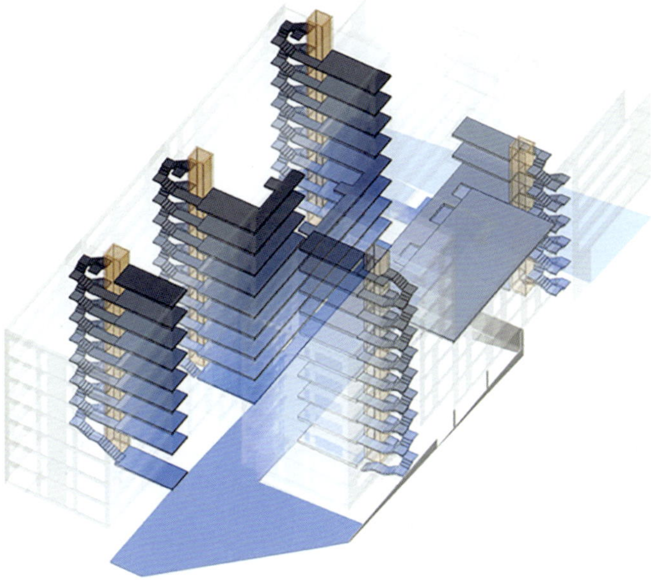

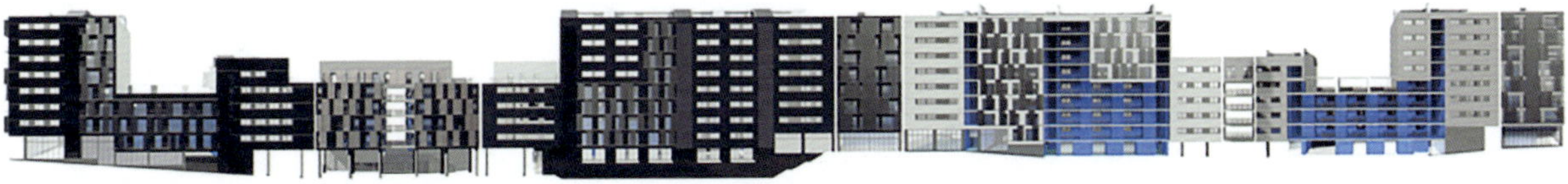

Union

MA+HG Architects

Multi-generational Housing
Vancouver, British Columbia
2020

GFA
5,800 ft² [540 m²]

Site area
6,100 ft² [567 m²]

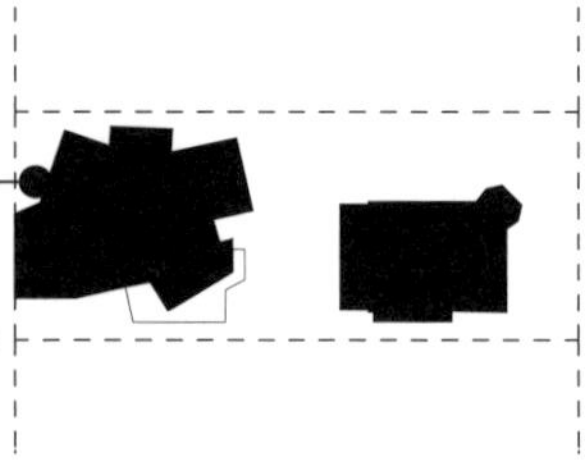

Floor area ratio
0.95

Covered area
40%

Efficiency [Gross/net]
100%

Unit types

Bedrooms	2	2	2	0
Storeys [within units]	2	3	0	0

Parking stalls 3

Units

63% Average unit
1132 ft² [105 m²]

25% Smallest unit
452 m² [42 m²]

122% Largest unit
2195 m² [204 m²]

Typology

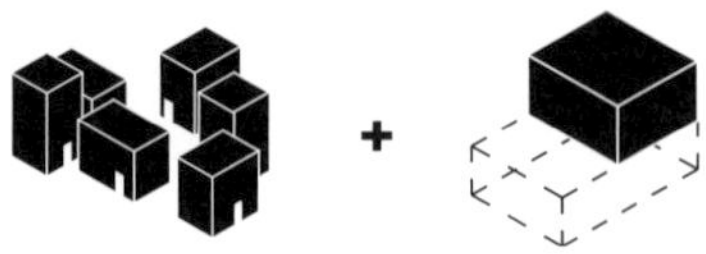

Occupancy

Residential
90%

Live / Work
10%

Construction

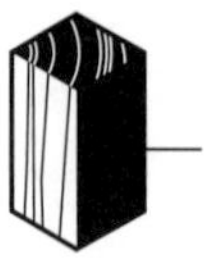

Existing & new
- Structure
- Interior walls

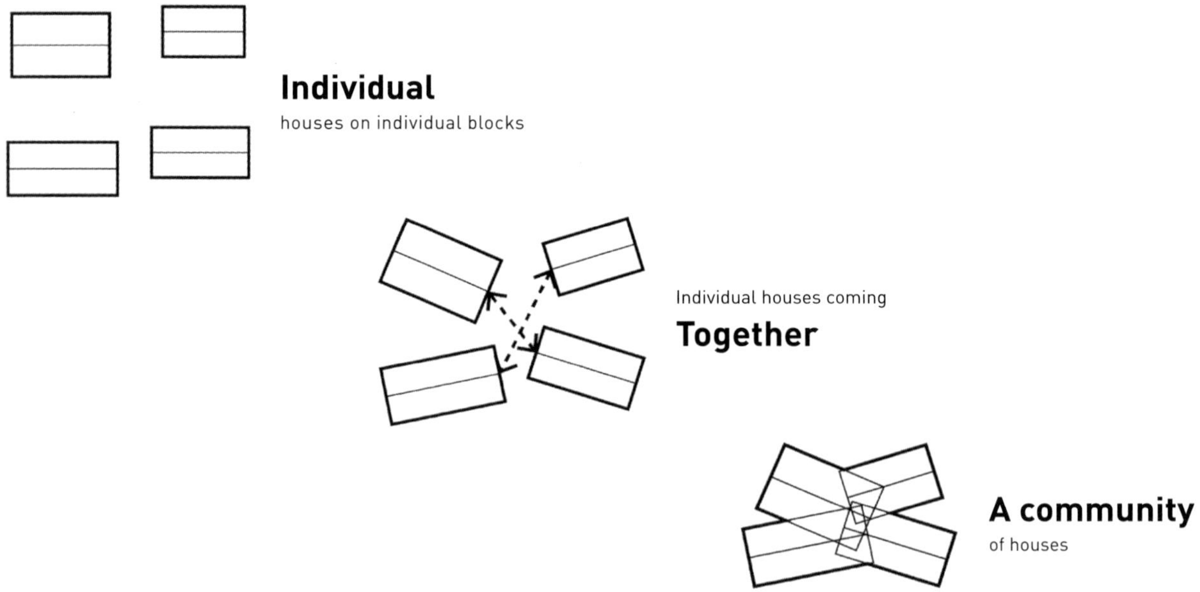

In Vancouver, where new buildings are constructed at an unprecedented pace, the ongoing preservation and the imaginative rehabilitation of heritage buildings enables the city to recognize and maintain places of shared memory and history. At the same time, heritage buildings also offer unique opportunities for "soft density" through adaptive re-use.

Saving heritage buildings is one MA+HG Architects key strategies for social density. The Union Street project is a multi-family project that rehabilitates an existing heritage building and includes additional residential units in a new construction. Located in the established and eclectic Strathcona neighbourhood, the site is a double-wide lot upon which sits a Victorian home with a colourful and storied past, constructed at the turn of the twentieth century. The character home (commonly referred to as the "Big House") is justified along the western edge of the spacious site. The project restores and slightly expands this existing structure to accommodate a multi-generational family.

Together with the new three-unit construction at the rear of the existing building, the site is transformed to operate as a shared community of homes. The "Big House" is renovated and lifted to create a new artist live-work space below, while a communal patio space between the buildings encourages interaction both between tenants and between the buildings and the streetscape beyond. This variety of spaces are also intended to host interior and exterior events for the Vancouver art community.

The infill building responds in scale and form to its surroundings. Its height and form connect to the surrounding traditional gable formed homes while allowing for variety of views. While its angular geometry is artful, it is also functional. The direction of views obliquely away from both the "Big House" and its surrounding neighbours eliminates overlook issues while allowing for increased glazing area, natural daylight, and a variety of indirect views. The infill building employs modest and robust materials: wood siding at the base matches the surrounding buildings with low-maintenance metal siding above.

The project is achieved with great support from the community at large, as well as the City of Vancouver, as an example of a "Missing Middle" project that promotes increased density, community interaction, heritage preservation and character retention.

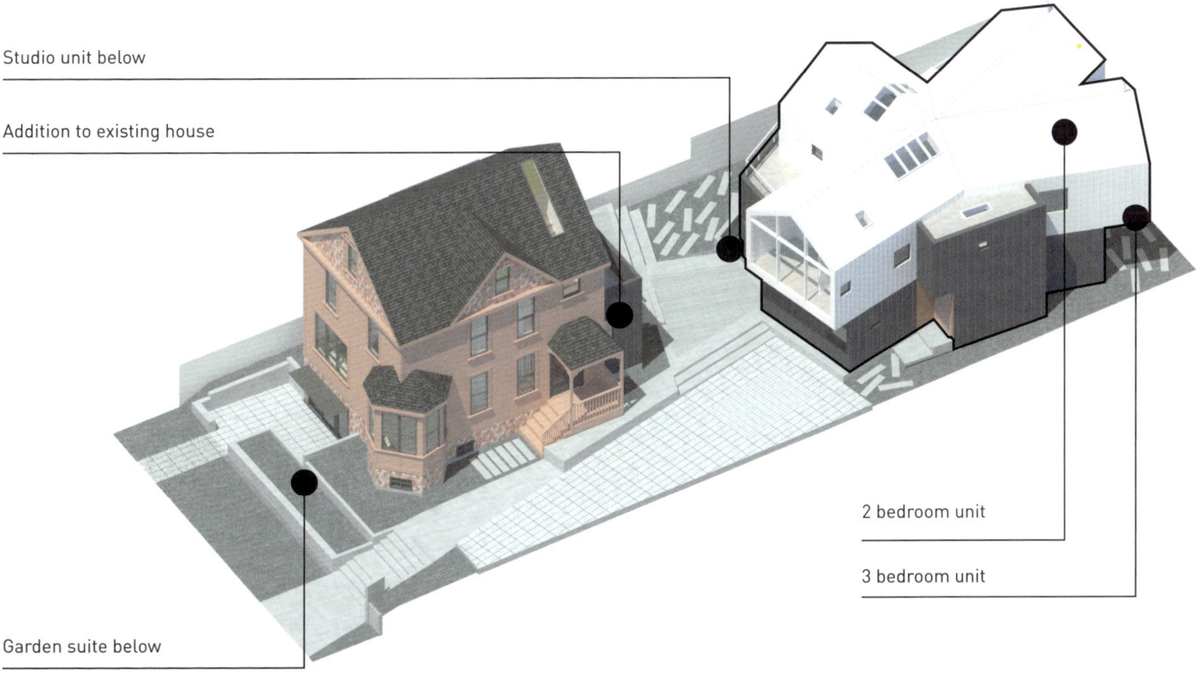
Studio unit below
Addition to existing house
2 bedroom unit
3 bedroom unit
Garden suite below

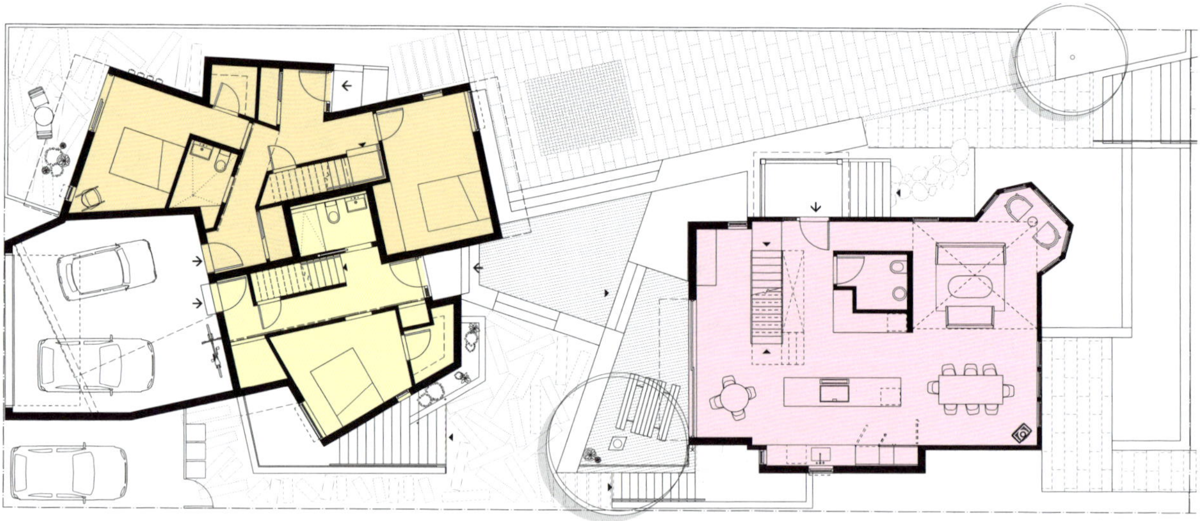

3 bedroom
2 bedroom
Heritage renovation

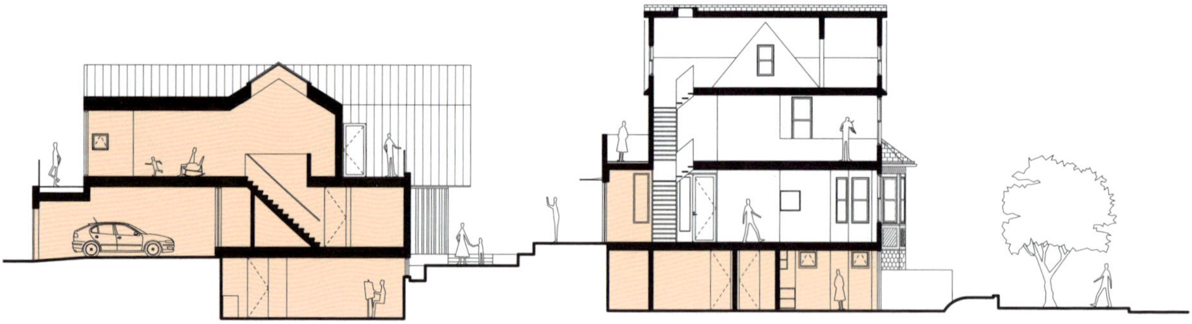

New construction
Existing house

BAUHAUS

Independence Library + Apartments

John Ronan Architects

Affordable seniors housing + library
Chicago, Illinois
2019

GFA
65,000 ft² [6,040 m²]

SITE AREA
32,785 ft² [3,046 m²]

Floor area ratio
2.59

Covered area
89%

Efficiency [Gross/net]
90%

Unit types

Bedrooms	36	8	1	0
Storeys [within units]	44	3	0	0

Parking stalls 29

Units

Average unit (34%)
617 ft² [57 m²]

Smallest unit (30%)
535 ft² [49.5 m²]

Largest unit (46%)
824 ft² [76.5 m²]

Typology

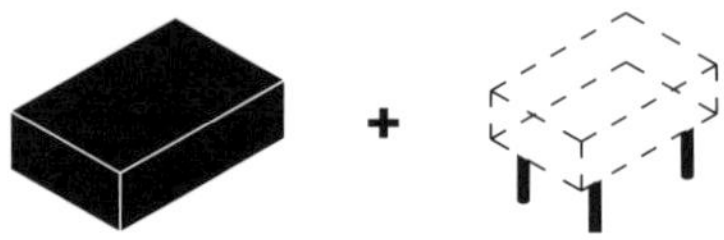

Occupancy

Residential
75%

Library
25%

Cost

$290/ft²

Construction

The Independence Library and Apartments is a 65,000 square foot hybrid library and affordable housing project located in the Irving Park district of Chicago. The project emerged from a 2016 design competition initiated by former mayor Rahm Emanuel in conjunction with the Chicago Housing Authority and the Chicago Public Library. The intent of this city-led initiative was to co-locate housing and libraries in order to bring shared community spaces together with the individuals they are intended to serve.

The program combines a 16,000 square foot branch library with a 44-unit affordable housing development for seniors. Clad in polished, pre-cast concrete panels, the two-storey library block slides toward the street to better engage the public realm, with an extensive glazed portion running along the length of the sidewalk. The residential block, clad in a mix of white corrugated and perforated metal cladding, hovers at a setback from the street above. Both the library and the apartments are entered through an at-grade courtyard with on-site parking accessed from the rear alley. The library can also be entered directly from the street.

The library's main interior volume features a split-level scheme, which allows natural light in from both sides of the building while offering a mix of generous high-ceiling spaces and intimate gathering areas. The program includes reading and learning areas for all age groups, as well as a community multi-purpose room for public lectures, gatherings and events.

The second level of the library extends outside to form a semi-public terrace that serves as an amenity space for the apartment dwellers while acting to cover the at-grade parking. Although this space was not an explicit part of the program, JRA recognized it as an opportunity for added design and lived value.

For affordable housing projects, the construction process must be made as efficient as possible. In the case of Independence Library, there was also strong political pressure for the library to open before an upcoming election. Using a hybrid structure, with a concrete podium and a steel structure above, offers an ease of construction that is both cheaper and faster than alternative building systems. As a result, the building construction was completed in only 17 months.

The structural grid must also be fine-tuned to negotiate the organizational requirements of the parking, library and apartments above. Within this rigorous system, JRA was able to generate a mix of one and two bedroom unit types that would meaningfully accommodate a wide range of occupants. The apartments are distributed above the library in four levels. The terrace forms a soft intersectional space, a sort of social condenser or urban room between the two constituencies. Each apartment features a distinctly and brightly-coloured balcony embedded within the façade that speaks to individuality among the collective.

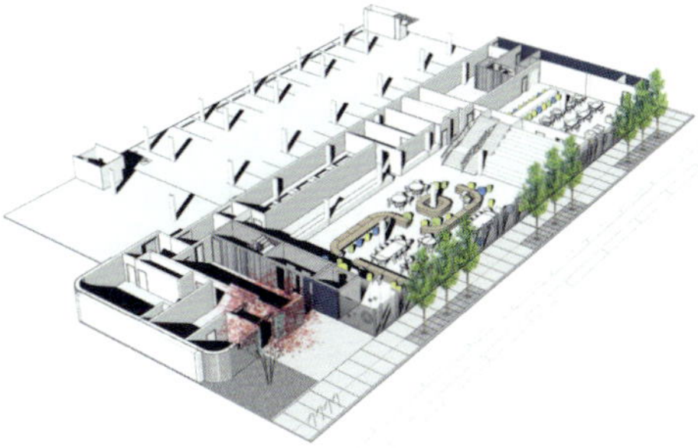

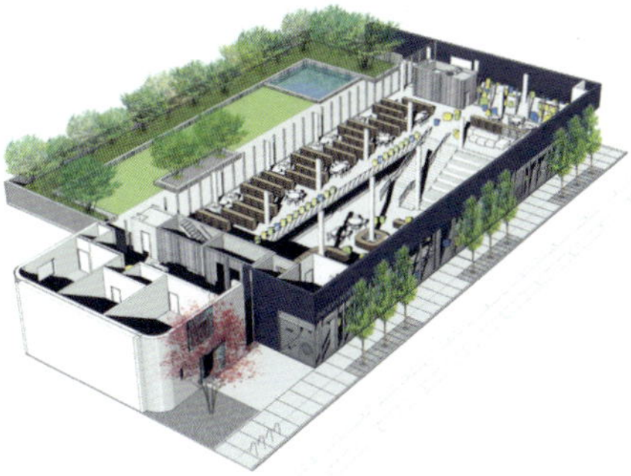

INDEPENDENCE

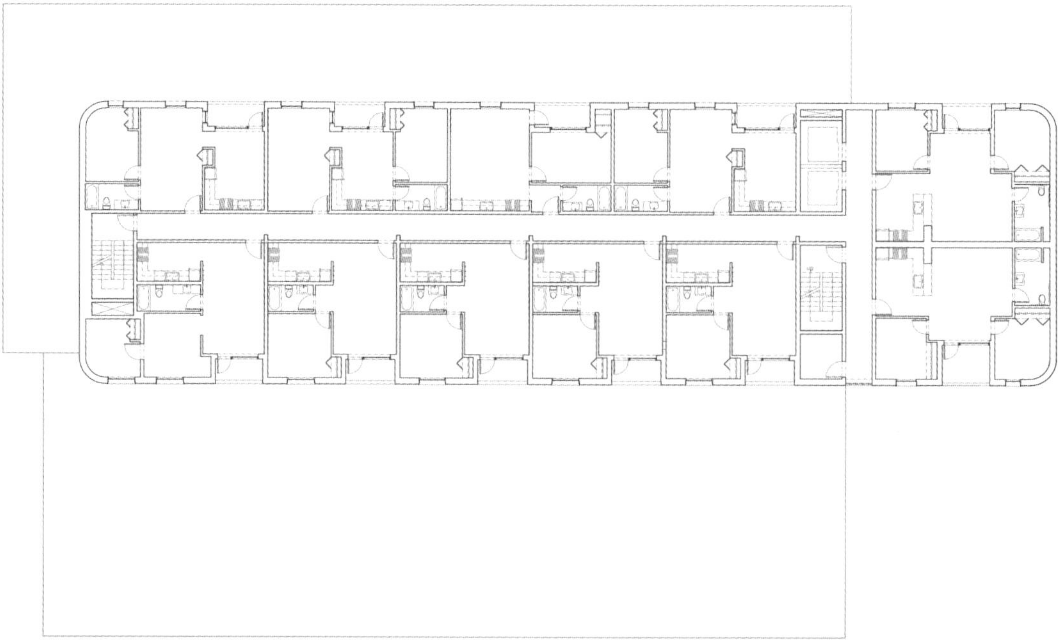

Level 2 Plan

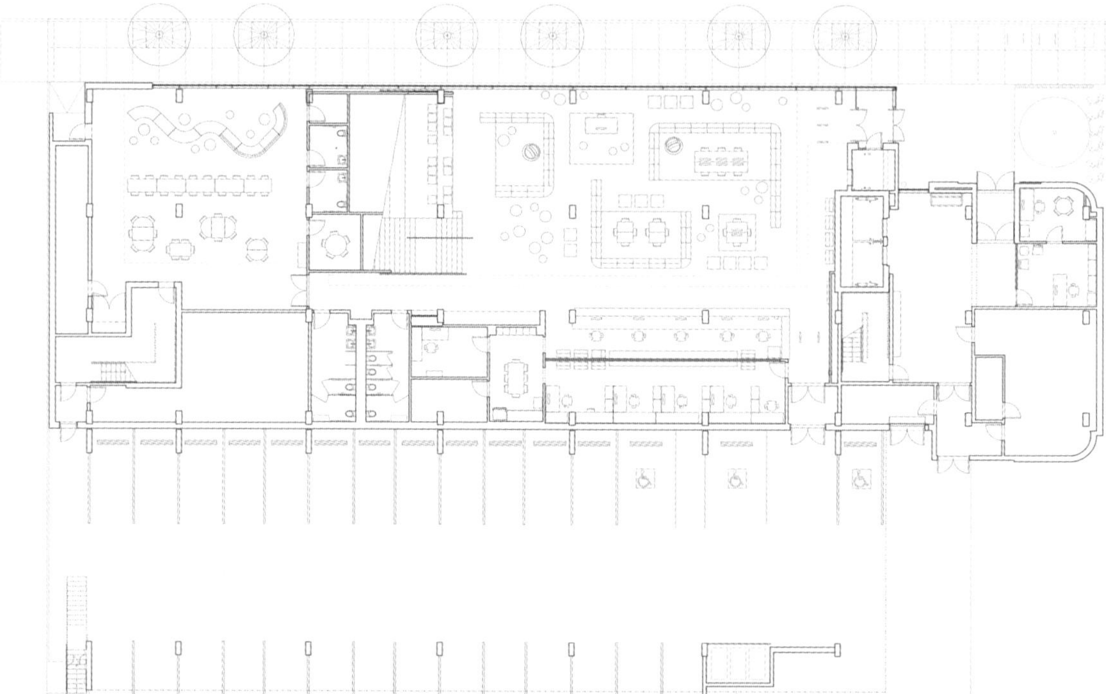

Site Plan

4022

Edison

KANVA

Student Housing
Montreal, Quebec
2014

Site area
3,871 ft² [360 m²]

GFA
8,506 ft² [790 m²]

Floor area ratio
2.20

Covered area
57%

Efficiency [Gross/net]
86%

Unit types

Bedrooms	30	0	0	0
Storeys [within units]	30	3	0	0

Parking stalls 0

Units

Average unit 7%
128 ft² [12 m²]

Smallest unit 7%
123 ft² [11.5 m²]

Largest unit 7%
131 ft² [12.5 m²]

Typology

Occupancy

Residential
100%

Cost

$128/ft²

Construction

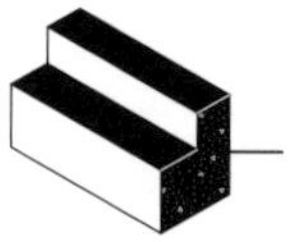

Concrete structure

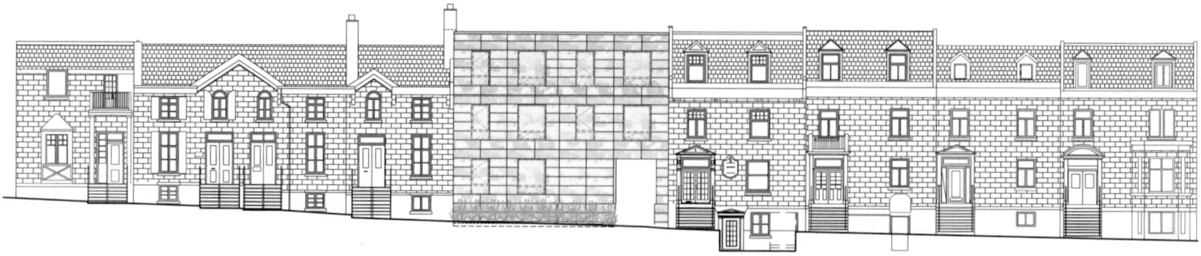

Edison is a university residence in Montreal that embodies KANVA's commitment to total architecture. The project, which includes 30 residential units complemented by communal living and dining areas, was envisioned, developed, financed, constructed, marketed, sold and operated by KANVA. Located on a double-lot among a series of row houses on the northern edge of McGill University, the project exists at the intersection of overlapping zones impacted by a myriad of complicated building requirements. Under normal circumstances, these restrictions would prescribe the construction of a building to match the form and type of those adjacent.

The design draws from an intimate understanding of the site's educational and historical contexts. The inclusion of a ground floor communal space demonstrates a familiarity with the needs and behaviours of students – many of KANVA's team members are McGill University alumni and are familiar with the particular desires of the student population. The design is also didactic; the site and program formed the basis for an architectural design studio led by KANVA at the university while the built work serves as an ongoing case study and reference for design and construction innovation in close physical proximity to the architecture department.

The building is composed to respect its context and to take advantage of existing setbacks and a public rear garden to create new relationships between the campus and the community. The building is entered along its side, beneath the front-most of two volumes whose massing matches the rhythm of adjacent buildings. The required side setback and setback of the adjacent property are merged to create a semi-public outdoor zone and passageway beyond the entrance that leads to a garden beyond.

A cocoon-like semi-private gathering space is located just inside the entry while more private living spaces are distributed on the floors above. Constructed entirely of concrete with concrete interior finishes throughout allowed for rapid construction, high quality acoustic separation and ease of longterm maintenance.

The site's history is recast through the façade as a means to integrate the new project with its storied environment. In the early 20th century, an historic stone house on the site was claimed by fire. Photoengraved concrete panels present the narratives of both the fires of early 20th century Montreal and the emergence of motion pictures. A sequence of stills from the 1901 film *Montreal Fire Department on Runners* by Thomas Edison, for whom the project is named, are etched into the concrete façade and window glazing, bringing the building to life as a performer in its urban context.

Since KANVA was able to execute all key roles in the project's development, the project retained its architectural and narrative qualities throughout construction. However, due to its unprecedented typological qualities, there were also significant perceived risks for potential buyers. Ultimately, KANVA's expertise and architectural vision paid off – the Edison project stands as a bold yet successful example of an architect-led, creative risk-reward strategy for housing that is durable, financially sound, respectful of its context, architecturally robust, technologically innovative and rooted in its community.

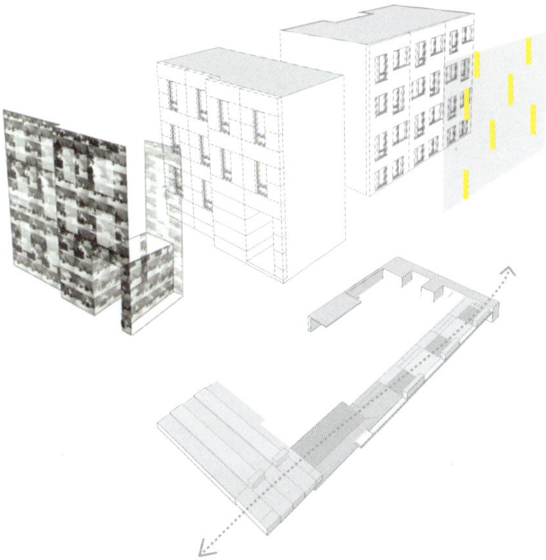

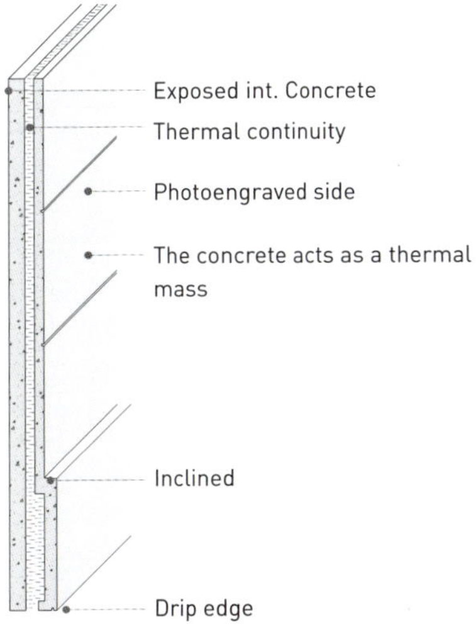
Exposed int. Concrete
Thermal continuity
Photoengraved side
The concrete acts as a thermal mass
Inclined
Drip edge

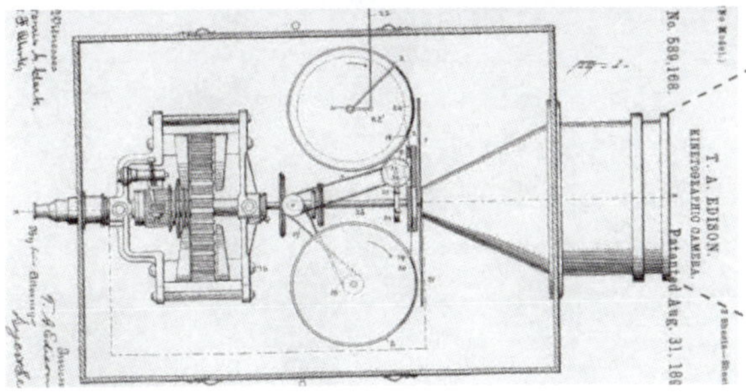
No. 589,168.
T. A. EDISON.
KINETOGRAPHIC CAMERA.

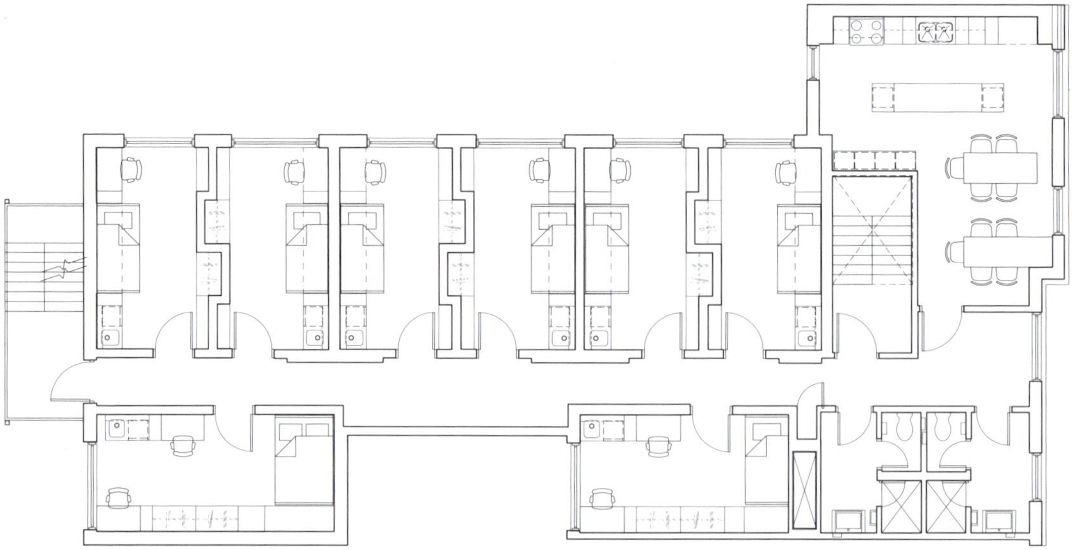

L1 plan

630 N. Franklin

Brininstool + Lynch

Apartments + Condominiums
Chicago, Illinois
2006

GFA
226,200 ft²
[21,015 m²]

SITE AREA
24,000 ft²
[2,230 m²]

Floor area ratio
9.43

Covered area
85%

Efficiency [Gross/net]
95%

Unit types

Bedrooms	80	88	0	0
Storeys [within units]	168	0	0	0

Parking stalls 135

Units

44% Average unit **796 ft²** [74 m²]

31% Smallest unit **550 ft²** [51 m²]

58% Largest unit **1050 ft²** [97.5 m²]

Typology

Occupancy

Residential
95%

Retail / Commercial
5%

Cost

$115/ft²

Construction

Pre-cast concrete

PARK

630 N. Franklin is a contemporary mid-rise containing 165 units. The building is located in Chicago's vibrant River North neighbourhood.

As industrial lofts in Chicago's River North neighbourhood were developed, they incorporated the most efficient and effective structural systems of their day. Their architecture reflects these systems, delineated in masonry and glass. Today's multi-residential developments require an equivalent economical solution: pre-cast concrete, which provides structural capability for integrating parking within the buildings, as well as acoustic performance and fire protection.

The pre-cast structural system is combined with other economical systems and materials to create a more refined architectural aesthetic. Pre-cast elements in the building's exterior float within the glazing systems, and so extending the residential units and enclosing a multi-story parking facility. The lobby continues this approach with a composition of pre-cast concrete, stone, wood and metal set below a luminous ceiling.

Level 2 plan

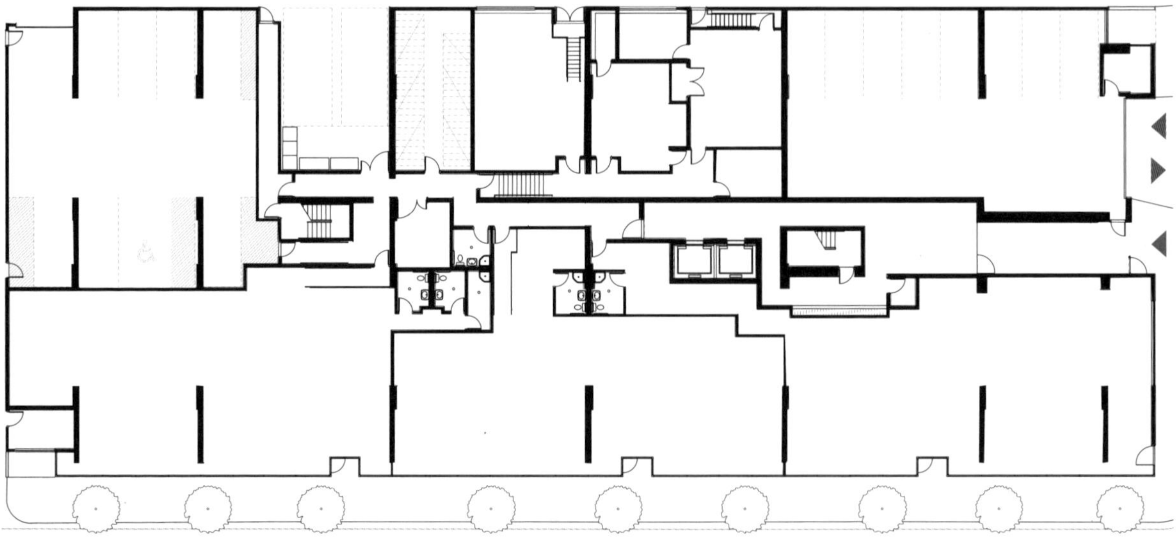

Site plan

REFLECTION

REFLECTION

5468796 Architecture

"Architecture is a political act. We talk about what's important to us and what we value through what we choose to build."

Marianne Amodio
MA+HG Architects

To us, these words embody the shared passion for housing that was conveyed by everyone involved in making the "platform.MIDDLE" symposium a reality. We choose to build homes for people.

Trevor Boddy uses the term "housing cultures" to refer to the distinct personalities and ideas, typologies and technologies, economic opportunities and social frameworks that unite the architectural community in cities. The symposium held at the IIT Campus made for Chicago's housing culture to be a natural focal point for conversation. Many of the participants call the city their own and dedicate themselves to the wellbeing of its citizens and communities.

Traveling west to east across Canada, the cities of Vancouver, Calgary, Saskatoon, Winnipeg and Montreal were also represented, each with their own unique challenges and opportunities for growth. With an emphasis on sharing economies and community building, all of the Canadian practices that spoke are serving an invaluable niche market in their respective locales, one that will hopefully become the norm and not the exception.

Since the event, we have had an opportunity to reflect on the work of our practice as well as the lessons that were shared at the symposium. We've attempted to compile and disseminate the common themes that unite the presentations and roundtable discussions into a cohesive picture of contemporary practice.

What can we do to have a lasting impact? What traits can we foster, what expanded roles can we take on, what can we ask of our politicians and policy makers? We hope the following principles help lay the groundwork for a path forward toward a more equitable and sustainable housing architecture.

Shift policy

"When you're designing affordable housing, there are these filters that your design has to pass through: federal, state, local. They make the project more expensive. It's actually more expensive to build affordable housing than it is to build market."

John Ronan
John Ronan Architects

"Our cost structure for affordable housing isn't that different from luxury housing. Building inner city affordable housing is impossible without new policy."

Rich Sciortino
Brinshore Development LLC

The regulatory framework put in place to support the creation of social housing ultimately makes it more expensive. When affordable housing can cost as much or more than luxury housing, there is a greater issue at play that cannot be addressed without a dramatic policy shift in the United States and Canada.

Advocate for change

"For me, it's impatience. I don't want to sit around and wait. It takes so long for these changes to come around. I really want to be involved in pushing the city and advocating for this change that is really needed."

Marianne Amodio
MA+HG Architects

MA+HG Architects is impactful in Vancouver with thoughtfully considered housing interventions that are sensitive to place while pushing the boundaries of a given site. Marianne's passion for her city has led her to join a number of advisory committees. Through her efforts, she inspires others to meet the challenge of affordability head on, not just as an architect but through advocacy and policy making.

Reform regulations

"When you have a low density city and you need to increase the density and bring more people within its boundaries, you have to fight the good fight over and over again. We have to take a stand as architects against sprawl."

Trevor Boddy
Writer + Curator

"Zoning by-laws are the invisible hand that define what is and is not possible on a given site."

Curtis Olson
Shift Development

Without zoning reform, it will always be cheaper to build on the edges in low density cities. In high density cities, it can be equally challenging to achieve missing middle infill when mature neighbourhoods adopt a NIMBY stance, even when so-called single family homes often contain multiple households to meet the rising cost of living. We operate in an environment where there are regulatory roadblocks at every turn, making it difficult to bring much needed housing projects to reality

Take a seat

"As an architect you have to know more than design. You have to understand the regulatory framework, politics, construction costs, and many other things that have nothing to do with design in the strict sense."

John Ronan
John Ronan Architects

Through his firm's work in Chicago, John Ronan has proven that hybrid affordable housing typologies make a dynamic model for sustainable living possible. In order to get a seat at the table, Ronan suggests that we must become experts in all of contextual issues that touch architecture.

Control cost

"As land prices rise, where is the give? There is a lot of pressure to keep the construction cost at a point that makes sense to the market."

David Brininstool
Brininstool + Lynch Ltd

"It's really about cost containment. That's where this is all headed – trying to find ways to deliver something that is appealing, while at the same time holding down costs."

Rich Sciortino
Brinshore Development LLC

To deliver market-rate multi-family projects on downtown infill sites, David identifies the need for efficient construction methods and a relationship with the contractor from the outset in order to avoid the effects of value engineering. A project can only afford a finite amount of big moves. Designs need to be boiled down to their essence. Working together with developers and contractors, we can find the synergies that will ultimately lead to more robust design outcomes.

Harness data

"Traditionally, planners don't make decisions based on data. We believe numbers tell a story and we use them as a critical tool in assessing the success or failure of a specific initiative, both in our work and in understanding the context we operate in."

Curtis Olson
Shift Development

In Saskatoon, Shift Developments has focused their efforts on a single neighbourhood in transition. Olson uses data to advocate for policy reform at City Hall and support design initiatives in his developments. In our role as architects, we need to learn the language of numbers and think like economists in order to work alongside developers and inspire policy changes.

Think sustainably

"Despite the contemporary challenges of population density, energy resource depletion and material consumption, through architectural innovation we can make positive progress toward a world that is a better-balanced place for all living things."

Arathi Gowda
Skidmore, Owings & Merrill LLP

Using the vast resources of their interdisciplinary team, SOM is able to commit their expertise to a wide range of future-focused research initiatives centred on environmental sustainability. This research then gives back to their daily practice, enabling a feedback loop of information gathering, dissemination and testing through built work. By researching, understanding and ultimately implementing new technologies and approaches, you can advocate for their adoption and drive up availability. Thinking sustainably also means learning to live with less and enjoy shared space more, concentrating on quality over quantity and finding opportunities for in-between spaces and social connection.

Respect history

"Where possible, we advocate for keeping and renovating existing public housing projects as opposed to demolishing them due to their negative stigma. With the right approach, moments of beauty may be found, brought out or invented."

Rich Sciortino
Skidmore, Owings & Merrill LLP

In great cities, the architectural layering of different eras of history show that the past and present can coexist and lead to richer urban experiences. Winnipeg has an invaluable historic building stock of post and beam warehouses, which have proven to be highly adaptable and changeable over time, a lesson we can all carry forward as we consider how to design for the present while considering the needs of the future.

Know your context

"Would it be possible for us to do residential projects in any other city but our own? Without that knowledge of a city, can you participate without being generic?"

Rami Bebawi
KANVA

There is a comfort and confidence that arises from practicing in a place you know well, especially when it comes to understanding city processes and approval timelines, as well as neighbourhood sentiments and pressure points. As an architect operating in a new city, it is important to embed yourself in the local culture. Where possible, forming close partnerships with local architects who know the issues firsthand will allow you to act with insight and intention.

Study precedents

"We went about identifying the typological solutions in different cities to answer the question: what have we learned?"

Curtis Olson
University of Houston

For Rafael Longoria, travel and research have contributed to a deep understanding of housing typologies and the urban development of Ibero-American cities. Through his work, he is able to share knowledge of the high quality design elements and common themes that result in successful projects. We can all learn and benefit from this approach, seeking precedents in our own locales and the work of our peers, while being inspired by projects from across the globe.

Be patient

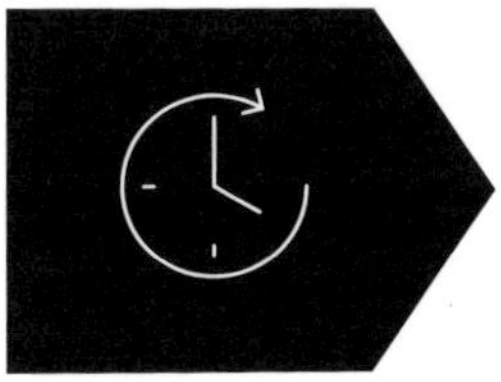

"Maybe it's good that it's slow, maybe it's good because it gives you a chance to learn, to see what other people are doing, and you don't have one big mistake that's compounded."

Peter Landon
LBBA

LBBA takes a hands on approach to practice in Chicago, immersing themselves in the communities they serve with a focus on social housing. Landon describes the nature of their work as cumulative. By building lasting, intimate relationships with clients, one project leads to the next through a natural evolution of iteration and growth. While progress may be slow, there is value in learning over time.

Be a risk taker

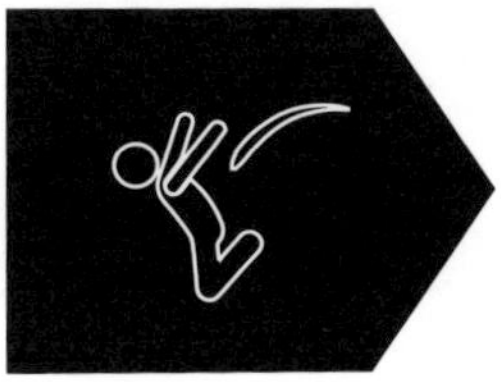

"Really what it takes to be a developer has very little to do with mathematics and everything to do with a lack of risk aversion."

Rafael Longoria
Univeristy of Houston

In Montreal, KANVA practices their philosophy of "total architecture" to realise projects that might not otherwise come to fruition. A deep understanding of building processes – from design all the way through to construction and tenant management – allow them to take creative risks and create work from unique circumstances.

Share more

"There is a movement to be more collective. Instead of something small, create something substantial."

Peter Landon
LBBA

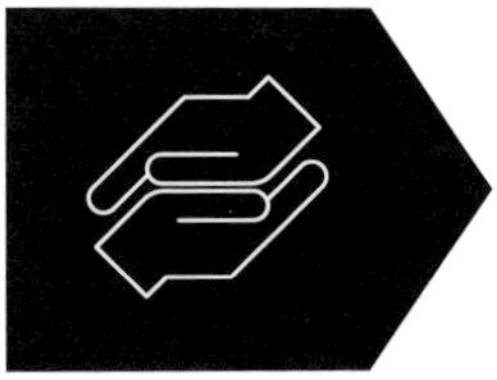

Amenities are better when they are shared. As homes get smaller, shared space deserves proportional growth. We need to consider how we can weave opportunities for social activities from the micro to the macro scale, and from inside to outside.

Build less

"People are questioning how much space they really need – it's about economics and the environment. The best way to save money and have a smaller carbon footprint is to simply build less."

Marianne Amodio
MA+HG Architects

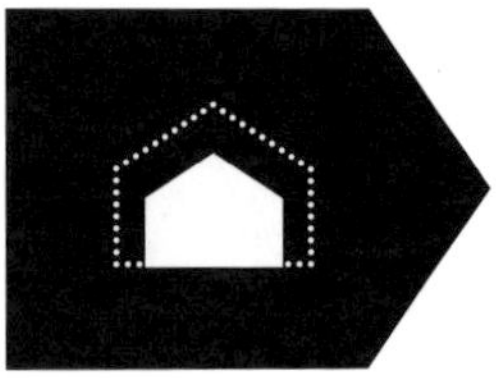

In Canada and the United States, the demographic share of one-person households and two-person non-family households is increasing at a fast pace. At the same time, Canadians and Americans live in approximately three times the square footage as the rest of the world. To meet the call for a sustainable future, we must challenge preconceived notions about how much space we really need to live comfortably.

Find the cracks

"We always try to find the cracks that people have overlooked because there is too much friction or an unknown."

Curtisn Olson
Shift Development

Often, it is the most challenging contexts that provide the most inspiring opportunities for innovation. From busy traffic corridors, industrial surroundings or a lack of views, to atypical lot proportions and restrictive zoning by-laws – if we tap into the latent potential of sites that might otherwise appear undesirable, we can prove that sustainable opportunities for living are possible.

Repair the holes

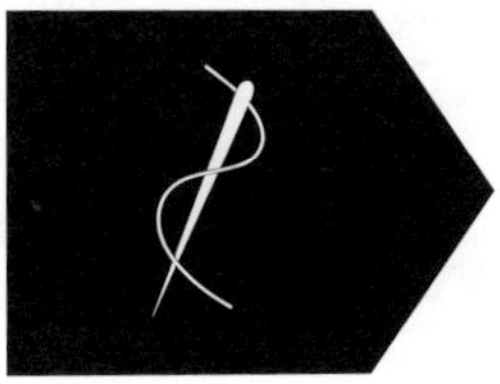

"We believe that in order to repair a hole in the urban fabric, one must reach beyond the boundaries of a single building in order to strengthen the surrounding areas."

Peter Landon
LBBA

To understand our role in neighbourhood revitalisation, it is important to look beyond the statistics and make direct connections with community groups through consultation and civic engagement. One building cannot fix a neighbourhood, but small interventions and moments of connection can create the ripple effects that lead to lasting change.

Meet the neighbours

"We seek out amenity space for the building in the larger community, in order to support a symbiotic relationship between residents and small businesses, reinforcing connections and promoting walkability."

Alkarim Devani
RNDSQR

In Calgary, RNDSQR builds connections with like-minded entrepreneurs in order to strengthen the relationship between their buildings and the surrounding small business community. When square footage is at a premium, the neighbourhood coffee shop, the local gym and the pocket park all become an extension of our private living spaces. Hand in hand with building less, when you have amenities and public spaces just beyond your front door, you can expand your social circle and foster relationships with the neighbourhood that ultimately lead to happier citizens and healthier cities.

Create a network

"The more open we are, the better we are. Nothing is ever lost through sharing information."

Trevor Boddy
Writer + Curator

There is immense value in architects being open with one another and with the public. Invite people into your work. Initiate conversations that lead to growth and new perspectives. While there may appear to be competition between designers, sharing knowledge is imperative for us all to do better and serve the common good. We need to take down barriers between architecture and the public and be receptive to advice and critique from our peers.

Tell the story

"When we have meetings for finance, insurance or construction, we ask that everyone gives us five minutes and we tell them the narrative. That sharing of the story actually brings the risk down. Everyone is willing to commit on a whole new level."

Rami Bebawi
KANVA

If we share the project narrative, we can inspire a mutual passion for the project's success. Stories are a powerful tool to communicate with the public. We often under-estimate how people who are not embedded in the profession can appreciate the project's goals and ambitions. When we take the time to explain the thought process behind the design and the care that's required to bring it to fruition, people can take more ownership over the end product.

Find beauty

"You have to draw people in with beauty, imagination and the potential for a lifestyle that you cannot get anywhere else."

Curtis Olson
Shift Development

As we fight uphill battles at City Hall, as we strive for efficiency at all costs, it is important not to lose sight of beauty and moments of delight. Architecture is an expression of culture. Beauty exists in things that are built for their intended purpose, at the right size in their context and in harmony with their neighbours, whether it be traditional or a modern counterpoint.

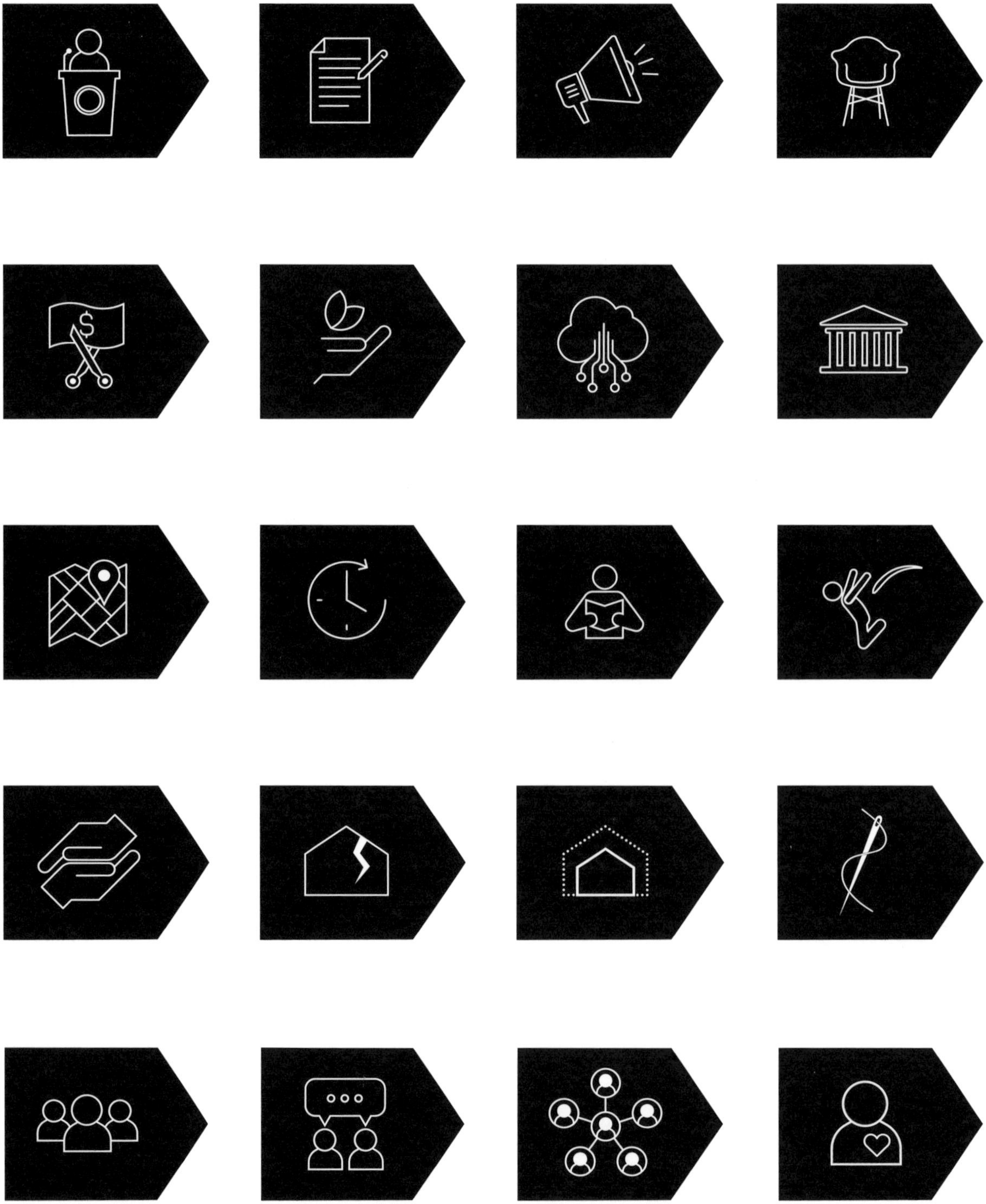

Looking forward

In 2019, we gathered together at Crown Hall with a shared spirit of inquiry, openness and collaboration. In 2020, a pandemic upended all of our lives and businesses. The effects have been profound and evolving. The aftershocks will be felt for years and decades to come.

At the same time, the profession of architecture has proven its essentialness. Covid-19 had highlighted in sharp relief the deeply rooted inequities in our society and the demand for housing the 99% has only grown more acute. If we can extract any meaningful lessons from this global shift, it is that what we already know to be true has become even more relevant. Multi-family housing is about more than proforma calculations or density targets. At its heart, architecture is for people. Quality design at all scales is essential. Homes need access to light, air and views. People need outdoor spaces to gather and linger.

Above all, housing is a human right. The ability to stay home is an emblem of privilege, one that is starkly divided along socio-economic and racial lines. As architects, we must expand our repertoire to meet the housing crisis with the urgency it demands.

One of the biggest questions we had grappled with is whether life would "return to normal" or if the effects of this period would inspire a broad change. Our hope is that there would be a renewed appreciation for the shared experience of living in cities and all of the messiness and beauty it entails. We will continue to advocate for housing architecture that supports community building and the power of tangible connections in physical space.

post.SCRIPT

Notes

GOOD DESIGN IS FOR EVERYONE

1 Jonah Newman, "Half of Chicago Renters Can't Afford Their Housing." The Chicago Reporter, June 01, 2015. https://www.chicagoreporter.com/half-of-chicago-renters-cant-afford-their-housing/.

HOUSING REVISITED

1 Jonas Salk and Jonathan Salk, *World Population and Human Values a New Reality* (New York: Harper & Row, 1981).

2 Donella H. Meadows, Dennis L. Meadows, Jorgen Randers and William W. Behrens, III, *The Limits of Growth*. (New York, New York: Universe Books, 1972).

TAKING CHARGE

1 Charlie Smith, "Report Forecasts 1.1 Million Population Rise in Lower Mainland by 2041, Requiring 500,000 New Housing Units." *The Georgia Straight*, January 22, 2019, https://www.straight.com/news/1191291/ areport-forecasts-11-million-population- rise-lower-mainland-2041-requiring-500000-new.

TOTAL ARCHITECTURE

1 Jon Townsend, "Rinus Michels and the Total Football Rebellion," *These Football Times*, January 28, 2016, https://thesefootballtimes.co/2016/01/28/rinus-michels-and-the-total-football-rebellion/.

FORM FOLLOWS FINANCE

1 While the LIHTC compliance period expires in year 15, every State requires extended affordability periods of at least 30 years.

Image credits

14, 15 "platform.MIDDLE" symposium (2019). Photograph by 5468796 Architecture.

18 From top to bottom: Tierra Linda. Photograph by Mark Ballogg. Courtesy of LBBA. – Independence Library + Apartments. Drawing by JRA. Courtesy of JRA. – futureHOME 2050. Rendering © SOM. Courtesy of SOM. – Co-. Rendering by MA+HG Architects. Courtesy of MA+HG Architects. – Pop-up installation prior to Edison. Photograph by KANVA. Courtesy of KANVA.

19 From top to bottom, left column: Marina Crescent by James Cheng Architects. Photo by James Cheng. Courtesy of James Cheng. – Barcelona Ensanche courtyard. Photograph by Rafael Longoria. Courtesy of Rafael Longoria. – Two Twenty. Photograph provided by Shift Developments. Courtesy of Shift Developments. – Legends South. Photography by Brinshore Development. Courtesy of Brinshore Development. – LIFE. Photograph by RNDSQR. Courtesy of RNDSQR.

From top to bottom, right column: 120 Dwellings. Photograph by José Hevia. Courtesy of Sio2 Arch. – Union. Photograph by Janis Nicolay. Courtesy of MA+HG Architects. – Independence Library + Apartments. Photography by James Florio. Courtesy of JRA. – Edison. Photograph by Marc Cramer. Courtesy of KANVA. – 630 N. Franklin. Photograph by Darris Lee Harris, Padgett & Company. Courtesy of Brininstool + Lynch.

24-25 "platform.MIDDLE" symposium (2019). Photograph by KANVA. Courtesy of KANVA.

28, 29 Woodlawn Park. Photographs by Mark Ballogg; diagram by LBBA. Courtesy of LBBA.

30, 31 Terrace 459 at Parkside of Old Town. Drawing by LBBA; photograph by David Schalliol. Courtesy of LBBA.

32 -33 Legends South Development. Photograph by LBBA. Courtesy of LBBA.

34 LBBA Projects in Chicago (2016). Map by LBBA. Courtesy of LBBA.

35 Tierra Linda. Photograph by Mark Ballogg. Courtesy of LBBA.

36-37 "platform.MIDDLE" symposium (2019). Photograph by KANVA. Courtesy of KANVA.

40, 41 Perth Amboy High School (2003). Renderings by John Ronan Architects. Courtesy of John Ronan Architects.

42, 45 South Shore High School. Photographs by Larry Okrent. Courtesy of John Ronan Architects.

44, 45 Independence Library + Apartments. Collage by John Ronan Architects; photograph by James Florio. Courtesy of John Ronan Architects.

50, 51 "platform.MIDDLE" symposium (2019). Photograph by KANVA. Courtesy of KANVA.

54-57 futureHOME 2050. Drawings, diagrams and renderings by SOM (Full project team includes: Brian Lee, Jeffrey McCarthy, Andrew Obendorf, Arathi Gowda, Aaron Mazeika, Michael Pfeffer, Michael Waldo, Cyril Marsollier, Yukun Xu, Michael Charters, Leif Eikevik; Additional team: Jaime Velez, Rodrigo Buelvas, Giacomo Tinari, Brandon Vieth, Billy Raleigh, Jacob Gay, Sung Jin Cho). Courtesy of © SOM.

58-59 AMLI 900+. Rendering and diagrams by SOM (Full project team includes: Brian Lee – Design Partner, Jonathan Stein – Managing Partner, Andrew Obendorf – Architectural Associate Director, Kevin Rodenkirch – Architectural Associate Director, Anthony Dombrowski – Sr. Architectural Professional, Brian Poling – Architectural Professional, Lanye Luo – Architectural Professional, Yang Yu– Architectural Professional, JongNyoung Park – Architectural Assistant, Zhexiong Chai – Architectural Professional, Benton Johnson – Structural Engineering Associate Director, Luke Leung – Director of Sustainable Engineering, Arathi Gowda – Sustainable Engineering Specialist, Associate Director, Marzia Sedino – Mechanical Engineer, Associate Director, Stephen Ray – Sr. Licensed Mechanical Engineering Professional). Courtesy of © SOM.

60 AMLI 900. Photographer unknown (left). AMLI 900+. Rendering by SOM (Full project team noted above). Courtesy of © SOM.

61 AMLI 900+. Rendering by SOM (Full project team noted above). Courtesy of © SOM.

64-65 S. R. Crown Hall, IIT. Photograph by Johanna Hurme. Courtesy of 5468796 Architecture.

69 Zoning map (Vancouver, March 1990). Map by City of Vancouver. Courtesy of Open Government Licence - Vancouver: https://opendata.vancouver.ca/pages/licence/.

70-71 Tomo. Elevation drawing, rendering and diagram by MA+HG Architects. Courtesy of MA+HG Architects.

72-75 Co-. Renderings and diagrams by MA+HG Architects. Courtesy of MA+HG Architects.

80 "platform.MIDDLE" symposium (2019). Photograph by 5468796 Architecture. Courtesy of 5468796 Architecture.

81 Teaching at IIT. Photograph by 5468796 Architecture. Courtesy of 5468796 Architecture.

86 Fabbrica. Photographs by Marc Cramer. Courtesy of KANVA.

87 Irene. Photographs by Jimmy Hamelin; rendering by KANVA. Courtesy of KANVA.

88 Edison. Photographs by Marc Cramer. Courtesy of KANVA.

89 Elää. Photograph by Alex St.Jean; diagrams by KANVA. Courtesy of KANVA.

90 archigraphik. Photograph/Triptych by KANVA. Courtesy of KANVA.

91 Pop-up installation prior to Edison. Photograph by KANVA. Courtesy of KANVA.

92 Irene construction. Photograph by KANVA. Courtesy of KANVA.

93 Edison residence photoengraving. Photograph by KANVA. Courtesy of KANVA.

98-99 "platform.MIDDLE" symposium (2019). Photograph by Hugh Taylor. Courtesy of 5468796 Architecture.

102 [600 Block West] Hastings Street looking East from Granville Street, Vancouver, B.C. (ca. 1902). Photograph (silver gelatin print, 19x24 cm) by Richard Henry Trueman. Courtesy of Trueman Photo, Vancouver, BC, Accessed from City of Vancouver Archives: https://searcharchives.vancouver.ca/600-block-west-hastings-street-looking-east-from-granville-street-vancouver-b-c.

103 Project 56 conceptual sketch elevation (1955). Sketch by Arthur Erickson. Courtesy of Arthur Erickson. Arthur Erickson fonds, Canadian Architectural Archives, University of Calgary. Accession: 4A/76.13.

105 Marinaside Crescent by James Cheng Architects. Photograph by James Cheng. Courtesy of James Cheng.

106 River Green by James Cheng Architects. Photograph by James Cheng. Courtesy of James Cheng.

107 Formal typological studies. Diagrams by University of British Columbia students. Courtesy of Trevor Boddy.

108 Waterfall Building by Arthur Erickson. Photograph by Gerry Kopelow. Courtesy of Nick Milkovich Architects Inc.

109 Michael Green Architects' Ronald McDonald House. Photograph by Ema Peter. Courtesy of MGA | Michael Green Architects.

110 Vancouver House. Photograph by Laurian Ghinitoiu. Courtesy of BIG Architects.

Alberni Tower. Rendering by Kengo Kuma. Courtesy of Kengo Kuma & Associates.

Terrace House, Shigeru Ban Architects. Rendering by Portliving. Courtesy of Portliving.

112-113 S. R. Crown Hall. Photograph by Johanna Hurme. Courtesy of 5468796 Architecture.

116 Dellekamp Arquitectos CB 29 building. Photograph by Óscar Necoechea. Courtesy of Dellekamp Arquitectos.

117 Quinta Monroy. Photographs by Cristóbal Palma (top) and Elemental (bottom). Courtesy of Elemental.

118 Carabanchel Social Housing (17 July 2008). Photograph by Alejandro García González & Francisco Andeyro / CC BY 3.0.

119 Edificio 111 (2011). Photograph by Duccio Malagamba. Courtesy of Flores & Prats.

Walden 7 (2013). Photograph by Rafael Longoria. Courtesy of Rafael Longoria.

120 Barcelona Ensanche courtyard (2012). Photograph by Rafael Longoria. Courtesy of Rafael Longoria.

121 Pan-American Studio investigating Eixample blocks. Drawings by Andrew Sharkody, Pan-American Studio, University of Houston 2013. Courtesy of Rafael Longoria.

122 "platform.MIDDLE" symposium (2019). Photograph by Hugh Taylor. Courtesy of 5468796 Architecture.

123 Teaching at IIT. Photograph by Johanna Hurme. Courtesy of 5468796 Architecture.

126 Two Twenty (2014). Photograph provided by Shift Development. Courtesy of Shift Development.

127 Riversdale, Saskatoon, Saskatchewan. Map by Shift Development. Courtesy of Shift Development.

129-131 Element Urban Village (2018). Photographs by Taylor Summach; Advertisement by Brandon Webber. Courtesy of Shift Development.

132-133 "platform.MIDDLE" symposium (2019). Photograph by Hugh Taylor. Courtesy of 5468796 Architecture.

136 Legends South (2006). Photograph by Brinshore Developments. Courtesy of Brinshore Developments.

137 Hyacinth Place (2009). Photograph by Brinshore Developments. Courtesy of Brinshore Developments.

138-139 Dorchester Art Housing Collaborative (2015-2016). Photograph (left) by Mark Ballogg; photograph (right) by Brinshore Developments. Courtesy of Brinshore Developments.

140-141 "platform.MIDDLE" symposium (2019). Photograph by KANVA. Courtesy of KANVA.

144-145 Life. Illustrations and photographs by RNDSQR. Courtesy of RNDSQR.

153-155 102 Dwellings. Photographs by José Hevia; renderings by Sio2 Arch. Courtesy of Sio2 Arch.

157-161 Union. Photographs by Janis Nicolay; drawings and diagrams by MA+HG Architects. Courtesy of MA+HG Architects.

163-167 Independence Library + Apartments. Photographs by James Florio; drawings and diagrams by John Ronan Architects. Courtesy of John Ronan Architects.

169-175 Edison. Photographs by Marc Cramer; drawings and collage by KANVA. Courtesy of KANVA.

175-179 630 N. Franklin (2005-2007). Photograph (175) by Christopher Barrett, Hedrich Blessing; photograph (p. 176, left and p. 177, bottom) by Darris Lee Harris, Padgett & Company; photograph (p.168, middle and right, p.179) by Barbara Karant, Karant & Associates, Inc.; photograph (p. 177, top 6 photos) by Brininstool + Lynch; sketch and drawings by Brininstool + Lynch. Courtesy of Brininstool + Lynch.

platform.MIDDLE: Architecture for Housing the 99%
5468796 Architecture
First edition, 2023
ISBN 978-607-8880-19-5

platform.MIDDLE

© 5468796 Architecture Inc.
Winnipeg, MB
Canada

© Arquine, SA de CV
Ámsterdam 163 A
Colonia Hipódromo, 06100
Ciudad de México

Texts
© 5468796 Architecture
© John Ronan Architects, John Ronan
© KANVA, Tudor Radulescu and Rami Bebawi
© LBBA Architects, Peter Landon
© MA+HG Architects, Marianne Amodio
© Rafael Longoria
© Illinois Institute of Technology, Reed Kroloff
© Brinshore Development LLC, Rich Sciortino
© RNDSQR, Alkarim Devani
© Shift Development, Curtis Olson
© Skidmore, Owings & Merrill, Arathi Gowda
and Andrew Obendorf
© Trevor Boddy

Images
© Authors specified on the image credits page

5468796 Architecture

Original layout and Editorial Management
Johanna Hurme, Sasa Radulovic, Ken Borton, Shannon Wiebe, Ainsley Johnston and Hugh Taylor

Content production
Emeil Alvarez, Pablo Batista, Jordy Craddock, Donna Evans, Teresa Garside, Ben Greenwood, Ralph Guitierrez, Jeffrey Kachkan, Matthew Kurtas, Andrew Lawler, Kelsey McMahon, Mohammad Massoumi, Colin Neufeld and Amanda Reis.

Past collaborators: Sharon Ackerman, Mandy Aldcorn, Maria Amagasu, Apollinaire Au, Brandon Bergem, Eric Decumutan, Jason Ejzenbart, Michelle Heath, Aynslee Hurdal, Caroline Inglis, Lucretia Ionescu, Andriy Ivanystskyy, Eva Kiss, Stanislav Klas, Lindsey Koepke, Grant Labossiere, Justin Lieberman, Jayne Miles, Royce O'Toole, Zach Pauls, Simone Prill, Sean Radford, Erin Riediger, Helia Saadat, Shannon Scott, Hasan Shurrab, Renee Struthers, Trent Thompson, Matthew Trendota, Alan Vamos, Jennifer Yablonowski and Dazhong Yi.

Arquine

Director
Miquel Adrià

Editorial Director
Brenda Soto Suárez

Editorial Assistants
Ana Luz Valencia and Karina Reyes

Layout
María Marín de Buen, Yavanna Latapí and Regina Sierra
(Estudio María Marín de Buen)

Proofreading
Quentin Pope

Prepress
Offset Rebosán

5468796.ca
arquine.com

platform.MIDDLE is generously supported by the College of Architecture at the Illinois Institute of Technology.

The architects and publishers have made every effort to identify ownership in the use of images and copyrighted material. In the event of an inadvertent omission or error, please notify the publisher.

No part of this publication may be reproduced, stored in a retrieval system, or transmitted in any form or by any means, electronic, mechanical, photocopying, recording or otherwise, without prior and express written permission of the owners of the intellectual property rights and of the publishers.

platform.MIDDLE is one of four volumes in the publication *platform. MIDDLE: Architecture for Housing the 99%*. The other volumes include: platform.MACRO, platform.MICRO and projects.MODELLING.

platform.MIDDLE: Architecture for Housing the 99% was printed and bound in September 2023 by Artron Art Printing Ltd. in China. It was printed on 100 g IKPP paper and set in typefaces of the DIN family. The print run was 1,300 copies.

5468796 Architecture

platform.MACRO

platform.MACRO

platform.MACRO looks at the larger scale of housing production that falls outside the traditional scope of the architect alone. **Divest / invest** clarifies the definitions of affordable and social housing, explores other metrics that influence affordability and paints a broad picture of the current state of social and public housing in Canada and the United States. **Restrict / restructure** examines the ramifications of land use policy on housing affordability and supply. **Commodity / community** considers the global impact of the commodification of housing, as well as strategies being implemented to counteract its effects. **Formulaic / formative** describes current housing forms, the push for missing middle and mid-rise infill, and the opportunities for innovation that can be found within them.

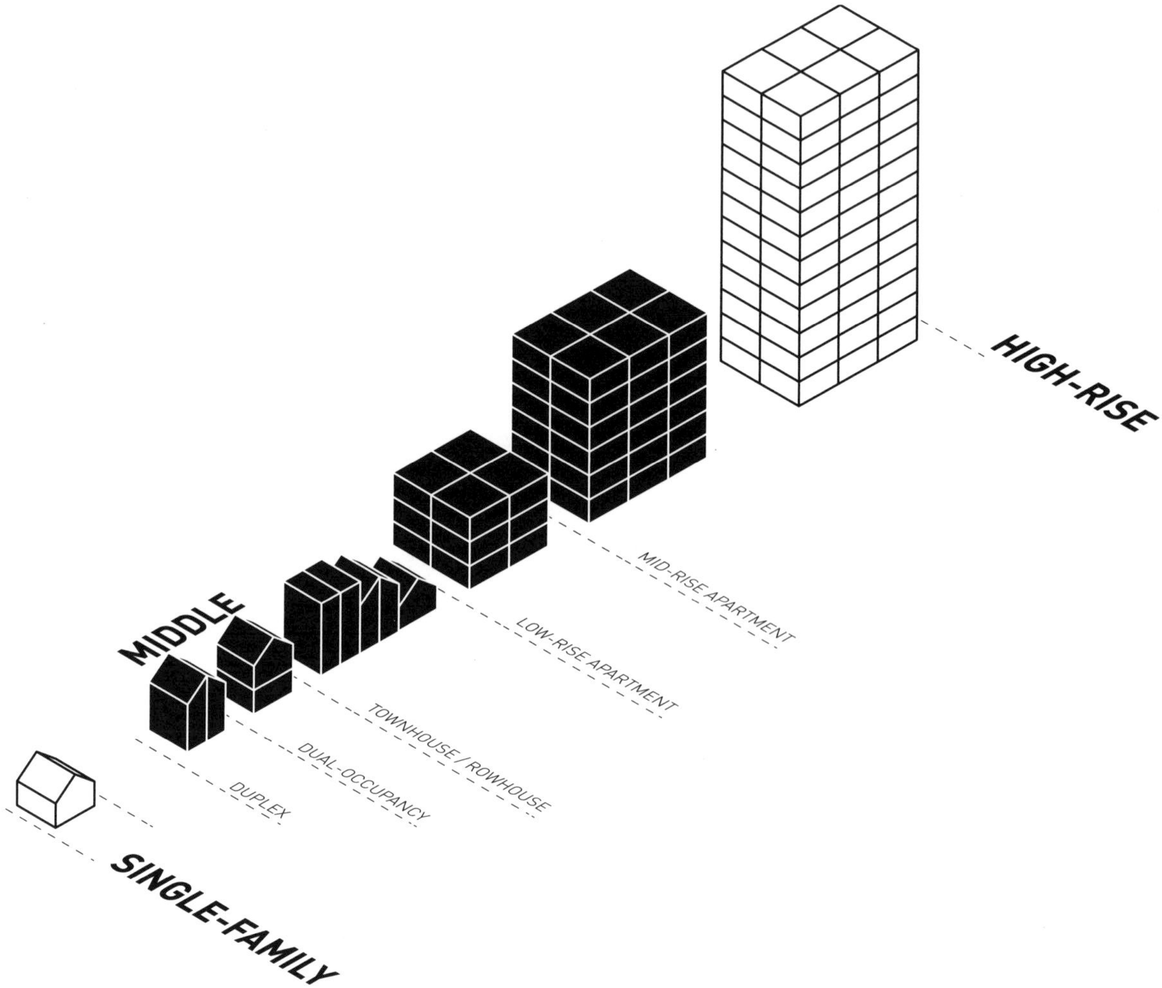
HIGH-RISE
MID-RISE APARTMENT
LOW-RISE APARTMENT
TOWNHOUSE / ROWHOUSE
DUAL-OCCUPANCY
DUPLEX
MIDDLE
SINGLE-FAMILY

INTRODUCTION

In the context of urbanized North America, multi-family housing is often perceived as the least attractive and most mundane of architectural typologies – yet by its very nature, it is one of the most sustainable and socially conscious of architectural briefs.

The work and research of 5468796 Architecture has focused on missing middle and mid-rise housing in its many forms and ownership models, from refugee and social housing to market-rate condominiums. The following chapters build on this work, and on a manifesto for housing, "Add via Edit: A Decade of Housing," which was first published by Canadian Architect in 2018.[1]

Issues of housing and affordability vary widely from one city to another and from one economic reality to the other, as demonstrated by the breadth of individual practice experiences that were discussed at the "platform.MIDDLE" Symposium. In urban centres like Toronto, Vancouver, San Francisco or New York, affordability is tied to land costs and offshore investor policy loopholes, rendering the majority of existing and near-future housing stock unaffordable for the average population. In midwestern cities like Winnipeg and Chicago, architects and planners must contend with low density and sprawl as a result of cheap land values that in turn create unsustainable economies and enormous infrastructure deficits.

The gap between a sustainable city building model and the current condition is especially wide where the urban landscape still reflects the ideals of mid-century planning based on car culture and the segregation of activities, epitomized by the proliferation of suburbs and single-family dwellings. In response, much needed housing density is concentrated in high-rise buildings where the view is prioritized over connection to the ground plane or shared outdoor space.

Multi-family housing is one architectural typology that can have a significant impact on ordinary people going about their daily lives. With the condominium boom taking hold across the continent, the number of residential units passing across an architect's desk is unprecedented. As a result of the typology's inherent repetition and potentially banal programme – as well as the private sector's pursuit of profit, often at the expense of quality and livability – the margin in which architecture can operate is very narrow. It is therefore incredibly important that as architects we respond to the challenges of this typology with the rigour that it deserves. Given the current affordable housing shortage, the dramatic shift towards smaller family units in North America, and the adoption of multi-family housing as an acceptable form of living, the opportunity to do so is now.

Climate crisis

It's impossible to discuss architecture or urban design without addressing the climate crisis. Buildings are currently responsible for 33% of global energy consumption and 39% of greenhouse gas emissions.[2] Architects and allied professionals must profoundly change the way we design and construct for the world of tomorrow if we are to slow, stop or reverse climate change.

Buildings are responsible for...

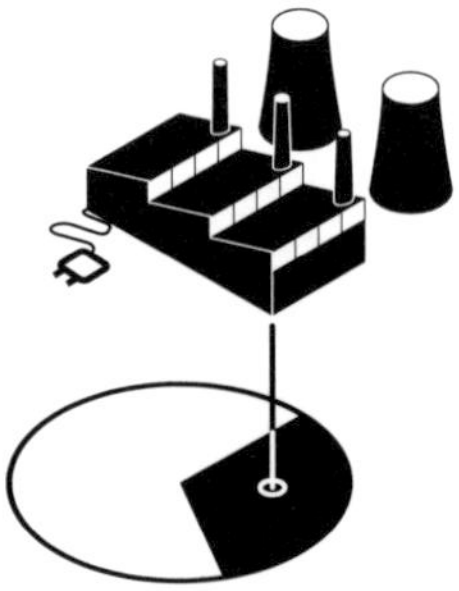

33%

of global energy consumption

39%

of greenhouse gas emissions

There is little doubt that climate change is the defining issue of our time. According to the manifesto published by Canada's chapter of Architects Declare (AD), an international network organizing for transformative change to address the climate crisis, "the world is already 1 °C warmer than it was in pre-industrial times and our current infrastructure will take us past 1.5 °C by mid-century. The next ten years are pivotal. In order to avoid 2 °C of warming – widely understood as the tipping point into ecological catastrophe – we must dramatically reduce greenhouse gas emissions."[3] A sufficient response requires a rapid paradigm shift in thought and action for everyone working as designers and builders of our built environment.

As stated by Seth Klein, Director of Strategy with the Climate Emergency Unit, the time for incentives is well past, and the speed and scale required for an adequate response far exceeds the current climate targets set by most, if not all governments. We are truly dealing with a crisis that requires a crisis-level response. If we don't act now, the effects will be drastic and irreversible.

The majority of contemporary literature on sustainable building practices centres on strategies to reduce emissions and carbon in new buildings. To a lesser extent, there is also a growing recognition that, as famously stated by Carl Elefante, "the greenest building is the one that's already built." What seems to be missing from the conversation, or even the green building certification programs, are any specific per capita targets to reduce the size and scale of buildings, measured against a baseline.

The average North American occupies...

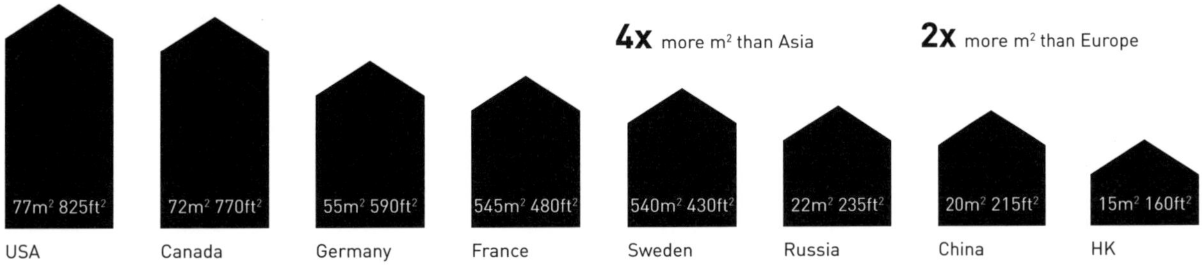

For example, a typical newly built suburb of single detached houses in Winnipeg has an average density of five dwellings per acre. In fact, 62% of Winnipeg's housing stock consists of single detached homes.[4] By comparison, only 7.7% of Helsinki's population lives in single-family houses.[5] Similarly, the density of a newly built, median Northern European residential neighbourhood is at least four or five times greater, at 20-30 dwellings per acre, and includes a mix of multi-family apartment buildings, row houses and duplexes, in addition to an occasional detached home. As a measure of street frontage alone, it is easy to understand why servicing 20-30 homes versus five on the same land area is that much more sustainable.

Examining household size statistics in Canada reveals that single person households are the largest and fastest growing demographic, at 28% of total households for the first time.[6] Similar statistics apply to the United States, as well as the majority of the developed world. Generally speaking, the average family unit size has been shrinking from 4 persons in the 1950's to less than 2.5 today. The opposite is true for average home size, which has increased from approximately 1,000 ft^2 in 1930 to around 2,600 ft^2 in 2015. This discrepancy means that every individual citizen occupies an ever increasing personal footprint, up from about 250 ft^2 in 1950 to about 900 ft^2 in 2015. Compared to the rest of the world, the average Canadian or American occupies about four times more residential floor space per capita than the average person in Asia and about twice as much as the average European.[7]

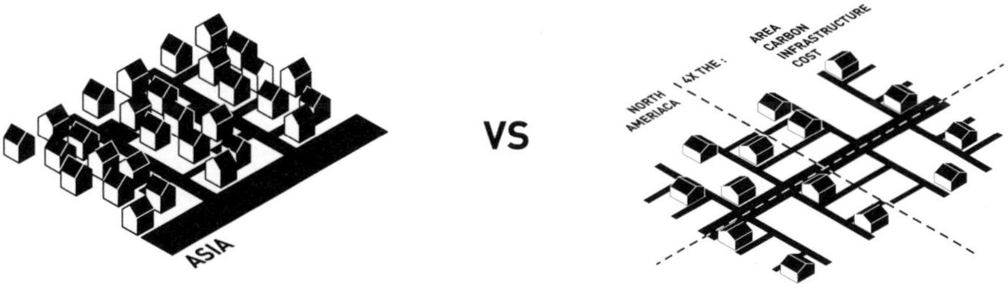

DIVEST / INVEST

The terminology for affordable and social housing can vary widely from one country to another and from one jurisdiction to the next. "Affordable housing" in Canada and the United States is defined as housing that costs less than 30% of a household's total gross income, expressed as the shelter-cost-to-income ratio (STIR). We use the term "affordable housing" to mean a variety of ownership types, not just developments that are owned by the government or a public housing agency.

On the other hand, social housing (Canada) or public housing (United States) is any rental housing which may be owned and managed by the province or state, by non-profit organizations, or by a combination of the two, usually with the aim of providing affordable housing. Social housing can also be seen as a potential remedy to housing inequality. Although the common goal of social housing is to provide affordable housing, the details, terminology, definitions of "poverty" and other criteria for allocation vary within different contexts.

Targeted / universalist

According to the Organization for Economic Co-operation and Development (OECD), social housing systems can be classified as targeted or universalist.

In Canada and the United States, targeted models concentrate on low-income and vulnerable populations. In contrast, Northern European countries like Denmark have universalist models that are open to a broad cross section of the population and do not set an income threshold to determine eligibility. As a result, "it is no coincidence that these countries have the biggest social housing sectors."[1]

In Canada, 4% of households (628,700 of 14.8 million) live in social and affordable housing.[2] In the United States, over 2 million residents live in slightly more than 1 million public housing units out of 139 million total housing units, accounting for only 0.7% of the total housing stock.[3] In Denmark, social housing accounts for 24% of the total housing stock. The country uses the term general housing to reflect "its theoretical aim to house a broad range of the Danish population."[4] Units are provided at cost-based rents through over 760 public interest housing associations, regulated by central government policies.[5] A cost-based approach means that rent levels are determined in part by the cost of building the dwelling, thus allowing for long-term cost recovery.

In the Netherlands, 4 million people live in 2.4 million social housing units, which accounts for 32% of the housing stock.[6] There are over 425 non-profit social housing corporations that finance housing for those at the bottom of the economic pyramid.[7] Such corporations provide 44% of the housing stock in Amsterdam and over 50% in Rotterdam.[8] Universalist criteria was only changed in 2015 to focus on individuals with a social disadvantage, and housing organizations are now required to rent 80% of vacancies to households with incomes below a set threshold.

Comparing the numbers between North America and Europe highlights a broader issue that is rooted in the fundamental value system of each nation – one of individual responsibility versus collective well-being and equity.

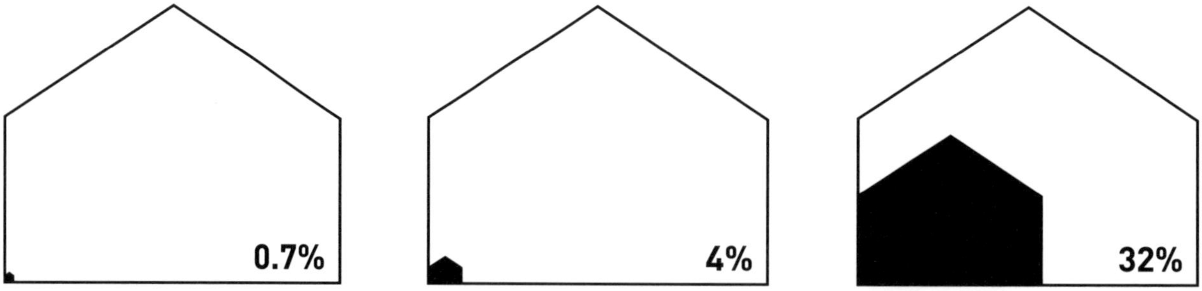

United States — Canada — The Netherlands

Cost of housing provision

The cost of constructing new housing generally consists of land costs, construction costs and government imposed costs.

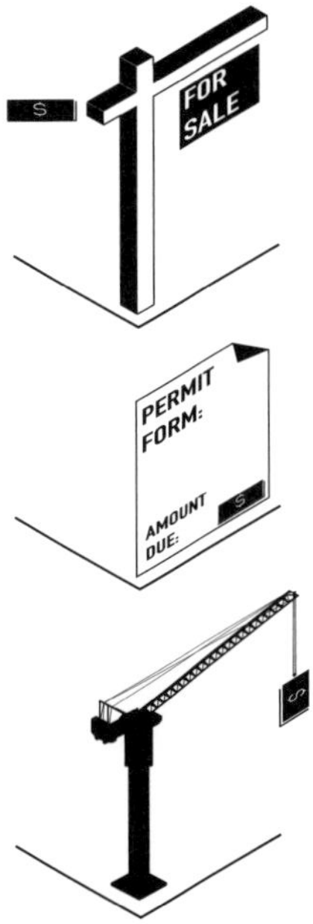

Government-imposed charges – including taxes, fees and infrastructure charges – are a significant component of any new construction project, accounting for upward of 12% of the total cost for typical low-rise and high-rise developments in Canadian cities.[9] In the United States, state and local regulations "account for nearly 20% of the cost of building a single-family home."[10] While land costs vary significantly from one jurisdiction to another, construction costs are somewhat similar across the continent (with the exception of the far north, where access, limited labour markets and higher transportation costs add significant up-charge).

It is obvious that the private sector alone cannot adequately fulfill existing and future needs under current policy frameworks, especially for those with the greatest need. In order for a private developer to create profitable rental housing in one of Canada's major urban centres, for example, a large one-bedroom or small two-bedroom unit has to fetch approximately $1,500 per month in rent. Using 30% of gross monthly income as an affordability benchmark, a household has to earn $60,000 annually to afford a market-rate rental unit.

Cost of transportation

The link between housing affordability and transportation costs is an indirect but significant factor that adds to the overall cost of living, especially given the pervasiveness of greenfield developments and associated long commutes.

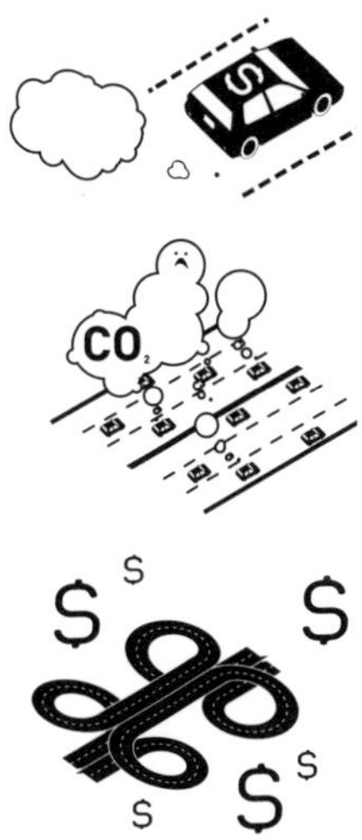

With further thought, it seems obvious that locating affordable housing away from job centres, which serves to increase the demand for car ownership, only deepens the inequity between low-and-high-income earners. Outside of Canada, jurisdictions are beginning to take an expanded view of affordability, one that combines housing and transportation costs. Generally, 15% of income for transportation is added to the 30% affordable housing threshold, for a benchmark of no more than 45%.[11]

In Canada, we do not have a regular, rigorous survey that captures this combined metric. Prolonged commutes have an obvious negative impact on government infrastructure and limit the progress of environmental goals, such as increased transit ridership and reduced emissions. A recent Metro Vancouver study measured the combined cost of housing and transportation for the region. The study found that renter households earning less than $50,000 can spend up to 67% of their pre-tax income on housing and transportation costs.[12]

A brief history

Canada's housing authority, the Canadian Mortgage and Housing Corporation (CMHC), was created during World War II in response to a housing shortage for returning veterans, in order to fund the construction of public housing and guarantee private mortgages.

A period of exponential growth in social housing investment carried through to the 1970's, which saw the creation of a National Housing Act that spurred the development of housing co-ops and provided additional stimulus for construction projects.

Canada's more recent history of social housing investment is one of neglect and decline. The economic recession of the 1980's led to a retreat from interventionist government policy and the introduction of more stringent austerity measures, including the outright elimination of the Cooperative Housing Program. By the 1990's, the federal government withdrew all support from the social housing sector. The CMHC no longer directed funds to municipalities and responsibility was offloaded to cash-strapped provinces, many of whom responded by cutting their own programs due to financial pressures.

Of all social and affordable housing structures in the country, only 5.2% have been built since 2000.[13] As noted by the Advocacy Centre For Tenants Ontario in 2014: "Between 1985 and 1989, the federal government helped fund 5,356 units of social housing per year. If Ottawa had continued to fund social housing at this rate, between 1994 and 2013, some 107,120 homes could have been built."[14]

As described by housing policy expert Greg Suttor, "on a per capita basis, the United States creates more subsidized rentals per year, and offers more subsidies. Canada's peak period for social housing was a generation ago."

The United States public housing sector began in earnest with the 1934 Housing Act and the creation of the Federal Housing Administration (FHA), an agency responsible for insuring mortgages for low-and-moderate income homebuyers to private lenders. The 1937 Housing Act that followed was implemented to target slums and the exodus of middle-class Americans to the suburbs. Under the act, the federal government paid development costs and subsidized rents for new public housing projects, which were run by local housing authorities. The act was renewed and expanded in 1949 as a postwar campaign to revitalize American cities.

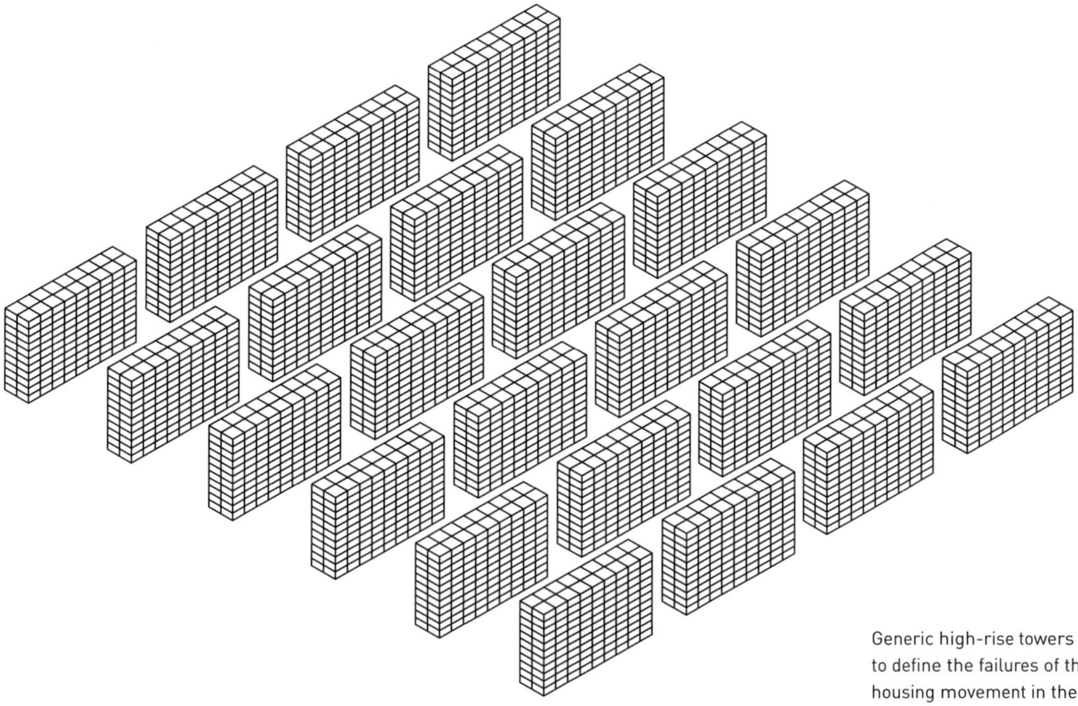

Generic high-rise towers came to define the failures of the social housing movement in the U.S.

Although the Housing Act had major achievements, it was also besieged by controversies. Under the guise of urban renewal, drastic neighbourhood clearance projects displaced people from their communities, tenants were segregated by race and class and troubled high-rise developments fell into a steep decline.

The FHA perpetuated segregation by "refusing to insure mortgages in and near African-American neighbourhoods... At the same time, the FHA was subsidizing builders who were mass-producing entire subdivisions for whites – with the requirement that none of the homes be sold to African-Americans."[15] The term "redlining" was used to describe the process by which areas with large populations of Black people were outlined in red ink as a warning to mortgage lenders.[16]

The demolition of Pruitt-Igoe in 1972 signalled the beginning of the end for the Housing Act. In 1974, a moratorium was placed on public housing expenditures and the program was suspended, to be replaced by the Housing and Community Development Act, which encouraged the private sector to construct affordable homes and supported low-income families with a broad system of housing allowances. A dramatic reduction in funding for the Department of Housing and Urban Development (HUD) followed in the 1980's, when federal spending on subsidized housing "dropped by $26 billion to $8 billion, barely enough to maintain the government's existing stock of public units."[17] Instead, the government intensified its efforts to create incentives for the private sector.

In 1986, the Low Income Housing Tax Credit (LIHTC) was created to encourage private sector investment in the creation of affordable housing. In a typical arrangement, developers sell tax credits to investors to raise equity for the project, enabling them to borrow less and charge lower rents.[18] The program is now responsible for 90% of all affordable housing in the country.

Today, both the United States and Canada have a serious social housing deficit. According to the Urban Institute, for every 100 extremely low-income households in the United States in need of an affordable apartment, only 29 units are available.[19] Researchers at the Harvard Joint Centre for Housing Studies found that 37 million households are cost burdened according to the STIR metric, representing 30% of all households nationwide.[20] The 2018 Canadian census revealed that one in ten Canadian households live in core housing need, defined as "living in an unsuitable, inadequate or unaffordable dwelling, and not able to afford alternative housing in their community."[21]

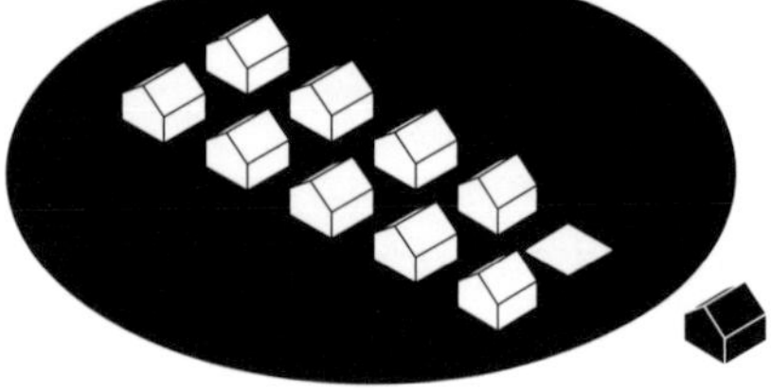

1 in 10

Canadian households live in core housing need.

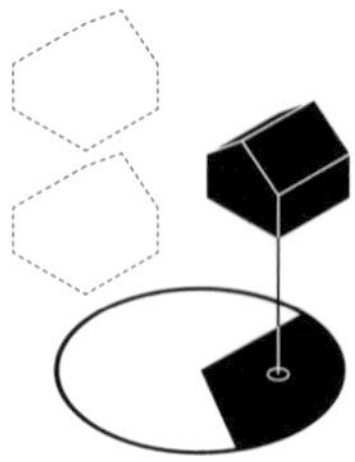

30%

of US households are cost-burdened.

In order to address the affordability crisis, new promises and policies have been announced by federal leadership in both countries. In the United States, President Biden's Build Back Better (BBB) Act was an infrastructure bill that included a historic infusion of $170 billion for housing to support the construction, rehabilitation and preservation of over 1 million affordable housing units and increase funding for federal housing vouchers.[22]

In 2017, Canada's federal government announced the country's first-ever National Housing Strategy: a 10-year, $70 billion plan in partnership with CMHC to "help reduce homelessness and improve the affordability, availability and quality of housing for Canadians in need."[23] Specific goals include building 160,000 new homes and modernizing 300,000 existing homes. As part of this initiative, a federal "Right to Housing" legislation was signed into law, setting Canada apart as one of the few countries in the world with a legally binding agreement in place. Another feature of the legislation is that future governments will be required to maintain and renew the program. This new legislation is an incredibly important step, the long-term impacts of which have yet to be fully realised.

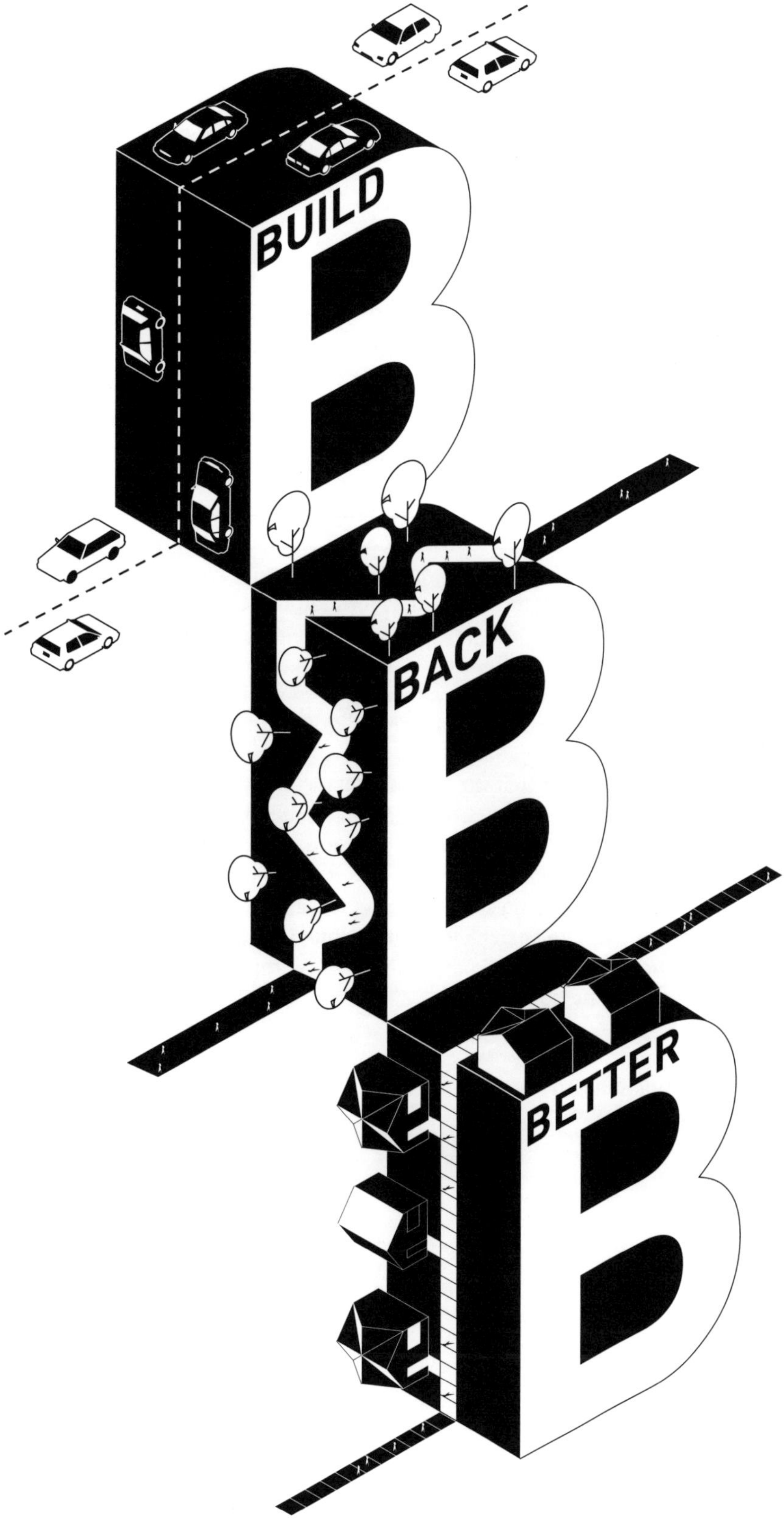

The Build Back Better budget reconcilation was a transformative legislative framework proposed by USA President Joe Biden in 2020. It sought to invest trillions of US dollars into social, infrastructural and environmental programs, including education, healthcare, housing and the climate emergency.

RESTRICT / RESTRUCTURE

At a basic level, urban planning should make positive contributions to the resolution of complex issues like housing affordability. However, there is ample evidence to suggest that the impact of such high-level decision making is more nuanced, especially when the success or failure of a specific policy change can only be studied and measured in hindsight.

In reference to the invaluable research conducted by Andy Yan into Vancouver's current housing crisis, planning professor Patrick Condon concludes that "every planning effort the city undertook in the past ten years has made things worse."[1] Yan's statistical analysis indicates that new community plans for mature neighbourhoods intended to address housing affordability have instead increased property values due to speculative development significantly in the last few years, sometimes well before any of the plans or upgrades were actually realised. At the same time, Yan identifies that land values in the unplanned parts of the city have dropped during the same period.[2]

In his article, Condon states that the primary focus of any citywide policy should be to plan for affordability and that all other issues "need to be only viewed through the lens of housing for our people." It is hard to argue otherwise, especially as "Right to Housing" legislation is adopted by a number of national and international constitutions. However, it is much more challenging to determine the right mechanisms through which this goal can be achieved in the United States and Canada, where the vast majority of housing is produced by the private sector and few processes exist to create projects led by the public sector.

This section considers a variety of planning tools – including up-zoning, inclusionary zoning and soft density strategies – that are intended to increase housing supply for marginalized communities, and some of the challenges and opportunities inherent in each.

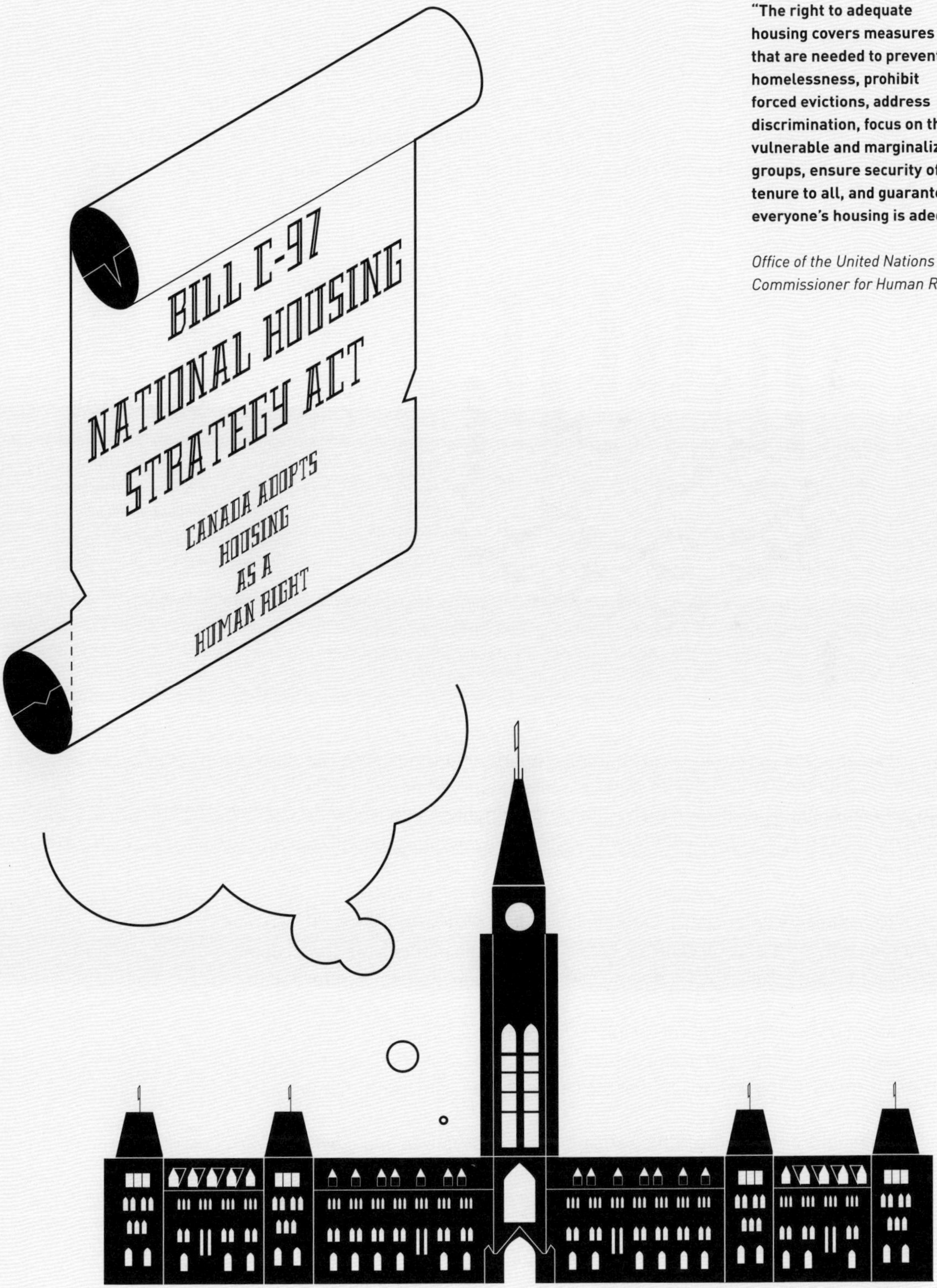

"The right to adequate housing covers measures that are needed to prevent homelessness, prohibit forced evictions, address discrimination, focus on the most vulnerable and marginalized groups, ensure security of tenure to all, and guarantee that everyone's housing is adequate."

Office of the United Nations High Commissioner for Human Rights

Up-zoning

One of the most common strategies making its way through legislatures across the United States and Canada is the introduction of up-zoning policies in high-growth urban centres, in order to reduce regulatory barriers and permit multi-family housing in areas currently restricted to single-family houses.

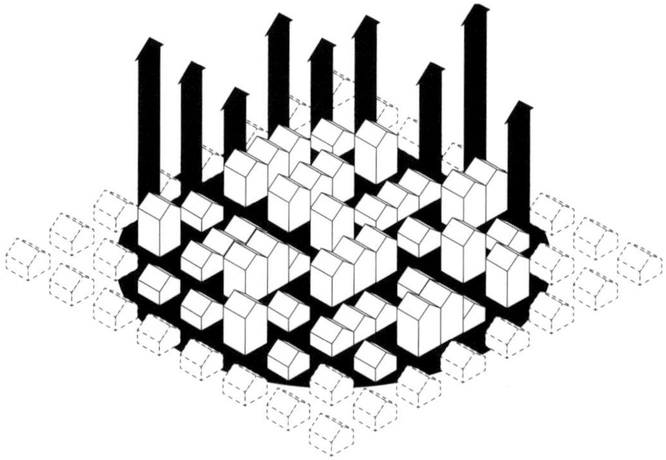

Up-zoning

policies are intended to increase opportunities for missing middle housing developments in mature neighbourhoods.

For decades, land use regulations throughout Canada and the United States have favoured private single-family houses on large plots of land, promoting urban sprawl through persistent patterns of low density and car dominant neighbourhoods. On 75% of land in many American cities, a detached single-family home is the only permitted building type.[3]

The intention behind the up-zoning movement is to add more housing closer to existing transportation networks and job centres, based on the logic that denser construction will increase housing supply, thus reducing competition and increasing affordability.[4] The approach has been polarizing, embraced by density and affordability advocates and contested by local governments. Concerned citizens have also protested the measures, either as a means to protect so-called neighbourhood character or out of concern that new development won't meet the needs of their community demographic.

In 2018, Minneapolis became the first city to eliminate restrictive zoning by-laws with a new comprehensive plan that permits the development of three-family dwellings on existing single-family lots, among other policy changes. The state believes that through up-zoning they will be able to house their growing population at a more affordable rate. "Neighbours for More Neighbours" became the rallying anthem used by supporters.[5] In 2019, Oregon became the first state to ban restrictive single-family zoning codes.[6]

California made similar attempts to pass a bill permitting the development of new high-density housing near transit stations. However, the bill failed to get enough votes to advance and lost support from the same low-income residents it aimed to help, who felt it was overly broad and feared the expansion of housing in this manner would displace them from their communities.[7] In Virginia, a bill to legalize duplex housing was shut down by the Land Use subcommittee, who raised concerns about allowing the state to exercise more influence over zoning, which is traditionally under the jurisdiction of local governments who believe they can best tailor policy to local market demands.[8]

Rick Jacobus, an American expert on affordable homeownership, describes the importance of understanding that the housing market is segmented, not just by region and neighbourhood but also by type and value. While we might be tempted to argue that more housing supply will invariably lead to lower housing costs overall, the economic divide between luxury developments and buildings targeted toward low-and-middle income households is too great. If up-zoning legislation results in developers building more luxury condominiums, the price of other units of a similar quality might decrease, but the trickle down effect to low-cost housing units is marginal at best. Instead, these policies can have the effect of enriching property owners and investors, leaving voters inclined "to stand in the way to keep the market from doing harm."[9]

Jacobus suggests that we need to look at increasing housing supply from the bottom up: "Instead of (or in addition to) focusing on changes that support development in general, we should identify the policies that change who benefits from new development and we should stress that aspect when we explain these policies to the public."[10]

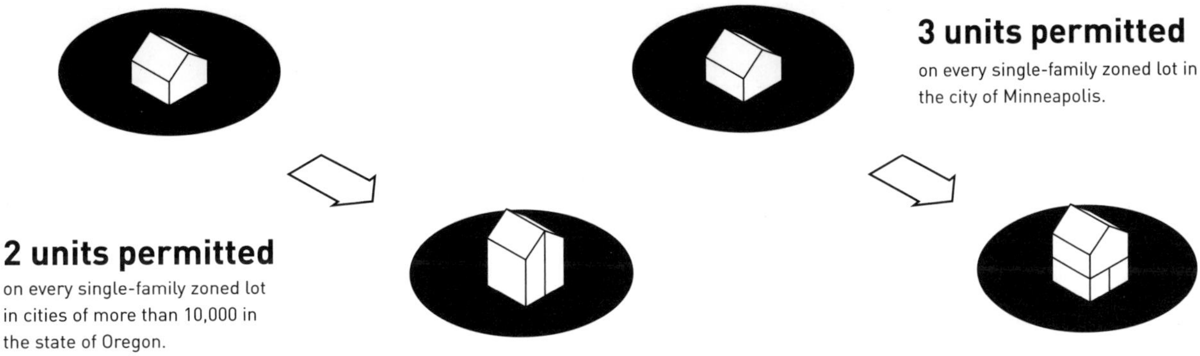

Inclusionary zoning

If increasing allowable density may have the effect of reducing affordability, then any supported increase in density should have an associated social benefit, a concept known as "inclusionary zoning."

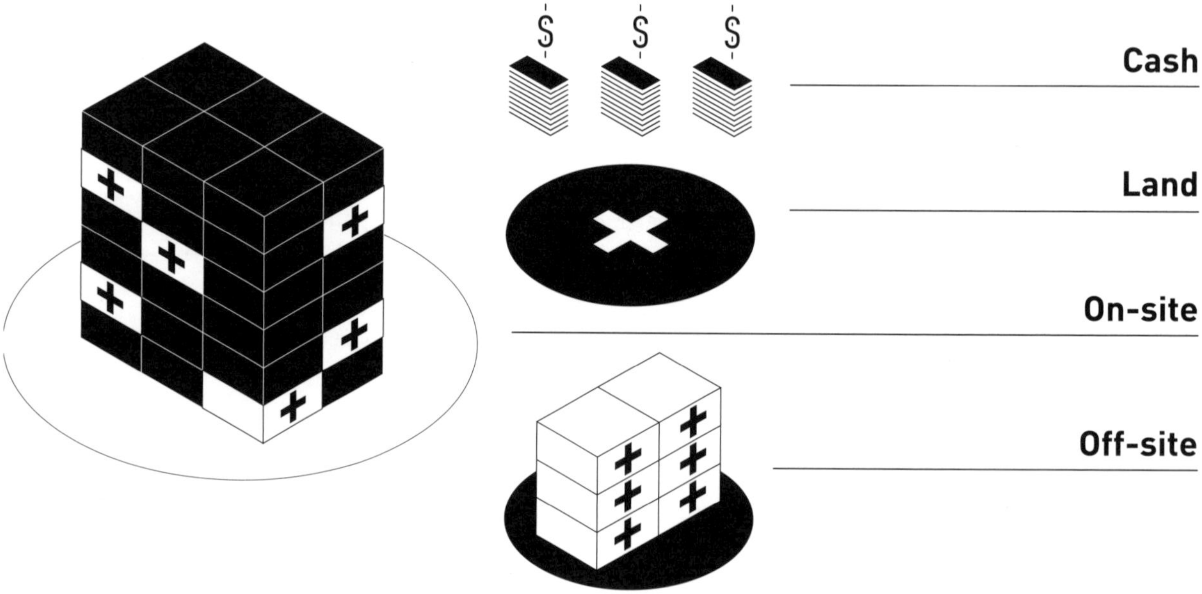

In *The New Urban Crisis*, Richard Florida reinforces the need for zoning, building code and tax policy reforms, citing "a growing chorus of so-called market urbanists" who argue that restrictive zoning and building codes "limit the market's ability to build as needed."[11] He also points out that while clustering drives growth, it also drives up the cost of land which in turn makes housing more expensive, pushing out the very people the reforms are intended to serve.[12]

Inclusionary zoning refers to a range of strategies in which private developers are offered cost saving incentives by the government to incorporate affordable or social housing as part of market driven developments, in order to reduce gentrification and provide opportunities for disadvantaged families to move to low-poverty areas. The affordable housing might be part of the same development or built elsewhere, or developers might contribute cash or land for the production of social or affordable housing in lieu of construction.[13] The popularity of this approach has experienced exponential growth, with hundreds of jurisdictions across the US and Canada implementing new policies.

In Canada, Vancouver has the longest standing inclusionary housing requirements for large development sites. First introduced in 1988, the policy mandates that a minimum of 20% of new residential floor space be provided as affordable housing, with flexibility in how that housing is delivered. In 2017 a new 10-year plan increased the minimum to 30%, in order to incorporate an additional 10% requirement for moderate income housing.[14] Montreal's approach, adopted in 2005, requires that all new large residential developments provide a minimum of 30% of new units as affordable housing, split equally between social housing and affordable rental or ownership units.[15] Toronto is in the process of adopting its own inclusionary zoning official plan.[16]

30% affordable

units required for large sites in Vancouver and Montreal.

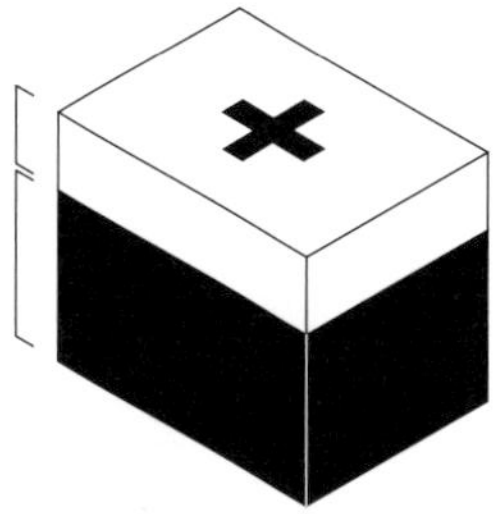

Some cities are also implementing inclusionary zoning policies for smaller scale projects. Portland's new zoning by-law includes a provision that allows up to six dwelling units on all residentially zoned lots in the city, but developers must ensure that three of the units remain affordable to average wage earners.[17]

Inclusionary zoning is not without its drawbacks. Subsidies typically have an expiration date, resulting in the affordable units being converted back to market-rate housing in a 10 to 15 year time period. In addition, a change in government and thus ideology can impact whether these subsidies will be renewed as expected. For inclusionary zoning to be successful, it is also important that any proposed policies have sufficient oversight.

Although Winnipeg does not have a mandated inclusionary zoning policy, a downtown Tax Increment Financing (TIF) stimulus program is intended to serve a similar function, providing subsidies to developers in exchange for 10% affordable housing units. In 2018, a large mixed-use project came under fire for seeking an exemption to the TIF requirement for affordable housing. Through the efforts of local housing advocates and city councillors, the developer agreed to return 10% of the new municipal property taxes incurred from the towers to the city to support an affordable housing grant.[18]

6 units permitted

on every single-family zoned lot in the city of Portland if 3 remain affordable.

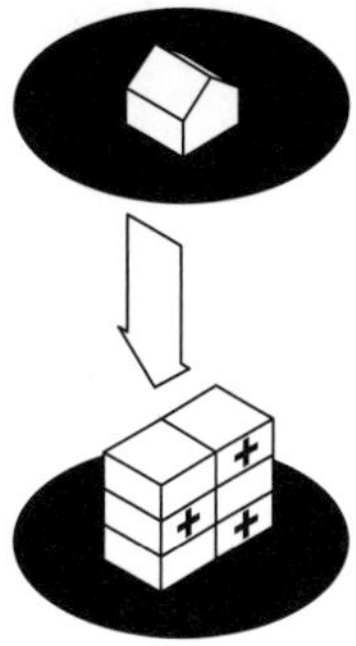

In Chicago, a recent study found that after five years of up-zoning efforts, property values rose without significant additional development. One theory behind the lack of measurable success is the option for developers to opt out of inclusionary zoning requirements (ensuring 10% of units be affordable) by paying cash in lieu towards an Affordable Housing Fund. Although the fund was intended to help subsidize rental costs for low-income residents, the study found that $4.5 million put into that fund between 2003 and 2017 remains unaccounted for and there is no metric to determine which neighbourhoods received the funding.[19]

As Richard Florida notes, and as evidenced by these examples, inclusionary zoning works best in expensive real estate markets where there is already incentive for developers to "build affordable units in exchange for the ability to build taller buildings. But in other types of cities, these policies can cause developers to build less than they otherwise might."[20]

Soft density

Finer grain solutions – sometimes referred to as "gentle densification" or "soft density" – include the introduction of accessory dwelling units (ADUs) or laneway houses and the removal of parking minimums to support redevelopment in the inner city. These strategies are often more accessible in smaller cities where inclusionary zoning might deter development.

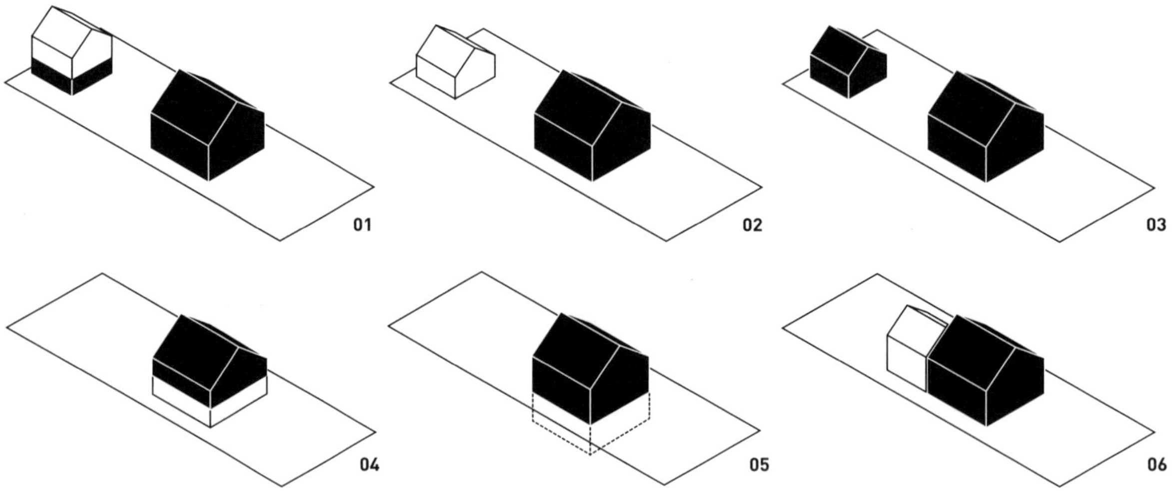

The City of Edmonton has taken progressive strides to address their affordable housing shortage and bring density back to the city centre through a major overhaul of their zoning by-law. In 2019, a series of revisions were passed as part of their Missing Middle Zoning Review, including the ability for homeowners to introduce both a basement suite and garden suite on the same lot. [21] In June of 2020, city council voted unanimously to end minimum parking requirements.[22] In addition to boosting support for small scale developer led interventions, these revisions give some power back to homeowners in existing single-family neighbourhoods, allowing them to densify their communities and provide supplemental income at a scale that is more amenable to neighbours.

As a launching point for this initiative, Edmonton held an ideas competition to encourage and excite citizens about infill in the city's mature communities. The challenge presented by the competition brief was to create innovative and engaging solutions that did not alter neighbourhood character in a significant way. Edmonton's approach to public engagement could inspire other jurisdictions to tackle an often contentious subject matter with both sensitivity and creativity.

Types of ADUs

01 Above Garage
02 Detached
03 Converted garage
04 Internal
05 Basement
06 Attached

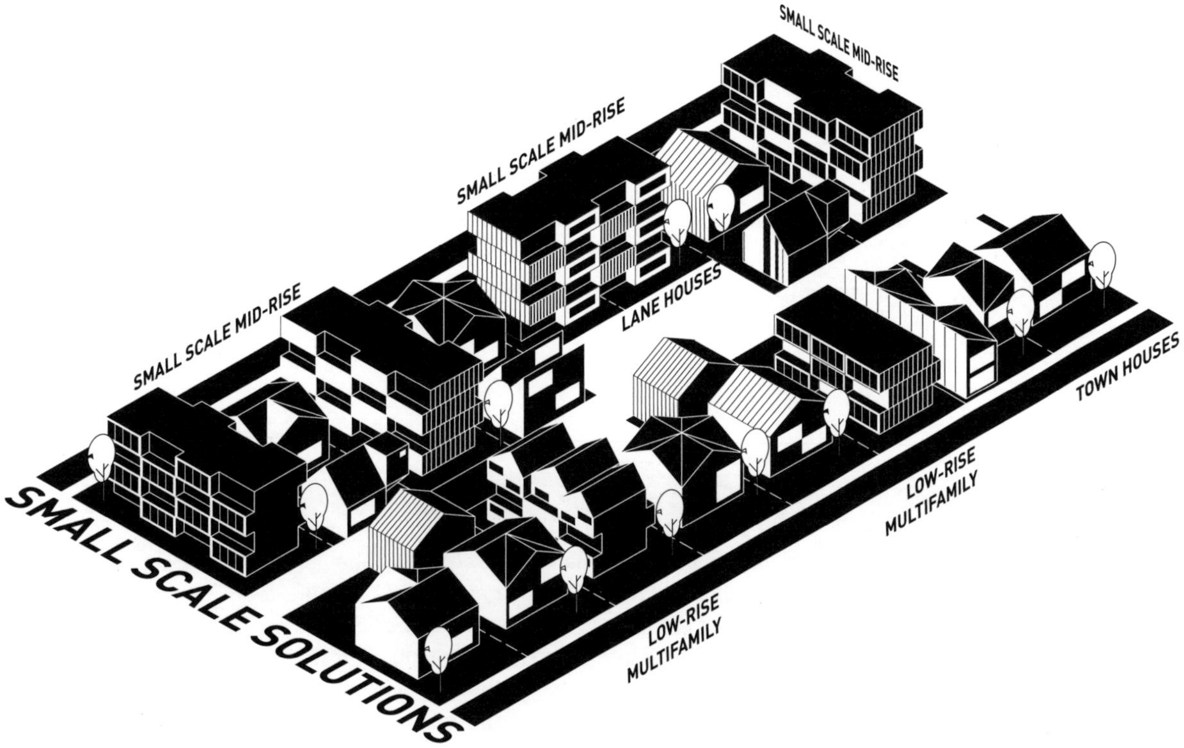

As cities scramble to implement zoning and density reforms, it is clear that there is no silver bullet solution, and that there will always be both eager proponents and fierce detractors for any proposed policy changes. There are new articles published every day by progressive urbanists touting the bold visions being passed by governments and city councils with the hope that these strategies will put homes into the hands of the people who need them most.

As demonstrated by the high-level and fine grain approaches described, although the long-term outcomes of these new policies have yet to be measured, they represent an important procedural step. One thing is certain: the status quo is not working. Zoning is a powerful tool to enact change and decisive land use policy is needed if we are to address the housing affordability crisis.

COMMODITY / COMMUNITY

While cities struggle to increase housing supply for marginalized communities, global capital markets continue to push housing out of reach even for average wage earners. Expensive, vacant properties used primarily as financial instruments create a vacuum in the urban fabric, driving up the price of much needed housing for hundreds of thousands of households beyond a threshold of affordability.

Referred to as the financialisation or commodification of housing, "this phenomenon occurs when housing is treated as a commodity – a vehicle for wealth and investment – rather than a social good."[1] As of 2020, the value of global real estate is approximately US$270 trillion and rising.[2] In 2000, the Commission on Human Rights created a Special Rapporteur with a mandate on the right to adequate housing. Their appointee, Leilani Farha, believes that housing is at the centre of an historic structural transformation in global investment and has found "patterns of systemic exclusion" resulting from the role of international finance in housing systems. She also notes that "corporate tax havens that generate massive amounts of profit immune from taxation, estimated at 30 percent of global gross domestic product, are particularly attracted to housing and real estate." Fahra's report found that these global financial factors have contributed to greater income inequality, spatial segregation, inadequate housing provision and growing homeless populations.[3]

This section considers the broader impact of the financialisation of housing on the life of cities and some of the measures intended to counteract these effects, including government funding strategies, hybrid housing models and alternative forms of homeownership.

HOUSING
IS NOT A
COMM
ODITY
Wholesale BOOT and SHOES

Impact on cities

The treatment of housing as a commodity has long-term consequences in the form of high-vacancy rates in cities where a significant portion of the population struggles to afford a place to live or where a high-level of homelessness occurs.

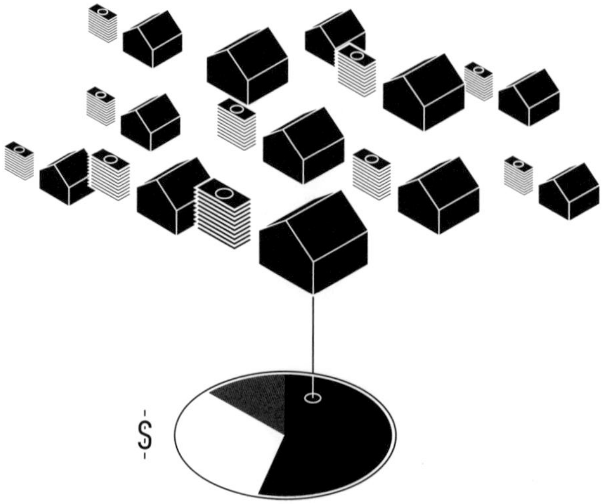

60%

of global assets are real estate. 75% of this amount is residential.

Urban planner Peter Marcuse and sociologist David Madden expand on this subject in their book, *In Defense of Housing*: "The commodification of housing means that a structure's function as real estate takes precedence over its usefulness as a place to live. When this happens, housing's role as an investment outweighs all other claims upon it..."[4] Marcuse and Madden go on to describe what they see as our current age of hyper-commodification, where "all of the material and legal structures of housing – buildings, land, labour, property rights – are turned into commodities. In the process, the capacity of a building to function as a home becomes secondary."[5]

If we look to Vancouver and similar west coast cities, we see how the myriad factors that contribute to the financialisation of housing have been compounded: offshore investment is rampant, housing costs are exorbitant, countless homes sit empty and even rental accommodations have become unattainable.

According to a 2019 report by the Canadian Housing Statistics Program, almost half of all condominiums and nearly one in five detached homes in Vancouver are not owner occupied. This percentage has gone up substantially in the past decade.[6] Based on data analysis of the 2016 census, the city had over 25,000 dwelling units that were either unoccupied or occupied by temporary or foreign residents, serving as wealth storage or secondary residences. An empty homes tax of 1% was implemented in 2018 and tripled to 3% in 2021. Since the tax was implemented, the City of Vancouver said it has reduced the number of empty homes in the city by 25%.[7]

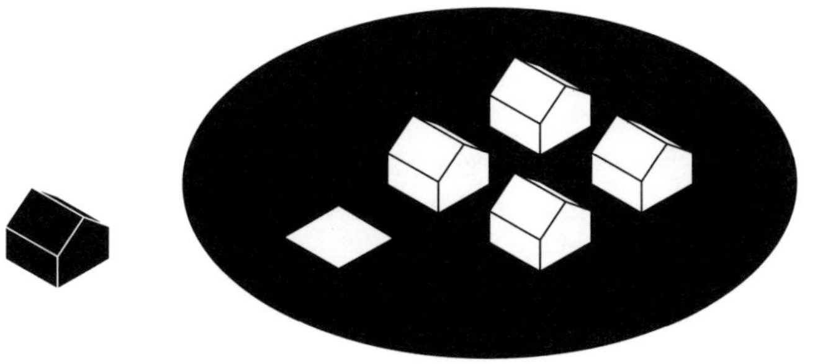

1 in 5

detached homes in Vancouver are not owner occupied.

In Vancouver, as in other high-land value cities, homes represent a disproportionately large share of their owners' wealth. These owners then rely on high-market valuations as retirement savings, leaving them understandably reluctant to accept policies – such as changes to the capital gains tax exemption on principal residences – that would begin to return the value of their properties to local income level norms. In 1995, an average detached house in Vancouver cost $400,000 – by 2015 it was $1.8 million, a 450% increase. Average incomes in Vancouver increased only 14% in the same period.[8] At this rate of inflation, it would take two decades for millennials who save 20% of their incomes to afford a down payment in Vancouver.[9] As a result, finding rental accommodations in the city has itself become a competition, with people outbidding one another in order to access housing.

In cities across North America, the exponential growth rate of short-term rentals has led to thousands of accommodations being taken off the long-term market. In *Icebergs, Zombies, and the Ultra Thin*, Matthew Soules examines the impact of finance capitalism on urbanism and architecture. He describes the effect of neighbourhoods existing in a state of reduced occupancy as zombie urbanism: "These areas mix present populations with absent populations, exhibiting an eerily low level of vitality in relation to their scale. They are not dead, but they are also not quite alive."[10]

When multi-family buildings fill with short-term tenants and investment units sit empty, it is difficult to establish a community and it becomes even more difficult to house the people who need these homes the most. There are alternative funding and ownership models that increase housing supply and combat the effects of aggressive commodification.

Government funding

The merits of strong government investment in affordable housing cannot be overstated – if housing is to be de-commodified, then government must play a greater role in withdrawing units with respect to profit-oriented speculative real-estate markets.

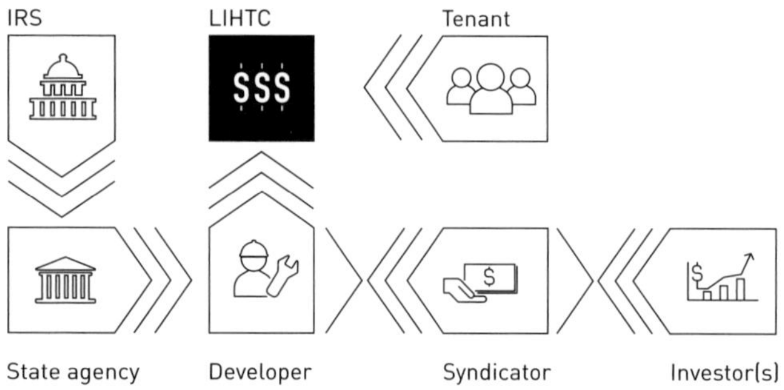

LIHTC
Funding structure (USA)

In the United States, there are countless examples of programs and funds anchored by the Low Income Housing Tax Credit (LIHTC), which supports the majority of all affordable rental housing created in the country.

The city of Denver has also implemented a number of progressive strategies to address its housing shortage that are worth highlighting. In 2015, they replaced their inclusionary housing ordinance with a revolving affordable housing loan fund that provides gap financing for affordable housing developers. The program leverages state and city funds to direct $10 million over the next ten years to encourage take-up of the LIHTC program. In its first year, the fund was instrumental in supporting the completion of three housing developments, which added nearly 300 new affordable units to the city.[11] With so much success bringing in new projects and as loans are paid back into the capital pool over time, the city continues to expand support and has become a national reference point for similar endeavours.

In addition, Denver has seen success with a Regional Transit Oriented Development (TOD) Fund that leverages federal grants as well as private and philanthropic support to acquire land or property near mass transit for use as affordable housing and encourage holistic development. On a smaller scale, a two year pilot "buy-down" program was launched in 2018 to put vacant market-rate apartments within financial reach of workers who are at risk of being priced out of the city. The subsidy is targeted toward working families who "make just enough that they don't qualify for programs but still have incredible rent burdens."[12] Denver recently created the Department of Housing Stability to gather all of these programs under one umbrella.

In Canada, federal support for affordable housing was withdrawn in 1994, leaving each province to establish their own policies and frameworks. Two projects from the early years of our practice demonstrate the level of government commitment required to achieve affordable infill developments in this fiscal context: **Welcome Place** and **Ross Avenue** Housing. Both projects were supported by the HomeWORKS! program, which was introduced in 2009 as Manitoba's long-term housing strategy and policy framework under the former NDP government. The program was managed through Manitoba Housing, with a mandate to increase the supply of affordable housing and improve existing building stock.

Following a shift to conservative leadership in 2016, Manitoba has been without a provincial housing strategy and the government has begun to privatize its portfolio to address rising costs.[13] As of 2018, nearly 950 social housing units have been transferred to non-profit agencies and the private sector. Between 2016 and 2019, the province sold off 94 properties owned by Manitoba Housing.[14] Despite a waitlist in the thousands for affordable units, the province has signalled that it "wants to transition to the role of funder and regulator of public housing, rather than landlord."[15]

In 2017, Canada's National Housing Strategy was created in part to bolster the country's affordable housing sector. The Affordable Housing Innovation Fund encourages the development of new finance models and innovative building techniques. Up until the time of writing, the program has supported the development of over 17,600 affordable units, with an additional funding promise of $600M and 12,700 units announced in the 2021 federal budget.

Welcome Place

Completed in 2010, Welcome Place is a mixed-use facility that provides a range of transitional services for refugees. The $4.4 million complex was financed by all three levels of government, receiving more than $3 million in shared funding under the HOMEWorks! program, with additional support from the City of Winnipeg and the federal Homelessness Partnering Strategy (HPS). In 2019, the organization lost the federal grant that made up one third of its annual operating budget, requiring extensive layoffs and program restructuring.[16] This major funding loss demonstrates the tenuous nature of non-profit organizations like Welcome Place, whose ability to provide housing is tied to financial sources that may lack long-term stability.

Ross Avenue

Ross Avenue Housing is a 10-unit affordable condominium project in Winnipeg's inner city, designed in collaboration with the Winnipeg Housing Rehabilitation Corporation (WHRC). Funding for the building, which cost $2.1 million to construct and was completed in 2012, was supported by the HOMEWorks! initiative and the City of Winnipeg. The remaining balance was bridge-financed through WHRC, prior to the units being sold. In a unique model, WHRC committed to managing the project for the first five years in order to facilitate condominium ownership education and provide support for first time home buyers at an extremely affordable rate. Units must remain owner-occupied as a criteria of resale.

projects.MODELLING: Welcome Place (p. 68), Ross Avenue (p. 88)

Hybrid housing

In order to make our communities more resilient, new buildings and infill developments must do more within a given footprint. A maximum return on investment – both financial and social – can be achieved when affordable housing is considered in tandem with a complementary, or sometimes unexpected, civic use.

Mixed-use buildings are not a new concept by any means. They have been championed by Jane Jacobs and many urbanists after her. Following post-war planning trends that emphasized car culture and separation of functions, a renewed emphasis on this building typology has been critical in drawing people back to the inner city. In their typical configuration, mixed-use buildings are arranged vertically, defined by ground floor commercial or office space with residential suites above. Mixed-use can also be spread horizontally over several buildings or even a city block. The relaxation of outdated zoning laws have helped new mixed-use concepts come to fruition and inspired cities to ask pointed questions about how best to put these spaces to use.

Within this context, a civic-minded form of mixed-use development has emerged that considers how affordable housing can be co-located with social amenities and essential services – from libraries and community centres to fire halls and healthcare facilities. Co-location supports the intensification of existing sites, especially when the land is publicly owned and thus does not require new acquisitions. This approach is particularly valuable in cities with high-land-values where vacant properties are scarce and land cost can present a significant barrier to the provision of affordable housing.

Across Canada, many major cities have adopted policies that support co-location as part of their affordable housing mandates. In Calgary, the Corporate Affordable Housing Strategy indicates that city assets should no longer be built for a single purpose. Instead, priority has been given to integrated civic facilities where municipal services are co-located with housing, community space and other amenities in order to support vibrant neighbourhoods. Metro Vancouver's 10-Year Housing Plan and Toronto's Housing TO 2020-2030 Action Plan also emphasize opportunities to co-locate affordable rental housing with civic facilities wherever possible.

In the United States, San Francisco was an early champion of this approach, combining their first new library branch in the last 40 years with a community meeting space, an adult day health centre and affordable senior housing. Chicago followed suit, forming an atypical partnership between their public library and housing authorities to create a series of hybrid projects under former mayor Rahm Emanuel.

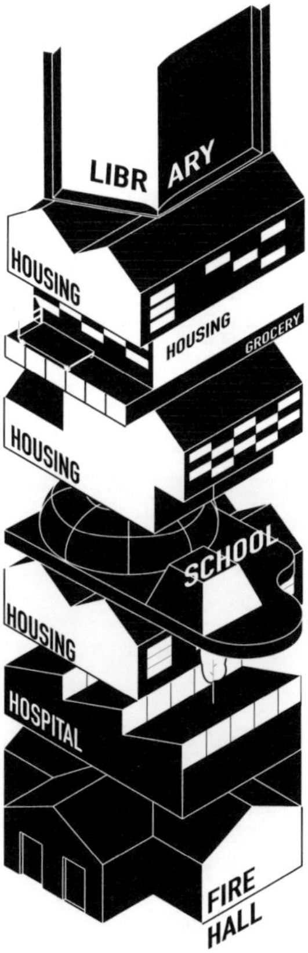

Co-location

pairs affordable housing and civic amenities on the same site.

Joining forces and integrating functions provides opportunities for governments and the non-profit sector to work together to address the affordable housing shortage, making it possible to invest public dollars and leverage additional funds for projects that can serve their constituents in a myriad of ways. These buildings act as civic anchors to strengthen the social fabric, make better use of finite public resources and ensure long-term affordability through capital and operational cost savings. Additional benefits include the potential for shared infrastructure, amenity spaces and onsite support services, especially when they are intended for high-needs populations. As noted by New York Times architectural critic Michael Kimmelman in a summary of Chicago's co-location efforts, this approach can also be strategic: "the library helped sway community groups resistant to public housing in their neighbourhoods."[17]

Co-location also presents a particular set of challenges for designers as disparate user groups are brought together under one roof, each with their own unique identities and programmatic needs. Development approval timelines and the stakeholder engagement process also become more complex as more parties require a seat at the table. Regarding the architectural outcome of a fire hall and social housing hybrid project in Vancouver, "issues around security, privacy, shared facilities and combined services were some of the complications which were addressed during the design."[18]

At their best, mixed-use hybrid housing projects have the potential to become dynamic and inclusive gathering places that contribute to a strong sense of community pride and neighbourhood character, remaining active throughout the day while supporting human connection and well-being.

Alternative ownership

To counteract the effects of commodification, some individuals are taking matters into their own hands, pursuing alternative models for housing ownership and low-impact living that places housing above profit. Cooperatives, community land trusts, and co-housing communities are some of the people-driven models being implemented in cities across the US and Canada.

2200 Co-ops	**92,500** Units	**Canada**
6400 Co-ops	**1,200,000** Units	**United States**

There are two main types of cooperatives: **Market Rate (MRC)** and **Limited Equity (LEC)**. In both versions, residents come together as shareholders rather than owning their unit outright. Communities are self-managed by an elected board, with members taking an active role in day-to-day maintenance. In Canada and the United States, the cooperative housing sector is estimated to represent approximately 0.7% and 1% of each country's total housing stock respectively, compared to 22.8% in Sweden and 14% in Norway.[19]

In an MRC, shareholders are able to build equity as the value of the property increases. An LEC allows low-income eligible members to purchase shares at below market prices. Members are then subject to limitations on the amount of profit they can receive on their unit's resale, in order to preserve affordability in perpetuity for future tenants. LECs can offer low-income households autonomy and limited asset building, but often require fiscal support from government to succeed, including construction subsidies and low-interest financing.

With the **Community Land Trust (CLT)** model, a household retains ownership of its dwelling unit while a non-profit organization retains title to the underlying land. While CLTs can provide stability and access to affordable homeownership, they often require households to qualify for conventional loans, which can exclude some segments of the low-income population.

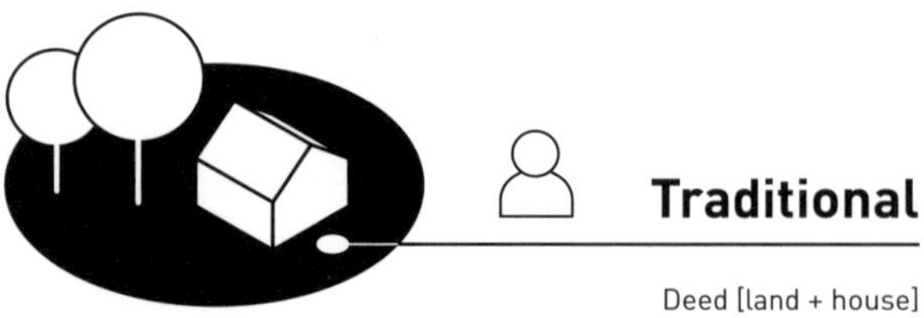

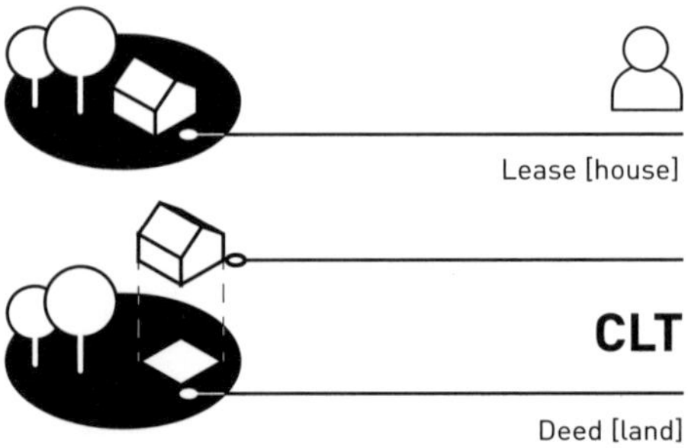

Co-housing

- Communal kitchen
- Event room
- Play area
- Workshop
- Garden
- Shared yard

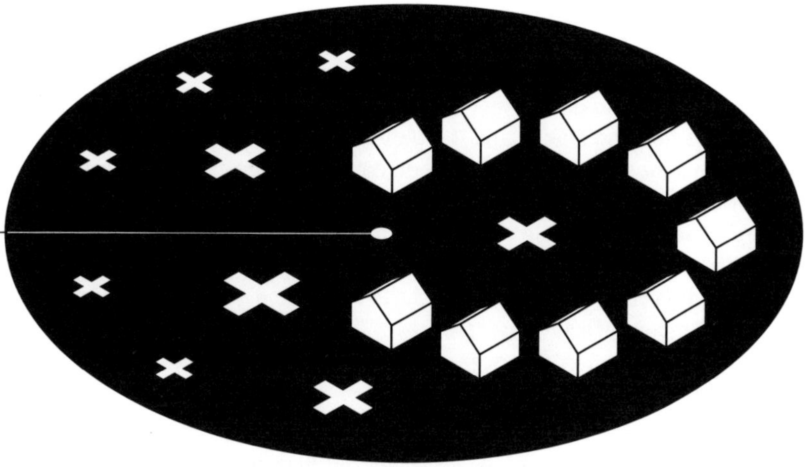

Co-housing is another intentional community model that is popular in Europe and slowly becoming adopted in North America. Co-housing is a collaborative, mutually supportive model in which owners work together in a participatory design process to buy land, plan the project, and manage it together once it is built. Private homes are supplemented by shared amenities . As participants in co-housing are typically people who can afford to buy their own homes, the cost is approximately market-rate.

The Grounded Solutions Network – an American non-profit that promotes housing solutions focused on long-term affordability – describes the national housing industry as being "caught on a hamster wheel." While investment is funnelled toward new affordable housing stock, the legal price restrictions on buildings that are only two decades old are expiring. In the next 10 years, over a million publicly financed housing units will be returned to market rate.[20] The organization supports the shared equity housing sector and CLTs specifically because they create homes that remain permanently affordable.

A shared desire for affordability, safety and long-term stability unites each of the alternative housing models described above. In addition, due to the strict criteria placed on membership and resale, as well as through the oversight of elected boards, external forces that can lead to a reduced state of occupancy are deterred. These developments require a personal shift in how individuals envision their role as tenants, as well as a cultural shift in the value we place on community. As the dream of single-family home ownership moves further out of reach, a grassroots resurgence of communal living is taking hold.

There is a profound disconnect between the efforts of planners and policy makers to increase housing supply and the global forces at play that turn them into investment vehicles, often before they ever come to market. People are not commodities, and nor should the roof over one's head be. Having a place to call home has a profound and measurable impact on the mental health and physical wellbeing of individuals and families. Housing for all represents good social policy – studies have demonstrated clear links between access to housing and reduced burdens on healthcare systems, improvements in early childhood education outcomes, reduced expenditures on social assistance and employment insurance, among countless other long-term benefits.[21]

As described by Greg Suttor: "Affordable housing is not about intrepid local groups doing a project here or there, with disjointed layers of public funding at different periods. It's about implementing policies to sustain a system of capital funding, mortgages, and rent subsidies (plus support services for people with disabilities) on a scale that makes a difference."[22]

We cannot leave the provision of adequate housing entirely to the market. Housing is a social good that calls for strong and sustained public investment, one that should not be fractured by a change in political ideology. We have a responsibility to one another and to the betterment of our communities to advocate for stronger policies from all levels of government.

HOUSING
IS A
HUMAN
RIGHT

FORMULAIC / FORMATIVE

The forms that we build have a real impact on the environment, long-term affordability and our overall quality of life. Most new housing exists in one of two extremes: high-rise towers or single-family homes. Many urbanists believe that the solution lies in the gap between these scales, in the form of missing middle and mid-rise housing.

In "Rethinking Values in Designing Architecture," Ashok Lall suggests that building tall – where non-combustible construction methods and additional mechanical and electrical systems are required and need to be maintained – actually increases per-unit construction and maintenance costs, which in turn decreases long-term affordability.[1] At the same time, new suburban communities of detached single-family homes put an enormous strain on municipal resources, pulling much-needed funds away from services citywide.

As zoning legislations are reconsidered and regulatory constraints are reduced, we can begin building more density into established neighbourhoods in order to support the sustainable life of cities. The term "Missing Middle Housing" was coined by Daniel Parolek in 2010 to identify a range of multi-family building types, including duplexes, fourplexes and townhomes, all of which are typically no more than three storeys. Parolek believes that these housing options can bridge the divide between new communities of detached single-family homes that demand large infrastructural expenditures and high-rise towers in the inner city that require expensive long-term upkeep.[2] In contrast, Missing Middle Housing fits more naturally into existing neighbourhoods and provides custom-fit solutions along a spectrum of affordability. Furthermore, ground-oriented developments increase opportunities for shared outdoor amenities that can support family life and multi-generational communities.

This section covers ways that form can be used as a response, ranging in size from the multi-family house to large scale urban planning.

Stumpies

Mid-rise housing can be defined as structures between three and eight storeys in height. In recent years, developers have gravitated to this building scale in order to achieve a maximum return on investment in the face of rising construction costs, regulatory burdens and a lack of skilled labour. Typically constructed as rental apartments or condominiums near suburban commercial centres, these blocks often occupy the absolute maximum of a given site.

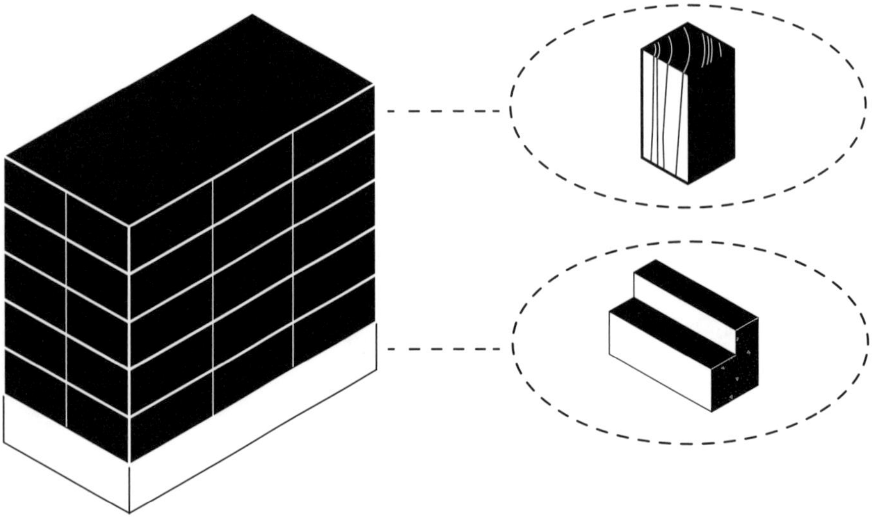

5 over 1

Five floors of residential units in light-frame wood construction over one floor of parking or commercial space in concrete, with a central elevator core.

Based on this data alone and the urgent need for action, design professionals should advocate not only for the construction of more compact cities at a macro scale, but also strive to usher in new models for more diverse housing options, while supporting a drastic reduction in square footage per person at a micro scale.

Improvements in building technology and the introduction of fire retardants and sprinkler systems through amendments to the building code have together supported the construction of taller wood frame construction over time. In turn, this has allowed for significantly lower construction and labour costs, which are often 20% to 40% cheaper than alternative construction in concrete, steel or masonry. While the burgeoning acceptance of mid-rise wood construction could hold great architectural promise, many developers have turned to a less innovative model.

The most common construction of this type is a blocky six storey building composed of five floors of residential units constructed in light-frame wood over one floor of structured parking or commercial space in concrete, with a central elevator core. Widely referred to as "stumpies," these buildings have become pervasive throughout North American cities over the past few decades.

With the stumpy model, wood-stick frame construction sits behind an inexpensive façade of low-quality fibre cement, metal, stucco or brick, designed with the intention of breaking up the monolithic appearance of the structure and giving the impression of smaller buildings at street level. The units, often reused from project to project, are optimally sized along double-loaded corridors and strung together in U, E, or S shapes with two and three-bedroom units at corners. If present, high-end finishes are restricted to the interiors of apartment units rather than the exterior façade. The repetition of these buildings can have a negative effect on the visual variety of the city and, over time, its overall character.

A recent criticism by Bloomberg columnist Justin Fox states that "these structures' proliferation is one of the most dramatic changes to the country's built environment in decades."[3] Stumpies are popular with developers due to their uncompromising efficiency, simple construction methods, inexpensive materials and predictable market absorption. Despite their pragmatic appeal and the density they afford, the widespread adoption of stumpies has become a visual blight on the urban landscape.

Matthew Soules expands on the ubiquitous presence of generic mid-rise buildings, making a direct link to the global affordability crisis. He outlines how "the financialisation of architecture necessitates its simplification in order to make it easier to own and trade as an asset. This process standardizes, homogenizes, and physically disengages architecture, yet, paradoxically, attempts to render it unique and locally specific... as architecture is simplified for investment purposes, it is propelled toward materials and forms that minimize the burdens of maintenance."[4]

The stumpies typology emerged at the intersection between market forces, developer preference, labour availability as well as restrictive zoning and building code regulations that limit architectural scope and vision. Growing regulatory burdens, operating in tandem with rising construction costs and a lack of skilled construction labour, make it difficult to propose alternatives to the dependable five-over-one type. At the same time, the growing presence of institutional housing development finance firms with both public and private investment can occlude any architectural innovation that might lie outside of this often banal model.

Much can still be done to improve livability within the existing stumpie parameters, including integrating this typology into urban spaces with more creativity to build better cities. Reorganizing parking spaces in between can help prioritize shared outdoor space over utility and ensure connections. An attractive network of public space weaves through the otherwise normative typology.

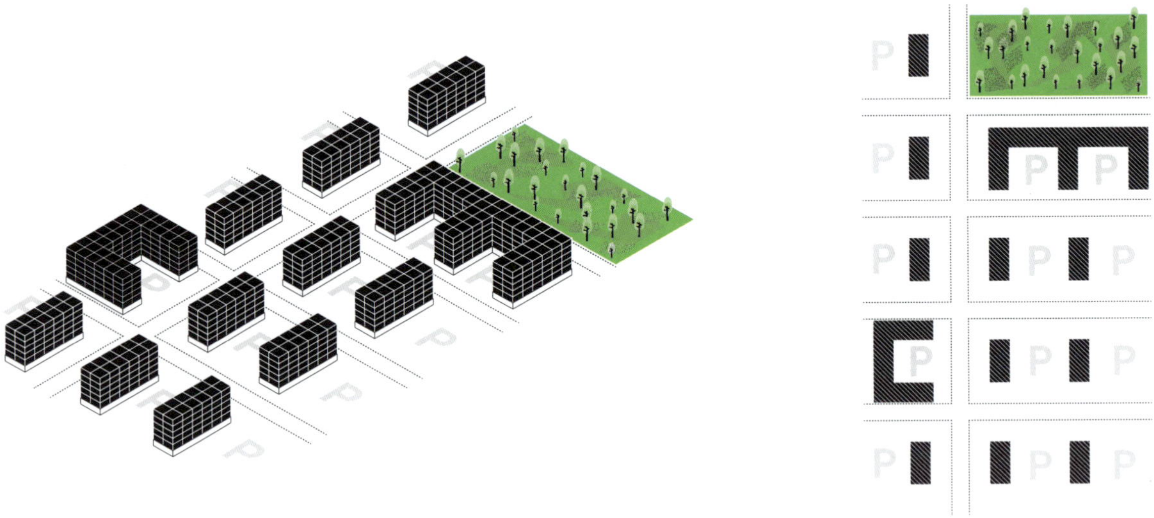

Stumpies: North American city grid

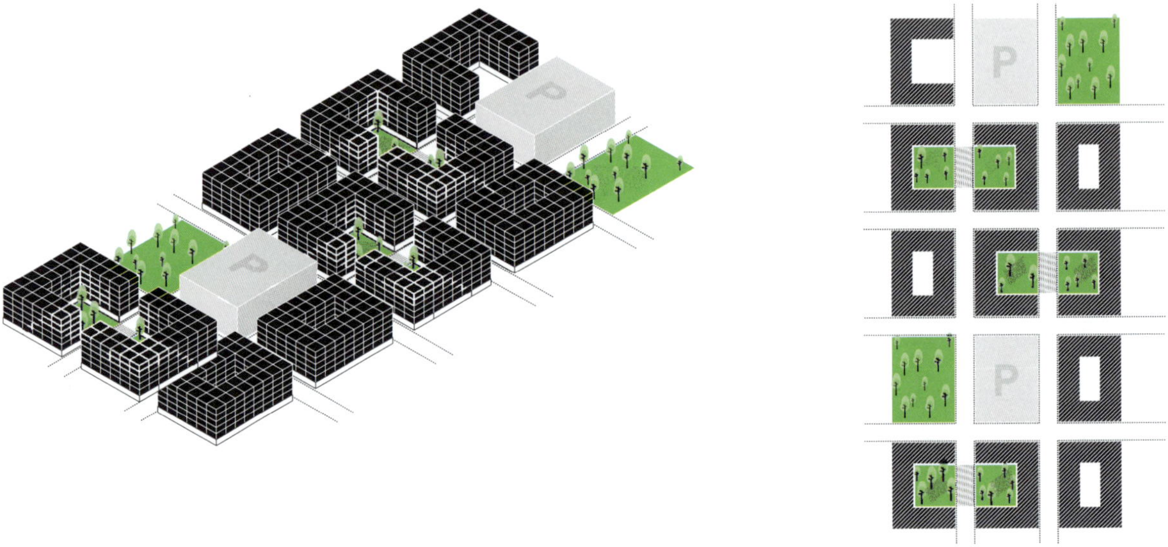

Stumpies: European city grid

Adaptive reuse

Conversion and renovation projects – especially within protected heritage buildings – provide a rich context to engage with and draw inspiration from. They also represent an irreplaceable asset in the downtown core of many cities, speaking to the layered history of a place through their scale and presence, materiality and texture, with a quality of workmanship that cannot be replicated using today's construction standards.

Adaptive reuse projects offer unique opportunities as well as an array of challenges, many of which are not evident at the outset of the design process.

Adaptive reuse of heritage buildings requires strong support from government. The architectural profession can only do so much and it is critical that regulators and policy makers stand behind us to pave the way. Winnipeg has a large stock of excellent heritage buildings in its historically protected Exchange District. Rehabilitating projects of this typology marks an extremely large and important sector in shaping the future of our city's downtown.

We've had the opportunity to contribute to this signature neighbourhood from our inception, with one of our first projects being the commercial rehabilitation of **315 Pacific Avenue** followed by the residential conversion of **230 Princess Street** for the same owner. This project was one of the first in Winnipeg to successfully apply the Richardson Report to ensure the life safety of occupants while not prescriptively meeting the building code, which was not possible as a five storey combustible building.

The Richardson Report is a unique document developed by the City in response to the demand for repurposing these post and beam warehouses within the limits of the building code. The Report supports heritage preservation and rehabilitation goals with fire safety alternatives, and facilitates their change of use from warehouse to commercial or residential occupancy. The report outlines alternatives and their separate risk indices, providing a quantitative method for architects, builders or the AHJ to determine if sufficient fire protection has been provided. The use of these indices allows for heritage features such as century old timber columns and beams to remain exposed and celebrated, among other important benefits.

We have worked on a number of other complex conversions of protected heritage buildings into residential use – including **The Avenue** on Portage, **The Porter Building**, **Warehouse 1885** and **90-100 Alexander** – all of which are high-rise wood frame structures with unique building code challenges.

projects.MODELLING: The Avenue (p. 76), Warehouse 1885 (p. 104), 90-100 Alexander (p. 116)

Mid-rise strategies

As large parcels of empty urban land are redeveloped, the repetition of homogenized building forms in a sea of surface parking will come to define an era of lackluster housing development in Canada and the United States. Together with landscape architecture partner Scatliff Miller Murray, 5468796 is currently implementing two masterplans for multi-acre sites in Winnipeg and Calgary that take a decidedly different approach.

Railside

Commissioned by the Forks North Portage Development Corporation, Railside at The Forks reimagines two existing surface parking lots in downtown Winnipeg. Where a previous scheme proposed five residential towers in order to meet density targets, we were able to achieve the same density in a mixed-use micro development, breaking the 11 acre parcel into 35 smaller pieces. Rather than depending on a single or even a handful of developer(s) or architects, the Railside model is well-suited to a slow growth city like Winnipeg. The mid-rise building scale paired with manageable lot sizes helps reduce investor risk and ensure that a variety of developer and architect teams can engage with the project, resulting in a diverse and more organic mix of architectural interventions. This model also provides a means of emulating the rich layering of architectural experiences that typically take many years to emerge. As it takes shape over the next two decades, Railside has the potential to accommodate up to 1200 residential units, with a targeted density of 80 to 100 units per acre.

Chroma East

Together with the Calgary Municipal Land Corporation (CMLC), RNDSQR, and planning consultant Civic Works, we established a mixed-use master plan for the former site of the David D. Oughton (DDO) School. The eight acre property represents a prime redevelopment parcel and unique city-building opportunity intended to catalyze the revitalization of Calgary's East Central region.

According to requirements for City-owned Municipal Reserve lands, the project was required to dedicate 2.41 acres for use as a public park. Instead of simply portioning off one third of the site, we divided up the reserve into four smaller parcels, mixed in among the housing blocks, in order to provide a finer grain development with more intimate public spaces. Obtaining approval for these smaller parcels represented a major achievement, as the Municipal Reserve had never been split in this way before.

In a geographic area primarily occupied by new Canadians, DDO is an inclusive community that will provide approximately 200 new townhomes and almost 500 apartment units, with opportunities for young families, multi-generational housing and aging in place that would not otherwise be accessible to this demographic. Although the buildings are not designed in their entirety at the concept plan stage, layouts for all of the unit types were tested in principle in order to demonstrate their viability.

 projects.MODELLING: Railside (p. 26), Chroma East (p. 40)

In both proposals, people-oriented public spaces are prioritized and as such render the quality of individual architectural responses within the site less impactful. Connected spaces and network of alleys, plazas, pocket parks and squares offer a rich environment where building architecture is subservient to the in-between, and even the typical stumpie can support vibrant urban life.

Railside

Vehicles are permitted for service access and visitor parking only, supporting a comfortable environment for pedestrians and cyclists, like the *woonerfs* or "living streets" of the Netherlands. Service access is allowed and encouraged throughout the site via front doors to avoid large dedicated loading zones that are detrimental to the streetscape continuity. In the case of **Railside**, at-grade parking is supplied in small, distributed pockets to minimize their impact on the pedestrian experience. Five parking stalls per building are intended to accommodate accessible stalls and car share spaces. For **Chroma East**, in addition to parallel and pocket surface parking stalls at grade, two or three underground parking areas would be supplied by the developer.

Chroma East

As the majority of our projects have been constructed on small inner city infill lots, larger land areas provide opportunities to make a more substantial contribution to the supply of new housing. There is also a greater potential for failure, demonstrated by the placeless towers of the modernist era. At this scale of development, it takes significant buy-in from government officials and policy makers to get projects off the ground. Once completed, the hope is that Railside and Chroma East will provide tangible examples to both the public and private sector, demonstrating the potential of innovative, mid-rise building patterns on underused sites in urban areas.

Our interest in mid-rise planning strategies has also extended to a theoretical densification plan for Winnipeg to meet the city's 25-year growth projection of 80,000 new homes by 2040. It includes an analysis of leftover urban parcels along existing arterial roads, further detailed in our contributing chapter to "Innovative Solutions for Creating Sustainable Cities," edited by Sylvie Albert in 2019. Leftover land is different from areas flagged as major redevelopment opportunities, as they represent untapped potential for urban densification, with the majority of necessary infrastructure already in place. Similar to **Railside** and **Chroma East**, these parcels can demonstrate the effectiveness of a mid-rise building scale in achieving much needed infill density.

Winnipeg: leftover land case study

*** Excerpt from the "Business Case for Compact Cities" chapter written by Johanna Hurme and Shannon Wiebe for *Innovative Solutions for Sustainable Cities*, (edited by Sylvie Albert, 2019)**

Winnipeg is one of the least dense cities in the world with a population of over 500,000. With the projected 25-year growth numbers at the forefront of recent discussions in Winnipeg's development community, a myth has been perpetuated that the city is running out of developable land and that the only viable option for new residential development is the outlying greenfield areas at the city's perimeter.

While simply dividing the population of a city by its land area is not the most comprehensive way to assess urban density, the statistic does give a clear synopsis of the main root of Winnipeg's problem: the city's footprint is too large and its population density is too low to support efficient delivery of municipal services into new and existing communities.

Nearly 75% of Winnipeg's annual $1.1 billion budget is dedicated to infrastructure maintenance and municipal service delivery. Road renewal, transit, waste collection, water, sewer, snow removal, police and fire paramedic services, libraries, parks, and insect control – all of these services are directly linked to the physical distance between points (i.e. kms of road, meters of sewage pipe, distance driven, etc.). It is therefore logical that a more compact city would yield a multitude of efficiencies and long-term savings. In other words, directing all new growth into the downtown core, mature neighbourhoods, and along established infrastructure routes or near existing community services is key to maximizing the benefit to Winnipeg's bottom line.

The Halifax regional municipality recently calculated that their annual service cost per household is $1,416 for an urban dwelling versus $3,462 for a suburban household, representing a savings of over $2,000 a year. Assuming that these figures would be comparable to Winnipeg and in light of the city's expected need for 80,000 new residences over the next 25 years, the opportunity to capitalize on directing this growth into urban areas could be in excess of $4 billion dollars – a portion of which could be invested in developing policy frameworks to support and incentivize infill development. While Winnipeg may be running out of cheap developable bare land, it should not justify further expansion of the city's unsustainable footprint. As previously discussed, simply examining the citywide density numbers provides evidence for the need to move in the opposite direction – increasing density within the existing core area and along existing and developing transit routes.

The densification strategy could consist of a variety of approaches, including increasing the density of existing neighbourhoods through the introduction of secondary suites, increasing density targets of infill lands already slated for development, identifying "**leftover**" parcels along existing infrastructure routes, rezoning larger existing single-family lots in strategic locations to accommodate mid-rise infill and turning a portion of city-owned surface parking lots into developable lands. Together, these strategies will provide an increase in the city's tax base and sufficient land supply to accommodate the 25-year growth projection. Note that with the exception of the downtown core, the examples provided do not rely on density achieved through high-rise construction, but rather through ground oriented, mixed-use development.

Leftover land on Grant Avenue in Winnipeg.

A review of the city's existing footprint indicates that there are several city-owned parcels of land along existing arterial roads that are much wider than necessary. In some cases, there is enough land that a development on the scale of Railside could be accommodated on these left-over parcels. One such area exists along Grant Avenue, just off Pembina Highway. At 4.5 acres of land, it could accommodate 450 new suites at no more than a four to six storey multifamily development pattern while effectively providing a buffer zone towards the single-family detached neighbourhood on either side. Considering the site's location along an arterial road, very little would be required in terms of new road infrastructure or transit routing. In fact, bringing in a higher density of residents would warrant more efficient use of transit and potentially allow for increased frequency of existing bus services.

One of the more radical ways to incentivize infill of this type would be to give away these leftover parcels for $1 to a private developer committed to the target density. The typical land cost in Winnipeg of about $30,000 per unit door for serviced land would generate $15M of value that the developer could then use to overcome any infill specific challenges, such as upgrading utility services, repaving public lanes or constructing new street approaches to the arterial road. As is, the city would be hard-pressed to see even a fraction of the value of this type of land being offered through a traditional sale to the private sector. In fact, following the Halifax service costs example, even at full value, the payback on such investment to the city would take less than 17 years.[5] In addition to the much lower municipal service costs within the mature city over time, the return on investment for Winnipeg will come immediately upon completion of the development in the form of future property taxes and new transit users, rendering it a much more feasible proposal than continuing to build out to greenfield sites on the fringes.

$2,000 x 450 suites x 25 years = $22,500,000

The research conducted by our practice concluded that there are approximately 400+ acres of City of Winnipeg-owned "leftover land" within the city boundaries. At 100 units / acre (based on our previous density target of four to six storey building heights) this would yield 40,000 new residential suites – or about half of the 25 year citywide growth target. The remainder, as identified in the following diagram, can be achieved with a strategic and incentivized deployment of existing densification approaches.

It's clear the commodification of housing and the need for mid-rise housing in North America has funnelled many developers toward uninspiring building types. In contrast, we believe that economically viable, highly livable, and architecturally inspiring alternatives are entirely possible while embracing the inherent efficiencies in the five-over-one building type, as further outlined in "platform.MICRO." There are countless opportunities for innovation within the various forms of Missing Middle Housing.

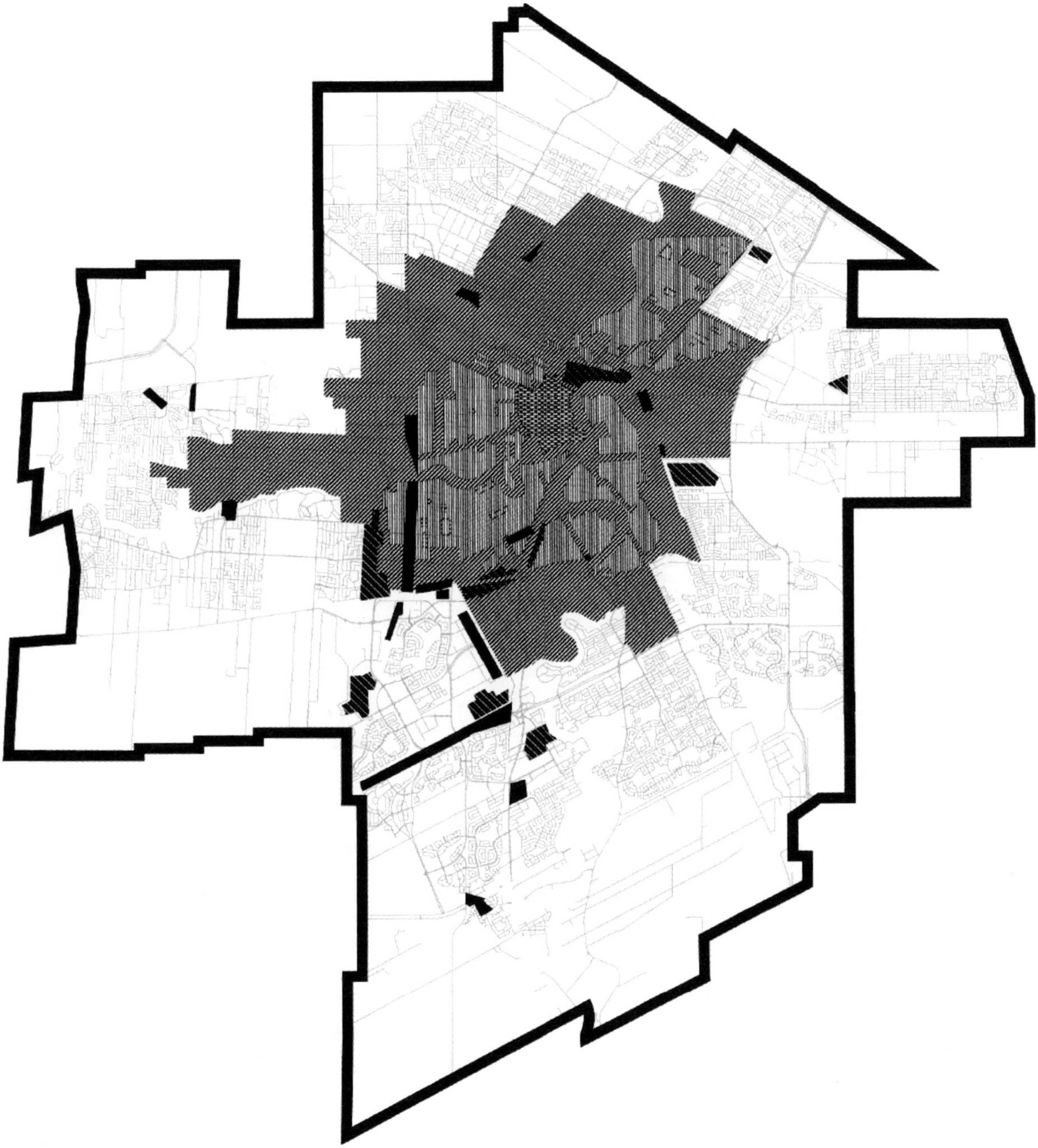

Major redevelopment sites	20,000 units
Leftover land	40,000 units
Mid-rise infill	7,500 units
Secondary suites	5,000 units
Downtown parking lots	7,500 units
	80,000 units

The map identifies five strategies for densification through infill in Winnipeg's existing footprint in order to meet the 25-year growth targets.

post.SCRIPT

Notes

INTRODUCTION

1 Canadian Architect, December 4, 2018. https://www.canadianarchitect.com/add-via-edit-a-decade-of-housing/.

2 Lilly Cao, "Urgent Issue: 10 Strategies to Decarbonize Architecture," *Archdaily*, July 27, 2020, https://www.archdaily.com/938866/urgent-issue-10-strategies-to-decarbonize-architecture.

3 Geoffrey Turnbull, David Constable, Jessica Piper, "Manifestos on the Climate Crisis," November 1, 2020, https://www.canadianarchitect.com/manifestos-on-the-climate-crisis/.

4 Statistics Canada, "Census in Brief: Dwellings in Canada", 2017, https://www12.statcan.gc.ca/census-recensement/2016/as-sa/98-200-x/2016005/98-200-x2016005-eng.cfm.

5 Helsingin Kaupunki. Kaupunkisuunnitteluvirasto, 2007, https://www.hel.fi/static/liitteet/kanslia/aluerakentaminen/kehittyvakerrostalo/Julkaisut/kerrostalojen-kehittaminen-talotyyppiselvitys.pdf.

6 Statistics Canada, "Families, households and marital status: Key results from the 2016 Census," 2016, https://www150.statcan.gc.ca/n1/daily-quotidien/170802/dq170802a-eng.htm.

7 Lindsay Wilson, "How Big is a House?," *Shrink That Footprint*, April, 2013, http://shrinkthatfootprint.com/how-big-is-a-house.

DIVEST / INVEST

1 Organization for Economic Co-operation and Development (OECD), Employment, Labour and Social Affairs Policy Briefs, *Social Housing: A Key Part of Past and Future Housing Policy*, https://www.oecd.org/social/social-housing-policy-brief-2020.pdf, 5.

2 Statistics Canada, "Results from the Canadian Housing Survey: 2018," November 22, 2019, https://www150.statcan.gc.ca/n1/daily-quotidien/191122/dq191122c-eng.htm.

3 Jeff Andrews, "Affordable Housing is in Crisis. Is Public Housing the Solution?," *Curbed*, January 13, 2020, https://archive.curbed.com/2020/1/13/21026108/public-housing-faircloth-amendment-election-2020.

4 OECD, *Social Housing*, 6.

5 Future Distributed, "Social Housing in Denmark: The Tenant Democracy," June 1, 2021, https://futuredistributed.org/stories/social-housing-denmark/.

6 Government of the Netherlands, "Basics on Dutch Housing," 2012, https://www.government.nl/topics/investing-in-dutch-housing/basics-dutch-housing.

7 Housing Europe, "Social Housing in Europe: The Netherlands," March 27, 2010, https://www.housingeurope.eu/resource-117/social-housing-in-europe.

8 Amelyn Ng, "Amsterdam Social Housing: A Primer," *Assemble Paper* #10: Housing (October 2018), https://assemblepapers.com.au/2018/12/13/amsterdam-social-housing-a-primer/.

9 Canadian Home Builders Association, "New Report Offers Insight on How to Improve Municipal Processes, Fees and Charges," https://www.chba.ca/CHBA/News/ Municipal_Benchmarking_Study.aspx.

10 Katy O'Donnell, "How Biden Hopes to Fix the Thorniest Problem in Housing," *Politico Magazine*, April 10, 2021, https://www.politico.com/news/2021/04/10/biden-housing-plan-480676.

11 Center for Neighborhood Technology (CNT), *Housing and Transportation Index*, https://www.cnt.org/tools/housing-and-transportation-affordability-index.

12 Metro Vancouver, *The Metro Vancouver Housing and Transportation Cost Burden Study: A New Way of Looking at Affordability*, 2015, http://www. metrovancouver.org/services/regional-planning/PlanningPublications/HousingAndTransportCostBurdenReport2015.pdf.

13 Statistics Canada, "Canada's Core Public Infrastructure Survey," October 9, 2018, https://www150.statcan.gc.ca/n1/daily-quotidien/181009/dq181009a-eng.htm.

14 Greg Suttor, "Lessons from the Past on a National Housing Strategy," *Policy Options*, March 27, 2017, https://policyoptions.irpp.org/magazines/march-2017/lessons-from-the-past-on-a-national-housing-strategy/.

15 Terry Gross, "A Forgotten History of How the U.S. Government Segregated America," *NPR*, May 3, 2017, https://www.npr.org/2017/05/03/526655831/a-forgotten-history-of-how-the-u-s-government-segregated-america.

16 Andre M. Perry and David Harshbarger, "America's Formerly Redlined Neighborhoods have Changed, and so Must Solutions to Rectify Them," October 14, 2019, https:// www.brookings.edu/research/americas-formerly-redlines-areas-changed-so-must-solutions/.

17 Chris Roberts, "The Great Eliminator: How Ronald Reagan Made Homelessness Permanent," *SFWeekly*, June 29, 2016, https://www.sfweekly.com/news/the-great-eliminator-how-ronald-reagan-made-homelessness-permanent/.

18 HUD USER, "What Happens to LIHTC Properties After Affordability Requirements Expire?," https://www.huduser.gov/portal/pdredge/pdr_edge_research_081712.html.

19 Urban Institute, "Features, The Cost of Affordable Housing: Does it Pencil Out?," https:// apps.urban.org/features/cost-of-affordable-housing/.

20 Joint Center for Housing Studies of Harvard University, "The State of the Nation's Housing: 2020," https://www.jchs.harvard.edu/sites/default/files/reports/files/Harvard_ JCHS_The_State_of_the_Nations_Housing_2020_Report_Revised_120720.pdf.

21 Statistics Canada, "One in Ten Canadian Households Living in Core Housing Need in 2018," *The Daily*, October 2, 2020, https://www150.statcan.gc.ca/n1/daily-quotidien/201002/dq201002a-eng.htm.

22 Taylor Locke, "Build Back Better includes $170 billion for Affordable Housing – Here's Where it Would Go," November 24, 2021, https://www.cnbc.com/2021/11/24/build-back-better-includes-170-billion-for-housing.html.

23 Government of Canada, "Canada's National Housing Strategy: A Place to Call Home," January 30, 2018, https://www.placetocallhome.ca/-/media/sf/project/ placetocallhome/pdfs/canada-national-housing-strategy.pdf.

RESTRICT / RESTRUCTURE

1 Patrick Condon, "Uh oh. I'm a Planner and Planning Makes Housing More Expensive," *The Tyee*, February 26, 2019, https://thetyee.ca/Analysis/2019/02/26/Planning-Expensive/.

2 Condon, "Uh oh."

3 Emily Badger and Quoctrung Bui, "Cities Start to Question an American Ideal: A House With a Yard on Every Lot," *The New York Times*, June 18, 2019, https://www.nytimes.com/interactive/2019/06/18/upshot/cities-across-america-question-single-family-zoning.html.

4 Diana Budds, "Will Upzoning Neighborhoods Make Homes More Affordable?" *Curbed*, January 30, 2020, https://archive.curbed.com/2020/1/30/21115351/upzoning-definition-affordable-housing-gentrification.

5 Erick Trickey, "How Minneapolis Feed Itself from the Stranglehold of Single-Family Homes," *Politico Magazine*, July 11, 2019, https://www.politico.com/magazine/story/2019/07/11/housing-crisis-single-family-homes-policy-227265/.

6 Laurel Wamsley, "Oregon Legislature Votes to Essentially Ban Single-Family Zoning," *NPR*, July 1, 2019, https://www.npr.org/2019/07/01/737798440/oregon-legislature-votes-to-essentially-ban-single-family-zoning.

7 Conor Dougherty, "California, Mired in a Housing Crisis, Rejects an Effort to Ease It," *The New York Times*, January 30, 2020, https://www.nytimes.com/2020/01/30/business/economy/sb50-california-housing.html.

8 Ally Schweitzer, "An Ambitious Housing Proposal in Virginia is Dead – For Now," *WAMU*, January 23, 2020, https://wamu.org/story/20/01/23/an-ambitious-housing-proposal-in-virginia-is-dead-for-now/.

9 Rick Jacobus, "Why Voters Haven't Been Buying the Case for Building," *Shelterforce*, February 19, 2019, https://shelterforce.org/2019/02/19/why-voters-havent-been-buying-the-case-for-building/.

10 Jacobus, "Why Voters."

11 Richard Florida, *The New Urban Crisis: How Our Cities Are Increasing Inequality, Deepening Segregation, and Failing the Middle Class – and What We Can Do About It* (New York: Basic Books, 2017), 192.

12 Florida, *The New Urban Crisis*, 21.

13 The World Bank, "Inclusionary Zoning," https://urban-regeneration.worldbank.org/node/46.

14 City of Vancouver, "Housing Vancouver: 10 Year Affordable Housing Delivery and Financial Strategy," 2017, https://vancouver.ca/files/cov/affordable-housing-delivery-and-financial-strategy.pdf.

15 Marian Scott,"Proposed By-law Aims to Fix Affordable Housing Dilemma in Montreal," *Montreal Gazette*, June 12, 2019, https://montrealgazette.com/news/local-news/city-presents-housing-by-law.

16 City of Toronto, "Inclusionary Zoning Policy," https://www.toronto.ca/city-government/planning-development/planning-studies-initiatives/inclusionary-zoning-policy/.

17 Patrick Condon, "Portland Just Showed Vancouver How to Fix Its Housing Crisis," *The Tyee*, August 28, 2020, https://thetyee.ca/Analysis/2020/08/28/Portland-Showed-Vancouver-Fix-Housing-Crisis/.

18 Bartley Kives, "True North Square Deal Now Includes Grant for Affordable Housing," *CBC News*, September 20, 2018, https://www.cbc.ca/news/canada/manitoba/true-north-square-financing-affordable-housing-1.4831490.

19 Paris Schutz, "Report: City Misuses Affordable Housing Funds," *WWTW News*, March 28, 2017, https://news.wttw.com/2017/03/28/report-city-misuses-affordable-housing-funds.

20 Florida, *The New Urban Crisis*, 202.

21 City of Edmonton, "Missing Middle Zoning Review," https://www.edmonton.ca/city_government/urban_planning_and_design/medium-scale-housing-review.aspx.

22 John Pattison, "Lessons from Canada: How to End Mandatory Parking Minimums," *Streetsblog USA*, November 23, 2020, https://United States.streetsblog.org/2020/11/23/lessons-from-canada-how-to-end-mandatory-parking-minimums.

COMMODITY / COMMUNITY

1 Leilani Farha, United Nations, "Report of the Special Rapporteur on Adequate Housing as a Component of the Right to an Adequate Standard of Living, and on the Right to Non-Discrimination in This Context," January 18, 2017, https://digitallibrary.un.org/record/861179?ln=en.

2 Research and Markets, Global Real Estate Market Report 2021, March 18, 2021, https://www.prnewswire.com/news-releases/global-real-estate-market-report-2021-market-is-expected-to-grow-from-2687-35-billion-in-2020-to-3717-03-billion-in-2025---forecast-to-2030--301250151.html.

3 Farha, 2017.

4 David Madden and Peter Marcuse, *In Defense of Housing: The Politics of Crisis* (Verso Books: New York, 2016), 17.

5 Madden, 26.

6 John Mackie,"Not-Owner-Occupied Property Skyrockets in Vancouver," *Vancouver Sun*, June 14, 2019, https://vancouversun.com/news/local-news/not-owner-occupied-property-skyrockets-in-vancouver.

7 Alyse Kotyk, "Vancouver's Empty Home Tax is Increasing to 3% Next Year," *CTV News*, November 25, 2020, https://bc.ctvnews.ca/vancouver-s-empty-home-tax-is-increasing-to-3-next-year-1.5204533.

8 Brian Carney, "The Big Reason We're Not Serious About Tackling Housing Affordability," *The Tyee*, December 30, 2019, https://thetyee.ca/Opinion/2019/12/30/Housing-Unaffordability-Big-Reason/.

9 Andra Hopulele, "Millennials Study: Down Payment Delay Homeownership by up to 35 Years," *Point2 Homes*, August 27, 2018, https://www.point2homes.com/news/canada-real-estate/millennials-down-payments-delay-homeownership-35-years.html.

10 Matthew Soules, *Icebergs, Zombies, and the Ultra Thin: Architecture and Capitalism in the Twenty-First Century* (New York: Princeton Architectural Press, 2021), 50.

11 Diana Elliott and Tanaya Srini, Carl Hedman, Shiva Kooragayala, Cary Lou, "Denver and the State of Low- and Middle-Income Housing: Strategies to Preserve Affordability and Opportunities for the Future," *Urban Institute*, May 19, 2017, https://www.urban.org/research/publication/denver-and-state-low-and-middle-income-housing.

12 Donna Kimura, "Denver Approves Bold Rent Program," *Affordable Housing Finance*, July 16, 2018, https://www.housingfinance.com/policy-legislation/denver-approves-bold-rent-program_o.

13 Lynne Fernandez, ed., "Change Starts Here: Manitoba Alternative Provincial Budget 2020," *Canadian Centre for Policy Alternatives*, March 3, 2020, https://www.policyalternatives.ca/mbapb2020.

14 Austin Grabish, "Province Has Sold Off 94 Manitoba Housing Properties Since 2016, Documents Show," *CBC News*, December 2, 2019, https://www.cbc.ca/news/canada/manitoba/manitoba-housing-properties-sold-off-1.5381628.

15 Ian Froese, "Wait List Soars for Manitoba Housing Units – and So Do The Vacancies," *CBC News*, October 12, 2020, https://www.cbc.ca/news/canada/manitoba/manitoba-housing-unit-vacancies-wait-list-grows-1.5745816.

16 Rachel Bergen, "Welcome Place to Lose One-Third of Budget After Federal Funding Cut," *CBC News*, August 17, 2019, https://www.cbc.ca/news/canada/manitoba/welcome-place-funding-1.5251191.

17 Michael Kimmelman, "Chicago Finds a Way to Improve Public Housing: Libraries," *The New York Times*, May 15, 2019, https://www.nytimes.com/2019/05/15/arts/design/chicago-public-housing.html.

18 Canadian Architect, January 15, 2021. https://www.canadianarchitect.com/jda-designs-vancouvers-first-fire-hall-and-housing-colocation-project/.

19 CMHC, "Housing Research Report: New Models for Co-operative Housing," January, 2018, https://4bfebv17goxj464grl4a02gz-wpengine.netdna-ssl.com/wp-content/uploads/2019/01/Canada-CHMC-new_models_for_co-op_housing.pdf.

20 Sasha Hauswald and Stephanie Reyes, "Lasting Affordability is the Path to Resilience," *Shelterforce*, August 2, 2020, https://shelterforce.org/2020/08/02/lasting-affordability-is-the-path-to-resilience/.

21 Tom Carter and Chesya Polevychok, "Housing is Good Social Policy," Canadian Policy Research Networks (CPRN), Research Report F|50, December, 2004, http://www.urbancenter.utoronto.ca/pdfs/elibrary/CPRN_Housing-Good-Soc-Polic.pdf.

22 Greg Suttor. "Lessons from the Past on a National Housing Strategy." *Policy Options*. https://policyoptions.irpp.org/magazines/march-2017/lessons-from-the-past-on-a-national-housing-strategy/ March 27, 2017.

FORMULAIC / FORMATIVE

1 Ashok B. Lall, "Rethinking Values in Designing Architecture," *Tekton* 5, no. 1 (March 2018). https://tekton.mes.ac.in/issues/volume-5-issue-1/practice/.

2 Daniel Parolek, *Missing Middle Housing: Thinking Big and Building Small to Respond to Today's Housing Crisis* (Washington, D.C.: Island Press, 2020).

3 Justin Fox, "Why America's New Apartment Buildings All Look the Same," *Bloomberg*, February 13, 2019, https://www.bloomberg.com/news/features/2019-02-13/why- america-s-new-apartment-buildings-all-look-the-same.

4 Matthew Soules, *Icebergs, Zombies, and the Ultra Thin: Architecture and Capitalism in the Twenty-First Century* (New York: Princeton Architectural Press, 2021), 130-136.

5 Smart Prosperity Institute. "Infographics: The Cost of Sprawl." (2013). https://institute.smartprosperity.ca/library/publications/infographics- cost-sprawl.

platform.MIDDLE: Architecture for Housing the 99%
5468796 Architecture
First edition, 2023
ISBN 978-607-8880-19-5

platform.MACRO

© 5468796 Architecture Inc.
Winnipeg, MB
Canada

© Arquine, SA de CV
Ámsterdam 163 A
Colonia Hipódromo, 06100
Ciudad de México

Texts and images
© 5468796 Architecture

5468796 Architecture

Original layout and Editorial Management
Johanna Hurme, Sasa Radulovic, Ken Borton, Shannon Wiebe, Ainsley Johnston and Hugh Taylor

Content production
Emeil Alvarez, Pablo Batista, Jordy Craddock, Donna Evans, Teresa Garside, Ben Greenwood, Ralph Guitierrez, Jeffrey Kachkan, Matthew Kurtas, Andrew Lawler, Kelsey McMahon, Mohammad Massoumi, Colin Neufeld and Amanda Reis.

Past collaborators: Sharon Ackerman, Mandy Aldcorn, Maria Amagasu, Apollinaire Au, Brandon Bergem, Eric Decumutan, Jason Ejzenbart, Michelle Heath, Aynslee Hurdal, Caroline Inglis, Lucretia Ionescu, Andriy Ivanystskyy, Eva Kiss, Stanislav Klas, Lindsey Koepke, Grant Labossiere, Justin Lieberman, Jayne Miles, Royce O'Toole, Zach Pauls, Simone Prill, Sean Radford, Erin Riediger, Helia Saadat, Shannon Scott, Hasan Shurrab, Renee Struthers, Trent Thompson, Matthew Trendota, Alan Vamos, Jennifer Yablonowski and Dazhong Yi.

Arquine

Director
Miquel Adrià

Editorial Director
Brenda Soto Suárez

Editorial Assistants
Ana Luz Valencia and Karina Reyes

Layout
María Marín de Buen, Yavanna Latapí and Regina Sierra
(Estudio María Marín de Buen)

Proofreading
Fionn Petch

Prepress
Offset Rebosán

5468796.ca
arquine.com

The architects and publishers have made every effort to identify ownership in the use of images and copyrighted material. In the event of an inadvertent omission or error, please notify the publisher.

No part of this publication may be reproduced, stored in a retrieval system, or transmitted in any form or by any means, electronic, mechanical, photocopying, recording or otherwise, without prior and express written permission of the owners of the intellectual property rights and of the publishers.

platform.MACRO is one of four volumes in the publication *platform. MIDDLE: Architecture for Housing the 99%*. The other volumes include: platform.MIDDLE, platform.MICRO and projects.MODELLING.

platform.MIDDLE: Architecture for Housing the 99% was printed and bound in September 2023 by Artron Art Printing Ltd. in China. It was printed on 100 g IKPP paper and set in typefaces of the DIN family. The print run was 1,300 copies.

5468796 Architecture

platform.MICRO

platform.MICRO

platform.MICRO covers the network of responsibilities falling on the architect in planning and building housing projects. **Practice ecosystem** grounds the work of 5468796 in contemporary discourse, recognizing that an architect's role in challenging contexts must increasingly intersect with politics, economics, civic governance, social activism, and other forms of cultural and scholarly research. The **Toolkit** works through a series of strategies developed by the office over years of experience, highlighting: critical opportunism, adaptability + resilience, building between and promoting livability, ultimately leaning on an informed optimism that serves as a wake-up call to rise above the status quo.

PREFACE

Johanna Hurme

Having summarized the 2019 IIT symposium content into "platform.MIDDLE," we realized that as a practice we had more to contribute to the conversation – not just through individual projects that we get to design and build in the future, but as a set of strategies that could potentially be universally applied by our colleagues or anyone participating in the production of housing across North America and possibly beyond. As such, it is our earnest intent that the following volume and the accompanying "projects.MODELLING" catalogue not be a monograph of our work, but rather, that it might act as a guide or toolkit for others.

We operate in a context where the vast majority of the housing stock is produced by the private sector and is driven by profit. As teachers and lecturers in North America, we find these realities and financial proformas generally absent in the curriculums of universities across the continent. It seems particularly important to us to share how we've carved out room for design from the often predetermined spectrum of formulas.

We attempt to combine common sense, real-life solutions with an ambitious architectural agenda: the project samples are not simply "appropriately scaled" or "comfortable in their context," but in nearly all cases, peer recognized for their design quality with various awards and publications. With students, academics, young practitioners and practitioners not previously engaged in housing architecture, or any non-or for-profit organization producing housing in mind, it is our hope that the following micro strategies and solutions will allow others to leapfrog the lessons we have spent uncovering since 2007. This head start will hopefully allow more of us to take on the housing and environmental crises on a larger scale through the mid-scale multi-family building typology, and give architects some practical, straightforward options to increase livability and quality of the spaces they design, while still meeting the financial goals of their clients.

What arose from a desire and commitment to disseminate the information that was presented at the "platform.MIDDLE" symposium has grown to encapsulate the systemic issues that have shaped this discourse, our own personal ideology and how the three overlap and intertwine.

PRACTICE ECOSYSTEM

Design competitions
Political pursuit
Design giving
Financial success
Design activism
Exhibitions
Thought leadership
Awards + publications
Academic pursuit
Design juries
Collaboration
Take a seat

The role of the architect

Starting a practice in Winnipeg – a city one architectural margins of the Canadian midwest – may not seem like an obvious choice for two European-born immigrants hoping to push the boundaries of architecture. Yet it is perhaps the specific challenges of this context that have inspired a broader understanding of an architect's social and civic responsibilities. In this environment, an architect's scope of work stretches deep and wide, necessitating a parallel stream of architectural activism in order to challenge the status quo and create opportunities for critical practice.

Our focus on missing middle and mid-rise housing arose as a direct result of our decision to stay in Winnipeg at a time when many of our colleagues left for greener architectural pastures. As the suburbs continued their uncompromising sprawl, downtown development remained stagnant and cultural projects were in short supply. In this environment, some private multi-family housing developers saw an opportunity to obtain affordable land in the city centre. Still, economic realities and the high cost of construction presented a substantial challenge, combined with the existing stigma imposed on these sites. Projects needed to stand out as a desirable place to live, and in many cases a community needed to emerge from within while the surrounding context caught up.

A handful of these risk-takers knocked on our door and became some of our first clients. Our location in a so-called "second city" provided a quick feedback loop – from design to construction to response to critique – and a context to visibly stand out or fail in. Serendipity and connections played a role as well. Like most architects starting out, we were shaped by the type of projects we were given, before we could shape the work.

The office has grown at a pace that far exceeded our initial expectations, from those first months working at the kitchen table to the first years renting progressively larger office spaces for our emerging practice. Each new challenge required exponential growth. In response, members of the team have developed individual strengths that, when brought together, enable us to innovate and challenge presupposed solutions. The power of our collaborative partnership is our greatest resource. With more knowledge, we are more open to embracing change and reacting in a way that improves the project outcome.

In the aftermath of the 2008 financial crash, the ability to create something out of nothing in our local context became even more relevant on the global stage. During the ceremony we attended for **Bloc_10** at the 2012 AR Awards for Emerging Architecture, editor Catherine Slessor described the current state of architecture in the world as being both sobering and heartening. Sobering because of the acute impact the economic crisis has had on the profession, but heartening because the selected works represented a crucial sense of creative resilience, an architectural direction that was no longer about novelty.

Over the years, we have come to see that a more holistic view of practice is required to address the current challenges of providing multi-family housing – especially in conservative contexts. The definition of architecture (and an architect) must be broadened to that of a strategy (and a strategist). The role of a strategist is not limited to skillful form-making, technical achievement, or satisfying the client's financial targets. It also includes concern for making good spaces for people both inside and outside of the program, weaving the project into the existing city fabric, being environmentally sustainable and meeting the challenge of affordability. As strategists, we are also responsible for fostering the connections between key players, potential sites and available funding sources in order to facilitate projects and help get them off the ground.

To accomplish these goals, our definition of a successful practice has expanded and evolved. With every new project we undertake, we are inspired to broaden our approach.

Migrating Landscapes, 2012.

projects.MODELLING: Bloc_10 (p. 72), Migrating Landscapes (p. 12)

Advocacy + activism

We believe that by inspiring colleagues, public and municipal decision-makers, it is possible to re-establish a strong design culture in our city and beyond. Design advocacy is an ongoing pursuit to improve the recognition of our profession's value in the eyes of the public and private sector, as well as with the government agencies that ultimately make decisions about how contracts are awarded and funds are spent.

We gain insight from one another via our day-to-day office environment and interactions. We have invited colleagues and clients to take a temporary seat and add their voice to the conversation. The Winnipeg Architecture Foundation – a local non-profit with a mandate to educate the public about the city's architecture – now has a permanent home within our office.

In addition to practice, it is important that we continue to measure ourselves against others via international competitions and through participation with design juries. We pursue awards and publications to remind ourselves that "good enough" is not good enough, and as a means to reach the right kind of collaborators and gain future opportunities. In recent years, this has been one of our main vehicles to attract new clients as they come across our work.

We have personally pursued board positions and become more politically active to instigate change and advocate for quality-based procurement practices, where lowest fee is not the common denominator and the value of design is recognized. Through advocacy work – including exhibitions, publications and public events – we can communicate the value of design in order to support innovation and risk taking, with the ultimate goal of creating better buildings and cities.

In 2012, 5468796 co-curated **Migrating Landscapes** with Jae-Sung Chon, Canada's official submission to the Venice Biennale in Architecture. Migrating Landscapes explored the settling-unsettling dynamic of im/migration, featuring video narratives and architectural scale models of dwellings by young Canadian designers. The work was selected by a jury and displayed in regional exhibitions before traveling to Venice.

We also remain connected to academia via teaching to remind ourselves of the power of youthful energy, to gain insight from the brilliance of our colleagues, and to support the next generation of designers by demonstrating that opportunities for innovation exist beyond the confines of the classroom or studio.

At the same time, we must also be smart business people. Financial success allows us to share wealth with the broader design community through giving initiatives. It also supports our ability to create future opportunities through competitions and design advocacy, while continuing to pay staff fairly, valuing their work and ability.

All of these aspects play an important role in what we consider to be our practice ecosystem, considering the role of the architect to expand beyond its traditional scope.

Please see projects.MODELLING for a selection of our Advocacy + Activism projects starting on page 11

Practice ecosystem

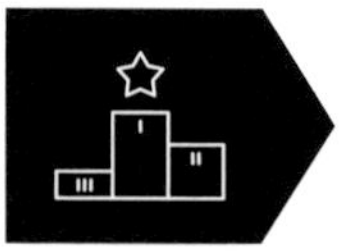

Design competitions: Participation in design competitions offers an opportunity to test new ideas freely and measure one's skill set against other architects around the world. Both open and invited competitions offer a unique opportunity for architects to compete with ideas rather than based on experience with a particular typology or by fee. 546 builds design competitions into our annual budget. Past competition ventures include: Old Market Square [Winner], Canadian Canoe Museum [Finalist], Arkansas Attainable Housing Competition [Winner, Site 3], Helsinki Guggenheim, Bibliotheque et Espace Culturel du Coeur-Nomade [Finalist], Art Gallery of Greater Victoria [Shortlist, WAF Future Project of the Year], International Peace Garden Tower Competition [Runner-up], Bentway Waterfront Reconnect [Winner], Edmonton Infill Competition [Winner, Open Category].

Design giving: We believe that in order to build a better design culture, we have to invest in it. These causes have included supporting student publications, graduations, non-profit architectural organizations and foundations, various one-off design events and initiatives, as well as in-kind work and volunteer efforts, helping to design an orphanage in Tuxpan, Mexico and offering a substantial donation to a girl's orphanage in Mexico City though the second edition of "One Bucket at a Time" in Winnipeg in 2018.

Design activism: Our 2013 Professional Prix de Rome project Table for Twelve attempted to uncover what creates architecture culture, what sustains it and who and what are the critical players for it to thrive. Almost all of our activism initiatives through the years have attempted to build and participate in building what we saw as missing design culture in our city. Architecture had fallen off the cultural radar, and for our work to have value, we believed, and continue to believe, that we must build the culture in order for our practice to succeed and to live in a better environment. Projects in this arena also include Architecture Fringe Festival, On the Boards Sessions, Table for 1200, Chair Your Idea, Winnipeg Design Quarter, One Bucket at a Time, Walk-Winnipeg, Windsock 1+2, Bijou Box and Re-Tree Winnipeg.

Political pursuit: Architects with a social conscience should take an active role in advocacy and politics – including running for elected office. Being an active part of finding solutions and crafting policies that can respond to the environmental crises or alleviate the housing crises is incredibly important and urgently needed. Members of 546 have held numerous board positions in the community, most notably Johanna's Chairmanship at the helm of the Winnipeg Chamber of Commerce and her subsequent activism in municipal politics.

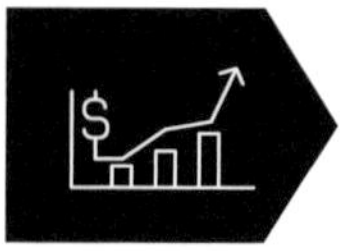

Financial success: In the architectural community it is often believed that to be considered a serious practice with a high design ambition one must sacrifice financial stability for the "art of architecture," that morally and artistically financial and architectural success cannot go hand-in-hand. The reality is quite different. Architects, like any professionals, sell time, and time allows us to do our work properly, with care and in the service of better performing, long-lasting buildings that are good for our souls, our environment and the overall well-being of our fellow human beings. Furthermore, for the profession to be valued, for design and architecture to be valued, and for us to value ourselves and the people who work with and for us, we must be fairly compensated. Architects should not be ashamed of being equally innovative in business as we are in our core practice.

Exhibitions: Creating architectural exhibitions engages a wider public in architectural discourse. A selection of 546's exhibitions to date include: "Migrating Landscapes" Canada's representation at the Venice Biennale in Architecture in 2012 [and a 7-city Canadian tour prior]; "Table for 12," exploring 546's housing projects in 2013, exhibited both at College of Architecture at Urbana Champagne, IL, and at Daniels school of Architecture; "Build" exhibition at the University of Manitoba, "Tapped/Untapped" for Toronto Design Festival in 2017 and "Outside the Box" Toronto Offsite Design Festival Wanted Design NYC, 2015.

Thought leadership: 546 has written and participated in several articles and publications, including *Innovative Solutions for Sustainable Cities*, edited by Sylvie Albert in 2019, and *Future Urban Habitation: Transdisciplinary Perspectives, Conceptions, and Designs* edited by Oliver Heckmann in 2022.

Academic pursuit: We believe that being active in academia alongside our practice is important. It gives us a chance to share our knowledge with future architects and designers, while at the same time holds us accountable for what we pursue in our practice and reminds us about the greater dialogue in architecture. A certain naiveté that comes along with working with students in a studio environment finds its way back into our own work setting – the belief in possibilities, opportunities and asking, "why not?" At the same time, we can help students understand how proformas, technical details or advocacy are all integral to their design work. Our past teaching engagements include the University of Manitoba, Daniels School of Architecture in Toronto, University of Montreal, College of Architecture at the Illinois Institute of Technology in Chicago and Art, Architecture and Planning at the Cornell University in New York.

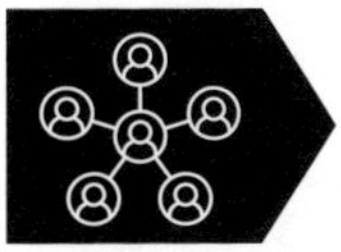

Collaboration: The team at 546 has always sat around one continuous table with the thought that ideas are exchanged freely and valued for their quality, not author, while at the same time learning through passive listening, or "osmosis." While at times challenging for work tasks requiring concentration, the learning value has been enormous, especially for junior or new members of the team.

Awards + publications: Applying for awards or pursuing publication opportunities in industry magazines allows us to find a broader audience for the work, often leading to future opportunities, whether it be directly by new clients, repeat work with clients who see a value in recognition, or through invitations to limited competitions that may result in commissioned work. More altruistically, sharing projects, ideas, and research is important in the broader discourse of architecture, and the ability to learn through others' work is a critical part of growth for our practice.

Design juries: Not unlike participating in Design Competitions, being invited to jury design and architectural awards or competitions makes us inspired by our colleagues to think critically about the future of architecture and the important questions of our time. The perspective gained from such experiences can clarify one's position, add nuance to understanding, or motivate new areas of interest. A healthy level of professional envy that may come from reviewing colleagues, work often also spurs new ambition to simply do better. Our past jury participations have included both international [WAF, PAs], North American [AIA NYC, Denver], Canadian [Governor General's Medals, RAIC Awards, Canadian Architect] and regional awards and competitions.

Take a seat: Our office space and shared table has opened up for various external collaborators and like-minded organizations over the years to further entice idea exchange and create serendipitous encounters. At the time of writing, we have shared our space with Winnipeg Architecture Foundation for more than eight years, with their exhibits and events regularly expanding into our office. Similarly, 546 has also welcomed researchers, developers, scholars and executive directors of design-focused organizations to work at our table or temporarily run their operations from our office. These include Storefront MB, Design Quarter Winnipeg, RNDSQR, Greenseed Development Corp., Steelcase and a number of independent academics.

TOOLKIT

building.

CRITICAL OPPORTUNISM

It is easy to be skeptical about the narrow definition within which capital "A" Architecture operates in North America today. Houses for the 1% and the luxury towers shaping the ever-expanding skylines of large metropolises do not meet the growing need for well built and well planned cities, nor do they provide access to carefully considered and designed places for the vast majority of the population.

In the face of a global affordability crisis, our profession needs to position itself as an indispensable creative resource. Within our practice, we have identified the role of "critical opportunism" – the ability to harness opportunities for innovation in both building design and project delivery – as an integral component of our practice ecosystem.

The vast majority of housing in North America is constructed by the private sector, where the market-driven formula for success tends to be limited. In the world of private development, architecture is a commodity that is expected to bend to the pressures of net-to-gross floor area ratios. All too often, the results fail to impress: fat floor plates with deep, tunnel-like units off double-loaded corridors, no cross-ventilation and a single narrow window face at the perimeter. As members of a profession founded on creative thought and concern for the greater good, we have to do better. It falls on the architect to broaden these parameters – early on and without additional expense.

In a three-storey walk-up project like **youCUBE** the formula is simple: individual doors at grade result in a 100% buildable-to-sellable efficiency ratio, with no space or cost devoted to indoor public corridors or exit stairs. As a trade-off, developers are able to reallocate a portion of the budget towards the outdoor public realm – a shared space that allows life to extend beyond the confines of individual suites and becomes part of the network of public spaces in the city. With mid-rise buildings, the inclusion of skip-stop corridors (**CY33** and **OZ**) or the redefinition of budget priorities (**62M** and **The Avenue**) have allowed us to re-invest a portion of our client's budget and incorporate public spaces or civic presence into the project's proforma.

WATERFRONT
HISTORY

Pumphouse

Our efforts on the revitalization of the historic **James Avenue Pumping Station** demonstrate the holistic nature of this approach on a larger scale, from knowledge of city processes to harnessing funding sources and facilitating partnerships. Although these aspects of project development are not typically considered part of an architect's purview, they are an essential component of our expanded role as strategists.

Slated for demolition after at least a dozen previous attempts to revive the historic structure over more than a decade had failed, 5468796 developed the financial proforma for the historic building and presented it to an existing client, bringing them to the table with Centre Venture (a municipally-funded downtown development agency) leading to its successful preservation through private investment. While the existing foundation was not capable of supporting the construction of additional floors on top of the Pumphouse, an existing gantry crane capacity allowed for a new commercial tenant floor within the building.

Analysis of the building revealed two independent structural systems: one for the building shell and the other for two gantry cranes. By permanently fixing the existing gantry crane system in place, the structure's initial capacity to move 20,000 lbs across the crane foundation and rail beams was repurposed for the construction of a floating floor within the historic structure. As a result, the pumps on the main floor could remain free and clear of complicated programming, as proposed in previous revitalization attempts. Instead, this adaptive reuse project celebrates the existing utilitarian beauty of the space while offering a viable future life for the building.

The uncovered potential of the existing structure allowed for the transformation of the Pumphouse into a financially feasible, contemporary mixed-use development that preserves the structure, pumps and pump hall through a combination of commercial and office spaces.

Furthermore, 546 brought in the future major tenant for the historic office space, enabling the developer to sign a multi-year lease and solidify the financial development plan.

In addition to the historic rehabilitation component of the development, the Pumphouse is book-ended by two modular, mid-rise housing structures. As part of the proforma analysis, 5468796 assessed the feasibility of incorporating housing on the east end of the site, an area that was not previously deemed suitable for development. By lifting the building up to preserve views of the heritage façade from Waterfront Drive, the front parcel was able to accommodate 28 apartment units, in addition to 63 units on the west parcel.

01 Unlocked potential

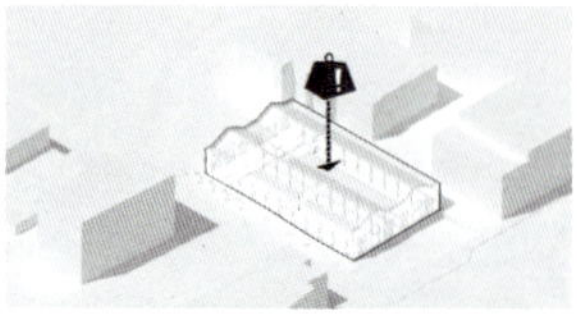

02 The gantry lift

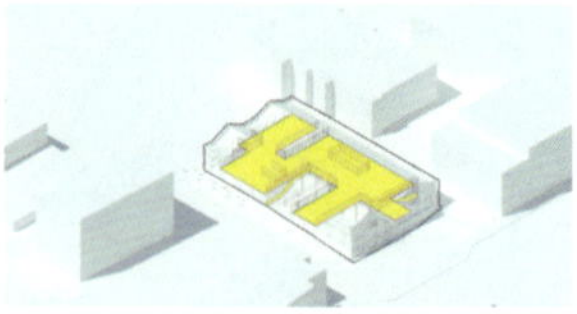

03 Historic activation

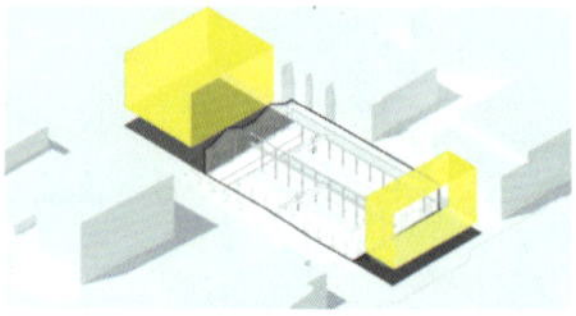

04 Buildable site

projects.MODELLING: Pumphouse (p. 112)

CROSSLEY BROTHERS LIMITED MANCHESTER
3

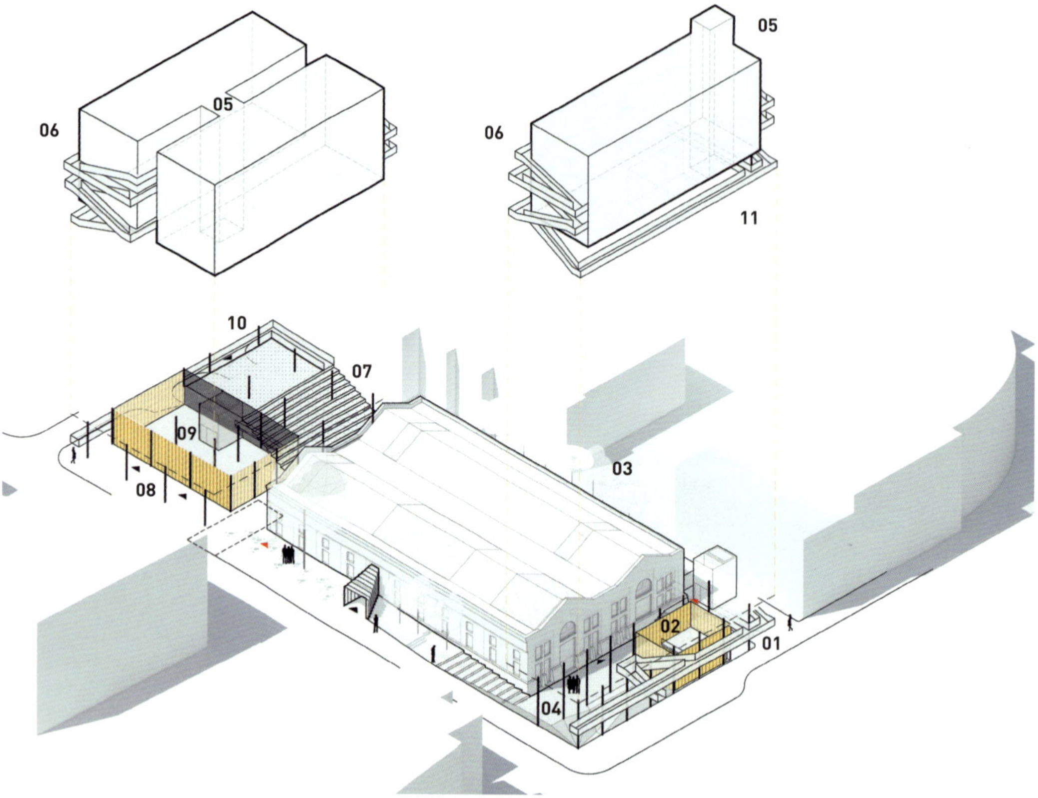

With additional developable land captured and square footage gained within the Pumphouse, the project proforma was able to support mid-rise construction, setting it apart from previous tower schemes. Significantly more affordable than high-rise construction in Winnipeg, this allowed for a buildable site to be designed in tandem, expanding the program and truly adapting the strengths of this early 20th century historic building into a feasible, contemporary mixed-use development.

Capped at six storeys in height, the new development consists of rental apartments, commercial use at ground level and underground parking. In keeping with the utilitarian nature of the original design, the new buildings subtly support its aesthetic through deliberately simple, modular forms. With views directed to the historical centre of the site, its storied past is highlighted and can be experienced in the approach to the site, the neighbouring exterior walkways, and the intimate alleyways formed between the old and new façades. Innovative connections between the historic building and the new program help strengthen the relationship between tenants, visitors and their local architectural history.

01 East entry
02 Commercial space 1
03 Skinny forest
04 Corner plaza
05 Elevator core
06 Exterior walkway + stair
07 Amphitheatre
08 Covered commercial entry
09 Commercial space 2
10 Parking roof
11 Raised exterior walkway

building.

ADAPTABILITY + RESILIENCE

In our practice, we see adaptability and resilience as multi-faceted and multi-scaled elements of design. When we are adaptable, we can acknowledge a changed reality and seek out new approaches. Through resilience, we find ways to respond and adjust. How do architects adapt to changing circumstances, expectations and political or social realities?

Architectural projects are invariably influenced by outside forces not present during the initial design phases. This is especially true with one of the most common client types for multi-family housing: the single entity owner-developer-builder, who can decide to modify any element at any time, and has the means to implement changes without further scrutiny. Remaining open to this evolution means treating each request as an opportunity to learn and improve. The inevitability of this process requires the courage to adapt and the conviction to pursue improvements at any stage of a project's development. The design process is liberating when allowed to evolve – details get tighter, concepts get leaner and projects get better.

Working in Winnipeg teaches us that architectural ideas will always be vetted against conventional or cheaper alternatives. In order to survive in this context, every design decision must be essential. Efficiency of means results in more robust projects that can resist the value engineering process, to the service of the client and end user – and ultimately to the benefit of the architectural outcome for all.

The Avenue

The Avenue on Portage demonstrates the evolutionary nature of the owner-developer-builder design process. The project started as a fast-track project as the owner acquired the historic Avenue Building and immediately began interior demolition and reinforcement of the structure while 5468796 was simultaneously tackling the schematic design of the project and running various proforma scenarios. Soon thereafter the project was expanded with the addition of the adjacent three-storey Hample Building. The owner then applied for and was granted a substantial Tax Incremental Finance grant requiring construction of 75 residential suites, some of which had to be affordable rentals.

Design development of the scheme was well underway when the owner determined that carving underground parking below both structures would make economic sense. At this time the basement floor had to be lowered by two feet, and the design had to accommodate a vehicular ramp at the back of the building in tight urban conditions. This was followed by an expanded need for commercial space at grade, as the owner secured a multi-year government tenant for the lower floors of the building. It quickly became clear that more floor space would be required to accommodate the new commercial tenant's space needs, displacing a portion of the 75 suites that were a requirement of the grant. These factors led to the need to add three storeys above the Hample Building, which in turn exceeded the structural capacity of the existing building foundation. The addition required an entirely new structure (piercing through the existing building) and new foundations (which could not interfere with the parking layout below or the existing footings). The design team shaped the new addition around the Avenue Building lightwell in part to reduce the bulk and weight of the addition, and pulled the façade back from the street to create the opportunity for inset balconies.

Compared to the sequential nature of the typical architectural process of schematic design, design development, construction documents, tender and construction phases services, working with owner-developer-builder often necessitates working in a much more fluid fashion and requires continuous decision making on-site, while at the same time maintaining a strong overall design vision.

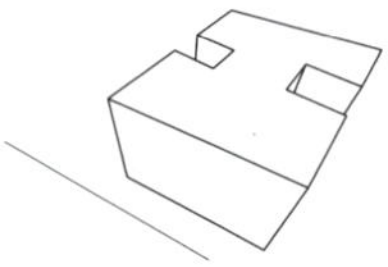

01

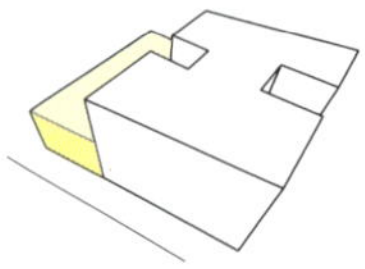

02

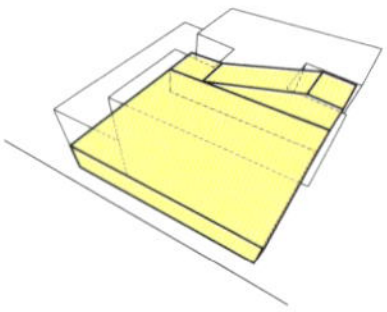

03

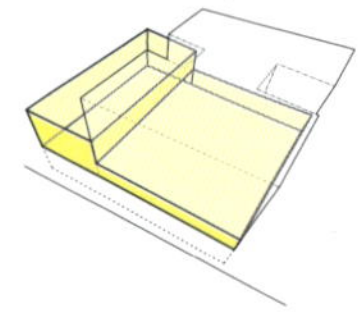

04

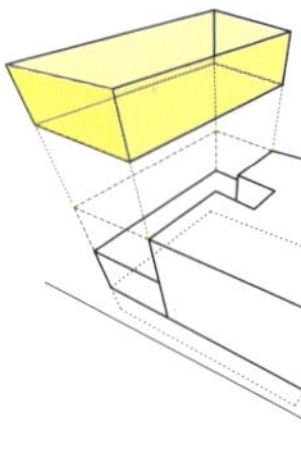

05

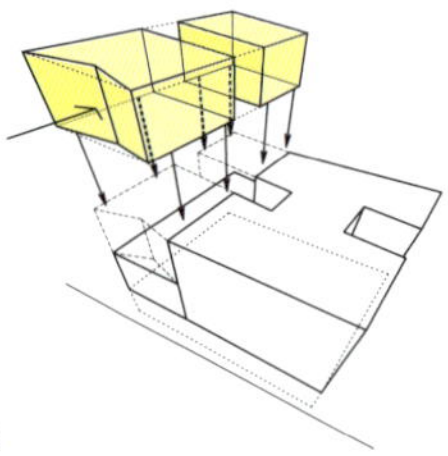

06

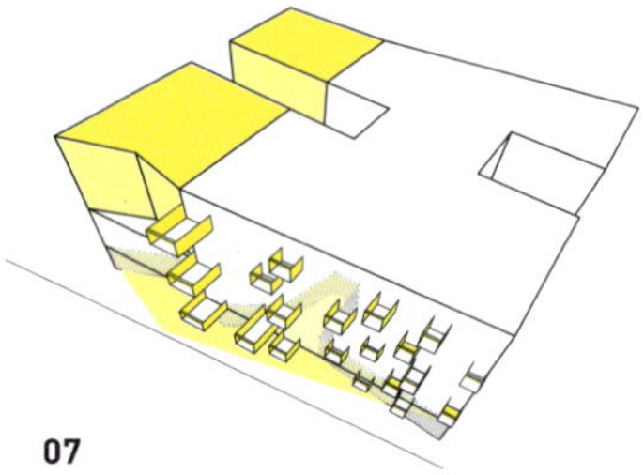

07

01 Avenue building
02 Hample building acquisition
03 Underground parking
04 Expanded commercial allocation
05 Displaced residential = addition required
[Exceeds structural capacity]
06 Addition is too heavy
[Requires subtraction + new structure]
07 Final project

projects.MODELLING: The Avenue (p. 76)

It is critical for adaptive reuse projects to make economic sense in the competitive world of private development. Together with the owner, it's important to analyze the costs and profits, as well as potential pitfalls and methods to compensate for these risks. Our cities become better and more dynamic places with every piece of history that we retain, rehabilitate and re-inhabit with daily life.

Future proof

As the global pandemic unfolded during 2020, urban cores in cities across North America and around the world experienced a dramatic shift in building occupancy. When downtown high rises emptied out of office workers and public amenities shut down, single-family dwellings with extra bedrooms became all the more appealing. Although a virtual work-from-home world is not the future we long for, the pandemic reinforced the need for buildings to adapt in order to increase their long-term life cycle and stand the test of time.

For **Railside** at the Forks and our award winning **attainable housing submission for NW Arkansas**, the size of developable blocks and depth of floor plates have been limited to support a range of uses. If businesses are unsuccessful, housing can take its place and vice versa. These masterplans focus on happy places for people, disconnected from modes of transport that may change over time.

The **Parkade of the Future** in Calgary represents another forward-focused hybrid project that asks what a future without parking garages might look like. If we continue to invest money in building parkades underground, they have no future function if and when car use becomes obsolete. To counteract this effect, Parkade of the Future is an aboveground parkade, with access to light and natural ventilation in order to serve a secondary function. The project has been designed to support structural loads for housing or office use in the future, with a generous floor-to-ceiling height to facilitate redevelopment. The seven storey building program includes a 50,000 square foot innovation centre, a publicly accessible sport court, an outdoor event rental space, as well as over 510 parking stalls and 100 bicycle stalls.

Future proofing can also apply to more small scale design considerations and interventions. Exterior corridors are one such example, heightened as a key design strategy to maximize ventilation and access to fresh air with a direct connection between inside and out. Although this feature might raise some eyebrows in cold climates, it has serendipitously been the right decision for a number of our projects, including **62M** and **Pumphouse**.

 projects.MODELLING: Railside (p. 26), 62M (p. 96), Pumphouse (p. 112)

EAST

Parkade of the Future

Calgary Municipal Land Corporation [CMLC] and the Calgary Parking Authority commissioned 5468796 Architecture as Design Architects together with Kasian Architecture, Interior Design and Planning as Architect of Record in late 2016 to design a "parkade of the future" for a 2.25 acre site on 9th Avenue in Calgary's East Village.

The project consists of a 510-stall parkade in addition to speculative commercial and residential towers for future development. The team was asked to not only provide a parkade concept that could be converted to other uses in the future when the need for parking stalls may decrease, but also to transform the parkade user experience from utilitarian to one that inspires its patrons and the public at large and contributes to the urban street edge along 9th Avenue.

The design deploys continuous narrow floor plates at a 1% slope, higher than average floor-to-floor heights and increased structural capacity to ensure that the building can be converted to residential, commercial and / or community uses in phases or at once. In addition, a disciplined and systematic structural grid within the parkade allows for flexibility. The "pipe" cladding was designed with the same future proofing in mind: recycled aluminum extrusions are fastened to a rail system through a pressure-based clip system, currently acting as a guardrail, but with the option to be repositioned or removed and reused or recycled.

Pedestrian circulation is directed immediately away from the drive aisle to horizontal and vertical circulation spaces that offer access to natural light, views, greenery, and in some instances other uses such as art, physical activity zones or incubator spaces.

9th Ave
Library
40 Ft Platform
Clear span floors
40 Ft Courtyard
Informal street
40 Ft Platform
Clear span floors
Rail

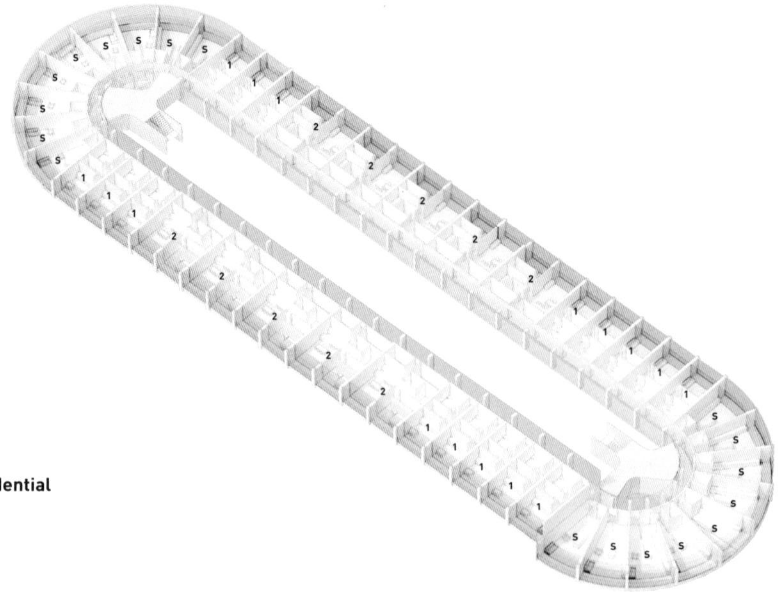

Conversion plan: Residential
S Studio
01 1 Bed
02 2 Bed

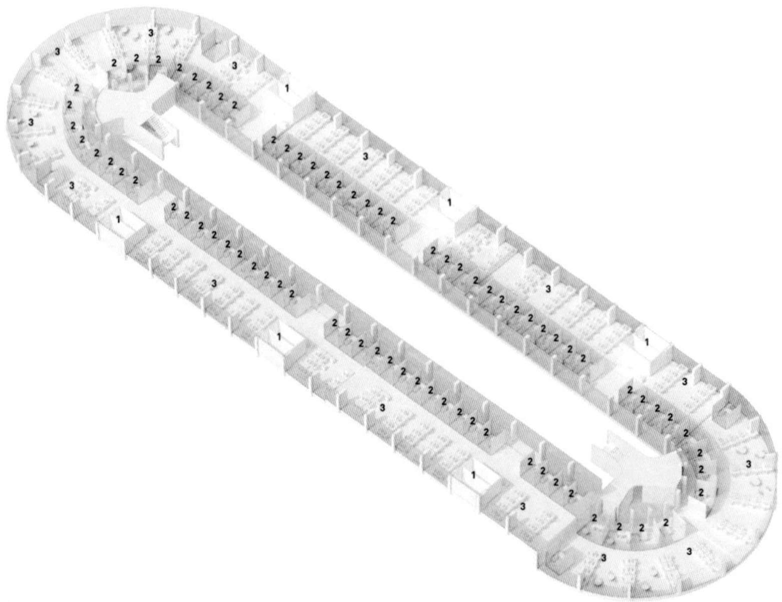

Conversion plan: Office
01 Meeting room
02 Work pods
03 Open work space

01 Living
02 Kitchen / dining
03 Restroom
04 Bedroom

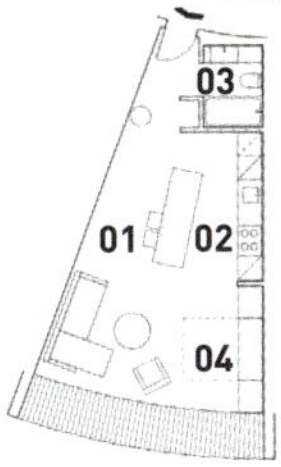

Studio [450 sqft]

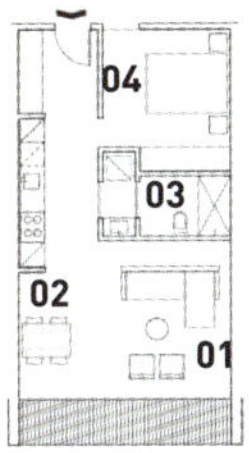

1 Bedroom [550 sqft]

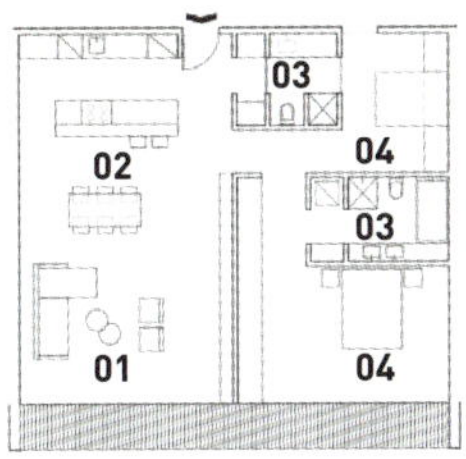

2 Bedroom [1100 sqft]

building.

BETWEEN

Communities are built on connections. As Danish architect and urban design innovator Jan Gehl says, "it is not buildings, but people and events, that need to be assembled. Concepts like floor area / site ratio and building density say nothing conclusive about whether human activities are adequately concentrated."

There are numerous design tools and strategies that can help support and foster connection. Beyond quantities such as square footage or number of bedrooms, the qualitative aspects of a place are what will attract people and encourage them to stay. Our research into this typology has been centred on the relationships between dwellings and ultimately between people, with an overarching mandate to create something of lasting value.

While the parameters vary widely from one project to another, we always focus on finding a way to include public spaces within each project's framework. The majority of our missing middle and mid-rise housing projects are characterized by one or a series of gathering places that expand the individual living space in order to support community building and weave the project into the existing urban fabric. We believe that these spaces are key ingredients in the creation of a successful project, as well as a vibrant and sustainable city.

In a European courtyard city like Barcelona, pushing multi-family buildings to the property line frees up the centre of the block for open space and shared uses. In North America, high efficiency targets paired with standard setback requirements often result in standalone pavilions surrounded by leftover strips of land that are too small to be programmed or even landscaped in a meaningful way. Beyond the lobby or a few small amenity rooms in buildings that can afford them (or where zoning by-laws require them), tenants have limited opportunities to connect with one another.

(Left) Johanna and her best friend Johanna Knekt sitting at their shared Piha circa 1980; (right) Johanna and her brother Jani Hurme ready to participate in the kids cross-country skiing competition on the Piha organized by their building complex's resident association.

Piha

Johanna Hurme

Five years into our practice, I was asked to speak at an inaugural PechaKucha storytelling event in Winnipeg. Having seen a few such presentations online, I wanted to share something personal rather than just show our recent projects. Through this process of reflection, it became clear to me what we had been doing out of instinct from the beginning – infusing shared public outdoor space into every housing project we had been commissioned to design, even if it was not part of the original brief.

This in-between space was something that both Sasa and I grew up with and became a defining element of our childhood experiences. Neither of us has ever lived in a single-family detached house, even after moving to Canada.

In my hometown of Helsinki, this place is called the *kortteli piha*, which roughly translates to a shared yard between apartment buildings. Consisting of a sandbox, swing set, play structures, some forest or garden space, benches, laundry lines and sports goals, it is the place where neighbourhood life unfolds. In winter the piha is transformed with ice skating rinks, snow piles for playing king of the hill and a Christmas tree decorated by the tenant board. This is the place where parents would feel comfortable leaving their children to play without supervision, where we would be called home for dinner through kitchen windows, where senior folk would sit and watch life go by, where cross-country skiing competitions would be held, where sleigh rides took place on special occasions and where families would gather for a leaf raking bee in the autumn.

European residential land use (left) versus North American (right).

The piha was the place where my identity was shaped, where I forged lifelong friendships and where I came to understand something about a territory that I felt ownership over, where safety was implied and perceived not with fences but through collective responsibility, and where my sense of community was closely connected to these physical boundaries. It was not mine or my family's, yet it was ours. In the Finnish language, you would say that you were from that piha (yard), not the building.

When I immigrated to Winnipeg on a more permanent basis in 1995, I lived in a very similar condominium complex made up of two buildings that were three storeys each. Yet the space between these buildings did not have play structures or grass to run on, no gardens or benches and certainly no identity – what it did have was a garbage enclosure and a parking lot.

In some ways these differences in approach are indicative of the values that each context and culture places on collective space. The lack of in-between space in North America perpetuates the devaluation of multi-family housing as a legitimate full lifecycle housing form – not just something acceptable for students, young professionals and seniors. As a practice we now believe that the piha is a missing ingredient that makes multi-family housing feasible on a larger scale.

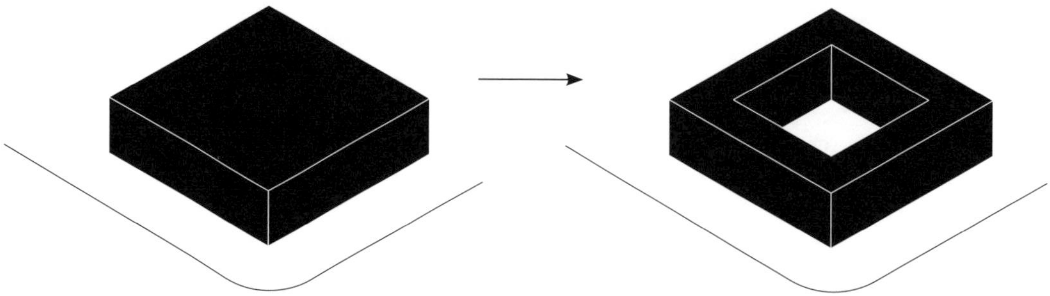

Carve for livability

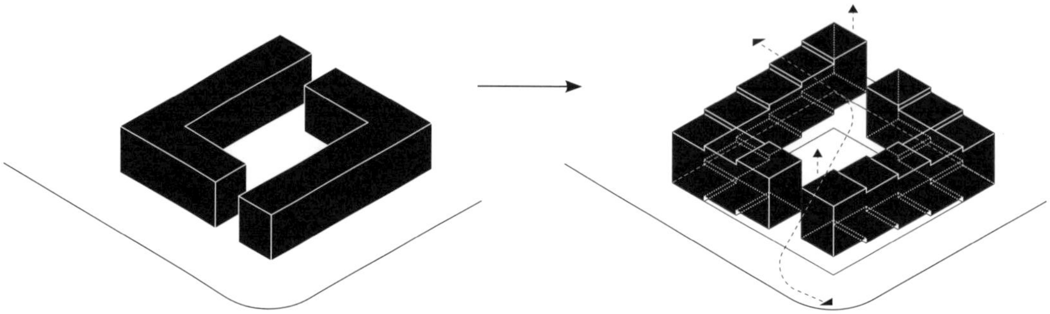

Facilitate access to shared spaces

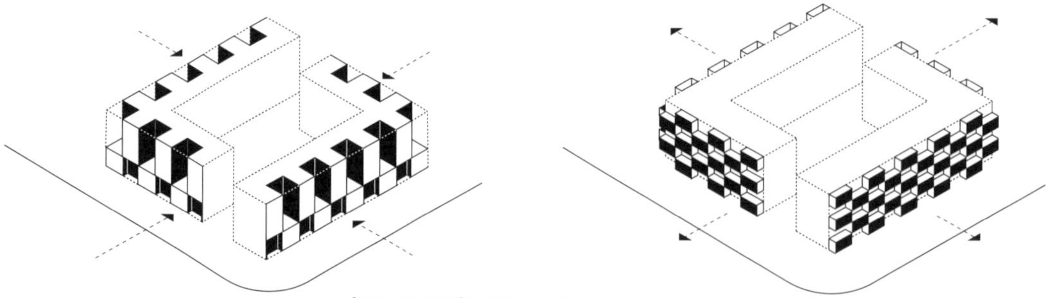

Increase perimeter + capture more space

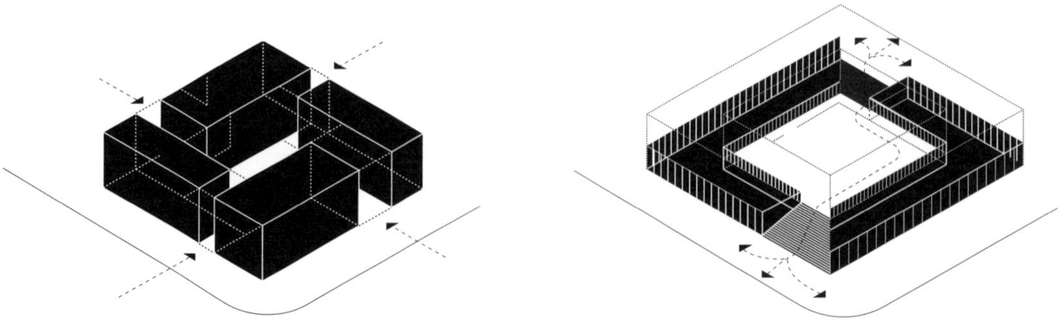

Expand public realm

In-between

Building the in-between is about capturing space for life to happen: space within, space below, space above, and space beyond the boundaries of a given site or setback condition.

From the shared courtyards of **Centre Village**, **Ross Avenue**, **BGBX** and **CY33** to the elevated block party of **youCUBE**'s rooftop patios, each project seeks out opportunities for social connection through specific design interventions. While **Bloc_10** provides an intimate interstitial space sheltered behind a wooden screen wall, **The Avenue** explores the potential for neighbourly connections while standing on dynamic projected balconies over one of Winnipeg's most iconic streets. **62M** and **Pumphouse** both shape shared experiences, redefining exterior circulation space as an opportunity for chance encounters with one another and with the city skyline by exposing dramatic urban views. At **90-100 Alexander**, a series of cuts through the ground plane draws the city in, creating moments to linger and exposing everyday occurrences to occupants and urban visitors.

When **Webbsite** was completed in 2005, the small seven-unit condominium development was one of the first downtown interventions of new infill housing in decades. We were on site taking photographs when the new owners came out of their homes one by one into the urban courtyard and started chatting. Soon enough they were on their way to share dinner at a nearby restaurant.

True communities are not built overnight. Once a project is sold and occupied, it takes on a life of its own, the outcome of which is hard to predict and is dependent on a range of factors, including building management and maintenance, the individual personalities of tenants, and market conditions.

Upon reflection, we can acknowledge that the communities we designed for have not always emerged, or they have emerged in ways that were unexpected. At the same time, we have witnessed first hand the beauty of what can happen when spaces are designed for connection to occur. The following pages consider a range of interventions – from intimate courtyards to grand staircases – and some of the inherent challenges and opportunities of each approach in turn.

Courtyards + plazas

A hidden sanctuary, a place to rest, a slice of nature or a private patio. Courtyards in their many forms and scales allow us to create a sense of enclosure and intimacy. They provide refuge from the urban milieu, and are particularly important for families with young children.

In the design of courtyards, solid and void come together and the shape of one informs the other. Through programming, landscaping and surface treatments – and through the furnishings and remnants of daily life that residents accumulate over time – each space develops its own unique yet evolving character. This character is also intrinsically tied to the architecture that surrounds it.

As our practice has evolved from small scale infill to larger mixed-use developments, these spaces have also grown in scale and complexity.

Clear and well defined courtyards are captured at the centre of **Ross Avenue**, **CY33** and **BGBX** housing projects, as well as on the southern portion of **Centre Village**, where the surrounding building mass acts to form the boundary of the shared outdoor space. At **90-100 Alexander**, **Pumphouse**, and at **youCUBE** the definition of the courtyards and plazas is more nuanced, consisting of a sequence of connected spaces that open and compress to accommodate pedestrian movement and activities within. Finally, at **Webbsite**, the common space is created with the help of an existing building face. Together the two projects form a well-defined, multi-functional courtyard within the larger urban fabric.

projects.MODELLING: CY33 (p. 108), 90-100 Alexander (p. 116), Centre Village (p. 64), Pumphouse (p. 112), youCUBE (60), Ross Avenue (p. 88), Webbsite (p. 52), BGBX (p. 56)

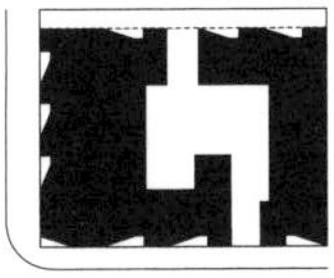

CY33

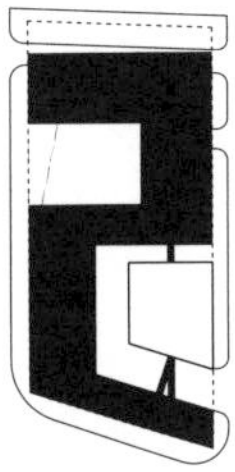

90-100 Alexander

Centre Village

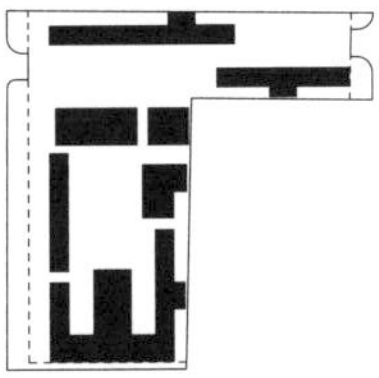

Pumphouse

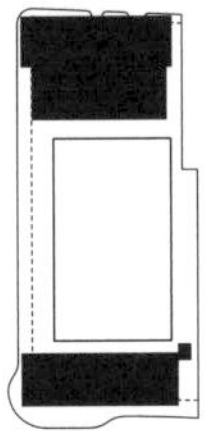

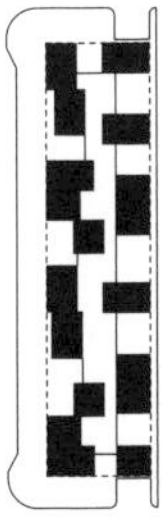

youCUBE

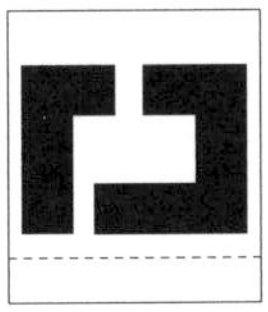

Ross Avenue

Webbsite

BGBX

Terraces + cutouts

Terraces, balconies and cutouts of the general building mass offer opportunities for private and shared outdoor spaces when larger common gathering areas may not be possible in tighter urban conditions. Generally, terraces, balconies and cutouts almost always add costs to the overall construction budget, yet provide value in livability for the end user, offsetting the costs of the developer in additional rent or sale price. In affordable housing scenarios, the livability value remains equally important, but may become more difficult to justify if the additional cost results in fewer suites or less interior square footage per suite.

OZ includes both inset balconies and cutout terraces through the building mass to notionally weave the city into the building and to strategically reduce the total interior building area of some of the suites' mezzanines to meet code. At **Bloc_10**, the terraces are located behind a unifying cedar screen. The individual terraces "cascade" on the façade to allow for interaction between neighbours, creating a semi-common outdoor space for the residents. **1885 Warehouse** features an external frame to support individual balconies. The building façade was pushed back from the street edge to create an entry porch for the commercial space beyond, allowing the weathering steel frame to rest on the original foundation. **The Avenue** balconies project out of the existing building face by as much as nine feet. Structurally, the balcony frame is supported by the existing floor plate that acts as a diaphragm, and diagonal steel members extend from the tip of the balcony to the maximum height of the guardrail at the exterior wall.

OZ

Bloc_10

Warehouse 1885

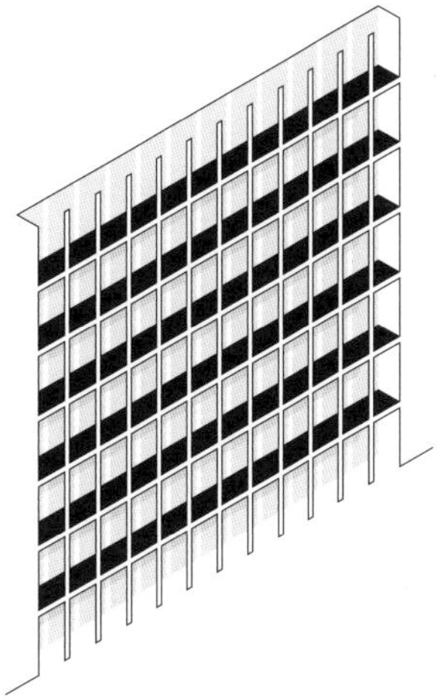

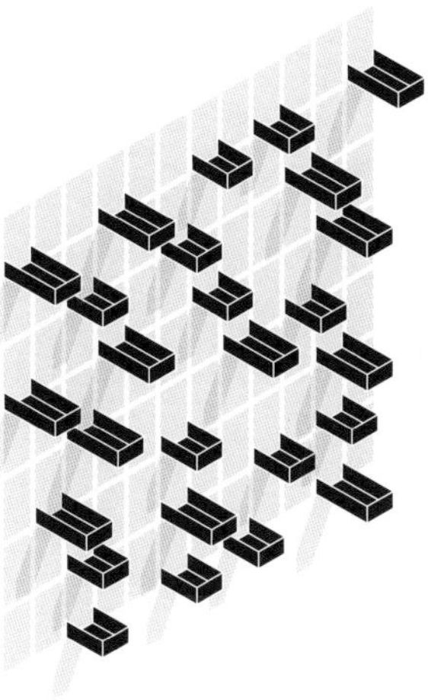

The Avenue

Roofs

Utilizing rooftops beyond the scope of mechanical equipment is an important consideration when space is at a premium. Green space on rooftops can combat the heat island effect, and in a multi-family scenario, provides a natural space for communal outdoor space.

When rooftop access is provided directly off an adjoining indoor floor area and the floor structure is continuous, insulation required on the roof area almost always results in a step-up scenario from the inside out, like the **BGBX** individual rooftop terraces. Providing a level access between the two requires more forethought and investment. Dropping the floor structure for the roof area in relation to the adjoining indoor floor space, or raising the indoor floor structure with additional frame are both possible, but more costly and more complicated propositions. At **90-100 Alexander**, the top floor elevator stop is set to a foot higher than the majority of the adjoining interior floor area to provide level access to the common rooftop. The interior corridor off the elevator then ramps down at 5% slope to also accommodate universal access to the residential suites.

A simpler scenario is presented by rooftops that involve very limited or no adjoining indoor floor space, as the height differential caused by insulation is effectively eliminated. This is the case with **62M**'s common rooftop terrace and **youCUBE**'s individual rooftop terraces.

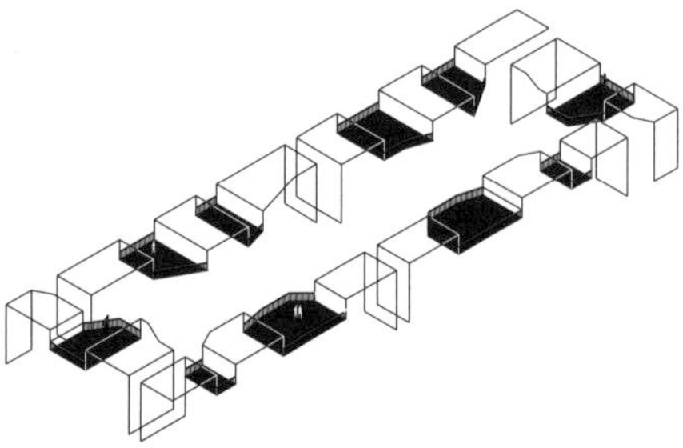

90-100 Alexander

BGBX

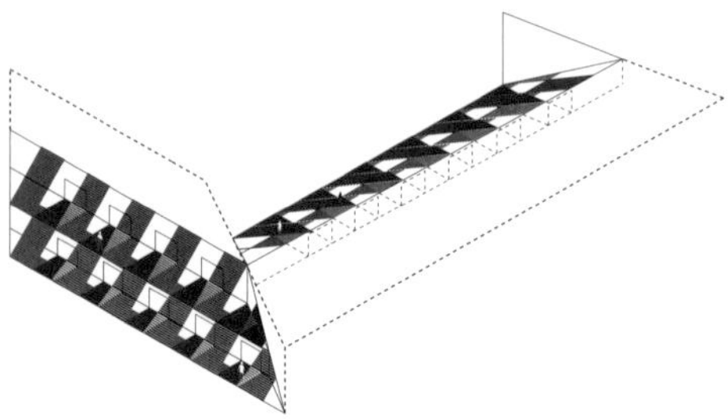

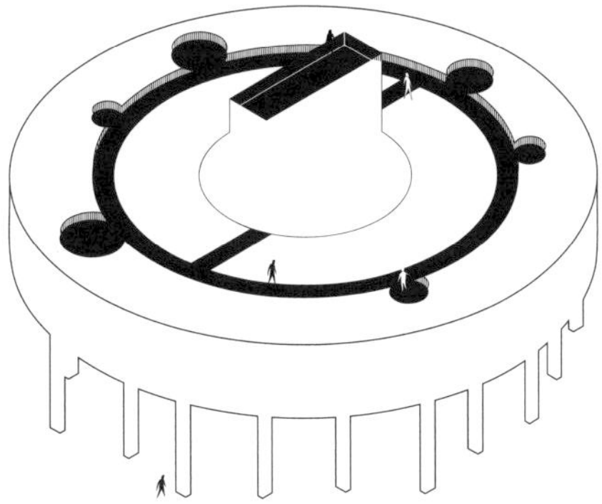

62M

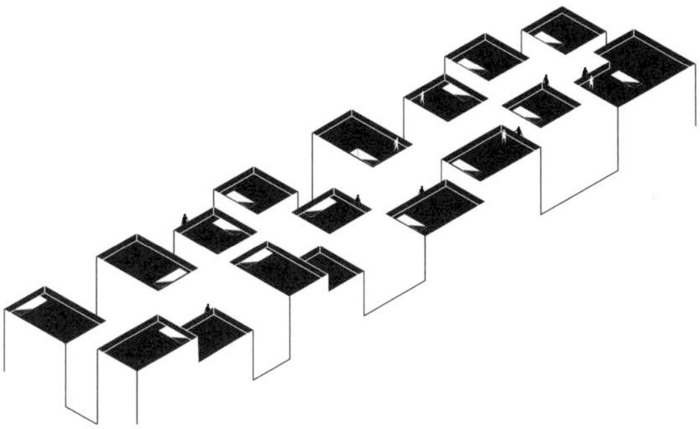

youCUBE

Passages + stairs

In tight urban conditions, almost any passage provides an opportune framework for interaction between neighbours, for kids to play, or for a welcome relief from indoor environments.

At-grade passages share similarities with courtyards. At **Webbsite**, a mews enhances the existing adjoining courtyard and provides residents with a multi-modal common outdoor space that accommodates vehicular access with four parking stalls, private patios and a common access "porch" animated by mature trees and greenery. **Centre Village** features a multi-use, multi-modal access path through the project connecting two adjoining streets, and due to its curbless, single-surface treatment, it fosters play and gathering. At **youCUBE**, the elevated exterior passageway not only acts as the access to all suites, but widens out on several locations to provide areas for gathering among neighbours, housing barbecues, planters and benches. Similarly, the generous landscape stairs leading to the common courtyard at **CY33** provides opportunities to pause and observe the street life while surrounded by planted greenery.

Higher up the building, exterior corridors and stairs can both perform the necessary exit functions and offer additional connection points for neighbours [**62M**, **CY33**], and an opportunity to enjoy extended views to the surrounding neighbourhood that are not typically offered by interior corridor or stair configurations [**Pumphouse**, **90-100 Alexander**].

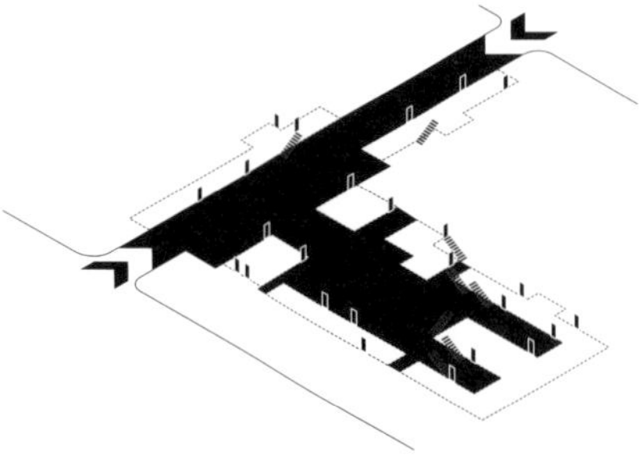

Centre Village

Webbsite

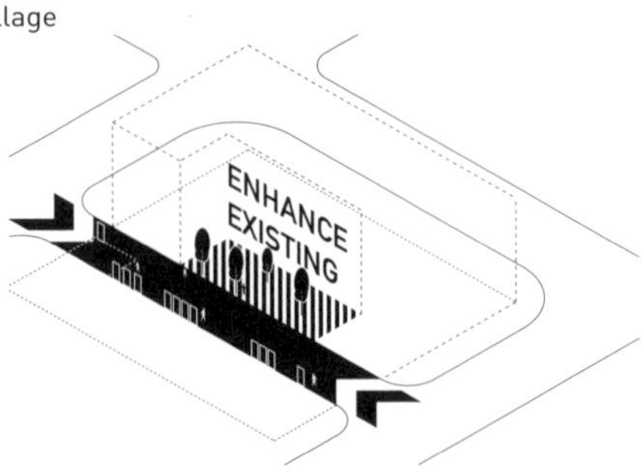

projects.MODELLING: Webbsite (p. 52), Centre Village (p. 64), 62M (p. 96), youCUBE (p. 60)

62M

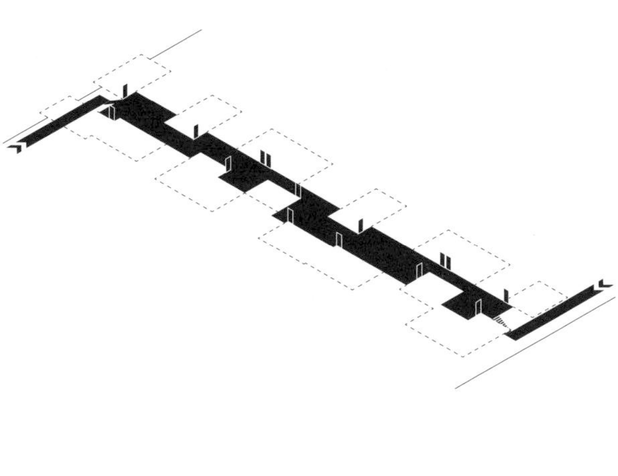

youCUBE

90-100 Alexander

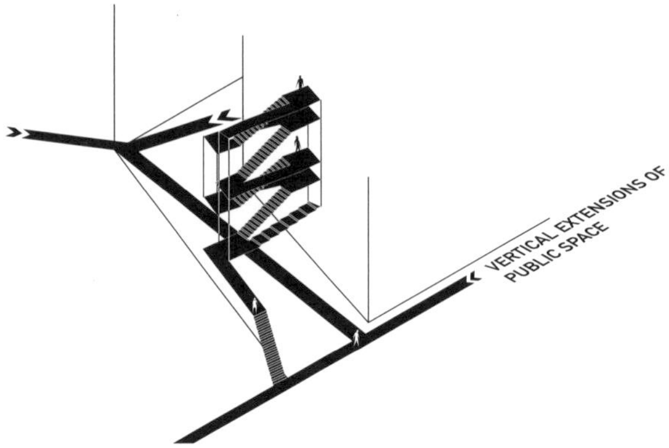

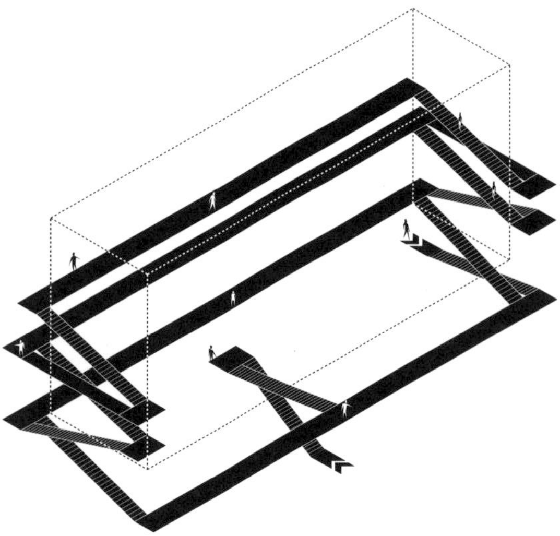

Pumphouse

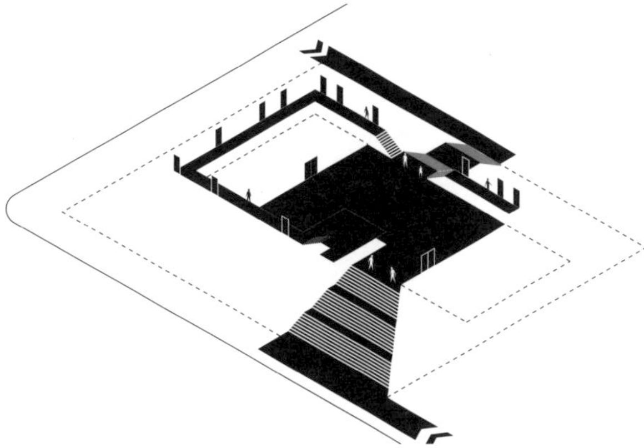

CY33

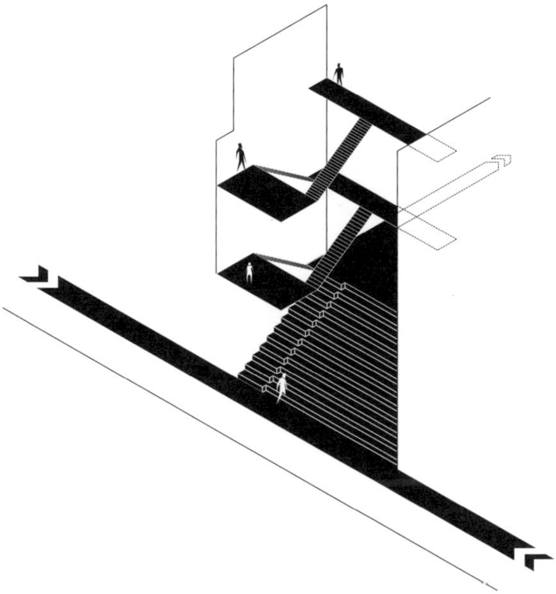

CY33

building.

LIVABILITY

Every design exploration that we undertake adds to a growing repertoire of planning strategies and tools that support our ability to create high-quality housing. Although our work began in Winnipeg with a series of small infill projects ranging from 10 to 25 units in scale, we are now operating in jurisdictions across Canada on multi-family projects with upwards of 700 units.

This section shares the broad lessons we have learned about where best to allocate resources and how to achieve an optimal result from the conflicting interests of efficiency versus quality of living. Although similar challenges and constraints exist in the United States, we have focused on Canada as it is the jurisdiction where we have the most firsthand knowledge and experience, providing an in-depth analysis of site conditions and a comparative study of projects that we have designed and completed to date.

As stewards of high-quality housing design, our profession must develop new strategies in order to overcome evolving challenges and constraints. Throughout this section, we list issues and potential solutions, and highlight a cross-section of micro design outcomes that have been tested by our practice in response to various missing middle and mid-scale housing briefs.

None of these individual solutions are especially ground-breaking, and may even seem rather obvious in some instances. However, we hope that gathering and sharing this learning might allow fellow practitioners to hit the ground running – and as a result, be able to spend their time providing the quality and innovation that is desperately needed to make mid-scale multi-family an attractive and attainable choice for more North Americans. Furthermore, perhaps these micro solutions can demonstrate that housing – even with its considerable limitations and "proven developer formulas" – can be challenged to carve out room for architecture, and ultimately, provide value for the built environment of our cities.

Without adequate policies or requirements in place by the authority having jurisdiction, the desire to create high-quality suites is often in direct conflict with the core reason that the private sector engages in development in Canada: profit.

As a result, efficiency targets must meet or exceed a typical minimum of 85% rentable or sellable square footage of the total building area. The traditional outcome of this proforma objective is very deep units with limited access to natural light and operable windows. This is particularly true with smaller multi-family units that generally require more corridor space for access, when compared to larger suites at the corners of building plates that enable the corridor to be shorter and thus more efficient.

In New South Wales, Australia, an Apartment Design Guide (developed in collaboration with council, industry partners and community members) sets a benchmark for better practice in the design of multi-family buildings. The document encourages and mandates that architects and developers strive for innovation and improve the

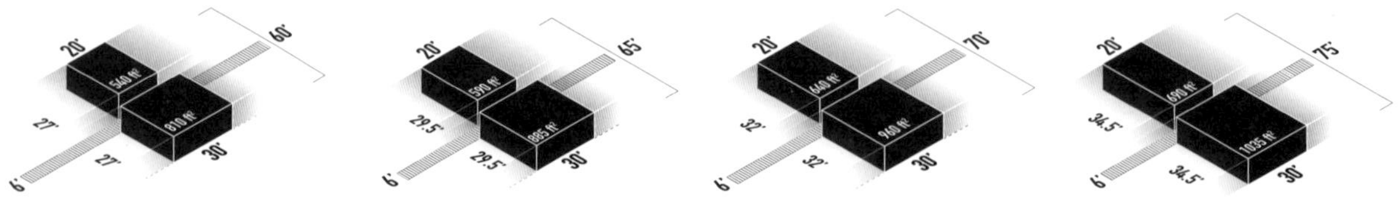

Maintaining access to natural light increases dwelling size when increasing building depth.

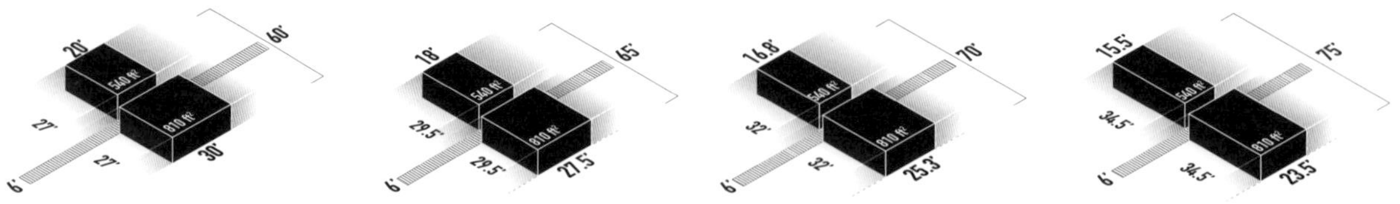

Maintaining dwelling sizes reduces access to natural light when increasing building depth.

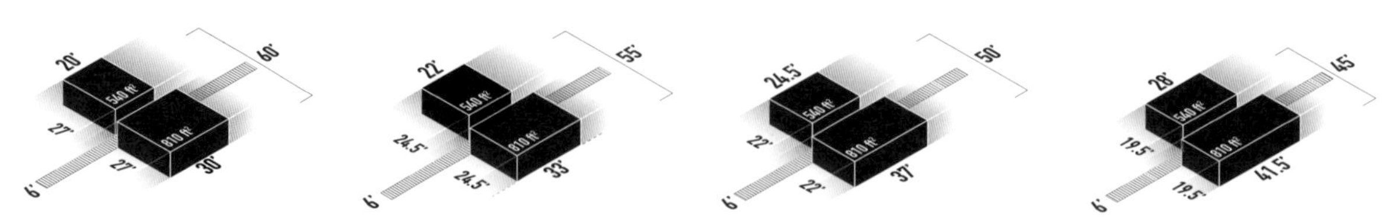

Maintaining dwelling sizes increases access to natural light when decreasing building depth.

livability of units with an emphasis on layout efficiencies, apartment depth and ceiling heights, solar access, natural ventilation and visual privacy. Additional focus is placed on enhanced amenity offerings both inside and outside the building.

Although some Canadian jurisdictions have mandated basic design standards for social or affordable housing, they are typically focused on cost effectiveness and efficient project delivery. Despite the leadership efforts of our national voices for architecture and housing, the Royal Architectural Institute of Canada (RAIC) and the Canada Mortgage and Housing Corporation (CMHC), there is currently no governing document with the specific goal of advancing design excellence and best practice for multi-family housing developments.

To fill this gap, a trio of Canadian academics (together with industry experts) created the Multi-Unit Residential Building (MURB) Design Guide for design professionals, in order to enhance livability and provide benchmarks for multi-family housing in a Canadian context. The document has not been formally adopted and the authors acknowledge that it is only intended as a "knowledge map" or cognitive framework toward a more integrative approach, one that will hopefully have more influence in the future with adequate political support. In its epilogue, the authors also point out that architecture education in Canada does not currently include multi-unit residential building design as part of the core curriculum, despite the growing prevalence of this building typology in professional practice.

In Canada, the National Building Code (NBC) defines egress requirements for multi-family developments. Individual provinces can then propose amendments and create their own provincial codes. In British Columbia and Manitoba, every bedroom requires an operable window or exterior door, except where the building is sprinklered. In Ontario, an egress window need only be supplied on the floor level where the bedroom is contained. The results can be mixed on both ends of the spectrum. In some cases, bedrooms receive limited or no access to natural light. In others, the requirement for bedroom windows can result in layouts where the living room and bedroom are jammed together at the perimeter and both rooms are below standard in width, making furniture placement difficult and resulting in excessively dark utility areas at the back of the suite.

Another limiting design factor that is largely unique to Canada (and the United States) is the requirement for two exit stairs, whereas in many circumstances in much of Europe and elsewhere permits a single exit stair. The provision of two exit stairs generally results in double loaded corridors, making it difficult, if not impossible, to incorporate double aspect units with proper cross ventilation and access to light on opposite façades.

These three parameters present a series of challenges for architects hoping to achieve a fundamental quality of living for the end user: deep suite plans resulting from the private sector's focus on profit and efficiency, a lack of governing policy, and the requirement for two exits.

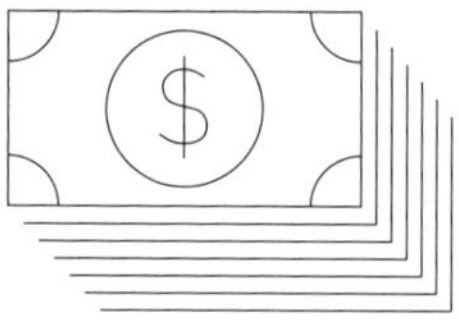

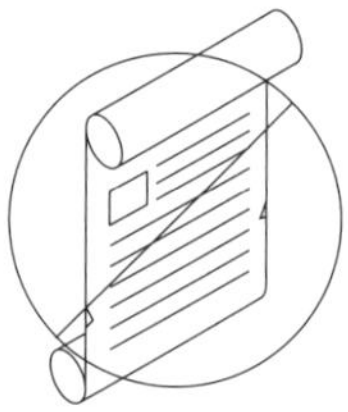

There are multiple factors at play in the demands of site planning and zoning requirements as well. There is a notable contrast between high and low land value cities and how they accommodate each element in turn. Land costs and parking requirements often dictate how buildings can be shaped and what area is left for recreation and enjoyment. In high land value cities like Vancouver, Toronto and Calgary, construction costs and underground parking requirements necessitate an efficient parking grid that often dictates the general measurements of the building plates – and in some cases, the suite demising walls above unless a transfer slab is implemented. In low land value cities like Winnipeg, and in places where the water table and soil conditions make it very expensive to build underground parking, surface parking requirements can take up the majority of the site area aside from the building footprint.

Indoor and outdoor amenity areas present another point of departure. The inclusion of indoor amenity space in low land value cities is often dictated by market demands and thus typically reserved for the luxury condominium market where buyers are willing and able to pay for shared fitness centres or rooftop patios, and may choose one building over another based on the amenities that are available. In high land value cities, indoor and outdoor amenity requirements are often mandated as part of

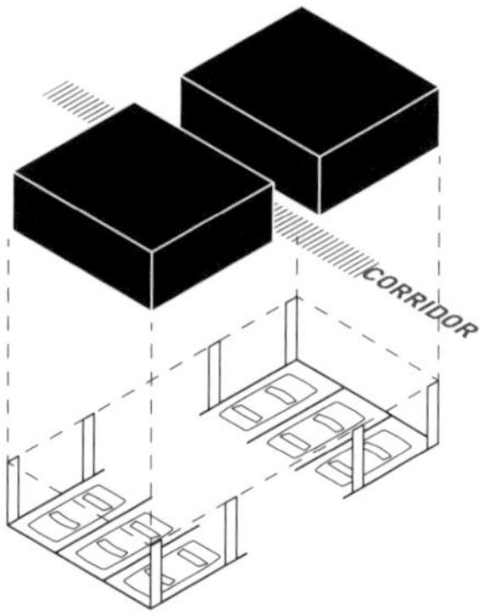

Parking grid vs building plate

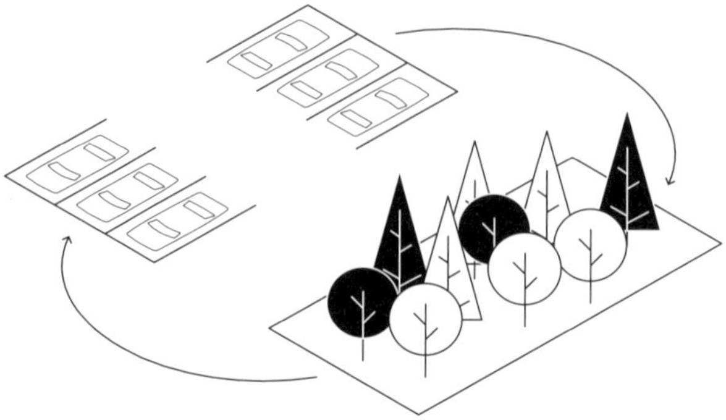

Surface parking vs public space

the zoning by-law and calculated as a square footage requirement per dwelling unit. Some cities, including Surrey and Calgary, also require the inclusion of balconies for all dwelling units in a multi-family project of a certain scale. Similar requirements do not exist in Winnipeg, where margins are tight and developers would balk at any square footage demands that might impact their bottom line.

In high land value areas where public green space is prioritized as part of planning conditions, by-law requirements for landscaped areas support the design team's ability to build in common shared outdoor amenity space. In Winnipeg, landscape requirements are reduced to shrub and tree planting for street edges in required setbacks. As a result, elements like internal courtyards must be integral to the building design, so that they do not present an extra cost for the developer.

Generally speaking, achieving quality inside and out in a multi-family housing project is a battle for building perimeter.

More exterior envelope equals more space for windows and thus access to natural light, but not so much that the envelope costs become excessive. The battle extends to frontage and extended views: buildings on property lines are not useful as they do not provide additional window frontage. In the case of infill conditions, corner lots are always more advantageous than mid block.

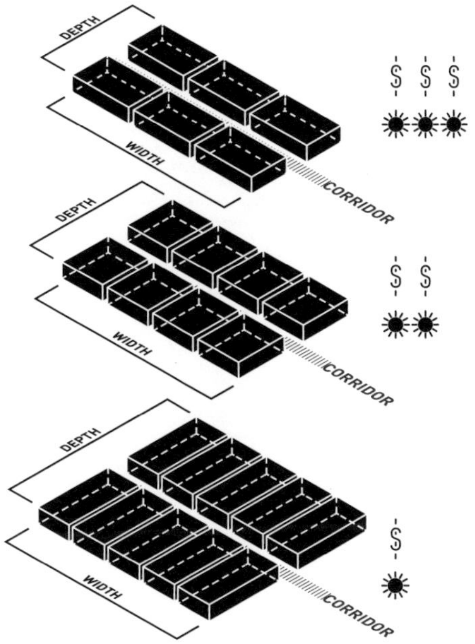

Battle for building perimeter

Challenging contexts

As cities evolve and industries shift away from core areas or downsize in physical scale due to digitization, leftover industrial parcels and more challenging sites will need innovative solutions to transform them into attractive residential uses.

The past few decades have produced multiple well-published examples of such large scale transformations. As densification efforts in urban centres mature, the fight for more land and building area will continue to put pressure on land values and building heights, to the detriment of mid-scale infill. In all likelihood, more and more odd or tight slivers of land with limited exposure or street frontage will become prime development sites for missing middle housing.

We've determined five distinct responses that all attempt to creatively address their immediate site condition: **Lift**, **Flip**, **Stagger**, **Undulate** and **Gather**.

Context for 62M and youCUBE in 2012 (above) and 2022 (below).

Lift

Located at the foot of an elevated freeway, **62M** is entirely land-locked behind an industrial building and the blank party wall of another infill project.

The project began with the development group asking whether or not the site could be feasible for housing. Lifting the residential floors off the ground and above the freeway is certainly not a classic case for city making, but felt necessary in the context of a rather hostile urban condition. The move also supported the developer's proforma requirement for a 1:1 ratio of surface parking, now located below the underbelly of the elevated housing.

The resulting circular form arose in direct response to the need for trade off cost saving measures. The round shape offered a 30% reduction in envelope from a traditional orthogonal plan. Limiting the building to three storeys under the NBC made it possible to construct the residential floors above the initial platform out of prefabricated wood elements, true modularity lending itself to construction efficiencies. The continuous window face offers panoramic views of downtown Winnipeg, the river and the neighbourhoods beyond, elevating residents above previously compromised views.

62M

Flip

youCUBE, the next door neighbour to **62M**, was the first residential project to be built at the edge of this slowly transforming industrial area.

In addition to the shared outdoor deck that doubles as a roof for the parking stalls below, the simple individual suite volumes of two, three, and four levels each contain vertically arranged interior spaces, essentially one room per floor. On the initiative of the young developer, the typical townhouse style arrangement was turned upside down for half of the suites, allowing the living room the best view over the industrial context. Every suite culminates with a rooftop terrace.

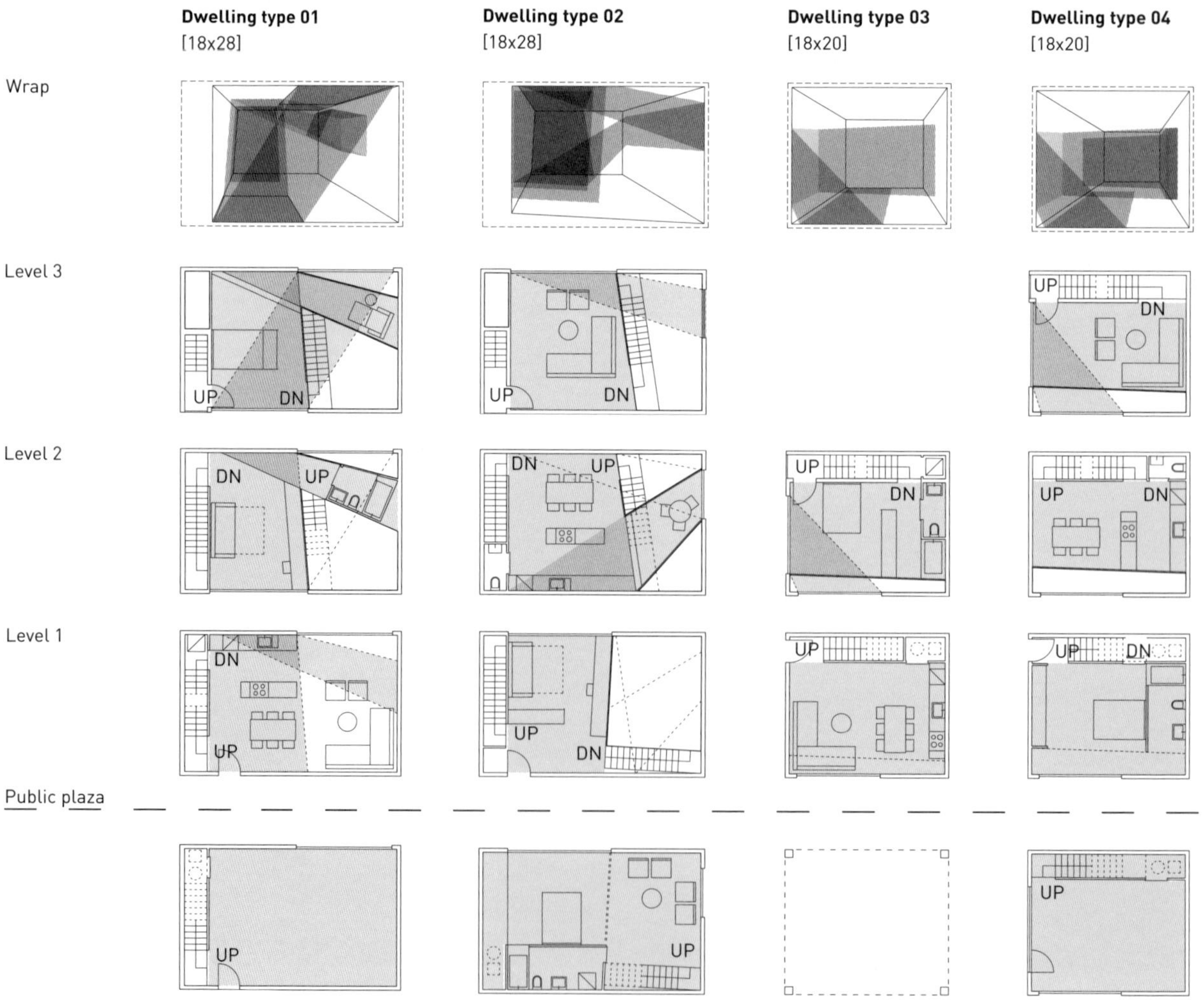

youCUBE

Stagger

Located on the site of a former gas station on a busy arterial street, **Bloc_10** was tied to an existing zoning agreement that allowed for ten suites.

Due to the 100-foot street frontage, a simple double aspect townhouse arrangement was not feasible as it would have limited each suite to a ten foot width. In this instance, breaking the allowable building mass into 30 blocks, 15 per building face, and connecting them internally with a central stair and utility spine allowed each three storey unit to be a more generous 18 feet in width, while maintaining exposure to both sides of the building. Interestingly, this "jenga" arrangement also made eight of the ten units into corner suites with triple exposure.

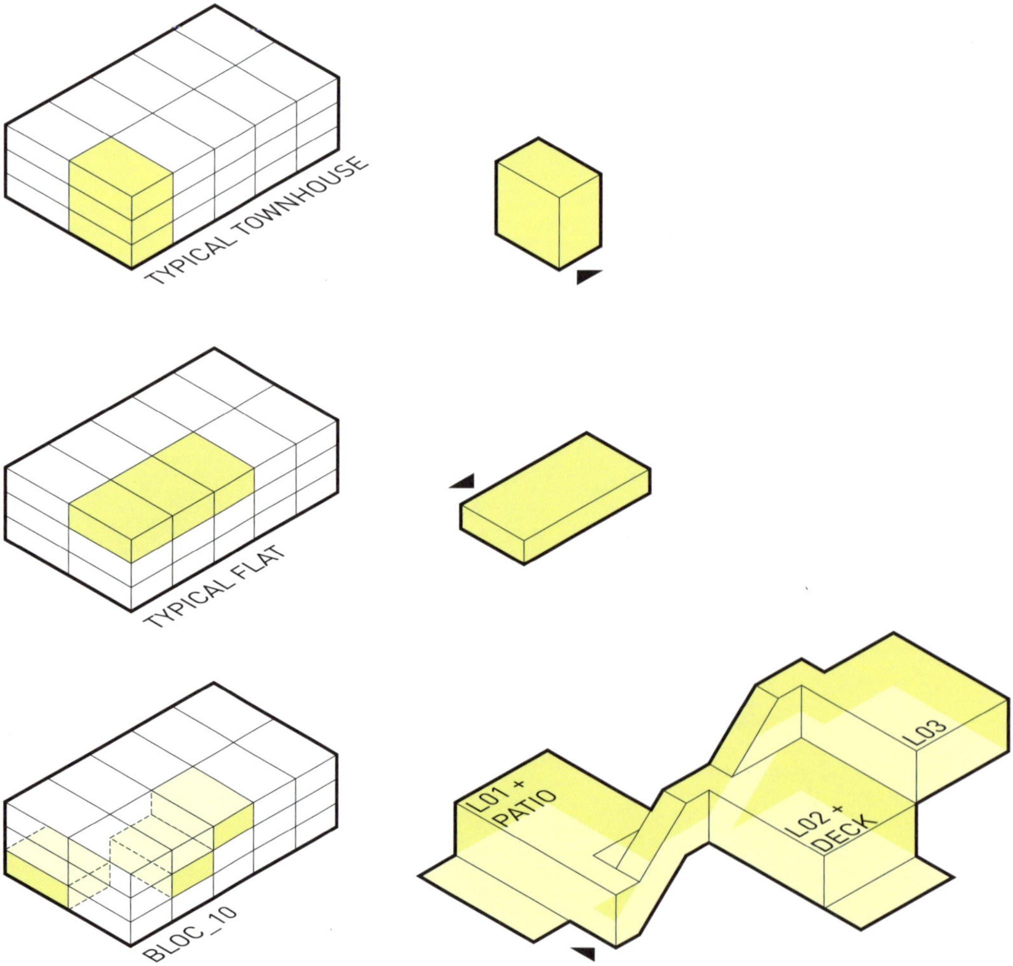

 projects.MODELLING: Bloc_10 (p. 72)

Bloc_10 key plans

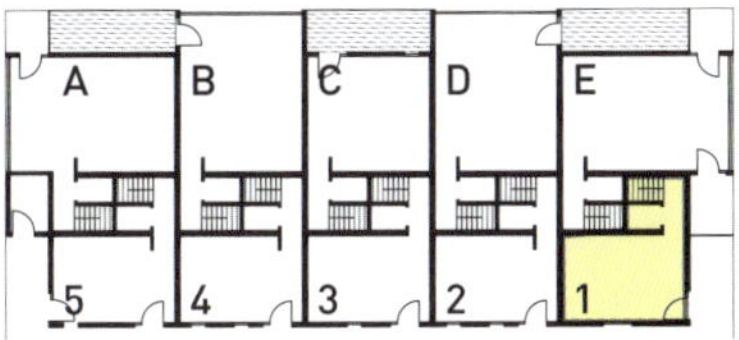

Level 3

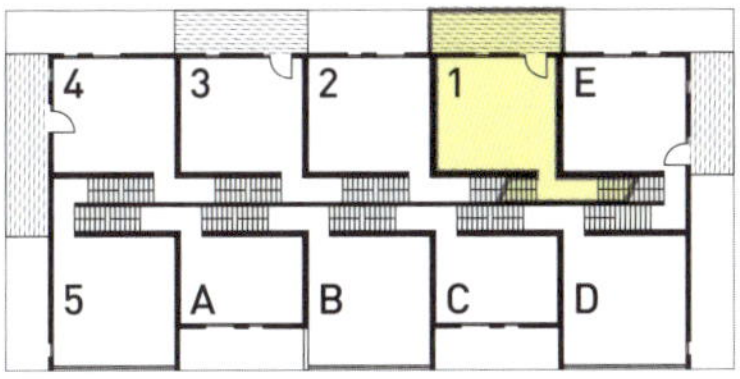

Level 2

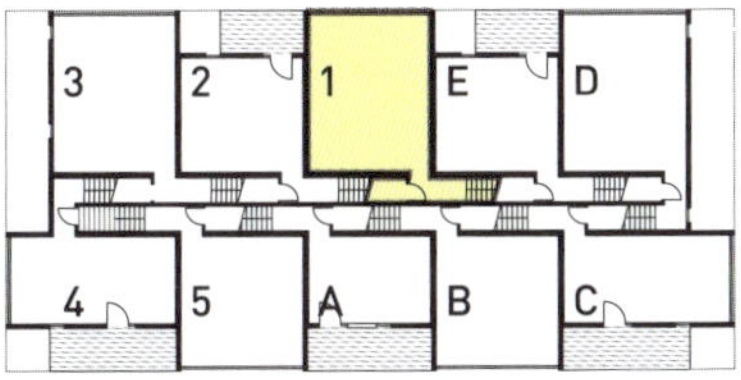

Level 1

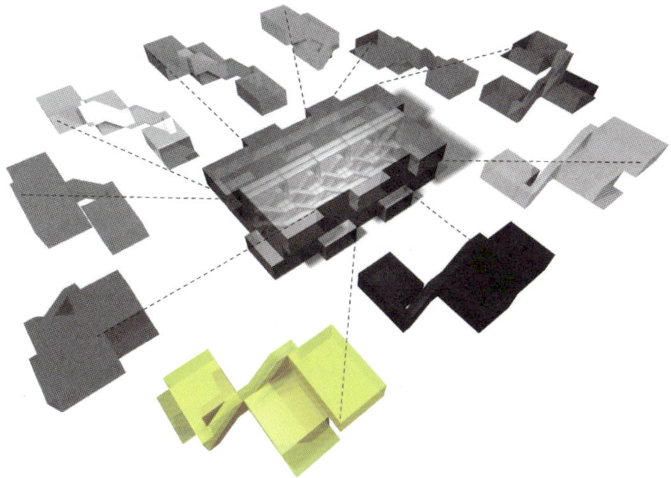

Bloc_10

Undulate

Typical mid-block infill projects contend with a plot depth that is not optimal for mid-rise housing.

The 100-135 foot depths found in mature neighbourhoods across Canada make it difficult to optimize sites for multi-family housing, considering 60-foot-deep floor plates are required for adequate unit layouts. Due to these constraints, full potential of infill sites is rarely realized and land cost per unit remains high.

LIFE uses a similar, but simplified packing strategy to **Bloc_10**. The limited frontage of this mid-block site is expanded for necessary window exposure to accommodate the required 84 one and two bedroom suites through the undulating façade and seven open-air lightwells along the common corridor.

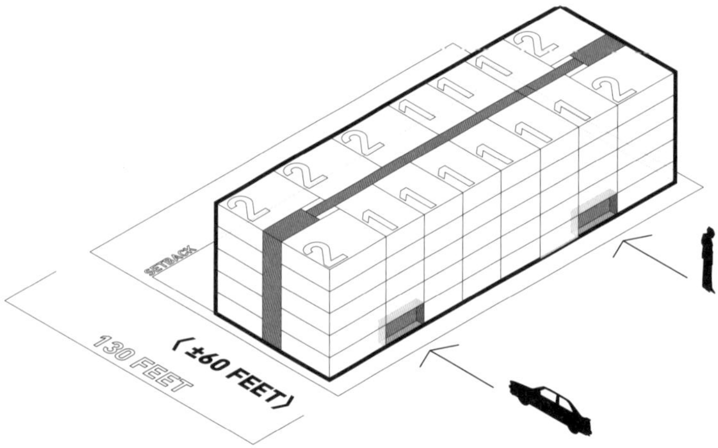

Typical scenario
Building footprint: 10,800 sf

The test scenario shows 15 units per floor [6 two-bed and 9 one-bed] for a total of 70 suites [after lobbies, elevators, utility rooms and entrances are accommodated].

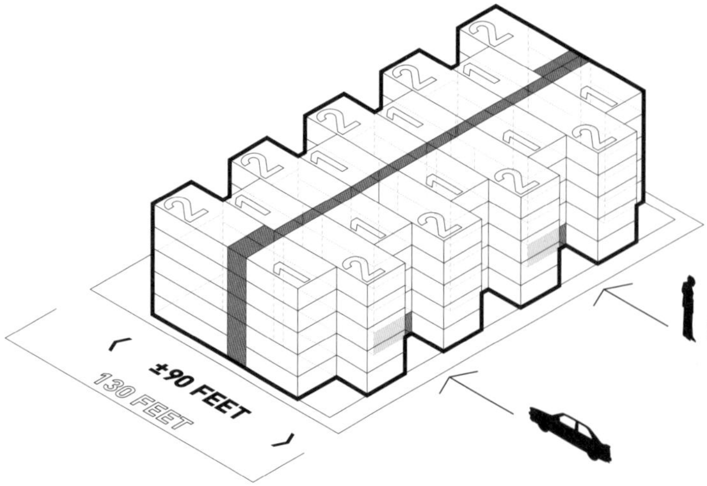

LIFE scenario
Building footprint: 13,800 sf

Undulating the façade creates 18 units per floor for a total of 84 suites [9 two-bed and 9 one-bed], a 20% increase from the typical scenario.

LIFE

Gather

In some instances creating "defensible" exterior space at grade makes the most sense when the context presents challenges in either real or perceived security.

In the instance of **Ross Avenue** Affordable Housing, the site is located in a low income inner city neighbourhood with a number of social housing projects in the immediate context. Through the community consultation process, it became clear that a courtyard arrangement would provide an additional layer of protection for individual at-grade suite entrances with the oversight of the neighbours, and the courtyard communal space could lend itself well for play and gathering by kids, families and seniors.

The required building mass is organized into two L-shaped blocks around the site's perimeter, which forms a built-in enclosure around the 56x32 foot semi-private courtyard at the centre of the blocks. The two access points into the courtyard lead to the sidewalk along Ross Street, and a public back lane where at-grade parking and garbage collection are located. While not always necessary, the client, a non-profit community organization, opted to include a gate at each entry point for added protection.

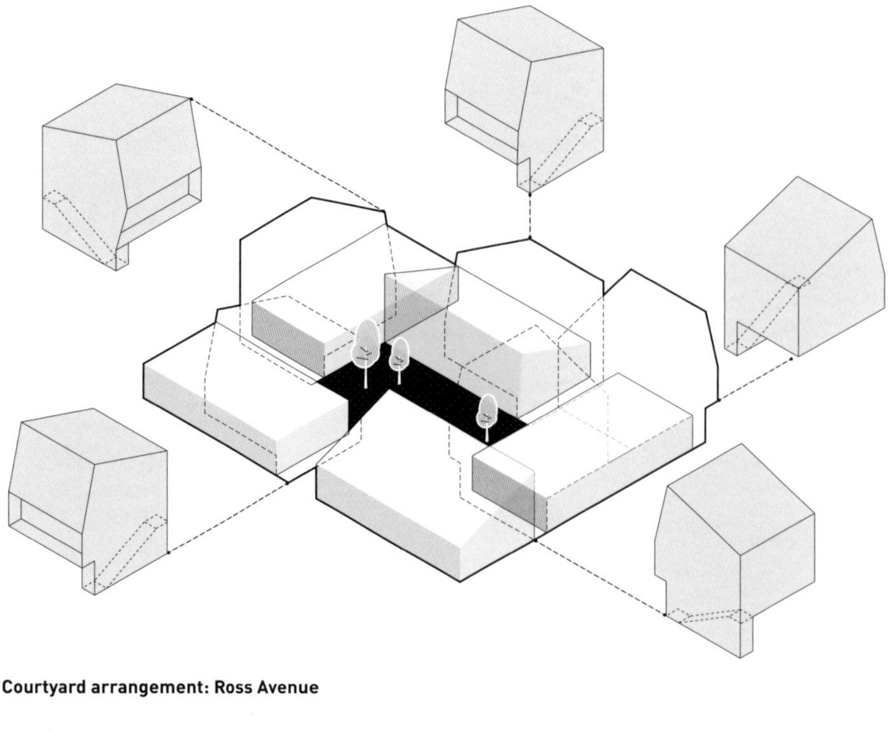

Courtyard arrangement: Ross Avenue

projects.MODELLING: Ross Avenue (p. 88)

Ross Avenue

More levels (OZ)

More units (548 Stradbrook)

Increased area (Bloc_10)

Step back strategies (CY33)

Intelligent zoning

Hand-in-hand with efficiency, it is often necessary to maximize the allowable zoning envelope of any given site, or even exceed it, in order to meet the client's proforma and carve out room for architectural quality elsewhere.

Considering an architect's ethical and civic responsibilities, these are not straightforward decisions and often paint the picture that architects have little concern for the immediate neighbours. At the same time, the creative introduction of infill density in urban locations has much wider and broader benefits to the community and city as a whole.

Some of the zoning strategies that have allowed us to creatively add density, increase building area or reset formal expectations without needing to apply for re-zoning or re-classification fall under four categories: **More levels**, **More units**, **Increased area** and **Step back strategies.**

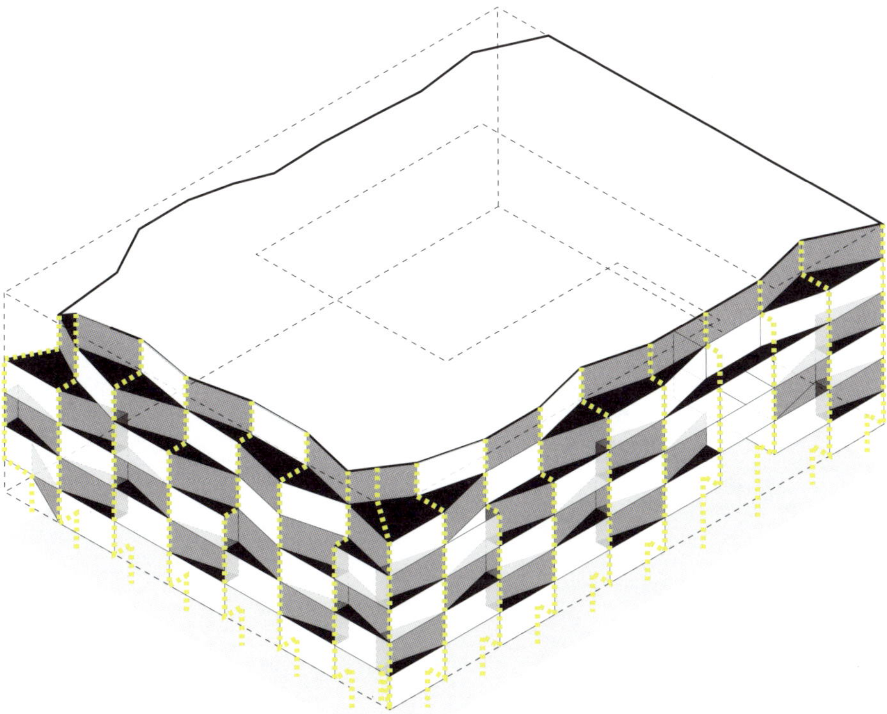

More levels

When building storeys are limited by zoning by-laws or local area plans, other strategies can be employed to increase buildable square footage.

For **OZ** Condominiums, it was possible for us to achieve seven building levels within a site classification that allowed for a maximum of five storeys or 60 foot building height, through the use of two mezzanine levels within the building. While we exceeded the 60 foot height limitation by 5%, this was minimal enough to be dealt with as an internal administrative process by the planning department. Naturally, increasing the building capacity of the site with two additional levels not only improved the client's proforma by amortizing land costs over more sellable square footage, but also allowed for a greater variety of suite types within the building, emphasized by the dimensional checkboard setback composition and effectively paying for the loft areas required for the mezzanines.

At **youCUBE**, the nine housing units that face the street include an atypical basement level two feet below grade and six feet above, which is not considered an additional storey under the National Building Code – another play for increased efficiency.

For **CY33**, although the Marda Loop neighbourhood's Area Redevelopment Plan (ARP) dictated a four-storey building for this gateway intersection, by incorporating the public courtyard, we were able to obtain approval for a six-storey building in exchange for this community benefit.

Unit composition: OZ
A Townhouse
B Flat
C Loft
D Penthouse

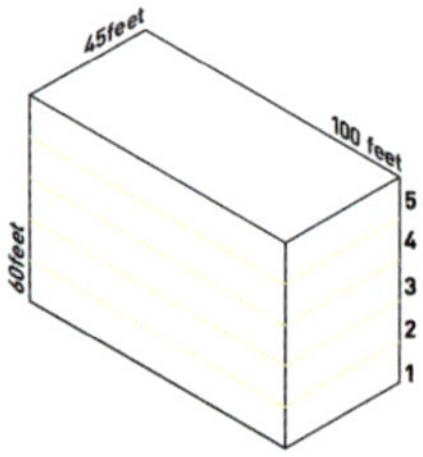

01 Site zoning classification permits a maximum of 5 storeys.

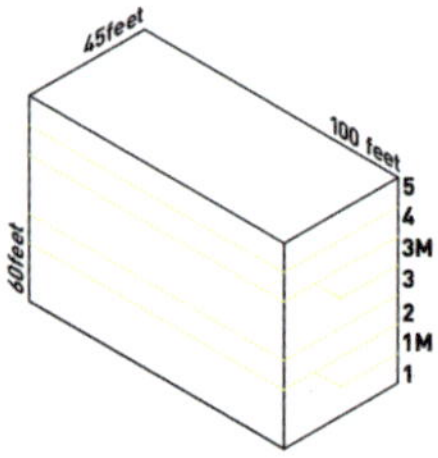

02 Introducing mezzanines on 2 levels improves client's proforma.

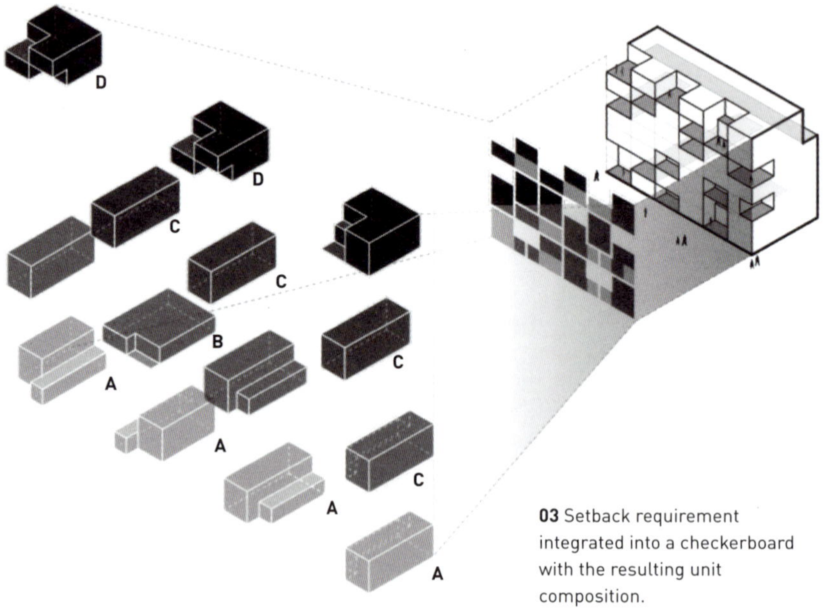

03 Setback requirement integrated into a checkerboard with the resulting unit composition.

 projects.MODELLING: OZ (p. 84), youCUBE (p. 60), CY33 (p. 108)

OZ

More units

Similarly, it has been possible for us to incorporate additional units where the zoning by-law mandated a maximum unit count.

For **548 Stradbrook**, a vacant single-family residence was replaced by an eight-unit condominium building. Based on the maximum permitted density calculated as a factor of square feet of lot area per dwelling unit, only six units were initially supported by the planning department. As a result, while the number of units required a conditional use, the allowable zoning envelope remained the same regardless of how many units the volume contained. In essence, the only adverse effect on the surrounding mature mixed-use neighbourhood of single-family homes, commercial businesses and apartment blocks was increased density and the potential for a few more cars accessing the back lane – parking for which was accommodated on site at a 1:1 ratio. As a result, we were able to obtain the necessary approvals to supply eight reasonably sized suites (six two-bed flats and two three-bed lofts) within the same envelope.

At **Welcome Place**, only 23 units were permitted by zoning, although the organization's true housing needs were much greater. The project uses a similar strategy to 548 Stradbrook in that the increased unit count did not impact the overall building massing, but merely allowed the client group to better respond to the changing needs of the incoming refugee population. The use of the common vestibule for two adjoining suites made it possible to accommodate a variety of family sizes at any given time, turning 23 units into 30 smaller suites as needed.

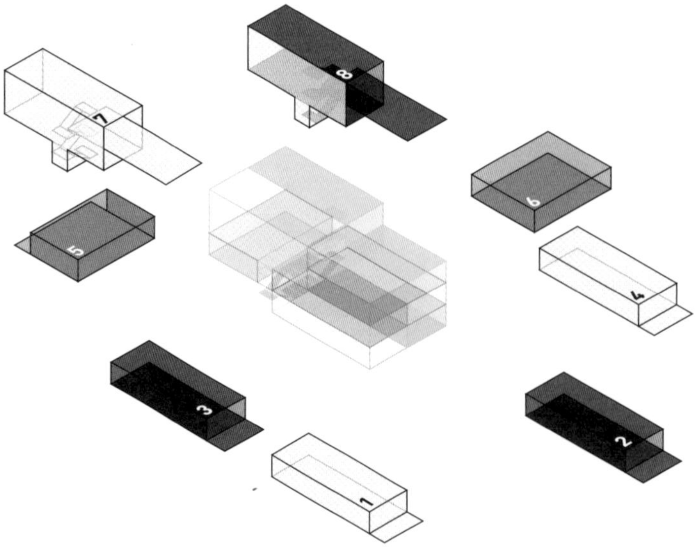

Unit composition: 548 Stradbrook

 projects.MODELLING: 548 Stradbrook (p. 80), Welcome Place (p. 68)

Increased area

On a smaller scale, zoning by-laws can also provide room for creative thought within their limitations.

For **Bloc_10**, a clause that permitted a specific percentage of bay-window projections into the front yard setback was used to expand the living areas in a checkerboard pattern across the façade that increased the recaptured building area.

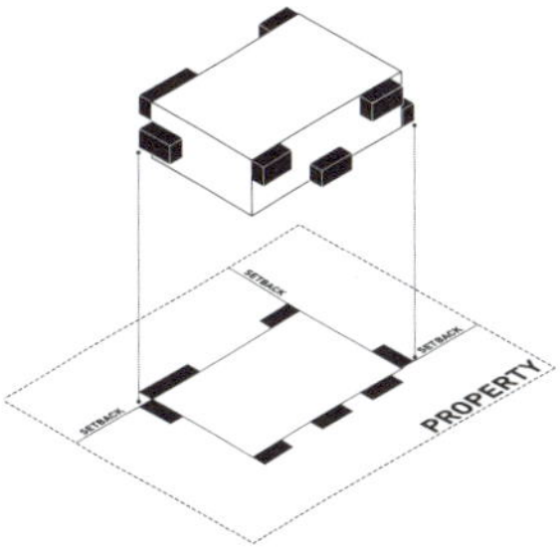

Bloc_10

Step back strategies

A widely used zoning strategy in many jurisdictions involves some type of step back requirement for higher building levels, alleviating any adverse effects on neighbouring properties from shadowing and/or an imposing building mass.

These requirements often result in a rather banal and unimaginative cake-layering effect. We have been able to reinterpret the by-law in order to avoid an expected outcome.

The zoning rules for **CY33** in Calgary required a progressive setback of the top two floors on the street façade of the six-storey building, as well as a 45° angle on the back lane, measured 7.5 meters up from the far edge. Here we masked the step back requirement through the folding, checkered pattern of the façade, derived from the alternating balcony and window configuration on the lower levels, aimed at giving sky back to the city.

LIFE is a mid-rise rental housing project in Calgary, featuring 84 tightly packed one and two bedroom suites in a mid-block site over five storeys. The project maximizes its allowable FAR on a heavily sloped site while folding back the top four storeys of the building mass, reducing its appearance on the street and lane.

OZ Condominiums present a basic trade off. The neighbourhood design guidelines dictated that a certain portion of the upper levels must be stepped back. Instead of simply sloping the top of the building to suit, we met the requirement by crenelating the top two floors, turning the in-between spaces into terraced balconies.

Setbacks: OZ

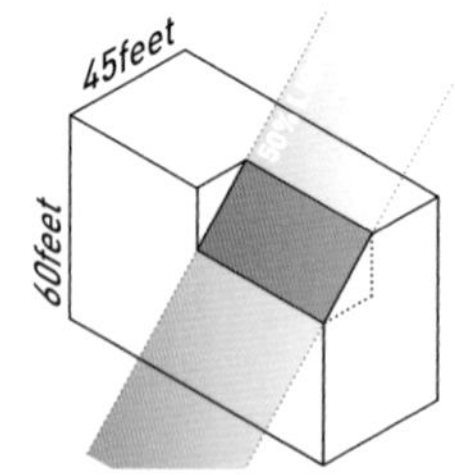

01 50% of upper 2 storeys must be setback from street.

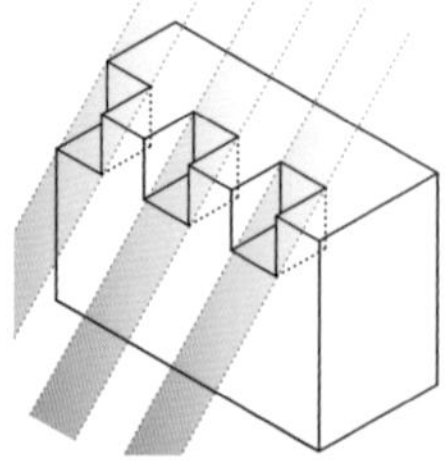

02 Setback requirement is integrated into building

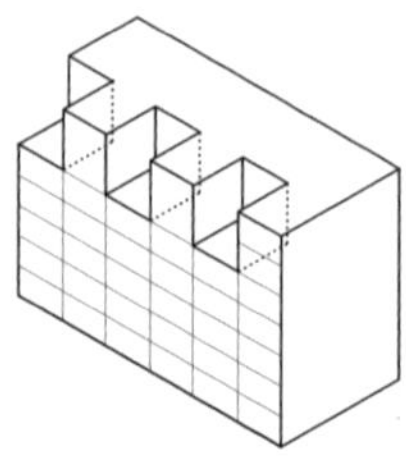

03 Checkerboard is carried through all levels.

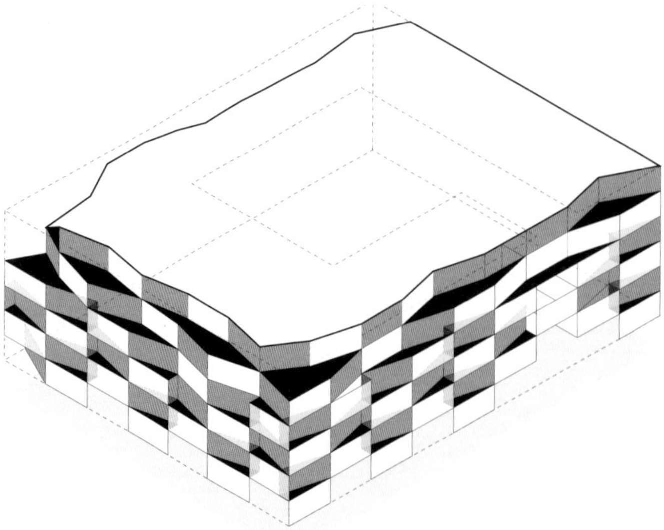

Setbacks: CY33

CY33

Structural alignment (62M)

Minimize parking (Centre Village)

Surface quilt (Rundle)

Dual-purpose plaza (youCUBE)

Parking potential

Parking requirements tend to put various pressures on mid-scale housing, especially when zoning dictates a minimum quantity of stalls based on proposed suite counts. Fortunately, many jurisdictions across North America are moving away from minimum parking requirements in lieu of letting developers and market conditions determine the appropriate number of stalls. There is also a push for increased bicycle parking and electric car charging stations in an effort to build more sustainable transportation into projects.

In low land value cities, especially when soil conditions present a challenge, required parking often ends up on the surface adjacent to the building, taking up the majority of any remaining site area. This is especially true when local by-laws lack requirements for on-site landscaping or maximum lot coverage. Accessory surface parking is, of course, the low cost alternative to structured or underground parking, but generally detrimental to the quality of on-site spaces for people as well as the surrounding urban environment.

Structured parking carries a significant price tag, in the region of $35,000 - $50,000 per stall in Winnipeg and Calgary at the time of writing. As a result, it is essential to consider the distance between any new affordable/attainable housing and nearby employment opportunities or services, as well as proximity to public transit, cycling networks or car co-op programs, in order to reduce the need for vehicle ownership over the long-term.

The various ways we have dealt with the design realities and additional cost of parking, whether structured, covered or on surface, include four subsections: **Structural alignment**, **Minimize parking**, **Surface quilt** and **Dual-purpose plaza.**

Structural alignment

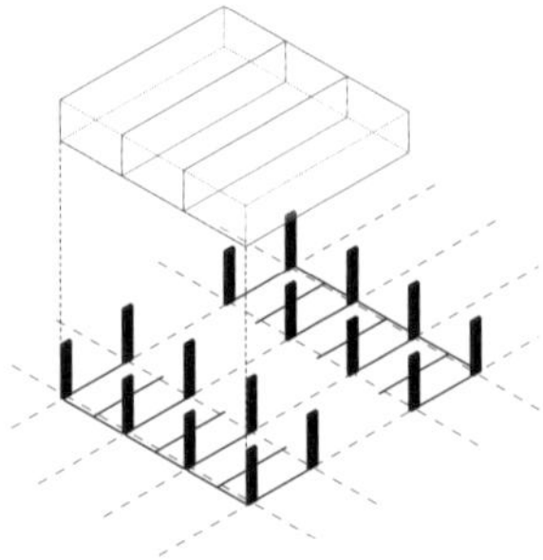

LIFE rental housing is located in a South Calgary neighbourhood where local by-laws still dictate a minimum parking count. The site is also heavily sloped, enabling level street access to a below grade garage. Due to the slope and the split level arrangement of the design, the excavation of the garage for 55 stalls remains relatively shallow, keeping costs moderate.

The project is situated in a well connected neighbourhood and the allowances for reduced parking was possible due to proximity to existing transit, as well as a proposed increase to the supplied number of bicycle stalls and the provision of two car share stalls, and including two flex stalls that can be converted from visitor to car share in the future. Architecturally, the key to keeping overall costs down was to align all of the suite demising walls with the parking bays below and keep all suites to a consistent 20 foot frontage, avoiding complexity and the cost associated with more expensive structural solutions like transfer slabs. Our hope is that this approach demonstrates the architectural outcome of such a scheme does not need to be mundane.

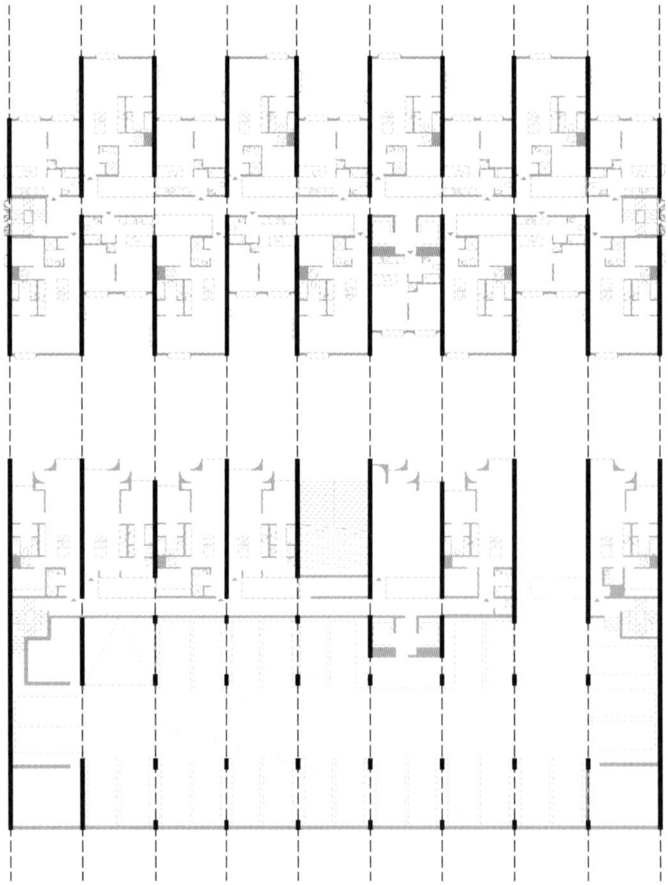

LIFE structural alignment with parking, spanning for two floors below.

 projects.MODELLING: LIFE (p. 100)

Dual-purpose plaza

youCUBE is located at the edge of downtown Winnipeg, close to Waterfront Drive. While no minimum parking requirements exist in the core area, the developer felt that in order to respond to market demands, a 1:1 parking ratio would be needed for uptake of this mixed ownership project. Parking is provided beneath an open-air concrete platform, which also serves as a shared public plaza for the residents above. The plaza also serves as an exterior passageway for all of the suites, meaning that the entry doors of individual units are accessed via this common deck. The deck is located only six and a half feet above the adjoining street level, making the transition from the street to the semi-private zone easier and more natural. The long street façade of the building is aligned with the housing units and flex suites (including commercial), masking the sunken parking area behind.

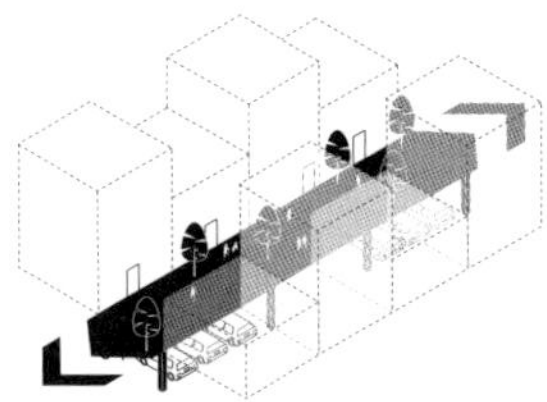

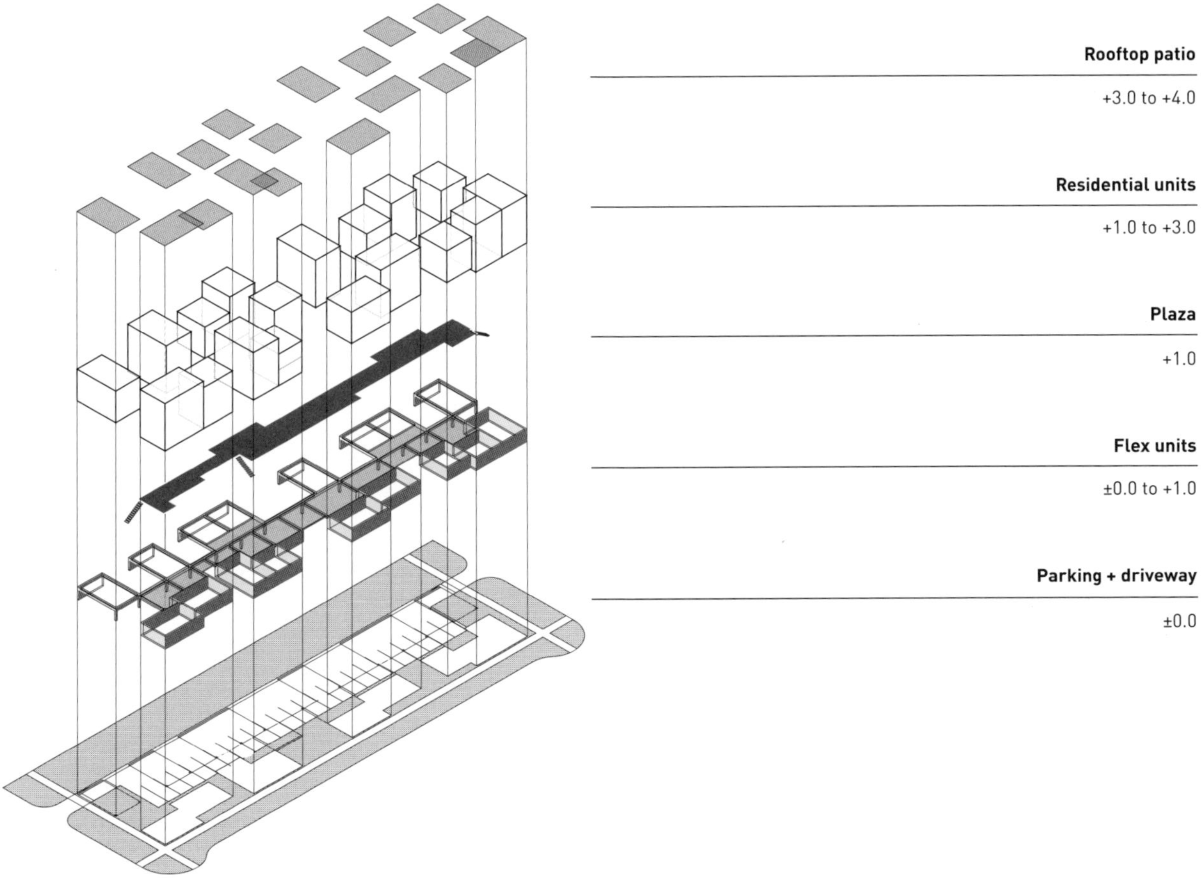

Surface quilt

Rundle is an affordable rental housing project in a northeast Calgary neighbourhood. With half of the 145 suites at the low end of market rate and the other half affordable, the client (Calgary Housing Company) deemed that at least 1:1 ratio of parking would be required, even with transit reductions. In this instance, it was clear from the start of the project that anything but surface parking would be too expensive to accommodate. At the same time, the total number of required stalls was varying between 145 and 170 well into the design process as various city departments continued to weigh in. The design response consists of a surface quilt strategy, where a parking stall size module repeats across the full site. The modules are then rendered in various materials and uses, from a ground cover greenery, trees, and shrubs to play surfaces, BBQ spots, benches, paths, hardscaping and of course, actual parking stalls. The major benefits of this scheme are that the impact of a contiguous paved parking area is broken into smaller pockets, the number of stalls provided can vary throughout the design process and should the need for parking reduce in the future, it is simple to reclaim any superfluous stalls.

 projects.MODELLING: Rundle (p. 120)

Minimize parking

Some owners and development groups are willing to supply dramatically less parking. **Porter House**, which converted an historic warehouse into rental housing in the Exchange District, provides zero stalls on site. This does not sound like an achievement for large urban centres, but continues to be very rare in car-centric cities like Winnipeg and Calgary.

In **90-100 Alexander** or **Railside** at The Forks, the inclusion of on-site car-share vehicles and priority stalls is a key strategy to support the reduction of the unit-to-parking ratio. 90-100 Alexander features just 30 stalls per 206 housing units, a 14.5% ratio, whereas Railside includes approximately 150 stalls – 5 per building – for between 1,000 and 1,200 housing units, or a 12.5% – 15% ratio. The hope is that projects like these will demonstrate their feasibility through market uptake and act as catalysts for more people-centric future developments.

A Covered parking
B Carshare parking

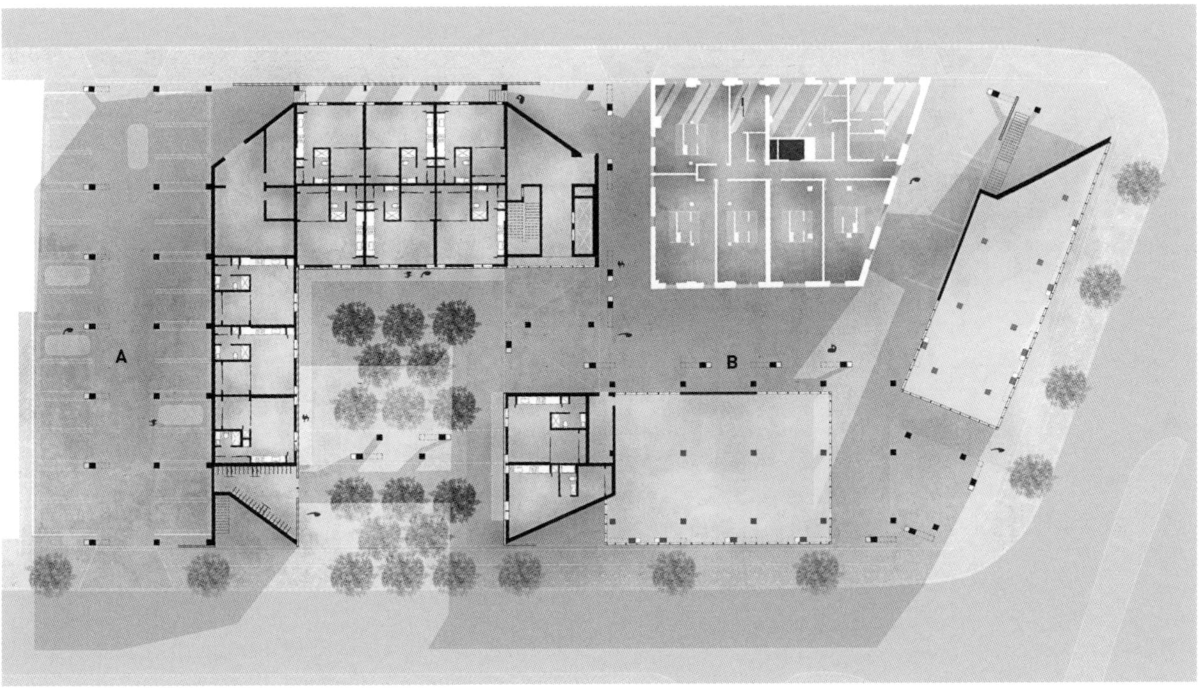

90-100 Alexander (p. 116), Railside (p. 26)

Three-storey walk-up (BGBX)

At-grade entrance (548 Stradbrook)

Skip-stop corridor (Pumphouse)

Sharing exit stairs (3319 Douglas)

Efficiency

Efficiency drives the vast majority of basic design decisions in multi-family housing, in both public and – to an even larger extent – private projects. The typical 85% minimum efficiency target of usable or leasable space often dictates everything from basic building mass to depth of floor plates.

In simple terms, and partially due to the fact that in North America dual fire exits are required by building codes, the deeper the floor plate, the more efficiency is to be gained. This requirement is in direct conflict with livability and access to natural light and ventilation that would tend to favour shallower plates. The strategies to increase efficiency include: elimination of all tare area (possible in a **three-storey walk-up** scenario), elimination of public corridor at-grade in favour of individual **at-grade entrances** for a portion of the dwellings, inclusion of **skip-stop corridors** that can reduce public corridor space up to 50% and **sharing exit stairs** among two adjacent buildings.

Three storey walk-up

A three-storey walk-up model allows nearly 100% efficiency through the omission of shared corridors and common spaces.

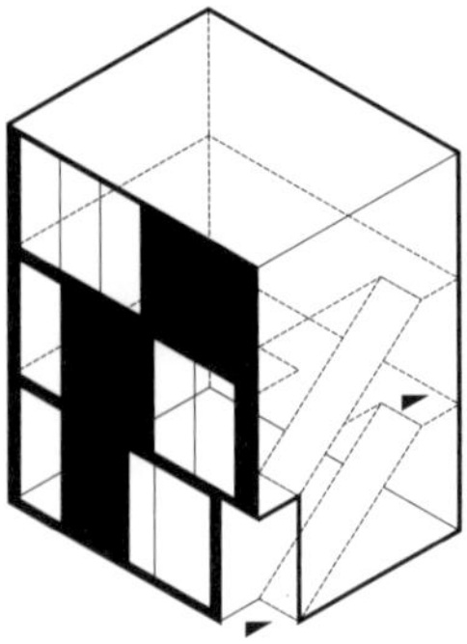

In low land value cities, this typology is one of the easiest solutions to increase efficiency. It is even possible to eliminate shared utility space as separate hot water tanks and HVAC units can be provided for each suite. The walk-up strategy also has the advantage of locating individual suite doors at grade, ideal for supporting the creation of community and giving residents a sense of ownership over adjoining shared outdoor spaces. Further benefits include through-unit designs and increased access to cross ventilation, which may also eliminate the need for air conditioning. In addition, projects that fall under Part 9 of the National Building Code of Canada (NBC) do not typically require sprinkler coverage or other more onerous fire protection measures, all resulting in reduced building costs overall.

Operating in Winnipeg, we have explored this building type through numerous projects in the early years of our practice, including **BGBX**, **youCUBE**, **Centre Village**, **Bloc_10**, and **Ross Avenue**. In addition, **Webbsite** Condominiums represents our earliest foray into this typology. It is worth noting that all of the above projects vary from the typical three-storey town or row house in that they have suites above one another and hence require unique fire-rating strategies.

In retrospect, these early experiments are all remarkably different from one another and quite playful within the boundaries of a rather rudimentary and low-cost typology. The mix includes anything from accessible single level family suites at **Ross Avenue** to three level townhomes at **Bloc_10**, to rather ambitious – and perhaps naive – four level loft units with 36′ ceiling heights at **youCUBE**.

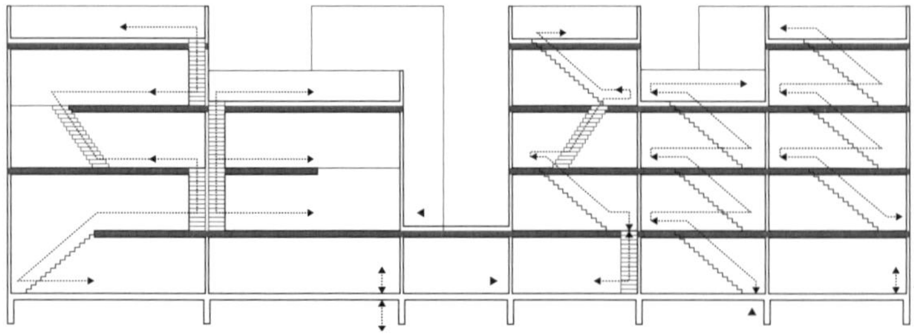

youCUBE

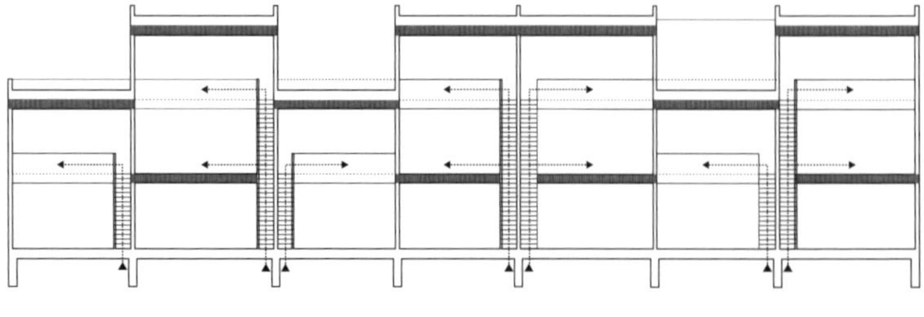

Webbsite

projects.MODELLING: BGBX (p. 56), youCUBE (p. 60), Centre Village (p. 64), Bloc_10 (p. 72), Ross Avenue (p. 88), Webbsite (p. 52)

youCUBE

At-grade entrance

Eliminating the common corridor at grade increases efficiency by providing the lowest suites with direct outdoor access.

When common lobby or corridor space and exiting is required, either due to additional storeys or units that have their entrance above the second level, 100% efficiency is no longer possible. In these cases it has been useful to increase efficiency by providing ground level suites their own exterior front doors (**Rundle, 90-100 Alexander, 548 Stradbrook**), thus eliminating the need for a common corridor on this level. Eliminating corridors on both the first and second storey – thus increasing efficiency further – becomes possible with the inclusion of two level townhomes with mezzanines at the base of the building (**OZ, Treehouse**).

Entry at grade

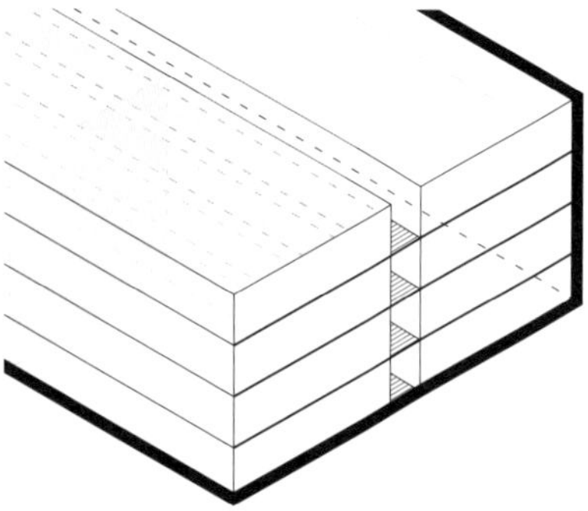

Most common

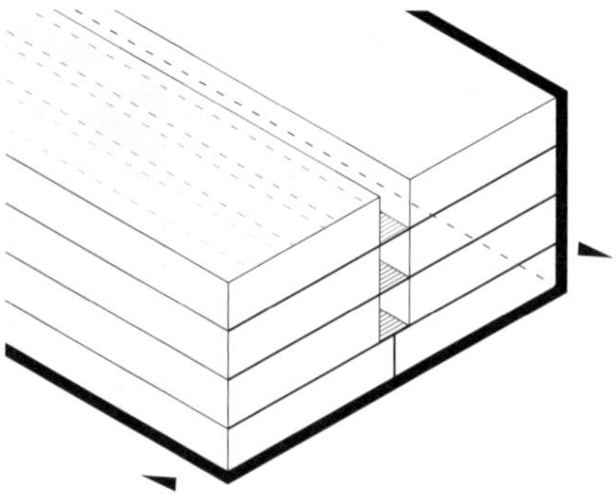

25% Less corridor
(individual access for ground floor suites)

Entry at grade + walk-up

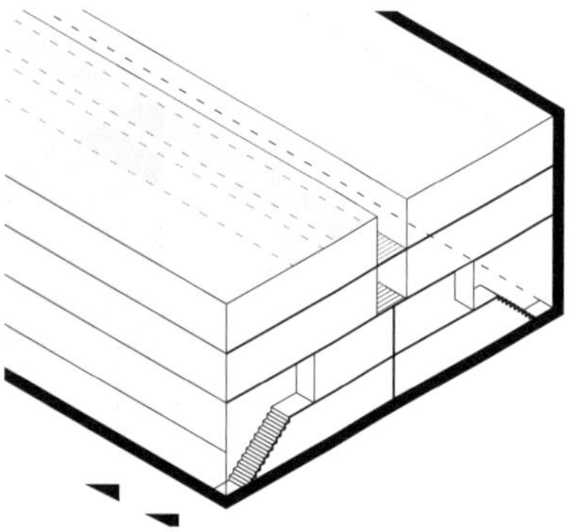

50% Less corridor

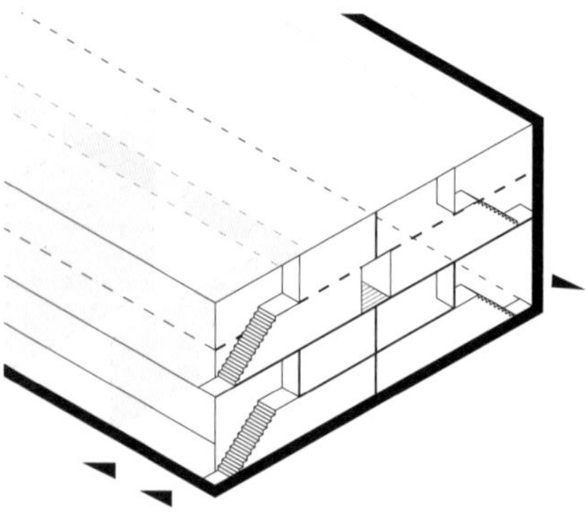

75% Less corridor

 projects.MODELLING: Rundle (p. 120), 90-100 Alexander (p. 116), 548 Stradbrook (p. 80), OZ (p. 84), Treehouse (p. 92)

OZ

Skip-stop corridor

For mid-rise buildings, the introduction of skip-stop corridors can improve efficiency on upper levels.

With Courtyard 33 (**CY33**), the 125'x150' site dimensions, 0' east side yard setback, target unit count and our desire to avoid "shotgun suites," pushed us to a dough-nut-shaped plan, although the lot width was not sufficient to accommodate a double loaded corridor on all sides of the building. To recover the lost efficiency resulting from single loaded corridors on two sides, we introduced a skip-stop corridor on levels three and five that would also serve suites on levels four and six. While the drawback of this strategy is that non-corridor suites have stairs within the suite and are therefore not universally accessible, the benefits include additional floor area for the suite and the possibility of through-units with windows on both building faces. This strategy is also deployed on the resident blocks of **Pumphouse**. In the case of **OZ** Condominiums, we achieved additional efficiency through two level mezzanine suites on the upper storeys of the building.

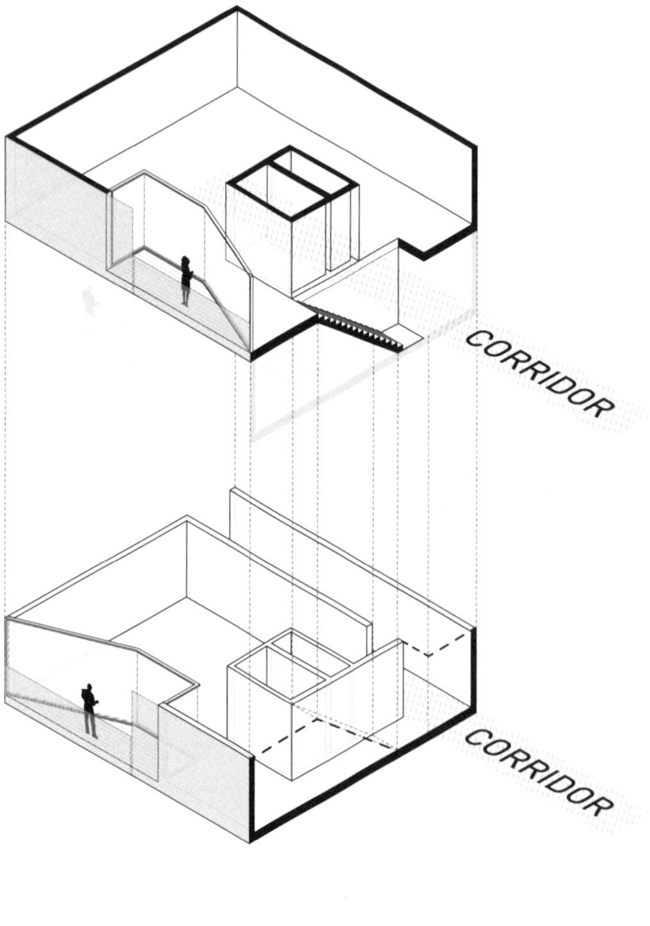

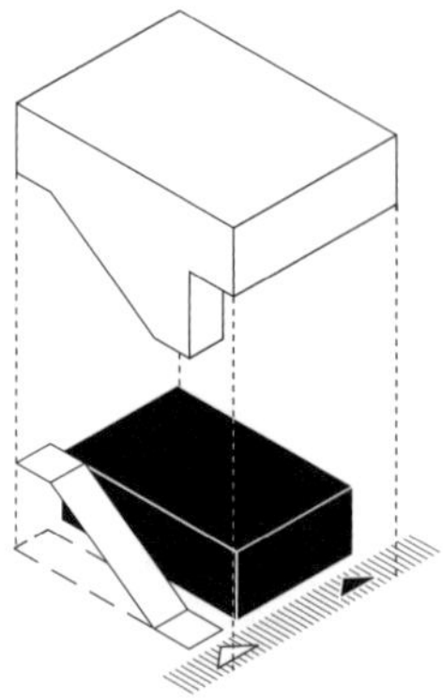

In CY33, the skip-stop corridor on floors 3 and 5 serve floors 4 and 6 to increase efficiencies as well as maximizing natural light and ventilation per suite.

projects.MODELLING: CY33 (p. 108), Pumphouse (p. 112), OZ (p. 84)

Pumphouse

Sharing exit stairs

Sharing exit stairs between adjacent, but separate buildings under the building code can offer significant savings in tare area, essentially cutting the requirement in half.

Admittedly, providing bridges or connections between the buildings will add some cost back to the equation, but when distances are limited or when other challenges are present [i.e. heritage buildings] utilizing "Horizontal Exiting" into another building under Canada's National Building Code has allowed us to creatively increase efficiency of our mid-scale multi-family projects without increasing costs or compromising occupant safety.

At **3319 Douglas** the project's two six-storey building blocks share two exterior exit stairs at each end of the buildings, allowing a 50% reduction of vertical exit circulation. The stairs further define a courtyard between the two buildings and shared by all residents.

The **Hedge** 55+ complex consisted of two distinct building masses in order to save a number of mature trees that were an important part of the project's overall objective and vision. The two separate buildings share two exits, each utilizing a horizontal exit into the other, effectively reducing the number of exit stairs from four to two. At **90-100 Alexander**, the existing heritage building included a single exit stair and new residential use would have required adding another means of exiting to the historic floor plate. Instead, a new exterior exit stair is placed between the new and the old, and shared by both buildings.

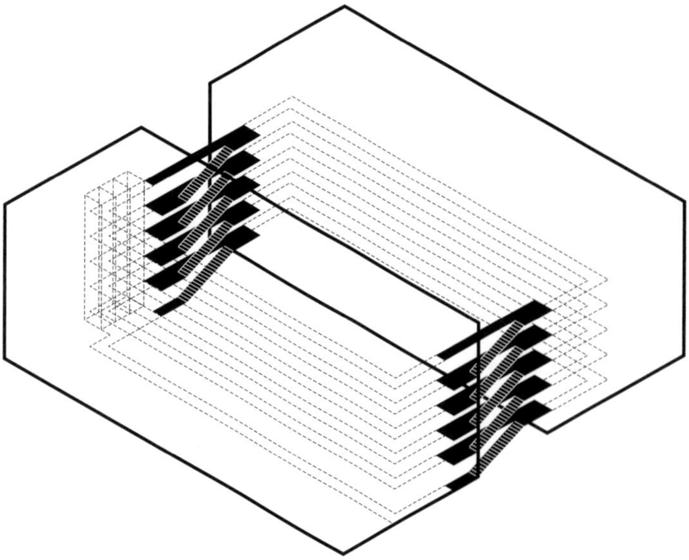

At 3319 Douglas, exterior staircases connect two buildings

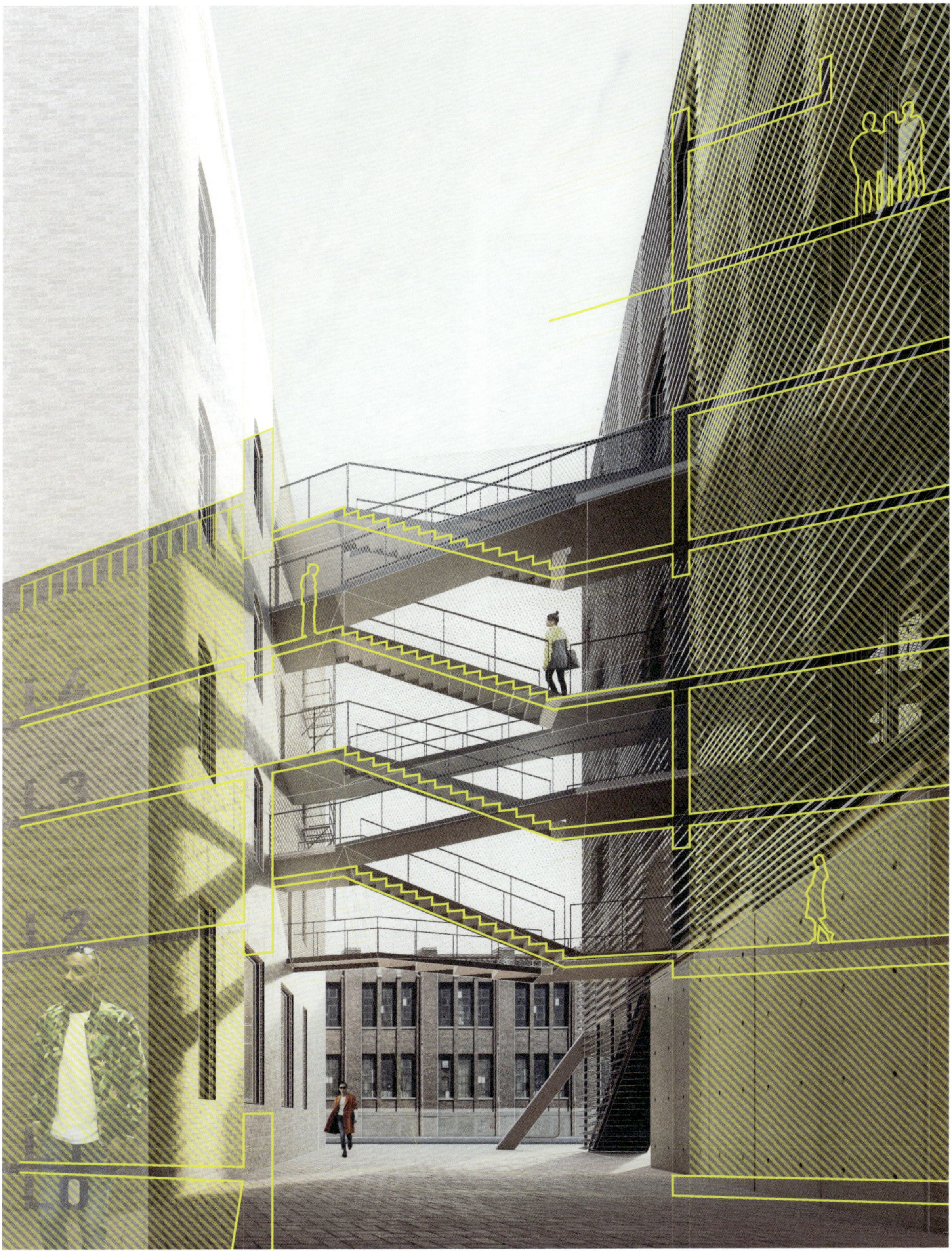

90-100 Alexander

Short-term flexibility (90-100 Alexander)

Programmatic flexibility (Webbsite)

Long-term flexibility (Welcome Place)

Unit flexibility (62M)

Flexibility

Flexibility in housing design is a well-covered topic in architecture, especially as a means to support long-term sustainability goals.

Although the ability to expand or contract an occupant's living space according to need is desirable, it can be difficult to execute, often resulting in overly ambitious proposals that either cost too much to build or are too cumbersome to change over time. Recognizing these realities, we have come to understand that in certain instances, designing flexibility into a project – either for the duration of the design process or for the life of the building – is valuable and necessary.

The examples of flexibility included in our sample projects are broken into the following subcategories: **Short-term flexibility**, **Programmatic flexibility**, **Long-term flexibility** and **Unit flexibility.**

Short-term flexibility

Flexibility during the design process can be useful as clients are still trying to assess the true market value of their development.

For **90-100 Alexander** and **Rundle**, incorporating interchangeable unit types enabled our clients to regularly fine-tune their suite ratios and keep their proforma flexible far into the design stage.

90-100 Alexander establishes a base one-bedroom suite module, with an optional 1/2 module add-on to form a standard two-bedroom suite. A mix of standard configurations and their reversed (mirrored) versions stack to create the oversized checkerboard façade while permitting a mix of one and two bedroom suites within the same load-bearing demising wall grid system. This strategy provided flexibility in design and regularity in construction without compromising the uniformity of the primary building grid.

 projects.MODELLING: 90-100 Alexander (p. 116), Rundle (p. 120)

90-100 Alexander

Programmatic flexibility

A lock-off flex room can be combined with adjacent suites (either next door or above) as the needs of occupants change over time.

In the case of **Webbsite** Condominiums and **BGBX**, the flex suites are on separate titles and can be sold independent of the adjoining larger suite. In both cases the flex rooms are located on the ground floor so that they lend themselves for use as home-based businesses, as granny-suites, or simply as an additional living area or bedroom. Similarly, **youCUBE** and **Bloc_10** incorporate ground-floor rooms that can be used independent of the living space above, and some of these are currently in commercial use.

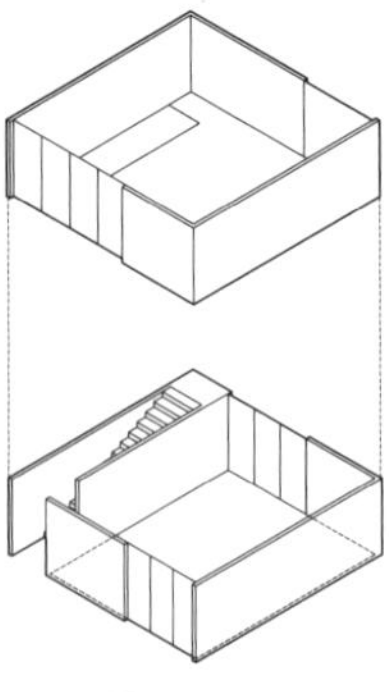

Flex space

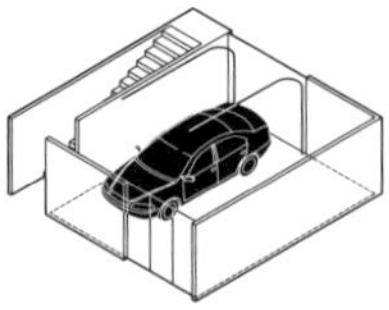

Flex space as garage

L3 plan

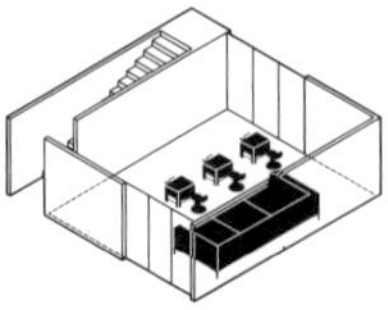

Flex space as studio

L2 plan

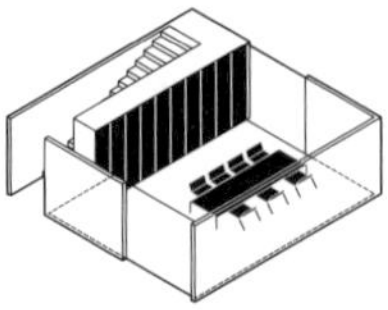

Flex space as dining

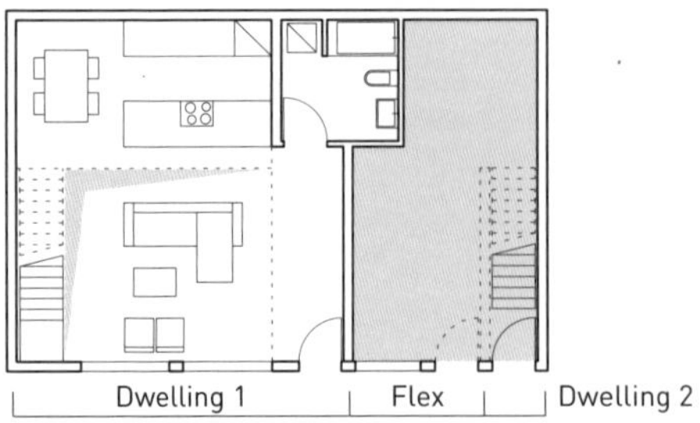

L1 plan

Webbsite flex suites

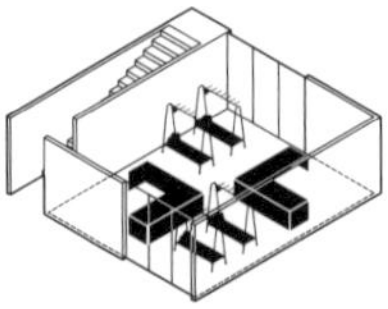

Flex space as pop-up

 projects.MODELLING: Webbsite (p. 52), BGBX (p. 56), youCUBE (p. 60), Bloc_10 (p. 72)

Webbsite

Long-term flexibility

Flexibility throughout the life of a building can be a basic necessity driven by the client's programmatic requirements.

For **Welcome Place**, the type of units that are needed varies widely depending on the origin country of the refugee population as well as the source of conflict. As a result, suites require adaptability in order to shift from housing individuals to supporting large families. Further adding to the pressure for flexibility is the fact that a typical stay at Welcome Place is only three weeks in duration. The design solution includes a simple vestibule with two unit doors (each of which are fire rated) that can be propped open to create a continuous suite for larger groups as needed.

L4 key Plan

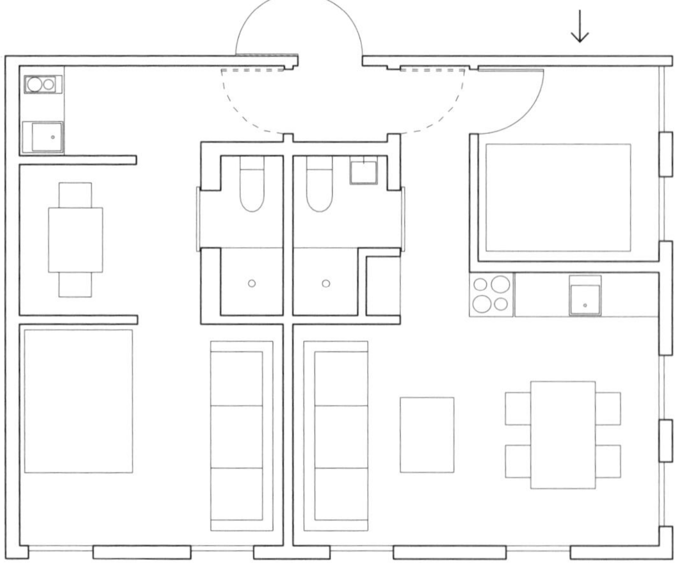

Two-bedroom flex suite
670 sf

Welcome Place

Unit flexibility

When suite dimensions are tight and building perimeter is at a premium, flexible bedrooms (both primary and secondary) can be incorporated. This strategy allows the living area of the suite to feel larger and increases access to window space when the bedroom is not in use.

In **62M**, every suite includes a Murphy bed. In some units a modest curtain track sections off the bedroom from the living area, and in others the bed simply folds away into a continuous utility band when not in use. In **90-100 Alexander** and **CY33**, the secondary bedroom is defined by folding wall panels that can be pulled closed when the area is used as a guest bedroom or left open to enlarge the living room.

Such conditions are of course not suitable for every user type or families with children where acoustic privacy is of primary concern. However, for singles or couples these simple solutions can provide a modest yet useful way to modify their space on a daily basis, on occasion for overnight guests, or when temporary visual privacy is needed.

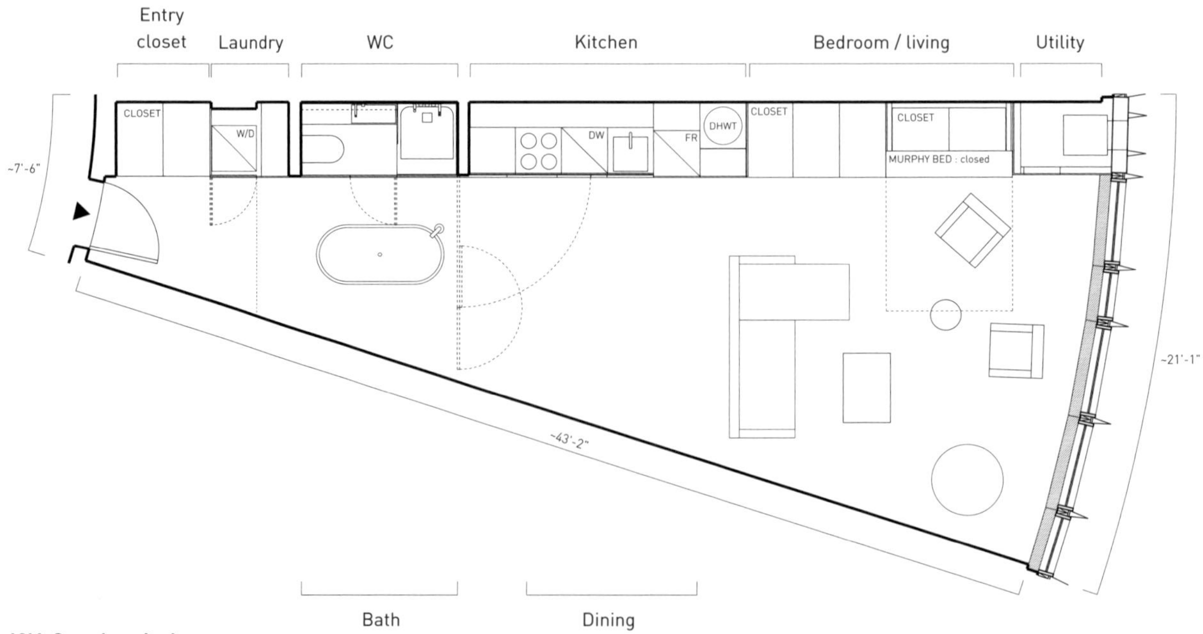

62M: Sample unit plan
TYPE 01 ~610 SQFT

 projects.MODELLING: 62M (p. 96), 90-100 Alexander (p. 116), CY33 (p. 108)

62M

Raised floor (Edge on Princess)

Insert balcony (Treehouse)

Splay plan (62M)

Lightwell (LIFE)

Deep units

In North America – where the private sector delivers the majority of new housing developments and inclusionary zoning strategies are still in their infancy in many jurisdictions – profit and efficiency drive housing design. Generally speaking, due to the length of corridor required, the deeper the building plate, the better the efficiency and resulting profit for the developer.

As previously discussed, access to natural light and ventilation are directly related to this formula. In the absence of codes or policies that require otherwise, it is critical for architects to use every skill in their arsenal to add quality and livability for the end user, while maintaining the required efficiency for their clients. This is true for both new construction as well as the rehabilitation of existing buildings where floor plate conditions are predetermined, potentially including an increased number of conversions of former office space into residential use.

Raised floor

When window access is limited, a raised floor at the back of the suite allows private rooms to receive light from the perimeter.

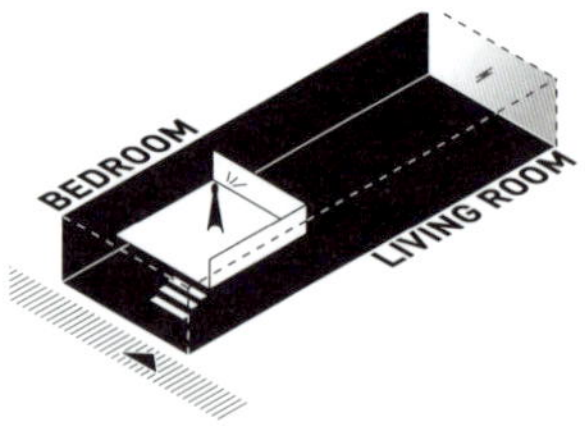

The **Edge on Princess** is an adaptive reuse project that transforms the historic Frost and Wood warehouse in Winnipeg's Exchange District into a multi-use building, with ground floor commercial and 36 rental units above. It is bound by another building with a zero property line condition on one of its long façades and features an existing historic stair – factors that dictated the location of vertical circulation and the typical floor plate. Furthermore, the target market for rental suites was the student body of the adjacent college, necessitating a majority of smaller studio and one bedroom suite types.

Given the historic façade, window locations were also predetermined with the exception of the public lane where new openings were possible in a few locations. Fortunately due to its previous use, the ceiling height of a typical floor was more generous at eleven feet. Given these conditions, the solution for a typical mid-block suite involved raising the bedroom area at the back of the layout by two or three feet so that it could receive some borrowed light from the single window face at the perimeter. The design strategy represents a modest improvement to a difficult condition enabled by the existing ceiling height. The same conditions were prevalent in **Warehouse 1885**, where we implemented the same strategy.

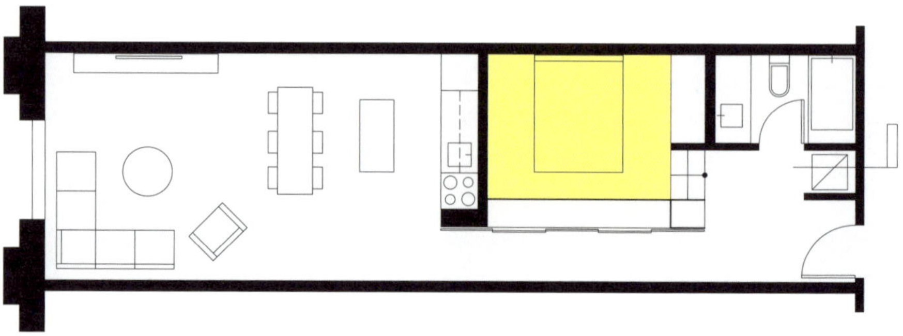

Suite plan

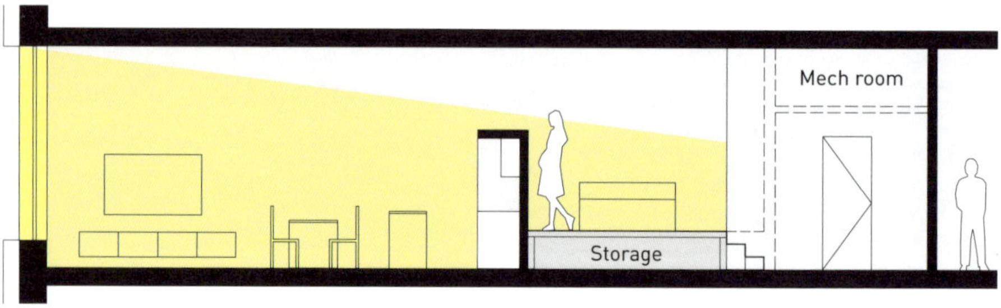

Suite section

 projects.MODELLING: Warehouse 1885 (p. 104)

Warehouse 1885

Inset balcony

In order to provide window access to a second bedroom while tightening the length of the required perimeter, a deep inset balcony can be incorporated.

The relationship between window perimeter and depth of building plate generally determines building efficiency. In addition, the width of façade available for each unit drives how many legitimate bedrooms can be included in a typical mid-block suite. Approximately 20 to 25 feet of exposure suggests a one bedroom, whereas 30 feet and up can begin to house a two bedroom suite, assuming that each room has its own window. One way to "cheat" these basic dimensions is through the inclusion of a deep inset balcony.

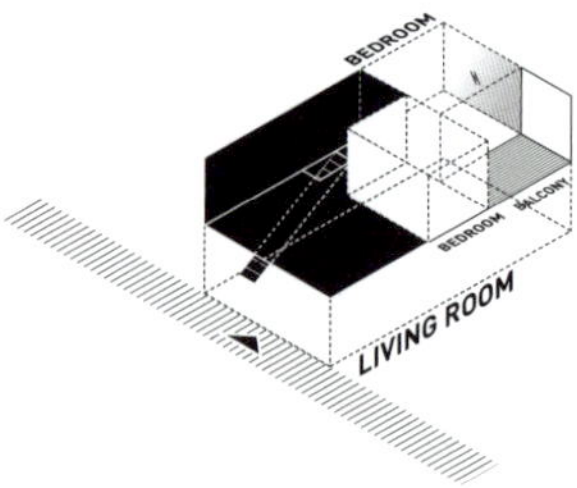

This strategy is perhaps best demonstrated by the speculative 750 square foot, two bedroom suites of various configurations developed for Great Gulf as part of a larger research project. In addition, **Treehouse** in Toronto deploys this strategy in order to pack the required 39 units within the constraints of the site and project parameters. It is worth noting that there is a significant cost and construction complexity associated with the inset balcony, due to additional undulation of the building perimeter, especially if the balconies are not vertically aligned. Furthermore, the light quality achieved for the bedroom or living space in question due to the deep set window face is likely less than ideal, especially for northern climates.

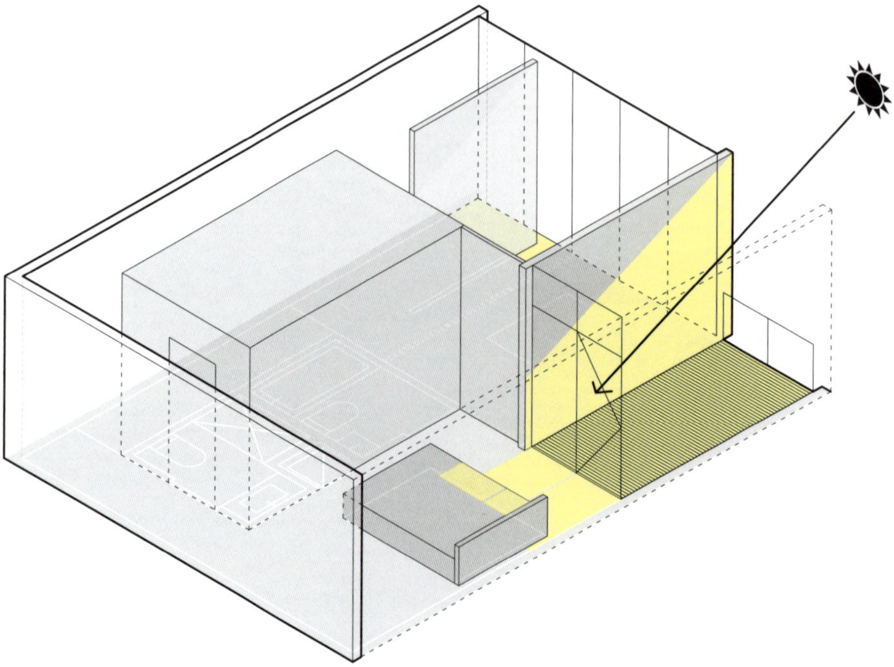

Inset balcony: Treehouse

Treehouse

Splay plan

For a variety of reasons – including grid-based urban plans, construction conventions and off-the-shelf building material availability – it is natural that the majority of modern housing design follows orthogonal geometry. Yet on some occasions, these conventions are worth questioning.

For **62M**, due to immediate site limitations, the design process led to raising the building on stilts – hence requiring that cost efficiencies be found elsewhere. Through numerous iterations, the team discovered that a circular building form resulted in 30% less envelope while still providing the same quantity of suites as an equivalent orthogonal plan. The resulting splayed plan carries the added benefit of minimizing the often oversized dark utility space at the back of the suite and maximizing the window perimeter on the façade, without unnecessarily increasing the overall square footage. Compared to a typical deep suite layout, the quantity and quality of natural daylight achieved in this scheme is far superior.

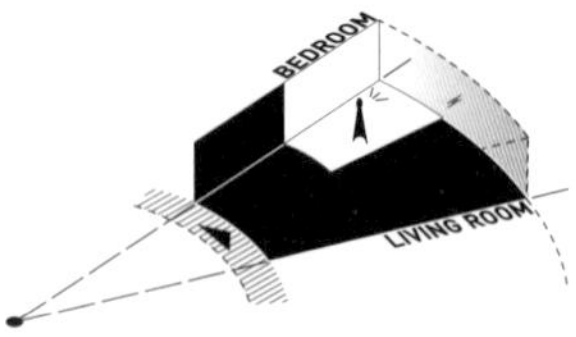

Due to building geometry, a similar splayed suite type has been repeated in the **Parkade of the Future** as the speculative conversion of the project into future housing.

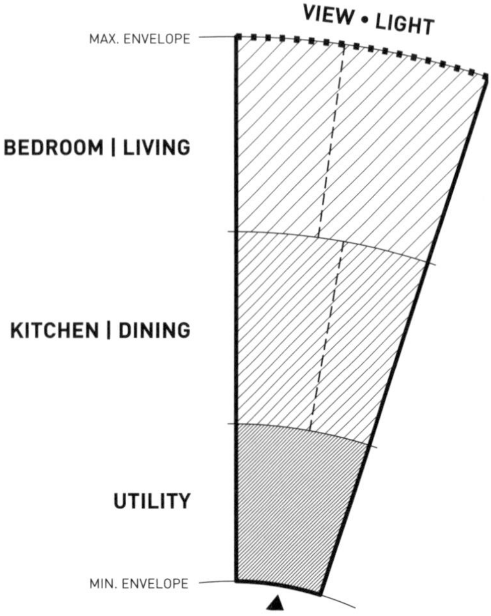

Schematic arrangement

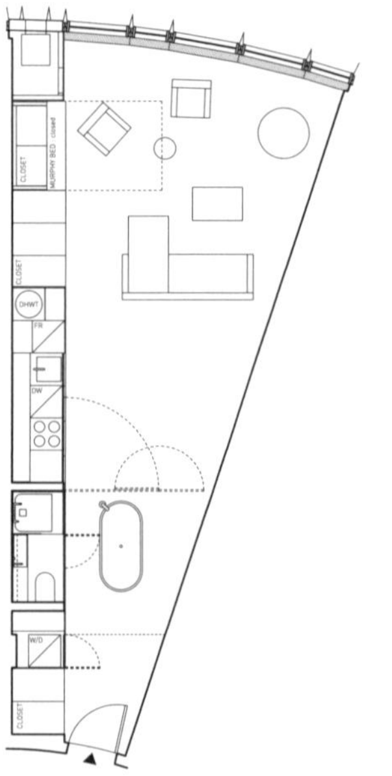

62M: suite type 01

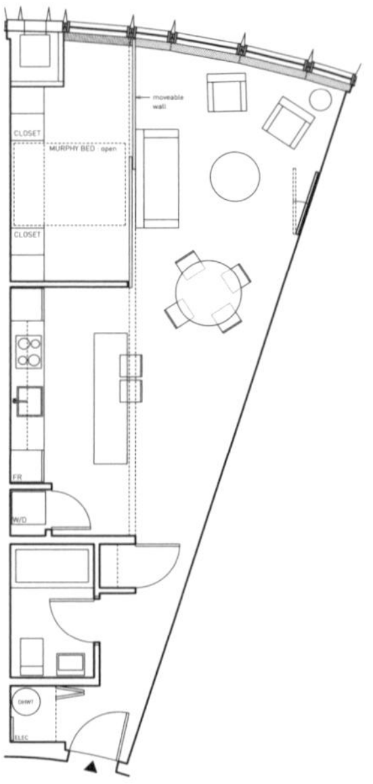

62M: suite type 02

62M

Lightwell

Another strategy to address long and deep suites in a new build condition is through the introduction of an internal lightwell.

LIFE in Calgary fits 84 suites within the given FAR and height restrictions, with building perimeter limited to two façades. In order to ensure that operable windows for the secondary bedroom would still be possible, seven open-air lightwells were introduced along the building corridor. In addition, the building façade steps back and forth horizontally, enabling window placement on all four faces of the two-bedroom suites, and on two facades of the one-bedroom suites. It is important to note that both the lightwells and increased perimeter of the undulating façade are the two major investments in the project's design quality – everything else remains straightforward and modest.

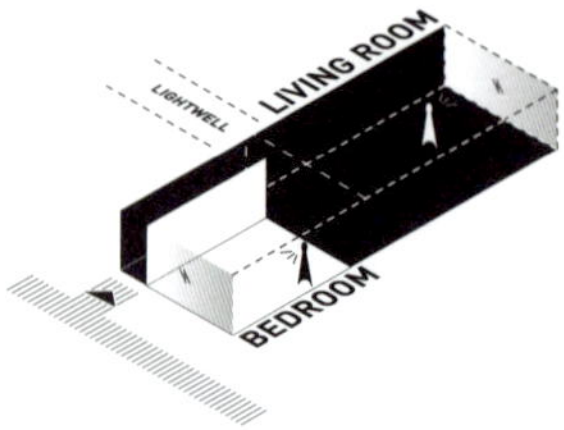

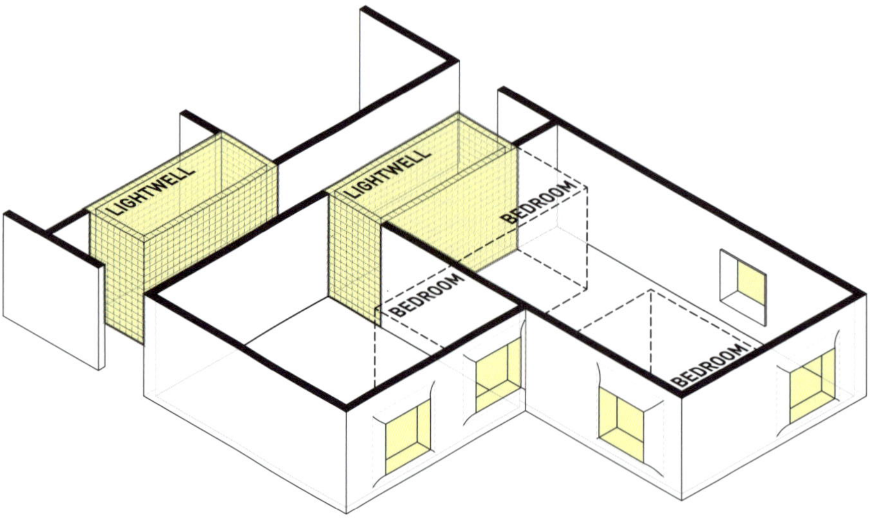

LIFE

Three storey walk-up (Ross Avenue)

Skip-stop corridor (Pumphouse)

Lightwell (LIFE)

Exterior passageway (62M)

Multi-aspect [cross ventilation]

Access to proper cross ventilation in the North American multi-family context is both rare and an under-appreciated benefit for the general well-being of future occupants.

Building code requirements for two exits severely limits the potential for double aspect suites in most multi-family housing projects. This prerequisite, together with efficiency targets that necessitate double-loaded corridors, make it difficult to support cross ventilation, which also perpetuates the need for air conditioning – even in cold climates – increasing base construction costs and adding to the building's environmental burden. A number of planning strategies reappear under this section as they also support opportunities for through-unit design: **Three storey walk-up**, **Skip-stop corridor**, **Exterior passageway** and **Lightwell**.

Three storey walk-up

In a three-storey walk-up building, common exits or corridor space are not required and operable windows are possible on both sides of the building. There are many traditional and contemporary townhouse examples from across the continent that demonstrate the myriad benefits of this typology, whenever land values allow.

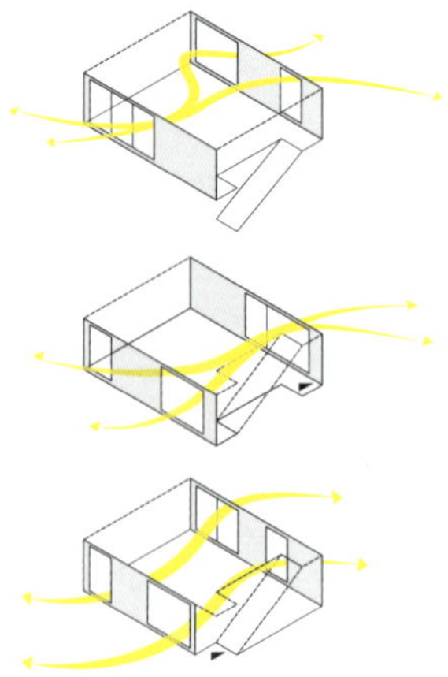

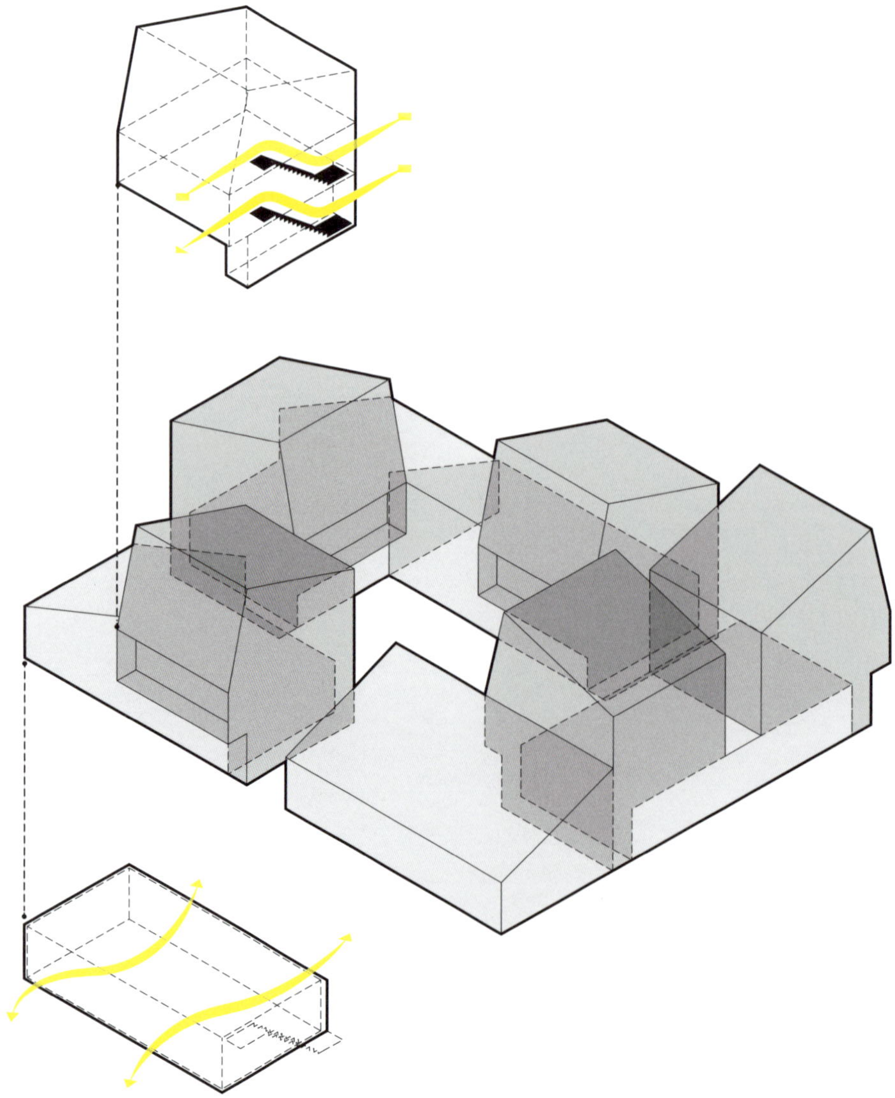

Ross Avenue Condominiums: three-storey walk-ups nested on sprawling ground-level units.

Skip-stop corridor

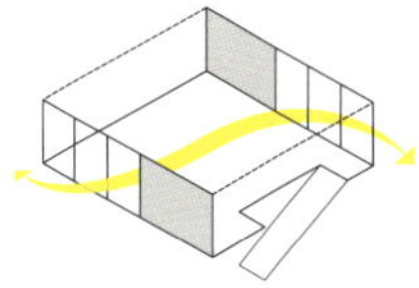

With skip-stop corridors, suites on non-corridor levels can extend from one building face to the other, as is the case with a number of suites on levels four and six of **CY33**. This configuration allows for operable windows on each end of the suite.

Similarly, at **90-100 Alexander**, the skip-stop strategy is used not only to reduce corridors and add efficiency, but also to enable through units at the top (seventh) floor.

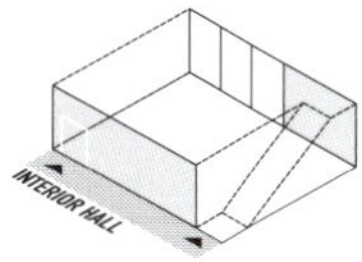

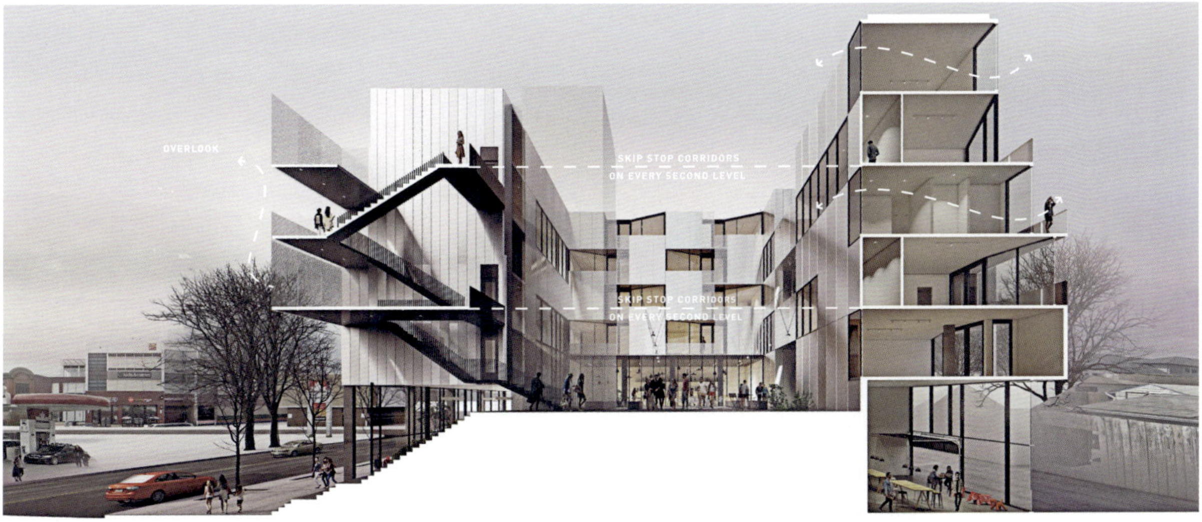

CY33 section of skip-stop corridors.

Lightwell

LIFE provides an opportunity for natural cross ventilation through the use of seven open-air lightwells along the central corridor. These lightwells provide an operable window for a secondary bedroom in a typical two-bedroom suite configuration, as well as an operable window for the typical one-bedroom kitchen, significantly improving the traditional double-loaded corridor typology for air flow and natural ventilation for nearly all suites [see page 111].

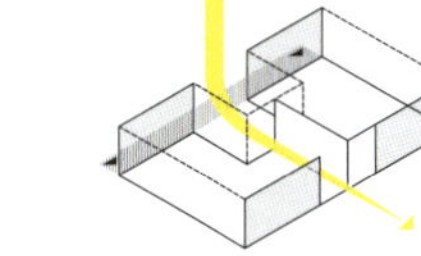

Exterior passageway

A through-unit can also be achieved via an exterior exit passageway. The **Pumphouse** residential component, which is divided between two buildings that together frame the historic pumping station, features both single and double loaded exterior corridor conditions, on the east and west façades respectively. Furthermore, the project utilizes skip-stop levels for both buildings, with access stairs provided on level two of the east building and levels two and five of the west building. While unprotected openings – in this case windows facing an exit corridor – can be permissible in an exterior passageway condition under the NBC, the Pumphouse suite windows that face the exterior corridors required sprinkler protection due to the unrated steel used to support the exterior stairs and passageways.

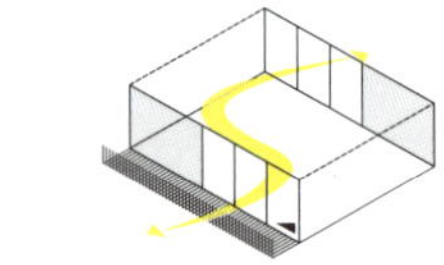

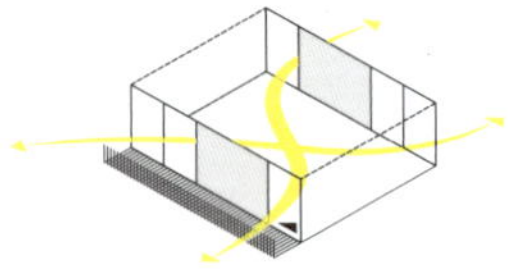

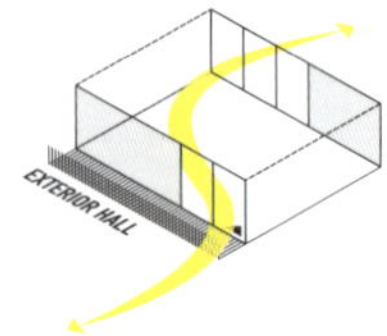

Pumphouse

62M

Systems thinking (Bloc_10)

Modularity + variation (90-100 Alexander)

Extreme affordability (Centre Village)

Local knowledge (youCUBE)

Low cost cladding (Webbsite)

Demystifying details (youCUBE)

Practical innovation

The concept of a holistic approach to design – where architecture is understood in tandem with structural, mechanical and electrical systems – is not new, nor is it in and of itself especially innovative. Architects, consultants and clients alike have touted the value of an Integrated Design Process (IDP) for decades. However, integrating all building systems from the outset is particularly important in the creation of attainable/social housing, in order to achieve high-quality with limited means.

Optimizing structural spans and modularity to reduce waste may be more inherent to high-rise construction where such decisions are amplified with each building storey, resulting in a large and visible impact on the bottom line. For this simple reason it is perhaps easier on a mid-scale building to let aesthetic decisions drive too much of the basic design thinking, to the detriment of simplicity, constructibility and cost. On occasion, we have certainly fallen into this trap ourselves. Conversely, chasing cost savings – with added pressures from clients and stakeholders – often results in banal design outcomes. The ultimate goal is to find cost effective ways to elevate the design of budget-driven projects, in order to invest any potential savings into user experience and architectural quality.

Systems thinking

As a white box development, the flexibility of plumbing, HVAC, and electrical systems was critical to the success of **Bloc_10**. These systems needed to support a variety of interior layouts while simultaneously providing efficient, coherent connection points to limit costs of future extensions and modifications of the system. Electrical distribution begins at the main floor in the stairwell wall and diagonally follows the stairwell ceiling to each floor connection. The main water supply and all drain lines run vertically within the plumbing walls. The supply of hot and cold water, along with tempered fresh air follows the ceiling of the staircase providing connection points to each floor. The air and hot water source both start at the third floor to allow access to the roof for combustion air, and fresh air supply. This arrangement situates the mechanical areas at the core of the building rather than the more coveted exterior.

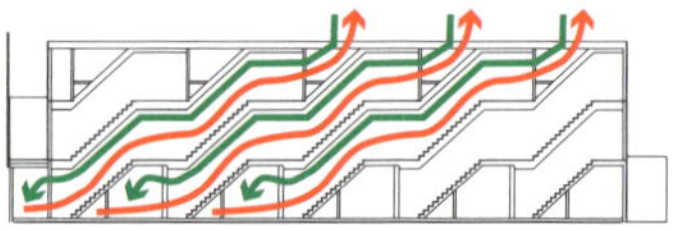

Air

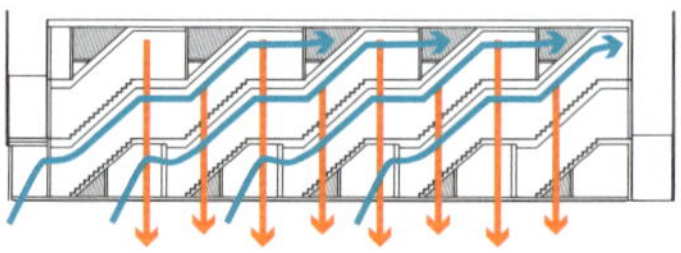

Water

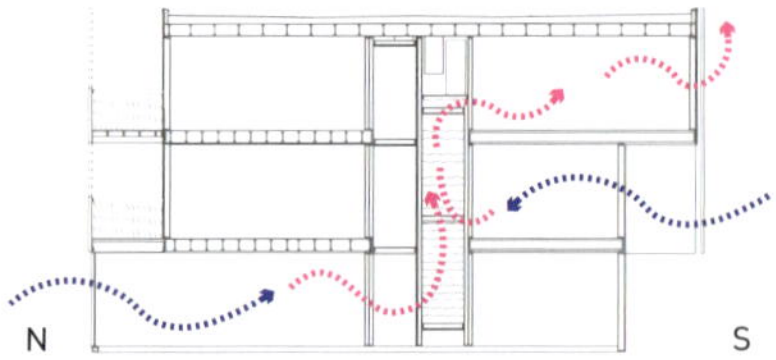

Natural ventilation

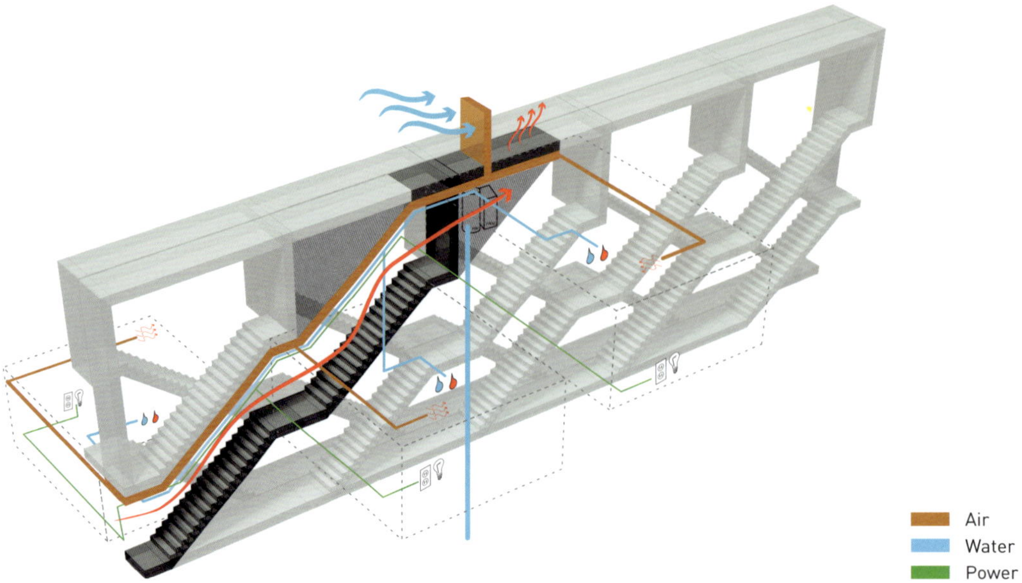

Bloc_10

BGBX is a 24-unit, three-storey walk-up housing complex on a busy industrial corridor. Early on, the client (an experienced small-scale developer) wanted to use precast concrete planks in combination with wood framing to achieve durability and an improved sound rating between the suites. The four-foot-wide precast module became the basic architectural module as well, and the maximum span of the plank dictated the maximum depth of the building. Similarly, all of the suite wet spaces backed onto a one-foot-wide vertical utility shaft, leaving a remaining three foot space for the stairs in each unit. Mechanically, heat was distributed from the vertical shaft through a single larger duct into the hollow core floor slabs, and run in the cores to the suite perimeter, minimizing visible ductwork and the labour associated with installation.

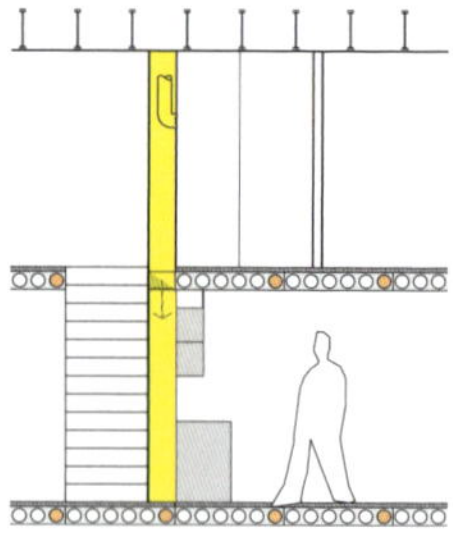

Stairs + mechanical shaft

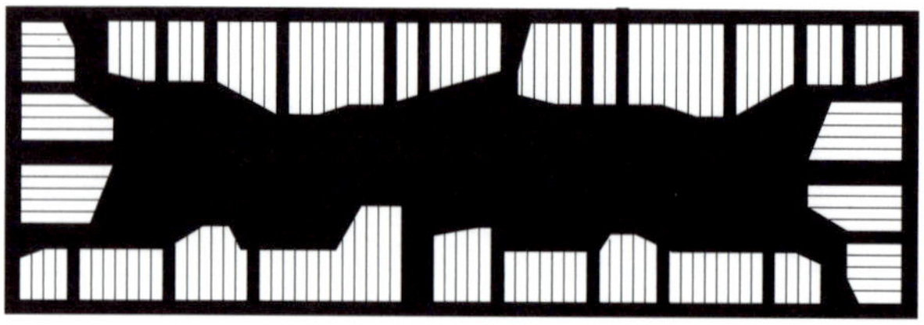

Structure

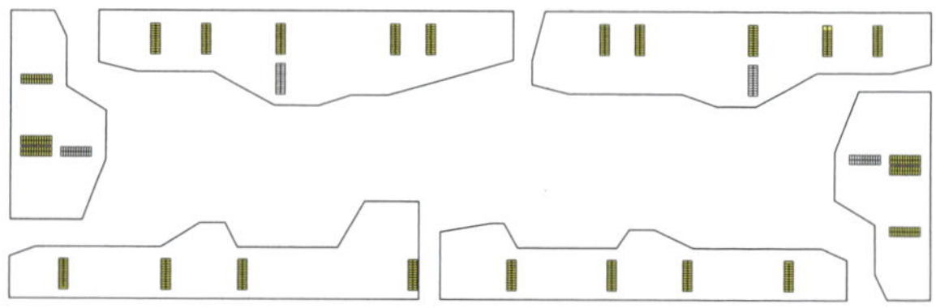

Stairs + mechanical shaft

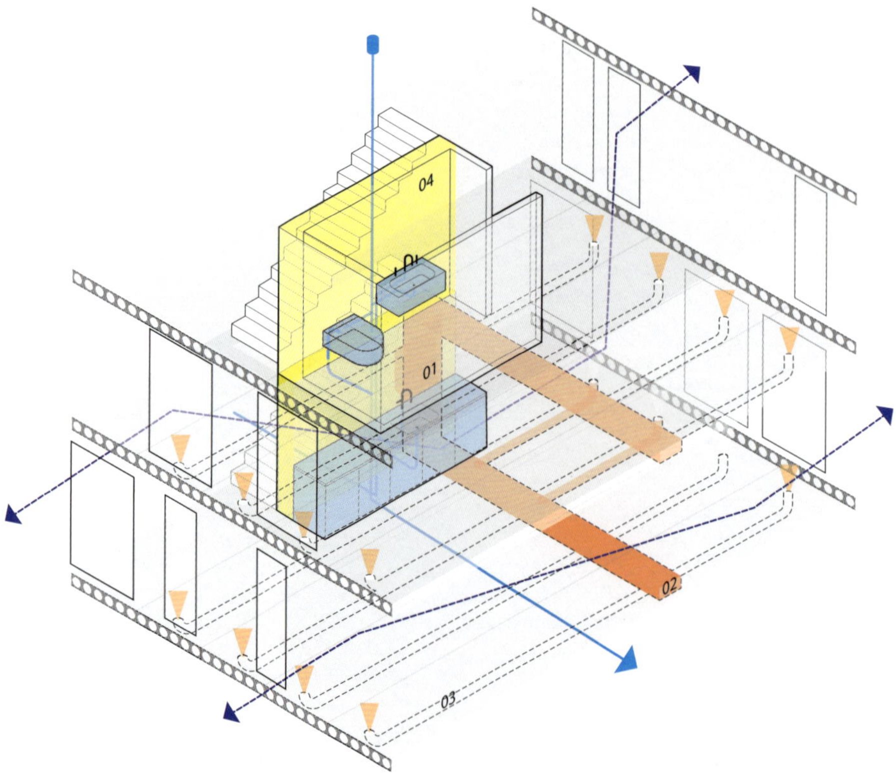

01 Furnace under stairs
02 Header duct
03 Hollowcore distribution
04 Mechanical shaft

BGBX

Modularity + variation

With multi-family housing design, repetition is a given and margins are famously tight. As a result, much of the potential architectural quality is closely tied to the relationship between the suites and the building façade.

As with other systems-based strategies, the aim is to ensure that by keeping the base construction cost low with straightforward structural and mechanical alignments, richness and variety of architectural expression can still be achieved.

Simple, interchangeable unit modules described under "Flexibility" were further considered in the planning of individual suites at **90-100 Alexander**. The plumbing wall alignment and ability to mirror various suite layouts gives the façade a checkered pattern, as opposed to a typical "stumpy" where units are stacked one on top of another and windows align vertically in a predictable and often banal arrangement. **62M** also uses this unit flipping strategy to a simpler extent, as all plumbing is positioned at strategic common points along the centreline of the suite. Similarly, mirroring units results in a more blended façade treatment from one floor to the next.

LIFE disguises its "stumpiness" in a different way. While all of the suites repeat from floor to floor, the façade undulates so that each two-bedroom suite opens to four façades (one of which is a lightwell), allowing for greater variety of window placement on the public building face, regardless of the internal suite alignment from floor to floor.

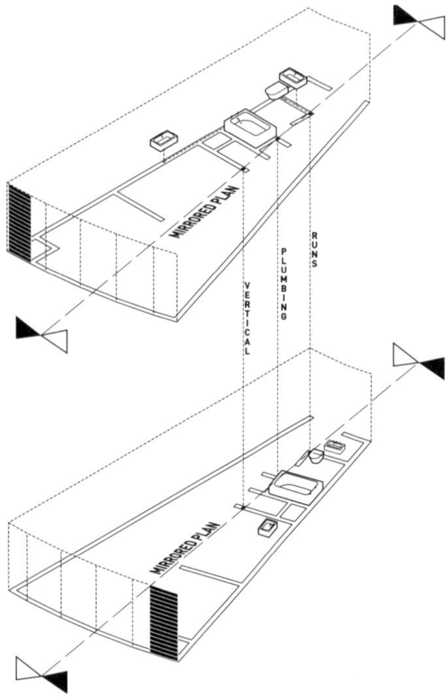

90-100 Alexander

62M

LIFE

Extreme affordability

Low-income housing developments highlight the need for very stringent cost constraints, from initial capital costs to long-term operational and maintenance realities. Meeting these constraints allows the client to pass on acutely needed monthly cost savings to the end user.

Since the beginning of 546, we've been engaged in housing projects intended for underprivileged communities. This work has included transitional housing for former youth sex workers, recent immigrants or refugee populations, along with other social and affordable housing projects.

In the case of **Centre Village**, one of the strategies to keep costs very low was to use only dimensional lumber for construction – in other words, the wood framing does not even include basic engineered wood products, such as TJIs. The largest framing member is a 2x10 joist. This was possible due to the design consisting of room modules that are organized along an eight foot wide "spine," with occasional six-foot cantilevers as needed to house wider master bedrooms and living spaces. This strategy allowed us to keep dimensions tight and structural spans to a minimum.

Centre Village modules based on dimensional lumber.

 projects.MODELLING: Centre Village (p. 64)

Centre Village

Similarly, when it is essential to keep both capital construction and maintenance costs low in a very cold climate such as Winnipeg, using standard size PVC punched windows in lieu of larger expanses of glass has been a useful strategy for **Centre Village**, **Welcome Place** and **Ross Avenue** Condominiums. Of course reductions in window size must be carefully balanced with adequate access to natural light, but the trade off from a few large windows to a number of smaller ones – even if the glass area is the same – has proven to deliver modest savings. Interestingly, in cold climates, tangential winds along the window face play an important role in energy performance – so much so that the use of deeply set double pane windows has provided improved energy performance without increased costs.

With **Centre Village**, the savings from using dual instead of triple pane windows was traded off to afford the colourful window cowlings (in turn making them deep-set), which create a playful shadow pattern on the otherwise rudimentary façade. The windows provide more opportunities for informal surveillance over the shared courtyard and through street.

According to Stephanie Haight of the Winnipeg Housing Rehabilitation Corporation for Ross Avenue Condominiums: "Even an extra ten dollars can make or break a low-income family's monthly budget." At the same time, it is important to keep in mind that extremely affordable does not necessarily mean "cheap," but rather durable low-cost options, solutions that provide best long-term value.

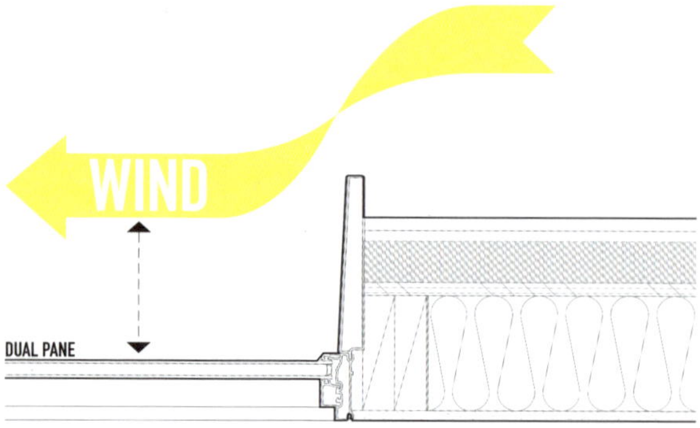

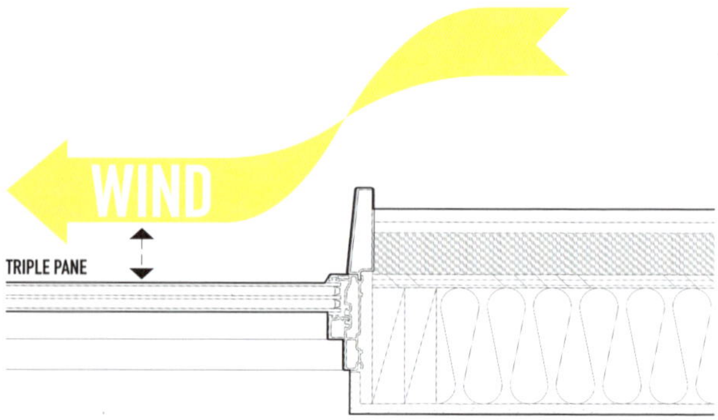

A dual pane window has a similar thermal performance to triple pane when inset into the external wall.

projects.MODELLING: Centre Village (p. 64), Welcome Place (p. 68), Ross Avenue (p. 88)

Welcome Place

Local knowledge

The availability of local trades and materials – as well as prevailing building traditions – have a big impact on construction costs.

Knowledge of these contextual issues, which vary across the country, is a major factor in understanding how to access and design for better pricing. In the context of Winnipeg, a lack of high-rise trades or competitive pricing for concrete, steel and masonry leads many developers to focus on smaller scale buildings and mid-rise construction methods. In the multi-family housing market, it is hard to imagine building cost-effective, mid-scale projects out of anything other than stick framing, where this construction method is widely used and competition is stiff. Conversely, cast-in-place concrete is standard fair on the Canadian coasts and even as close to us as Calgary. Curiously enough, this reality can be traced back to the days of mass immigration from Europe. The concentration of various populations and their prevailing building traditions have carried through generations, whether from Southern (masonry) or Eastern Europe (stick framing).

There is also a big difference in price between small-scale residential trades and so-called commercial trades. We were taught one such lesson early on by the young developer for **youCUBE**, who realized through the design process that breaking down the scale of his 18-unit housing project into single-family house-sized parts would allow him to access much cheaper residential builders. This would not have been possible if the project had been a more typical contiguous single-mass building.

In the case of **62M**, the construction type is true hybrid – the prefabricated concrete piers and the radial steel base merely form a "new ground plane" onto which a more traditional dimensional lumber frame could be constructed. Due to the three-storey building classification, using dimensional lumber became possible, presenting savings in construction costs and schedule. The prefabricated wood floor, wall and roof elements were constructed off site and hoisted up onto the platform for quick on-site assembly.

 projects.MODELLING: youCUBE (p. 60), 62M (p. 96)

Radial steel beams on tilt-up precast concrete columns and cast-in-place concrete core, with prefabricated floor sections & precast concrete corridor slabs during installation.

Low-cost cladding

Local knowledge of available and dominant cladding materials is equally valuable when it comes to achieving fair budgets.

Stucco, cementitious panels and off-the-shelf corrugated metals represent the most economical and durable cladding options in Winnipeg, depending on the application. The lowest cost stucco application, and the lowest cost cladding overall, is a standard textured treatment over traditional building paper and wire mesh. The untreated stucco remains breathable and due to the slight wrinkling of the paper when wet stucco is applied, creates a modest rain screen that in addition to natural evaporation allows driven rain to drain below the façade and contributes to the longevity of the building envelope. Of course, this is only effective in relatively dry continental climates with limited precipitation. With **youCUBE**, the façade design mixes low-cost stucco with larger windows framed out by powder-coated aluminum extensions for further visual impact.

As with **youCUBE**, **The Avenue**'s low-cost cladding choice provided a means to achieve a trade off for something more impactful. In this case, repointing and repainting the historic brick façade, as opposed to more extensive restoration or recladding, allowed the client to reinvest the $200,000 savings into the creation of twenty cantilevered balconies that provide the building's signature expression as well as an additional revenue source.

At **548 Stradbrook**, simple massing and interior volumes allowed for a more inventive façade treatment. For the glass cladding of **548 Stradbrook**, using the typical installation methods for downtown office towers, this application would result in $60-$80 CAD per square foot construction costs. Working together with a local glass supplier and installer, we were able to devise a system that cost $18 CAD per square foot. This value is transferred back to the project, providing a higher quality building for the community, street and owners.

projects.MODELLING: youCUBE (p. 60), The Avenue (p. 76), 548 Stradbrook (p. 80)

62M

youCUBE

The Avenue

548 Stradbrook

Demystify details

It is important to demystify any unusual or atypical building details in order to achieve fair pricing at construction tender.

All too often, innovative elements suffer a pricing up-charge unless the architect is able to remove the guesswork and convince potential bidders that a particular detail or application can be straightforward. This process may require an actual demonstration and some showmanship. For the custom cladding design at **Webbsite**, Johanna assembled a sample of the system in front of potential bidders prior to tender close.

Another avenue might involve additional drawing packages, axonometric assembly details, and digital or physical models. We have deployed all of these strategies at one time or another in order to overcome pricing barriers. For **youCUBE**, a physical framing scale model helped explain the seemingly complicated, but in reality relatively straightforward assembly to the construction team. With **BGBX**, an additional cladding detail package was issued after the initial pricing came back out of budget, resulting in the desired outcome.

youCUBE 1/4"= 1'-0" framing model helped the builder visualize the construction.

projects.MODELLING: Webbsite (p. 52), youCUBE (p. 60), BGBX (p. 56)

Custom fabrication / assembly

In an effort to keep costs down, it can be necessary to rethink off-the-shelf methods, which are typically too expensive.

Establishing ongoing and trusting relationships with builders and fabricators is invaluable when attempting to deliver quality for less, or in particular when testing new methods, assemblies, applications, details or materials. We have been fortunate to find collaborators that have allowed us to produce custom designs and specialized components for less.

Our work in this arena includes numerous cost-effective cladding systems, a hybrid projection screen, security wall and adjustable curtain, various privacy and sun shading screens, balconies, window cowlings, stairs, light shades, partition walls and an integrated floor slab/mechanical system – all leading to a growing library of locally conceived and manufactured design responses.

Melvin Kleinsasser of Klartech, a long-term collaborator of 546. Concord Hutterite colony just north of Winnipeg has tested and fabricated numerous components and entire cladding systems for 546's projects.

Custom fabrication: case study 90-100 Alexander

Custom cladding was developed as a reinterpretation of masonry detailing and interlocking evident in the surrounding historic buildings. Cladding is approached from a perspective of buildability, taking a rudimentary six-inch deep brake shape "flashing"and deploying across all façades in a straightforward and unique way. Using repeatable lengths, the installation pattern allows for the creation of more intense overlaps around windows, creating a modern interpretation of quoining at the corners of the building. The system had to be able to satisfy a variety of conditions from turning inside / outside corners to stretching along different lengths of property line. The same cladding system acts as a guardrail on rooftop patios as well as a screening of all rooftop mechanical equipment (supported by a lightweight galvanized steel frame).

A Typical Cladding Module [17 part version shown]
B Support clip provides stiffness and helps reduce gauge of main component
C Finger-joint overlap of cladding modules
D Open system conceals mechanical vents
E Vertical offset organized for finger-jointed overlap at all corners
F Cladding pattern extends to sloped steel frame at roof patio trellis
G Window pattern repeats as openings in roof patio trellis
H Shaped screening at grade using standard components on open steel frame

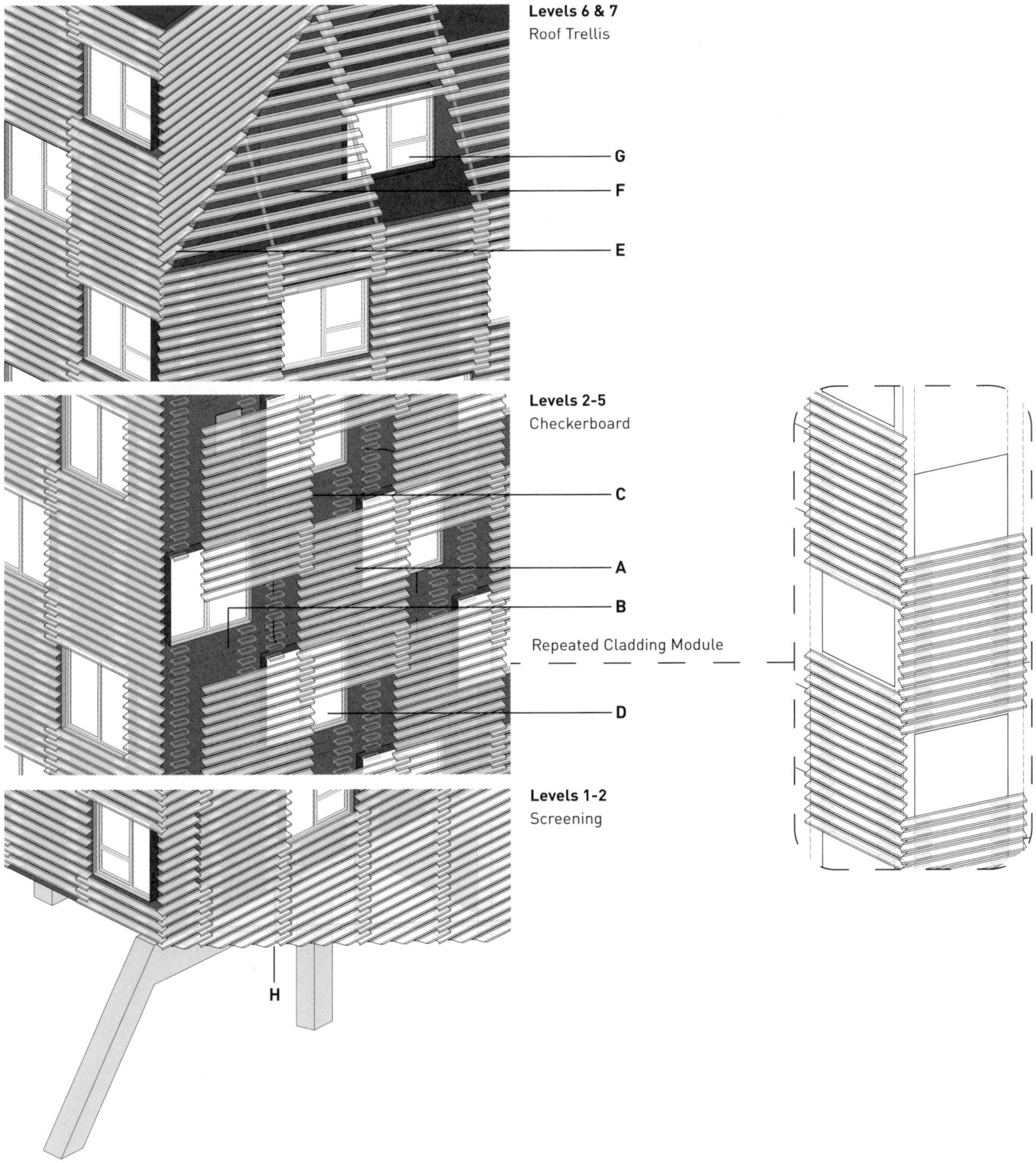
Levels 6 & 7
Roof Trellis
G
F
E
Levels 2-5
Checkerboard
C
A
B
Repeated Cladding Module
D
Levels 1-2
Screening
H

Custom fabrication: case study 62M

A "circular" building should read as a "circle." Aiming to avoid the "facets" typical of other low-budget curved buildings, the design team worked with the builder and custom sheet metal fabricators to find innovative ways to build a non-standard building form using standard methods. A gradual transition from orthogonal to curvature is achieved with the approximate 10 inch maximum curve depth in each suite.

A series of custom formed one foot deep pre-finished steel fins are placed at each window frame to help conceal the faceted window systems [2.5 facets per suite], the seams in fascia panels and the associated connectors.

This approach to detail is carried through to the structure where precast concrete columns utilize two types of blocking to create a multitude of column shapes. The resulting ledges and niches create light and shadow patterns on the smooth concrete surfaces while providing extra space for parking and ledges for soffit focused lighting.

01 Full height, wall to wall **windows** give each suite approx. 200 sf of continuous glazing. With no budget for standard curtain wall, large fibreglass windows are used instead. Five window widths create unique fenestration combinations for each unit while adhering to a standard repeatable and stackable system.
02 A continuous **recessed chase** along the windows provides concealed heating and contributes to the visual extension of the suite interior through to the tree canopy & city beyond.
03 A simple **wood frame structure** perpendicular to the trusses [top and bottom] forms the framework for the shallow fascia curvature.
04 Heavy gauge aluminum **window sill** flashing with curved leading edge and integrated drip.
05 **Rolled weathering steel panels** act as flashing, cladding and fin connectors. Combining functions reduces install time in a hard to access area.
06 Custom formed pre-finished **steel fins** conceal panel breaks, fasteners and window facets while providing shade and façade variation.
07 Two layers of thin **plywood substrate** smooth out the faceted wood system.
08 A heavy rolled aluminum **perimeter angle** finishes the soffit and presents a continuous round edge from below.
09 Pre-finished black diamond shingle soffit cladding.
10 Radial steel beams support a simple wood truss **floor structure**. Steel beams are supported by the CIP concrete core and by precast concrete columns.

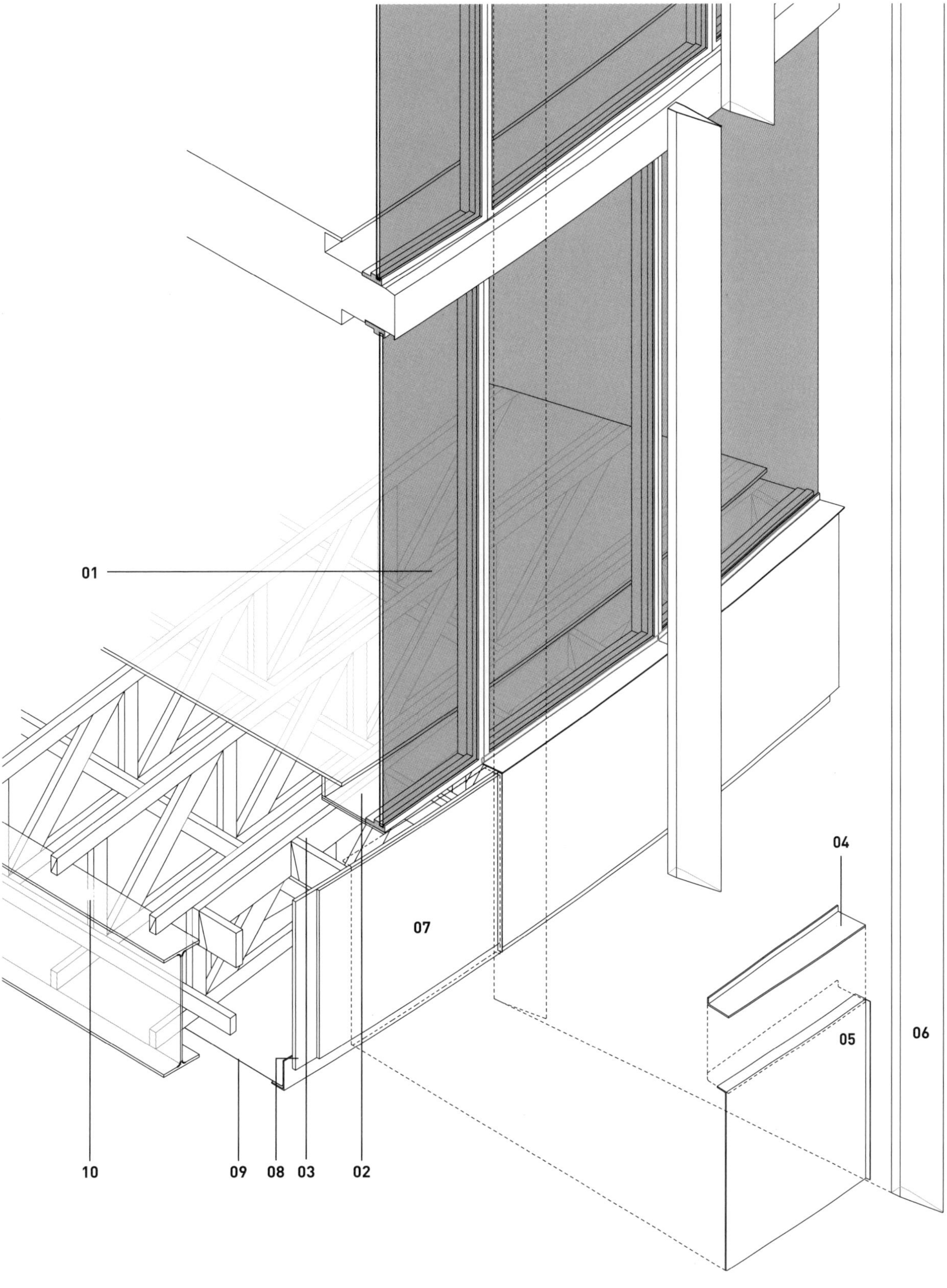
01
04
05
06
07
10
09
08
03
02

Custom assembly: case study
548 Stradbrook

The shingled glass façade of Stradbrook Condominiums is composed of reflective panels and a pre-finished aluminum clip system. The façade is a rainscreen application.While the panels themselves shed the majority of rainwater, the true water barrier is achieved through the use of a heavy, UV-resistant water resistive barrier [WRB] inboard of the glass. An approximately one-inch airspace separates the WRB and the finished panels, allowing sufficient space for air circulation, drainage and evaporation off the surface of the membrane. The aluminum clip system is fastened through the sheathing into the studs beyond at regular intervals for additional support. The glass panels are applied in a shingle pattern, overlaid both vertically and horizontally across the entire building. The tempered panels follow a simple grid pattern that allows them to be easily substituted for windows wherever necessary. The window surrounds, sills and headers are wrapped in stainless steel sheet edging to ensure that all glass panels are consistent in size and no cut-offs are required. The mirror-like finish and subtle angling of the glass creates an ephemeral interplay of reflections and light during the day and transforms the building into a glowing apparition at night.

01 Finished flooring
5/8" Tongue and groove plywood
14" TJI Joists @ 1'-4" o.c.
Acoustical batt insulation
1/2" Resilient channel @ 2'-0" o.c.
5/8" Type X gypsum board [2 layers]
02 Continuous pressure treated blocking @ all clip locations
03 Pressure treated blocking typ. @ all panel locations
04 1/8" Aluminum panel
05 Prefinished flashing typ. @ all window heads
06 Glass panel beyond
07 Spray foam insulation typ. all sides of windows
08 1/2" laminated & tempered glass cladding [reflective coating]
UV resistive WRB, black
7/16" OSB sheathing
2X6 Wood studs @ 1'-4" o.c.
Continuous P.T. wood blocking
R22 Batt insulation
6 mil. Poly air & vapour barrier
5/8" Type X gypsum board, painted
09 4"x1/4" SS Lag bolts
10 1/4" Gap typical @ all corners
11 1x4 Pressure treated vertical furring every second column of clips.
Carry WRB over furring strips, typ.
12 Mill finished aluminum glass edge fitting clips
13 Gypsum board return typ. @ all window & door locations
14 Pressure treated wood closure painted black, angle cut to match glass angle, typ. @ all window & door jambs

 projects.MODELLING: 548 Stradbrook (p. 80)

El. 128'-3 3/8"
Top of subfloor mezzanine

El. 126'-11"
U.S. of finished ceiling level 3

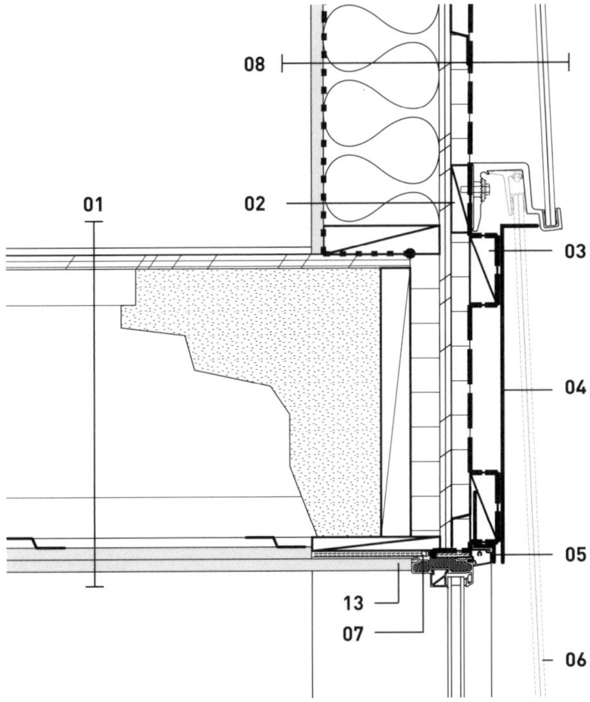

Section: Window detail

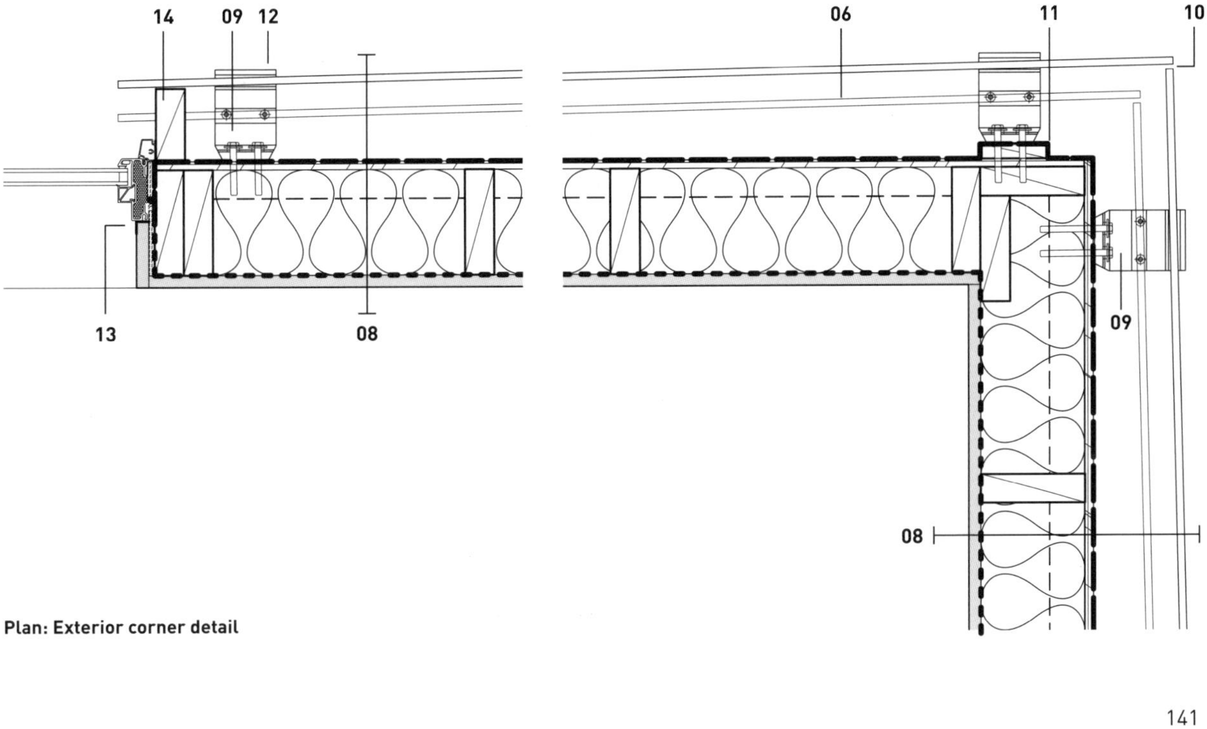

Plan: Exterior corner detail

Custom assembly: case study
Hedge

The building is clad in corrugated weathering steel, giving added depth through the addition of a standard chainlink mesh screen that spans vertically between deep flashing angles. These are spaced to create an eight-inch gap between steel and mesh where planters are placed. The mesh itself is modulated in density, creating additional depth and texture on the façade, but also ensuring safety where French balconies open onto the screen. The mesh visually screens parking along the street level, and serves as the guardrail along the bridges. Three strains of ivy grow from the planters and extend up and through the mesh, creating a third, vegetal layer of depth. Two varieties provide colourful blossoms, while the third retains its green foliage year-round (a welcome anomaly in the Winnipeg context). The façade is thus conceived as a green wall that gives soft life and depth to the building.

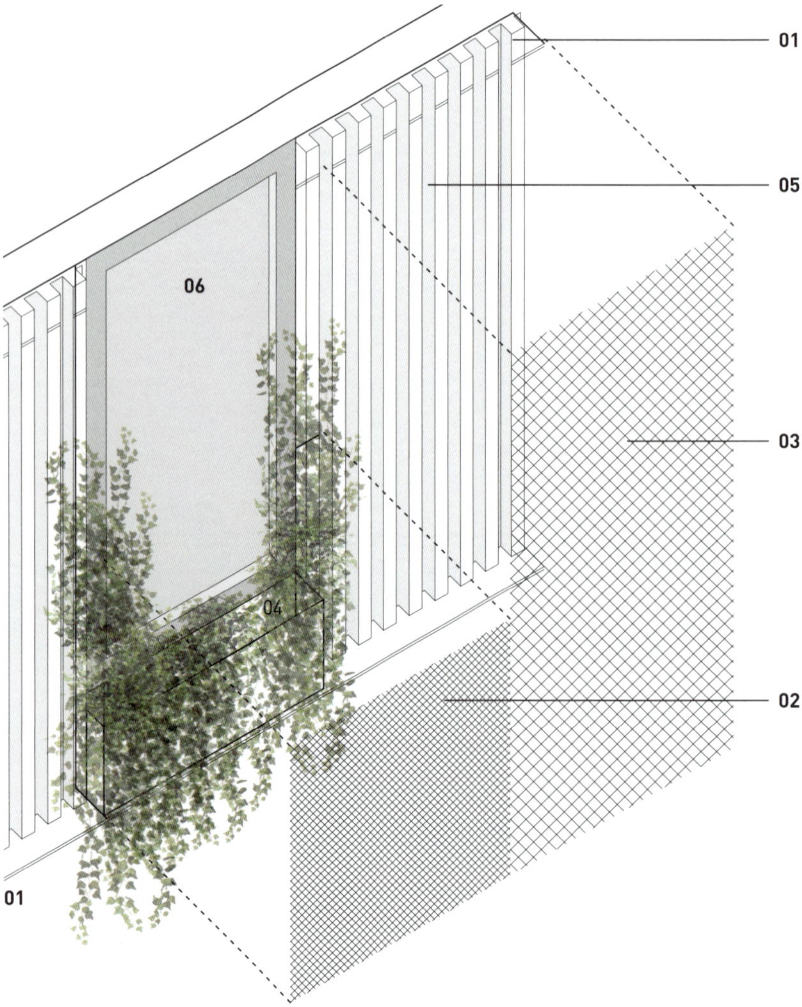

Hedra - mix 70%

Clematis - mix 15%

Lonicera - mix 15%

01 Flashing angle
02 Mesh guardrail
03 Mesh large weave
04 Planters box
05 Corrugated weathering steel
06 Windows

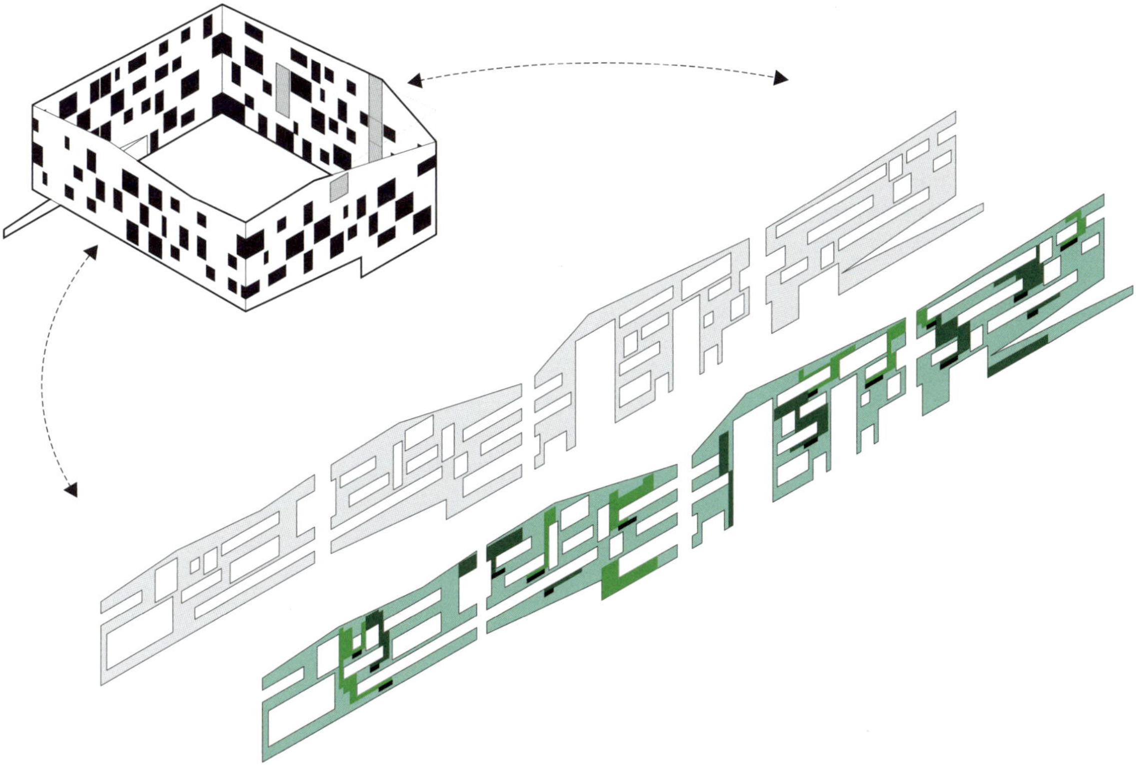

North building

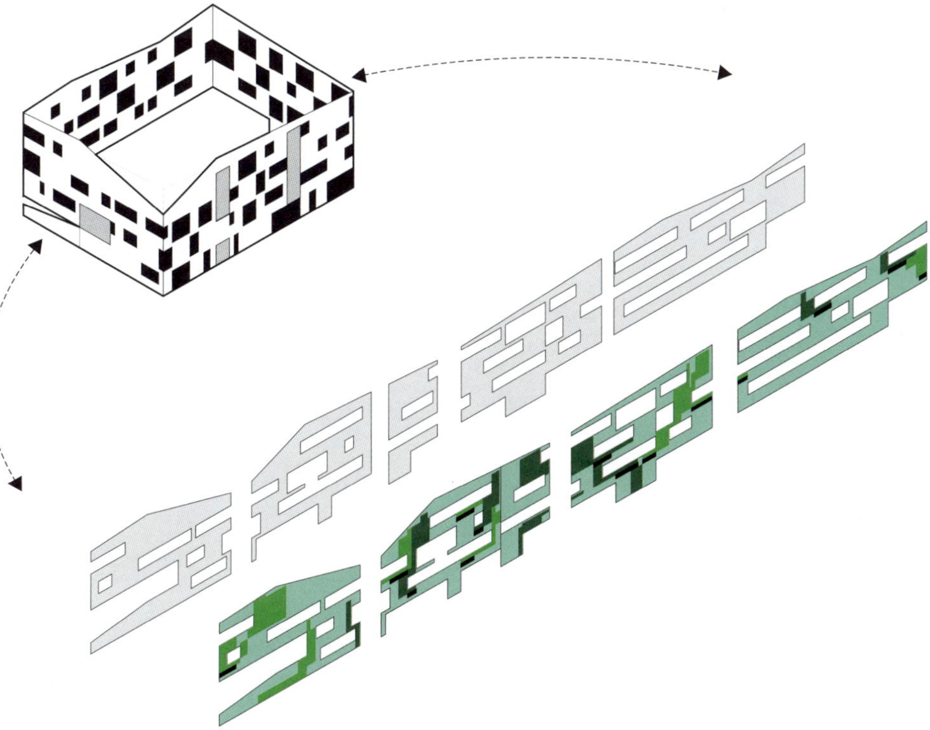

South building

Custom assembly: case study Pumphouse

The new interior partitions and floor assembly of the James Avenue Pumphouse pay homage to the utilitarian origins of the existing heritage building around it. The rudimentary material palette consists of exposed painted steel studs, spaced at two-feet on centre, and 1/4" tempered glass panels, that span two feet and act as a guardrail. The two-foot wide panels are light and easy to handle for added ease of construction. A custom brakeshape at the base of the stud enables fastening of the system to the face of the adjoining floor plate. As such, the entire glazed assembly became more economical than a traditional gypsum board partition, avoiding the labour associated with multiple rounds of taping, mudding, sanding and painting on site.

The new floor, suspended above the historic equipment, is supported on the old gantry crane beams, with the original gantry crane used to install and service the original fire suppression pumps. The new steel structure is supported on these existing beams, and in turn, supports a back to back three inch deep steel deck with a cast concrete finish floor. Black fibre board panelling on ceilings and walls replaces a typical gypsum board, while simultaneously addressing sound transfer and attenuation within the new office interior.

Ceiling and wall assembly

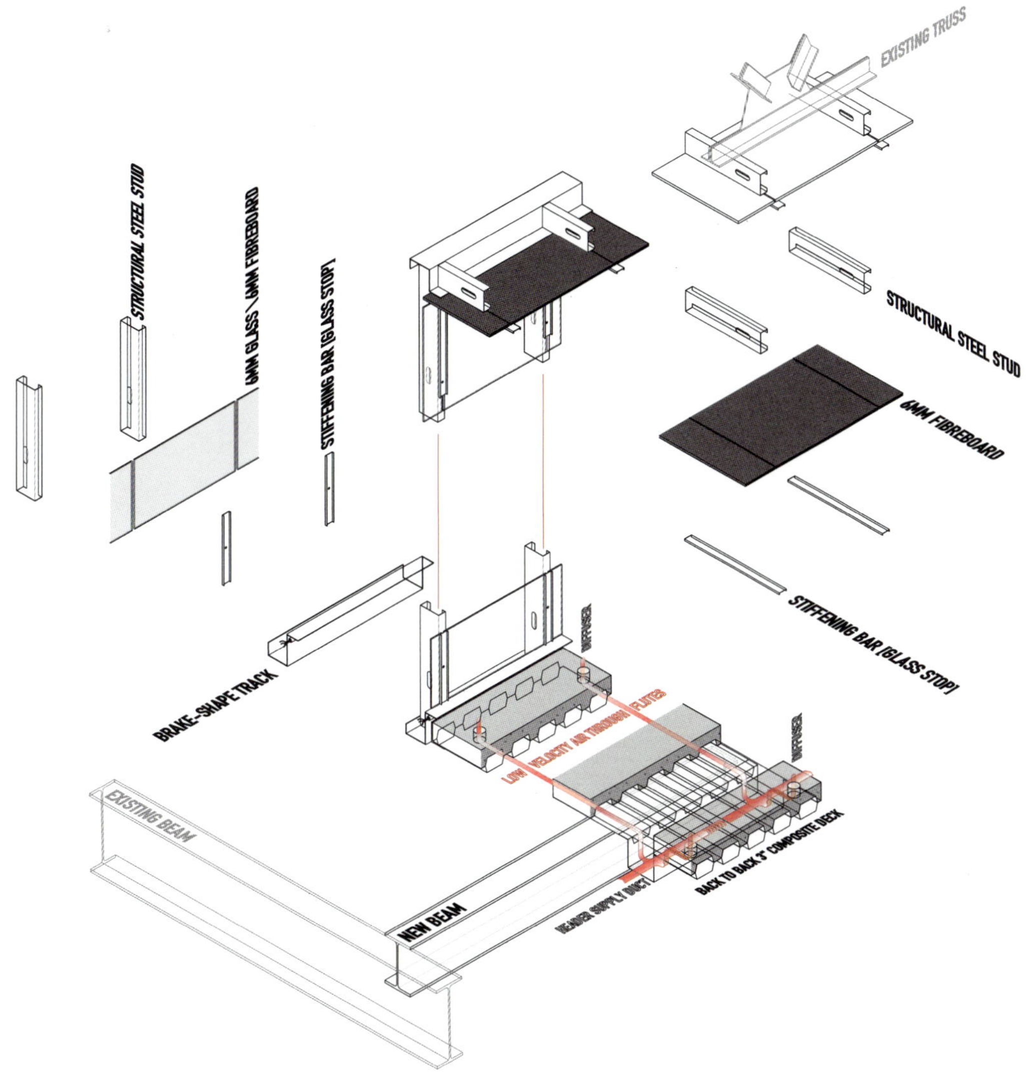

Floor and wall assembly

A	B	C	D	E	F
Custom brake-shape	Structural steel stud	Stiffening bar	6mm glass	6mm fibreboard	3" corrugated metal

Kit of parts
Forming floors + walls + ceiling within existing structure

building.

OPTIMISM

While by no means do we feel that we have all the answers, our experience has armed us with a set of convictions resulting from the particular realities of our own context and circumstance. Through our quest for conceptual clarity and robustness, we strive to remain nimble and curious in order to capture opportunities that can unlock a project's potential beyond a profit line.

Taking time to define the parameters early on in the design process allows us to distill a project to its fundamental core. This creates a roadmap that establishes the right hierarchy of design ideas and priorities for the duration of the project. Regardless of the turbulence that inevitably follows as a project matures and external pressures increase, this roadmap encourages us to hang on to what we have collectively deemed to be the most important aspects of each design. With this clarity, we can react to changes without losing sight of the whole.

For us, one sign of a great project is when the final outcome is far removed from our initial inclinations. This does not mean that we suppress intuition. Rather, we try to engage in an iterative, open-ended and flexible process that allows our ideas to evolve as we react to various conditions, clients and end users. Letting go of preconceived notions opens the door to innovation, or even true invention. Flexibility is necessary to allow projects to mature and improve with each obstacle, instead of eroding as issues arise. Our most successful interventions are ones that have transformed from their original diagram or sketch into a detailed narrative that directly supports the project's core architectural values.

In the face of challenging global circumstances, it is all too easy to grow complacent and default to the common denominator. If we can conclude this publication with a singular call to action, it is that we must approach our work as architects with unrelenting optimism in the face of what at first might appear to be insurmountable odds. It is in fact these challenges that make a project great. With adaptability and resilience, through advocacy and community building, we can meet the demands of a changing world.

68

post.SCRIPT

Bibliography

Ally Schweitzer, "An Ambitious Housing Proposal in Virginia is Dead – For Now," *WAMU*, January 23, 2020, https://wamu.org/story/20/01/23/an-ambitious-housing-proposal-in-virginia-is-dead-for-now/.

Alyse Kotyk, "Vancouver's Empty Home Tax is Increasing to 3% Next Year," *CTV News*, November 25, 2020, https://bc.ctvnews.ca/vancouver-s-empty-home-tax-is-increasing-to-3-next-year-1.5204533.

Amelyn Ng, "Amsterdam Social Housing: A Primer," *Assemble Paper* #10: Housing (October 2018), https://assemblepapers.com.au/2018/12/13/amsterdam-social-housing-a-primer/.

Andra Hopulele, "Millennials Study: Down Payment Delay Homeownership by up to 35 Years," *Point2 Homes*, August 27, 2018, https://www.point2homes.com/news/canada-real-estate/millennials-down-payments-delay-homeownership-35-years.html.

Andre M. Perry, David Harshbarger, "America's formerly redlined neighborhoods have changed, and so must solutions to rectify them," *Brookings Metro*, October 14, 2019, https://www.brookings.edu/research/americas-formerly-redlines-areas-changed-so-must-solutions/.

Andy Sullivan and Jarrett Renshaw, "Biden Seeks to Ease Housing Shortage with $5 billion 'carrot, no stick' approach," *Reuters*, April 8, 2021, https://www.reuters.com/article/us-United States-biden-infrastructure-zoning-idUSKBN2BV1CX.

Ashok B. Lall, "Rethinking Values in Designing Architecture." *Tekton* 5, no. 1 (March 2018). https://tekton.mes.ac.in/issues/volume-5-issue-1/practice/.

Austin Grabish, "Province Has Sold Off 94 Manitoba Housing Properties Since 2016, Documents Show," *CBC News*, December 2, 2019, https://www.cbc.ca/news/canada/manitoba/manitoba-housing-properties-sold-off-1.5381628.

Bartley Kives, "True North Square Deal Now Includes Grant for Affordable Housing," *CBC News*, September 20, 2018, https://www.cbc.ca/news/canada/manitoba/true-north-square-financing-affordable-housing-1.4831490.

Brian Carney, "The Big Reason We're Not Serious About Tackling Housing Affordability," *The Tyee*, December 30, 2019, https://thetyee.ca/Opinion/2019/12/30/Housing-Unaffordability-Big-Reason/.

Canadian Home Builders Association, "New Report Offers Insight on How to Improve Municipal Processes, Fees and Charges That are Affecting Housing Affordability and Supply in Canada," https://www.chba.ca/CHBA/News/Municipal_Benchmarking_Study.aspx.

Catherine Slessor and Rob Gregory, "Emerging Architecture and Creative Resilience," *The Architectural Review*, November 23, 2012, https://www.architectural-review.com/awards/emerging-architecture-and-creative-resilience.

Center for Neighborhood Technology (CNT), Housing and Transportation Index, https://www.cnt.org/tools/housing-and-transportation-affordability-index.

Charlie Smith. "Report Forecasts 1.1 Million Population Rise in Lower Mainland by 2041, Requiring 500,000 New Housing Units." *The Georgia Straight*, January 22, 2019, https://www.straight.com/news/1191291/report-forecasts-11-million-population- rise-lower-mainland-2041-requiring-500000-new.

Chris Roberts, "The Great Eliminator: How Ronald Reagan Made Homelessness Permanent," *SFWeekly*, June 29, 2016, https://www.sfweekly.com/news/the-great-eliminator-how-ronald-reagan-made-homelessness-permanent/.

City of Edmonton, "Missing Middle Zoning Review," https://www.edmonton.ca/city_government/urban_planning_and_design/medium-scale-housing-review.aspx.

City of Toronto, "Inclusionary Zoning Policy," https://www.toronto.ca/city-government/planning-development/planning-studies-initiatives/inclusionary-zoning-policy/.

City of Vancouver, "Housing Vancouver: 10 Year Affordable Housing Delivery and Financial Strategy," 2017, https://vancouver.ca/files/cov/affordable-housing-delivery-and-financial-strategy.pdf.

CMHC, "Affordable Housing Innovation Fund," https://www.cmhc-schl.gc.ca/en/professionals/project-funding-and-mortgage-financing/funding-programs/all-funding-programs/affordable-housing-innovation-fund.

CMHC, "Housing Research Report: New Models for Co-operative Housing," January, 2018, https://4bfebv17goxj464grl4a02gz-wpengine.netdna-ssl.com/wp-content/uploads/2019/01/Canada-CHMC-new_models_for_co-op_housing.pdf.

Conor Dougherty, "California, Mired in a Housing Crisis, Rejects an Effort to Ease It," *The New York Times*, January 30, 2020, https://www.nytimes.com/2020/01/30/business/economy/sb50-california-housing.html.

Co-operative Housing International, "Housing Cooperatives Worldwide: United States of America," https://www.housinginternational.coop/co-ops/united-states-of-america/.

Daniel Parolek, *Missing Middle Housing: Thinking Big and Building Small to Respond to Today's Housing Crisis* (Washington, D.C.: Island Press, 2020).

David Madden and Peter Marcuse, *In Defense of Housing: The Politics of Crisis* (Verso Books: New York, 2016), 17, 26.

Diana Budds, "Will Upzoning Neighborhoods Make Homes More Affordable?" *Curbed*, January 30, 2020, https://archive.curbed.com/2020/1/30/21115351/upzoning-definition-affordable-housing-gentrification.

Diana Elliott and Tanaya Srini, Carl Hedman, Shiva Kooragayala, Cary Lou, "Denver and the State of Low- and Middle-Income Housing: Strategies to Preserve Affordability and Opportunities for the Future," *Urban Institute*, May 19, 2017, https://www.urban.org/research/publication/denver-and-state-low-and-middle-income-housing.

Donella H. Meadows, Dennis L. Meadows, Jorgen Randers and William W. Behrens, III. *The Limits of Growth*. New York, New York: Universe Books, 1972.

Donna Kimura, "Denver Approves Bold Rent Program," *Affordable Housing Finance*, July 16, 2018, https://www.housingfinance.com/policy-legislation/denver-approves-bold-rent-program_o.

Emily Badger and Quoctrung Bui, "Cities Start to Question an American Ideal: A House With a Yard on Every Lot," *The New York Times*, June 18, 2019, https://www.nytimes.com/interactive/2019/06/18/upshot/cities-across-america-question-single-family-zoning.html.

Erick Trickey, "How Minneapolis Feed Itself from the Stranglehold of Single-Family Homes," *Politico Magazine*, July 11, 2019, https://www.politico.com/magazine/story/2019/07/11/housing-crisis-single-family-homes-policy-227265/.

Future Distributed, "Social Housing in Denmark: The Tenant Democracy," June 1, 2021, https://futuredistributed.org/stories/social-housing-denmark/.

Government of Canada, "Canada's National Housing Strategy: A Place to Call Home," January 30, 2018, https://www.placetocallhome.ca/-/media/sf/project/placetocallhome/pdfs/canada-national-housing-strategy.pdf.

Government of the Netherlands, "Basics on Dutch Housing," 2012, https://www.government.nl/topics/investing-in-dutch-housing/basics-dutch-housing.

Greg Suttor, "Lessons from the Past on a National Housing Strategy," *Policy Options*, March 27, 2017, https://policyoptions.irpp.org/magazines/march-2017/lessons-from-the-past-on-a-national-housing-strategy/.

Housing Europe, "Social Housing in Europe: The Netherlands," March 27, 2010, https://www.housingeurope.eu/resource-117/social-housing-in-europe.

HUD USER, "What Happens to LIHTC Properties After Affordability Requirements Expire?" https://www.huduser.gov/portal/pdredge/pdr_edge_research_081712.html.

Ian Froese, "Wait List Soars for Manitoba Housing Units – and So Do The Vacancies," *CBC News*, October 12, 2020, https://www.cbc.ca/news/canada/manitoba/manitoba-housing-unit-vacancies-wait-list-grows-1.5745816.

Ivo Balmer and Tobias Bernet, "Housing as a Common Resource? Decommodification and Self-Organization in Housing – Examples from Germany and Switzerland," Birkhauser, Urban Commons: Moving Beyond State and Market, 2020, https://www.semanticscholar.org/paper/Housing-as-a-common-resource-Decommodification-and-Balmer-Bernet/4cf6121be2aeafcd5bb7973bd8c13483467844ae.

Jan Gehl, *Life Between Buildings: Using Public Space* (Washington, DC: Island Press, 2011), 81.

Jeff Andrews, "Affordable Housing is in Crisis. Is Public Housing the Solution?," *Curbed*, January 13, 2020, https://archive.curbed.com/2020/1/13/21026108/public-housing-faircloth-amendment-election-2020.

John Mackie, "Not-Owner-Occupied Property Skyrockets in Vancouver," *Vancouver Sun*, June 14, 2019, https://vancouversun.com/news/local-news/not-owner-occupied-property-skyrockets-in-vancouver.

John Pattison, "Lessons from Canada: How to End Mandatory Parking Minimums," *Streetsblog USA*, November 23, 2020, https://UnitedStates.streetsblog.org/2020/11/23/lessons-from-canada-how-to-end-mandatory-parking-minimums/.

Jonah Newman, " Renters Can't Afford Their Housing." *The Chicago Reporter*, June 01, 2015. https://www.chicagoreporter.com/half-of-chicago-renters- cant-afford-their-housing/.

Jonas Salk and Jonathan Salk. *World Population and Human Values a New Reality* (New York: Harper & Row, 1981).

Jon Townsend. "Rinus Michels and the Total Football Rebellion," *These Football Times*, January 28, 2016, https:// thesefootballtimes.co/2016/01/28/rinus-michels-and-thew- total-football-rebellion.

Joint Center for Housing Studies of Harvard University, "The State of the Nation's Housing: 2020," https://www.jchs.harvard.edu/sites/default/files/reports/files/Harvard_JCHS_The_State_of_the_Nations_Housing_2020_Report_Revised_120720.pdf.

Justin Fox, "Why America's New Apartment Buildings All Look the Same," *Bloomberg*, February 13, 2019, https://www.bloomberg.com/news/features/2019-02-13/why- america-s-new-apartment-buildings-all-look-the-same.

Katy O'Donnell, "How Biden Hopes to Fix the Thorniest Problem in Housing," *Politico Magazine*, April 10, 2021, https://www.politico.com/news/2021/04/10/biden-housing-plan-480676.

Laurel Wamsley, "Oregon Legislature Votes to Essentially Ban Single-Family Zoning," *NPR*, July 1, 2019, https://www.npr.org/2019/07/01/737798440/oregon-legislature-votes-to-essentially-ban-single-family-zoning.

Leilani Farha, United Nations, "Report of the Special Rapporteur on Adequate Housing as a Component of the Right to an Adequate Standard of Living, and on the Right to Non-Discrimination in This Context," January 18, 2017, https://digitallibrary.un.org/record/861179?ln=en.

Lynne Fernandez, ed., "Change Starts Here: Manitoba Alternative Provincial Budget 2020," *Canadian Centre for Policy Alternatives*, March 3, 2020, https://www.policyalternatives.ca/mbapb2020.

Marian Scott, "Proposed By-law Aims to Fix Affordable Housing Dilemma in Montreal," *Montreal Gazette*, June 12, 2019, https://montrealgazette.com/news/local-news/city-presents-housing-by-law.

Matthew *Soules, Icebergs, Zombies, and the Ultra Thin: Architecture and Capitalism in the Twenty-First Century* (New York: Princeton Architectural Press, 2021), 50.

Metro Vancouver, "The Metro Vancouver Housing and Transportation Cost Burden Study: A New Way of Looking at Affordability," 2015, http://www.metrovancouver.org/services/regional-planning/PlanningPublications/HousingAndTransportCostBurdenReport2015.pdf.

Organization for Economic Co-operation and Development (OECD), "Employment, Labour and Social Affairs Policy Briefs, Social Housing: A Key Part of Past and Future Housing Policy," https://www.oecd.org/social/social-housing-policy-brief-2020.pdf, 5, 6.

Paris Schutz, "Report: City Misuses Affordable Housing Funds," *WWTW News*, March 28, 2017, https://news.wttw.com/2017/03/28/report-city-misuses-affordable-housing-funds.

Patrick Condon, "Portland Just Showed Vancouver How to Fix Its Housing Crisis," *The Tyee*, August 28, 2020, https://thetyee.ca/Analysis/2020/08/28/Portland-Showed-Vancouver-Fix-Housing-Crisis/.

Patrick Condon, "Uh oh. I'm a Planner and Planning Makes Housing More Expensive," *The Tyee*, February 26, 2019, https://thetyee.ca/Analysis/2019/02/26/Planning-Expensive/.

Postmedia News, "City Launching Consultation on Proposed Redevelopment of Varsity Fire Station," *Calgary Herald*, January 16, 2018, https://calgaryherald.com/news/local-news/city-launching-consultation-on-proposed-redevelopment-of-varsity-fire-station.

Rachel Bergen, "Welcome Place to Lose One-Third of Budget After Federal Funding Cut," *CBC News*, August 17, 2019, https://www.cbc.ca/news/canada/manitoba/welcome-place-funding-1.5251191.

Research and Markets, "Global Real Estate Market Report 2021," March 18, 2021, https://www.prnewswire.com/news-releases/global-real-estate-market-report-2021-market-is-expected-to-grow-from-2687-35-billion-in-2020-to-3717-03-billion-in-2025---forecast-to-2030--301250151.html.

Richard Florida, *The New Urban Crisis: How Our Cities Are Increasing Inequality, Deepening Segregation, and Failing the Middle Class – and What We Can Do About It* (New York: Basic Books, 2017), 21, 192, 202.

Rick Jacobus, "Why Voters Haven't Been Buying the Case for Building," *Shelterforce*, February 19, 2019, https://shelterforce.org/2019/02/19/why-voters-havent-been-buying-the-case-for-building/.

Sasha Hauswald and Stephanie Reyes, "Lasting Affordability is the Path to Resilience," *Shelterforce*, August 2, 2020, https://shelterforce.org/2020/08/02/lasting-affordability-is-the-path-to-resilience/.

Statistics Canada, "Canada's Core Public Infrastructure Survey," October 9, 2018, https://www150.statcan.gc.ca/n1/daily-quotidien/181009/dq181009a-eng.htm.

Statistics Canada. "First Results from the Canadian Housing Survey: 2018," November 22, 2019, https://www150.statcan.gc.ca/n1/daily-quotidien/191122/dq191122c-eng.htm.

Statistics Canada, "One in Ten Canadian Households Living in Core Housing Need in 2018," *The Daily*, October 2, 2020, https://www150.statcan.gc.ca/n1/daily-quotidien/201002/dq201002a-eng.htm

Ted Kesik, Liam O'Brien and Terri Peters, "MURB Design Guide: Enhancing the Liveability and Resilience of Multi-Unit Residential Buildings," February 2019, https://pbs.daniels.utoronto.ca/faculty/kesik_t/PBS/Kesik-Resources/MURB-Design-Guide-v2-Feb2019.pdf.

Terry Gross, "A 'Forgotten History' Of How The U.S. Government Segregated America," Fresh Air, *NPR*, May 3, 2017, https://www.npr.org/2017/05/03/526655831/a-forgotten-history-of-how-the-u-s-government-segregated-america.

The World Bank, "Inclusionary Zoning," https://urban-regeneration.worldbank.org/node/46.

Tom Carter and Chesya Polevychok, "Housing is Good Social Policy," Canadian Policy Research Networks (CPRN), Research Report F|50, December, 2004, http://www.urbancenter.utoronto.ca/pdfs/elibrary/CPRN_Housing-Good-Soc-Polic.pdf.

Urban Institute, "Features, The Cost of Affordable Housing: Does it Pencil Out?," https://apps.urban.org/features/cost-of-affordable-housing/.

Image credits

All photographs are by James Brittain Photography and property of 5468796 Architecture unless otherwise indicated.

12 Migrating Landscapes (2012). Photograph by Lisa Stinner-Kun.

23 (top right, bottom left) Pumphouse. Photographs by 5468796 Architecture.

30 Parkade of the Future. Photograph by RedPoint Media.

36 Piha. Photographs by Johanna Hurme. Courtesy of Johanna Hurme.

37 Piha. Map data taken from Google Earth, year unknown.

47 62M. Photograph by James Florio.

51 62M. Photograph by Johanna Hurme.

56 62M. Aerial photography. Copyright Pictometry Canada Corp. 2021.

68 Bloc_10. Photograph by Lisa Stinner-Kun.

82 BGBX and Pumphouse. Photographs by 5468796 Architecture.

92 Webbsite and 62M. Photograph and collage by 5468796 Architecture.

Welcome Place. Aerial photography. Copyright Pictometry Canada Corp. 2021.

102 Edge on Princess. Photograph by 5468796 Architecture.

62M. Aerial photography. Copyright Pictometry Canada Corp. 2021.

112 62M. Photograph by James Florio.

147 Table for 1200. Photograph by Jacqueline Young | Station-point Photographic.

platform.MIDDLE: Architecture for Housing the 99%
5468796 Architecture
First edition, 2023
ISBN 978-607-8880-19-5

platform.MICRO

© 5468796 Architecture Inc.
Winnipeg, MB
Canada

© Arquine, SA de CV
Ámsterdam 163 A
Colonia Hipódromo, 06100
Ciudad de México

Texts
© 5468796 Architecture

Images
© Authors specified on the image credits page

5468796 Architecture

Original layout and Editorial Management
Johanna Hurme, Sasa Radulovic, Ken Borton, Shannon Wiebe, Ainsley Johnston and Hugh Taylor

Content production
Emeil Alvarez, Pablo Batista, Jordy Craddock, Donna Evans, Teresa Garside, Ben Greenwood, Ralph Guitierrez, Jeffrey Kachkan, Matthew Kurtas, Andrew Lawler, Kelsey McMahon, Mohammad Massoumi, Colin Neufeld and Amanda Reis.

Past collaborators: Sharon Ackerman, Mandy Aldcorn, Maria Amagasu, Apollinaire Au, Brandon Bergem, Eric Decumutan, Jason Ejzenbart, Michelle Heath, Aynslee Hurdal, Caroline Inglis, Lucretia Ionescu, Andriy Ivanystskyy, Eva Kiss, Stanislav Klas, Lindsey Koepke, Grant Labossiere, Justin Lieberman, Jayne Miles, Royce O'Toole, Zach Pauls, Simone Prill, Sean Radford, Erin Riediger, Helia Saadat, Shannon Scott, Hasan Shurrab, Renee Struthers, Trent Thompson, Matthew Trendota, Alan Vamos, Jennifer Yablonowski and Dazhong Yi.

Arquine

Director
Miquel Adrià

Editorial Director
Brenda Soto Suárez

Editorial Assistants
Ana Luz Valencia and Karina Reyes

Layout
María Marín de Buen, Yavanna Latapí and Regina Sierra
(Estudio María Marín de Buen)

Proofreading
Fionn Petch

Prepress
Offset Rebosán

5468796.ca
arquine.com

The architects and publishers have made every effort to identify ownership in the use of images and copyrighted material. In the event of an inadvertent omission or error, please notify the publisher.

No part of this publication may be reproduced, stored in a retrieval system, or transmitted in any form or by any means, electronic, mechanical, photocopying, recording or otherwise, without prior and express written permission of the owners of the intellectual property rights and of the publishers.

platform.MICRO is one of four volumes in the publication *platform. MIDDLE: Architecture for Housing the 99%*. The other volumes include: platform.MIDDLE, platform.MACRO and projects.MODELLING.

platform.MIDDLE: Architecture for Housing the 99% was printed and bound in September 2023 by Artron Art Printing Ltd. in China. It was printed on 100 g IKPP paper and set in typefaces of the DIN family. The print run was 1,300 copies.

5468796 Architecture

projects.MODELLING

projects.MODELLING

projects.MODELLING is a reference catalogue, breaking down a selection of 5468796 projects in **Advocacy + activism**, **Urban design** and **Multi-family housing** that are discussed throughout each volume. The following project sheets offer extended background information, statistics and specify building particulars that set each project apart.

Project matrix

Advocacy + activism

Migrating Landscapes
2012

Table for 12 + 1200
2013

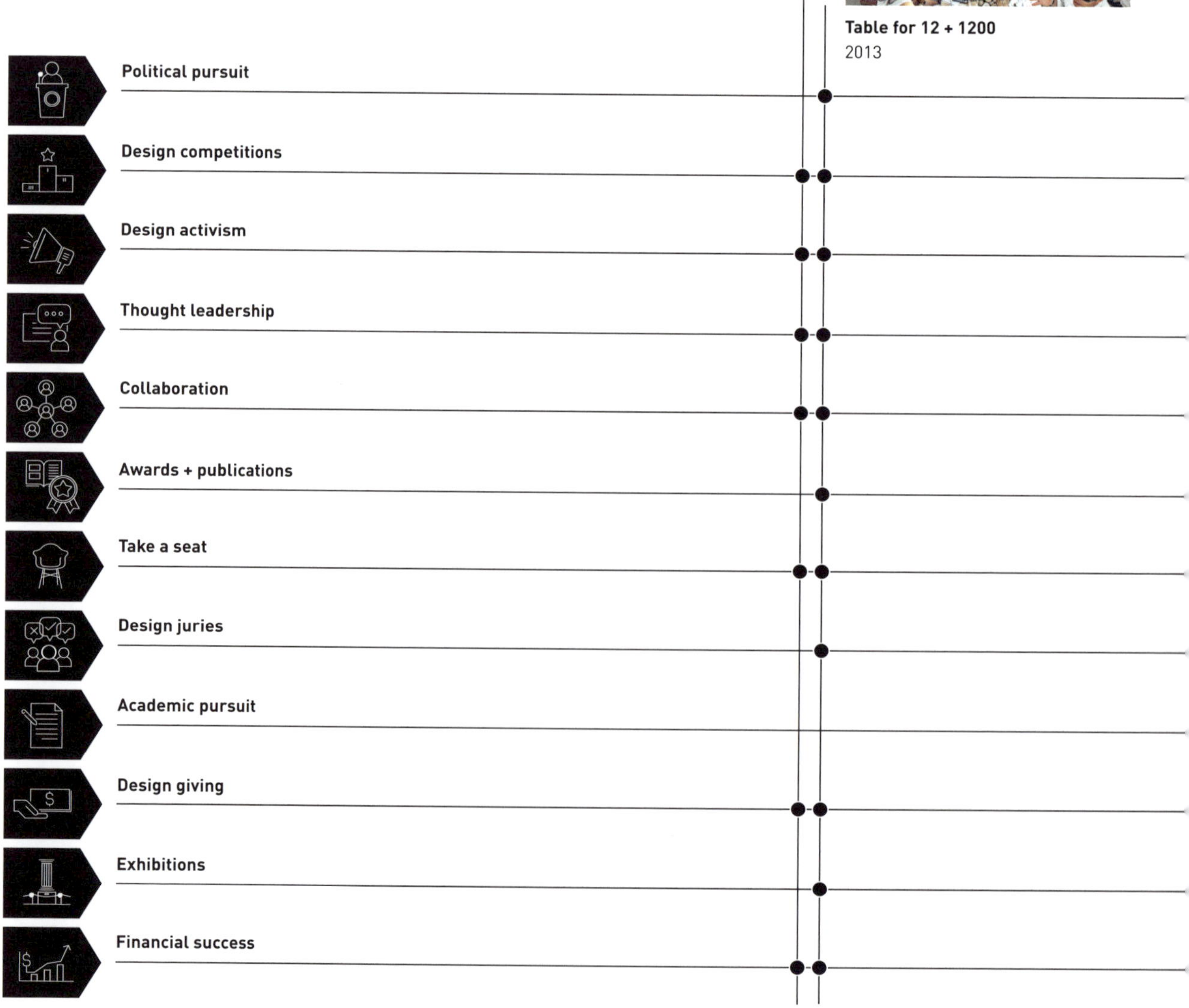

Chair Your Idea
2015

Design Quarter
2016

One Bucket at a Time
2017

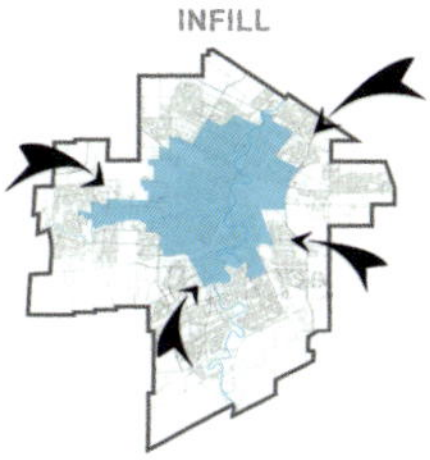

Food for Thought
2017

Walk Winnipeg
2019

ReTree
2021

Project matrix

Urban design + multi-family housing

Webbsite

Welcome Place

BGBX

Bloc_10

Railside

youCUBE

The Avenue

Chroma East

Centre Village

548 Stradbrook

	Chroma East	Railside	Webbsite	BGBX	youCUBE	Centre Village	Welcome Place	Bloc_10	The Avenue	548 Stradbrook
Type										
New construction	●	●	●	●	●	●	●		●	●
Adaptive reuse									●	
Ownership										
Market rate condominiums	●	●	●	●	●		●			●
Subsidized condominiums										
Market rate rental	●	●			●				●	
Subsidized rental	●	●				●			●	
Supportive housing	●	●					●			
Typology										
Low-rise [3 storeys or less]	●	●	●	●	●	●	●			
Mid-rise [3 storeys and more]	●	●					●		●	●
Use / occupancy										
Housing only						●	●			●
Mixed-use	●	●	●	●	●		●		●	
Parking										
Enclosed parking		●							●	
Covered parking		●		●	●					●
Surface parking	●	●	●	●		●	●			●

OZ

Ross Avenue

Treehouse

62M

LIFE

Warehouse 1885

CY33

Pumphouse

90-100 Alexander

Rundle

Catherine

3319 Douglas

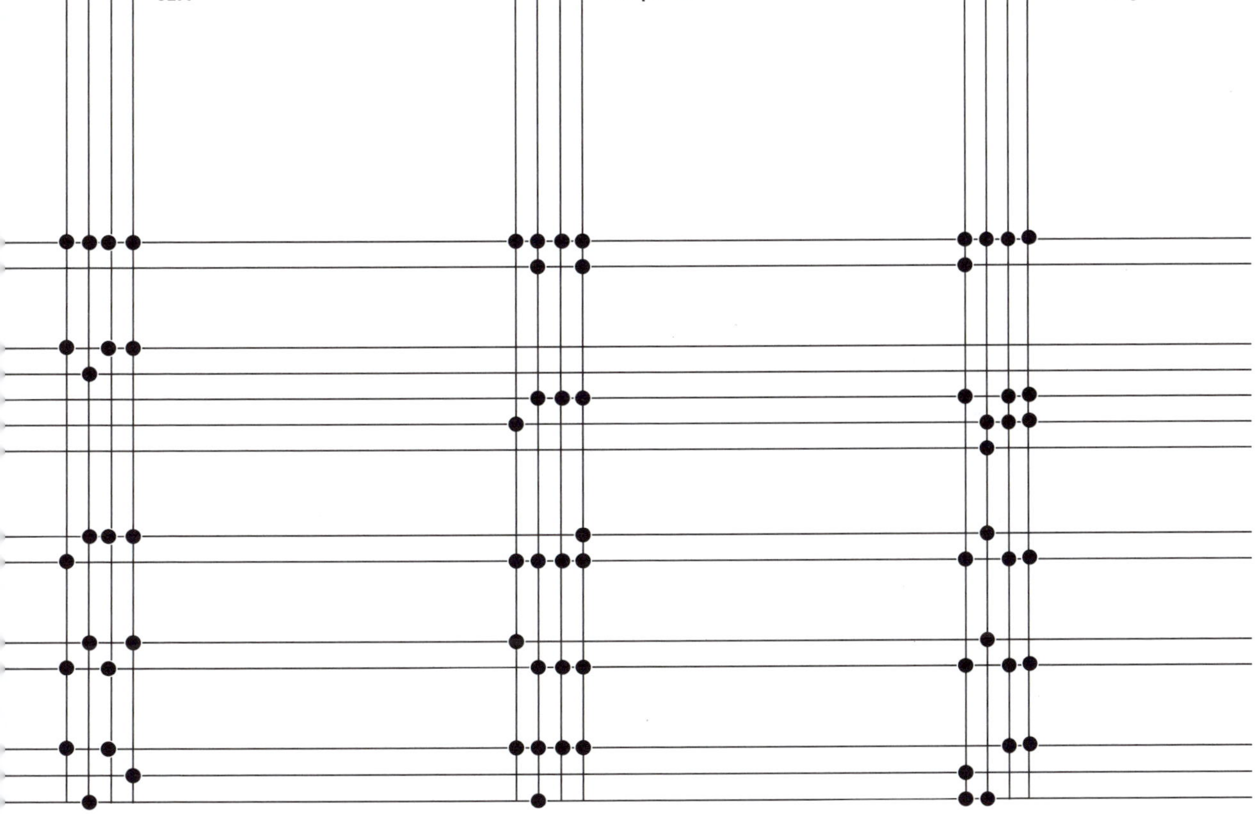

ADVOCACY + ACTIVISM

Migrating Landscapes

Migrating Landscapes was Canada's official submission to the 2012 Venice Biennale in Architecture.

Migrating Landscapes was Canada's official submission to the 2012 Venice Biennale in Architecture. The exhibition explored the settling-unsettling dynamic of im/migration, acting as a forum for Canadian designers to investigate and expose the unique manifestations of cultural memory that overlay our country. With eight exhibitions across the country before a final stop in Venice, Migrating Landscapes helped reawaken Canada's architectural and development community. Countless volunteers committed hundreds of hours, and invaluable corporate and private sponsors committed thousands of dollars to help make the project possible.

Through Migrating Landscapes, the team came to understand that while Canada is one of the most culturally rich countries in the world, it may be specifically because of this diversity that a strong architectural identity does not seem to exist. The exhibition represented our attempt to rediscover this cultural richness as a strength. The Venice Biennale became a platform through which we were able to not only draw the architectural community together, but also to engage a singular and relevant conversation, that of a bolder – and perhaps more independent – approach to architectural thinking in Canada.

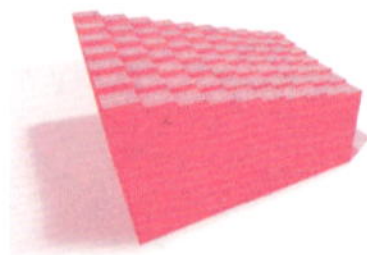

Table for 12 + 1200

In 2013, 546 won Canada's Professional Prix de Rome in Architecture with a project proposal "Table for 12." The project was intended to examine architecture culture in eight cities across the world.

Holding dinner parties for an intimate group of experts at architectural epicenters around the world was intended to help us identify the drivers behind a strong design culture. In other words, what creates appreciation of architecture and design, what are the entities or policies that sustain it and what lessons could be learned about and extracted from each location. The logistical premise of the project was to rely on a pre-existing relationship with a local host who could identify the right mix of invitees from politicians to media and policy makers, architects, planners, thinkers, educators, theoreticians and heads of key organizations. Aided by great food and wine, the resulting dinner conversation was much more candid than a typical formal interview with participants engaging in vigorous debate around the issues. The discussion was recorded and produced into a regular blog on Archinect. At the core of the project was to also understand if any of these strategies could be reproduced or built on in our own locale in Winnipeg or in Canada at large.

Table for 1200

As a finale to the year-long project, we collaborated with a Winnipeg-based design advocacy group Storefront Manitoba to create a non-profit design and dining event in our home city. With the ambition of creating the world's longest continuous dinner table, the original Table for 1200 involved setting-up logistics to maneuver 1200 people for a pop-up style dinner at a the secret location, the recruitment of the "Table Captains" to manage the table design competition and communication with participants, and on-boarding best local chefs for the project, as well as engaging sponsors and creating a "celebrity" head table for the event.

Drawing inspiration from "Dîner en Blanc" in Paris for its dress code, the inaugural Table for 1200 was a non-profit initiative aiming to make design [and dinner] accessible to the broader public. Also acting as a host to the 2014 Royal Architectural Institute of Canada RAIC conference closing event, the original Table for 1200 was setup against the backdrop of the then new Canadian Museum for Human Rights. Stretching the length of the Esplanade Riel pedestrian bridge, it aimed to draw attention to urban design issues, build community spirit and connect the general public, politicians, prominent business people and the media with the creative industries.

Outcome

Through its innovative concept and visual power, Table for 1200 became an overnight success, drawing national and international attention and is now an annual event – in part fulfilling the original objective of Table for 12.

The Assiniboine

Chair Your Idea

Chair Your Idea was a crowdsourced and crowdfunded open competition that sought to generate 1000+ tactical urban design ideas from the general public and $30,000 to realize the winning idea. People from all walks of life were invited to submit small-scale urban design ideas, possible to realize within a $30,000 budget. The ideas were to be expressed in short form – in 140 characters or less to be exact, the max Twitter message length at the time – in exchange for a $25 competition registration fee.

The same ideas were also printed on white chairs temporarily located on sidewalks and public spaces in front of partnering businesses or private homes, with the aim that the ideas could be seen, read, and further debated by anyone talking a seat or passing by. At the same time, the additional seating in the public realm encouraged people to enjoy a pause, talk to their fellow citizens, and inhabit public outdoor spaces. The Twitter thread allowed people to take part in the discussion and express their ideas whether they were formally participating in the competition or not.

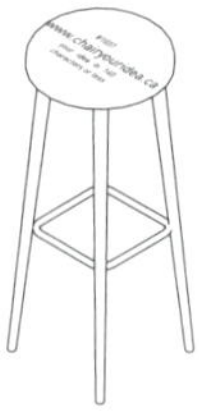

Outcome
At the end of the three-week installation period, an invited jury gathered to review the ideas and select an overall winning idea, which was subsequently realized the following Fall.

The rest of the ideas were collected together and presented City Hall and the mayor of Winnipeg as an idea bank for future consideration. The competition announcement took place at the City Hall in a form of a street party – championed by the Mayor himself.

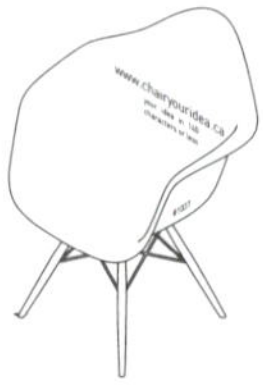

Design Quarter

In 2016, 5468796 created, developed and acquired start-up funding and key partnerships for the establishment of Design Quarter Winnipeg [DQW], a non-profit organization aimed to support creative businesses from the city's core, including art organizations and design-focused experience providers in the food and hospitality sectors.

Based on similar Design Districts around the world, Design Quarter Winnipeg not only helps its members thrive through collective promotion, marketing and programming; but promotes vibrancy and walkability within its boundary. The ultimate objective of the Quarter is to position Winnipeg as a true design city, to increase local and tourist visitorship to the core area, promote business-to-business networking and collaboration through collective marketing and events, and to cater to an ever-growing demographic of design-conscious consumers.

The Design Quarter is a member based organization with a volunteer board and a full time Executive Director. In addition to membership fees, its operations are funded through strategic partnerships and event sponsorships. Bi-annually, the DQW publishes a printed guide map distributed through the city's tourism offices and member venues and promotes its member organizations, events and campaigns through its website and social media.

Outcome
In its first two years of operations, the DQW acquired and maintained an active membership of about 60 businesses in the core area [Downtown, The Exchange District and the Forks]. Within the first year it had distributed over 15,000 maps, including the Canada Summer Games, International Downtown Association Conference, and Winnipeg Chamber of Commerce Luncheons. DQW organized number of public events and pop-ups, member-to-member programs and gatherings, and experience tours through the area, promoted walkability and outdoor vibrancy through its patio blanket and lighting campaigns, as well as introduced the member businesses and area to travel writers and media across the world, generating over $550,000 in earned media value.

DESIGN
QUARTER
WINNIPEG

One Bucket at a Time

In 2017, 546 was invited to collaborate with Factor Eficiencia to build a temporary pavilion for MEXTRÓPOLI Festival (Latin America's largest annual architectural festival) in Mexico City. The project is a response to the "viene viene": entrepreneurs who function outside of government oversight, bribing local police, using common painter's buckets to claim a piece of the street and charge hopeful drivers looking for a parking spot with an additional fee in exchange for access to their illegal stall.

By using the same buckets as the building blocks for an interactive pavilion, we hoped to highlight and question the pervasive condition of holding public space hostage, and also empower people of Mexico City to reclaim ownership over their public space, One Bucket at a Time.

Connecting the buckets via a grid of ropes, the installation is a malleable surface that the public is encouraged to freely explore. The surface can be rolled, pulled together or up to a point or along a line taking on different forms. People can sit, run, play, stand, lounge, and participate in the act of taking over the public realm.

Outcome

The pavilion remained in place for the duration of the MEXTRÓPOLI Festival and was extremely well used by passersby as piece of interactive art. It was also widely consumed on social media, receiving over 25,000 Instagram likes within a matter of 24 hours. After having been in place for three days, the installation then came down within a few hours by releasing the ropes. The individual buckets were absorbed by eager community members back into their original purpose as ordinary containers with a variety of household uses.

Subsequently, the team was invited by Storefront MB to rebuild the pavilion in Winnipeg as part of the Winnipeg Design Festival later that year. With the original reference to the "viene viene" making less sense in the new context, the design team decided to use the buckets as a vehicle to raise much needed funds for a Mexican girl's orphanage, effectively re-establishing a connection to its place of origin and making a tangible difference in the lives of a group of underprivileged children. Each of the buckets could be claimed for $20 CAD, and figuratively sent back to Mexico City full of hope. The campaign garnered much needed attention to the cause, raised $10,000 and provided evidence of the power of architecture to create positive change in a very direct way.

Food for Thought

In 2017, after several years on the Board, Johanna was appointed as the Chair of the Board of Winnipeg Chamber of Commerce, one of Winnipeg's oldest and most respected organizations representing the interests of local businesses to all three levels of government. In the Chamber's 150-year history, she was only the third architect to be given the honour.

Through her position as Chair, Johanna instigated a conversation about urban design and better city building at the Chamber and to the Chamber's membership, framing it around a better business case, in a language that the business and political audience best understands: money and numbers. As part of the strategy, she convinced the Chamber's well-established monthly luncheons to include a new segment, a "Food for Thought from the Chair," a short visual and passionate presentation on various design topics that Johanna delivered at each monthly event attended by a 1000+ business and political elite of the city. The segments presented important city building issues based data and economics and intentionally not as an architectural argument.

She also spearheaded the Chamber's task force on City of Winnipeg's new Planning Document "Our Winnipeg" and used her platform to advocate for value of people-centric design through events, speaking opportunities and the Chamber's newsletter.

Outcome
The "Food for Thought" segments became a widely popular part of Chamber's monthly luncheons, generating many fans and heated debate among the membership. The segments were quoted and shared widely on social media and around office water coolers. Johanna's Chairmanship contributed to Winnipeg's business membership's understanding that good urban design is good business and under her leadership, the Chamber issued its own policy paper in response to the "Our Winnipeg" planning process. She is regularly asked to address city council on important urban design issues, and has lent her expertise and 546 produced urban strategies research to many city councillors and political community events as a guest speaker.

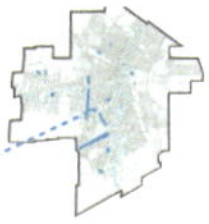

There are another 400+ acres of leftover land within the city. At **100 units / acre** that's

40,000

potential new residential units.

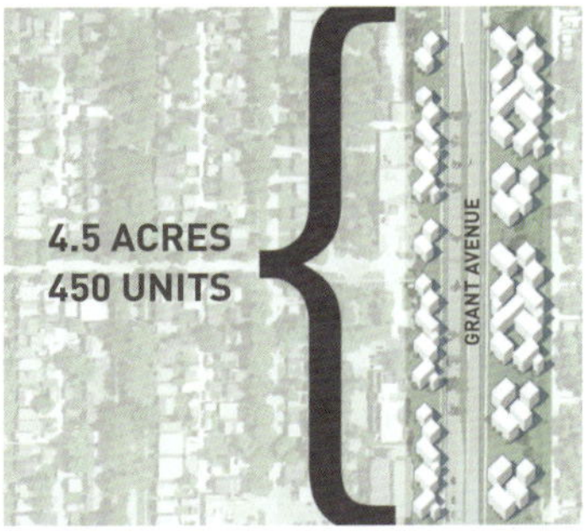

450 residential units

x $30,000 door

[typical cost of land per unit]

=$15M

towards **supporting development** costs that would otherwise be spent on land costs

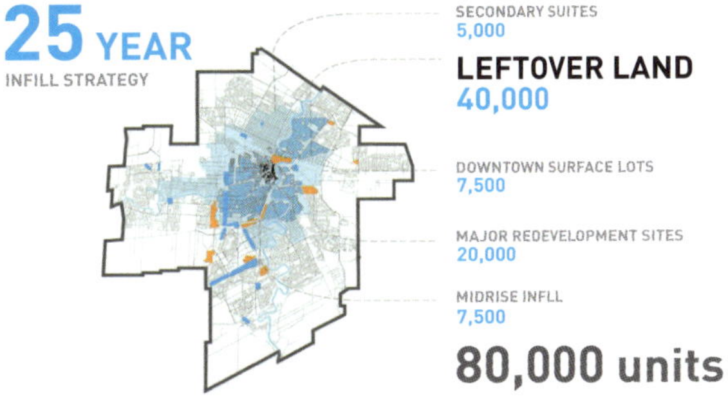

When complete, The **Railside** development at **The Forks** will provide **+- 1,200 residential units** over **12 acres.** That's an average density of

100 units/acre

with a building height of 4-6 storeys.

In the 2016 Census, **one-person households** became the **most common type** of household in Canada for the first time, accounting for

28%

of all households.

2016 Statistics Canada Key Results

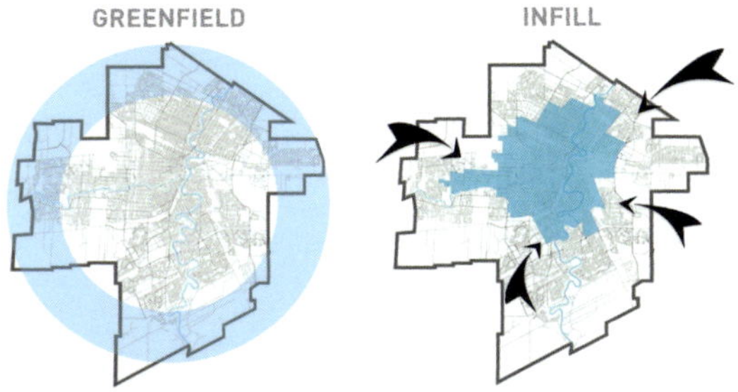

2018 State of the Infrastructure Report pegs our infrastructure deficit at **$6.9 billion** over the next **10 years**

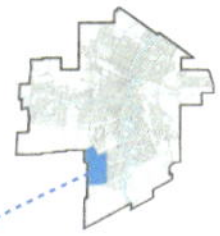

If built to a more reasonable density of even just 30 units/acre, the 2,900-acre **Waverley West** could have fit

80,000±

residential units and met the City of Winnipeg's **entire** projected growth for the **next 25 years**.

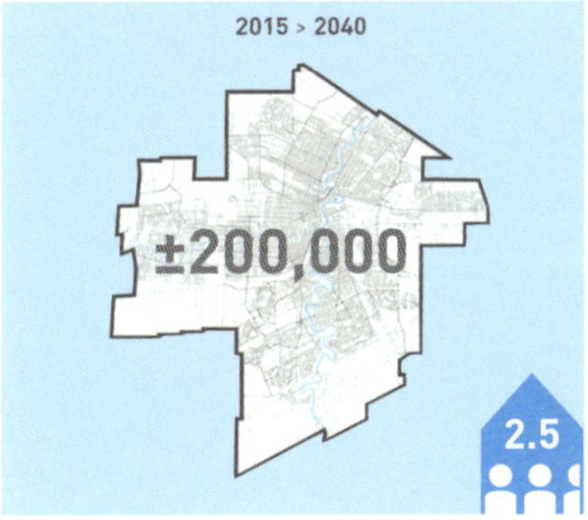

Winnipeg is projected to grow by about **±200,000 new residents** in the **next 25 years**. With an average of **2.5 persons per household** this means that

80,000±

new homes would need to be built.

Walk Winnipeg

In 2019, 546 organized a guerrilla campaign to install walk guides across Winnipeg's core area. The signs were intended to encourage foot traffic and walkability within Winnipeg's downtown, Exchange District and The Forks by simply indicating the distance to the next point of interest by the number of minutes it would take to walk. The campaign was modelled after "Walk Raleigh" and hoped to demonstrate the benefits of the initiative without the hurdles and expense of a public funding and approvals process.

The team mapped out distances and important intersections and locations for the signs, designed and produced plaques, and organized the 546 staff into seven teams to install the signs across the core area. The two-to-three person volunteer teams collectively installed nearly 300 signs over a four hour time frame during a single evening in June of 2019. The authorship of the project was intentionally hidden in part to avoid possible fines for non-permitted signs, and in part to let public reception determine their need and usefulness.

Outcome

Over the next several weeks the signs were noticed by a number of people passers by, actively discussed in social media and the origin of the signs was widely speculated upon. Canada's national media outlet CBC covered the story and interviewed several urban design activists and experts, further speculating on the origins of the signs. Almost without exception, the reception was positive and enthusiastic. Finally, in August 2019 the Manager of Transportation at the City of Winnipeg had traced the origins of the campaign back to 546 and contacted us with a plan to formalize the signs and make them permanent.

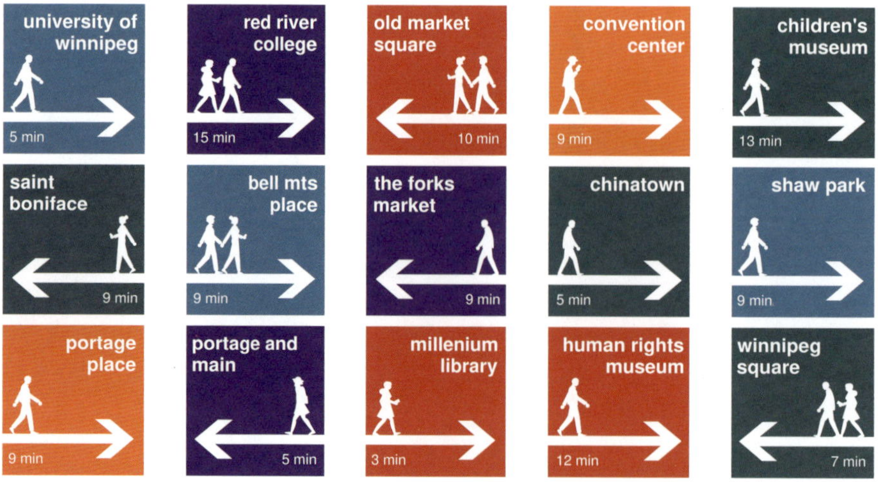

ReTree

ReTree WPG is a call to action to plant more trees in Winnipeg. In 2021, 546 was chosen as an guest artist to create an installation for Cool Gardens, an annual competition where in addition to one selected invitee, winning proposals are built for the summer season at The Forks.

Instead of building a singular installation, 546 chose to use the opportunity to draw attention to Winnipeg's disappearing tree canopy due to severe weather, invasive pests, urban development and disease, and spent the honorarium in acquiring hundreds of trees and handing them to willing citizen to plant on their own properties across the city. In addition, 546 collaborated with various businesses and building locations to install substantial colourful ribbon markers to draw attention to the campaign and the cause.

Outcome
The campaign hosted its own Instagram account and attracted wide local media coverage, including several TV and radio interviews as well as newspaper and social media stories. The available trees were distributed to enthusiastic community members in a matter of hours. 546 is currently assessing the feasibility of further afterlife for the campaign.

01 This tree is a gift! please take me home and plant me.
02 Turn sheet over for full planting instructions.
03 After planting, make a triangle from the ribbon provided.
04 Share a photo of your tree / triangle on social media!
05 Pay it forward and encourage others to plant.

01

02

03

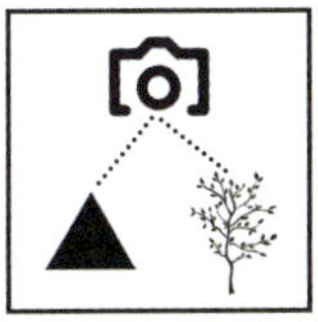

04

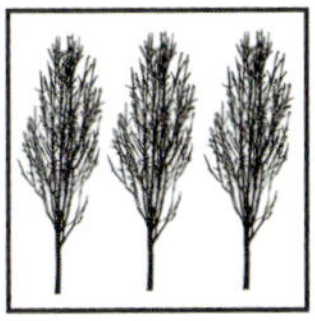

05

URBAN DESIGN

Railside

Mixed-use development
Winnipeg, Manitoba
2014 -

Railside is a 1,000-1,200 unit concept plan for a walkable, pedestrian-first residential and commercial community at The Forks in the heart of Winnipeg. Planned on an 11-acre surface parking lot against elevated rail lines and next to the city's most vibrant recreational area and major tourist attraction, this multi-developer and multi-decade concept plan aims to deliver high density, mixed-use and ownership housing, both market and subsidized, in a mid-rise format that prioritizes shared public space, local developers and retailers, slower modes of transit and environmental care. The project is organized around central plazas, includes only five stalls of parking per building, and is powered by a district geothermal system.

Background
5468796, together with Scatliff, Miller, Murray, has been engaged by The Forks North Portage Development Corporation to act as advisors for The Forks lands located at the junction of the Red and Assiniboine Rivers in the heart of Winnipeg. The Forks North Portage Development Corporation is embarking on the development of turning approximately 550,000 square feet of lands into 1.5 million square feet of mixed-use development with a major focus on housing.

5468796 has facilitated workshops, carried out public consultations, envisioned key qualities and financial parameters for the project, outlined the detail development vision, created guidelines for desirable urban design qualities and set parameters for development, as well as acted as design advisors for the selected developer's architectural teams.

Concept
The aim of the Railside development is to create a model for a complete community with vibrant, high-quality public spaces mixed with residential and commercial.

The overarching concept of the plan was to break a previously proposed development plan for five large residential towers into 35 smaller projects. This proposal had several objectives and advantages: making development more accessible to local [small] developers, creating design variety [vs. homogeneity], responding to Winnipeg's slow absorption rate and allowing for smart phasing, creating more building perimeter = vibrant edge at at grade, keeping development to four-to-six-storeys in height at the same time as maintaining the same density of housing units as the pervious tower plan, approximately 100 units/acre.

Furthermore, the concept is premised around outdoor plazas and alleys – scaled to match some of the successful human-scaled precedents from Northern Europe – that are organized on an "off-set grid" pattern at 45 degrees due south to create microclimates that extend the outdoor season in a winter city and create a sense of place and enclosure, or "urban rooms," which are largely still missing in Winnipeg's existing fabric. The concept plan treats the ground plane as a single surface without curbs or sidewalks, still welcoming vehicular service traffic, while reducing speed and prioritizing pedestrian movement through the site.

The commercial activity is intentionally organized onto the ground floor, and buildings are to be treated as 360-degree prime façades without any dedicated loading areas or opaque frontage to ensure continuity of the pedestrian realm and to create a vibrant and active public edge throughout the entire development. The entire development is connected to a district geothermal loop system.

Units
To test the development scenario, 546 created a full set of building models as a proof of concept for the potential developers. These plans were set on the proposed masterplan footprints, designed on 10/20 foot grids to ensure post-and-beam construction would remain feasible, and included a full spectrum of suite sizes and types and run through a relatively rigorous financial proforma.

Particulars
The aim of the Forks Railside Concept Plan is to forge truly new ground in its exploration of sensible density and human scale development, aiming to provide a locally appropriate response to a complex set of urban design issues.

Clustering six-storey buildings provides the same density as a few high-rise buildings.

All of the buildings act together to frame and define public spaces. Accordingly, every façade is of high importance, with equally strong design emphasis on all sides of each building.

Mid-rise buildings paired with smaller lot sizes can lessen investor risk and ensure that a variety of developers and architects can engage with the project, resulting in a diverse and more organic mix of development solutions.

Railside incorporates an offset grid inspired by some of the most livable urban districts in the northern hemisphere. The offset condition creates an effective barrier for wind, visual termini for vistas through the site, enhancing sense of enclosure and comfortable human scale.

The grid is oriented approximately 45 degree south, ensuring optimal solar orientation for residential development for cold climates. By offering short walking distances between plazas with natural places to pause, multiple routes to choose from, and points of discovery along the way, Railside encourages a vibrant pedestrian environment.

Multiple layers of buildings are maintained from east to west (as opposed to a single row) to enhance the village atmosphere and create attraction points at the end of each block and around the plazas.

The mixing of short streets and plazas also enables the creation of microclimates within the development, a factor that is critically important for outdoor enjoyment, especially in winter cities. Since buildings do not directly face each other, overlap conditions are minimized and almost all residential units have extended views between buildings into open spaces beyond.

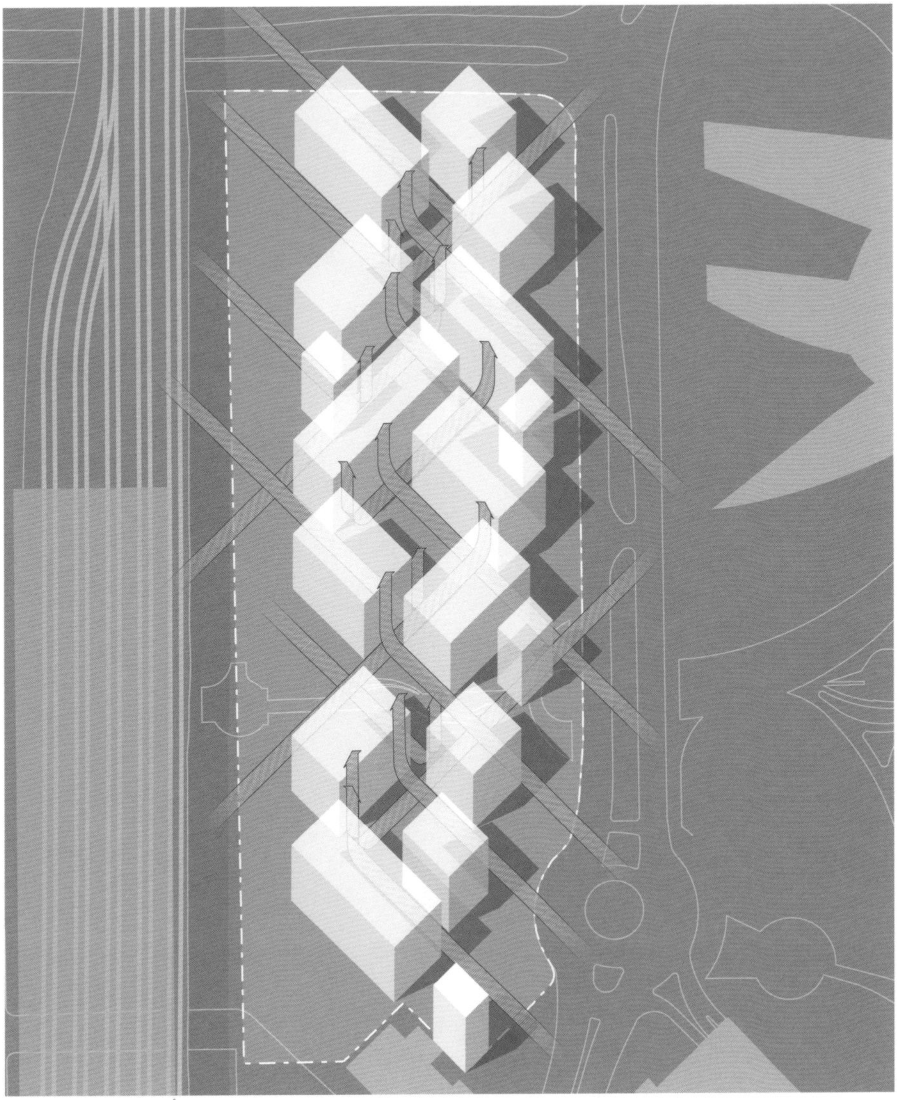

The public realm belongs to everyone

Similar to The Forks Market, all development on the ground floor of Railside must be accessible and in service to the general public. Ground floor uses will actively contribute to the public realm through physical and visual vibrancy. With the exception of limited work-live units in designated areas, no private residential development will occur at grade, but rather on levels two to six.

The increased building perimeter offered by smaller parcels creates more ground floor street frontage for retail and commercial storefronts, creating the conditions necessary for a vibrant, pedestrian-friendly public environment where people are encouraged to linger and explore.

At grade, the tenant units should generally be limited to maximum 20' width per business to encourage variety of the streetscape and to provide small grain business frontage for local, independent retailers, hospitality businesses and artisan grocers. Larger operations may be permitted, but it is recommended that these tenancies would be located over two levels [1-2] to maintain narrower widths and variety at grade. The tenant mix will be curated in collaboration with the FRC and subject to approval by the Railside Design Advisory Committee.

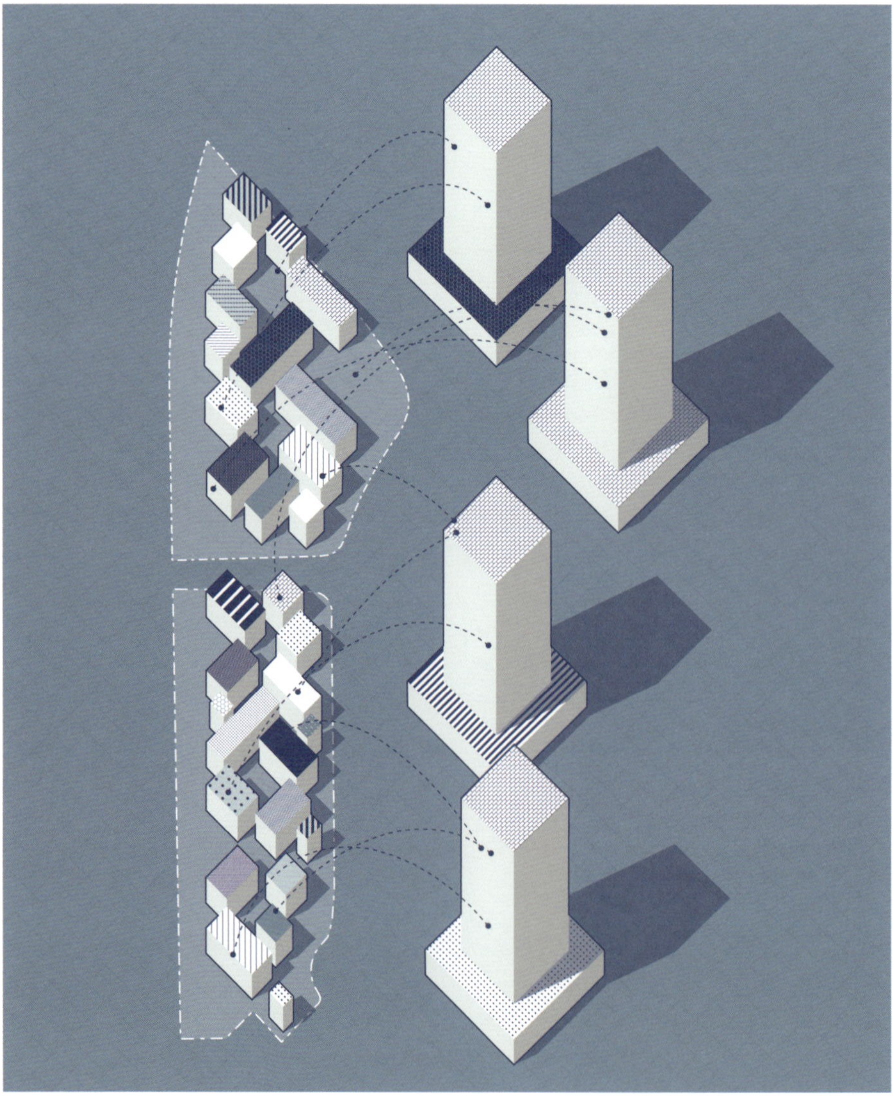

The Railside concept plan is somewhere between a village and historic downtown, attuned to Winnipeg's incremental growth and socio-economic context.

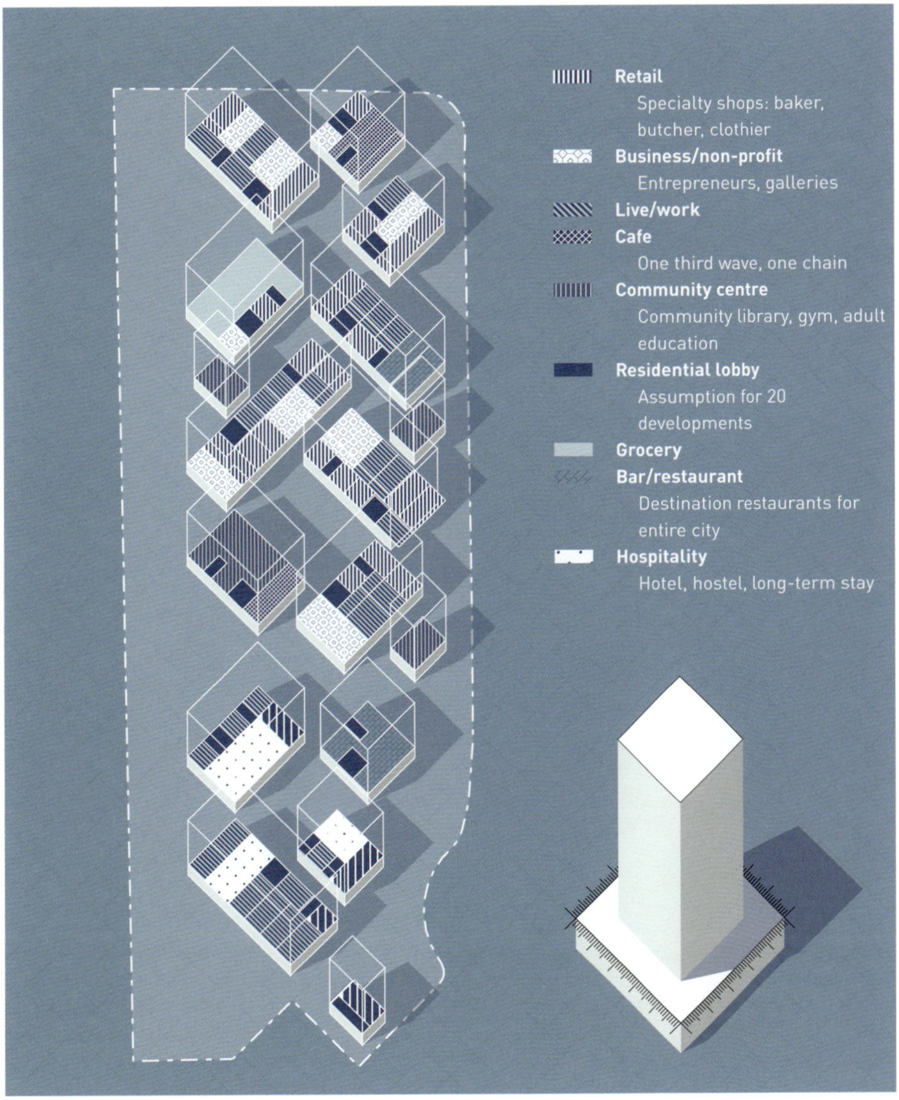

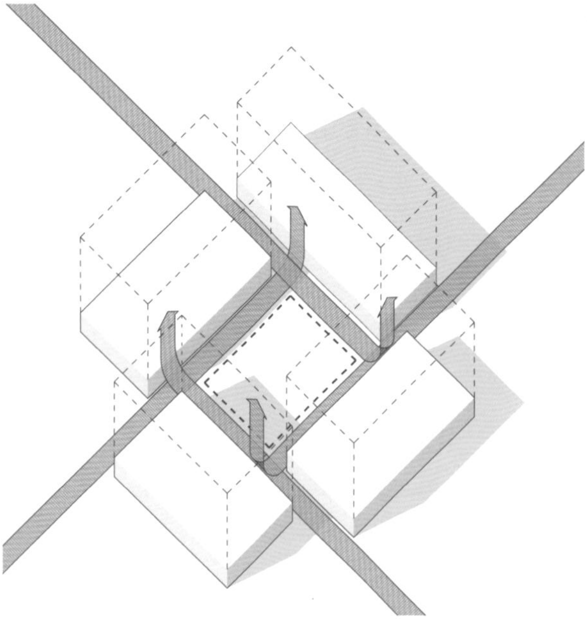

Enclosure: The offset grid will create a physical and psychological sense of enclosure – a series of urban rooms – that will not only be effective barriers for wind, but provide terminus for vistas through the site. This is important in creating a rich, interesting and comfortable human experience.

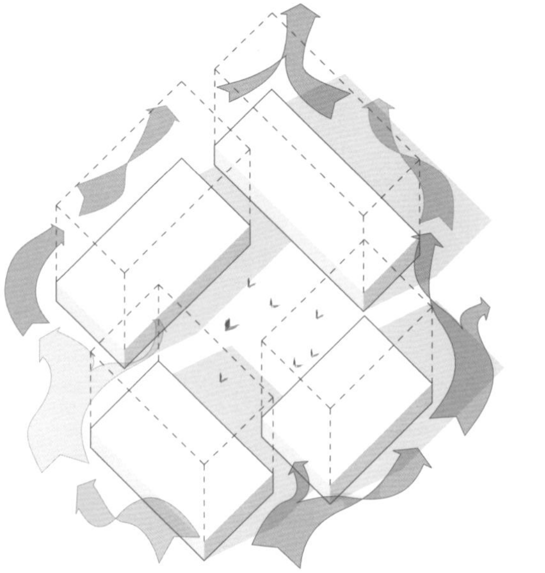

Microclimate: The proposed orientation and size of the buildings contribute to the creation of microclimates and help break up the wind and shelter the inner squares.

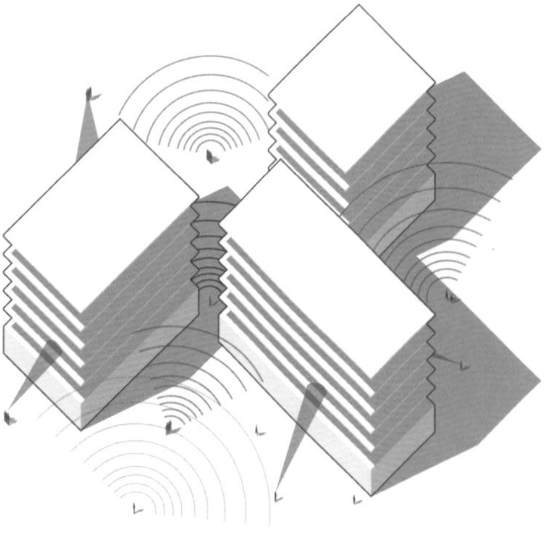

Multisensory: Multisensory experiences will be sought through careful curation of programmes, buildings, architecture and materials.

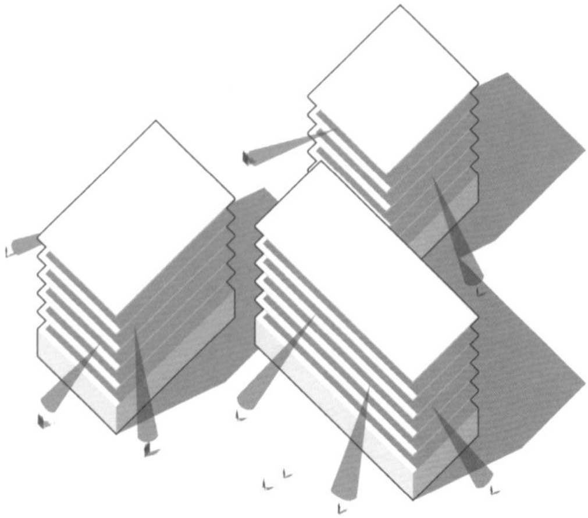

Eyes on the street: Individual buildings should be designed with ample windows on all façades providing "eyes on the street" for all adjoining public spaces at Railside. The presence of permanent residents 24/7 over the public realm will provide an added and effective measure of security.

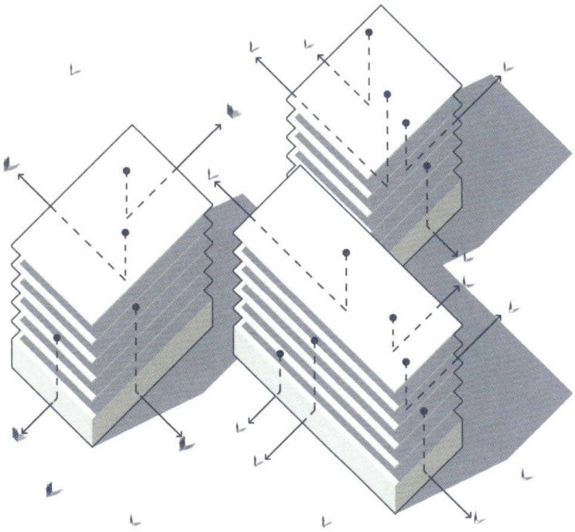

Scale: Mid-rise buildings, up to six storeys, contribute to the creation of a comfortable human scale, evident in most successful urban environments around the world.

Access to sky: While public spaces will feel protected from wind and create an intimate sense of enclosure, the size and continuous nature of the network of squares and alleys provides access to the sun and sky.

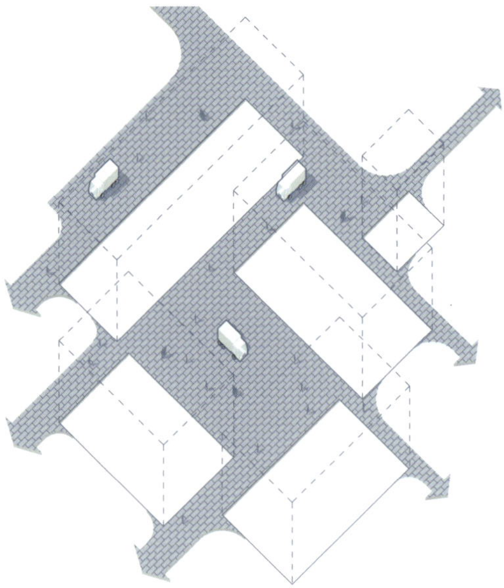

Equal grounds: The Concept Plan calls for a curbless, single surface without the traditional separation of pedestrian and vehicular activity. This continuous surface is intended to increase accessibility, prioritize pedestrian activity and slow down vehicular [service] traffic, while encouraging a mix amongst all modes.

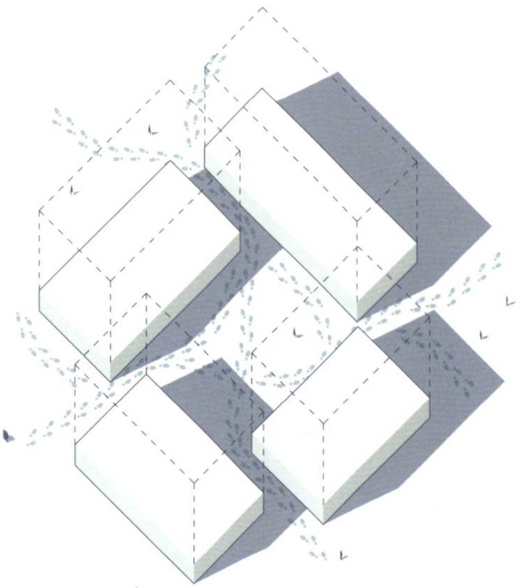

Multiple journeys: The physical configuration of the development will provide opportunities for multiple routes through the site providing a desire to explore the rich environment but also renewed interest for those coming back to visit.

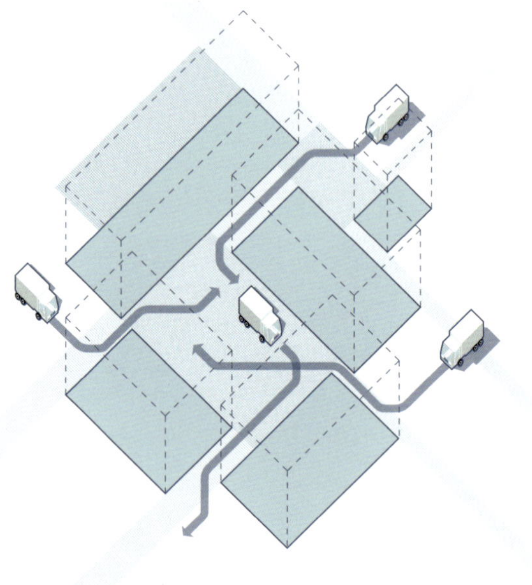

Service access: A network of squares and alleys connects to the surrounding major vehicular routes and provides convenient access for smaller service vehicles. Service should occur through front doors in smaller quantities/frequency, as opposed to large loading zones that interrupt the pedestrian environment.

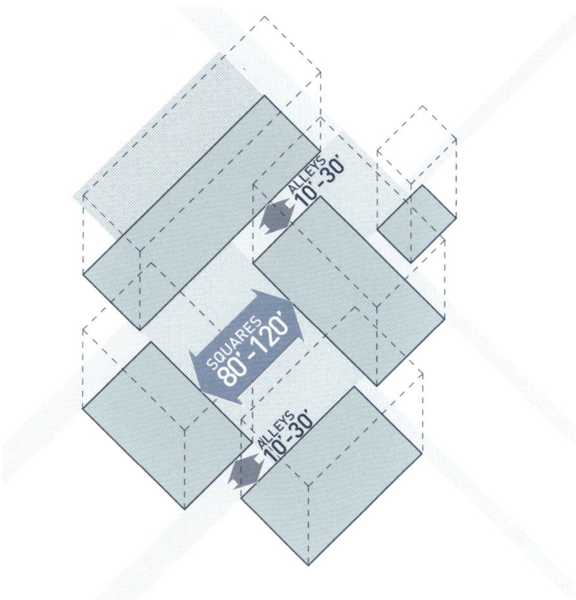

Urban dimension: The proposed positioning of buildings will assure that narrow alleys are very short and always connect to wide urban spaces providing a sense of discovery throughout Railside.

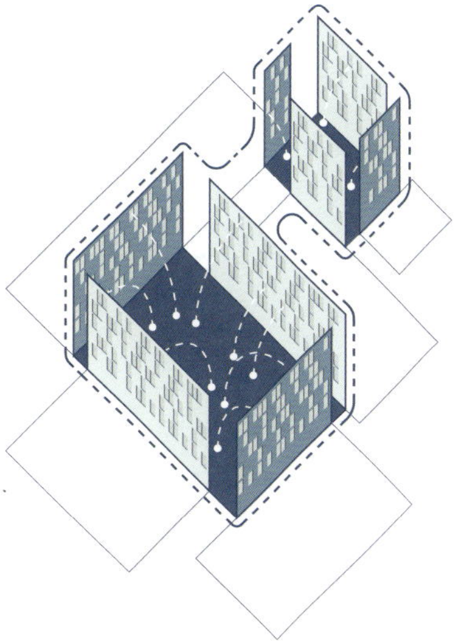

Defensible space: A visual connection between buildings [residents] and those in the public spaces at grade plays a critical role in creating a sense of safety and comfort. Research shows that above the 6th storey this audio and visual connection is lost.

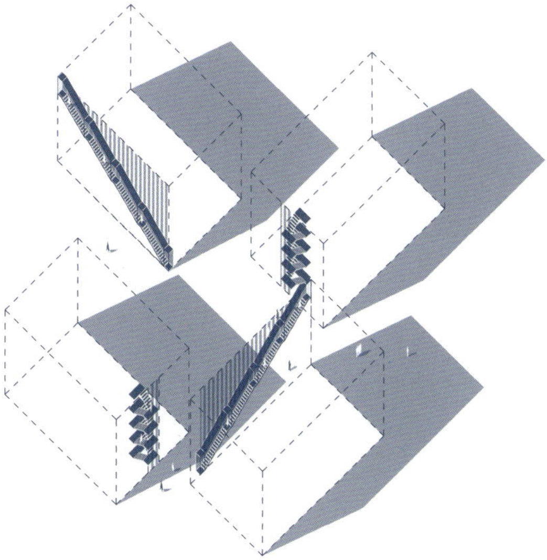

Visible stairs: The inclusion of glazing on the required exit stairs of individual buildings is highly encouraged. The building façades and therefore the public realm of the entire Railside Development can be further activated by the visible activity in the vertical circulation routes. Providing access to natural light in the exit stairs will also promote their use and support active lifestyles in lieu of taking the elevator.

Relief at grade: Ground floor of all buildings should be designed to allow for convenience of pedestrian movement. Such modulation will further reinforce sense of comfort at grade.

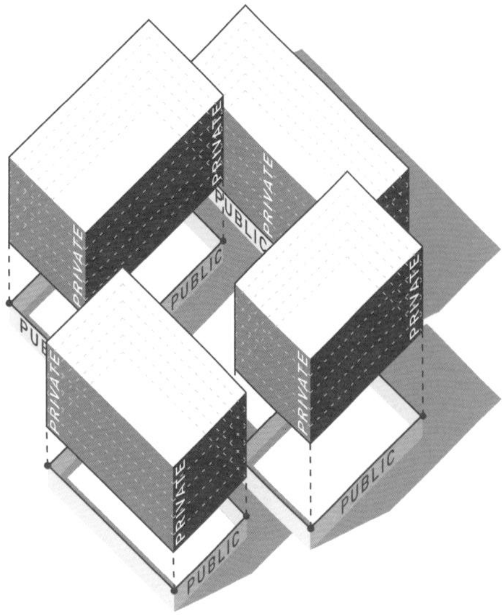

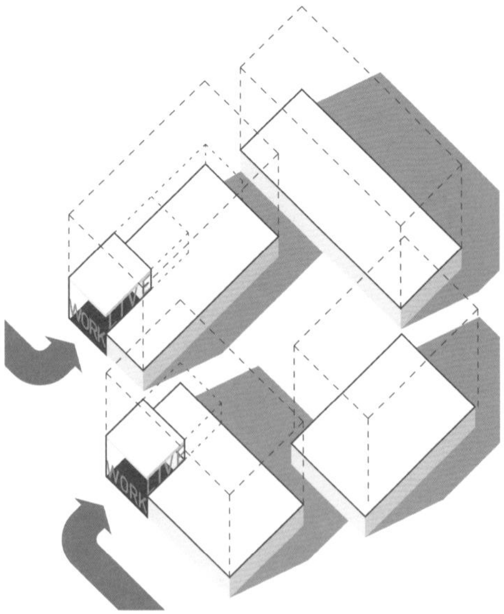

Public/private: The ground floor of each building must be comprised of uses and spaces that help activate the public realm and are generally accessible by the public. Floors above grade are envisioned as non-public uses, the majority of which will be dedicated for residential development.

Live/work: Supported ground floor uses include retail, restaurants, cafes, community spaces, active commercial and workshop spaces, and active live/work spaces. The live/work areas at grade must be limited to designated areas away from main squares and alleys.

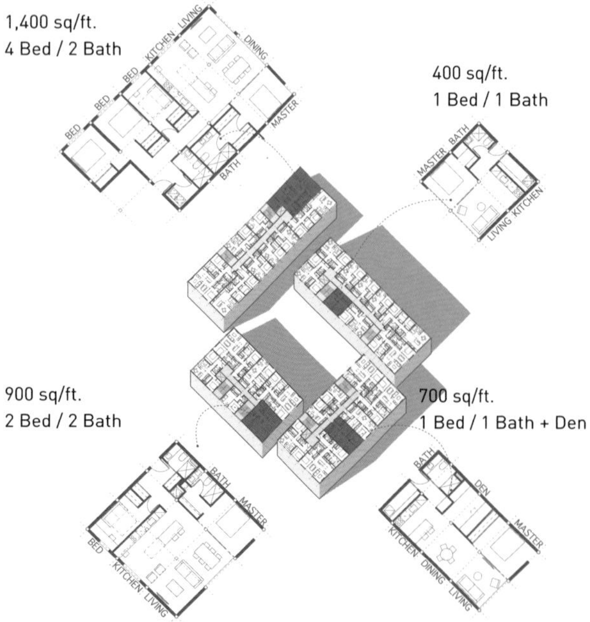

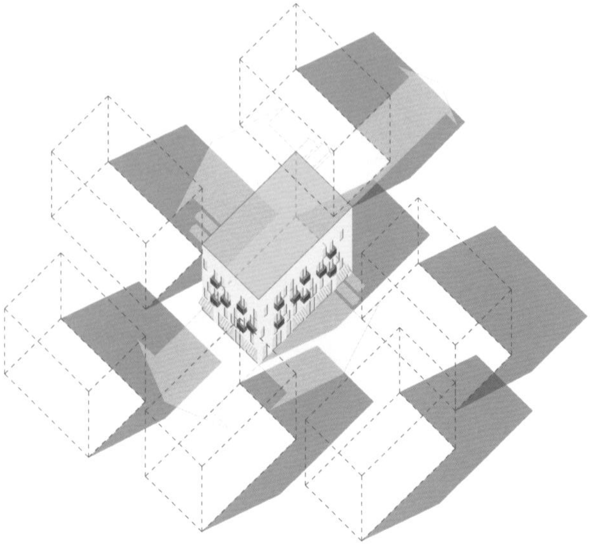

Proforma: The sample building sizes were tested through design and livability [access to light and views] as well financial proforma [efficiency + cost] in order to demonstrate the viability of the configurations.

Balconies: Balconies and French balconies are an important device to further articulate and activate building façades, but also extend the private interior spaces and provide extended views over the neighbourhood. Balcony projections are encouraged on façades facing public squares and wider dimensions between buildings, whereas French balconies may be more desirable in narrower alley conditions.

Environmental sustainability

The Forks has an aspirational goal to achieve zero garbage, zero water waste and zero carbon emissions. Within the main site, they have implemented a series of strategies as a way to be good to the environment while saving money, including onsite composting, reuse of waste vegetable oil to operate site equipment, a comprehensive recycling program, and water conservation initiatives. Railside will be built upon the first district geothermal field in Winnipeg.

Social sustainability is targeted through a rich mix of uses, unit and tenure types within the development. These strategies include various ownership models [from condominiums, rental suites for all incomes and co-operatives to student and senior housing] and the inclusion of a variety of unit sizes and types conducive to a mix of demographics [families, couples, singles, students, seniors], as well as physically accessible and visitable suites.

Railside's planned urban grid is oriented 45 degrees south to take advantage of passive energy strategies by maximizing solar exposure and access to daylight for all residential suites.

Railside will strengthen the physical connection between The Forks and downtown.

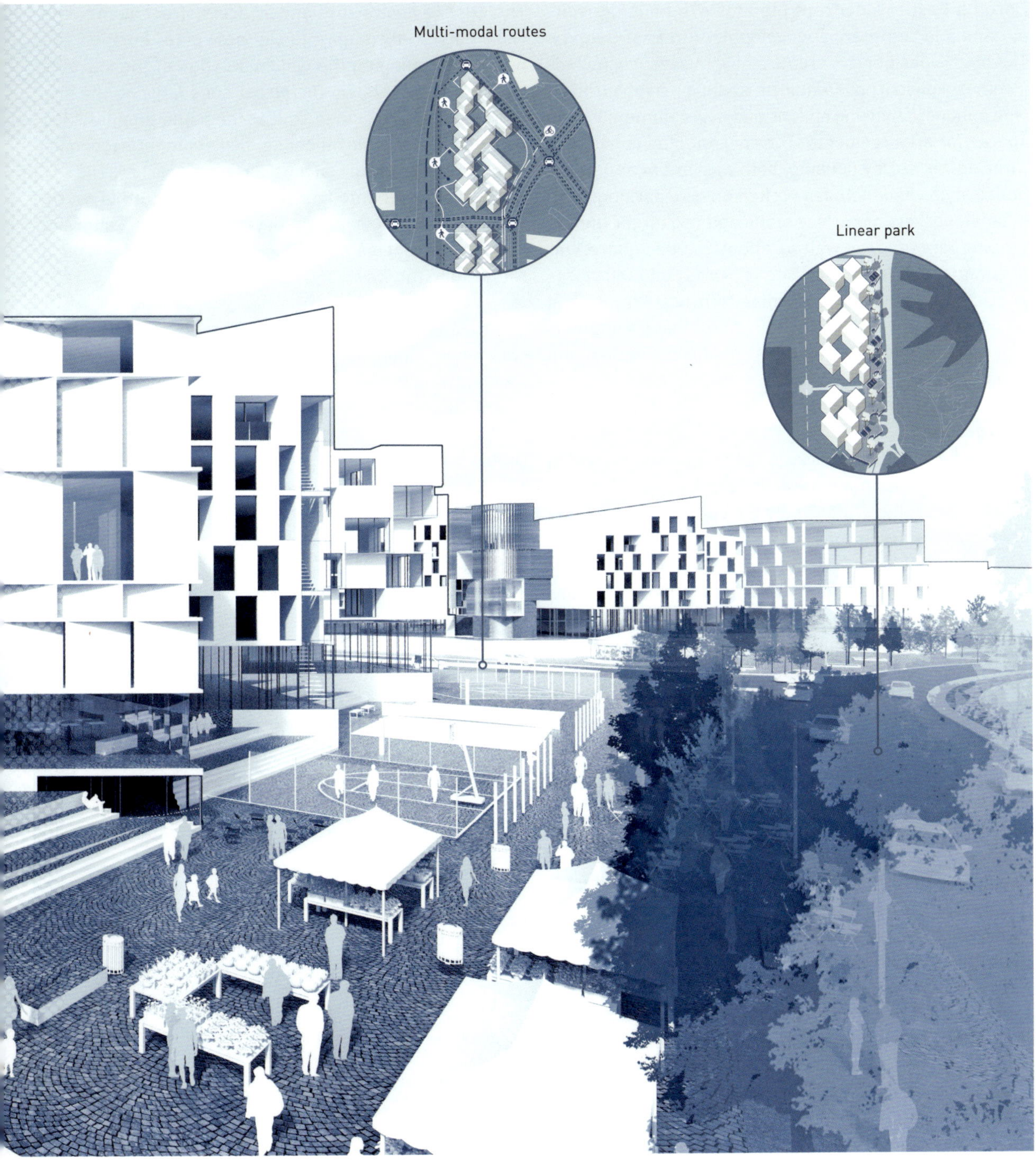
Multi-modal routes
Linear park

Chroma East

Mixed-use development
Calgary, Alberta
2018 -

Chroma East is a concept plan for 675 housing rental units and commercial development in East Calgary. The plan is designed to create a new mixed-use, mixed-income neighbourhood within an existing neighbourhood, with enhanced housing options and new community open spaces for area residents. The concept plan consists of three-to-six-storey housing, both apartment and townhouse styles and includes limited on-site parking, both in small pockets of surface stalls and two larger underground parkades, as well as about 25,000 square feet of commercial space. The site is broken into four larger parks and a network of pedestrian-first streets and pathways. The individual buildings or clusters of buildings also include smaller courtyards for communal and private uses.

Background

In 2019, 546 and Civic Works in Calgary were engaged to develop a concept plan for the former David D. Oughton (DDO) School site located in the East Calgary Community of Albert Park/Radisson Heights by a consortium of Calgary Municipal Land Corporation [CMLC] and RNDSQR. The objective of the project was to turn the eight-acre site into a variety of low-entry level multigenerational rental housing to serve the large immigrant population of the surrounding community. The programme also included about 25,000 square feet of commercial space to serve the future residents as a result of detailed market analysis. The city by-laws required that nearly half of the site be dedicated as a Municipal Reserve [MR], in other words, as a publicly accessible park.

Concept

The design team felt strongly that simply sectioning off one end or the other as a public park to meet the MR requirement was not the best use of available resources, but rather that the MR could be used as the "in-between tissue" to knit the new community into the existing one more effectively. Hence the team proposed that the total area of MR be split into four smaller parks within the site, creating mix of built and open space that in turn would support human scale, ground oriented development throughout.

The existing desire lines and adjacent street alignments were carried through into the new plan. Further, the public lane aligning the west side edge of the site was updated to slow down the street speed, giving the site more desirable frontage, and at the same time, making soft-density intensification, i.e. development secondary suites, more desirable on the adjacent properties. The site itself was broken into four phases, from south to north, and a total of nine separate development sites, allowing the development team(s) to assess market and absorption rates along the way.

Prioritizing pedestrian traffic, while also enabling local and vehicular service throughout was achieved by creating a curbless environment across the site's streets and plazas.

Units

The proposed buildings vary from six storey mid-rise buildings with underground parking to three storey townhome clusters. The plan was also designed with maximum flexibility in mind, so that it could contain only about 300 homes in total at the low end, and the maximum of 675 suites at the high end, in any case without losing its major qualities and objectives. This was achieved through the interchangeability of suite types, sizes and flexibility in number of floors [±1-2/building] built per each outlined building footprint. The unit types vary from a 1,800 square foot five-bedroom multigenerational townhome to an approximately 400 square foot one-bedroom apartment.

ROBSON CRESCENT SE
RAYNARD CRESCENT SE
12 AVE SE
RADISSON DR SE
ROULEAU CRESCENT SE
34 ST SE
14 AVE SE
16 AVE SE
TH
CY
PP
MR
AF
Legend
PP Pocket Park
AF Active Frontage
TH Townhouses
CY Courtyards
MR Municipal Reserve

Representative view showing the human scale proportions within the mews network

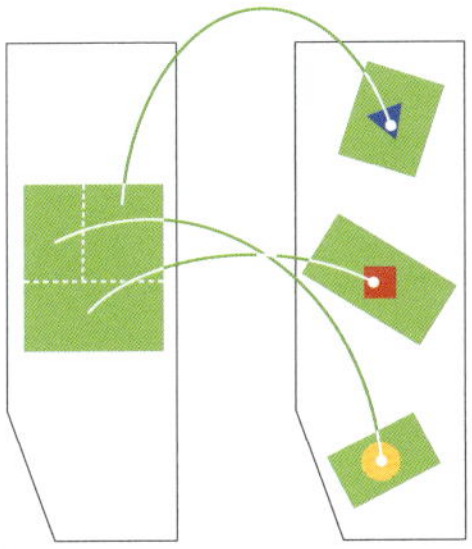

01

02

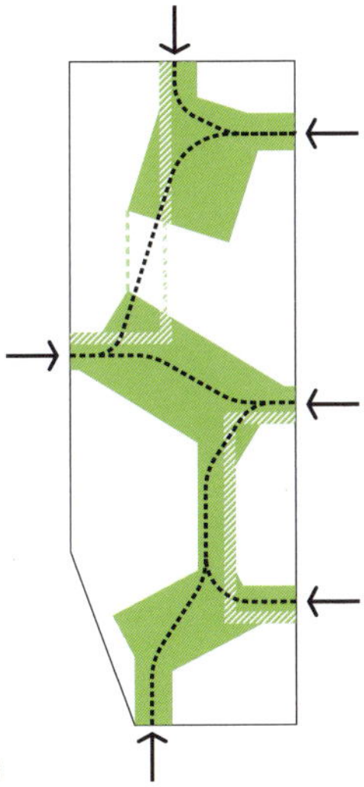

03

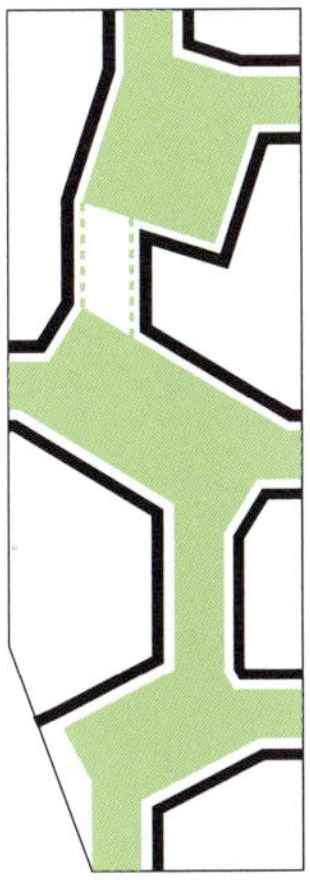

04

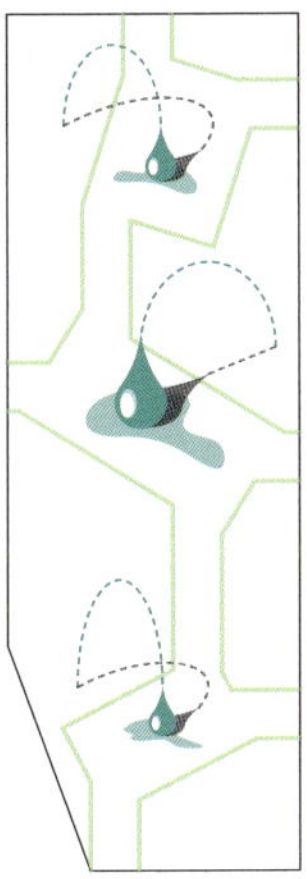

05

01 Multiple parks = multiple experiences

Goal: Maximize the distribution of and public access to open space and provide a wider variety of programming to serve all demographics.

Application: Divide and arrange Municipal Reserve requirement into distinct open space nodes.

02 Integrated + interconnected linking the neighbourhood

Goal: Create a comprehensive and connected public realm network with appropriate linkages among open spaces, streets, and other land uses.

Application: Support atypical Municipal Reserve parcels, where appropriate, to promote connectivity and the integration of the built form and public realm.

03 Crossings: extensions of the public realm

Goal: Recognize the role of streets and sidewalks as another means to provide amenity and recreation opportunities.

Application: Design open space that extends into the surrounding streetscape and allow access easements over Municipal Reserve.

04 Soft edges: framed open spaces

Goal: Maintain a human scale and enhance public realm vitality by designing for the proper enclosure, definition, and activation of open space.

Application: Delineate and reinforce Municipal Reserve through building design and "soft edges" on private lands - meaningfully designed transition zones where indoor and outdoor life interact.

05 Combined stormwater management

Goal: Manage stormwater in a manner that maintains the area's environmental, recreational, and aesthetic integrity.

Application: Where appropriate and in the interests of land efficiency, consider locating stormwater management facilities within Municipal Reserve lands.

The Plan applies several "Big Design Moves" that set the stage for the redevelopment's urban structure. These fundamental building blocks structure and guide the overall mews network, block pattern, community open space, building envelope and anticipated use across the Site.

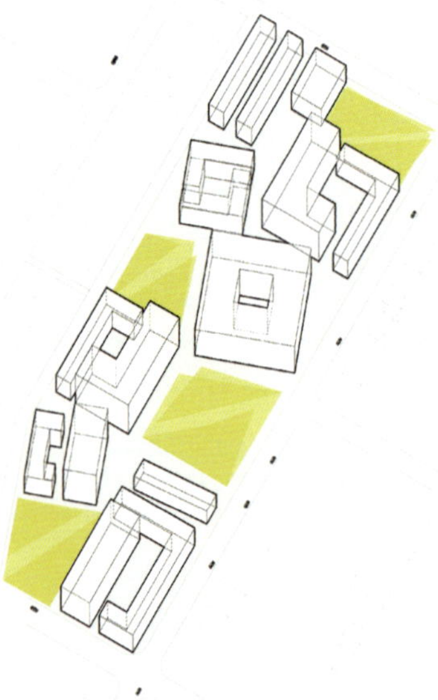

Multiple parks
Multiple experiences
Maximize the distribution of and public access to open space and provide a wider variety of programming to serve all demographics.

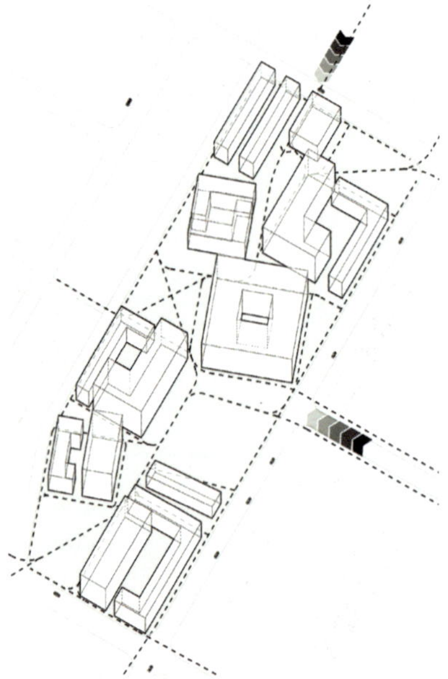

Interconnectivity
Linking the neighbourhood
Create a comprehensive and connected public realm network with appropriate linkages among open spaces, streets, and other land uses, promoting walkability.

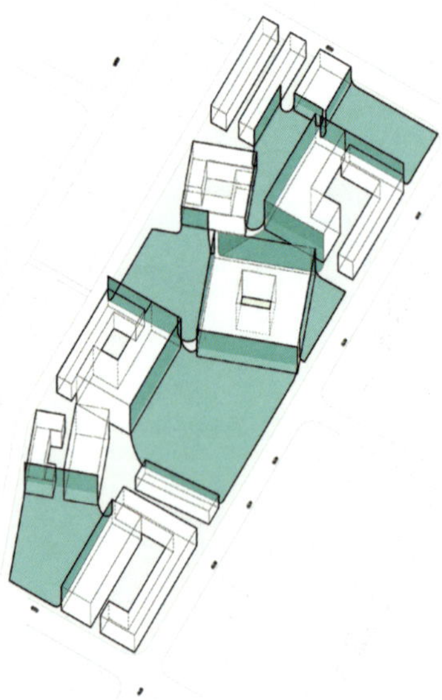

Framed open spaces
Better park edges
Maintain a human scale and enhance public realm vitality by designing for the proper enclosure, definition, and activation of open space.

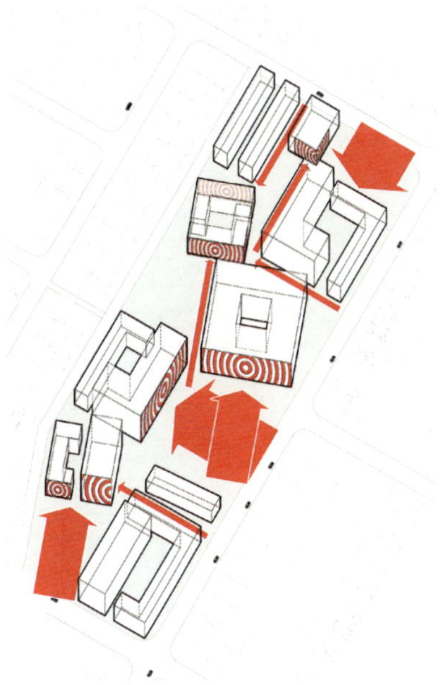

Terminal views
Urban drama
Evoke a sense of anticipation, surprise, and discovery with a network of streets and public spaces configured to create a succession of memorable experiences.

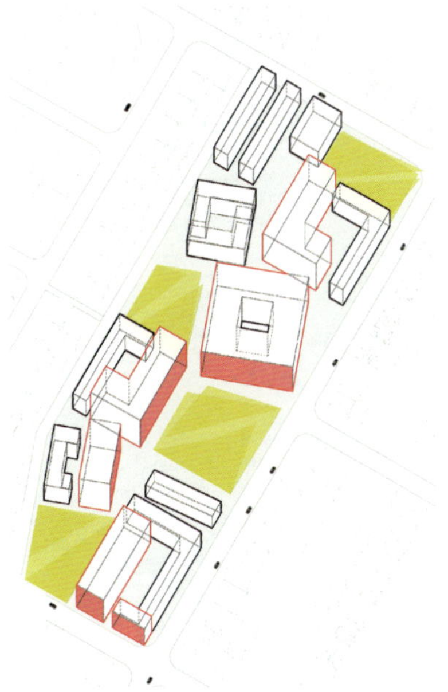

Mixed-use development
Use diversity
Combine different uses within the same building and provide for a variety of complementary and integrated uses within the development.

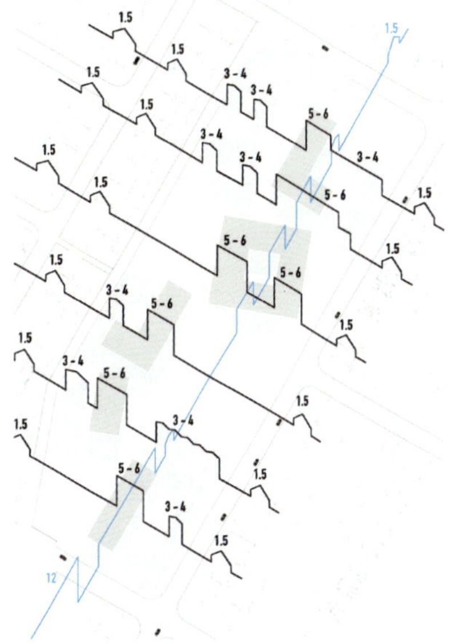

Transitional intensity
Built-form compatibility
Introduce appropriate transitions to adjoining residential areas that respect variations in scale, massing and land uses.

Representative view showing the human scale proportions within the mews network

Key design objectives and specific tactics have been used to craft the plan and by considering a hierarchy of scales: community; site; and open spaces & buildings.

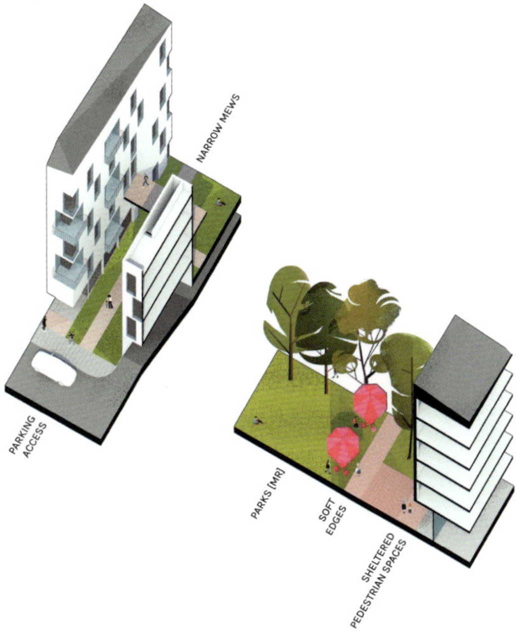

Smaller blocks and active edges
The vehicular navigation of a site comprised of carefully arranged series of smaller blocks has a traffic calming effect.

Building height
Carefully scale buildings from three to six-storeys in height.

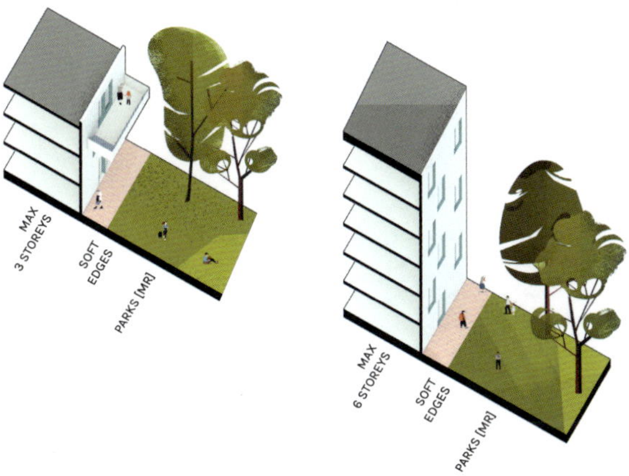

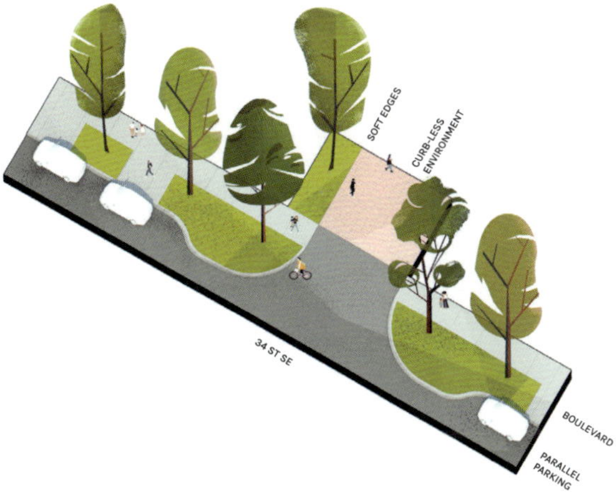

Carefully size people spaces
Right size open spaces create universally comfortable places for people.

Limit large surface parking areas
Surface parking is limited and interspersed in small clusters to ensure a pedestrian-oriented environment.

Narrow surrounding streets
Modifications to existing streets and intersections will calm traffic and create safe streets for pedestrians uses.

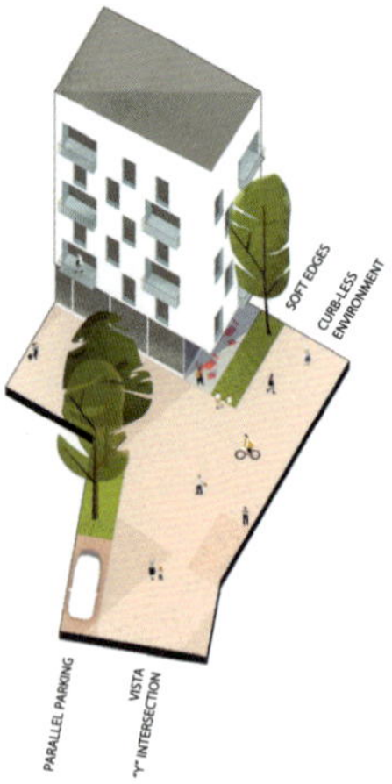

"Y" intersections + offset grid
A livable village-like place comes to life with use of "Y" intersections and an offset grid.

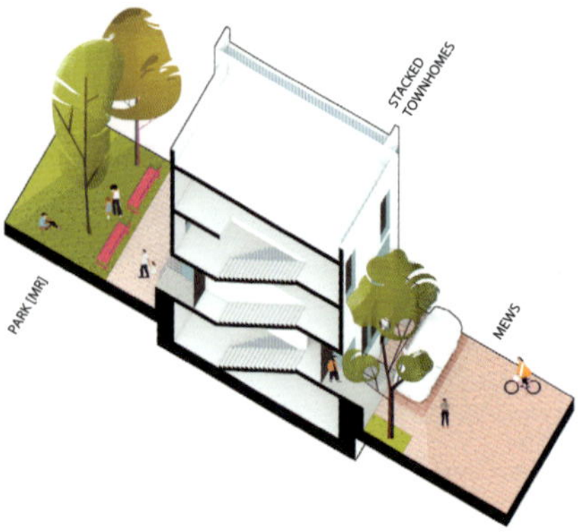

Transitions between public and private spaces
An intentional gradient and cues between public and private space are necessary to create an inviting environment for people.

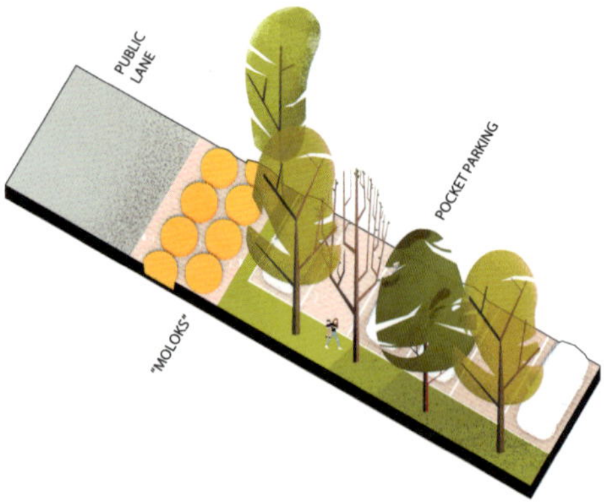

Communal waste + recycling
Common collection systems are efficient and can build a sense of community.

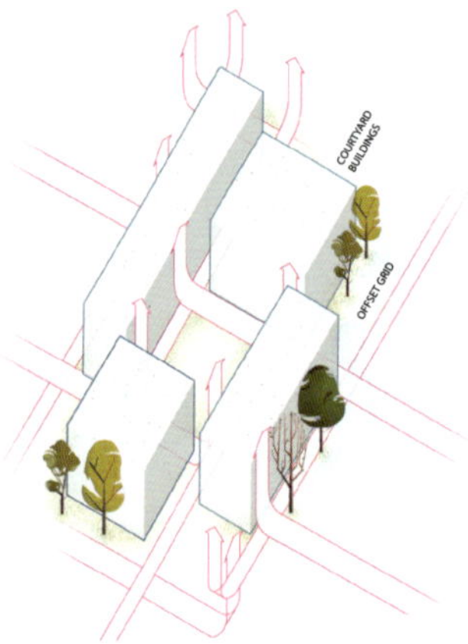

Courtyard buildings
More comfortable microclimates achieved using courtyard buildings.

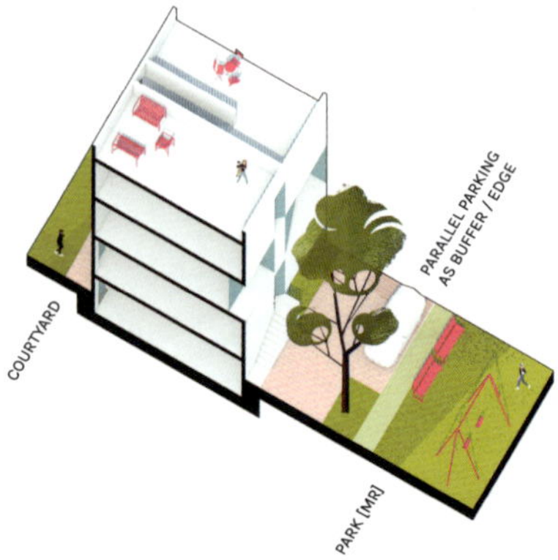

Dispersed surface parking
Narrow mews with active edges and parked cars calms traffic.

West view showing mews relationship with municipal reserve and active retail frontages

Northwest view showing city park framed by active retail frontages

MULTI-FAMILY HOUSING

Webbsite*

Condominiums
Winnipeg, Manitoba
2004 - 2006

Webbsite is a seven-unit urban condominium project located on an infill lot in downtown Winnipeg. This three-storey building also includes four "flex" spaces at grade with commercial and home-based business potential. The siting of the building takes advantage of the adjacent courtyard that expands the common amenity space at grade. The project also includes four surface parallel parking stalls, and a private balcony or patio space for each dwelling.

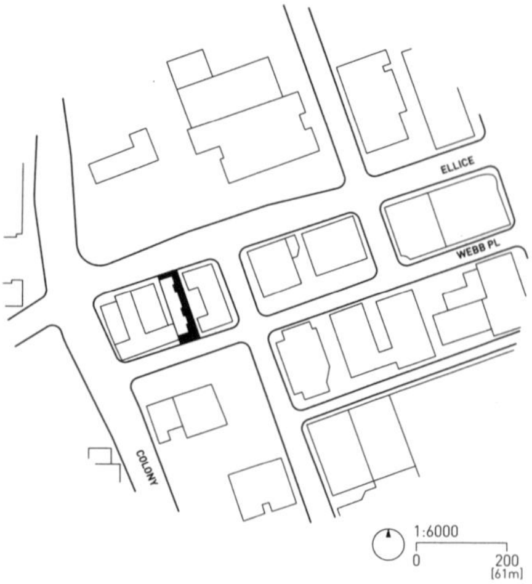

*Sasa Radulovic & Johanna Hurme completed while at Cohlmeyer Architecture.

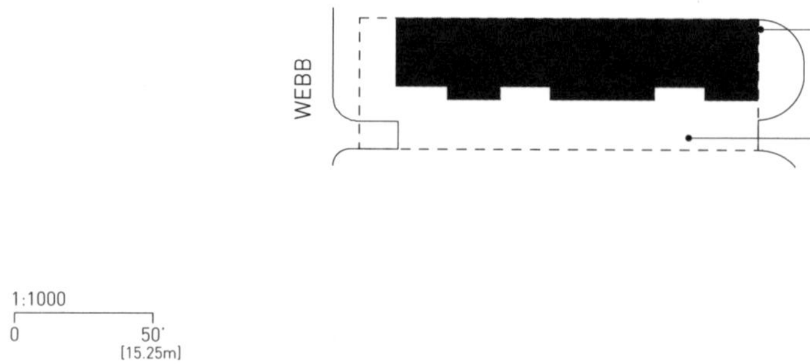

GFA
9,530 ft²
[885 m²]

SITE AREA
6,815 ft²
[633 m²]

COVERAGE

FLOOR AREA RATIO	COVERED AREA	EFFICIENCY [gross/net]
1.40	**48%**	**100%**

OCCUPANCY

RESIDENTIAL **100%**

TYPOLOGY

DENSITY

70 /ac [174/ha]

144 / ac [355/ha]

HEIGHT [STOREYS]

OF UNITS **7+4**

OF PARKING STALLS **4**

UNIT TYPES

bedrooms	0	**7**	**4**	0
storeys [within units]	**4** [flex]	**3**	**4**	0

UNIT SIZE* including flex units

AVERAGE UNIT (36%) **651 ft²** [60.5 m²]

SMALLEST UNIT (42%) **386 ft²** [35.9 m²]

LARGEST UNIT (56%) **1005 ft²** [93.4 m²]

COST

$118/ft²
[$1,265/m²]
(300 – 75)

CONSTRUCTION

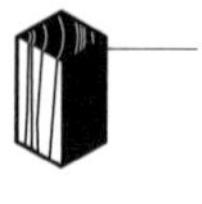

LIGHT WOOD FRAME
- WALLS
- FLOORS
- ROOF

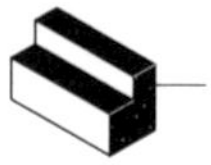

- FOUNDATION

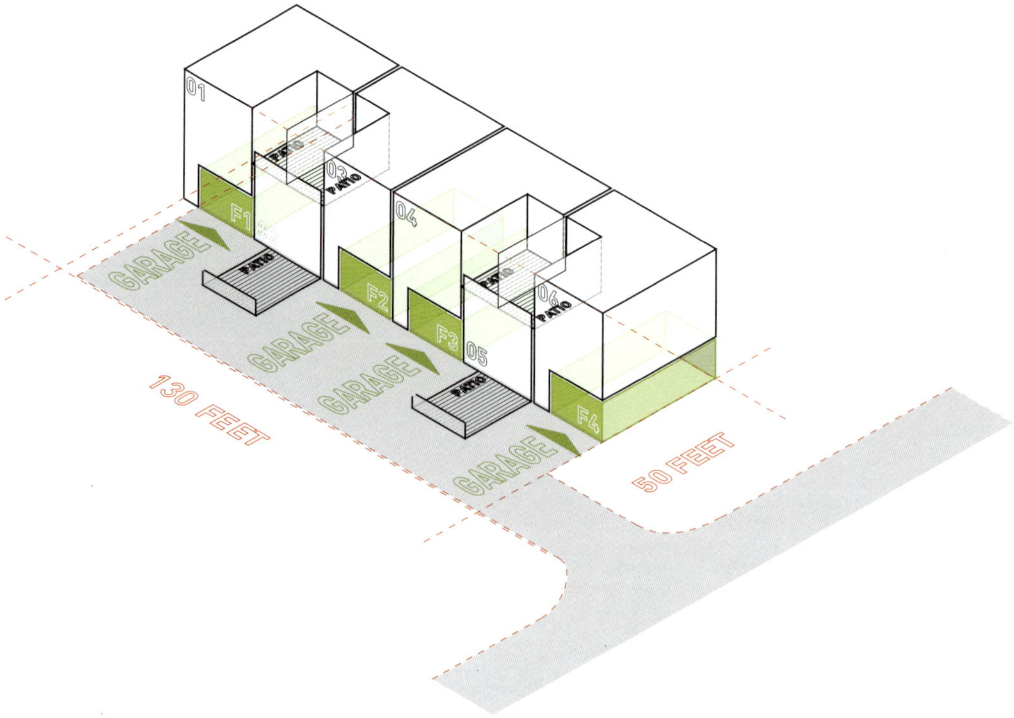

Background

In 2004, while still working at Cohlmeyer Architecture Limited, co-founders of 546, Sasa [project architect + design lead] and Johanna [junior designer] completed Webbsite Condominiums for Winnipeg's core area development agency, a quasi-public organization. The project was the first ever newly built condominium in the downtown core. The project's first challenge was the narrow 50x130 foot urban lot mid-block located between the existing Booth College and historic Raleigh apartment complex, facing two streets. The site had an existing single family home on it with large front and rear yard setbacks.

Concept

Design objectives – including sufficient access, pleasant views, and inviting outdoor spaces – were met by keeping the building's footprint shallow, stretching it between the two existing streets, and introducing a new through-mews. The building mass is positioned tight against the property line to Booth college, as made possible by zero setback allowances in the downtown district. The increased setback of the mews towards the Raleigh apartment block allows natural light to penetrate the units, and gives each dwelling a private entrance at grade.

Units

In order to maximize the available building area, the seven units and four flex spaces are nestled together to make 18-foot wide loft volumes. Four of the seven units are stacked two-storey blocks nestled on top of the lower suites, while two of the three ground floor suites are single level flats. The remaining ground floor suite is a two storey loft with its roof providing a large south facing deck to the adjacent upper suite. The concept of the 300 square foot flex space enables open-ended marketing for the two to three storey units; they can be resold, rented, or converted into a home office, additional bedroom, or connected suite.

Particulars

The modest project budget dictated the need for an envelope system that would challenge the economy of stucco. The exterior is clad in two-foot-wide precut cementitious panels of varying heights, secured in place with custom extruded aluminum clips. The result is a run of linear boards with a self generating pattern of clip pairs. The reveals between the boards break up large wall surfaces and reveal pre-finished aluminum facing around windows.

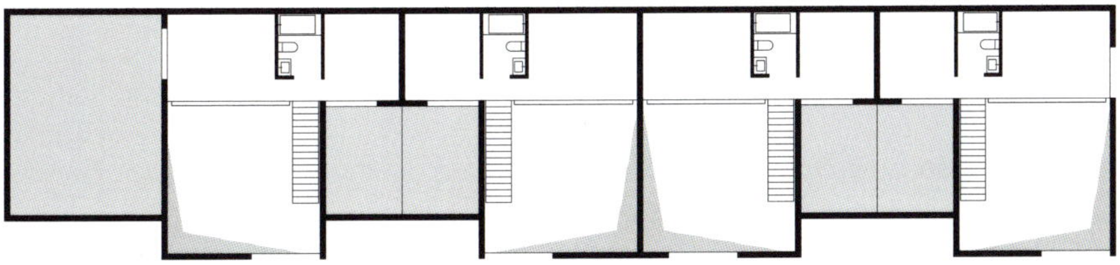

L3 Plan

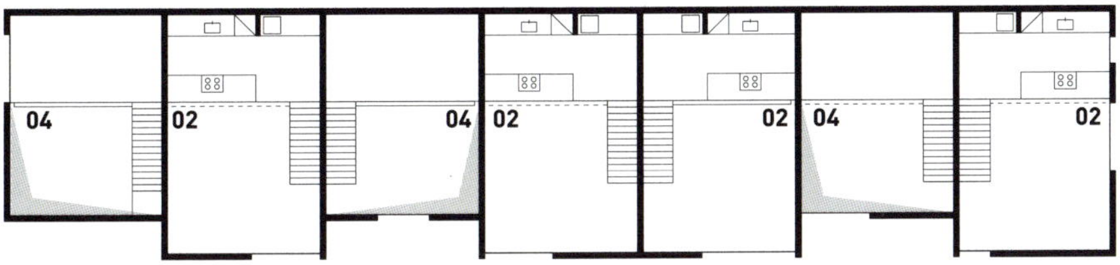

L2 Plan

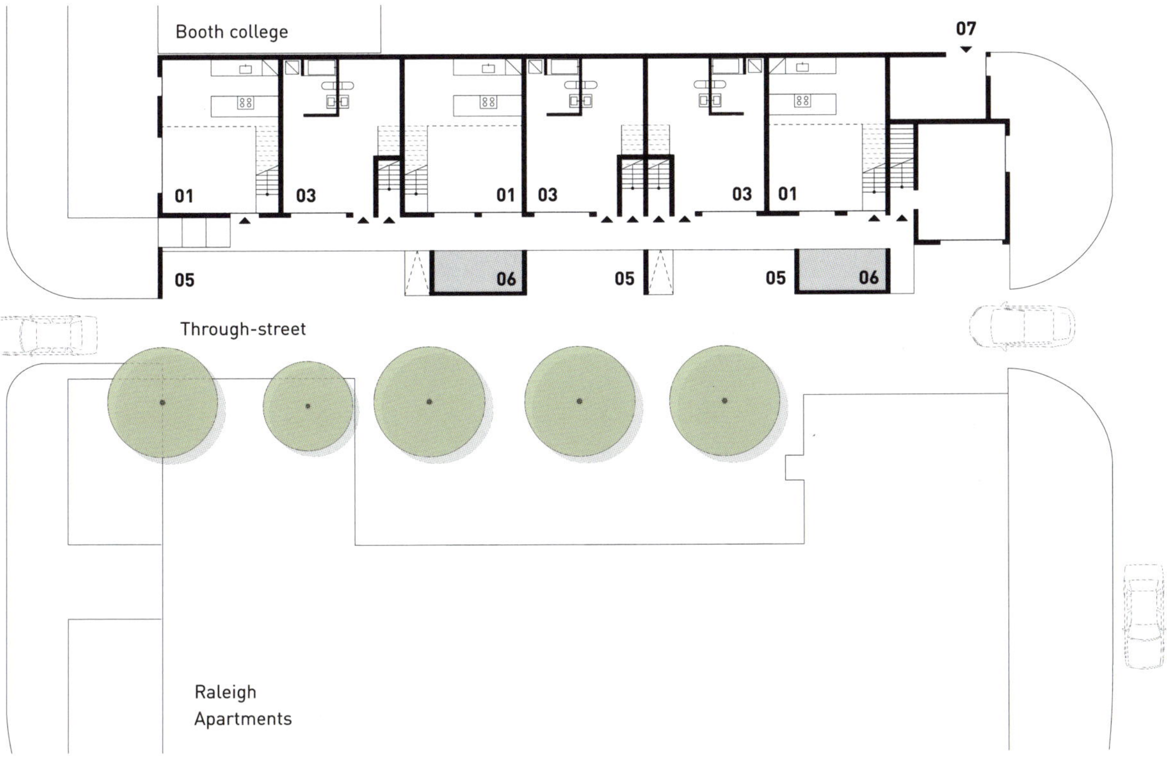

Site Plan

01 One-bedroom suite
02 Two-bedroom suite
03 Flex suite
04 Open to below
05 Surface parking
06 Terrace
07 Garbage

BGBX

Condominiums
Winnipeg, Manitoba
2008 - 2015 [West + north + south buildings]

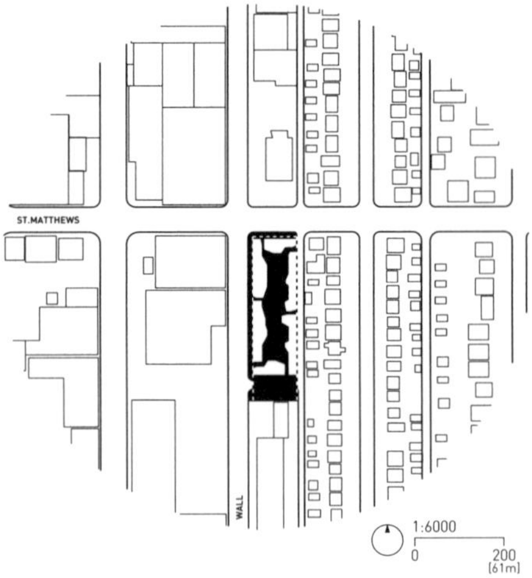

BGBX is a 27-unit market rate condominium project that includes seven ground floor flex spaces geared toward future cottage-industry / home base businesses or as extensions of the residential area. This three-storey new construction infill development consists of two storey townhouse style units and includes a very generous shared courtyard at the heart of the block. Individual outdoor spaces include a combination of porches along the street façades, private patios facing the courtyard and rooftop patios off the top floor. Parking consists of a surface lot on the south side of the property and [future] covered stalls below the yet-to-be-built Phase III off the public lane.

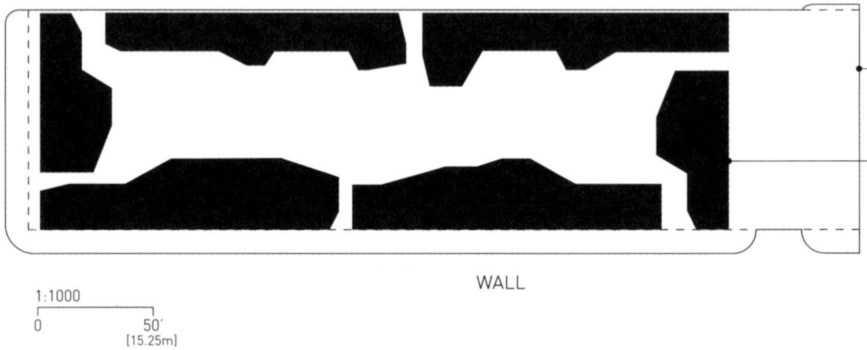

SITE AREA
34,210 ft²
[3,178 m²]

GFA
30,210 ft²
[2,807 m²]

COVERAGE

FLOOR AREA RATIO **0.88**

COVERED AREA **33%**

EFFICIENCY [gross/net] **100%**

OCCUPANCY

RESIDENTIAL **88%**

COMMERCIAL **12%**

TYPOLOGY

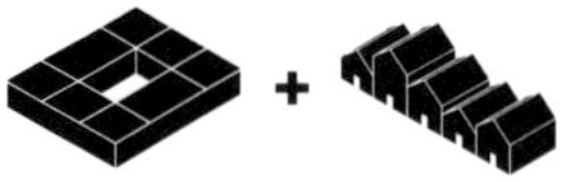

DENSITY

43 /ac [107/ha]

51 / ac [126/ha]

HEIGHT [STOREYS]

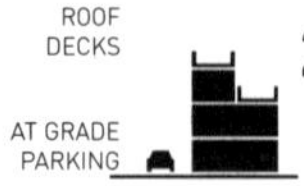

2-3

OF UNITS **27+7**

OF PARKING STALLS **15**

UNIT TYPES

bedrooms	29	2	0	0
storeys [within units]	10	24	0	0

UNIT SIZE* including flex units

AVERAGE UNIT (60%) **1078 ft²** [100 m²]

SMALLEST UNIT (27%) **485 ft²** [45 m²]

LARGEST UNIT (67%) **1,205 ft²** [112 m²]

COST

$155/ft²
[$1,673/m²]

CONSTRUCTION

ENGINEERED
- WALLS (LSL)
- L3 ROOF (TJI)

HOLLOWCORE
- FLOORS
- L2 ROOF

- FOUNDATION

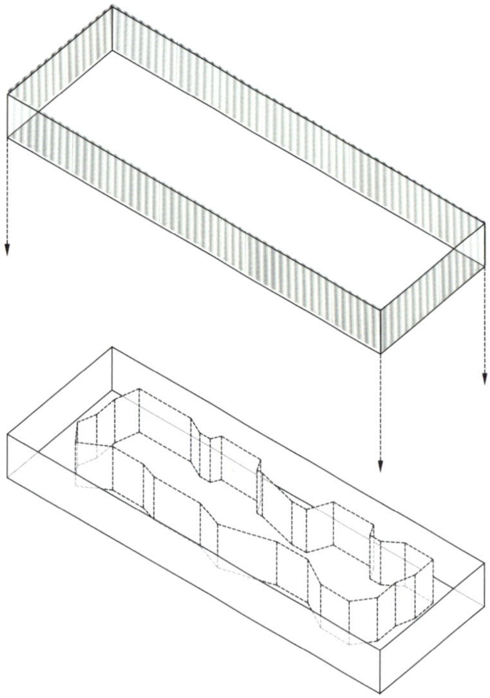

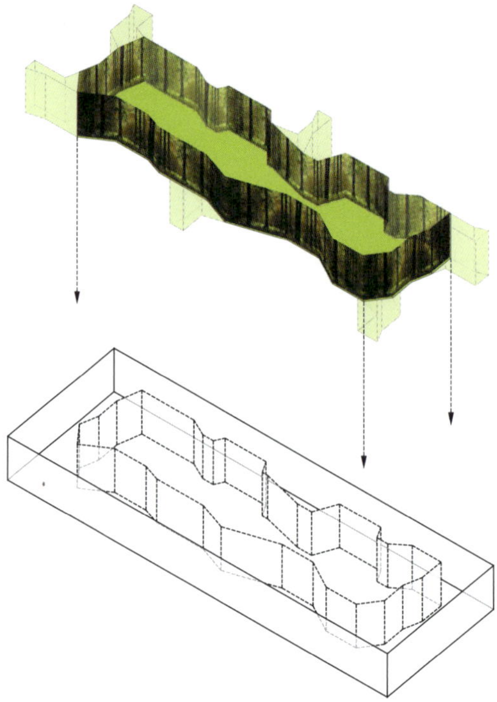

Background
In 2007, 546 was engaged by a private developer to design a townhouse development on a 100'x350' surface parking lot in an industrial corridor. The location and very affordable land cost drove the relatively low density pressure on the site. From the beginning, the developer wanted to use pre-cast concrete as the main floor assembly to provide a more robust sound barrier between living levels.

Concept
BGBX finds precedent in a big box design typology, transforming an existing parking lot on a hostile industrial corridor into a 27 unit housing development and public green space. Six separate blocks are arranged on the site, with two-storey residential loft units and small scale commercial flex spaces at grade.

The project begins as a white, non-descript box, a blank volume which is then strategically sliced at six points to reveal unexpected glimpses of lush foliage at the building's centre. This hidden courtyard cuts away at the box from the inside, creating a multi-facetted façade that is clad in a pixelated forest of green and yellow panels. On the exterior, a corrugated metal skin shields residents from the unyielding character of the street.

Units
Majority of the housing unit are two-storey loft style one and two bedroom suites with their living area either on the ground or on the second floor. Below the upper suites the project includes seven flex units at grade – individually titled and fire-separated rooms that can function and bought or sold as self standing studios suites and micro businesses, or be joined vertically or horizontally to adjoining condominium as a additional bedroom, home office or a granny suite.

Particulars
The design of BGBX is simplified through the integration of its building systems; despite the project's irregular shape, a module based on four-foot wide hollow core slabs determines the entire architectural, structural, and mechanical composition of the units. The systematic approach to the planning allows for considerable efficiencies in cost, material and overall interior aesthetic.

In the courtyard, abundant vegetation acts as lungs for the building, providing fresh air for residents. Gray water cisterns collect run-off from the roofs, and bioswales in the courtyard eliminate the need for catch basins.

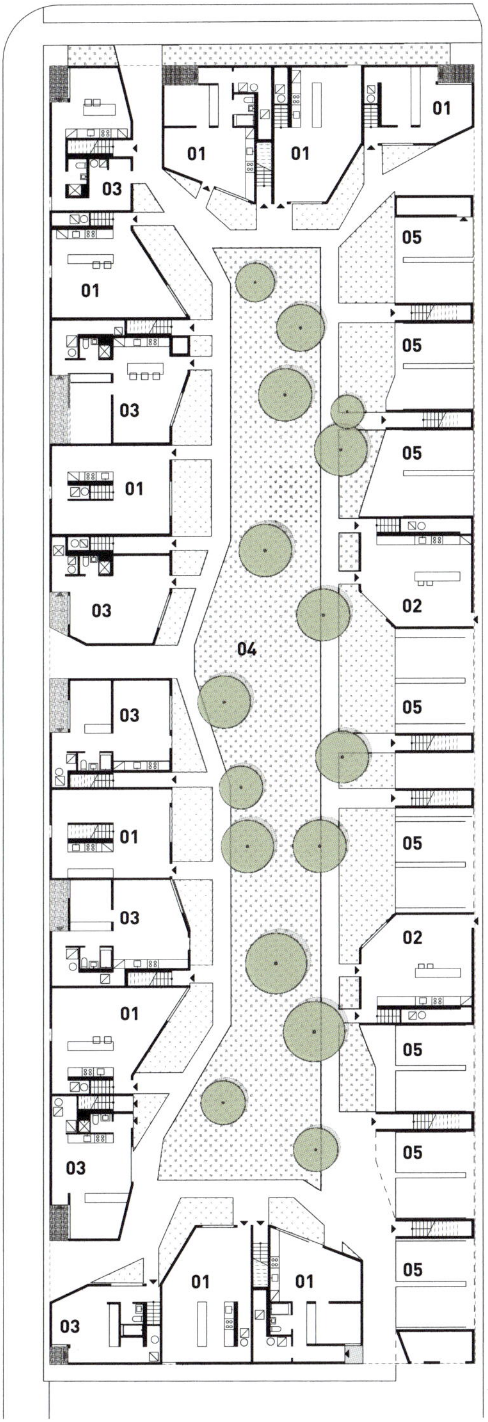

L1 Plan

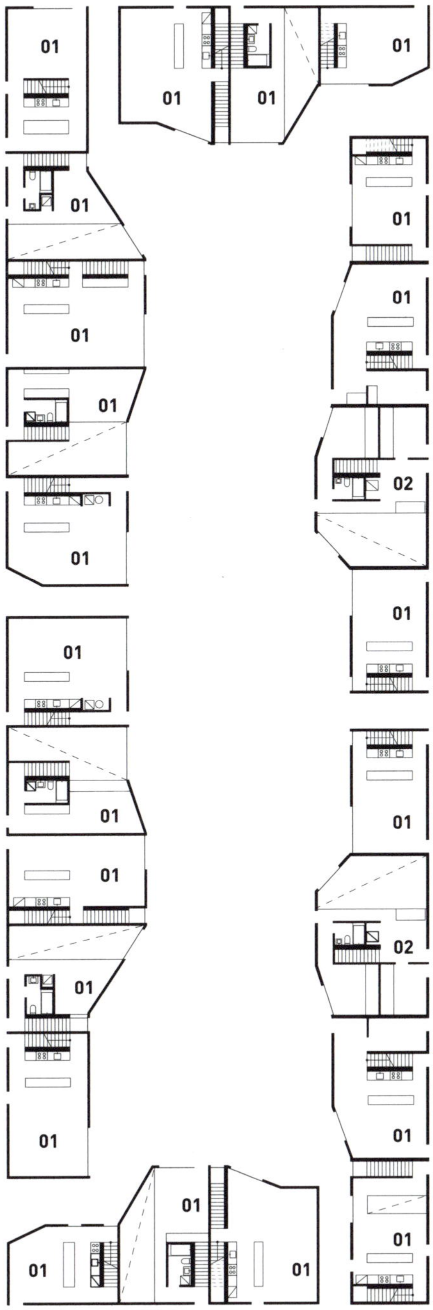

L2 plan

01 One-bed suite
02 Two-bed suite
03 Flex unit
04 Courtyard
05 Parking

youCUBE

Condominiums
Winnipeg, Manitoba
2009 - 2011 [phase 1], 2015 - 2020 [phase 2]

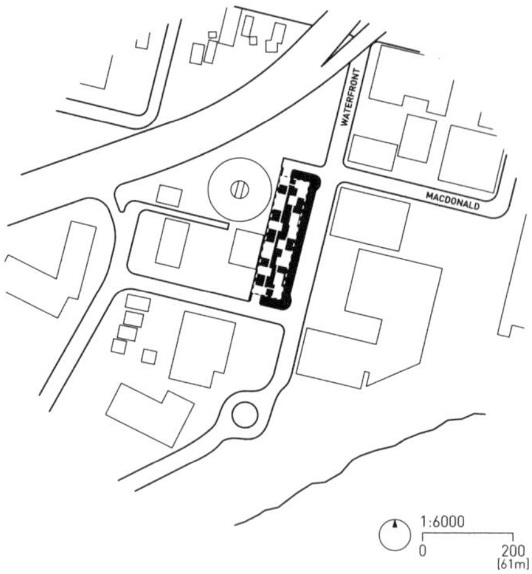

youCUBE is an 18-unit new construction market-rate condominium and rental housing cluster designed for a young private developer in a transitional neighbourhood. While technically considered a three-storey building, the development includes a slightly sunken lower floor that adds much needed square footage and essentially a highly usable forth floor to the development. A few commercial suites align the major street frontage and include retail and professional services. Parking is provided under a raised common plaza off grade at a 1:1 dwelling to stall ratio. A common elevated plaza and individual open rooftops provide outdoor space and opportunities for interaction among neighbours.

SITE AREA
17,550 ft² [1,630 m²]

GFA
21,725 ft² [2,018 m²]

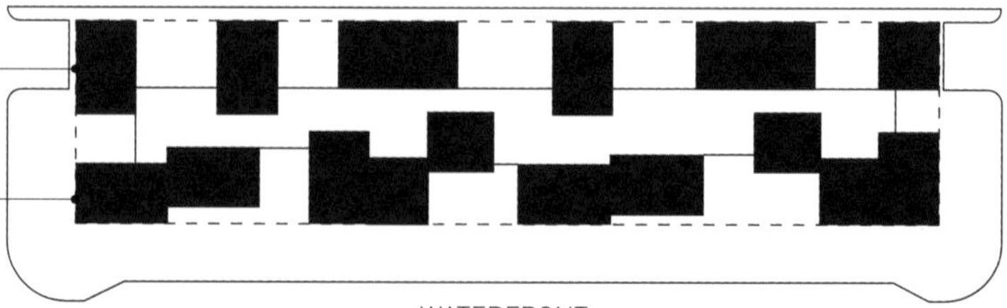

1:1000
0 — 50' [15.25m]

COVERAGE

FLOOR AREA RATIO	COVERED AREA	EFFICIENCY [gross/net]
1.24	**46%**	**97%**

\# OF UNITS **18** | # OF PARKING STALLS **19**

UNIT TYPES

bedrooms	**11**	**7**	0	0
storeys [within units]	0	**3**	**10**	**5**

OCCUPANCY

RESIDENTIAL **95%**

COMMERCIAL **5%**

TYPOLOGY

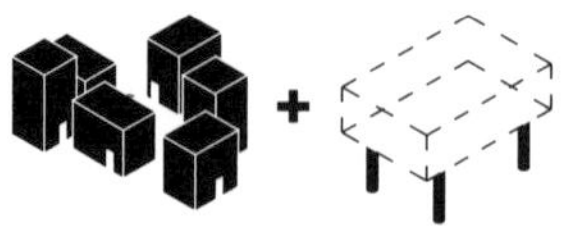

UNIT SIZE

AVERAGE UNIT (62%) **1,122 ft²** [104.3 m²]

SMALLEST UNIT (39%) **710 ft²** [66.0 m²]

LARGEST UNIT (91%) **1,635 ft²** [151.9 m²]

CONSTRUCTION

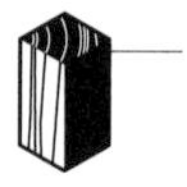

PRE-FAB LIGHT WOOD FRAME
- WALLS
- FLOORS
- ROOFS

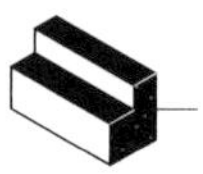

- LEVEL 1 WALLS
- LEVEL 1 FLOOR
- LEVEL 1 DECK
- FOUNDATION

DENSITY

45 /ac [111/ha]

78 /ac [192/ha]

HEIGHT [STOREYS]

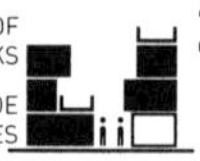

2-4

COST

$156/ft² [$1,684/m²]

530

Background

Located on the north end of Waterfront Drive, the project occupies a seemingly unremarkable 63'x264' urban lot with limited visibility of the nearby river and neglected, industrial surroundings. With a modest budget and a background in custom home building, the developer engaged 5468796 to produce a design that could be built using standard construction methods by residential contractors.

Concept

After testing a number of possibilities and massing options, the design team landed on a scheme that would break the required building mass/square footage into 18 individual blocks that could be perceived as individual homes. The final composition clusters three and four-storey townhouses together on a shared plaza [exterior passageway], which is elevated six feet above the sidewalk to suggest privacy and security without disengaging from the street. Additionally, lowering the lowest floor level two feet below the adjoining grade allowed the entire development to be classified as a small building, avoiding a number of building code requirements that would otherwise become applicable and result in additional expense.

The elevated plaza provides access to all of the suite entrances and shelters a new driveway for vehicular access and resident parking below. Each unit culminates in a rooftop patio with 360-degree vistas of the river and city skyline. Together, these two spaces lift residents above their industrial context, capturing formerly inaccessible views and carving a permanent community into a transitional setting.

Units

In order to keep the project cost effective, the design consists of two standard module sizes – 18'x20' or 18'x28' – that each have two interior layout options. The base modules vary from two to four levels, either beginning at two feet below grade or at the elevated plaza level, resulting in square footages that vary from 710 square foot one-bedroom lofts to 1635 square foot 3-4 bedroom townhomes. The first layout places the living spaces more traditionally on the main floor, while the other moves them to the upper levels for greater access to light and views. Inside, each unit is defined by an architectural "wrap," a design element that sculpts the interior into a fluid sequence of open plan rooms within a spacious, light-filled volume.

Particulars

Similar to a house, the basements are cast-in-place concrete, while the upper levels are traditional wood-frame assemblies. The cubes are clad in simple white stucco that reflects light into the plaza and provides a modern counterpoint to the neighbouring buildings. In addition to streamlining the construction process, the dwellings' vertical design also leaves more room for outdoor amenities along the sidewalk edge, incorporating pockets of green space, small patios and entrances to commercial suites that offer live-work opportunities for residents.

Touching only two walls at a time, the interior wrap delineates floors and mezzanines as it weaves through the space, creating dramatic overlooks to the spaces below. The wrap reacts with the walls of the cube by folding back onto itself, or continuing upward to form window openings. Ceiling heights soar up to 36 feet, filtering daylight from the top level all the way to the ground floor. The wrap becomes the mediator between the simplicity of the building's shell and the complexity of living that occurs within.

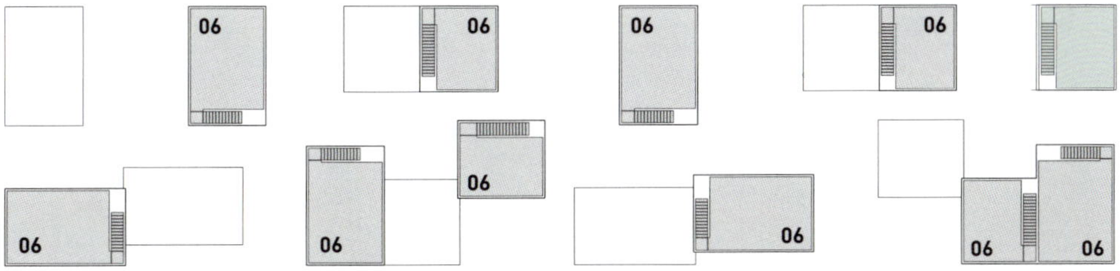

Roof Plan

L3 Plan

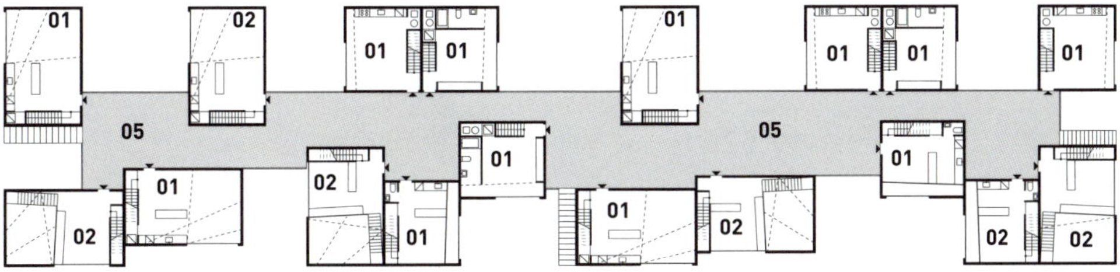

L2 Plan

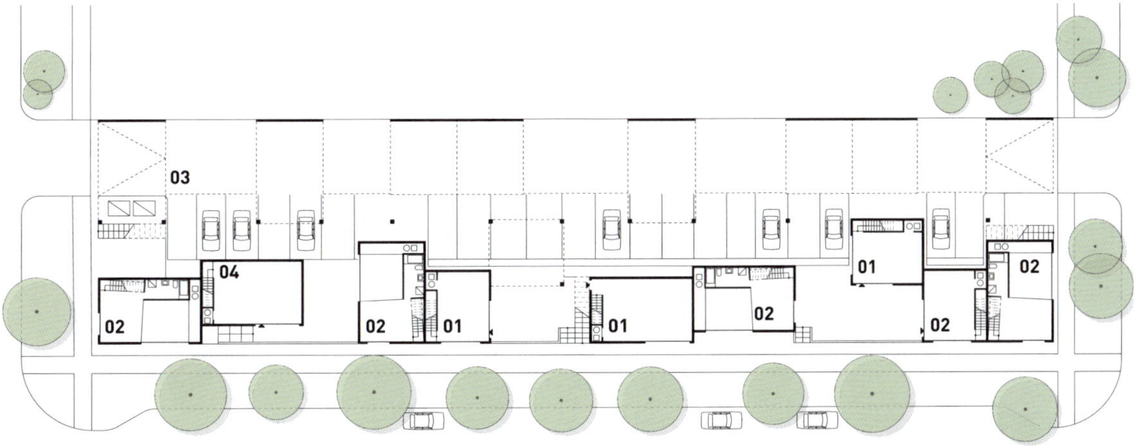

Site Plan

01 One-bed suite
02 Two-bed suite
03 Parking
04 Commercial space
05 Walkway
06 Rooftop patio

Centre Village

Rental housing
Winnipeg, Manitoba
2008 - 2010

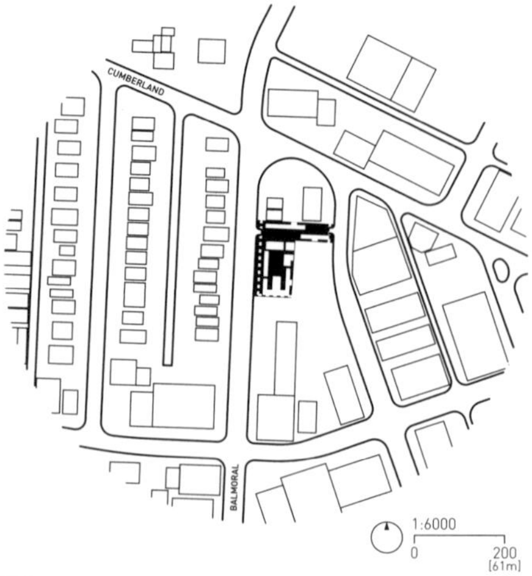

Centre Village is a 25-unit subsidized rental housing project on an infill lot in Winnipeg's inner city. The three-storey project consists of town-home type arrangement with all dwellings entered either directly at grade or via private stairs onto the second floor. The common areas include a shared courtyard and a mews connecting the two adjacent streets. The mainly pedestrian mews also contains the project's five surface parking stalls.

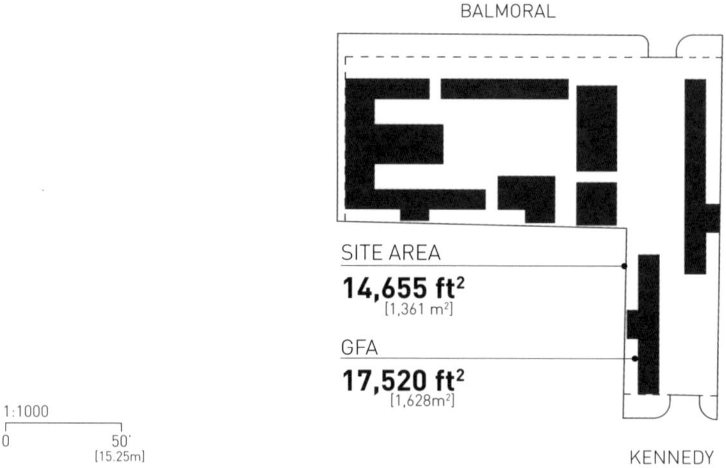

SITE AREA
14,655 ft²
[1,361 m²]

GFA
17,520 ft²
[1,628m²]

COVERAGE

FLOOR AREA RATIO **1.20**

COVERED AREA **46%**

EFFICIENCY [gross/net] **98%**

OCCUPANCY

RESIDENTIAL **100%**

TYPOLOGY

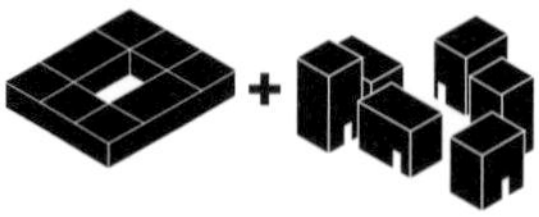

DENSITY

74 /ac [184/ha]

189 / ac [468/ha]

HEIGHT [STOREYS]

2-3

OF UNITS **25**

OF PARKING STALLS **5**

UNIT TYPES

bedrooms	8	10	5	2
storeys [within units]	5	9	11	0

UNIT SIZE

AVERAGE UNIT (38%) **688 ft²** [63.9 m²]

SMALLEST UNIT (20%) **370 ft²** [34.4 m²]

LARGEST UNIT (55%) **990 ft²** [92.0 m²]

CONSTRUCTION

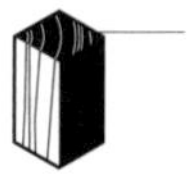

LIGHT WOOD FRAME
- WALLS
- FLOORS
- ROOFS

- FOUNDATION

COST

$137/ft²
[$1,472/m²]

CENTRE VILLAGE

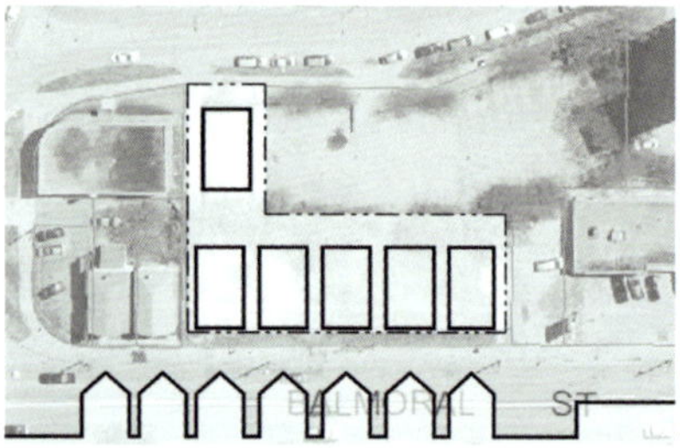
Original site - 6 house lots

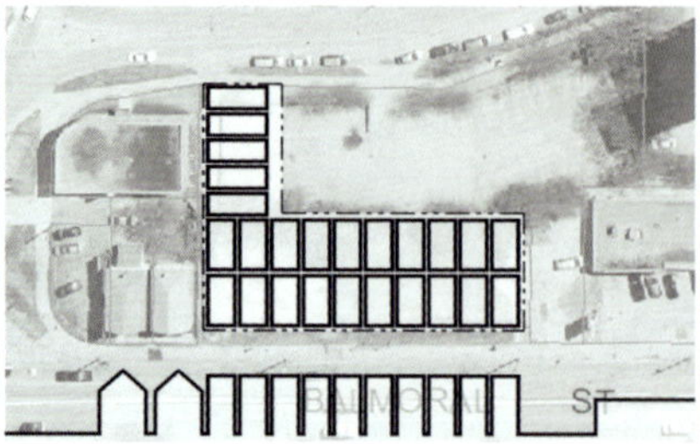
Required density - 25 units

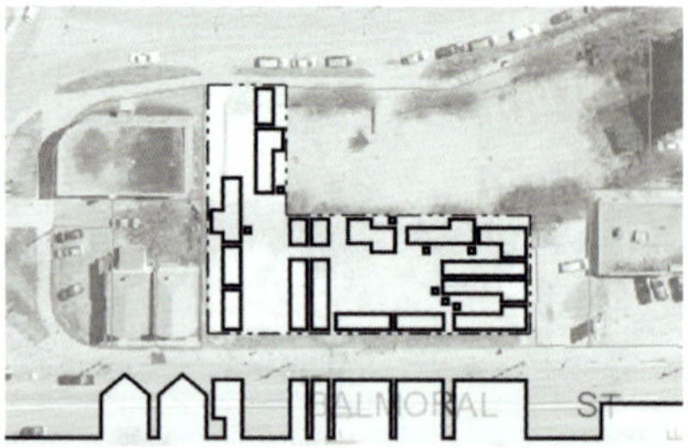
Centre Village

Background

In 2008, 546 was approached by project manger/development coordinator helping a non-profit client group realize a 25-suite subsidized rental housing project on a vacant infill lot. The design brief called for an extremely affordable project to serve the new muslim immigrant community and underprivileged families on a site that was zoned for six single-family houses.

Concept

The design team conceived the project from the inside out, intentionally challenging some of the North American preconceptions of space by using a minimum room dimension of 8 feet [2.4 m] as a the project's basic building block. In addition, inspired by the villages of the Arabic world, the design imagined much of the life occurring outside of the private realm in the communal shared spaces. As a result, the project is arranged onto eight-foot-wide "spines" that attempt to reduce the building's footprint at grade in order to maximize the shared outdoor areas. The completed project established a micro village of 25 dwellings within six three-storey blocks.

The blocks' arrangement both defines and animates two major public spaces – a through-street and a shared courtyard – that weave the city into the project and provide amenities for residents and neighbours. The landscaped courtyard offers a calm and protected place for children to play, and the new street is an informal meeting place. Each dwelling has its own entrance at grade or up an exterior staircase, reducing internal circulation and prompting residents to get to know one another.

Units

Designed to make the most of space, material and daylight, the dwellings have rich and playful compositions made from simple, compact and easy-to-build 8x12-foot modules and cantilevered 14x12-foot modules for larger living areas. The modules are stacked and interlocked to create diverse unit configurations that vary from 370 square feet for a one-bedroom unit, to 990 square feet for four-bedroom units. Since the rooms of each unit are distributed over several floors, even small apartments have plenty of privacy, which was an important factor since several of the intended residents were multigenerational families.

Particulars

The three-storey walk-up arrangement resulting in nearly 100% gross to rentable area, the short structural spans resulting from the eight-foot-wide "spines," and traditional stucco façade and double-pane standardized windows allow the construction to be extremely efficient and cost effective.

With entries and windows positioned on all sides of the blocks, there is no rear side to this project, thus improving the street quality and safety and security in all directions. A typical residence has eight or more windows on at least two sides of the building, providing ample and varied access to daylight and cross-ventilation. Deeply set, vibrant orange cowlings around the windows modulate privacy and views into the units, granting Centre Village a distinct identity in the city.

L2 plan

Site plan

01 One-bed suite
02 Two-bed suite
03 Three-bed suite
04 Four-bed suite
05 Courtyard
06 Mews
07 Patio

Welcome Place

Refugee housing + support services
Winnipeg, Manitoba
2008 - 2010

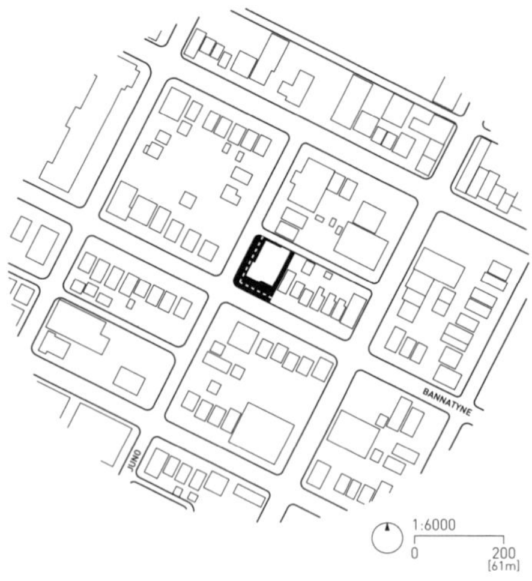

Welcome Place offers temporary supportive housing and transitional services for refugees arriving to Manitoba. The 25,000-square-foot project consist of 30 flexible housing units and approximately 10,000 square feet of support services. The newly constructed five-storey building is located on the corner of a quiet, residential street in Winnipeg's Centennial neighbourhood, and sunken half level down from grade to fit within the applicable zoning ordinances. The site includes only a single parking stall to accommodate the organization's transit van. Staff parking is located off site. The building includes generous common areas, including three indoor lounges, a multipurpose room, an outdoor forecourt and a rooftop patio.

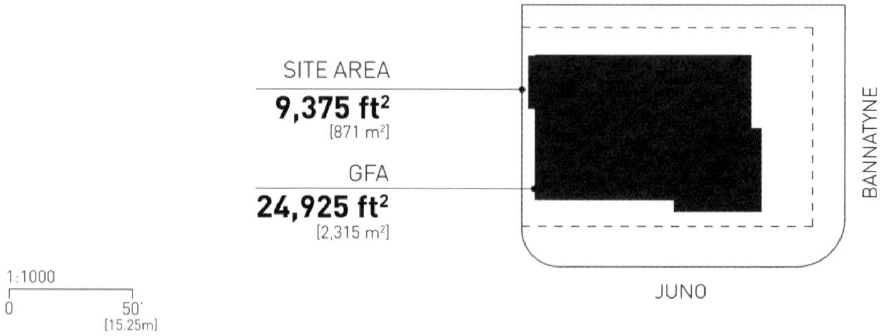

COVERAGE

FLOOR AREA RATIO **2.66**

COVERED AREA **53%**

EFFICIENCY [gross/net] **84%**

OCCUPANCY

RESIDENTIAL **65%**

COMMERCIAL **35%**

TYPOLOGY

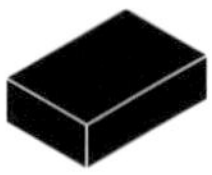

DENSITY

344 /ac [850/ha]

395 / ac [975/ha]

HEIGHT [STOREYS]

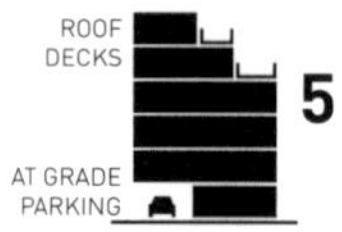

OF UNITS **30**

OF PARKING STALLS **1**

UNIT TYPES

bedrooms	**25**	**5**	0	0
storeys [within units]	**30**	0	0	0

UNIT SIZE

AVERAGE UNIT 22% **391 ft²** [36.4 m²]

SMALLEST UNIT 16% **285 ft²** [26.5 m²]

LARGEST UNIT 28% **505 ft²** [47.0 m²]

COST

$152/ft² [$1,635/m²]

300 / 75

CONSTRUCTION

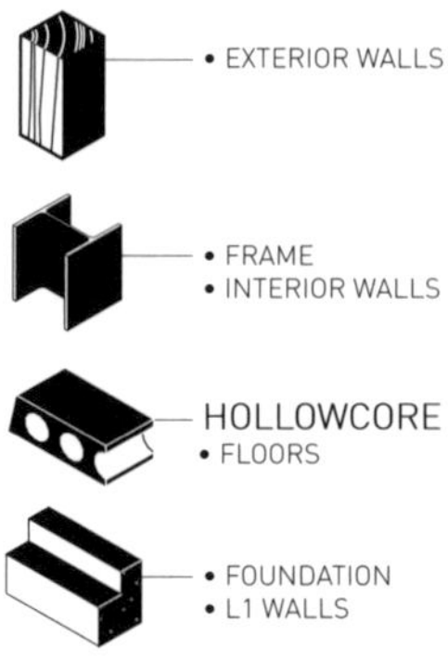

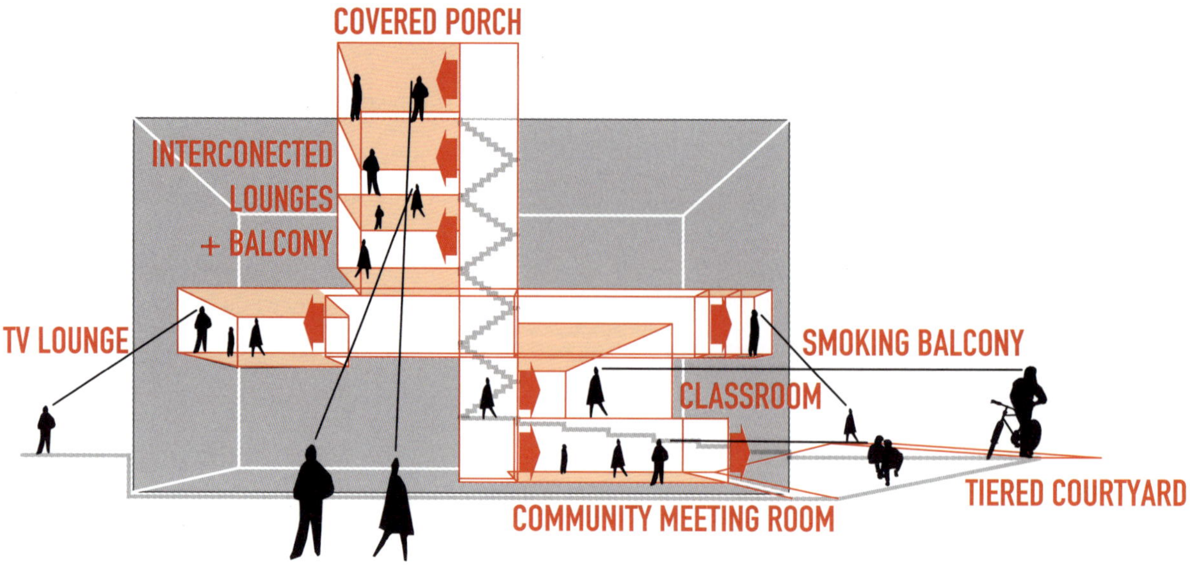

Background

In 2008, the Welcome Place management team engaged 546 to lead the design of their new facility, aiming for the first time to centralize the organization's support services and transitional housing under a single roof. As a former patron of Welcome Place from the Balkan war in the 1990's, 546 Principal Sasa Radulovic was uniquely positioned to understand the needs and distresses of refugees fleeing war-torn areas.

Concept

The project focuses on hope and refuge for residents and patrons, most of whom are coping with the emotional stress of being displaced from their homelands and are just beginning to form new lives in Canada. As a result, the design seeks to balance private rooms and spaces for social interaction, integrating the two on every level. The first two floors hold meeting rooms and administrative spaces, and the upper three floors contain the transitional housing. The concept of prospect and refuge shaped the thinking about the upper residential mass that aims to enclose and protect the patrons within, while simultaneously offering playful opportunities to peer out over the immediate context.

The design also seeks to balance the need for maximum possible square footage and residential suite total required for housing and the operations of the organization, while attempting to remain sensitive to the surrounding residential neighbourhood context and the prevailing zoning limitations.

Units

With an average stay of only three weeks, the 30 residential suites are designed with maximum flexibility in mind. Depending on the nature and location of the crises in the world, the type and size of the refugee family unit varies widely, necessitating constant shift in the type of residences needed at Welcome Place. A portion of the 30 base units can therefore be further combined into larger suites, to accommodate larger family units. Typical suite sizes vary from 285 to 505 square feet but some are increased up to 810 square feet when combined.

Particulars

The public area begins outside the building with a sunken courtyard that slopes down to the main entry doors, incorporating an accessible ramp and establishing a place for community functions. A separate residential entry is located at grade on the west façade. Interior public spaces are revealed through full-height glazing while the residences are defined by a random patterning of windows. These openings are small enough to be protective and numerous enough to provide ample access to views, daylight and fresh air. Inside, every floor includes wide corridors that might encourage conversation, as well as a public lounge or balcony. An array of vibrant paint colours charge these interiors with a positive energy, while private units are kept calm and neutral.

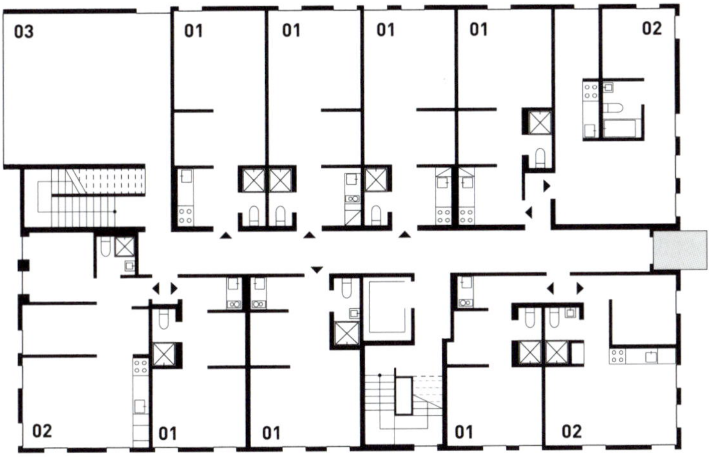

L3 Plan

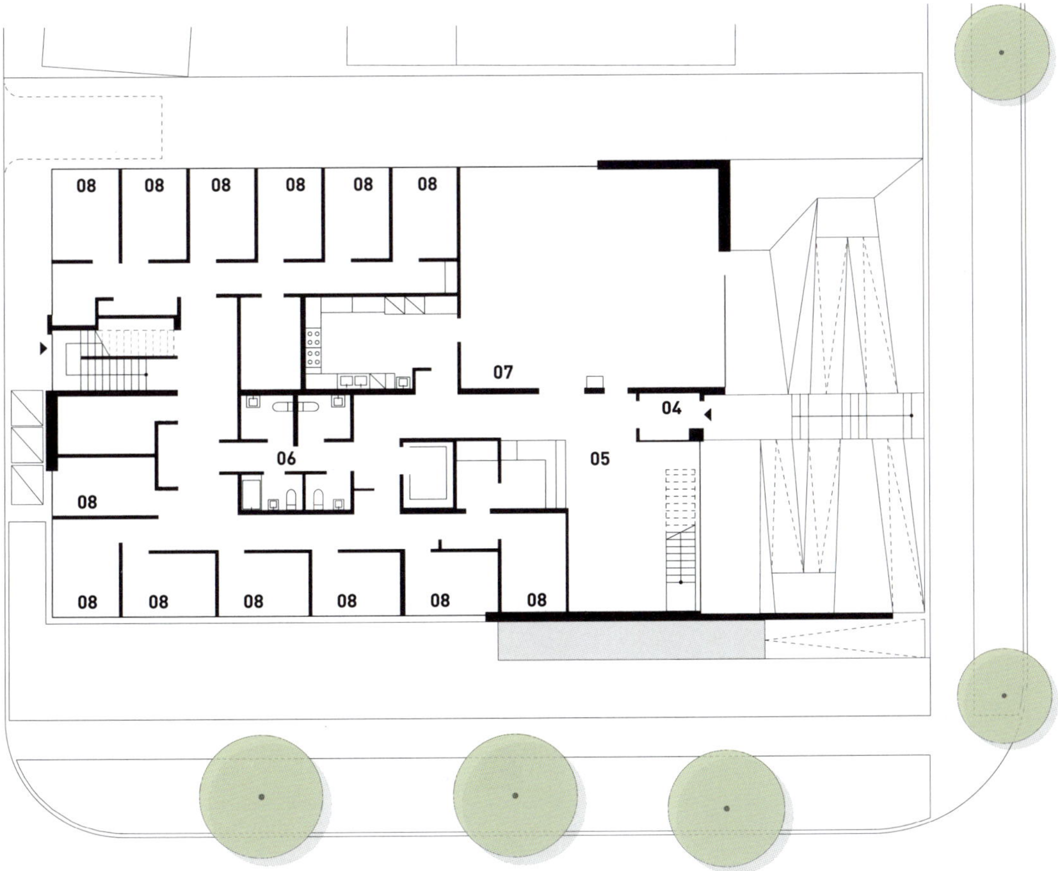

Site Plan

01 One-bed suite
02 Two-bed suite
03 Lounge
04 Entry
05 Lobby
06 Washroom
07 Multi-purpose room
08 Office

Bloc_10

Condominiums
Winnipeg, Manitoba
2009 - 2011

Bloc_10 is a 10-suite, market-rate condominium project built on an infill site within an existing mature neighbourhood. The new construction three-storey walk-up building is prefabricated in elements. The project includes a 14-stall surface parking area behind the building, and private, yet visually connected series of balconies and patios for all the suites.

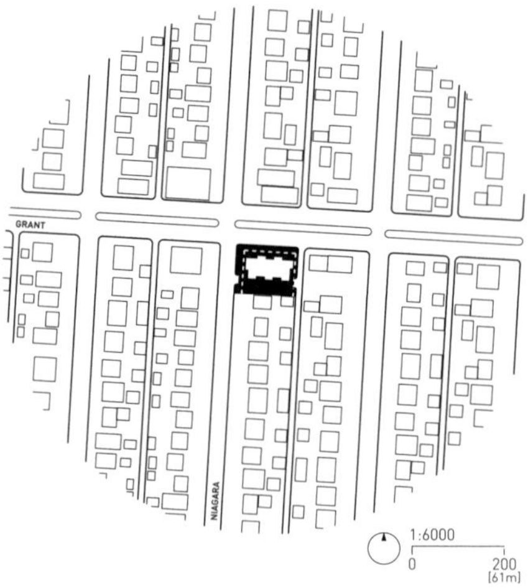

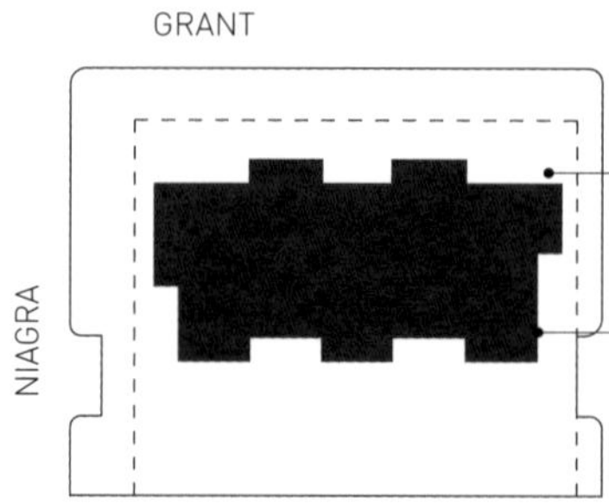

SITE AREA
11,135 ft² [1,034 m²]

GFA
12,145 ft² [1,128 m²]

1:1000
0 50' [15.25m]

COVERAGE

FLOOR AREA RATIO **1.09**
COVERED AREA **38%**
EFFICIENCY [gross/net] **100%**

OF UNITS **10**

OF PARKING STALLS **14**

UNIT TYPES

bedrooms	**8**	**2**	0	0
storeys [within units]	0	0	**10**	0

OCCUPANCY

RESIDENTIAL
100%

TYPOLOGY

UNIT SIZE

67% AVERAGE UNIT **1,210 ft²** [112.3 m²]

54% SMALLEST UNIT **965 ft²** [89.7 m²]

79% LARGEST UNIT **1,415 ft²** [131.5 m²]

CONSTRUCTION

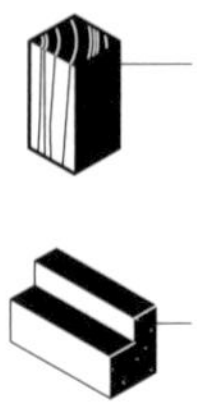

PRE-FAB LIGHT WOOD FRAME
- WALLS
- FLOORS
- ROOFS

- LEVEL 1 FLOORS
- FOUNDATION

DENSITY

39 /ac [97/ha]

59 / ac [145/ha]

HEIGHT [STOREYS]

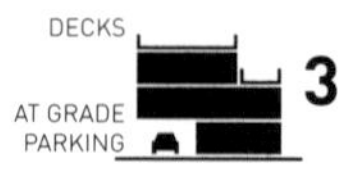

COST

$165/ft² [$1,773/m²]

CIMA

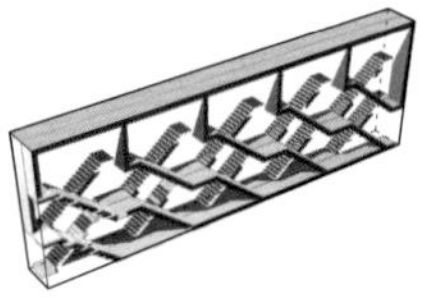

Solid core

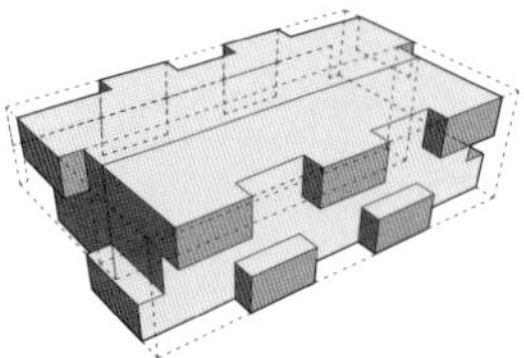

Flexible block

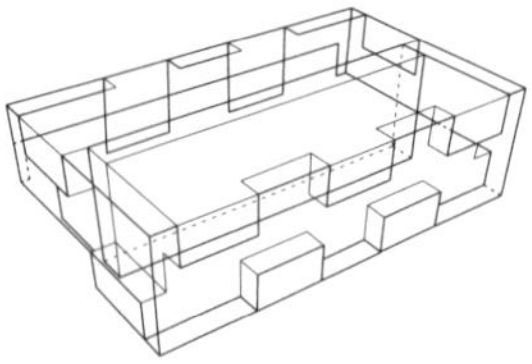

Habitable shell

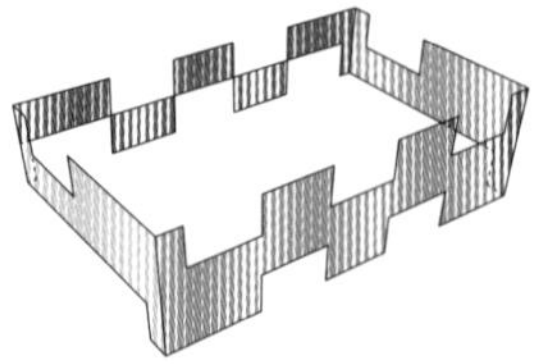

Thin screen

Background

On the site of a former gas station in Winnipeg's River Heights neighbourhood, the developer wanted a modestly priced building designed and constructed within 12 months. The 12-foot-wide site included an existing zoning agreement for 10 residential dwellings and in the interest of time, the developer did not wish to challenge the approved density further. The developer also requested that the building be designed as "white box": each buyer would purchase an unfinished unit with basic plumbing, heating and electrical systems. Buyers could decide which rooms they would like where, and would have the ability to personalize finishes to their own taste and budget.

Concept

The design team sought to re-imagine what a three-storey walk-up could be – in part due to the desire to ensure that all suites could face both the primary street and the backyard, providing opportunity for cross ventilation. At 100 feet wide it would have not been feasible to simply split the building in ten 10-foot-wide townhomes, so the team opted to divide the zoning envelope into thirty 18.5-feet-wide and 18-and-13-feet deep blocks instead, and connect them via a central utility/stair spine at the centre of the block. With this strategy each suite becomes double aspect, and traverses all three levels of the building.

Due to the site's former use as a gas station, the existing soil was encapsulated and isolated from the new building above. These site conditions further necessitated that the building be constructed without any basement or crawlspace below grade.

Units

All of the units (sized between 900 and 1,400 square feet) have their entry at grade and most have two balconies. As the apartments ascend, they cross from one side of the building to the other, resulting in 10 unique, interlocking layouts that feel like a hybrid between a condominium and a house. This arrangement provides views to the north and the south, and 8 of the 10 apartments have views in three directions. The rooms within the suites can be allocated according to the owners' preference. To rationalize the design of building systems, plumbing and utility connections are organized into the central spine as the only predetermined suite layout limitation.

Particulars

The building sits on a concrete structural slab and the wood frame was prefabricated off-site in wall, floor, and roof elements. The elements where then hoisted in place on site and rest of the construction followed standard building methods.

To take advantage of the maximum allowable mass for the development, cantilevered projections expand rooms within, create balconies and, at the same time, provide support for the wooden, vertical-slat privacy screen that wraps the building's exterior. The screen serves many purposes. It provides each homeowner with privacy and shade and yet by offering glimpses of neighbours, it also encourages community.

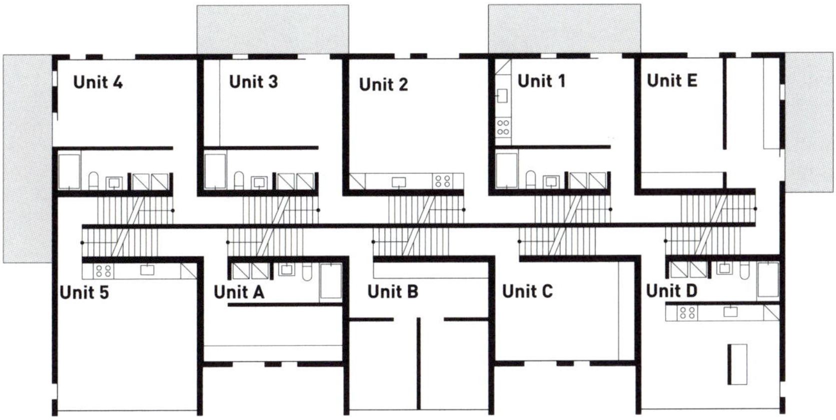

L2 Plan

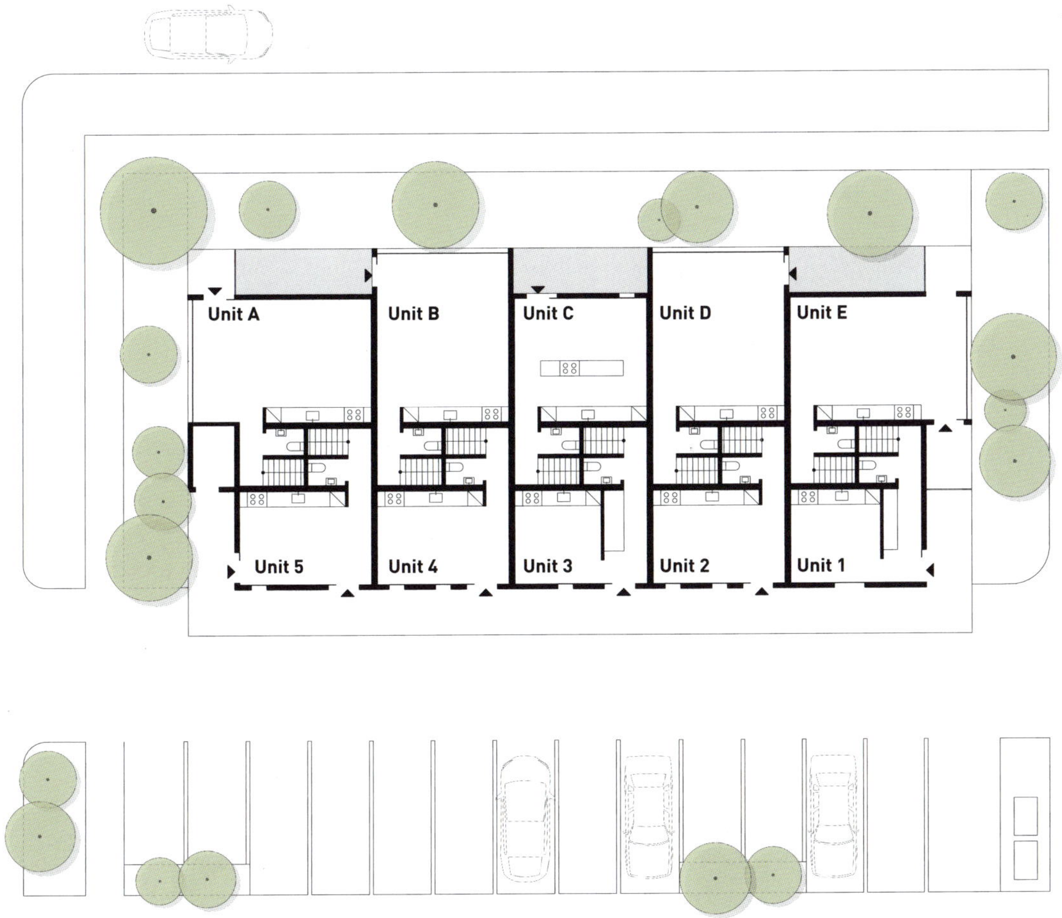

Site Plan

The Avenue

Mixed-use
Winnipeg, Manitoba
2011 - 2012

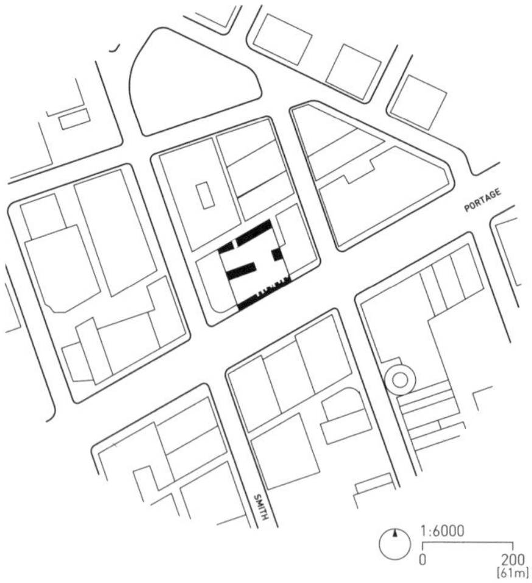

The Avenue on Portage is a six-storey adaptive re-use project converting two historic buildings into 75 housing units and 22,500 square feet of commercial tenant space for Manitoba Start, a public agency aimed to help professionally trained new Canadians find suitable employment. The project includes both market-rate rental and subsidized rental units. The on-site parking consists of 34 underground stalls that were created in the basement of the existing building footprints. The tenant amenities include common laundry room, a gym and an extensive rooftop patio.

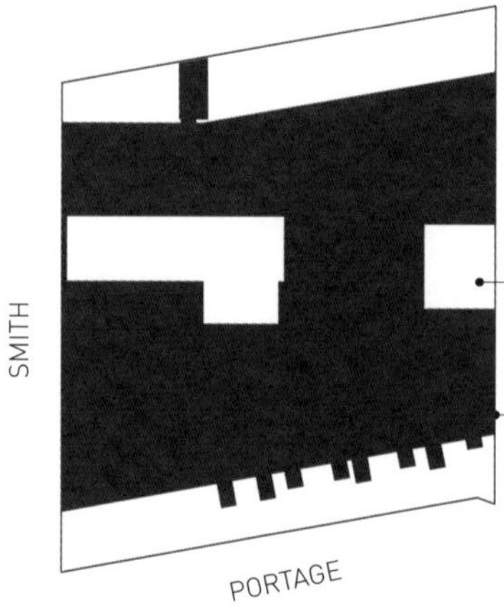

SITE AREA
16,780 ft²
[1,559 m²]

GFA
96,665 ft²
[8,981 m²]

1:1000
0 50' [15.25m]

COVERAGE

FLOOR AREA RATIO **5.76**

COVERED AREA **83%**

EFFICIENCY [gross/net] **81%**

OCCUPANCY

RESIDENTIAL **59%**

COMMERCIAL **25%**

PARKING **16%**

TYPOLOGY

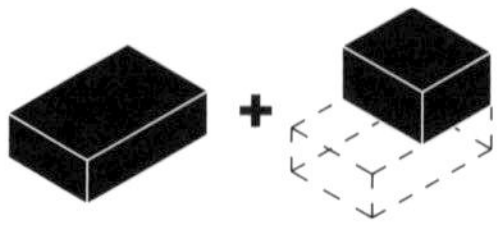

DENSITY

195 /ac [481/ha]

266 /ac [657/ha]

HEIGHT [STOREYS]

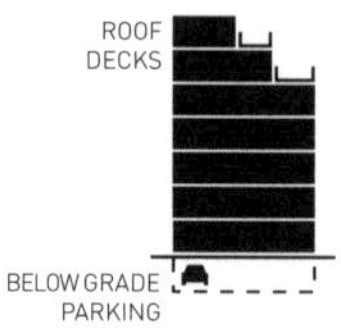

OF UNITS **75**

OF PARKING STALLS **34**

UNIT TYPES

bedrooms	**68**	**7**	0	0
storeys [within units]	**75**	0	0	0

UNIT SIZE

38% AVERAGE UNIT **685 ft²** [63.6 m²]

24% SMALLEST UNIT **425 ft²** [39.5 m²]

60% LARGEST UNIT **1,080 ft²** [100.3 m²]

COST

$131/ft²
[$1,414/m²]

CONSTRUCTION

EXISTING & NEW
- FLOORS
- STRUCTURE
- INTERIOR WALLS

EXISTING
- EXTERIOR WALLS

EXISTING & NEW
- FOUNDATION
- FLOORS[HAMPLE]
- STRUCTURE [HAMPLE]

PORTAGE
Visitor
Info
Parking
Route
42
NORTH
FULL FLOOR AVAILABLE
Start

Extending suites out into the city.

Entrance recedes back into the building.

Background

The Avenue on Portage revives two historic commercial buildings located one block west of Winnipeg's most famous corner, Portage and Main. Once major retail destinations in the city, the Avenue and Hample Buildings experienced a slow decline, becoming blights to the street and downtown. In 2010, a private development corporation purchased the site to develop the derelict properties into 75 rental apartments and 22,500 square feet of commercial space.

Concept

A series of formally simple moves dramatically transform the original façades, shifting public perception of the buildings from eyesores to a unified urban landmark. Hovering above the sidewalk, aluminum clad steel balconies cantilever from existing window openings and provide outdoor access for apartment dwellers. While the balconies push residents out beyond the façade, the main floor pulls pedestrians in, softening the boundary between the public streetscape and the private interiors.

Units

Inside, apartments sized between 425 and 1,080 square feet fill the upper four floors of The Avenue, as well as a new three-storey addition to the Hample. The majority of the units challenged the size expectations of the local market at the time, aiming to prove that well planned space could serve to reduce the required total square footage. In order to address the deep building footprint and provide windows for interior units, two existing light wells are carried down through all residential floors, while a third is extended into the new addition.

Particulars

At street level a wall of glass folds back into the building to create a deep, V-shaped entrance that broadens the width of the sidewalk. Overhead, a faceted, mirror-finish canopy unifies the two façades. Together, these elements draw the city into the building's expression.

L3 Plan

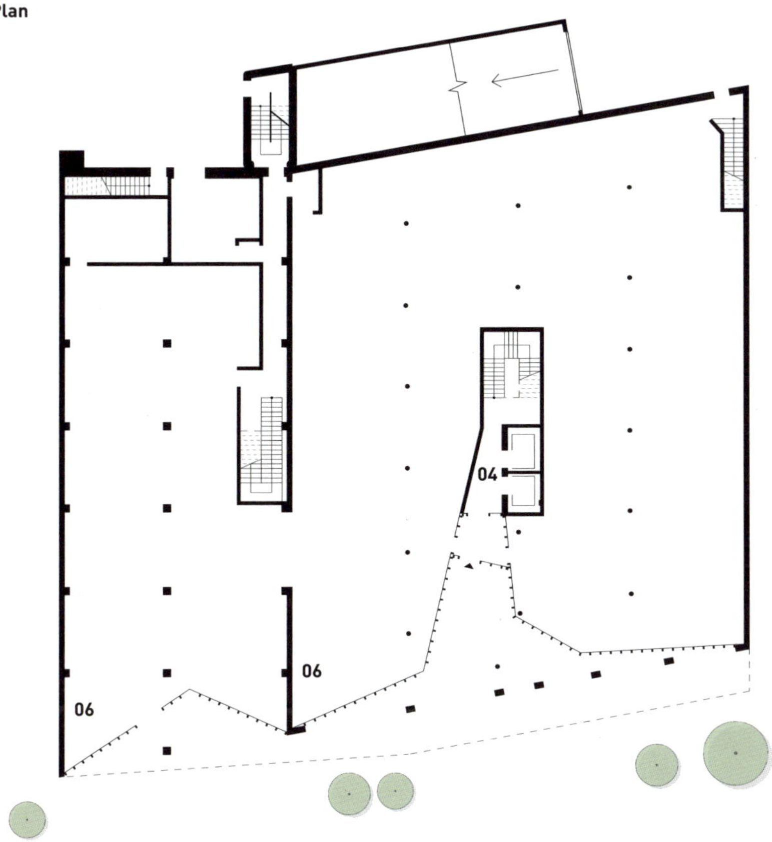

Site Plan

01 One-bedroom suite
02 Two-bedroom suite
03 Storage
04 Lobby
05 Light wall
06 Commercial

548 Stradbrook

Condominiums
Winnipeg, Manitoba
2012 - 2013

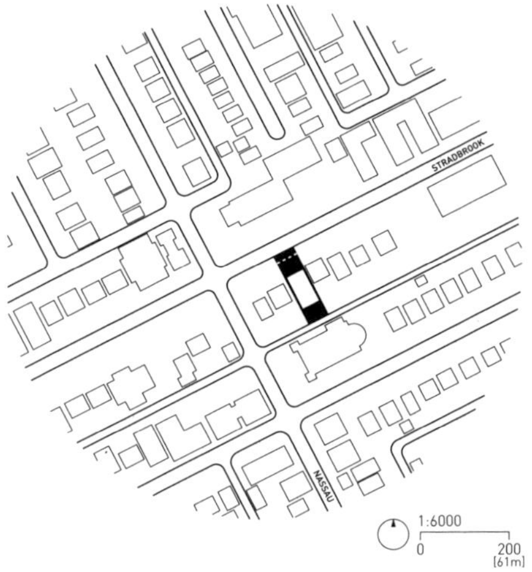

548 Stradbrook is an eight unit infill development occupying the site of a 50-foot wide x 120-foot deep single-family lot. Replacing a former fraternity house, this three and a half storey, market-rate condominium project includes a mix of eight covered and surface parking stalls accessed off the public lane at the rear of the project. Common space is limited to a relatively generous landscaped front yard and minimal circulation space for exiting.

SITE AREA
7,420 ft²
[690 m²]

GFA
9,200 ft²
[855 m²]

1:1000
0 50'
[15.25m]

COVERAGE

FLOOR AREA RATIO	COVERED AREA	EFFICIENCY [gross/net]
1.24	**32%**	**91%**

OCCUPANCY

RESIDENTIAL **100%**

TYPOLOGY

DENSITY

47 /ac [116/ha]

117 / ac [290/ha]

HEIGHT [STOREYS]

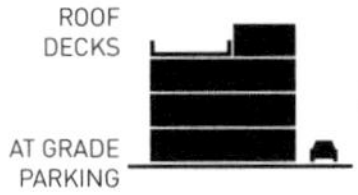

OF UNITS **8**

OF PARKING STALLS **8**

UNIT TYPES

bedrooms	0	**6**	**2**	0
storeys [within units]	**8**	0	0	0

UNIT SIZE

AVERAGE UNIT (59%)
1,066 ft² [99 m²]

SMALLEST UNIT (43%)
780 ft² [72.5 m²]

LARGEST UNIT (59%)
1,060 ft² [98.5 m²]

CONSTRUCTION

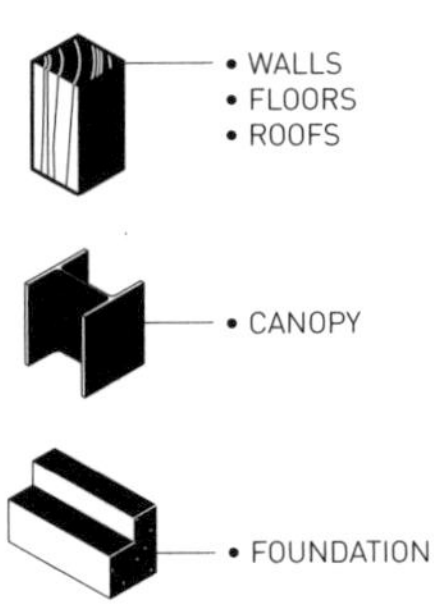

COST

$165/ft²
[$1,776/m²]

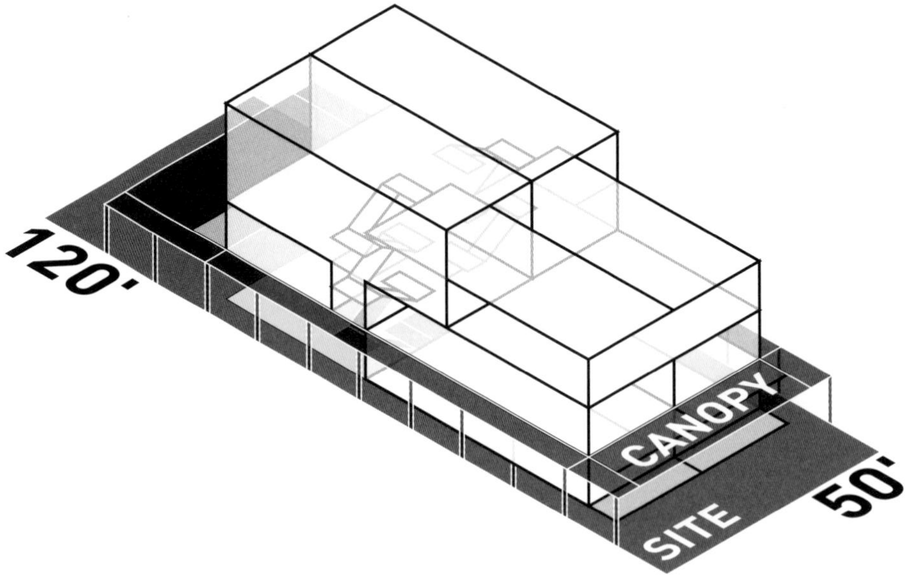

Background
Located in Winnipeg's Osborne Village neighbourhood on a mature residential street lined with turn-of-the-century homes, 100-year-old elm trees and an historic brick church, the 548 Stradbrook project is a result of a lengthy battle with the City of Winnipeg Planning Department to increase the allowed density of the site to eight residential suites, and to reduce the number of required parking stalls from a ratio of 1.5 to 1.0 per suite.

Concept
The project responds to existing zoning setbacks and massing constraints with a three-storey form that essentially maximizes the allowable zoning envelope, but in-turn is wrapped in a reflective glass shroud that allows it to be camouflaged with its character-filled surroundings.

An 8'x40' band incorporates all required exit stairs and the majority of public corridors. The area gained from reduced internal circulation is given back through generous private outdoor space for tenants, including ground floor patios, second-floor balconies as well as two large rooftop decks accessed from the third floor mezzanine level.

Units
The compact building form contains six two-bedroom flats and two three-bedroom loft units varying from 780 square feet to 1,060 square feet. Both of the ground floor flats are accessible off the building's side yards and have a private patios facing the street. Level 2 includes three flats off the common circulation, and entrances via stairs to Level 3 where the remainder of the units are located. Two out of the three of these suites extend upwards into mezzanines that in turn open onto a generous private rooftop patios.

Particulars
548 Stradbrook's cladding treatment draws direct inspiration from its historic context, embodying the high level of workmanship and careful attention to detail present in the construction of neighbouring heritage homes. The design reinterprets traditional lap siding with a custom, shingled glass façade of reflective panels that are overlaid like fish scales both vertically and horizontally across the entire building. The tempered panels follow a simple grid pattern that allows them to be easily substituted for windows wherever necessary. The mirror-like finish and subtle angling of the glass creates an ephemeral interplay of reflections and light during the day, and transforms the building into a glowing apparition at night.

At the second floor level, a metal canopy wraps the building's perimeter, supported by a colonnade of thin black columns that lightly touch the sidewalk below. Functionally, the canopy defines a front yard patio space and sheltered walking path for tenants. Aesthetically, the canopy provides a stable counterpoint and grounding element to balance the ever-changing nature of the glass façade above.

L4 Plan

L3 Plan

L2 Plan

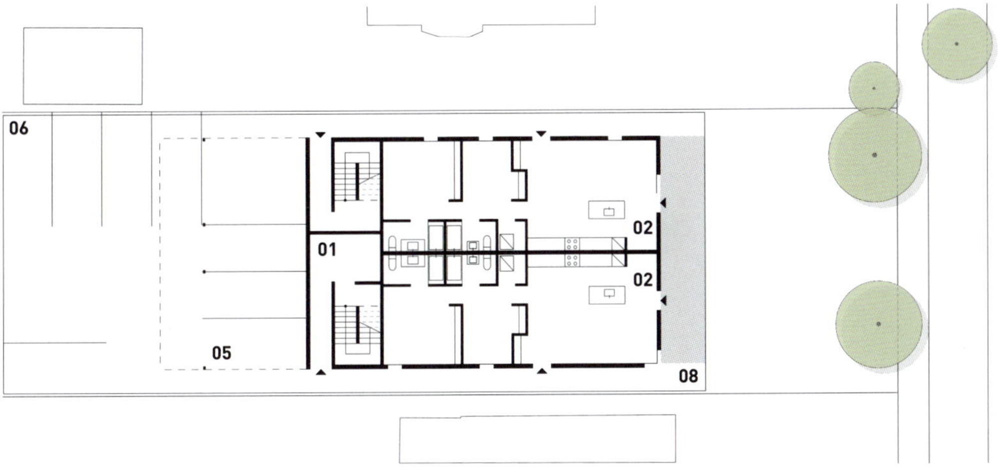

Site Plan

01 Lobby
02 Two-bedroom suite
03 Three-bedroom suite
04 Canopy
05 Covered parking
06 Surface parking
07 Rooftop patio
08 Ground-floor patio

OZ

Condominiums
Winnipeg, Manitoba
2012 - 2014

1:6000
0 200
[61m]

OZ is a 25-suite, high-end residential condominium development. Built on two single-family house lots the five-storey, seven-level project is an example of much needed urban intensification. The project includes a 30-stall enclosed parking garage for the residents, while other amenities are limited to private rooftop terraces, through-the-block patios, and more traditional balconies.

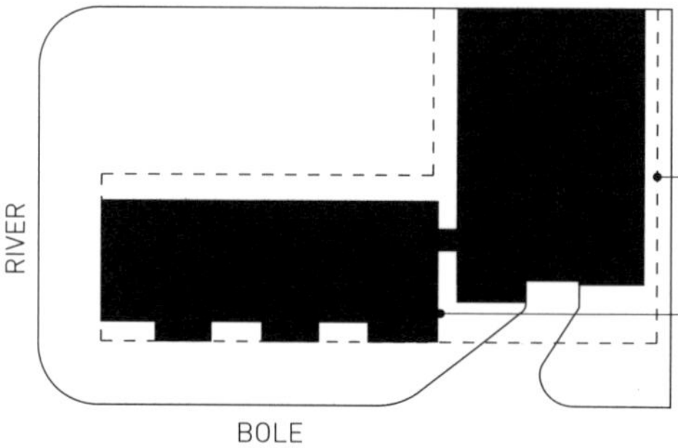

SITE AREA
11,545 ft²
[1,073 m²]

GFA
46,085 ft²
[4,281 m²]

1:1000
0 50'
[15.25m]

COVERAGE

FLOOR AREA RATIO **3.99**

COVERED AREA **75%**

EFFICIENCY [gross/net] **84%**

OCCUPANCY

RESIDENTIAL **80%**

PARKING **20%**

TYPOLOGY

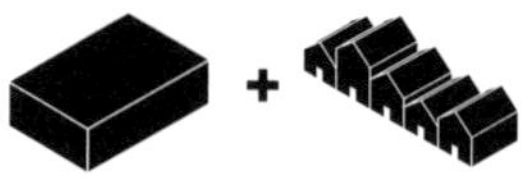

DENSITY

94 /ac [233/ha]

226 / ac [559/ha]

HEIGHT [STOREYS]

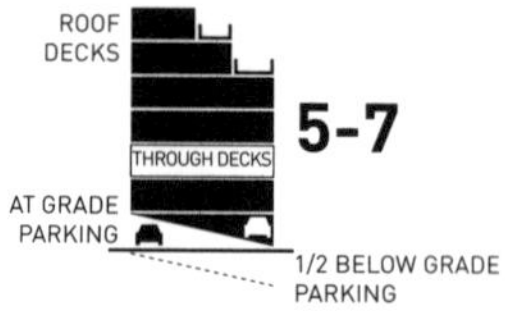

OF UNITS **25**

OF PARKING STALLS **30**

UNIT TYPES

bedrooms	2	23	0	0
storeys [within units]	8	17	0	0

UNIT SIZE

AVERAGE UNIT (64%) **1,160 ft²** [107.7 m²]

SMALLEST UNIT (48%) **870 ft²** [80.8 m²]

LARGEST UNIT (105%) **1,890 ft²** [175.4 m²]

COST

$152/ft²
[$1,635/m²]

CONSTRUCTION

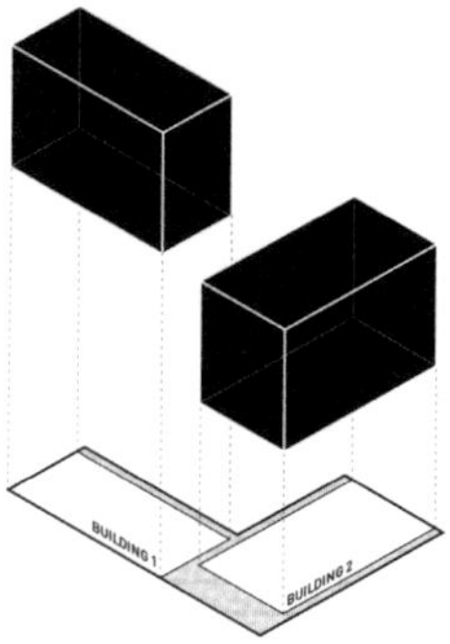

Site configuration

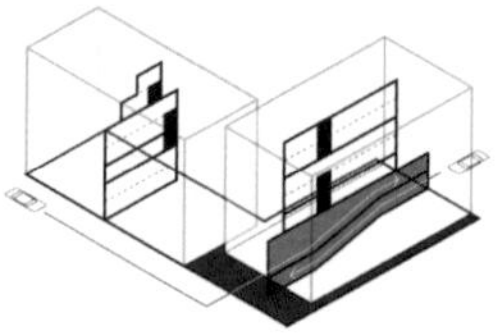
Sectional configuration

Background
In 2012, 546 was engaged by a private client consortium to maximize the development opportunity on a tight infill parcel located in the heart of Osborne Village, the densest and most walkable urban district in Winnipeg. The client's design brief also included enclosed, weather-protected parking for the residents, while the existing zoning regulations only allowed for a five-storey building and included significant reduction in building area on the higher floors.

Concept
Although zoning regulations initially limited the structure to five storeys as defined in the building code, by introducing mezzanines on two levels the project's saleable square footage was increased substantially while still conforming to the maximum allowable building height. In addition, the precise interlocking of a variety of one and two bedroom unit types served to reduce corridor areas and provide variety for potential buyers. Compared to a conventionally planned development, the OZ configuration significantly increases density efficiency and thus profit potential for the developer. The square footage gained from compact planning allowed for the creation of "horizontal courtyards" off the mezzanines that punch through the building and provide large exterior decks with expansive vistas for loft units.

Located on an L-shaped site, OZ is conceived as two distinct masses linked by a minimal glass entry and a shared elevator core. The first tower fronts on River Avenue, taking advantage of high traffic volumes with ground level townhouses that can accommodate small businesses. The second tower incorporate a two-level, 30-stall over/under parking garage that connects with the back lane.

The building area reduction requirement at the top of the complex was used as an opportunity to articulate how the building meets the sky – instead of employing step backs across the façade, the design team was able to acquire approval to alternate the façade with mass and void, still resulting in 50% reduction in mass across the two top floors.

Units
The suites consist of 23 two-bedroom dwellings and 2 one-bedroom suites. Seventeen of the 25 units are two-storey suites, either townhomes accessed through a private entry directly at grade, or two-storey lofts on upper levels. The balance are single level flats.

Particulars
Each building mass is wrapped in a cohesive skin of black metal cladding that is carved into and punctured through to introduce outdoor space, provide shelter for ground-floor entrances, reduce the building's shadow impact and respect setback restrictions. Breaking up the building mass in this way brings the building down to human scale, with the glass core and balcony cut outs further eroding the structure's monolithic nature.

The deeply fluted corrugated metal skin consists of a gradient of solid and perforated panels that create a subtle play of light across the façade. The perforations carry over windows that open into rooms where more privacy is desirable, providing filtered views out through a protective screen. Every component that is recessed behind or cut through the skin is rendered in white, further reducing the project's visual weight and reflecting daylight into the building's void spaces.

On the north façade, a reflective metal cowling frames a single floor-to-ceiling window that captures an impressive view of the river and the Legislative Building beyond.

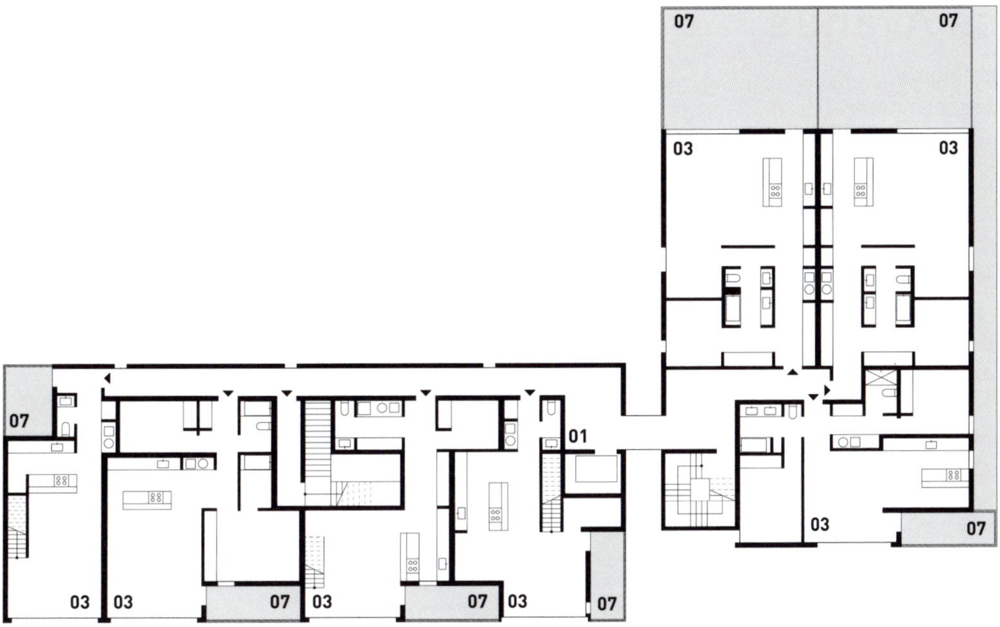

L3 plan

Site Plan

01 Lobby
02 Two-bedroom townhouse
03 Two-bedroom suite
04 Service room
05 Parkade
06 Ground floor patio
07 Terrace

Ross Avenue

Condominiums
Winnipeg, Manitoba
2012 - 2014

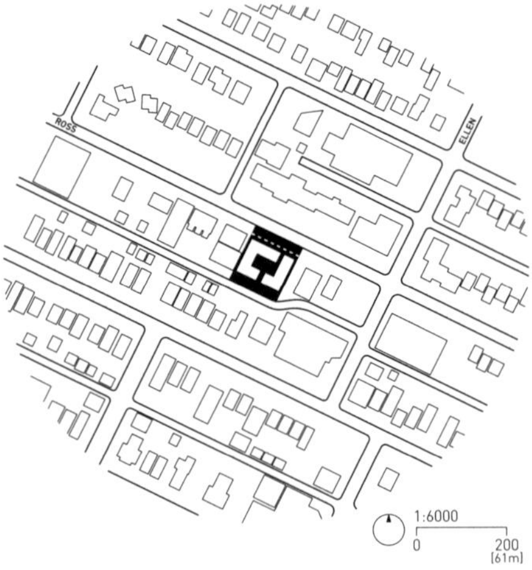

Ross Avenue is a subsidized condominium development on an inner city site built for public housing agency called Winnipeg Housing Rehabilitation Corporation. The project consists of 10 family-sized housing units, five of which are 'visitable' single-level suites at grade, and the other five are two-storey units perched on top. All units have their suite entry doors at grade. The project includes a common courtyard, two common utility rooms that double as additional storage for the residents and 10 surface parking stalls off the public lane at the rear of the project.

PUBLIC LANE

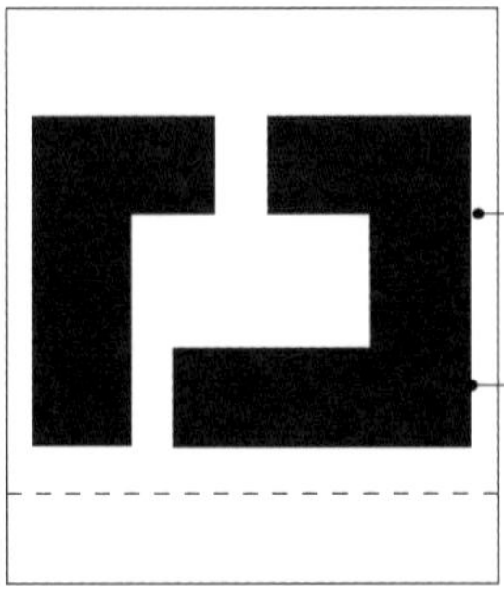

ROSS

SITE AREA
12,980 ft²
[1,206 m²]

GFA
10,915 ft²
[1,014 m²]

1:1000
0 50' [15.25m]

COVERAGE

FLOOR AREA RATIO **0.84**
COVERED AREA **43%**
EFFICIENCY [gross/net] **97%**

OCCUPANCY

RESIDENTIAL **100%**

TYPOLOGY

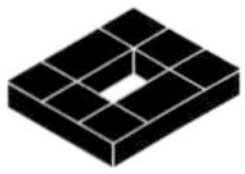

DENSITY

34 /ac [83/ha]
126 /ac [311/ha]

HEIGHT [STOREYS]

ROOF DECKS
AT GRADE PARKING
2-3

OF UNITS **10**

OF PARKING STALLS **10**

UNIT TYPES

bedrooms: 0, 0, **10**, 0

storeys [within units]: **5**, **5**, 0, 0

UNIT SIZE

AVERAGE UNIT (59%) **1,057 ft²** [98.2 m²]

SMALLEST UNIT (53%) **960 ft²** [89.2 m²]

LARGEST UNIT (67%) **1,200 ft²** [111.5 m²]

COST

$158/ft²
[$1,696/m²]
300
75

CONSTRUCTION

LIGHT WOOD FRAME
- WALLS
- FLOORS
- ROOFS

- FOUNDATION

422

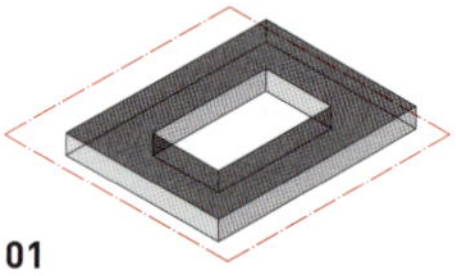

01

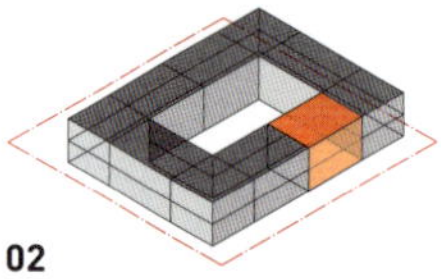

02

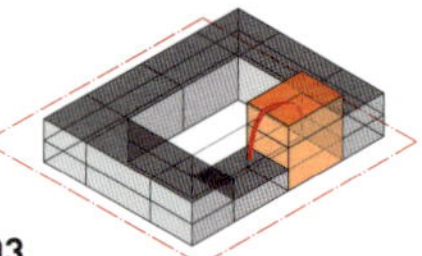

03

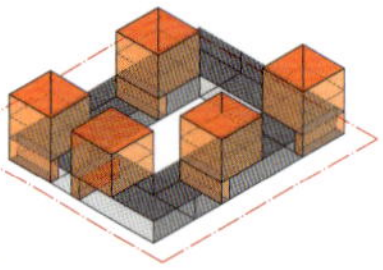

04

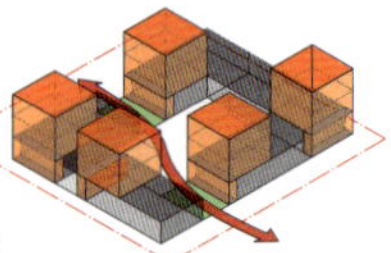

05

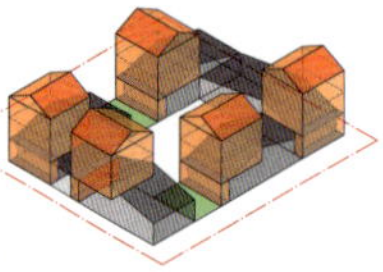

06

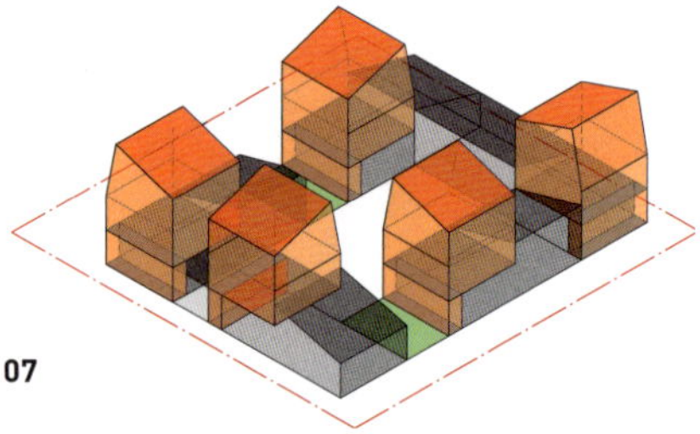

07

01 One-storey courtyard [not enough square footage]
02 Two-storey courtyard [10 units but none accessible]
03 Three-storey courtyard [allows stackable 1 + 2 storey units]
04 Configuration fits 10 units
05 Introduce paths to street + lane
06 Sloped roof allows for standard + affordable construction
07 Offset peaks create small village atmosphere

Background

In 2012, 546 was engaged to design a 10-unit subsidized condominium project by the Winnipeg Housing Rehabilitation Corporation (WHRC), a non-profit organization committed to developing safe, attainable and energy efficient homes for low income families. The project is located in Centennial, an inner-city neighbourhood where revitalization efforts are actively underway to to create a safe, vibrant and inclusive community with an expanding stock of quality subsidized housing developments.

Concept

Through consultation with community groups and the WHRC, the team selected a courtyard arrangement for its ability to address safety and security while contributing to a strong sense of community. In the courtyard, children can play under the watchful eye of their parents and neighbours, and everyone enters their home from this shared space, ensuring that it remains active at all times of day. Ground-level decks and second-floor balconies provide private outdoor space and eyes on all sides of the building, engaging with Ross Avenue and the side yards, as well as the back lane where parking is located. The project's peaked roofs emerged in response to the diverse mix of single family house styles on the street and affordability goals that relied on implementing construction friendly building materials and techniques.

Units

The design consists of stackable one and two-storey unit types arranged around the central courtyard. The suites range from 960-1,200 square feet and have three bedrooms to provide ample space for families. Half of the suites are located at grade on a single level and dimensioned to be "visitable" by persons with mobility issues. The remaining five suites are accessed from grade and perched on top of the ground floor in a two-storey arrangement.

Particulars

Every façade incorporates an array of variably-sized square windows, which are positioned at different heights above the floor to offer a variety of views. Large picture windows bring the outdoors in, while smaller windows are either kept low to provide lookouts for children, or raised up for access to light and air while maintaining privacy. All of the windows are operable to promote passive cross ventilation. To ensure that the homes have low operation and maintenance costs over the long-term, the project combines a high level of air tightness with efficient heating and ventilation equipment on the interior, and durable metal roofing and cement board siding on the exterior.

In order to meet the budget and schedule, the design uses typical residential construction materials and installation methods. As a result, all of the roofs consist of standard, repeatable wood truss assemblies. Variety is introduced with an atypical roof angle that is randomly rotated on each house block. The playfulness of the peaked roofs and the varied colour palette help emphasize individuality and create a small village atmosphere within the larger neighbourhood.

With unexpected rooflines, durable materials and generous access to outdoor space, the project challenges expectations of what affordable housing can be, and demonstrates that even with modest means a vibrant and socially responsive design is possible.

L2 Plan

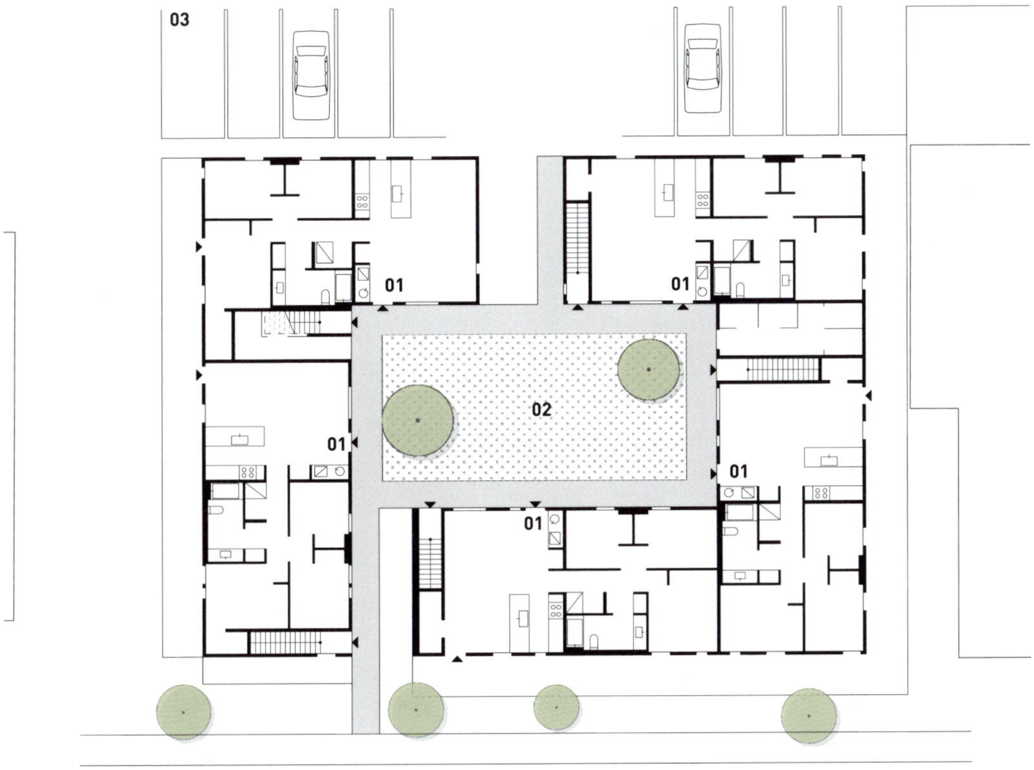

Site Plan

01 Three-bed suite
02 Courtyard
03 Parking

Treehouse

Condominiums
Toronto, Ontario
2014 - 2015
Not pursued

The Tree House is a new 37-unit low-rise townhome development in Toronto's emerging Birch Cliff neighbourhood. The new construction market-rate condominium project includes generous common garden spaces at grade, and a 54-stall underground garage. The project aims to offer ample sized, affordably priced homes and community spaces for first time homebuyers, particularly families, in the competitive Toronto market.

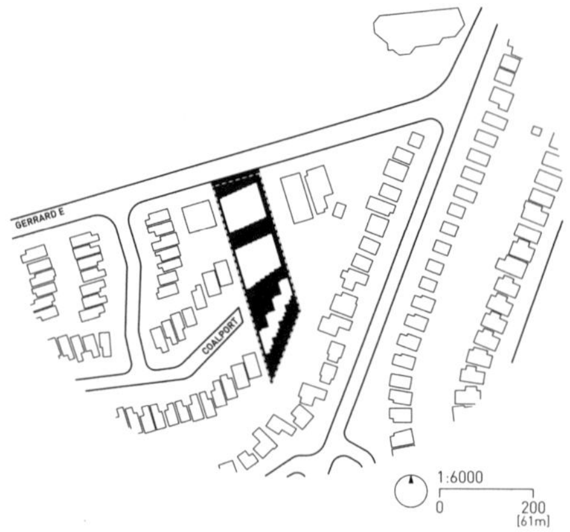

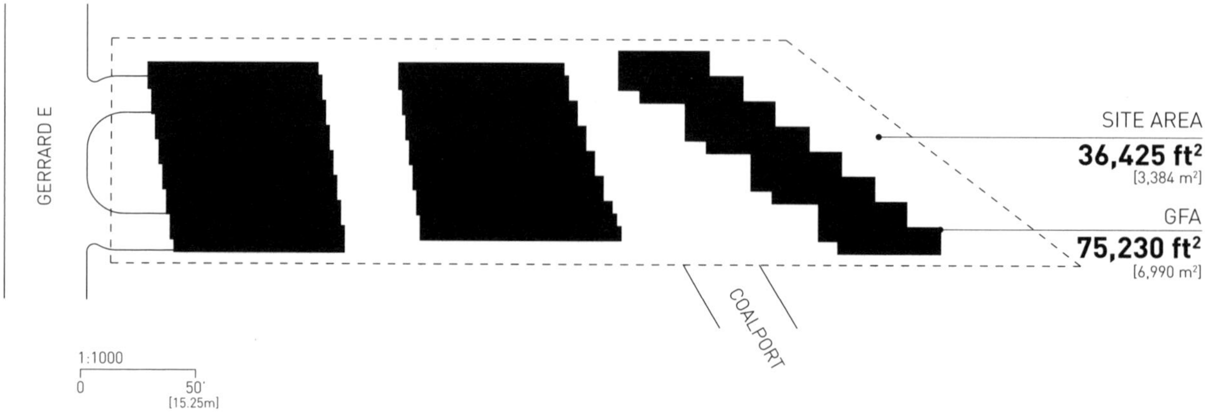

COVERAGE

FLOOR AREA RATIO **2.07**
COVERED AREA **48%**
EFFICIENCY [gross/net] **86%**

OCCUPANCY

RESIDENTIAL **67%**
PARKING **33%**

TYPOLOGY

DENSITY

44 /ac [109/ha]
133 / ac [329/ha]

HEIGHT [STOREYS]

ROOF DECKS
BELOW GRADE PARKING
2-3

OF UNITS **37**

OF PARKING STALLS **54**

UNIT TYPES

bedrooms	0	22	15	0
storeys [within units]	0	24	13	0

UNIT SIZE

AVERAGE UNIT (68%) **1,226 ft²** [114 m²]
SMALLEST UNIT (46%) **830 ft²** [77.1 m²]
LARGEST UNIT (74%) **1,325 ft²** [123.0 m²]

COST

$140/ft² [$1,502/m²]
300
75

CONSTRUCTION

LIGHT WOOD FRAME
• WALLS
• FLOORS
• ROOFS

• PARKING
• FOUNDATION

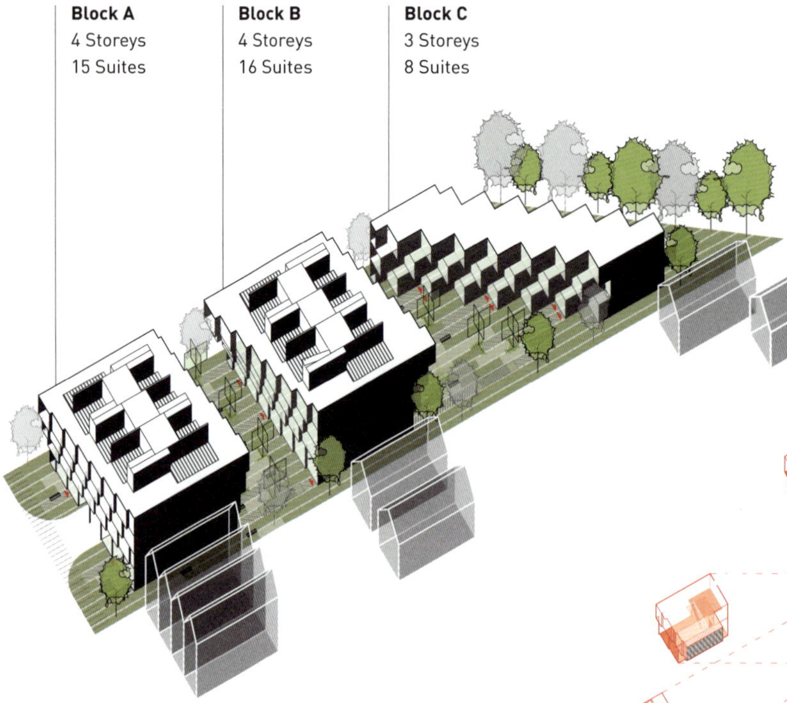

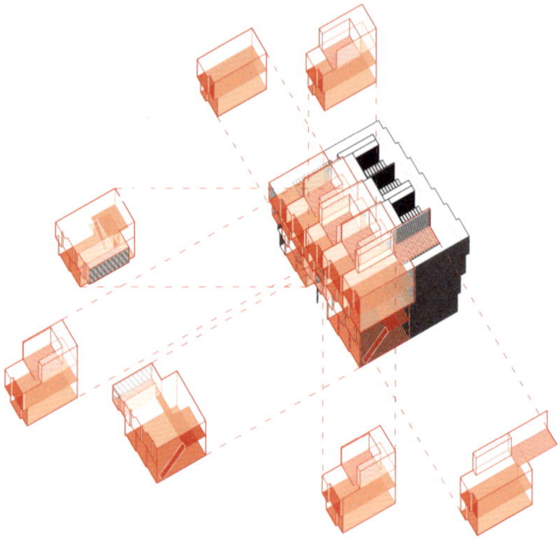

Background

In 2014, 546 was engaged by a private developer consortium to design a low-rise condominium project on an oddly shaped 37,000-square-foot site in Birch Cliff, Toronto. Located in a single-family detached home neighbourhood, the site included a one-storey industrial building that would become a sales centre for the project prior to its demolition and the commencement of construction of the new project.

Concept

Instead of a large residential building, The Tree House is composed of three separate blocks, with 37 townhomes in total, staggered to follow the property lines and maximize green space, with all required parking located underground. The three blocks are aligned with adjacent homes to ensure continuity and access to light and views from all the green spaces in between the blocks.

The rhythmic, staggered geometry of stacked unit cells creates an ever-changing interplay of void and solid, shadow and light across the façade. The Garden and Town Loft suites have been designed as shallow and wide layouts providing ample natural light, ventilation, and views towards landscaped courtyards, while at the same time ensuring that residents have the desired level of shelter and privacy. The upper floors and rooftops of the buildings feature sun-filled terraces and treetop views of their surroundings, while the lower floors have direct access to private patios and gardens at grade.

Units

The multi-level two and three bedroom units range in size from 830 square feet to 1,325 square feet. The project will appeal to buyers who desire both indoor and outdoor areas, with exterior access in the form of courtyards, private rooftop terraces, and gardens. The shared courtyards provide open communal space for residents, encouraging social engagement.

Particulars

The blocks are clad in anodized aluminum, which offers durability and modularity. The material's near-iridescent quality provides a unique surface to receive and reflect light and shadow. Based on the length of the anodizing process, different shades are applied to each of the blocks so that the overall aesthetic remains consistent while still allowing for variety across the site.

L3 Plan

L2 Plan

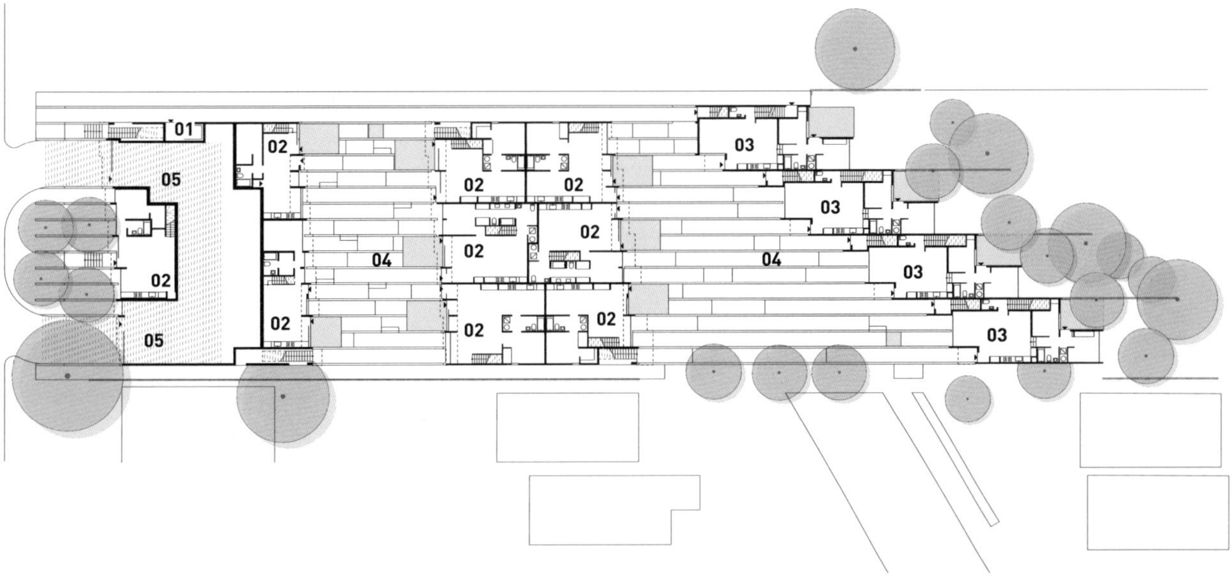

Site Plan

01 Lobby
02 Two-bed suite
03 Three-bed suite
04 Shared space
05 Parkade below

62M

Condominiums
Winnipeg, Manitoba
2010 - 2017

62M is a three-storey, 41-unit housing project consisting of both condominiums and market-rate rental units. The building hovers 35 feet in the air in response to difficult site conditions, allowing the underbelly to act as covered parking for majority of the 42 parking stalls at grade. Common tenant amenities are limited to a number of smaller-scale, forthcoming rooftop patios.

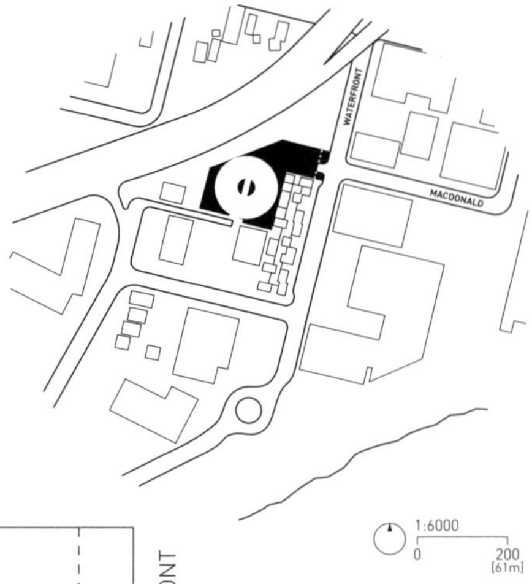

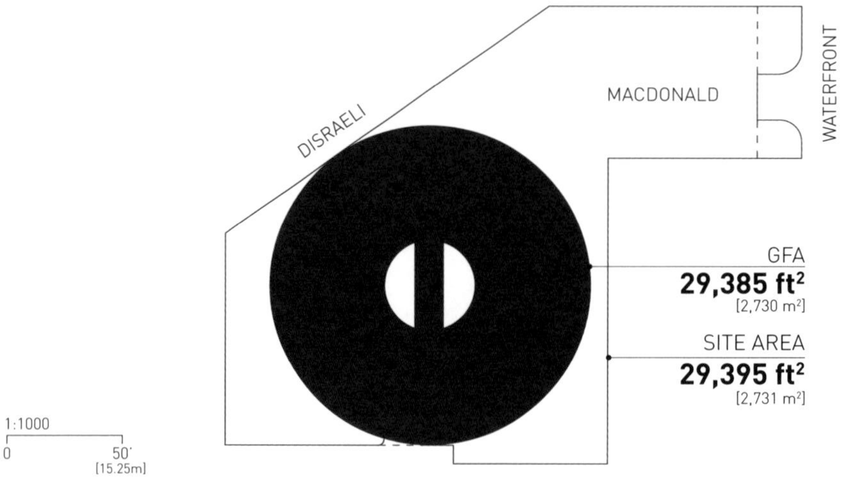

COVERAGE

FLOOR AREA RATIO	COVERED AREA	EFFICIENCY [gross/net]
1.00	47%	89%

 # OF UNITS 41

 # OF PARKING STALLS 42

UNIT TYPES

bedrooms	41	0	0	0
storeys [within units]	40	1	0	0

OCCUPANCY

RESIDENTIAL
100%

TYPOLOGY

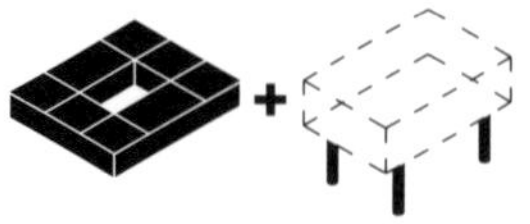

UNIT SIZE

AVERAGE UNIT (34%)
621 ft² [57.7 m²]

SMALLEST UNIT (34%)
610 ft² [56.7 m²]

LARGEST UNIT (46%)
830 ft² [77.2 m²]

CONSTRUCTION

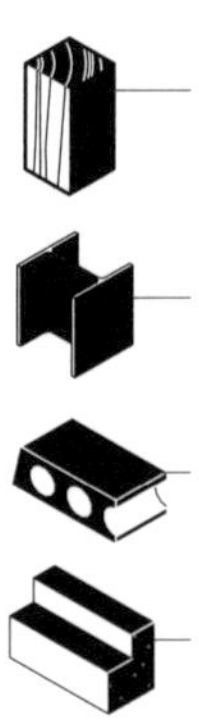

PRE-FAB LIGHT WOOD FRAME
- WALLS
- FLOORS
- FLOORS

- L1 STRUCTURE
- L1 COLUMNS
- CIRCULATION & SERVICE CORE

DENSITY

61 /ac [150/ha]

76 /ac [188/ha]

HEIGHT [STOREYS]

ROOF DECKS
3
AT GRADE PARKING

COST

$153/ft²
[$1,648/m²]

(scale: 75 – 300)

art upholstery

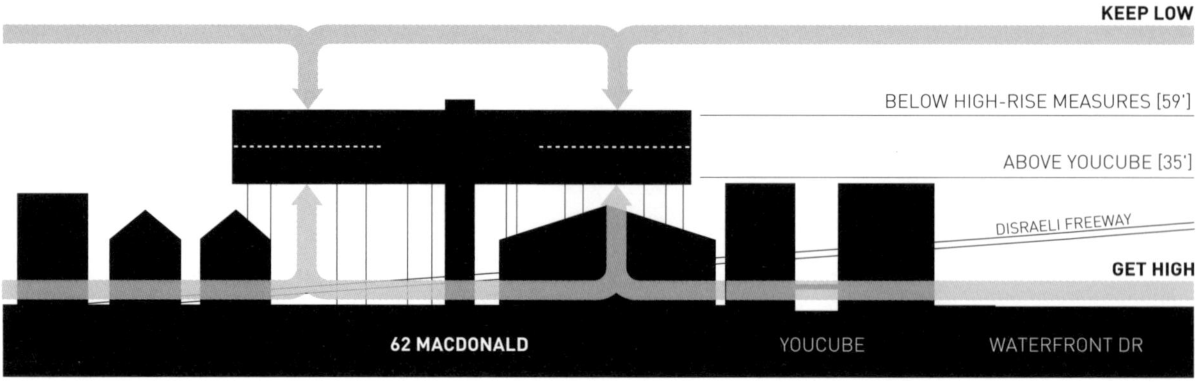

Background
546 was engaged by a private development consortium to answer the question whether entry level housing could be feasible on a site with difficult immediate site conditions. Compressed between a freeway and the backs of neighbouring properties, the site was considered undesirable due to restricted views and a lack of street frontage.

Concept
Early in the process, the design team determined that the bulk of the building should be lifted up on 35-foot-high stilts, allowing the project to overcome the limitations of its surroundings with an iconic form and unprecedented sightlines. Raising the building naturally resulted in additional construction costs and unexpectedly, the circular massing was a response to having to find savings to overcome this expenditure. As a corner-less plan, the circular building permits true modularity and consequently is both spatially efficient and cost effective. After exploring a number of schematics, the design team concluded that the envelope of the circular form is about 30% more efficient than more conventional orthogonal schemes, in other words, the 360-degree plan provides the widest possible perimeter for glass with the smallest amount of exterior envelope to construct.

Units
40 out of the 41 suites, 20 per level, have identical, 610 square foot pie-shaped footprint that simplifies construction. The unit layouts consist of two options, more conventional base option, and an upgrade. The base option is arranged so that the entry and utility spaces occupy the narrow end, closest to the circulation core. This configuration frees the remaining square footage for a flexible, open living area that culminates in an expansive wall of floor-to-ceiling glass. In the upgrade version all utilities are organized into a continuous millwork along the length of the suite, freeing the rest of the unit area as one open space with a free-floating tub and a large pivoting kitchen wall. The kitchen wall can be positioned to divide the tub area from the rest of the space.

Making use of every inch of available space within the core and its rooftop is the penthouse unit that was conceived by the architects while the building was already under construction. Rising unimpeded out of the top of the structure, it is outfitted as a fully functioning bachelor suite, surrounded by mirror-polished columns that enhance views of the city and the prairie horizon beyond. The suite is currently set-up as short-term rental to enable making it available pro-bono to special guests to the city, as film set, or an artist resident.

Particulars
Regardless of its height, 62M is classified as a three-storey building, consisting of the lobby level and two floors of housing. The penthouse addition is small enough to qualify as a "caretaker suite," not forming an additional "floor" under Canada's National Building Code. The classification as a three-storey building allows the residential floors to be constructed out of wood – combustible material, offering savings in cost, constructibility, schedule and carbon.

The cast-in-place concrete core that houses an elevator, exit stairs and a service shaft provides lateral stability for the structure and is surrounded by covered, open-air corridors. Leaving the corridors open to the elements reduces capital and operational costs, while allowing visibility across and between floors. The primary material palette consists of raw cast-in-place concrete, weathering steel and glass, rudimentary materials that are durable, straightforward and cost-conscious, while also moving away from expected off-the-shelf mid-rise developer specifications.

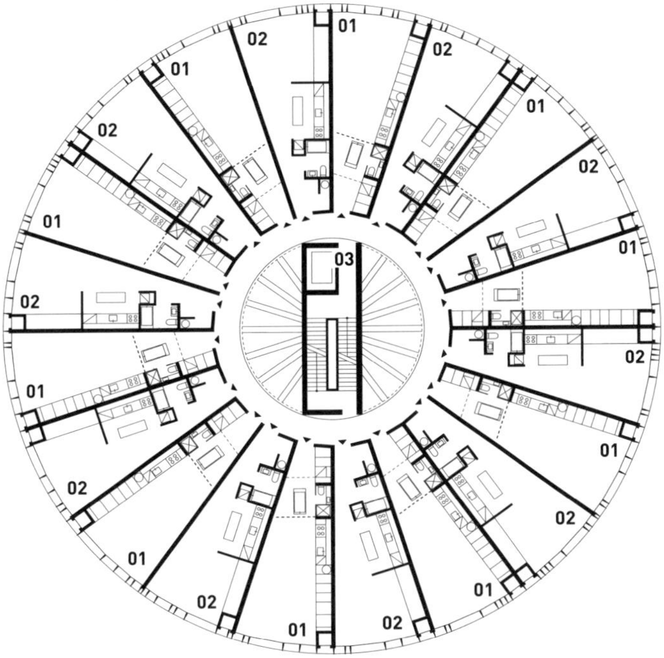

L2 + L3 Plan

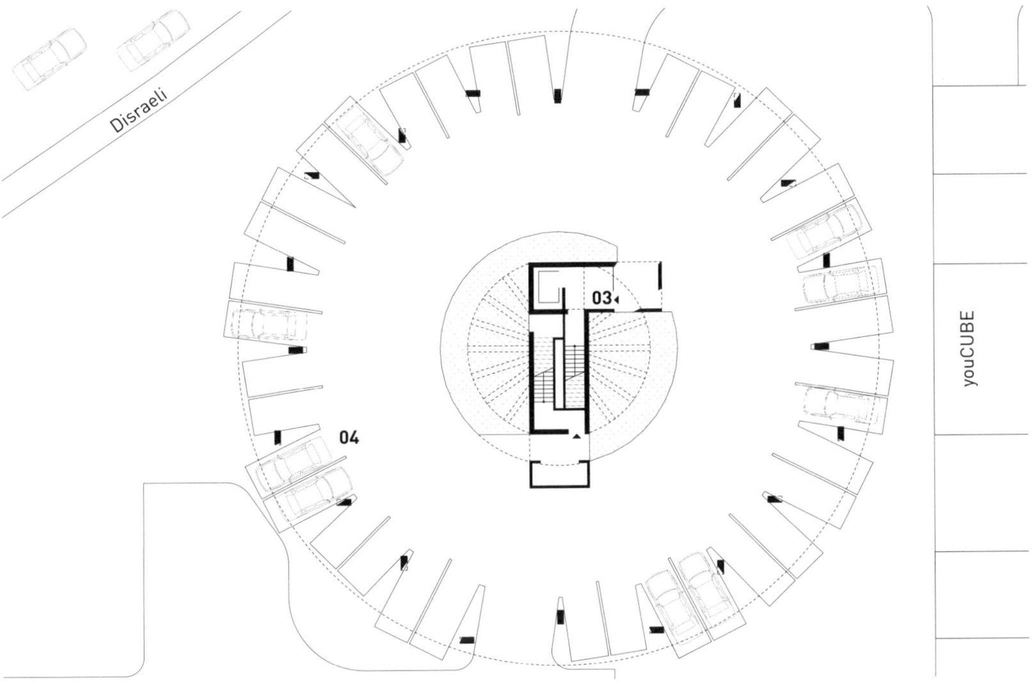

Site Plan

01 One-bed suite - type 1
02 One-bed suite - type 2
03 Lobby
04 Parking

LIFE

Condominiums
Calgary, Alberta
2018 -

LIFE is a six-storey market-rate rental housing project located in the South Calgary neighbourhood. The 84-suite project includes 55 enclosed parking stalls carved into the heavily sloped site. Common areas and amenities consist of unusually illuminated public corridors, indoor refuse and bike rooms, front and rear entry plazas, and a large rooftop patio. The suites on levels one and two also contain private outdoor space either as at grade patios or modest balconies.

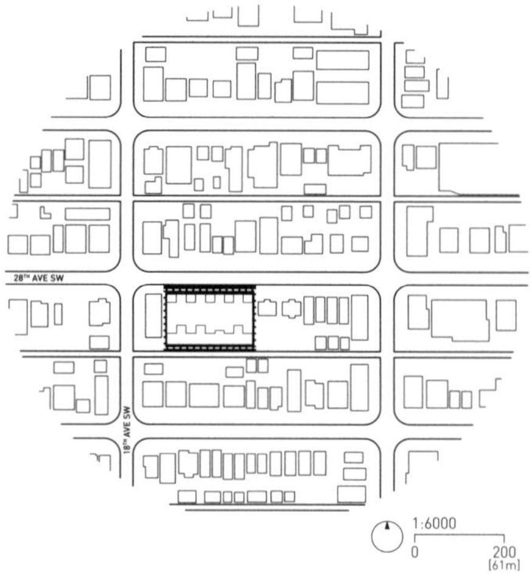

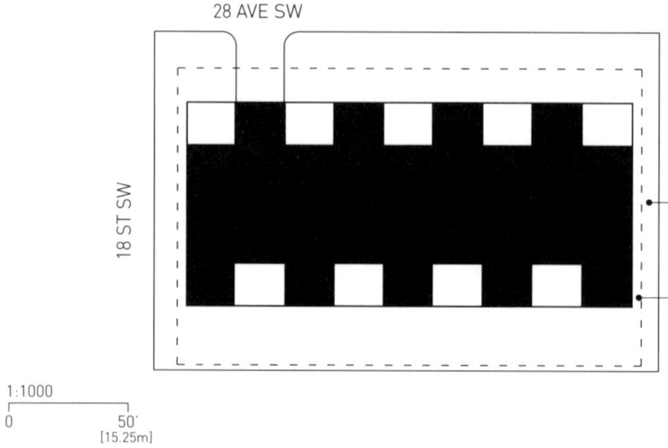

SITE AREA
24,460 ft²
[2,272 m²]

GFA
89,065 ft²
[8,275 m²]

COVERAGE

FLOOR AREA RATIO **3.64**

COVERED AREA **66%**

EFFICIENCY [gross/net] **86%**

OCCUPANCY

RESIDENTIAL **74%**

PARKING **26%**

TYPOLOGY

DENSITY

150 /ac [369/ha]

298 /ac [737/ha]

HEIGHT [STOREYS]

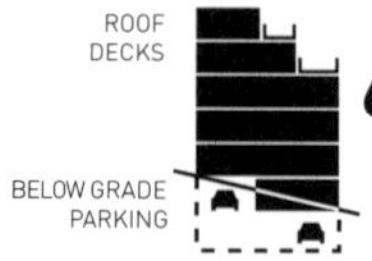

OF UNITS **84**

OF PARKING STALLS **55**

UNIT TYPES

bedrooms	**34**	**50**	0	0
storeys [within units]	**84**	0	0	0

UNIT SIZE

AVERAGE UNIT (35%) **634 ft²** [58.9 m²]

SMALLEST UNIT (25%) **455 ft²** [42.3 m²]

LARGEST UNIT (43%) **770 ft²** [71.5 m²]

COST

$222/ft²
[$2,386/m²]

300 / 75

CONSTRUCTION

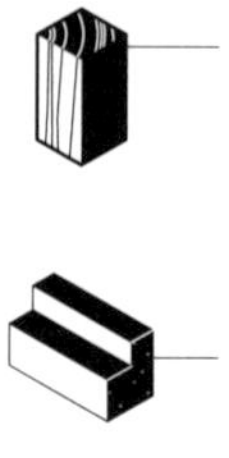

L2-L6 LIGHT WOOD FRAME
- WALLS
- FLOORS
- ROOFS

- L1 STRUCTURE
- PARKING
- FOUNDATION

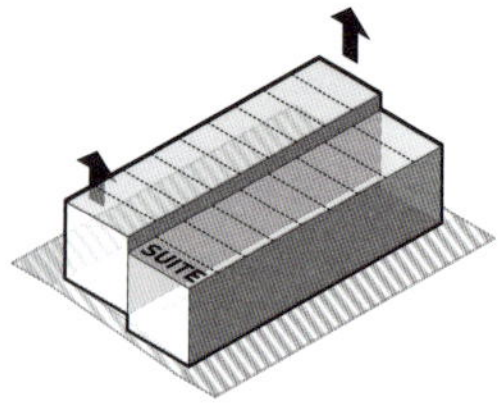

01 Shift + form

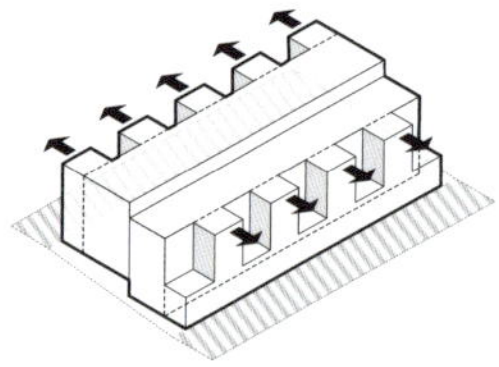

02 Undulate

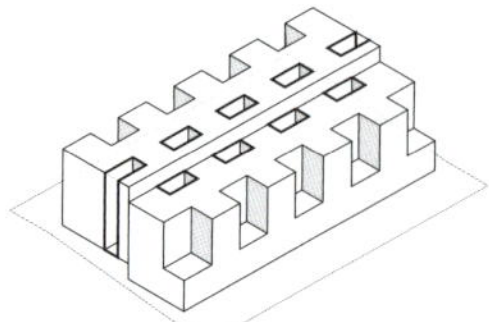

03 "Pierce" courtyards

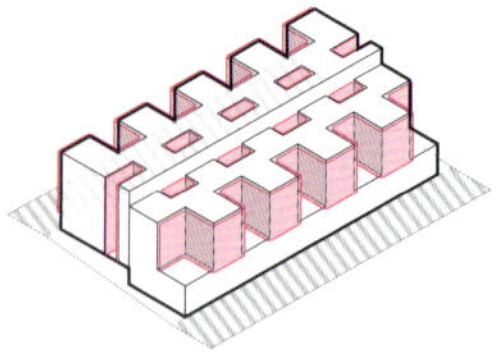

04 Increase perimeter

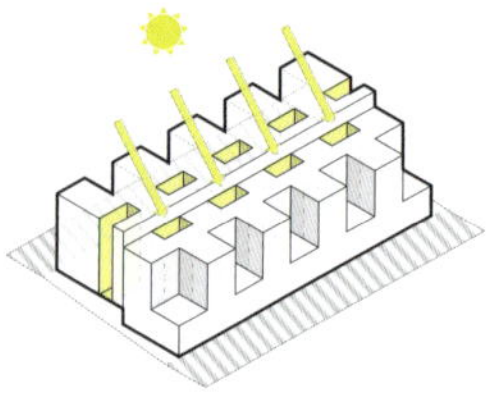

05 Light

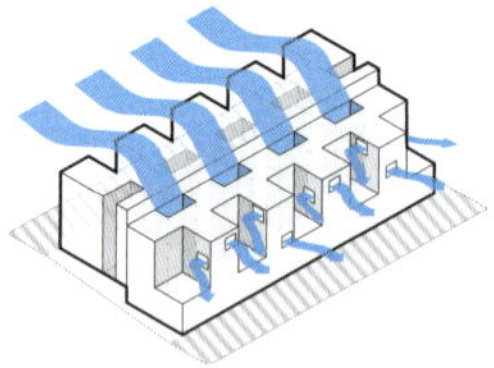

06 Cross ventilation

Background

546 was challenged by a private development corporation to up-zone a 200-foot wide mid-block parcel amalgamated from three smaller building lots, originally containing a single family home and two small apartment blocks; and to maximize the possible suite count on the site. The site location and the developer's proforma positioned the project at the low-end of the market rate rental offering.

Concept

Building configuration and design are a unique response to the quintessential multi-storey residential building shortcomings in which a corridor connects two exit stairwells resulting in single aspect residential suites with limited access to natural light and without cross-ventilation. The design takes advantage of a typical 120-foot deep inner-city lot served by a public lane through a series of alternating shifts of single-suite modules. These shifts produce several advantages – creating lightwells that provide for additional light access and cross ventilation, while reducing the perceived building mass on the street. The resulting undulating plan permits two-bedroom suites to take only 20 feet of frontage [typically this accommodates only a single bedroom suite] – all the while providing natural light to all bedrooms and living spaces. As an added benefit, the module width aligns with the parkade grid reducing structural complexity and cost.

The project is situated in a well-connected neighbourhood and the allowances for reduced parking (55 stalls, 84 units) was possible due to existing transit, proposed increased number of bicycle parking and two car co-op vehicles incorporated into the development scheme. The site is also heavily sloped, enabling level street access to a below grade garage. Due to the slope, and split level arrangement, the excavation of the garage remains relatively shallow, keeping costs moderate.

Units

The simple 20-foot wide unit modules are either shallow at 22 feet, or deep, at 30+ feet, providing a footprint for one and two-bedroom suites respectively. The inclusion of the light wells allow one-bedroom suites to be dual aspect and all two-bedroom suites quad aspect – resulting in much needed qualities that are unique for mid-rise residential buildings.

Particulars

The lightwells also filter natural light to corridors and ground floor. A public throughway at grade connects the street and public lane creating a public exterior space for residents and the community. Building services such as lobbies, mail room, bicycle room, and caretaker's office flank and activate the public throughway.

Architecturally, the key to keeping overall costs down was to align all above suite demising wall with the parking bays below, avoiding complexity and costs of any transfer slab or other structurally more expensive solutions. This was possible due to the consistent and straightforward 20-foot frontage for all suites, both one and two bedrooms – hopefully also demonstrating that the architecture of such a scheme does not need to be mundane as a result.

Typical Plan

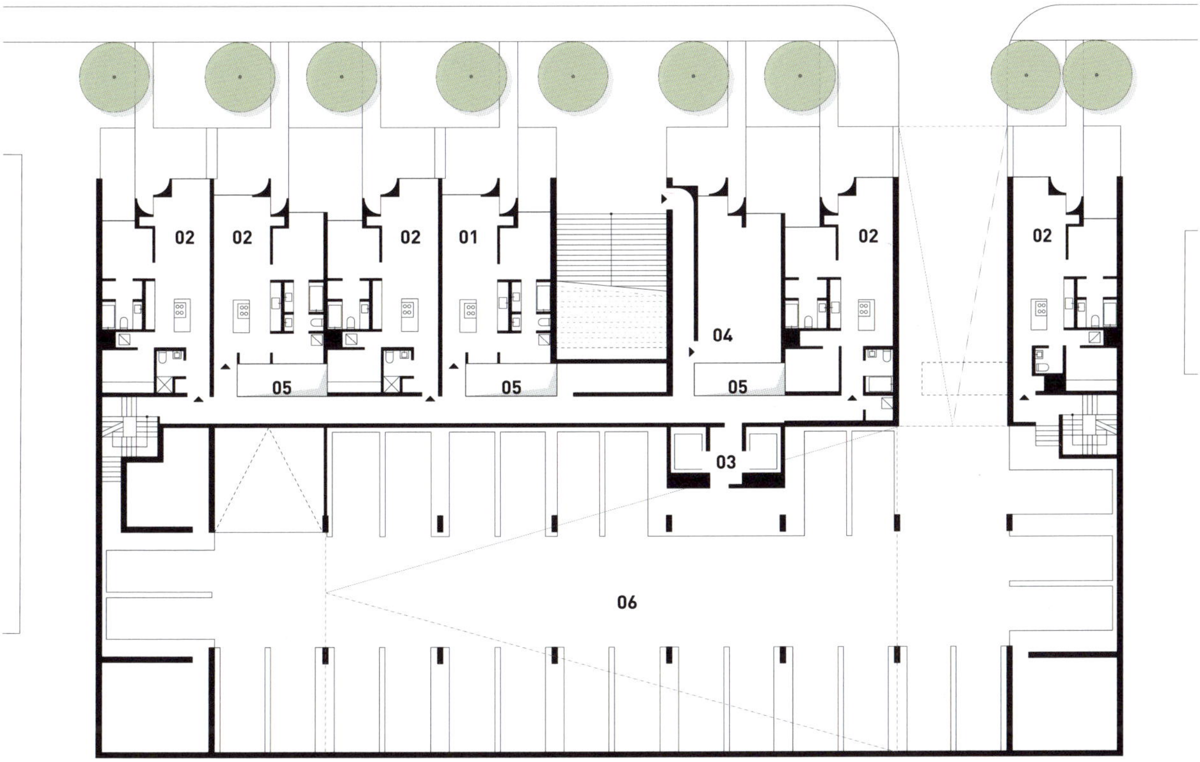

Site Plan

01 One-bed suite
02 Two-bed suite
03 Lobby
04 Office
05 Light well
06 Parkade

Warehouse 1885

Condominiums
Winnipeg, Manitoba
2018 - 2021

Warehouse 1885 is the major rehabilitation of two historic buildings into a mixed-use development. This five-storey project includes 39 rental apartments and 2,800 square feet of street-oriented commercial space. Parking consists of an existing surface lot at the rear of the site, as well as three newly constructed stalls at the basement level of the existing building footprint. Tenant amenities consist of a common rooftop patio, and eight private balconies facing Princess street.

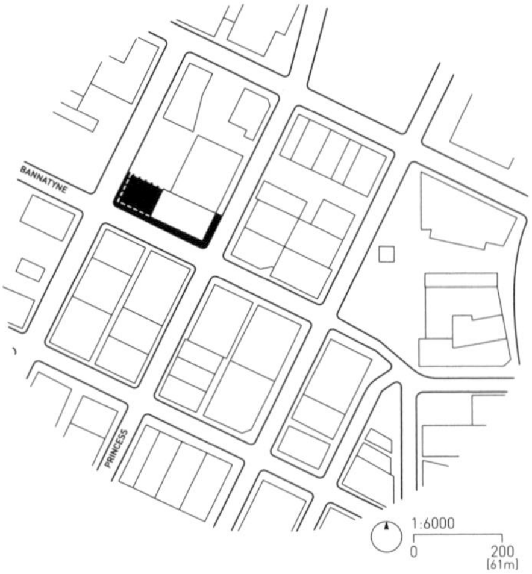

SITE AREA
7,105 ft²
[660 m²]

GFA
47,110 ft²
[4,377 m²]

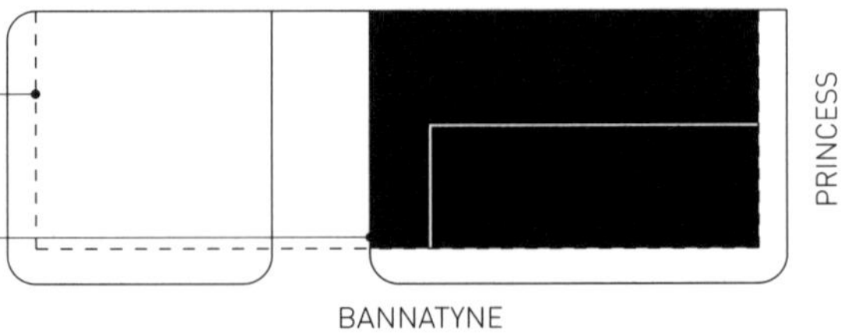

1:1000
0 50' [15.25m]

COVERAGE

FLOOR AREA RATIO **6.63**

COVERED AREA **95%**

EFFICIENCY [gross/net] **78%**

\# OF UNITS **39**

\# OF PARKING STALLS **16**

UNIT TYPES

bedrooms	29	10	0	0
storeys [within units]	34	5	0	0

OCCUPANCY

RESIDENTIAL **81%**

COMMERCIAL **8%**

PARKING **11%**

TYPOLOGY

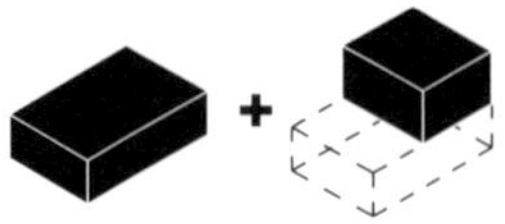

DENSITY

239 /ac [590/ha]

376 /ac [927/ha]

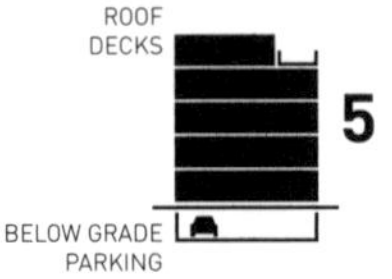

UNIT SIZE

37% AVERAGE UNIT **658 ft²** [61.1 m²]

23% SMALLEST UNIT **415 ft²** [38.6 m²]

48% LARGEST UNIT **855 ft²** [79.4 m²]

COST

$117/ft² [$1,260/m²]

300
75

CONSTRUCTION

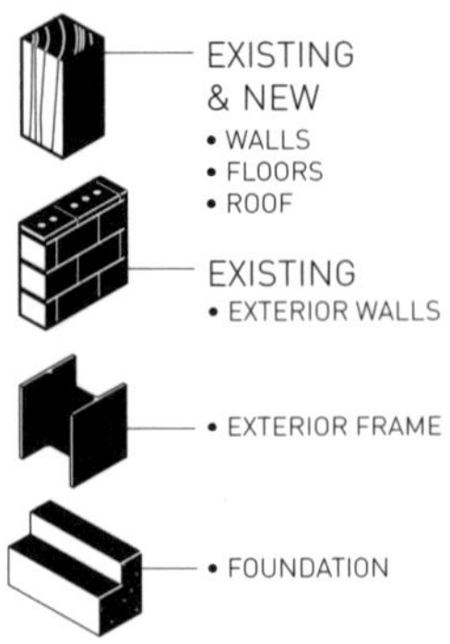

Background

Warehouse 1885 is the second project that Legatum, a private development group, commissioned 546 to undertake. The developer purchased the property located at the corner of Princess Street and Bannatyne Avenue in Winnipeg's Exchange District hoping to develop it into a housing and commercial space. The property consisted of a five-storey brick building at 104 Princess Street [south] and the adjacent two-storey warehouse at 108 Princess Street [north] – once twin building façades, before a massive fire in the 1940's destroyed the north section. The project team also brought along a commercial tenant for the ground floor with specific space and parking requirements.

Concept

While 104 Princess has heritage protection, the nondescript addition at 108 Princess does not, allowing for a modern L-shaped insertion into the historic streetscape. On the primary street the new façade of glass and black cementitious cladding is set back from a robust weathering steel grid that aligns itself with its neighbour. A three-storey addition on top of 108 Princess accommodates additional loft-style units and access to a new rooftop patio on 104 Princess, with unimpeded views of the downtown skyline.

Within the footprint of 104 Princess, the commercial tenant space is opened partially down into the lower level, making better use of the otherwise dark and low basement. This two-storey volume is in turn intersected with a "tube" – a corridor facilitating the residential entry off Bannatyne Avenue. The required underground stalls for the commercial tenant were carved into the basement level of 104 Princess, made feasible through a cross-access agreement for the use of an existing vehicle ramp with the adjacent condominium building.

Units

The residential portion of the project consists of 29 one-bedroom and 10 two-bedroom suites. The existing floor to floor ceiling height in the historic 104 Princess is a generous 10 feet, allowing for the typical one-bedroom suites to have a raised bedroom area away from perimeter of the suite, while still enjoying access to natural light. This arrangement enables efficient suite configuration that works with the existing window openings. In 108 Princess, additional mezzanines could be included for the top floor's five suites, while maintaining the existing snow shadow conditions due to the deep parapet height of 104, and savings in floor depth due to use of nail laminated timber floors.

Particulars

The grid of 108 Princess façade draws its horizontal arrangement from the cornice and brick banding lines of 104 Princess, while the new columns create five equal bays that mimic the spacing of the original façade. The steel structure also supports eight new balconies that animate the street and provide outdoor space for residents.

Together, the contrast between contemporary and historic, steel and brick bring renewed vibrancy to this important intersection and extend the building's narrative into its next century of life.

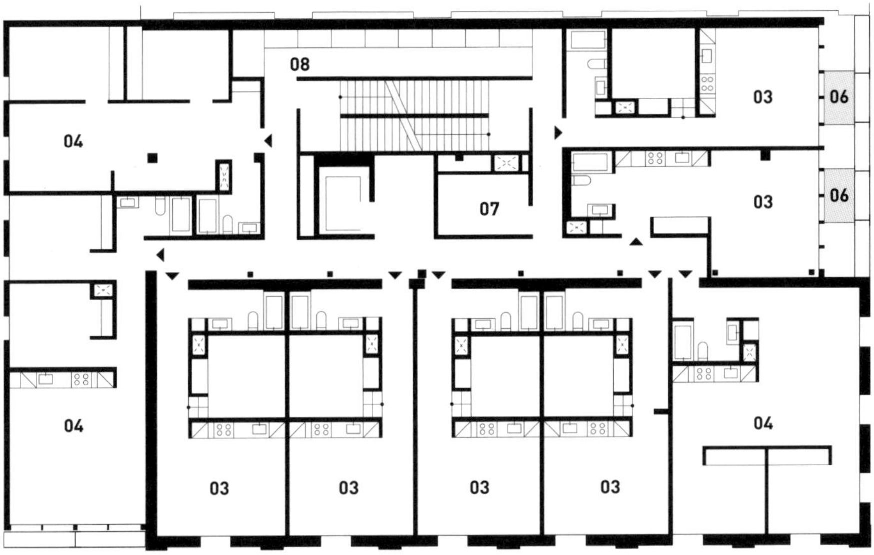

L2-L4 Plan

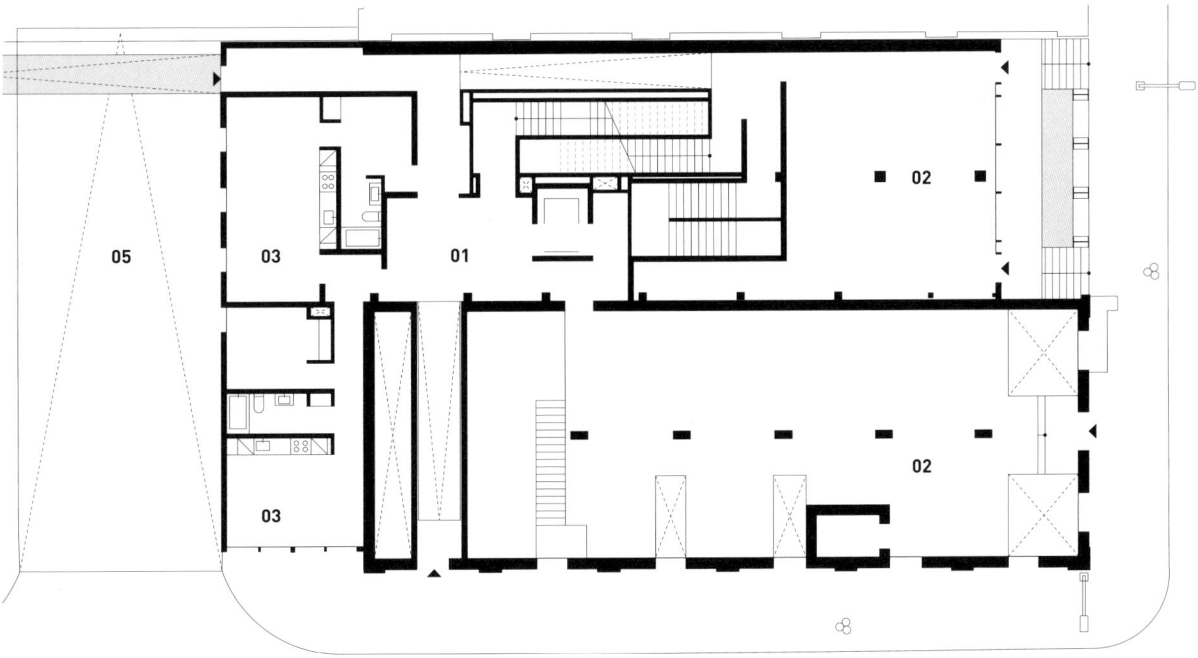

Site Plan

01 Elevator lobby
02 Commercial suite
03 One-bedroom suite
04 Two-bedroom suite
05 Parkade ramp
06 Balcony
07 Service room
08 Storage

CY33

Condominiums
Calgary, Alberta
2017 - 2021

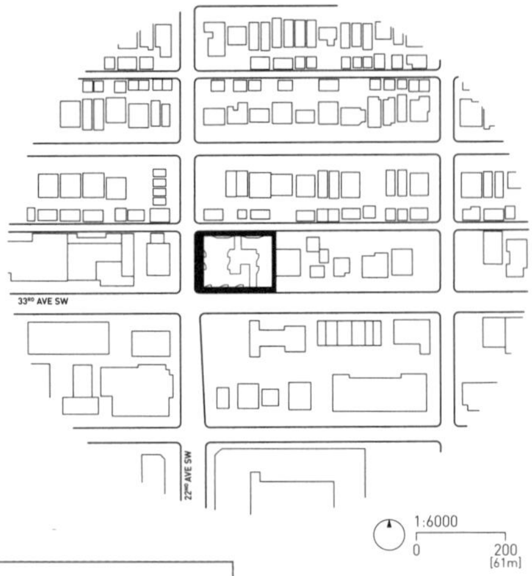

CY33 is a 56-unit market-rate rental housing project with 14,860 square feet of retail and commercial space at grade and off the elevated public courtyard. This six-storey building also includes two levels of underground parking with total of 87 parking stalls for both the tenants/visitors and for commercial use. Common tenant amenities include the before mentioned shared courtyard, generously sized public stairs with seating and planting leading to the courtyard and modest overlooks forming part of the outdoor exit stairs.

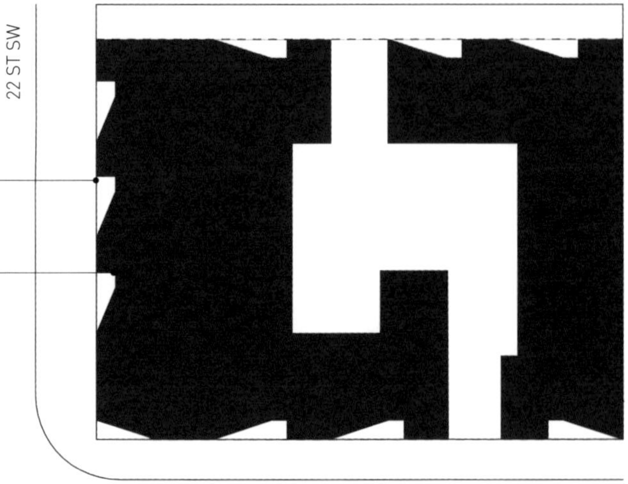

SITE AREA
18,670 ft² [1,734 m²]

GFA
112,170 ft² [10,421 m²]

1:1000
0 — 50' [15.25m]

COVERAGE

FLOOR AREA RATIO	COVERED AREA	EFFICIENCY [gross/net]
6.01	**84%**	**86%**

OCCUPANCY

RESIDENTIAL **50%**
COMMERCIAL **16%**
PARKING **34%**

TYPOLOGY

DENSITY

131 /ac [323/ha]
268 /ac [663/ha]

HEIGHT [STOREYS]

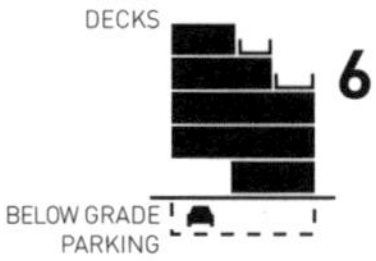

OF UNITS **56**

OF PARKING STALLS **87**

UNIT TYPES

bedrooms	**20**	**36**	0	0
storeys [within units]	**56**	0	0	0

UNIT SIZE

AVERAGE UNIT (46%) **837 ft²** [77.7 m²]
SMALLEST UNIT (32%) **570 ft²** [53 m²]
LARGEST UNIT (54%) **965 ft²** [89.7 m²]

CONSTRUCTION

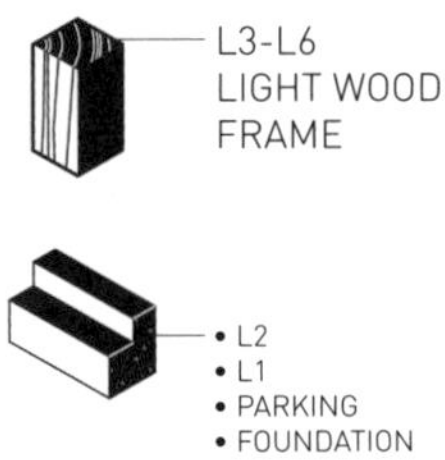

COST

$214/ft² [$2,303/m²]
300 — 75

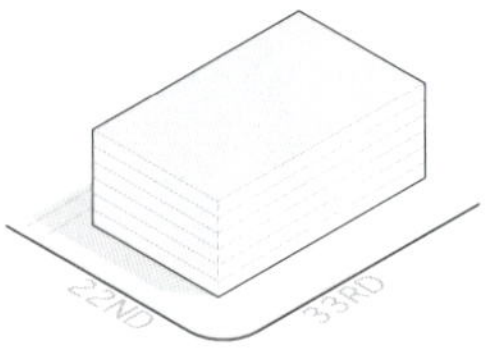

01 Select

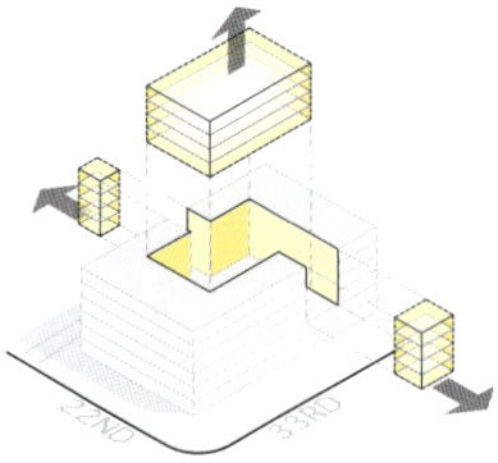

02 Carve

03 Welcome

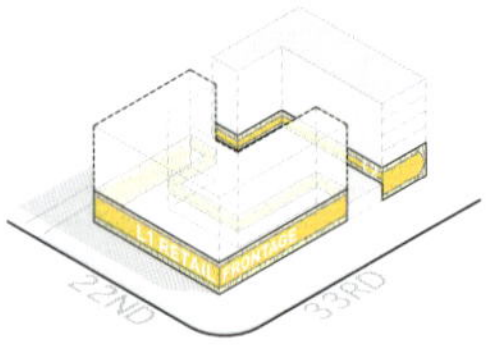

04 Activate

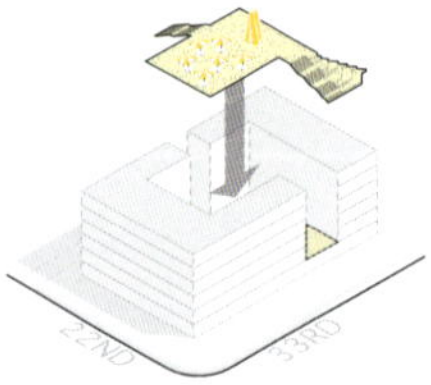

05 Create

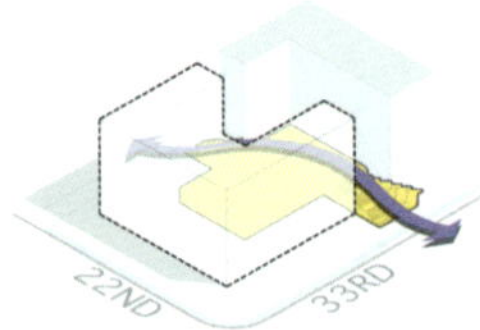

06 Invite

Background

In 2016, 546 was engaged by a private developer to work in collaboration with a local planning outfit to challenge the existing zoning classification of a site at a gateway intersection to the emerging Marda Loop neighbourhood of Calgary. The site amalgamates three former single-family lots into one 150-foot-wide by 120-foot-deep development parcel aligned by two streets to the south and west, a public lane to the north and a property line to the east.

Concept

In exchange for two additional storeys – from allowable four to six – the design of the proposed mixed-use building centres on the extension of the public realm and an increased commercial frontage. The 120-foot lot depth is also too deep for typical residential use without sacrificing user experience and overwhelming the scale of the neighbourhood. Carving into the large mass at the second-floor level, an elevated courtyard is introduced, spilling out onto the adjacent streetscape. This move is critical to providing residents with both through-route and gathering space, while also drawing neighbourhood life into the interior volume.

The public courtyard is accessed via two staircases: one from the main thoroughfare and one from the public lane. The primary cascading staircase is treated as a grand entrance with a mix of landscaping and bleacher-style seating, linking the two sides of the property with the surrounding community. Two additional commercial spaces open onto the courtyard.

The developer has a unique community-forward brand that has built partnerships and connected new commercial tenants and residents with over 100 different businesses in the surrounding area through a sharing platform. This platform enables and encourages new residents to tap into the vibrant life of Marda Loop through prearranged engagements that include fitness, wellness, and lifestyle opportunities [e.g. each resident gets four free coffees at the local coffee shop included in their rent each month].

Units

Residential units vary from one-bedroom suites to two-bedroom homes, providing attainable housing options for both individuals and small family units. Innovation and efficiency come through the implementation of a skip-stop corridor design. While multi-family buildings are typically designed as double-loaded corridors, the skip-stop strategy incorporates two-storey, through-units accessed via private staircase. This arrangement serves to eliminate corridors on alternating floors and increases saleable area, while also improving cross-ventilation and access to daylight in many of the suites.

Particulars

A variety of conditions are necessary to meet setback requirements on each façade. The checkered [cellular] approach – achieved through alternating composition of balconies and solid walls on all façades – permits inflections at each cell, allowing the design to meet zoning by-laws while maintaining the uniformity of design expression. Increasing setbacks on upper levels, inset alternating balconies, and exterior exit stairs also serve to reduce the overall building mass and allow more daylight into the courtyard and on the streets.

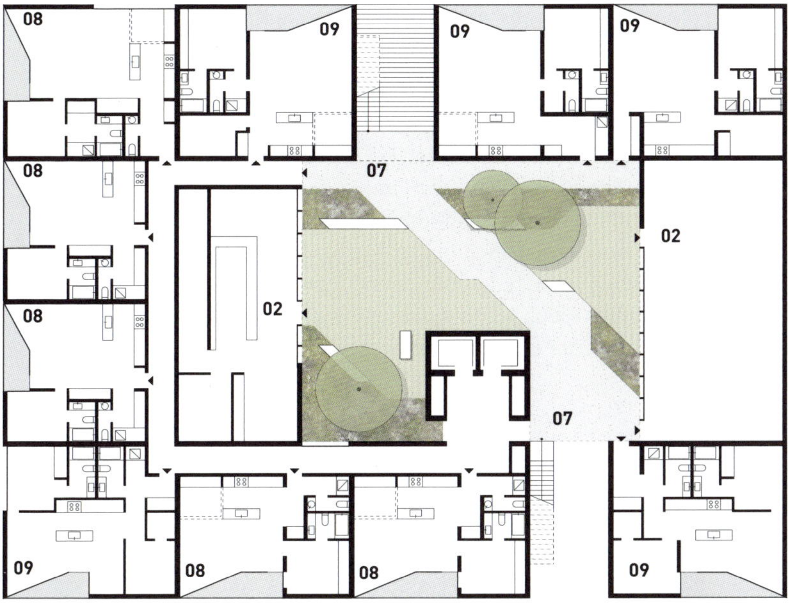

L2 Plan

Site Plan

01 Public stair
02 Commercial space
03 Studio space
04 Refuse
05 Parking access
06 Lobby
07 Courtyard
08 One-bedroom suite
09 Two-bedroom suite

Pumphouse

Condominiums
Winnipeg, Manitoba
2015 - 2023

Consisting of 93 residential dwellings and total of 15,500 square feet of commercial space and a 30-stall underground garage, the Pumphouse is a complex adaptive reuse and new-built revitalization of a historic pumping station building and site. The residential portion of the project consists of three six-storey prefab building slabs, each containing 28 to 35 dwellings. The common areas include generous outdoor passageways, ground-floor plazas and urban bleacher area above the underground parking ramp.

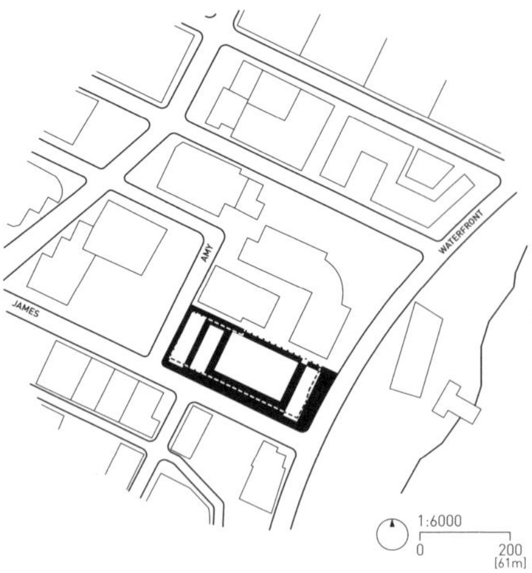

SITE AREA
39,375 ft^2
[3,658 m^2]

GFA
76,515 ft^2
[7,108 m^2]

1:1000
0 50' [15.25m]

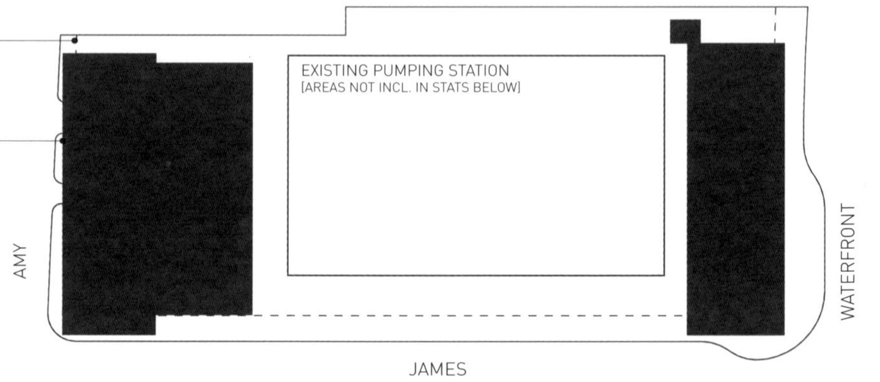

COVERAGE

FLOOR AREA RATIO **4.82**
COVERED AREA **74%**
EFFICIENCY [gross/net] **90%**

OCCUPANCY

RESIDENTIAL **83%**
COMMERCIAL **4%**
PARKING **13%**

TYPOLOGY

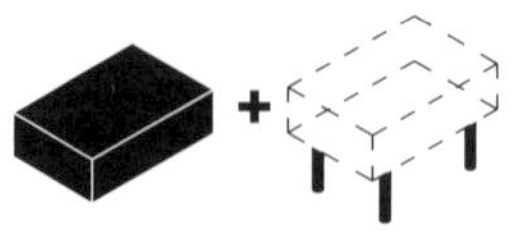

DENSITY

255 /ac [630/ha]
360 / ac [890/ha]

HEIGHT [STOREYS]

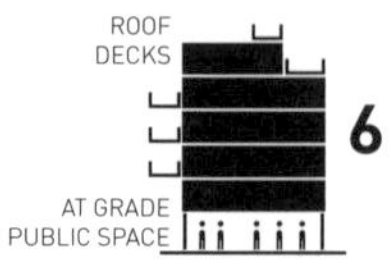

OF UNITS **93**

OF PARKING STALLS **30**

UNIT TYPES

bedrooms	81	12	0	0
storeys [within units]	86	7	0	0

UNIT SIZE

AVERAGE UNIT **604 ft^2** [56 m^2] (34%)
SMALLEST UNIT **515 ft^2** [48 m^2] (29%)
LARGEST UNIT **1,185 ft^2** [110 m^2] (66%)

COST

$211/$ft^2$
[$2,270/$m^2$]
*including structured parking & commercial
(300 / 75)

CONSTRUCTION

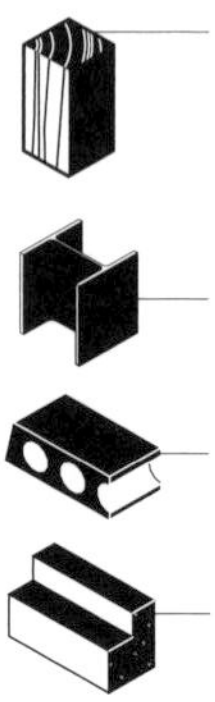

L2-L6 PRE-FAB WOOD FRAME
- WALLS
- FLOORS (NLT)
- ROOFS (NLT)

- L2
- L1
- WALKWAYS

- WALKWAY SLABS
- SERVICE SPACE
- PARKING

- L1
- FOUNDATION

HISTORY

Background

In 2015, 546 produced a financial proforma, approached their existing client and connected them with Centre Venture Development Corporation, the municipally funded downtown development agency to set up the James Avenue Pumping Station project. The historic building was slated for demolition after 17 attempts by various parties to revive the structure over 14 years.

Concept

While the existing building's foundation was not capable of supporting the construction of additional floors on top of the Pumphouse, the design team discovered that the existing gantry crane capacity allowed for a new floor within the historic building, turning Pumphouse from a financial liability to an income-generating asset. Incorporated as tenancy, this left the pumps on the main floor free and clear of complicated programming as proposed in previous revitalization attempts, and instead distinguished its adaptive reuse as one that celebrates the existing while creating a viable future life.

The other major piece of financial feasibility was turning the 40-foot wide parcel in front of the Pumphouse into a residential opportunity. The previous project schemes had deemed this land area too small to accommodate meaningful development. The single-loaded residential building designed for the site provides spectacular views over the Red River and the deliberately simple modular building form is repeated twice on the larger development pad at the opposite end of the Pumphouse, this time with double loaded circulation shared between the two building slabs.

The new residential buildings are spaced approximately 20 feet away from the existing building and from one another creating new "streets" and expand the ground floor store frontages. The east building's mass is additionally carved away at the street level, allowing the historic façade of the Pumphouse remain visible to the street and giving space to an intimate urban plaza below the building. The faces of the plaza are animated by the commercial uses opening onto it – a 3,000-square-foot restaurant within the lowest level of the Pumphouse and a 1,240 square foot barbershop to the north, below the east residential building.

Units

The 15-foot-wide one and two-bedroom wood-framed and prefabricated residential dwellings are vertically stacked into each slab, seven units per floor. The majority of the suites are single-storey flats off an exterior corridor, either directly level or via individual stair via a skip-stop arrangement. The river-facing building also contains seven, two-storey, two-bedroom suites with generous rooftop patios.

Particulars

The residential suites are accessed through open-air corridors. Leaving the corridors open to the elements reduce capital and operational costs further, while allowing double aspect suites on all levels, and in turn, access to natural light and ventilation on both ends of the space.

The unit floors are constructed with nail-laminated-timber [NLT] – dimensional lumber nailed together into a solid slab that allows the floor to span across the 15-foot suite bay without additional support. Concrete topping above the NLT completes the necessary fire assembly between floors so that the wood ceiling can be left exposed, adding a sense of warmth to the interiors.

The simple building mass resulting from the straightforward stacking of the prefabricated residential suites is further articulated by exterior exit stairs and corridors that wrap around the blocks, clad in perforated corrugated metal that doubles as guard rail.

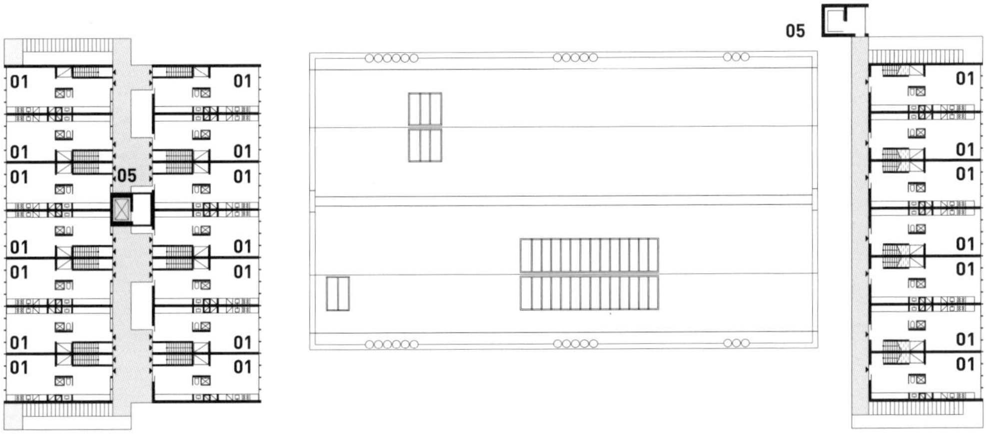

L2 + L4 + L5 Plan

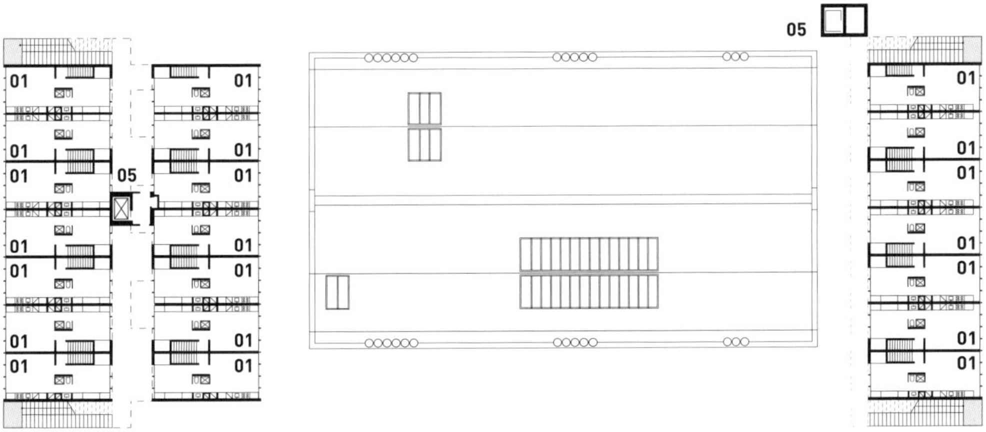

L3 + L6 Plan

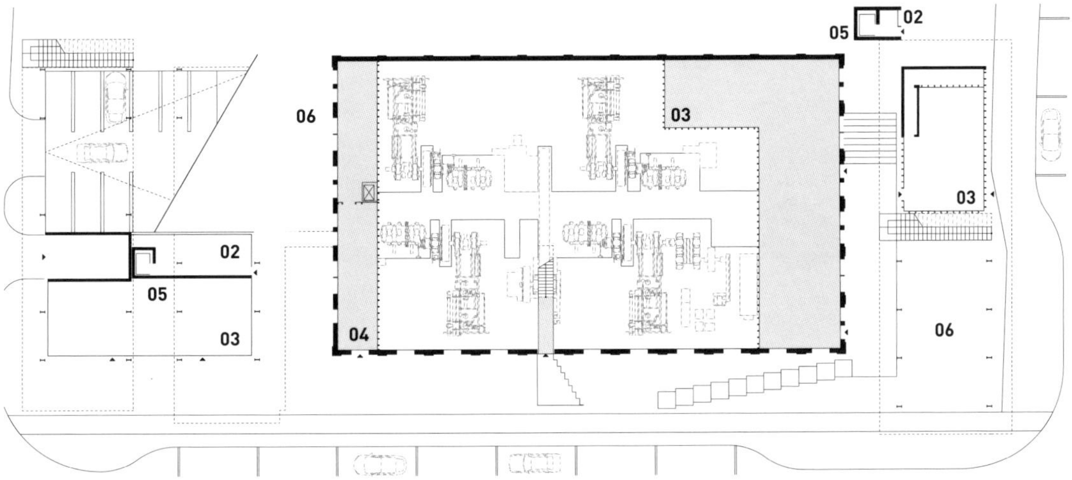

Site Plan

01 One-bedroom suite
02 Lobby
03 Commercial space
04 Amenity
05 Elevator
06 Public space

90-100 Alexander

Condominiums
Winnipeg, Manitoba
2018 - 2023

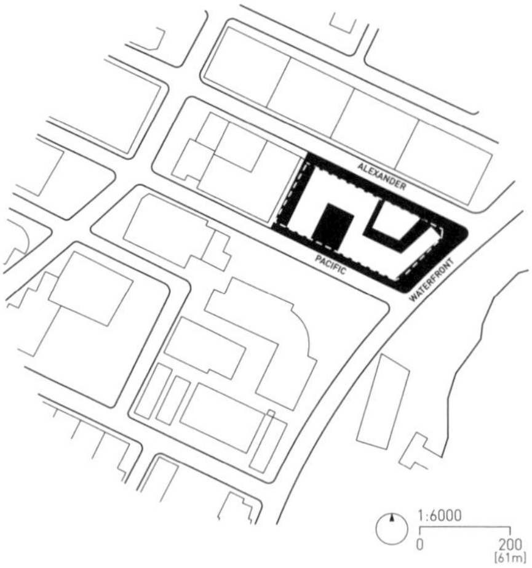

90-100 Alexander is both a new-built and an adaptive reuse development. The project consists a four-storey historic building, as well as a seven-storey newly built undulating mass, containing a total of 206 residential rental suites and 6,000 square feet of commercial space at grade, divided into two separate blocks to promote porosity of the ground floor. The site includes only 30 parking spaces, a combination of covered and surface stalls, two of which are intended for car-share vehicles. Common amenities include a large courtyard, outdoor mews and alleys through the site, indoor bike and refuse rooms and shared rooftop patios.

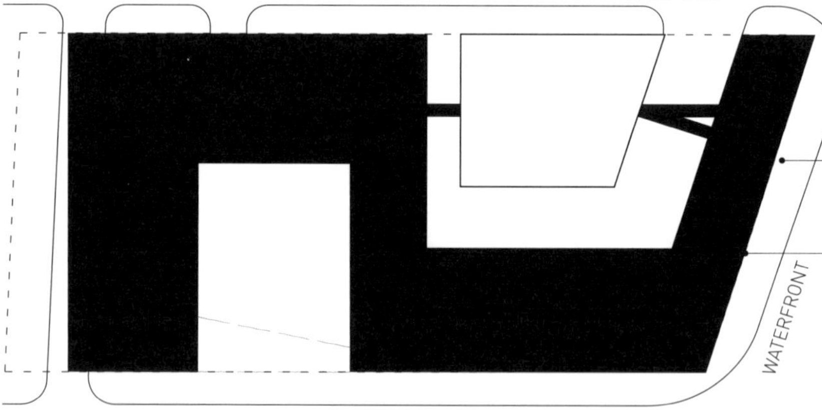

1:1000
0 50' [15.25m]

SITE AREA
47,080 ft² [4,374 m²]

GFA
179,000 ft² [16,630 m²]

COVERAGE

FLOOR AREA RATIO **3.80**

COVERED AREA **69%**

EFFICIENCY [gross/net] **83%**

OCCUPANCY

RESIDENTIAL **95%**

COMMERCIAL **5%**

TYPOLOGY

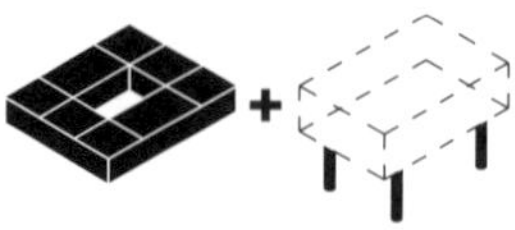

DENSITY

191 /ac [471/ha]

285 / ac [702/ha]

HEIGHT [STOREYS]

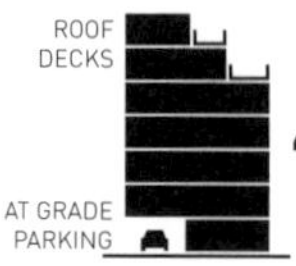

4-7

OF UNITS **206**

OF PARKING STALLS **30**

UNIT TYPES

bedrooms	**166**	**40**	0	0
storeys [within units]	**205**	**1**	0	0

UNIT SIZE

37% AVERAGE UNIT **668ft²** [62.1 m²]

28% SMALLEST UNIT **500 ft²** [46.5 m²]

50% LARGEST UNIT **900 ft²** [83.6 m²]

COST

$190/ft² [$2,045/m²]

300
75

CONSTRUCTION

- DEMISING WALLS

LIGHT FRAME
- EXTERIOR
- INTERIOR WALLS

HOLLOWCORE
- FLOORS
- ROOFS

- L1 WALLS
- COLUMNS
- FOUNDATION

Background

Representing the first project in Winnipeg for 546's Calgary based client, 90-100 Alexander is a continuum of the redevelopment of Waterfront Drive, the riverfront along the Red River at the edge of Winnipeg's Exchange District. Over the past several decades, development of the neighbourhood has adapted to support mixed-use residential projects. The client was excited to acquire the 47,080 square foot site do to its proximity to the river, to other successful developments along the waterfront, and as it contained a historic asset, a four-storey warehouse building suited for redevelopment. The developer's design brief called for maximizing the development opportunity, while remaining vague on the specific suite split due to unfamiliarity of the new market and potentially changing needs due to a long project span.

Concept

An S-shaped newly constructed building mass wraps around the existing heritage building in an attempt to contrast and highlight it. Its porous ground floor, designed to favour the pedestrian, offers views through to the heritage building from Waterfront Drive and Pacific Avenue, to the Red River from within the site and along multiple paths into two intertwined plazas from all directions. The series of shared spaces acts as an amenity to tenants and functions as public space, with commercial edges spilling out to activate the streetscape for residents, visitors and passersby.

Above, the ubiquitous black mass is supported and anchored to the pedestrian scale through a carefully articulated latticework of concrete beams, and sloping and vertical columns. Residential floor plates are kept shallow [40 foot single loaded to 55 foot double loaded] for increased natural light and air movement. Terracing and sloping at the sixth and seventh levels aligns the building wall height with the Historic Building, lowering the scale closer to grade and extending daylighting into shared spaces and surrounding streets.

Units

The first four residential floors are made up of stacked one and two bedroom modules. The basic suite module is designed to maximize the perception of open space and access to exterior by pushing the bedroom area deeper into the unit and providing a glazed partition between living and sleeping rooms. All of the one-bedroom modules are designed with a central plumbing wall that allows the suite to flip on itself from floor to floor without affecting the simplicity of plumbing alignment, while enabling the checker pattern of the exterior façade.

The unit modules were also designed to allow for maximum flexibility of the unit mix during the design and construction documents phase to help the developer to continuously assess the market needs well into the process. The 22-foot wide one-bedroom module expands to 33 feet as a two-bedroom suite to account for an additional master bedroom bay. This allows 2 x one-bedroom suites to structurally align with 3 x one-bedroom suites, making them interchangeable right until construction.

Dwellings on the two top levels [accessed from the same sixth floor plate to maximize usable area on the seventh and stay under high-rise measures] expand onto outdoor decks sheltered behind slanted rooflines, creating a semi-private, exterior mansard.

Particulars

Custom cladding of the new building was developed as a reinterpretation of masonry detailing and interlocking evident in the surrounding historic buildings. Cladding is approached from a perspective of buildability, taking a rudimentary eight-inch deep break shape "flashing" and deploying across all façades in a straightforward and unique way. The installation pattern / strategy allows for the creation of more intense overlaps around windows, creating a modern interpretation of quoining at the corners of the building. The system had to be able to satisfy a variety of conditions from turning inside / outside corners to stretching along different lengths of property line. The same cladding system acts as a guardrail on rooftop patios as well as a screening of all rooftop mechanical equipment [supported by a lightweight galvanized steel frame]. A unified approach is achieved through the repetition of a lightweight modular element in 95% of conditions. The basic module can easily be handled and cut to size on site, eliminating the need for complex coordination.

L2-L5 Plan

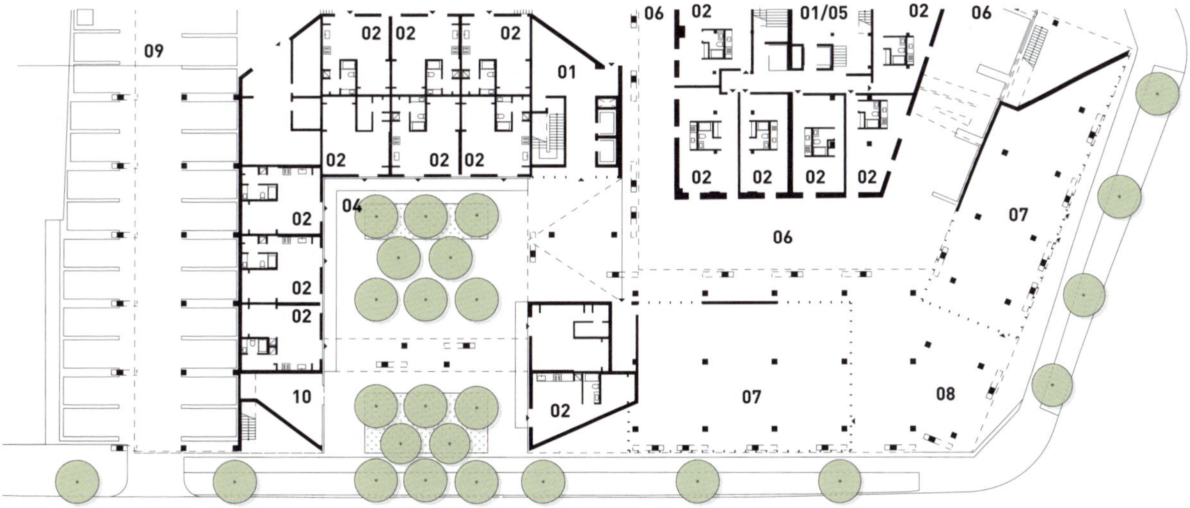

Site Plan

01 Residential lobby
02 One-bedroom suite
03 Two-bedroom suite
04 Courtyard

05 Heritage renovation
06 Heritage laneway
07 Commercial space
08 Public plaza

09 Surface parking
10 Bike parking
11 Elevated walkway

Rundle

Affordable rental housing
Calgary, Alberta
2019 - 2024

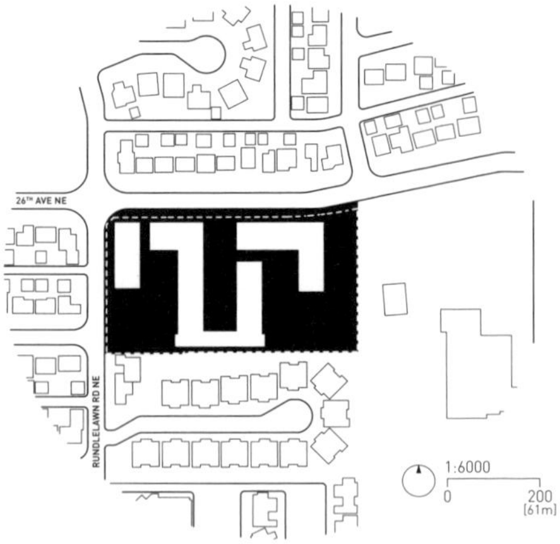

Rundle is a 135-unit subsidized and low-end rental housing project in a suburban neighbourhood of Calgary, Alberta, geared towards low income families. The three-storey new construction is organized around two exterior courtyards, each with direct access to a community amenity room on the ground floor. The site includes 156 surface stalls to meet the demand for resident and visitor parking.

SITE AREA
156,490 ft²
[14,538 m²]

GFA
140,920 ft²
[13,092 m²]

1:1500
0
100'
[30.5m]

COVERAGE

FLOOR AREA RATIO	COVERED AREA	EFFICIENCY [gross/net]
0.90	**21%**	**86%**

\# OF UNITS **135**

\# OF PARKING STALLS **156**

UNIT TYPES

bedrooms	35	88	6	6
storeys [within units]	135	0	0	0

OCCUPANCY

RESIDENTIAL **100%**

TYPOLOGY

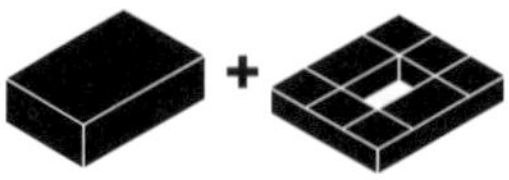

UNIT SIZE

48% AVERAGE UNIT **860 ft²** [80 m²]

31% SMALLEST UNIT **560 ft²** [52 m²]

72% LARGEST UNIT **1300 ft²** [121 m²]

CONSTRUCTION

L2-L3 LIGHT WOOD FRAME
- STRUCTURE
- WALLS
- FLOORS
- ROOFS

- L1 STRUCTURE

- FOUNDATION

DENSITY

38 /ac [93/ha]

88 / ac [217/ha]

HEIGHT [STOREYS]

AT GRADE PARKING **2-3**

COST

$304/ft² [$3,269/m²]

300
75

Background

In 2020, 546 and Stantec Architecture Calgary were selected by Calgary Housing Corporation to design 145 unit [scaled back to 135 units during the design process] housing project in the Rundle neighbourhood, a suburban community, to replace an existing low-density subsidized townhouse complex. The existing buildings were deemed to be in poor condition and the project was also aimed to intensify land use in this low-density neighbourhood. The design had to follow relatively strict Calgary Housing guidelines in all aspects of design, including dimensional, material and operational standards, as well as provisions for sustainability. Fifteen percent of the total suites were to be fully accessible. The project intends to serve low income families and individuals, while also including 50% of market rate rental housing. The two housing types are fully mixed within the building mass, and there is no difference in the level of finish from subsidized to market-rate suites by design. The client dictated a number of parking stalls required and that anything beyond surface parking would be too expensive to accommodate.

Concept

The building mass is organized around two exterior courtyards in an attempt to reduce scale and create protected common outdoor space and a sense of identity and ownership for the residents. Further, the final design scheme aims to minimize the perception of a large surface parking lot dictated by client's parking requirements and to keep the building as low-rise as possible given its detached single family home context and affordable construction.

The treatment of the ground plane as a "quilt" allowed the design team to break the parking surface into smaller pockets and blend the required stalls within landscape and amenity elements. The resulting three-storey building mass snakes around the site to reduce the perceived scale of the building, spaces in between and the surrounding parking areas. The continuous mass optimizes resources needed for exiting and circulation, while also lifting off the ground at selected points for vehicular and pedestrian access. The building programme's required 1,500 square feet of resident amenity space – multipurpose community room[s] – is split into two, located at grade and open directly onto the two courtyards, thus serving to extend the shared public space from indoors to out.

Units

The dwelling units reflect the project's objective to cater to a full spectrum of tenant types, families with children, single parents, couples without children and single individuals, and include suites from one-bedroom to four-bedroom types. Fifteen percent of all suites, across the range of types, are dimensioned to be fully accessible for those with mobility issues. All of the suites on the ground floor open directly onto the exterior and vast majority of them also have access to private patio space. The upper floor suites include either private balconies or a small interior flex nook, easily customizable by the tenant for their needs. In addition, the building includes two common balconies for the use of tenants on the upper floors who do not have access to private outdoor space.

The suite types consists of two "depths" of suites, balancing out cost with livability and allowing variety in the width of building blocks.

Particulars

A number of design decisions were made to break down the scale of the building to suit the single family housing in the surrounding neighbourhood. This included the building's undulating roofline, the screen at the base of the building that reaches to grade at points and reflects the roofline, the colour variation of the building blocks from black to white and the seemingly randomized window pattern to avoid a stacked façade effect.

The façade system was designed to include a flexible metal edge at windows openings to ensure that panels never required cutting to suit – promoting ease of construction, aesthetic appeal and long-term durability.

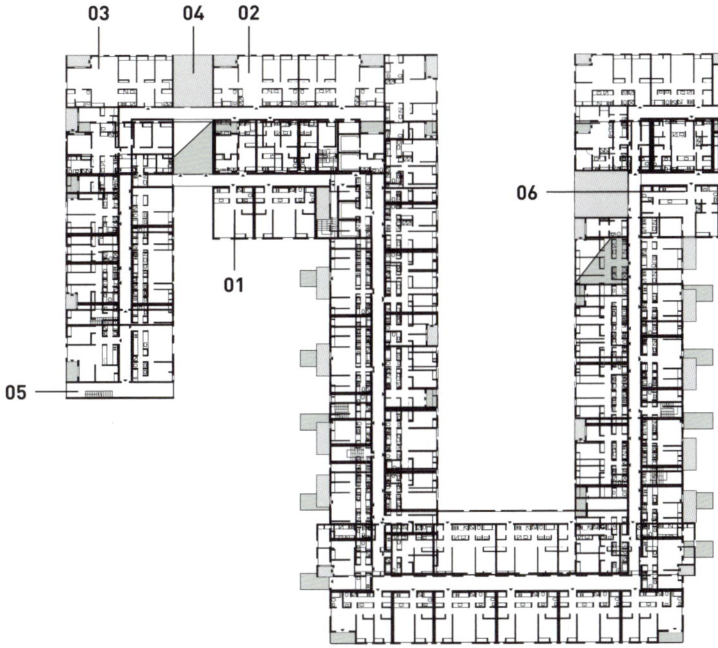

L2 Plan

Site Plan

01 One-bedroom suite
02 Two-bedroom suite
03 Three-bedroom suite
04 Outdoor amenity
05 Exterior stairs
06 Connection
07 Courtyard
08 Parking

Catherine

Rental housing
Victoria, British Columbia
2020 - 2024

Catherine Street is a 31-unit rental housing project located in West Victoria, British Columbia. This three and four-storey new build intensification project offers a combination of market rate and affordable housing suites and limited number of covered parking stalls below a central courtyard that also doubles as communal amenity for the residents.

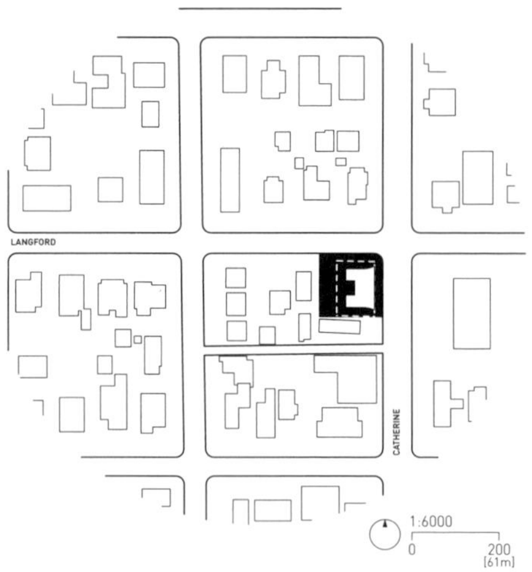

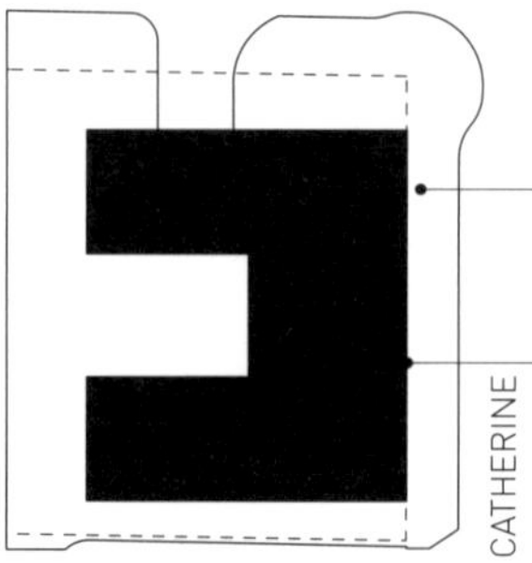

SITE AREA
10,800 ft²
[1,003 m²]

GFA
31,465 ft²
[2,923 m²]

1:1000
0 50'
[15.25m]

COVERAGE

FLOOR AREA RATIO **2.91**

COVERED AREA **69%**

EFFICIENCY [gross/net] **81%**

\# OF UNITS **31**

\# OF PARKING STALLS **13**

UNIT TYPES

bedrooms	16	15	0	0
storeys [within units]	31	0	0	0

OCCUPANCY

RESIDENTIAL **78%**

COMMERCIAL **6%**

PARKING **16%**

TYPOLOGY

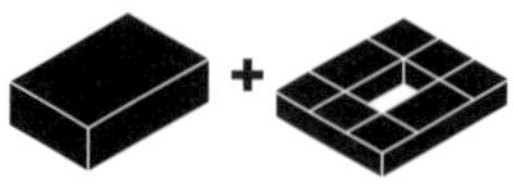

UNIT SIZE

AVERAGE UNIT **615 ft²** [57.1 m²] (34%)

SMALLEST UNIT **395 ft²** [36.7 m²] (22%)

LARGEST UNIT **890 ft²** [82.7 m²] (49%)

CONSTRUCTION

DENSITY

125 /ac [309/ha]

228 / ac [563/ha]

HEIGHT [STOREYS]

2-3

COST

$300/ft²
[$3,230/m²]

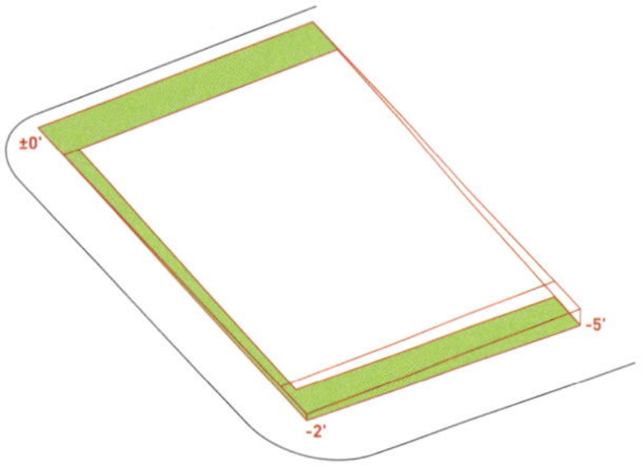

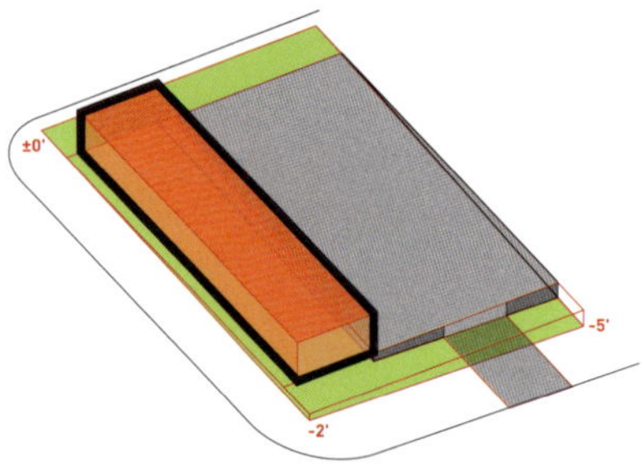

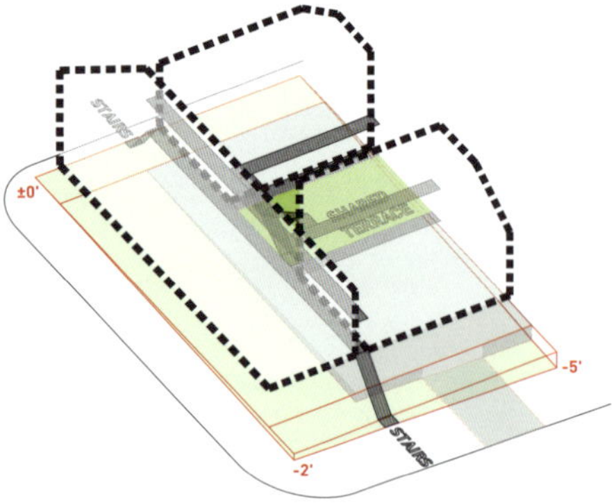

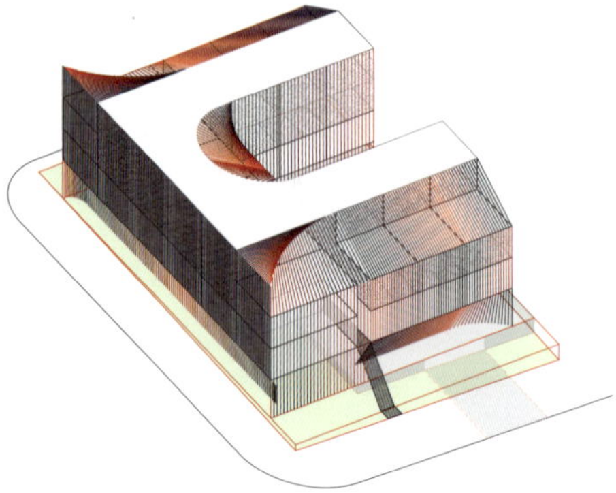

Background

In 2021, a private development group engaged 546 to design a number of housing projects in Victoria. The Catherine Street Development is the first of these ventures with this client. The site is located in West-Vic neighbourhood is aligned by three streets and a public lane, and situated in a largely single-family detached home context. The new project is intended to replace a former small apartment building in an effort to intensify the neighbourhood and provide affordable housing options in the future. One of the project's challenges for the developer was to provide relocation services for the existing residents and to continue providing rent controlled suites within the new project proforma.

Concept

The building mass wraps around the site in a U-shape, creating views and frontage to three sides of the site and stepping down from four storeys to three towards the adjacent single family homes. The top of the building also tapers back at the forth floor in a mansard-like fashion to further reduce the building's mass on the street. The site dimensions, the urban context and project objectives lended themselves to single-loaded configuration, where all circulation is managed through exterior passage ways and exit stairs to reduce capital and operational costs and to enable double aspect suites throughout the project.

The relatively aggressive parking-to-unit ratio [13:31] is compensated by increased supply of bicycle stalls. Both are located below the first residential level, and the roof of the covered parking area doubles as a common outdoor courtyard for the residents.

Units

The unit mix consists of bachelor, one-bedroom and two-bedroom suites, and due to the exterior exit passage ways, majority of the suites open to two façades, promoting natural ventilation and better access to light.

Particulars

The façade consists of custom metal shingles that are intended as a modern interpretation of the Victorian wood shingle cladding common in the surrounding neighbourhood. The shingles include a two-inch projecting "tab" to create depth and shadow play on the façade. While the units remain stacked for ease of construction, the façade pattern travels in a slight diagonal to avoid stacked façade effect and maintain the object-like character of the building mass.

L2-L4 Plan

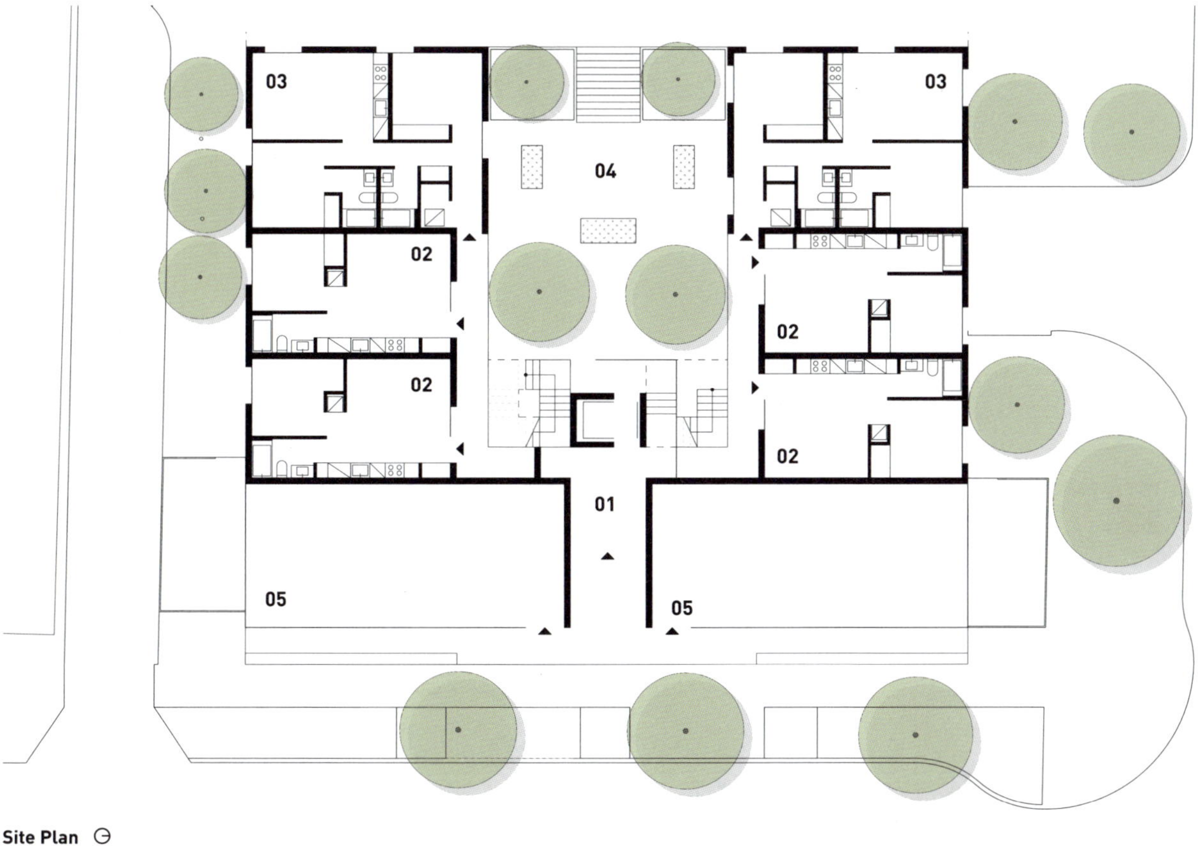

Site Plan ⊖

01 Residential lobby
02 One-bedroom suite
03 Two-bedroom suite
04 Courtyard
05 Commercial space

3319 Douglas

Mixed-use
Saanich, British Columbia
2021 -

The 3319 Douglas Street is a mixed-use development including 169 residential units, 8,000 square feet of street-oriented commercial space and two levels of enclosed parking in Saanich, BC. The six-storey building includes a large central courtyard above the 118-stall structured parking area and an extensive common roof deck area for the residents. 100% of the rental suites are designated as income secured homes in partnership with BC Housing's Housing Hub program. The project also includes one car share stall and over 200 bicycle stalls.

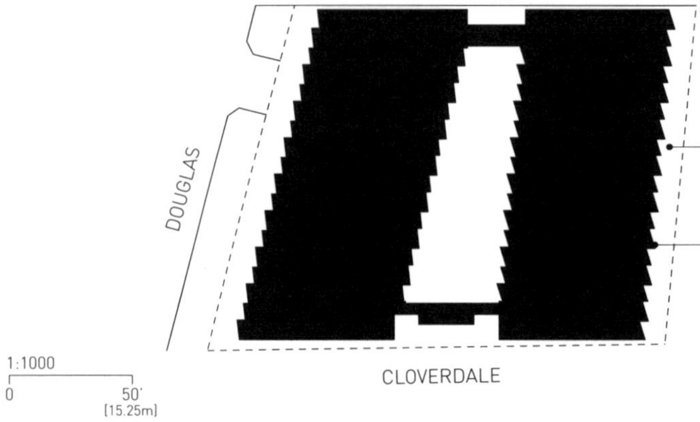

SITE AREA
27,500 ft²
[2,555 m²]

GFA
169,520 ft²
[15,749 m²]

COVERAGE

FLOOR AREA RATIO **4.4**

COVERED AREA **92%**

EFFICIENCY [gross/net] **87%**

OCCUPANCY

RESIDENTIAL **60%**

COMMERCIAL **5%**

PARKING **34%**

TYPOLOGY

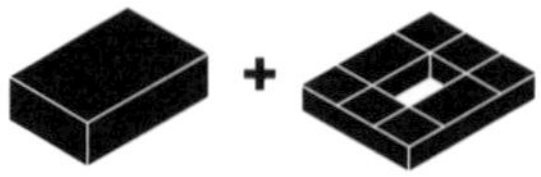

DENSITY

268 /ac [661/ha]

323 / ac [797/ha]

HEIGHT [STOREYS]

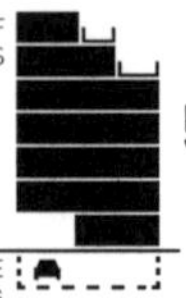

5-6

\# OF UNITS **169**

\# OF PARKING STALLS **118**

UNIT TYPES

bedrooms	154	15	0	0
storeys [within units]	169	0	0	0

UNIT SIZE

AVERAGE UNIT (32%)
571 ft² [53.0 m²]

SMALLEST UNIT (26%)
460 ft² [42.7 m²]

LARGEST UNIT (58%)
1050 ft² [97.5 m²]

CONSTRUCTION

LIGHT WOOD FRAME
- FLOORS
- WALLS
- ROOF

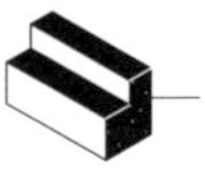

- L1 STRUCTURE
- PARKING
- FOUNDATION

Background

In 2020, 546 was engaged to design a a rental housing project by a private developer in Saanich, BC. One of the most dynamic areas of Saanich, the Uptown Douglas Corridor offers some of the most regionally significant transportation routes and is home to a variety of shops and services that employ more than 10,000+ people throughout the Greater Victoria region. While currently consisting of mostly low-rise building stock, the long-term vision for Uptown Douglas Corridor calls for building heights up to 50 metres [12-18 storeys], so surprisingly, the major challenge of the project originally was to convince both the local authorities and the client of the value of a mid-rise project in lieu of a tower design.

Concept

The building is conceived as two six-storey building blocks that frame the internal courtyard and pedestrian street. The six-storey height and massing represents a balance between the current streetscape and the future ambitions Uptown Douglas Corridor vision within the expected increased development over the next 20 years. Taking advantage of the site's shape, the building steps along the street frontage providing every unit with corner windows and extended views. The two building masses are connected via two exteriors stairs and corridors at either end of the project, presenting considerable savings for the project's capital and operational budget.

Due to a significant grade difference between the east and west property lines, the main level transitions from grade level commercial units to underground parking covered by the sloped grade of adjacent sites. This grade difference permits complete underground parking and six storeys above grade that remain under the the threshold of a "high building." This allows the project be built in a light wood frame, furthering its sustainable ambitions and affordability.

Units

The unit mix consists of studio, one-bedroom, one-bedroom and live-work suites, which open directly onto the common courtyard in the middle of the two building blocks. In an effort to provide more attainable housing solutions, the project will qualify as a 100% income restricted rental building under the BC Housing "Housing Hub" program, with all units intended to be leased for below market rents.

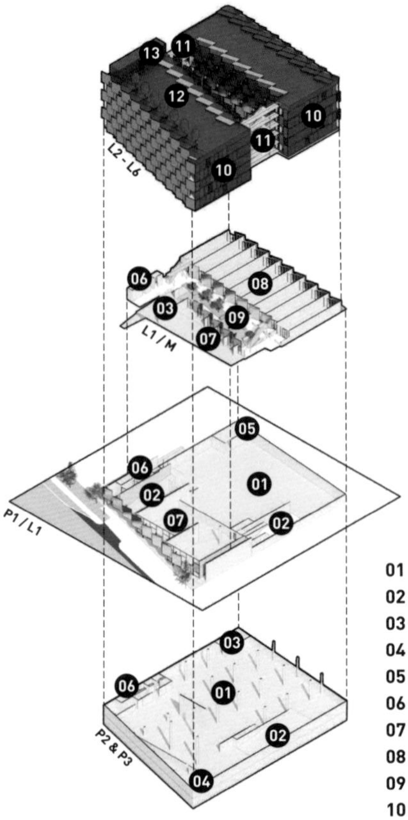

01 Vehicular parking
02 Ramp
03 Bicycle storage
04 Electrical substation
05 Garbage & recycling
06 Lobby
07 Commercial
08 Work/Live
09 Exterior courtyard
10 Residential
11 Link stair
12 Rooftop ammenity
13 Elevator penthouse

Particulars

The façade is composed of an alternating mosaic of solids and voids and is clad in aluminum foam panels that are both recycled and recyclable.

Accessed via a generous porte-cochere, a shared and public "pedestrian street" divides the building in two halves, and is lined by live-work units and a semi-private commercial patio. Open air stairways criss-cross this space and ascend up to a shared rooftop designed to provide an oasis from the busy street below.

Bike ramps on each end of the building allow pedestrians and cyclists to wheel right up from the street into the courtyard. Coupled with elevators and stairs, the proposed design allows for close integration of the Douglas Street frontage with the rest of the building. A wide path through the courtyard provides circulation through the space and to the individual work/live units. Built-in seating, a bike repair station, planters with small trees and raised patio area help this space feel welcoming and vibrant.

Typical level

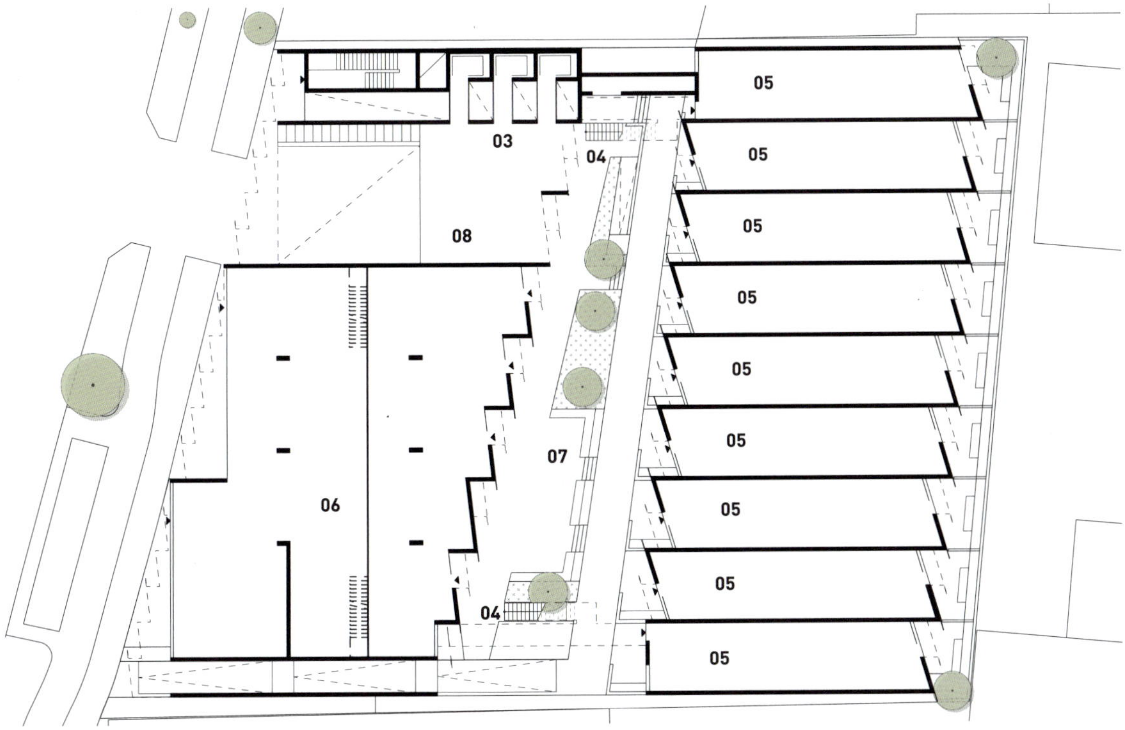

Site Plan

01 One-bedroom suite
02 Two-bedroom suite
03 Lobby
04 Exterior stairs
05 Live / work suite
06 Commercial space
07 Courtyard
08 Bicycle storage

post.SCRIPT

Key

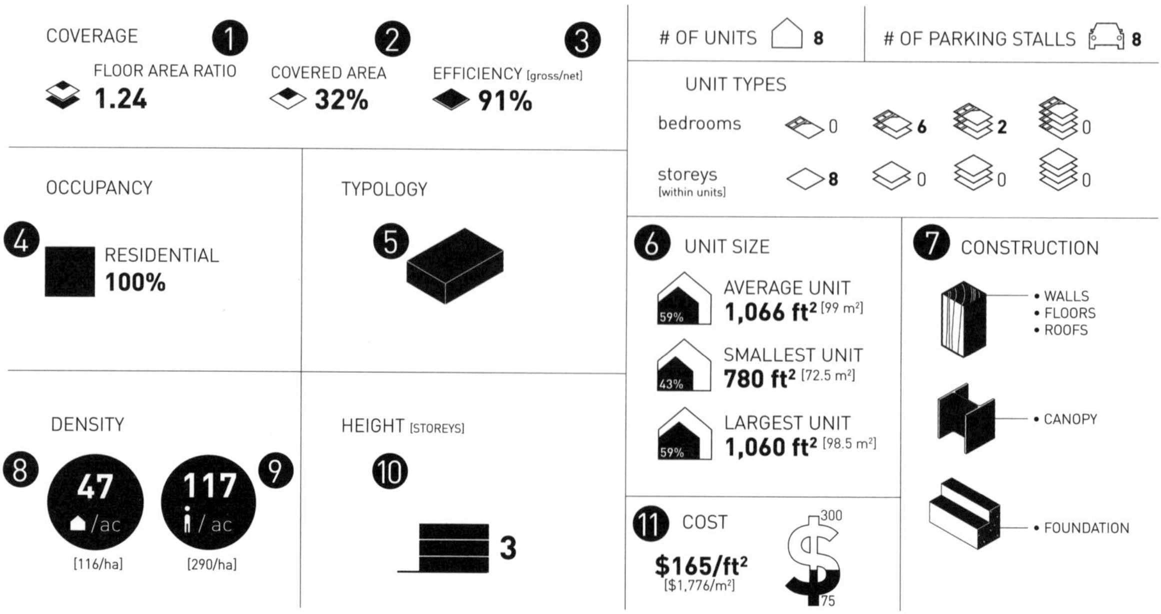
COVERAGE
1
FLOOR AREA RATIO
1.24
2
COVERED AREA
32%
3
EFFICIENCY [gross/net]
91%
OF UNITS 8
OF PARKING STALLS 8
UNIT TYPES
bedrooms 0 6 2 0
storeys [within units] 8 0 0 0
OCCUPANCY
4
RESIDENTIAL
100%
TYPOLOGY
5
6
UNIT SIZE
59%
AVERAGE UNIT
1,066 ft² [99 m²]
43%
SMALLEST UNIT
780 ft² [72.5 m²]
59%
LARGEST UNIT
1,060 ft² [98.5 m²]
7
CONSTRUCTION
• WALLS
• FLOORS
• ROOFS
• CANOPY
• FOUNDATION
DENSITY
8
47
/ac
[116/ha]
117
/ ac
[290/ha]
9
HEIGHT [STOREYS]
10
3
11
COST
$165/ft²
[$1,776/m²]
300
75

❶ FLOOR AREA RATIO = GROSS FLOOR AREA / SITE AREA

❷ COVERED AREA = SITE AREA - BUILDING FOOTPRINT

❸ BUILDING EFFICIENCY = GROSS FLOOR AREA / NET FLOOR AREA

❹ BUILDING OCCUPANCY BREAKDOWN BY PROGRAM TYPE

❺ BUILDING TYPOLOGY

BOX ADDITION ELEVATED COURTYARD VILLAGE TOWNHOUSE

❻ UNIT SIZE COMPARISON

 = AVERAGE CANADIAN HOME SIZE [NATURAL RESOURCES CANADA, 2020]
[1800 SQFT / 167 SQM]

❼ CONSTRUCTION MATERIALS

WOOD STEEL CAST IN PLACE CONCRETE PRE CAST CONCRETE MASONRY

❽ UNITS PER ACRE

❾ OCCUPANTS PER ACRE

OCCUPANTS BASED ON:
STUDIO= 1 OCC.
1 BR= 1.25 OCC.
2 BR= 2.50 OCC.
3 BR= 3.75 OCC.
4 BR= 5 OCC.

❿ BUILDING HEIGHT & CONDITIONS

⓫ CONSTRUCTION COST PER SQFT [NOT INCLUDING LAND OR SOFT COSTS] AT TIME OF BUILDING

Projects Appendix

Acknowledgements

5468796 Architecture

Emeil Alvarez
Pablo Batista
Ken Borton
Jordy Craddock
Donna Evans
Teresa Garside
Ben Greenwood
Ralph Guitierrez
Johanna Hurme
Ainsley Johnston
Jeffrey Kachkan
Matthew Kurtas
Andrew Lawler
Kelsey McMahon
Mohammad Massoumi
Colin Neufeld
Sasa Radulovic
Amanda Reis
Shannon Wiebe

Past collaborators

Sharon Ackerman
Mandy Aldcorn
Maria Amagasu
Apollinaire Au
Brandon Bergem
Eric Decumutan
Jason Ejzenbart
Michelle Heath
Aynslee Hurdal
Caroline Inglis
Lucretia Ionescu
Andriy Ivanystskyy
Eva Kiss
Stanislav Klas
Lindsey Koepke
Grant Labossiere
Justin Lieberman
Jayne Miles
Royce O'Toole
Zach Pauls
Simone Prill
Sean Radford
Erin Riediger
Helia Saadat
Shannon Scott
Hasan Shurrab
Renee Struthers
Hugh Taylor
Trent Thompson
Matthew Trendota
Alan Vamos
Jennifer Yablonowski
Dazhong Yi

platform.MIDDLE: Architecture for Housing the 99%
5468796 Architecture
First edition, 2023
ISBN 978-607-8880-19-5

projects.MODELLING

© 5468796 Architecture Inc.
Winnipeg, MB
Canada

© Arquine, SA de CV
Ámsterdam 163 A
Colonia Hipódromo, 06100
Ciudad de México

Texts
© 5468796 Architecture

Images
© 5468796 Architecture: 7 (Chair your Idea, Walk Winnipeg, ReTree), 8 (Webbsite, BGBX), 23, 53, 57, 93, 101, 105, 117, 121, 125, 129.
© James Brittain: 8 (youCUBE, Centre Village, Welcome Place, Bloc_10, The Avenue, 548 Stradbrook), 9 (OZ, Ross Avenue, 62M, Warehouse 1885, CY33, Pumphouse), 61, 65, 69, 73, 77, 81, 85, 89, 97, 106, 109, 113.
© Lisa Stinner-Kun: 6 (Migrating Landscapes), 12.
© Jacqueline Young | Stationpoint Photographic: 6 (Table for 12 + 1200), 13, 15.
© Jaime Navarro: 7 (One Bucket at a Time), 19.
© RNDSQR: 9 (LIFE). Courtesy of RNDSQR.
© Leif Norman: 16.
© Zephrya Vun: 17.

5468796 Architecture

Original layout and Editorial Management
Johanna Hurme, Sasa Radulovic, Ken Borton, Shannon Wiebe, Ainsley Johnston and Hugh Taylor

Arquine

Director
Miquel Adrià

Editorial Director
Brenda Soto Suárez

Editorial Assistants
Ana Luz Valencia and Karina Reyes

Layout
María Marín de Buen, Yavanna Latapí and Regina Sierra
(Estudio María Marín de Buen)

Proofreading
Quentin Pope

Prepress
Offset Rebosán

5468796.ca
arquine.com

The architects and publishers have made every effort to identify ownership in the use of images and copyrighted material. In the event of an inadvertent omission or error, please notify the publisher.

No part of this publication may be reproduced, stored in a retrieval system, or transmitted in any form or by any means, electronic, mechanical, photocopying, recording or otherwise, without prior and express written permission of the owners of the intellectual property rights and of the publishers.

projects.MODELLING is one of four volumes in the publication *platform.MIDDLE: Architecture for Housing the 99%*. The other volumes include: platform.MIDDLE, platform.MACRO and platform.MICRO.

platform.MIDDLE: Architecture for Housing the 99% was printed and bound in September 2023 by Artron Art Printing Ltd. in China. It was printed on 100 g IKPP paper and set in typefaces of the DIN family. The print run was 1,300 copies.